1989 SUPPLEMENT TO
CONSTITUTIONAL LAW
THE AMERICAN CONSTITUTION
CONSTITUTIONAL RIGHTS & LIBERTIES

Sixth Editions

By

William B. Lockhart
Professor of Law, University of California, Hastings
Dean and Professor of Law Emeritus, University of Minnesota

Yale Kamisar
Henry K. Ransom Professor of Law, University of Michigan

Jesse H. Choper
Dean and Professor of Law, University of California, Berkeley

Steven H. Shiffrin
Professor of Law, Cornell University

AMERICAN CASEBOOK SERIES®

WEST PUBLISHING CO.
ST. PAUL, MINN., 1989

ISBN 0–314–56402–0

(L.K.C. & S.) 1989 Supp. 6th Ed. ACB

Preface

This Supplement contains significant developments that have occurred between the end of the 1984–85 Supreme Court term—the "cutoff" date of the principal books—and the end of the 1988–89 Supreme Court term.

The editorial style of this Supplement follows that of the principal books. In designating the places in the principal books at which the supplementary material is to be inserted, the following abbreviations have been used:

Constitutional Law: Cases, Comments & Questions—CON LAW

The American Constitution: Cases & Materials—AMER CON

Constitutional Rights & Liberties: Cases & Materials—RTS & LIB

Chapter and section titles from the principal books have been reproduced in this Supplement to facilitate identification of the material to be inserted.

WILLIAM B. LOCKHART
YALE KAMISAR
JESSE H. CHOPER
STEVEN H. SHIFFRIN

July, 1989

*

Table of Contents

Table of Cases

The principal cases are in bold type. Cases cited or discussed in the text are roman type. References are to pages. Cases cited in principal cases and within other quoted materials are not included.

*

1989 SUPPLEMENT TO
CONSTITUTIONAL LAW
THE AMERICAN CONSTITUTION
CONSTITUTIONAL RIGHTS & LIBERTIES

*

Chapter

NATIONAL LEGISLATIVE POWER

SECTION 3: THE NATIONAL TAXING AND SPENDING POWERS

REGULATION THROUGH SPENDING

CON LAW: P. 153, after note 2

AMER CON P. 118, after note 2

SOUTH DAKOTA v. DOLE

483 U.S. 203, 107 S.Ct. 2793, 97 L.Ed.2d 171 (1987).

CHIEF JUSTICE REHNQUIST delivered the opinion of the Court.

[In 1984 Congress enacted 23 U.S.C. § 158, which directs the Secretary of Transportation to withhold 5% of the federal highway funds otherwise allocable to states in which purchase or public possession of any alcoholic beverage by a person less than 21 years of age is lawful. South Dakota, which permits persons 19 years of age or older to purchase 3.2% beer, sought a declaratory judgment that § 158 violates constitutional limits on congressional spending power and violates the twenty-first amendment. The District Court and Court of Appeals for the Eighth Circuit rejected these claims. The Supreme Court affirmed.]

[We] need not decide in this case whether [the twenty-first amendment] would prohibit an attempt by Congress to legislate directly a national minimum drinking age. Here, Congress has acted indirectly under its spending power to encourage uniformity in the States' drinking ages. As we explain below, we find this legislative effort within constitutional bounds even if Congress may not regulate drinking ages directly.

The Constitution empowers Congress to "lay and collect Taxes, Duties, Imposts, and Excises, to pay the Debts and provide for the common Defence and general Welfare of the United States." Art. I, § 8, cl. 1. Incident to this power, Congress may attach conditions on the receipt of federal funds, and has repeatedly employed the power "to further broad policy objectives by conditioning receipt of federal moneys upon compliance by the recipient with federal statutory and administrative directives." *Fullilove v. Klutznick* (Opinion of Burger, C.J.). The breadth of this power was made clear in *Butler*, where the Court, resolving a longstanding debate over the scope of the Spending Clause, determined that "the power of Congress to authorize expenditure of public moneys for public purposes is not limited by the direct grants of legislative power found in the Constitution."

1

Thus, objectives not thought to be within Article I's "enumerated legislative fields," may nevertheless be attained through the use of the spending power and the conditional grant of federal funds.

The spending power is of course not unlimited, *Pennhurst State School and Hospital v. Halderman*, 451 U.S. 1 (1981), but is instead subject to several general restrictions articulated in our cases. The first of these limitations is derived from the language of the Constitution itself: the exercise of the spending power must be in pursuit of "the general welfare." [Second,] we have required that if Congress desires to condition the States' receipt of federal funds, it "must do so unambiguously * * *, enabl[ing] the States to exercise their choice knowingly, cognizant of the consequences of their participation." *Pennhurst State School.* Third, our cases have suggested (without significant elaboration) that conditions on federal grants might be illegitimate if they are unrelated "to the federal interest in particular national projects or programs." *Massachusetts v. United States.* See also *Ivanhoe Irrigation Dist. v. McCracken*, ("[T]he Federal Government may establish and impose reasonable conditions relevant to federal interest in the project and to the over-all objectives thereof"). Finally, we have noted that other constitutional provisions may provide an independent bar to the conditional grant of federal funds. *Buckley v. Valeo.*

South Dakota does not seriously claim that § 158 is inconsistent with any of the first three restrictions mentioned above. [The] State itself, rather than challenging the germaneness of the condition to federal purposes, admits that it "has never contended that the congressional action [was] unrelated to a national concern in the absence of the Twenty-first Amendment." Indeed, the condition imposed by Congress is directly related to one of the main purposes for which highway funds are expended—safe interstate travel. This goal of the interstate highway system had been frustrated by varying drinking ages among the States. A presidential commission appointed to study alcohol-related accidents and fatalities on the Nation's highways concluded that the lack of uniformity in the States' drinking ages created "an incentive to drink and drive" because "young persons commut[e] to border States where the drinking age is lower." Presidential Commission on Drunk Driving, *Final Report* 11 (1983). By enacting § 158, Congress conditioned the receipt of federal funds in a way reasonably calculated to address this particular impediment to a purpose for which the funds are expended.

The remaining question about the validity of § 158—and the basic point of disagreement between the parties—is whether the Twenty-first Amendment constitutes an "independent constitutional bar" to the conditional grant of federal funds. Petitioner, relying on its view that the Twenty-first Amendment prohibits *direct* regulation of drinking ages by Congress, asserts that "Congress may not use the spending power to regulate that which it is prohibited from regulating directly under the Twenty-first Amendment." But our cases show that this "independent constitutional bar" limitation on the spending power is not of the kind petitioner suggests. *Butler*, for example, established that the constitutional limitations on Congress when exercising its spending power are less exacting than those on its authority to regulate directly.

We have also held that a perceived Tenth Amendment limitation on congressional regulation of state affairs did not concomitantly limit the range of conditions legitimately placed on federal grants. In *Oklahoma v. Civil Service Comm'n*, the Court considered the validity of the Hatch Act insofar as it was applied to political activities of state officials whose employment was financed in whole or in part with federal funds. The State contended that an order under this provision to withhold certain federal funds unless a state official was removed invaded its sovereignty in violation of the Tenth Amendment. Though finding that "the United States is not concerned with, and has no power to regulate, local political activities as such of state officials," the Court nevertheless held that the Federal Government "does have power to fix the terms upon which its money allotments to states shall be disbursed." The Court found no violation of the State's sovereignty because the State could, and did, adopt "the 'simple expedient' of not yielding to what she urges is federal coercion. The offer of benefits to a state by the United States dependent upon cooperation by the state with federal plans, assumedly for the general welfare, is not unusual." See also *Steward Machine Co.* ("There is only a condition which the state is free at pleasure to disregard or to fulfill"); *Massachusetts v. Mellon.*

These cases establish that the "independent constitutional bar" limitation on the spending power is not, as petitioner suggests, a prohibition on the indirect achievement of objectives which Congress is not empowered to achieve directly. Instead, we think that the language in our earlier opinions stands for the unexceptionable proposition that the power may not be used to induce the States to engage in activities that would themselves be unconstitutional. Thus, for example, a grant of federal funds conditioned on invidiously discriminatory state action or the infliction of cruel and unusual punishment would be an illegitimate exercise of the Congress' broad spending power. But no such claim can be or is made here. Were South Dakota to succumb to the blandishments offered by Congress and raise its drinking age to 21, the State's action in so doing would not violate the constitutional rights of anyone.

Our decisions have recognized that in some circumstances the financial inducement offered by Congress might be so coercive as to pass the point at which "pressure turns into compulsion." *Steward Machine Co.* Here, however, Congress has directed only that a State desiring to establish a minimum drinking age lower than 21 lose a relatively small percentage of certain federal highway funds. Petitioner contends that the coercive nature of this program is evident from the degree of success it has achieved. We cannot conclude, however, that a conditional grant of federal money of this sort is unconstitutional simply by reason of its success in achieving the congressional objective.

When we consider, for a moment, that all South Dakota would lose if she adheres to her chosen course as to a suitable minimum drinking age is 5% of the funds otherwise obtainable under specified highway grant programs, the argument as to coercion is shown to be more rhetoric than fact. * * *

Here Congress has offered relatively mild encouragement to the States to enact higher minimum drinking ages than they would otherwise choose. But the enactment of such laws remains the prerogative of the States not merely in theory but in fact. Even if Congress might lack the power to impose a national minimum drinking age directly, we conclude that encouragement to state action found in § 158 is a valid use of the spending power. * * *

JUSTICE BRENNAN, dissenting.

I agree with Justice O'Connor that regulation of the minimum age of purchasers of liquor falls squarely within the ambit of those powers reserved to the States by the Twenty-first Amendment. Since States possess this constitutional power, Congress can not condition a federal grant in a manner that abridges this right. The Amendment, itself, strikes the proper balance between federal and state authority. I therefore dissent.

JUSTICE O'CONNOR, dissenting.

[My] disagreement with the Court is relatively narrow on the Spending Power issue: it is a disagreement about the application of a principle rather than a disagreement on the principle itself. I agree with the Court that Congress may attach conditions on the receipt of federal funds to further "the federal interest in particular national projects or programs." *Massachusetts v. United States.* * * *

But the Court's application of the requirement that the condition imposed be reasonably related to the purpose for which the funds are expended, is cursory and unconvincing. We have repeatedly said that Congress may condition grants under the Spending Power only in ways reasonably related to the purpose of the federal program. * * * In my view, establishment of a minimum drinking age of 21 is not sufficiently related to interstate highway construction to justify so conditioning funds appropriated for that purpose. * * *

When Congress appropriates money to build a highway, it is entitled to insist that the highway be a safe one. But it is not entitled to insist as a condition of the use of highway funds that the State impose or change regulations in other areas of the State's social and economic life because of an attenuated or tangential relationship to highway use or safety. Indeed, if the rule were otherwise, the Congress could effectively regulate almost any area of a State's social, political, or economic life on the theory that use of the interstate transportation system is somehow enhanced. If, for example, the United States were to condition highway moneys upon moving the state capital, I suppose it might argue that interstate transportation is facilitated by locating local governments in places easily accessible to interstate highways—or, conversely, that highways might become overburdened if they had to carry traffic to and from the state capital. In my mind, such a relationship is hardly more attenuated than the one which the Court finds supports § 158. * * *

There is a clear place at which the Court can draw the line between permissible and impermissible conditions on federal grants. It is the line identifed in the Brief for the National Conference of State Legislatures et al. as *Amici Curiae*:

"Congress has the power to *spend* for the general welfare, it has the power to *legislate* only for delegated purposes * * *.

"The appropriate inquiry, then, is whether the spending requirement or prohibition is a condition on a grant or whether it is regulation. The difference turns on whether the requirement specifies in some way how the money should be spent, so that Congress' intent in making the grant will be effectuated. Congress has no power under the Spending Clause to impose requirements on a grant that go beyond specifying how the money should be spent. A requirement that is not such a specification is not a condition, but a regulation, which is valid only if it falls within one of Congress' delegated regulatory powers."

This approach harks back to *Butler*, the last case in which this Court struck down an Act of Congress as beyond the authority granted by the Spending Clause. There the Court wrote that "[t]here is an obvious difference between a statute stating the conditions upon which moneys shall be expended and one effective only upon assumption of a contractual obligation to submit to a regulation which otherwise could not be enforced." The *Butler* Court saw the Agricultural Adjustment Act for what it was—an exercise of regulatory, not spending, power. The error in *Butler* was not the Court's conclusion that the

Act was essentially regulatory, but rather its crabbed view of the extent of Congress' regulatory power under the Commerce Clause. The Agricultural Adjustment Act was regulatory but it was regulation that today would likely be considered within Congress' Commerce Power. See, e.g., *Katzenbach v. Mc-Clung; Wickard v. Filburn.*

While *Butler*'s authority is questionable insofar as it assumes that Congress has no regulatory power over farm production, its discussion of the Spending Power and its description of both the power's breadth and its limitations remains sound. The Court's decision in *Butler* also properly recognizes the gravity of the task of appropriately limiting the Spending Power. If the Spending Power is to be limited only by Congress' notion of the general welfare, the reality, given the vast financial resources of the Federal Government, is that the Spending Clause gives "power to the Congress to tear down the barriers, to invade the states' jurisdiction, and to become a parliament of the whole people, subject to no restrictions save such as are self-imposed." *Butler.* This, of course, as *Butler* held, was not the Framers' plan and it is not the meaning of the Spending Clause. * * *

SECTION: LIMITATIONS ON APPLYING NATIONAL POWERS TO STATE GOVERNMENTS: INTERGOVERNMENTAL IMMUNITIES

ORIGINS OF IMMUNITIES

CON LAW: P. 162, End of footnote j.

The latest such decision upheld a federal tax on private income from a class of state and municipal bonds, overruling *Pollock v. Farmers Loan and Trust Co.,* 157 U.S. 429, 15 S.Ct. 673, 39 L.Ed. 759 (1895). *South Carolina v. Baker,* considered at p. 9 of this Supplement. *Pollock* had not been challenged earlier, despite the 1938–41 revolutionary change in intergovernmental tax immunity, only because Congress had made no earlier effort to tax income from state bonds. Only O'Connor, J., dissented.

CON LAW: P. 162, before Part II.

Discrimination against other government's employees. In 1988 the Court applied intergovernmental immunity concepts to one government's discrimination against the other government's employees. DAVIS v. MICHIGAN DEPT. OF TREASURY, ___ U.S. ___, 109 S.Ct. 1500, 103 L.Ed.2d 891 (1989), held 8 to 1 that Michigan's income tax exemption for retirement benefits of former state and local government employees while taxing such benefits of resident former federal employees and all other Michigan residents receiving employment benefits, violated "the principles of intergovernmental tax immunity." The Court invoked the proposition that the "imposition of a heavier tax burden on [those who deal with one sovereign] than is imposed on [those who deal with the other] must be justified by a significant difference between the two classes. *Phillips Chemical Co. v. Dumas Independent School District,* 361 U.S. 376, 385, 80 S.Ct. 474, 4 L.Ed.2d 384 (1960)." In the light of intergovernmental immunity concerns, the Court found no "significant" justification. Stevens, J., dissented.

STATE IMMUNITY FROM FEDERAL REGULATION

CON LAW: P. 185, before note 6

AMER CON: P. 144, before note 5

The "procedural safeguards inherent in the structure of the federal system." A thoughtful article explores the possibilities of more meaningful judicial scrutiny of federal interference with state and local government operations through a "process-oriented analysis of the constitutional functions of federalism":

ANDRZEJ RAPACZYNSKI—FROM SOVEREIGNTY TO PROCESS: THE JURISPRUDENCE OF FEDERALISM AFTER GARCIA

1985 Sup.Ct.Rev. 341, 414–19.

The outcome of my discussion is that the process-oriented analysis of the constitutional functions of federalism, endorsed but not really carried out in the *Garcia* decision, leads to a more affirmative procedural role of the states within the federal system than suggested on the face of Justice Blackmun's opinion. Also, two important functions of the states—tyranny prevention and the provision of a space for participatory politics—are likely to be endangered by the national government and warrant a close judicial scrutiny of federal interference with state and local governmental operations. To some extent, then, my analysis confirms the accuracy of the insights implicit in *National League of Cities* by showing that its insistence on the protection of the political process of local governments, rather than on a guarantee of some exclusive state controls over the private sector, responded to the most fundamental desiderata of federalism, while also showing that some of these insights need not be viewed as incompatible with the *Garcia* approach.

Nevertheless, developing a constitutional theory of federalism does not automatically translate into a clear judicial doctrine specifying a set of genuinely manageable standards of review. In fact, it is the problematic character of such standards that occupies the bulk of the Court's opinion in *Garcia* and the unmanageability of the "traditional governmental functions" test laid down by *National League of Cities* seems to have been one of the main reasons for its overruling. What needs to be seen is whether the theory of federalism I have articulated can provide more reliable guidance for judicial application.

A full-fledged elaboration of the doctrinal implications of the process-oriented approach to federalism would probably be premature at this point. Given the collapse of *National League of Cities*, my aim has been to show that the process jurisprudence endorsed in *Garcia* does not signify an utter abandonment of a judicial role in this area. Nevertheless, a few preliminary observations on doctrinal matters may be in order.

To begin with, the delimitation of the protected processes of state governments with reference to traditional state functions—the road chosen by *National League of Cities*—is indeed deeply unsatisfactory. It is, of course, not a priori precluded that the traditional functions of state governments are also the very ones that are the most important from the point of view of the federalist concerns, although it is not clear why this should be so. On closer inspection, the traditional functions are much more likely to be a product of the historical role of the states in regulating the private sector and they are much more likely to have been shaped by outdated notions of state sovereignty and more modern ideas of governmental efficiency than by the more properly constitutional concerns with tyranny prevention and political participation.

At the same time, *Garcia*'s merciless critique of the criterion of tradition seems to evince a desire for watertight, mechanical tests of protected governmental functions that simply cannot be had in an area as complex as that of federalism. Constitutional adjudication is not, after all, a field in which simple standards predominate, and there can be no substitute for a painful case-by-case refinement and elaboration. Still, there are a number of ways in which the concerns of federalism may be intelligibly used as a guide for judicial review.

First, there are some state governmental functions so directly related to the federalist concern with preventing tyranny that they present rather easy cases for judicial intervention (though perhaps they are also, at this moment, the least likely to meet with serious interference). Under any approach, for example, federal interference with the agenda of the highest state legislative and executive organs is likely to undermine the overall autonomy of the political processes in the states and eliminate their constitutional role within the federal system. Similarly, an interference with the state electoral processes, insofar as it is not clearly related to the protection of individual rights but threatens to gerrymander the local districts in order to change the configuration of political forces in favor of the nationally powerful interests, would be clearly beyond the pale. A gradual subordination of state police forces to a federal command structure would cripple the states' ability to enforce their basic choices and resist tyrannical pressures from above. A radical limitation of the states' ability to tax would make their fiscal solvency a matter of federal grace and ultimately make a mockery of the federalist concerns.

It may be a little harder to come up with equally clearly unconstitutional instances of federal interference with the states' function of enhancing participation, especially since, as I have noted, it is mostly not the state governments themselves but rather their local emanations that provide the primary locus of direct citizen involvement in the political life in America. Even here, though, there may be clear enough cases. For example, given the special participatory mode in which school boards operate in most states, a federal education law that would attempt to transform those boards into an extension of the federal bureaucratic machinery would strike at the very core of participatory politics in the United States.[181]

Furthermore, it would be a mistake to think that cordoning off some areas of state governments from federal interference is the only possible method of implementing the principles of federalism. After all, if it is not the protection of state sovereignty that is at stake here but rather the basic functions of the states within the federal system, it is quite likely that the nature of the central intervention itself should be more determinative of its constitutionality than the local activity interfered with. Thus, for example, many federal laws that depend on state governmental machinery for their implementation attempt, though usually with only very modest success, to assure that the states open the administrative process to citizen involvement. Insofar as such programs attempt to open up state politics to citizen participation, without undermining those aspects of local representative systems that may be important to preventing tyranny, they may be subject to a looser form of control than laws that have

---

181. Even in the area of the enforcement of individual rights, where the courts have been quite willing to interfere with local control over schools to promote racial integration, they have stopped short of a radical transformation of the very structure of local school districting. *Milliken v. Bradley*.

the opposite effect. Similarly, federal laws that provide reimbursements for costs imposed on local governments may be more acceptable than those that constitute a serious drain on state fiscal resources.[183]

Finally, although *National League of Cities* concentrated exclusively on federal interference through a system of direct commands to local governments, federalist concerns also have some implications with respect to national action under the spending power. The common issue that is bound to arise in both contexts, but which was left unanalyzed by *National League of Cities* and its progeny, is the question of when the states are unconstitutionally induced by the national government into something that may impair their ability to fulfill their constitutional functions. In the context of the Commerce Clause, the question arose in *FERC v. Mississippi* as a result of Justice Blackmun's intimation that if the federal government had the power to preempt the states from the field of utility regulation, it could also condition its permission for the states to engage in the regulation of utilities on their acceptance of federally mandated standards and procedures. The ostensible explanation was that since the states were free to withdraw from the field altogether, they were not coerced by the federal requirements. Justice O'Connor's dissent in *FERC* disputed this approach but gave no real criteria for distinguishing incentives from coercion. It is this issue that becomes central when *National League of Cities'* concern with the federal coercion of the states is carried over to spending power legislation,[185] which constitutes the national government's main tool of securing state compliance with its demands. The reason why federalist concerns are usually ignored in the judicial review of spending power legislation is primarily related to the claim that the states are free to refuse to participate in the federal spending programs and thus are not really coerced into anything.[187] Nevertheless, while emphasis on the consent given by the states to the various conditions in federal grants (often quite unrelated to the purposes of the grant itself) may comport quite well with the idea of state sovereignty, the states' consent is often likely to be free in a rather Pickwickian sense. Even apart from coercion, the emphasis on consent may sometimes raise serious questions under the process analysis developed here. Even if the states should "consent" to measures that weaken their organizational capacity to resist tyrannical pressures from the national government or their ability to protect local participatory institutions, it is not clear that the Constitution allows the federal government to undermine its own democratic character by proposing such measures.

Clearly, the prospect of increased judicial control over the federal spending power raises problems of its own, and they are beyond the scope of this article. To recognize, however, the need for judicial concern, based in a well-thought-out theory of constitutional interpretation, does not necessitate an overly active judicial posture. Particularly in those areas in which the determinations required to assess the validity of federal enactments cannot, for some reason, be confidently made by the judiciary, it is always open for the courts to assume a more deferential posture to legislative assessments but to try to assure at the same time that the legislators themselves pay more attention to the factors that judges view as constitutionally important. This has been done in fact by the Court in some areas of Commerce Clause adjudication where judicial deference to a Congressional determination that a given activity concerned interstate

183. The *Garcia* Court mentioned this aspect of the federal legislation at issue there but discounted its relevance in a footnote. [N.] 21.

185. The issue was specifically left open in *National League of Cities*, n. 17.

187. This doctrine was spelled out in *Steward Machine* * * *

commerce was conditioned on the Congress's explicit statement to this effect or a requirement of a series of specific findings.[190] This kind of technique, particularly suited to *Garcia*'s confidence in political accountability, deserves more sustained consideration.

The historical reasons why our federalist jurisprudence has been for so long so barren of new thoughts are not very difficult to fathom. While the Framers had been very much aware that they were creating a new type of government, it was the sterile idea of state sovereignty, basically more appropriate to the old Confederation than the new Union, that came to dominate the thinking about the states. The Civil War, further shifting the balance of the federal system, and the New Deal, which relied so heavily on building up a national bureaucracy, made the old theories even more inadequate. At the same time, however, the best legal minds had little incentive to shore up the jurisprudence of federalism. "Progress" seemed to lie with centralization and chipping away at state rights; the defense of the states seemed to have too many reactionary and racist overtones.

It is time, however, to think again about federalism. Practically all the barriers that federalism once posed for the efficient national regulation of private activities have by now been swept away. One of the positive effects of *Garcia* was to put to rest the old ideas of state sovereignty. In the long run, however, unless we reassess the meaning of our dual system of government, we may not have any more federalism as we know it. This is not to say, of course, that the states will cease to exist altogether, but only that if the message of *Garcia* is misunderstood, the separateness of the state and national bureaucracies may be gradually undermined by ever more complex forms of national control over the local agencies of government. The era of weak national governments is clearly behind us. But for this very reason we should think twice before leaving behind us the era of strong local government as well. It is to be hoped that *Garcia* will come to be seen not as the last word on the subject of federalism but as the new and clean slate on which to inscribe the future jurisprudence of state-national relations.

Faulty national political process and interference with state governmental process. SOUTH CAROLINA v. BAKER, 485 U.S. 505, 108 S.Ct. 1355, 99 L.Ed.2d 592 (1988) rejected two efforts to fit tenth amendment claims into openings in the *Garcia* opinion. In the Tax Equity and Fiscal Responsibility Act of 1982 Congress sought to "reduce the ability of noncompliant taxpayers to conceal income and property from the reach of income, estate and gift taxes" by measures designed to ensure that federal, corporate and state and municipal bonds would be registered in the owners' names, which would provide records of sales and interest payments not feasible under the then-current bearer bonds and interest coupons. Section 110 required that U.S. bonds be so registered, imposed tax burdens on corporate bonds not so registered, and subjected to the federal income tax state and municipal bonds not so registered. *Baker,* per

---

190. See *United States v. Five Gambling Devices,* 346 U.S. 441, 74 S.Ct. 190, 98 L.Ed. 179 (1953) (registration and reporting provisions of a law prohibiting interstate shipment of gambling devices not applicable to local owners of such devices in the absence of spe-cific congressional findings); *United States v. Bass,* 404 U.S. 336, 92 S.Ct. 515, 30 L.Ed.2d 488 (1971) (narrow reading of a federal criminal statute). Cf. *Rewis v. United States,* 401 U.S. 808, 91 S.Ct. 1056, 28 L.Ed.2d 493 (1971) (narrow reading of the Travel Act).

BRENNAN, J., ruled that the latter provision did not violate the tenth amendment:[a]

"The Tenth Amendment limits on Congress' authority to regulate state activities are set out in *Garcia*. *Garcia* holds that the limits are structural, not substantive—i.e., that States must find their protection from congressional regulation through the national political process, not through judicially defined spheres of unregulable state activity. South Carolina contends that the political process failed here because Congress had no concrete evidence quantifying the tax evasion attributable to unregistered state bonds and relied instead on anecdotal evidence that taxpayers have concealed taxable income using bearer bonds. It also argues that Congress chose an ineffective remedy by requiring registration because most bond sales are handled by brokers who must file information reports regardless of the form of the bond and because beneficial ownership of registered bonds need not necessarily be recorded.

"Although *Garcia* left open the possibility that some extraordinary defects in the national political process might render congressional regulation of state activities invalid under the Tenth Amendment, the Court in *Garcia* had no occasion to identify or define the defects that might lead to such invalidation. Nor do we attempt any definitive articulation here. It suffices to observe that South Carolina has not even alleged that it was deprived of any right to participate in the national political process or that it was singled out in a way that left it politically isolated and powerless. Rather, South Carolina argues that the political process failed here because § 310(b)(1) was 'imposed by the vote of an uninformed Congress relying upon incomplete information.' But nothing in *Garcia* or the Tenth Amendment authorizes courts to second-guess the substantive basis for congressional legislation. Where, as here, the national political *process* did not operate in a defective manner, the Tenth Amendment is not implicated.

"The NGA argues that § 310 is invalid because it commandeers the state legislative and administrative process by coercing States into enacting legislation authorizing bond registration and into administering the registration scheme. They cite *FERC v. Mississippi,* which left open the possibility that the Tenth Amendment might set some limits on Congress' power to compel States to regulate on behalf of federal interests. The extent to which the Tenth Amendment claim left open in *FERC* survives *Garcia* or poses constitutional limitations independent of those discussed in *Garcia* is far from clear. We need not, however, address that issue because we find the claim discussed in *FERC* inapplicable to § 310.

"The federal statute at issue in *FERC* required state utility commissions to do the following: (1) adjudicate and enforce federal standards, (2) either consider adopting certain federal standards or cease regulating public utilities, and (3) follow certain procedures. The Court in *FERC* first distinguished *National League of Cities,* noting that the statute in *National League of Cities* presented questions concerning 'the extent to which state sovereignty shields the States from generally applicable federal regulations,' whereas the statute in *FERC* 'attempts to use state regulatory machinery to advance federal goals.' The Court in *FERC* then concluded that, whatever constitutional limitations might exist on the federal power to compel state regulatory activity, Congress had the power to require that state adjudicative bodies adjudicate federal issues and to

a. See fn. j p. 5 of this Supplement for the other ruling that the federal government may   tax private income from state and municipal bonds.

require that States regulating in a pre-emptible field consider suggested federal standards and follow federally mandated procedures.

"Because, by hypothesis, § 310 effectively prohibits issuing unregistered bonds, it presents the very situation *FERC* distinguished from a commandeering of state regulatory machinery: the extent to which the Tenth Amendment 'shields the States from generally applicable federal regulations.' Section 310 regulates state activities; it does not, as did the statute in *FERC*, seek to control or influence the manner in which States regulate private parties. The NGA nonetheless contends that § 310 has commandeered the state legislative and administrative process because many state legislatures had to amend a substantial number of statutes in order to issue bonds in registered form and because state officials had to devote substantial effort to determine how best to implement a registered bond system. Such 'commandeering' is, however, an inevitable consequence of regulating a state activity. Any federal regulation demands compliance. That a State wishing to engage in certain activity must take administrative and sometimes legislative action to comply with federal standards regulating that activity is a commonplace that presents no constitutional defect. After *Garcia*, for example, several States and municipalities had to take administrative and legislative action to alter the employment practices or raise the funds necessary to comply with the wage and overtime provisions of the Federal Labor Standards Act. Indeed, even the pre-*Garcia* line of Tenth Amendment cases recognized that Congress could constitutionally impose federal requirements on States that States could meet only by amending their statutes. See *EEOC v. Wyoming*, n. 2 (Burger, C.J., dissenting) (citing state statutes from over half the States that did not comply with the federal statute upheld by the Court). Under the NGA's theory, moreover, any State could immunize its activities from federal regulation by simply codifying the manner in which it engages in those activities. In short, the NGA's theory of 'commandeering' would not only render *Garcia* a nullity, but would restrict congressional regulation of state activities even more tightly than it was restricted under the now overruled *National League of Cities* line of cases. We find the theory foreclosed by precedent, and uphold the constitutionality of § 310 under the Tenth Amendment."

SCALIA, J., concurred in the judgment but not all of the opinion: "I do not read *Garcia* as adopting—in fact I read it as explicitly disclaiming—the proposition attributed to it in today's opinion that the 'national political process' is the States' only constitutional protection, and that nothing except the demonstration of 'some extraordinary defects' in the operation of that process can justify judicial relief. We said in *Garcia*: 'These cases do not require us to identify or define what affirmative limits *the constitutional structure* might impose on federal action affecting the States under the Commerce Clause.' I agree only that that structure does not prohibit what the Federal Government has done here."

Chapter

DISTRIBUTION OF FEDERAL POWERS: SEPARATION OF POWERS

SECTION: CONGRESSIONAL ACTION AFFECTING PRESIDENTIAL POWERS

APPOINTMENTS POWER

CON LAW: P. 205, after note 2

AMER CON: P. 161, after note 2

MORRISON v. OLSON

__ U.S. __, 108 S.Ct. 2597, 101 L.Ed.2d 569 (1988).

CHIEF JUSTICE REHNQUIST delivered the opinion of the Court.

This case presents us with a challenge to the independent counsel provisions of the Ethics in Government Act of 1978 (Act). We hold today that these provisions of the Act do not violate the Appointments Clause of the Constitution, Art. II, § 2, cl. 2, or the limitations of Article III, nor do they impermissibly interfere with the President's authority under Article II in violation of the constitutional principle of separation of powers.

Briefly stated, Title VI of the Act allows for the appointment of an "independent counsel" to investigate and, if appropriate, prosecute certain high ranking government officials for violations of federal criminal laws.[2] The Act requires the Attorney General, upon receipt of information that he determines is "sufficient to constitute grounds to investigate whether any person [covered by the Act] may have violated any Federal criminal law," to conduct a preliminary investigation of the matter. When the Attorney General has completed this

---

2. [T]he statute applies to violations of "any Federal criminal law other than a violation classified as a Class B or C misdemeanor or an infraction." * * * Section 591(b) sets forth the individuals who may be the target of an investigation by the Attorney General, including the President and Vice President, cabinet level officials, certain high ranking officials in the Executive Office of the President and the Justice Department, the Director and Deputy Director of Central Intelligence, the Commissioner of Internal Revenue, and certain officials involved in the President's national political campaign. Pursuant to § 591(c), the Attorney General may also conduct a preliminary investigation of persons not named in § 591(b) if an investigation by the Attorney General or other Department of Justice official "may result in a personal, financial, or political conflict of interest."

12

investigation, or 90 days has elapsed, he is required to report to a special court (the Special Division) created by the Act "for the purpose of appointing independent counsels."[3] If the Attorney General determines that "there are no reasonable grounds to believe that further investigation is warranted," then he must notify the Special Division of this result. In such a case, "the division of the court shall have no power to appoint an independent counsel." If, however, the Attorney General has determined that there are "reasonable grounds to believe that further investigation or prosecution is warranted," then he "shall apply to the division of the court for the appointment of an independent counsel." The Attorney General's application to the court "shall contain sufficient information to assist the [court] in selecting an independent counsel and in defining that independent counsel's prosecutorial jurisdiction." Upon receiving this application, the Special Division "shall appoint an appropriate independent counsel and shall define that independent counsel's prosecutorial jurisdiction."

With respect to all matters within the independent counsel's jurisdiction, the Act grants the counsel "full power and independent authority to exercise all investigative and prosecutorial functions and powers of the Department of Justice, the Attorney General, and any other officer or employee of the Department of Justice."[6] The functions of the independent counsel include conducting grand jury proceedings and other investigations, participating in civil and criminal court proceedings and litigation, and appealing any decision in any case in which the counsel participates in an official capacity. [T]he counsel's powers include "initiating and conducting prosecutions in any court of competent jurisdiction, framing and signing indictments, filing informations, and handling all aspects of any case, in the name of the United States." The counsel may appoint employees, may request and obtain assistance from the Department of Justice, and may accept referral of matters from the Attorney General if the matter falls within the counsel's jurisdiction as defined by the Special Division. The Act also states that an independent counsel "shall, except where not possible, comply with the written or other established policies of the Department of Justice respecting enforcement of the criminal laws." In addition, whenever a matter has been referred to an independent counsel under the Act, the Attorney General and the Justice Department are required to suspend all investigations and proceedings regarding the matter. * * *

Two statutory provisions govern the length of an independent counsel's tenure in office. The first defines the procedure for removing an independent counsel. Section 596(a)(1) provides:

> "An independent counsel appointed under this chapter may be removed from office, other than by impeachment and conviction, only by the personal action of the Attorney General and only for good cause, physical disability, mental incapacity, or any other condition that substantially impairs the performance of such independent counsel's duties."

If an independent counsel is removed pursuant to this section, the Attorney General is required to submit a report to both the Special Division and the

---

3. The Special Division is a "division of the United States Court of Appeals for the District of Columbia." The court consists of three Circuit Court Judges or Justices appointed by the Chief Justice of the United States. One of the judges must be a judge of the United States Court of Appeals for the District of Columbia, and no two of the judges may be named to the Special Division from a particular court. The judges are appointed for 2-year terms, with any vacancy being filled only for the remainder of the 2-year period.

6. The Attorney General, however, retains "direction or control as to those matters that specifically require the Attorney General's personal action under section 2516 of title 18."

Judiciary Committees of the Senate and the House "specifying the facts found and the ultimate grounds for such removal." Under the current version of the Act, an independent counsel can obtain judicial review of the Attorney General's action by filing a civil action in the United States District Court for the District of Columbia. Members of the Special Division "may not hear or determine any such civil action or any appeal of a decision in any such civil action." * * *

The other provision governing the tenure of the independent counsel defines the procedures for "terminating" the counsel's office. [The office terminates when counsel] notifies the Attorney General that he has completed or substantially completed any investigations or prosecutions undertaken pursuant to the Act. In addition, the Special Division may terminate the office [at] any time if it finds that "the investigation of all matters within the prosecutorial jurisdiction of such [counsel] have been completed or so substantially completed that it would be appropriate for the Department of Justice to complete such investigations and prosecutions."

Finally, the Act provides for Congressional oversight of the activities of independent counsels. An independent counsel may from time to time send Congress statements or reports on his activities. The "appropriate committees of the Congress" are given oversight jurisdiction in regard to the official conduct of an independent counsel, and the counsel is required by the Act to cooperate with Congress in the exercise of this jurisdiction. The counsel is required to inform the House of Representatives of "substantial and credible information which [the counsel] receives [that] may constitute grounds for an impeachment." In addition, the Act gives certain Congressional Committee Members the power to "request in writing that the Attorney General apply for the appointment of an independent counsel." The Attorney General is required to respond to this request within a specified time but is not required to accede to the request.

The proceedings in this case provide an example of how the Act works in practice. [The case arose when the House Judiciary Committee began an investigation into the Justice Department's role in a controversy between the House and the Environmental Protection Agency (EPA) with regard to the Agency's limited production of certain documents that had been subpoenaed during an earlier House investigation. At the time of this earlier investigation, appellee Olson was the Assistant Attorney General for the Office of Legal Counsel, appellee Schmults was Deputy Attorney General, and appellee Dinkins was the Assistant Attorney General for the Land and Natural Resources Division. The Judiciary Committee's Report suggested that Olson had given false and misleading testimony before a House subcommittee and that Schmults and Dinkins had obstructed the EPA investigation by wrongfully withholding certain documents. A copy of the Report was forwarded to the Attorney General with a request that he seek the appointment of an independent counsel to investigate the allegations against appellees.]

[The Attorney General chose to apply to the Special Division for the appointment of an independent counsel solely with respect to Olson, but also requested that independent counsel have authority to investigate "any other matter related to that allegation." Ultimately, pursuant to the Act's provisions, the Special Division appointed appellant as independent counsel with respect to Olson only, and gave her jurisdiction to investigate whether Olson's testimony, or any other matter related thereto, violated federal law. Appellant then asked the Attorney General to refer to her as "related matters" the Committee's allegations against Schmults and Dinkins. The Attorney General refused and the Special Division ruled that the Attorney General's decision not to seek appointment of an independent counsel with respect to the other appellees was final and unreviewable. But the court construed its original grant of jurisdiction as broad enough to permit inquiry into whether Olson had conspired with others, including Schmults and Dinkins, to obstruct the EPA investigation. Following this ruling, appellant caused a grand jury to issue subpoenas on appellees, who moved in Federal District Court to quash the subpoenas, claiming that the Act's independent counsel provisions were unconstitutional. The District Court upheld the Act's constitutionality, denied the motions to quash, and later ordered that appellees be held in contempt for continuing to refuse to comply with the subpoenas. The Court of Appeals reversed (2–1), holding that the Act violated the Appointments Clause of the Constitution, Art. II § 2, cl. 2; the limitations of Article III; and the principle of separation of powers by interfering with the President's authority under Article II.]

We now reverse. * * *

The Appointments Clause of Article II reads as follows:

"[The President] shall nominate, and by and with the Advice and Consent of the Senate, shall appoint Ambassadors, other public Ministers and Consuls, Judges of the supreme Court, and all other Officers of the United States, whose Appointments are not herein otherwise provided for, and which shall be established by Law: but the Congress may by Law vest the Appointment of such inferior Officers, as they think proper, in the President alone, in the Courts of Law, or in the Heads of Departments." U.S. Const., Art. II, § 2, cl. 2.

[As] we stated in *Buckley*, "[p]rincipal officers are selected by the President with the advice and consent of the Senate. Inferior officers Congress may allow to be appointed by the President alone, by the heads of departments, or by the Judiciary." The initial question is, accordingly, whether appellant is an "inferior" or a "principal" officer. If she is the latter, as the Court of Appeals concluded, then the Act is in violation of the Appointments Clause.

* * * We need not attempt here to decide exactly where the line falls between ["inferior" and "principal"] officers, because in our view appellant clearly falls on the "inferior officer" side of that line. Several factors lead to this conclusion.

First, appellant is subject to removal by a higher Executive Branch official. Although appellant may not be "subordinate" to the Attorney General (and the President) insofar as she possesses a degree of independent discretion to exercise the powers delegated to her under the Act, the fact that she can be removed by the Attorney General indicates that she is to some degree "inferior" in rank and authority. Second, appellant is empowered by the Act to perform only certain, limited duties. An independent counsel's role is restricted primarily to investigation and, if appropriate, prosecution for certain federal crimes. [The] grant of authority does not include any authority to formulate policy for the Government or the Executive Branch, nor does it give appellant any administrative duties outside of those necessary to operate her office. The Act specifically provides that in policy matters appellant is to comply to the extent possible with the policies of the Department.

Third, appellant's office is limited in jurisdiction. Not only is the Act itself restricted in applicability to certain federal officials suspected of certain serious federal crimes, but an independent counsel can only act within the scope of the jurisdiction that has been granted by the Special Division pursuant to a request by the Attorney General. Finally, appellant's office * * * is "temporary" in the sense that an independent counsel is appointed essentially to accomplish a single task, and when that task is over the office is terminated, either by the counsel herself or by action of the Special Division. [In] our view, [these factors] are sufficient to establish that appellant is an "inferior" officer in the constitutional sense.

This conclusion is consistent with our few previous decisions that considered the question of whether a particular government official is a "principal" or an "inferior" officer [and] with our reference in *United States* v. *Nixon* to the office of Watergate Special Prosecutor—whose authority was similar to that of appellant—as a "subordinate officer."

This does not, however, end our inquiry under the Appointments Clause. Appellees argue that even if appellant is an "inferior" officer, the Clause does not empower Congress to place the power to appoint such an officer outside the Executive Branch. They contend that the Clause does not contemplate congressional authorization of "interbranch appointments," in which an officer of one branch is appointed by officers of another branch. The relevant language of the Appointments Clause is worth repeating. It reads: "[but] the Congress may by Law vest the Appointment of such inferior Officers, as they think proper, in the President alone, in the courts of Law, or in the Heads of Departments." On its face, the language of this "excepting clause" admits of no limitation on interbranch appointments. Indeed, the inclusion of "as they think proper" seems clearly to give Congress significant discretion to determine whether it is "proper" to vest the appointment of, for example, executive officials in the "courts of Law." We recognized as much in one of our few decisions in this area, *Ex parte Siebold*, 100 U.S. 371, 25 L.Ed. 717 (1880).

We also note that the history of the clause provides no support for appellees' position. [In the course of drafting the Constitution,] there was little or no debate on the question of whether the Clause empowers Congress to provide for interbranch appointments, and there is nothing to suggest that the Framers intended to prevent Congress from having that power.

We do not mean to say that Congress' power to provide for interbranch appointments of "inferior officers" is unlimited. In addition to separation of powers concerns, which would arise if such provisions for appointment had the potential to impair the constitutional functions assigned to one of the branches, *Siebold* itself suggested that Congress' decision to vest the appointment power in the courts would be improper if there was some "incongruity" between the functions normally performed by the courts and the performance of their duty to appoint. [In] this case, however, we do not think it impermissible for Congress to vest the power to appoint independent counsels in a specially created federal court. We thus disagree with the Court of Appeals' conclusion that there is an inherent incongruity about a court having the power to appoint prosecutorial officers.[13] * * *

Congress of course was concerned when it created the office of independent counsel with the conflicts of interest that could arise in situations when the Executive Branch is called upon to investigate its own high-ranking officers. If it were to remove the appointing authority from the Executive Branch, the most

---

13. Indeed, in light of judicial experience with prosecutors in criminal cases, it could be said that courts are especially well qualified to appoint prosecutors. This is not a case in which judges are given power to appoint an officer in an area in which they have no special knowledge or expertise, as in, for example, a statute authorizing the courts to appoint officials in the Department of Agriculture or the Federal Energy Regulatory Commission.

logical place to put it was in the Judicial Branch. In the light of the Act's provision making the judges of the Special Division ineligible to participate in any matters relating to an independent counsel they have appointed, we do not think that appointment of the independent counsels by the court runs afoul of the constitutional limitation on "incongruous" interbranch appointments.

Appellees next contend that the powers vested in the Special Division by the Act conflict with Article III of the Constitution. We have long recognized that by the express provision of Article III, the judicial power of the United States is limited to "Cases" and "Controversies." As a general rule, we have broadly stated that "executive or administrative duties of a nonjudicial nature may not be imposed on judges holding office under Art. III of the Constitution." *Buckley*. The purpose of this limitation is to help ensure the independence of the Judicial Branch and to prevent the judiciary from encroaching into areas reserved for the other branches. With this in mind, we address in turn the various duties given to the Special Division by the Act.

Most importantly, the Act vests in the Special Division the power to choose who will serve as independent counsel and the power to define his or her jurisdiction. Clearly, once it is accepted that the Appointments Clause gives Congress the power to vest the appointment of officials such as the independent counsel in the "courts of Law," there can be no Article III objection to the Special Division's exercise of that power, as the power itself derives from the Appointments Clause, a source of authority for judicial action that is independent of Article III.[16] Appellees contend, however, that the Division's Appointments Clause powers do not encompass the power to define the independent counsel's jurisdiction. We disagree. In our view, Congress' power under the Clause to vest the "Appointment" of inferior officers in the courts may, in certain circumstances, allow Congress to give the courts some discretion in defining the nature and scope of the appointed official's authority. Particularly when, as here, Congress creates a temporary "office" the nature and duties of which will by necessity vary with the factual circumstances giving rise to the need for an appointment in the first place, it may vest the power to define the scope of the office in the court as an incident to the appointment of the officer pursuant to the Appointments Clause. This said, we do not think that Congress may give the Division *unlimited* discretion to determine the independent counsel's jurisdiction. In order for the Division's definition of the counsel's jurisdiction to be truly "incidental" to its power to appoint, the jurisdiction that the court decides upon must be demonstrably related to the factual circumstances that gave rise to the Attorney General's investigation and request for the appointment of the independent counsel in the particular case.

The Act also vests in the Special Division various powers and duties in relation to the independent counsel that, because they do not involve appointing the counsel or defining her jurisdiction, cannot be said to derive from the Division's Appointments Clause authority. These duties include granting extensions for the Attorney General's preliminary investigation; receiving the report of the Attorney General at the conclusion of his preliminary investigation; referring matters to the counsel upon request;[18] receiving reports from the

---

16. We do not think that judicial exercise of the power to appoint, per se, is in any way inconsistent as a functional matter with the courts' exercise of their Article III powers. We note that courts have long participated in the appointment of court officials such as United States commissioners or magistrates without disruption of normal judicial functions. * * *

18. In our view, this provision does not empower the court to expand the original scope of the counsel's jurisdiction; that may be done only upon request of the Attorney

counsel regarding expenses incurred; receiving a report from the Attorney General following the removal of an independent counsel; granting attorney's fees upon request to individuals who were investigated but not indicted by an independent counsel; receiving a final report from the counsel; deciding whether to release the counsel's final report to Congress or the public and determining whether any protective orders should be issued; and terminating an independent counsel when his task is completed, § 596(b)(2).

Leaving aside for the moment the Division's power to terminate an independent counsel, we do not think that Article III absolutely prevents Congress from vesting these other miscellaneous powers in the Special Division pursuant to the Act. As we observed above, one purpose of the broad prohibition upon the courts' exercise of "executive or administrative duties of a nonjudicial nature," *Buckley*, is to maintain the separation between the judiciary and the other branches of the Federal Government by ensuring that judges do not encroach upon executive or legislative authority or undertake tasks that are more properly accomplished by those branches. In this case, the miscellaneous powers described above do not impermissibly trespass upon the authority of the Executive Branch. [The] Act simply does not give the Division the power to "supervise" the independent counsel in the exercise of her investigative or prosecutorial authority. And, the functions that the Special Division is empowered to perform are not inherently "Executive"; indeed, they are directly analogous to functions that federal judges perform in other contexts, such as deciding whether to allow disclosure of matters occurring before a grand jury, deciding to extend a grand jury investigation, or awarding attorney's fees.

We are more doubtful about the Special Division's power to terminate the office of the independent counsel. [As] appellees suggest, the power to terminate, especially when exercised by the Division on its own motion, is "administrative" to the extent that it requires the Special Division to monitor the progress of proceedings of the independent counsel and come to a decision as to whether the counsel's job is "completed." It also is not a power that could be considered typically "judicial," as it has few analogues among the court's more traditional powers. Nonetheless, we do not, as did the Court of Appeals, view this provision as a significant judicial encroachment upon executive power or upon the prosecutorial discretion of the independent counsel.

We think that the Court of Appeals overstated the matter when it described the power to terminate as a "broadsword [and] rapier" that enables the court to "control the pace and depth of the independent counsel's activities." The provision has not been tested in practice, and we do not mean to say that an adventurous special court could not reasonably construe the provision as did the Court of Appeals; but it is the duty of federal courts to construe a statute in order to save it from constitutional infirmities, and to that end we think a narrow construction is appropriate here. The termination provisions of the Act do not give the Special Division anything approaching the power to *remove* the counsel while an investigation or court proceeding is still underway—this power is vested solely in the Attorney General. As we see it, "termination" may occur only when the duties of the counsel are truly "completed" or "so substantially completed" that there remains no need for any continuing action by the independent counsel. It is basically a device for removing from the public payroll an independent counsel who has served her purpose, but is unwilling to

General pursuant to [the Act]. At most, [the Act] authorizes the court simply to refer matters that are "relate[d] to the independent counsel's prosecutorial jurisdiction" as already defined.

acknowledge the fact. So construed, the Special Division's power to terminate does not pose a sufficient threat of judicial intrusion into matters that are more properly within the Executive's authority to require that the Act be invalidated as inconsistent with Article III.

Nor do we believe, as appellees contend, that the Special Division's exercise of the various powers specifically granted to it under the Act poses any threat to the "impartial and independent federal adjudication of claims within the judicial power of the United States." We reach this conclusion for two reasons. First, the Act as it currently stands gives the Special Division itself no power to review any of the actions of the independent counsel or any of the actions of the Attorney General with regard to the counsel. Accordingly, there is no risk of partisan or biased adjudication of claims regarding the independent counsel by that court. Second, the Act prevents members of the Special Division from participating in "*any* judicial proceeding concerning a matter which involves such independent counsel while such independent counsel is serving in that office or which involves the exercise of such independent counsel's official duties, regardless of whether such independent counsel is still serving in that office." (Emphasis added). We think both the special court and its judges are sufficiently isolated by these statutory provisions from the review of the activities of the independent counsel so as to avoid any taint of the independence of the judiciary such as would render the Act invalid under Article III.

We emphasize, nevertheless, that the Special Division has *no* authority to take any action or undertake any duties that are not specifically authorized by the Act. The gradual expansion of the authority of the Special Division might in another context be a bureaucratic success story, but it would be one that would have serious constitutional ramifications. The record in other cases involving independent counsels indicate that the Special Division has at times given advisory opinions or issued orders that are not directly authorized by the Act. [The] propriety of the Special Division's actions in these instances is not before us as such, but we nonetheless think it appropriate to point out not only that there is no authorization for such actions in the Act itself, but that the division's exercise of unauthorized powers risks the transgression of the constitutional limitations of Article III that we have just discussed.

We now turn to consider whether the Act is invalid under the constitutional principle of separation of powers. Two related issues must be addressed: The first is whether the provision of the Act restricting the Attorney General's power to remove the independent counsel to only those instances in which he can show "good cause," taken by itself, impermissibly interferes with the President's exercise of his constitutionally appointed functions. The second is whether, taken as a whole, the Act violates the separation of powers by reducing the President's ability to control the prosecutorial powers wielded by the independent counsel. * * *

Unlike both *Bowsher v. Synar* [p. 36 of this Supplement] and *Myers v. United States* [a primary antecedent for the ruling in *Bowsher*], this case does not involve an attempt by Congress itself to gain a role in the removal of executive officials other than its established powers of impeachment and conviction. The Act instead puts the removal power squarely in the hands of the Executive Branch; an independent counsel may be removed from office, "only by the personal action of the Attorney General, and only for good cause."[23] There is no

---

23. As noted, an independent counsel may also be removed through impeachment and conviction. In addition, the Attorney General may remove a counsel for "physical disability,

requirement of congressional approval of the Attorney General's removal decision, though the decision is subject to judicial review. In our view, the removal provisions of the Act make this case more analogous to *Humphrey's Executor* and *Weiner v. United States*, 357 U.S. 349, 78 S.Ct. 1275, 2 L.Ed.2d 1377 (1958), than to *Myers* or *Bowsher*. * * *

Appellees contend that *Humphrey's Executor* and *Wiener* are distinguishable from this case because they did not involve officials who performed a "core executive function." They argue that our decision in *Humphrey's Executor* rests on a distinction between "purely executive" officials and officials who exercise "quasi-legislative" and "quasi-judicial" powers. In their view, when a "purely executive" official is involved, the governing precedent is *Myers*, not *Humphrey's Executor*. And, under *Myers*, the President must have absolute discretion to discharge "purely" executive officials at will.

We undoubtedly did rely on the terms "quasi-legislative" and "quasi-judicial" to distinguish the officials involved in *Humphrey's Executor* and *Wiener* from those in *Myers*, but our present considered view is that the determination of whether the Constitution allows Congress to impose a "good cause"-type restriction on the President's power to remove an official cannot be made to turn on whether or not that official is classified as "purely executive." [27] The analysis contained in our removal cases is designed not to define rigid categories of those officials who may or may not be removed at will by the President, but to ensure that Congress does not interfere with the President's exercise of the "executive power" and his constitutionally appointed duty to "take care that the laws be faithfully executed" under Article II. *Myers* was undoubtedly correct in its holding, and in its broader suggestion that there are some "purely executive" officials who must be removable by the President at will if he is to be able to accomplish his constitutional role.[29] But, as the Court noted in *Weiner*,

> "The assumption was short-lived that the *Myers* case recognized the President's inherent constitutional power to remove officials no matter what the relation of the executive to the discharge of their duties and no matter what restrictions Congress may have imposed regarding the nature of their tenure."

At the other end of the spectrum from *Myers*, the characterization of the agencies in *Humphrey's Executor* and *Weiner* as "quasi-legislative" or "quasi-judicial" in large part reflected our judgment that it was not essential to the

mental incapacity, or any other condition that substantially impairs the performance" of his duties.

27. Indeed, this Court has never held that the Constitution prevents Congress from imposing limitations on the President's power to remove *all* executive officials simply because they wield "executive" power. *Myers* itself expressly distinguished cases in which Congress had chosen to vest the appointment of "inferior" executive officials in the head of a department. In such a situation, we saw no specific constitutional impediment to congressionally imposed restrictions on the President's removal powers. See also *United States v. Perkins*, 116 U.S. 483, 6 S.Ct. 449, 29 L.Ed. 700 (1886) (" 'The constitutional authority in Congress to thus vest the appointment [of inferior officers in the heads of departments] implies authority to limit, restrict, and

regulate the removal by such laws as Congress may enact in relation to the officers so appointed' ") (quoting the Court of Claims' decision in the case).

29. The dissent says that the language of Article II vesting the executive power of the United States in the President requires that every officer of the United States exercising any part of that power must serve at the pleasure of the President and be removable by him at will. This rigid demarcation—a demarcation incapable of being altered by law in the slightest degree, and applicable to tens of thousands of holders of offices neither known nor foreseen by the framers—depends upon an extrapolation from general constitutional language which we think is more than the text will bear. It is also contrary to our holding in *United States v. Perkins*, decided more than a century ago.

President's proper execution of his Article II powers that these agencies be headed up by individuals who were removable at will.[30] We do not mean to suggest that an analysis of the functions served by the officials at issue is irrelevant. But the real question is whether the removal restrictions are of such a nature that they impede the President's ability to perform his constitutional duty, and the functions of the officials in question must be analyzed in that light.

Considering for the moment the "good cause" removal provision in isolation from the other parts of the Act at issue in this case, we cannot say that the imposition of a "good cause" standard for removal by itself unduly trammels on executive authority. There is no real dispute that the functions performed by the independent counsel are "executive" in the sense that they are law enforcement functions that typically have been undertaken by officials within the Executive Branch. As we noted above, however, the independent counsel is an inferior officer under the Appointments Clause, with limited jurisdiction and tenure and lacking policymaking or significant administrative authority. Although the counsel exercises no small amount of discretion and judgment in deciding how to carry out her duties under the Act, we simply do not see how the President's need to control the exercise of that discretion is so central to the functioning of the Executive Branch as to require as a matter of constitutional law that the counsel be terminable at will by the President.

Nor do we think that the "good cause" removal provision at issue here impermissibly burdens the President's power to control or supervise the independent counsel, as an executive official, in the execution of her duties under the Act. This is not a case in which the power to remove an executive official has been completely stripped from the President, thus providing no means for the President to ensure the "faithful execution" of the laws. Rather, because the independent counsel may be terminated for "good cause," the Executive, through the Attorney General, retains ample authority to assure that the counsel is competently performing her statutory responsibilities in a manner that comports with the provisions of the Act.[32] Although we need not decide in this case exactly what is encompassed within the term "good cause" under the Act, the legislative history of the removal provision also makes clear that the Attorney General may remove an independent counsel for "misconduct." Here, as with the provision of the Act conferring the appointment authority of the independent counsel on the special court, the congressional determination to limit the removal power of the Attorney General was essential, in the view of Congress, to establish the necessary independence of the office. We do not think that this limitation as it presently stands sufficiently deprives the President of control over the independent counsel to interfere impermissibly with his constitutional obligation to ensure the faithful execution of the laws.

The final question to be addressed is whether the Act, taken as a whole, violates the principle of separation of powers by unduly interfering with the role

---

30. The terms also may be used to describe the circumstances in which Congress might be more inclined to find that a degree of independence from the Executive, such as that afforded by a "good cause" removal standard, is necessary to the proper functioning of the agency or official. It is not difficult to imagine situations in which Congress might desire that an official performing "quasi-judicial" functions, for example, would be free of executive or political control.

32. Indeed, during the hearings on the 1982 amendments to the Act, a Justice Department official testified that the "good cause" standard contained in the amendments "would make the special prosecutor no more independent than officers of the many so-called independent agencies in the executive branch." (Associate Attorney General Giuliani).

of the Executive Branch. Time and again we have reaffirmed the importance in our constitutional scheme of the separation of governmental powers into the three coordinate branches. [But], we have never held that the Constitution requires that the three Branches of Government "operate with absolute independence." *Nixon.* In the often-quoted words of Justice Jackson,

> "While the Constitution diffuses power the better to secure liberty, it also contemplates that practice will integrate the dispersed powers into a workable government. It enjoins upon its branches separateness but interdependence, autonomy but reciprocity." [*Steel Seizure* case] (concurring opinion).

We observe first that this case does not involve an attempt by Congress to increase its own powers at the expense of the Executive Branch. [It] simply does not pose a "dange[r] of congressional usurpation of Executive Branch functions." Indeed, with the exception of the power of impeachment—which applies to all officers of the United States—Congress retained for itself no powers of control or supervision over an independent counsel. The Act does empower certain members of Congress to request the Attorney General to apply for the appointment of an independent counsel, but the Attorney General has no duty to comply with the request, although he must respond within a certain time limit. Other than that, Congress' role under the Act is limited to receiving reports or other information and oversight of the independent counsel's activities, functions that we have recognized generally as being incidental to the legislative function of Congress.

Similarly, we do not think that the Act works any *judical* usurpation of properly executive functions. As should be apparent from our discussion of the Appointments Clause above, the power to appoint inferior officers such as independent counsels is not in itself an "executive" function in the constitutional sense, at least when Congress has exercised its power to vest the appointment of an inferior office in the "courts of Law." We note nonetheless that under the Act the Special Division has no power to appoint an independent counsel *sua sponte*; it may only do so upon the specific request of the Attorney General, and the courts are specifically prevented from reviewing the Attorney General's decision not to seek appointment. In addition, once the court has appointed a counsel and defined her jurisdiction, it has no power to supervise or control the activities of the counsel. [The] Act does give a federal court the power to review the Attorney General's decision to remove an independent counsel, but in our view this is a function that is well within the traditional power of the judiciary.

Finally, we do not think that the Act "impermissibly undermine[s]" the powers of the Executive Branch or "disrupts the proper balance between the coordinate branches [by] prevent[ing] the Executive Branch from accomplishing its constitutionally assigned functions," *Nixon v. Administrator of General Services.* It is undeniable that the Act reduces the amount of control or supervision that the Attorney General and, through him, the President exercises over the investigation and prosecution of a certain class of alleged criminal activity. The Attorney General is not allowed to appoint the individual of his choice; he does not determine the counsel's jurisdiction; and his power to remove a counsel is limited. Nonetheless, the Act does give the Attorney General several means of supervising or controlling the prosecutorial powers that may be wielded by an independent counsel. Most importantly, the Attorney General retains the power to remove the counsel for "good cause," a power that we have already concluded provides the Executive with substantial ability to ensure that the laws are "faithfully executed" by an independent counsel. No independent counsel may be appointed without a specific request by the Attorney General, and the

Attorney General's decision not to request appointment if he finds "no reasonable grounds to believe that further investigation is warranted" is committed to his unreviewable discretion. The Act thus gives the Executive a degree of control over the power to initiate an investigation by the independent counsel. In addition, the jurisdiction of the independent counsel is defined with reference to the facts submitted by the Attorney General, and once a counsel is appointed, the Act requires that the counsel abide by Justice Department policy unless it is not "possible" to do so. Notwithstanding the fact that the counsel is to some degree "independent" and free from Executive supervision to a greater extent than other federal prosecutors, in our view these features of the Act give the Executive Branch sufficient control over the independent counsel to ensure that the President is able to perform his constitutionally assigned duties.

In sum, we conclude today that it does not violate the Appointments Clause for Congress to vest the appointment of independent counsels in the Special Division; that the powers exercised by the Special Division under the Act do not violate Article III; and that the Act does not violate the separation of powers principle by impermissibly interfering with the functions of the Executive Branch. The decision of the Court of Appeals is therefore

Reversed.[a]

JUSTICE SCALIA, dissenting. * * *

The framers of the Federal Constitution * * * viewed the principle of separation of powers as the absolutely central guarantee of a just government. * * * Without a secure structure of separated powers, our Bill of Rights would be worthless, as are the bills of rights of many nations of the world that have adopted, or even improved upon, the mere words of ours.

The principle of separation of powers is expressed in our Constitution in the first section of each of the first three Articles. * * * But just as the mere words of a Bill of Rights are not self-effectuating, the framers recognized "[t]he insufficiency of a mere parchment delineation of the boundaries" to achieve the separation of powers. Federalist No. 73 (Hamilton). "[T]he great security," wrote Madison, "against a gradual concentration of the several powers in the same department consists in giving to those who administer each department the necessary constitutional means and personal motives to resist encroachments of the others. The provision for defense must in this, as in all other cases, be made commensurate to the danger of attack." Federalist No. 51. Madison continued:

> "But it is not possible to give to each department an equal power of self-defense. In republican government, the legislative authority necessarily predominates. The remedy for this inconveniency is to divide the legislature into different branches; and to render them, by different modes of election and different principles of action, as little connected with each other as the nature of their common functions and their common dependence on the society will admit. [As] the weight of the legislative authority requires that it should be thus divided, the weakness of the executive may require, on the other hand, that it should be fortified."

The major "fortification" provided, of course, was the veto power. But in addition to providing fortification, the founders conspicuously and very consciously declined to sap the executive's strength in the same way they had weakened the legislature: by dividing the executive power. Proposals to have multiple executives, or a council of advisors with separate authority were

a. Justice Kennedy took no part in the consideration or decision of this case.

rejected. Thus, while "[a]ll legislative Powers herein granted shall be vested in a Congress of the United States, which shall consist of a Senate *and* House of Representatives," U.S. Const., Art. I, § 1, cl. 1 (emphasis added), "[T]he executive Power shall be vested in *a President of the United States*," Art. II, § 1, cl. 1 (emphasis added).

That is what this suit is about. Power. The allocation of power among Congress, the President and the courts in such fashion as to preserve the equilibrium the Constitution sought to establish—so that "a gradual concentration of the several powers in the same department," Federalist No. 51 (J. Madison), can effectively be resisted. Frequently an issue of this sort will come before the Court clad, so to speak, in sheep's clothing: the potential of the asserted principle to effect important change in the equilibrium of power is not immediately evident, and must be discerned by a careful and perceptive analysis. But this wolf comes as a wolf. * * *

As a general matter, the Act before us here requires the Attorney General to apply for the appointment of an independent counsel within 90 days after receiving a request to do so, unless he determines within that period that "there are no reasonable grounds to believe that further investigation or prosecution is warranted." As a practical matter, it would be surprising if the Attorney General had any choice (assuming this statute is constitutional) but to seek appointment of an independent counsel to pursue the charges against the principal object of the congressional request, Mr. Olson. Merely the political consequences (to him and the President) of seeming to break the law by refusing to do so would have been substantial. How could it not be, the public would ask, that a 3,000-page indictment drawn by our representatives over 2½ years [referring to the Judiciary Committee's Report] does not even establish "reasonable grounds to believe" that further investigation or prosecution is warranted with respect to at least the principal alleged culprit? But the Act establishes more than just practical compulsion. Although the Court's opinion asserts that the Attorney General had "no duty to comply with the [congressional] request," that is not entirely accurate. He *had* a duty to comply unless he could conclude that there were "*no reasonable grounds to believe*," not that prosecution was warranted, but merely that "*further investigation*" was warranted, 28 U.S.C. § 592(b)(1) (emphasis added), after a 90-day investigation in which he was prohibited from using such routine investigative techniques as grand juries, plea bargaining, grants of immunity or even subpoenas. The Court also makes much of the fact that "the courts are specifically prevented from reviewing the Attorney General's decision not to seek appointment." Yes, but *Congress* is not prevented from reviewing it. The context of this statute is acrid with the smell of threatened impeachment. Where, as here, a request for appointment of an independent counsel has come from the Judiciary Committee of either House of Congress, the Attorney General must, if he decides not to seek appointment, explain to that Committee why. * * *

Thus, by the application of this statute in the present case, Congress has effectively compelled a criminal investigation of a high-level appointee of the President in connection with his actions arising out of a bitter power dispute between the President and the Legislative Branch. Mr. Olson may or may not be guilty of a crime; we do not know. But we do know that the investigation of him has been commenced, not necessarily because the President or his authorized subordinates believe it is in the interest of the United States, in the sense that it warrants the diversion of resources from other efforts, and is worth the cost in money and in possible damage to other governmental interests; and not even, leaving aside those normally considered factors, because the President or his authorized subordinates necessarily believe that an investigation is likely to unearth a violation worth prosecuting; but only because the Attorney General cannot affirm, as Congress demands, that there are *no reasonable grounds to believe* that further investigation is warranted. The decisions regarding the scope of that further investigation, its duration, and, finally, whether or not prosecution should ensue, are likewise beyond the control of the President and his subordinates.

If to describe this case is not to decide it, the concept of a government of separate and coordinate powers no longer has meaning. The Court devotes most of its attention to such relatively technical details as the Appointments Clause and the removal power, addressing briefly and only at the end of its opinion the separation of powers. As my prologue suggests, I think that has it backwards. Our opinions are full of the recognition that it is the principle of separation of powers, and the inseparable corollary that each department's "defense must [be] made commensurate to the danger of attack," Federalist No. 51 (J. Madison), which gives comprehensible content to the appointments clause, and determines the appropriate scope of the removal power. Thus, while I will subsequently discuss why our appointments and removal jurisprudence does not support today's holding, I begin with a consideration of the fountainhead of that jurisprudence, the separation and equilibration of powers.

First, however, I think it well to call to mind an important and unusual premise that underlies our deliberations, a premise not expressly contradicted by the Court's opinion, but in my view not faithfully observed. It is rare in a case dealing, as this one does, with the constitutionality of a statute passed by the Congress of the United States, not to find anywhere in the Court's opinion the usual, almost formulary caution that we owe great deference to Congress' view that what it has done is constitutional, and that we will decline to apply the statute only if the presumption of constitutionality can be overcome. That caution is not recited by the Court in the present case *because it does not apply.* Where a private citizen challenges action of the Government on grounds unrelated to separation of powers, harmonious functioning of the system demands that we ordinarily give some deference, or a presumption of validity, to the actions of the political branches in what is agreed, between themselves at least, to be within their respective spheres. But where the issue pertains to separation of powers, and the political branches are (as here) in disagreement, neither can be presumed correct. [The] playing field for the present case, in other words, is a level one. As one of the interested and coordinate parties to the underlying constitutional dispute, Congress, no more than the President, is entitled to the benefit of the doubt.

To repeat, Art. II, § 1, cl. 1 of the Constitution provides:

"The executive Power shall be vested in a President of the United States."

[T]his does not mean *some of* the executive power, but *all of* the executive power. It seems to me, therefore, that the decision [below] must be upheld on fundamental separation-of-powers principles if the following two questions are answered affirmatively: (1) Is the conduct of a criminal prosecution (and of an investigation to decide whether to prosecute) the exercise of purely executive power? (2) Does the statute deprive the President of the United States of exclusive control over the exercise of that power? Surprising to say, the Court appears to concede an affirmative answer to both questions, but seeks to avoid the inevitable conclusion that since the statute vests some purely executive power in a person who is not the President of the United States it is void.

The Court concedes that "[t]here is no real dispute that the functions performed by the independent counsel are 'executive,'" though it qualifies that concession by adding "in the sense that they are 'law enforcement' functions that typically have been undertaken by officials within the Executive Branch." The qualifier adds nothing but atmosphere. In what *other* sense can one identify "the executive Power" that is supposed to be vested in the President (unless it includes everything the Executive Branch is given to do) *except* by reference to what has always and everywhere—if conducted by Government at all—been conducted never by the legislature, never by the courts, and always by the executive. There is no possible doubt that the independent counsel's functions fit this description. She is vested with the "full power and independent authority to exercise all *investigative and prosecutorial* functions and powers of the Department of Justice [and] the Attorney General." 28 U.S.C. § 594(a) (emphasis added). Governmental investigation and prosecution of crimes is a quintessentially executive function.

As for the second question, whether the statute before us deprives the President of exclusive control over that quintessentially executive activity: The Court does not, and could not possibly, assert that it does not. That is indeed the whole object of the statute. Instead, the Court points out that the President, through his Attorney General, has at least *some* control. That concession is alone enough to invalidate the statute, but I cannot refrain from pointing out that the Court greatly exaggerates the extent of that "some" presidential control. "Most importan[t]" among these controls, the Court asserts, is the Attorney General's "power to remove the counsel for 'good cause.'" This is somewhat like referring to shackles as an effectve means of locomotion. As we recognized in *Humphrey's Executor*—indeed, what *Humphrey's Executor* was all about—limiting removal power to "good cause" is an impediment to, not an effective grant of, presidential control. * * * What we in *Humphrey's Executor* found to be a means of eliminating presidential control, the Court today considers the "most importan[t]" means of assuring presidential control. Congress, of course, operated under no such illusion when it enacted this statute, describing the "good cause" limitation as "protecting the independent counsel's ability to act independently of the President's direct control" since it permits removal only for "misconduct." H.R.Conf.Rep. 100–452.

Moving on to the presumably "less important" controls that the President retains, the Court notes that no independent counsel may be appointed without a specific request from the Attorney General. As I have discussed above, the condition that renders such a request mandatory (inability to find "no reasonable grounds to believe" that further investigation is warranted) is so insubstantial that the Attorney General's discretion is severely confined. And once the referral is made, it is for the Special Division to determine the scope and duration of the investigation. And in any event, the limited power over referral is irrelevant to the question whether, *once appointed*, the independent counsel exercises executive power free from the President's control. Finally, the Court points out that the Act directs the independent counsel to abide by general Justice Department policy, except when not "possible." The exception alone shows this to be an empty promise. Even without that, however, one would be hard put to come up with many investigative or prosecutorial "policies" (other than those imposed by the Constitution or by Congress through law) that are absolute. Almost all investigative and prosecutorial decisions—including the ultimate decision whether, after a technical violation of the law has been found, prosecution is warranted—involve the balancing of innumerable legal and practical considerations. Indeed, even political considerations (in the nonpartisan sense) must be considered, as exemplified by the recent decision of an independent counsel to subpoena the former Ambassador of Canada, producing considerable tension in our relations with that country. Another preeminently political decision is whether getting a convicton in a particular case is worth the disclosure of national security information that would be necessary. The Justice Department and our intelligence agencies are often in disagreement on this point, and the Justice Department does not always win. The present Act even goes so far as specifically to take the resolution of that dispute away from the President and give it to the independent counsel. In sum, the balancing of various legal, practical and political considerations, none of which is absolute, is the very essence of prosecutorial discretion. To take this away is to remove the core of the prosecutorial function, and not merely "some" presidential control.

As I have said, however, it is ultimately irrelevant *how much* the statute reduces presidential control. The case is over when the Court acknowledges, as it must, that "[i]t is undeniable that the Act reduces the amount of control or supervision that the Attorney General and, through him, the President exercises over the investigation and prosecution of a certain class of alleged criminal activity." It effects a revolution in our constitutional jurisprudence for the Court, once it has determined that (1) purely executive functions are at issue here, and (2) those functions have been given to a person whose actions are not fully within the supervision and control of the President, nonetheless to proceed further to sit in judgment of whether "the President's need to control the exercise of [the independent counsel's] discretion is *so central* to the functioning of the Executive Branch" as to require complete control (emphasis added), whether the conferral of his powers upon someone else "*sufficiently* deprives the President of control over the independent counsel to interfere impermissibly with [his] constitutional obligation to ensure the faithful execution of the laws" (emphasis added), and whether "the Act give[s] the Executive Branch *sufficient* control over the independent counsel to ensure that the President is able to perform his constitutionally assigned duties" (emphasis added). It is not for us to determine, and we have never presumed to determine, how much of the purely executive powers of government must be within the full control of the President. The Constitution prescribes that they *all* are.

The utter incompatibility of the Court's approach with our constitutional traditions can be made more clear, perhaps, by applying it to the powers of the other two Branches. Is it conceivable that if Congress passed a statute depriving itself of less than full and entire control over some insignificant area of legislation, we would inquire whether the matter was "*so central* to the functioning of the Legislative Branch" as really to require complete control, or whether the statute gives Congress "*sufficient* control over the surrogate legislator to ensure that Congress is able to perform its constitutionally assigned duties"? Of course we would have none of that. Once we determined that a purely legislative power was at issue we would require it to be exercised, wholly and entirely, by Congress. * * * We should say here that the President's constitutionally assigned duties include *complete* control over investigation and prosecution of violations of the law, and that the inexorable command of Article II is clear and definite: the executive power must be vested in the President of the United States.

Is it unthinkable that the President should have such exclusive power, even when alleged crimes by him or his close associates are at issue? No more so than that Congress should have the exclusive power of legislation, even when what is at issue is its own exemption from the burdens of certain laws. * * * No more so than that this Court should have the exclusive power to pronounce the final decision on justiciable cases and controversies, even those pertaining to the constitutionality of a statute reducing the salaries of the Justices. A system of separate and coordinate powers necessarily involves an acceptance of exclusive power that can theoretically be abused. * * * While the separation of powers may prevent us from righting every wrong, it does so in order to ensure that we do not lose liberty. The checks against any Branch's abuse of its exclusive powers are twofold: First, retaliation by one of the other Branch's use of *its* exclusive powers: Congress, for example, can impeach the Executive who willfully fails to enforce the laws; the Executive can decline to prosecute under unconstitutional statutes; and the courts can dismiss malicious prosecutions. Second, and ultimately, there is the political check that the people will replace those in the political branches [who] are guilty of abuse. Political pressures produced special prosecutors—for Teapot Dome and for Watergate, for example—long before this statute created the independent counsel.

The Court has, nonetheless, replaced the clear constitutional prescription that the executive power belongs to the President with a "balancing test." What are the standards to determine how the balance is to be struck, that is, how much removal of presidential power is too much? Many countries of the world get along with an Executive that is much weaker than ours—in fact, entirely dependent upon the continued support of the legislature. Once we depart from the text of the Constitution, just where short of that do we stop? The most amazing feature of the Court's opinion is that it does not even purport to give an answer. It simply *announces,* with no analysis, that the ability to control the decision whether to investigate and prosecute the President's closest advisors, and indeed the President himself, is not "so central to the functioning of the Executive Branch" as to be constitutionally required to be within the President's control. Apparently that is so because we say it is so. * * * Evidently, the governing standard is to be what might be called the unfettered wisdom of a majority of this Court, revealed to an obedient people on a case-by-case basis. This is not only not the government of laws that the Constitution established; it is not a government of laws at all.

In my view, moreover, even as an ad hoc, standardless judgment the Court's conclusion must be wrong. Before this statute was passed, the President, in taking action disagreeable to the Congress, or an executive officer giving advice to the President or testifying before Congress concerning one of those many matters on which the two branches are from time to time at odds, could be assured that his acts and motives would be adjudged—insofar as the decision whether to conduct a criminal investigation and to prosecute is concerned—in the Executive Branch, that is, in a forum attuned to the interests and the policies of the Presidency. That was one of the natural advantages the Constitution gave to the Presidency, just as it gave Members of Congress (and their staffs) the advantage of not being prosecutable for anything said or done in their legislative capacities. It is the very object of this legislation to eliminate that assurance of a sympathetic forum. Unless it can honestly be said that there are "no reasonable grounds to believe" that further investigation is warranted, further investigation must ensue; and the conduct of the investigation, and determination of whether to prosecute, will be given to a person neither selected by nor subject to the control of the President—who will in turn assemble a staff by finding out, presumably, who is willing to put aside whatever else they are doing, for an indeterminate period of time, in order to investigate and prosecute the President or a particular named individual in his administration. The prospect is frightening [even] outside the context of a bitter, interbranch political dispute. Perhaps the boldness of the President himself will not be affected—though I am not even sure of that. (How much easier it is for Congress, instead of accepting the political damage attendant to the commencement of impeachment proceedings against the President on trivial grounds—or, for that matter, how easy it is for one of the President's political foes outside of Congress—simply to trigger a debilitating criminal investigation of the Chief Executive under this law.) But as for the President's high-level assistants, who typically have no political base of support, it is as utterly unrealistic to think that they will not be intimidated by this prospect, and that their advice to him and their advocacy of his interests before a hostile Congress will not be affected, as it would be to think that the Members of Congress and their staffs would be unaffected by replacing the Speech or Debate Clause with a similar provision. It deeply wounds the President, by substantially reducing the President's ability to protect himself and his staff. That is the whole object of the law, of course, and I cannot imagine why the Court believes it does not succeed.

Besides weakening the Presidency by reducing the zeal of his staff, it must also be obvious that the institution of the independent counsel enfeebles him more directly in his constant confrontations with Congress, by eroding his public support. Nothing is so politically effective as the ability to charge that one's opponent and his associates are not merely wrong-headed, naive, ineffective, but, in all probability, "crooks." And nothing so effectively gives an appearance of validity to such charges as a Justice Department investigation and, even better, prosecution. The present statute provides ample means for that sort of attack, assuring that massive and lengthy investigations will occur, not merely when the Justice Department in the application of its usual standards believes they are called for, but whenever it cannot be said that there are "no reasonable grounds to believe" they are called for. The statute's highly visible procedures assure, moreover, that unlike most investigations these will be widely known and prominently displayed. * * *

In sum, this statute does deprive the President of substantial control over the prosecutory functions performed by the independent counsel, and it does substantially affect the balance of powers. That the Court could possibly conclude otherwise demonstrates both the wisdom of our former constitutional system, in which the degree of reduced control and political impairment were irrelevant, since *all* purely executive power had to be in the President; and the folly of the new system of standardless judicial allocation of powers we adopt today. * * *

Because appellant (who all parties and the Court agree is an officer of the United States) was not appointed by the President with the advice and consent of the Senate, but rather by the Special Division of the United States Court of Appeals, her appointment is constitutional only if (1) she is an "inferior" officer within the meaning of the above clause, and (2) Congress may vest her appointment in a court of law.

As to the first of these inquiries, the Court does not attempt to "decide exactly" what establishes the line between principal and "inferior" officers, but is confident that, whatever the line may be, appellant "clearly falls on the 'inferior officer' side" of it. The Court gives three reasons: *First,* she "is subject to removal by a higher Executive branch official," namely the Attorney General. *Second,* she is "empowered by the Act to perform only certain, limited duties." *Third,* her office is "limited in jurisdiction" and "limited in tenure."

The first of these lends no support to the view that appellant is an inferior officer. Appellant is removable only for "good cause" or physical or mental incapacity. By contrast, most (if not all) *principal* officers in the Executive Branch may be removed by the President *at will.* I fail to see how the fact that appellant is more difficult to remove than most principal officers helps to establish that she is an inferior officer. And I do not see how it could possibly make any difference to her superior or inferior status that the President's limited power to remove her must be exercised through the Attorney General.

[The] second reason offered by the Court—that appellant performs only certain, limited duties—may be relevant to whether she is an inferior officer, but it mischaracterizes the extent of her powers. As the Court states: "Admittedly, the Act delegates to appellant [the] '*full power and independent authority to exercise all investigative and prosecutorial functions and powers of the Department of Justice.*'" (Emphasis added).[2] Moreover, in addition to this general grant of power she is given a broad range of specifically enumerated powers, including a power not even the Attorney General possesses: to "contes[t] in court [any] claim of privilege or attempt to withhold evidence on grounds of national security." Once all of this is "admitted," it seems to me impossible to maintain that appellant's authority is so "limited" as to render her an inferior officer. The Court seeks to brush this away by asserting that the independent counsel's power does not include any authority to "formulate policy for the Government or the Executive Branch." But the same could be said for all officers of the Government, with the single exception of the President. All of them only formulate policy within their respective spheres of responsibility—as does the independent counsel, who must comply with the policies of the Department of Justice only "to the extent possible."

The final set of reasons given by the Court for why the independent counsel clearly is an inferior officer emphasizes the limited nature of her jurisdiction and tenure. Taking the latter first, I find nothing unusually limited about the independent counsel's tenure. To the contrary, unlike most high-ranking Executive Branch officials, she continues to serve until she (or the Special Division) decides that her work is substantially completed. This particular independent prosecutor has already served more than two years, which is at least as long as many cabinet officials. As to the scope of her jurisdiction, there can be no doubt that is small (though far from unimportant). But within it she exercises more than the full power of the Attorney General. The Ambassador to Luxembourg is not anything less than a principal officer, simply because Luxembourg is small. And the federal judge who sits in a small district is not for that reason "inferior in rank and authority." If the mere fragmentation of Executive responsibilities into small compartments suffices to render the heads of each of those compartments inferior officers, then Congress could deprive the President of the right to appoint his chief law-enforcement officer by dividing up the Attorney General's responsibilities among a number of "lesser" functionaries.

---

2. The Court omits the further provision that the independent counsel exercises within her sphere the "full power" of "*the Attorney General,* [with one minor exception relating to wiretap authorizations] and any other officer or employee of the Department of Justice[.]" 28 U.S.C. § 594(a). This is of course quite difficult to square with the Court's assertion that appellant is " 'inferior' in rank and authority" to the Attorney General.

More fundamentally, however, it is not clear from the Court's opinion why the factors it discusses—even if applied correctly to the facts of this case—are determinative of the question of inferior officer status. [T]he text of the Constitution and the division of power that it establishes [demonstrate] that the independent counsel is not an inferior officer because she is not *subordinate* to any officer in the Executive Branch (indeed, not even to the President). Dictionaries in use at the time of the Constitutional Convention gave the word "inferior" two meanings which it still bears today: (1) "[l]ower in place, * * * station, * * * rank of life, * * * value or excellency," and (2) "[s]ubordinate." In a document dealing with the structure (the constitution) of a government, one would naturally expect the word to bear the latter meaning— indeed, in such a context it would be unpardonably careless to use the word *unless* a relationship of subordination was intended. If what was meant was merely "lower in station or rank," one would use instead a term such as "lesser officers." At the only other point in the Constitution at which the word "inferior" appears, it plainly connotes a relationship of subordination. Article III vests the judicial Power of the United States in "one supreme Court, and in such *inferior* Courts as the Congress may from time to time ordain and establish." (Emphasis added). In Federalist No. 81, Hamilton pauses to describe the "inferior" courts authorized by Art. III as inferior in the sense that they are "subordinate" to the Supreme Court.

That "inferior" means "subordinate" is also consistent with what little we know about the evolution of the Appointments Clause. * * *

This interpretation is, moreover, consistent with our admittedly sketchy precedent in this area. [In] *Nixon* we noted that the Attorney General's appointment of the Watergate Special Prosecutor was made pursuant to the Attorney General's "power to appoint *subordinate officers* to assist him in the discharge of his duties." (Emphasis added). The Court's citation of *Nixon* as support for its view that the independent counsel is an inferior officer is simply not supported by a reading of the case. We explicitly stated that the Special Prosecutor was a "subordinate office[r]" because, in the end, the President or the Attorney General could have removed him at any time, if by no other means than amending or revoking the regulation defining his authority. Nor are any of the other cases cited by the Court in support of its view inconsistent with the natural reading that an inferior officer must at least be subordinate to another officer of the United States. * * *

To be sure, it is not a *sufficient* condition for "inferior" officer status that one be subordinate to a principal officer. Even an officer who is subordinate to a department head can be a principal officer. [But] it is surely a *necessary* condition for inferior officer status that the officer be subordinate to another officer.

The independent counsel is not even subordinate to the President. The Court essentially admits as much, noting that "appellant may not be 'subordinate' to the Attorney General (and the President) insofar as she possesses a degree of independent discretion to exercise the powers delegated to her under the Act." In fact, there is no doubt about it. As noted earlier, the Act specifically grants her the "*full* power and *independent* authority to exercise *all* investigative and prosecutorial functions of the Department of Justice" and makes her removable only for "good cause," a limitation specifically intended to ensure that she be *independent* of, not *subordinate* to, the President and the Attorney General. See H.R.Conf.Rep. No. 100–452.

Because appellant is not subordinate to another officer, she is not an "inferior" officer and her appointment other than by the President with the advice and consent of the Senate is unconstitutional.

I will not discuss at any length why the restrictions upon the removal of the independent counsel also violate our established precedent dealing with that specific subject. For most of it, I simply refer the reader to the scholarly opinion of Judge Silberman for the Court of Appeals below. I cannot avoid commenting, however, about the essence of what the Court has done to our removal jurisprudence today.

There is of course no provision in the Constitution stating who may remove executive officers, except the provisions for removal by impeachment. Before the present decision it was established, however, (1) that the President's power to remove principal officers who exercise purely executive powers could not be restricted, see *Myers,* and (2) that his power to remove inferior officers who exercise purely executive powers, and whose appointment Congress had removed from the usual procedure of presidential appointment with Senate consent, could be restricted, at least where the appointment had been made by an officer of the Executive Branch.[4]

The Court could have resolved the removal power issue in this case by simply relying upon its erroneous conclusion that the independent counsel was an inferior officer, and then extending our holding that the removal of inferior officers appointed by the Executive can be restricted, to a new holding that even the removal of inferior officers appointed by the courts can be restricted. That would in my view be a considerable and unjustified extension, giving the Executive full discretion in *neither* the selection *nor* the removal of a purely executive officer. The course the Court has chosen, however, is even worse.

[Since] *Humphrey's Executor*—which was considered by many at the time the product of an activist, anti-New Deal Court bent on reducing the power of President Franklin Roosevelt—it has been established that the line of permissible restriction upon removal of principal officers lies at the point at which the powers exercised by those officers are no longer purely executive. Thus, removal restrictions have been generally regarded as lawful for so-called "independent regulatory agencies," such as the Federal Trade Commission, [which] engage substantially in what has been called the "quasi-legislative activity" of rulemaking, and for members of Article I courts, such as the Court of Military Appeals, who engage in the "quasi-judicial" function of adjudication. It has often been observed, correctly in my view, that the line between "purely executive" functions and "quasi-legislative" or "quasi-judicial" functions is not a clear one or even a rational one. But at least it permitted the identification of certain officers, and certain agencies, whose functions were entirely within the control of the President. Congress had to be aware of that restriction in its legislation.

---

4. The Court misunderstands my opinion to say that "every officer of the United States exercising any part of [the executive] power must serve at the pleasure of the President and be removable by him at will" [fn. 29]. Of course, as my discussion here demonstrates, that has never been the law and I do not assert otherwise. What I *do* assert—and what the Constitution seems plainly to prescribe—is that the President must have control over all exercises of the executive power. That requires that he have plenary power to remove principal officers such as the independent counsel, but it does not require that he have plenary power to remove inferior officers. Since the latter are, as I have described, subordinate to, i.e., subject to the supervision of, principal officers who (being removable at will) have the President's complete confidence, it is enough—at least if they have been appointed by the President or by a principal officer—that they be removable *for cause,* which would include, of course, the failure to accept supervision. Thus, *Perkins* is in no way inconsistent with my views.

Today, however, *Humphrey's Executor* is swept into the dustbin of repudiated constitutional principles. "[O]ur present considered view," the Court says, "is that the determination of whether the Constitution allows Congress to impose a 'good cause'-type restriction on the President's power to remove an official cannot be made to turn on whether or not that official is classified as 'purely executive.'" What *Humphrey's Executor* (and presumably *Myers*) really means, we are now told, is not that there are any "rigid categories of those officials who may or may not be removed at will by the President," but simply that Congress cannot "interfere with the President's exercise of the 'executive power' and his constitutionally appointed duty to 'take care that the laws be faithfully executed.'"

One can hardly grieve for the shoddy treatment given today to *Humphrey's Executor,* which, after all, accorded the same dignity (with much less justification) to Chief Justice Taft's opinion 10 years earlier in *Myers* * * *. It is in fact comforting to witness the reality that he who lives by the *ipse dixit* dies by the *ipse dixit*. But one must grieve for the Constitution. *Humphrey's Executor* at least had the decency formally to observe the constitutional principle that the President had to be the repository of *all* executive power, which, as *Myers* carefully explained, necessarily means that he must be able to discharge those who do not perform executive functions according to his liking. [By] contrast, "our present considered view" is simply that *any* Executive officer's removal can be restricted, so long as the President remains "able to accomplish his constitutional role." There are now no lines. If the removal of a prosecutor, the virtual embodiment of the power to "take care that the laws be faithfully executed," can be restricted, what officer's removal cannot? This is an open invitation for Congress to experiment. What about a special Assistant Secretary of State, with responsibility for one very narrow area of foreign policy, who would not only have to be confirmed by the Senate but could also be removed only pursuant to certain carefully designed restrictions? Could this possibly render the President "[un]able to accomplish his constitutional role"? Or a special Assistant Secretary of Defense for Procurement? The possibilities are endless, and the Court does not understand what the separation of powers * * * is all about, if it does not expect Congress to try them. As far as I can discern from the Court's opinion, it is now open season upon the President's removal power for all executive officers, with not even the superficially principled restriction of *Humphrey's Executor* as cover. The Court essentially says to the President "Trust us. We will make sure that you are able to accomplish your constitutional role." I think the Constitution gives the President—and the people—more protection than that.

The purpose of the separation and equilibration of powers in general, and of the unitary Executive in particular, was not merely to assure effective government but to preserve individual freedom. Those who hold or have held offices covered by the Ethics in Government Act are entitled to that protection as much as the rest of us, and I conclude my discussion by considering the effect of the Act upon the fairness of the process they receive.

Only someone who has worked in the field of law enforcement can fully appreciate the vast power and the immense discretion that are placed in the hands of a prosecutor with respect to the objects of his investigation [quoting Justice Robert Jackson, when he was Attorney General under President Franklin Roosevelt].

Under our system of government, the primary check against prosecutorial abuse is a political one. The prosecutors who exercise this awesome discretion are selected and can be removed by a President, whom the people have trusted enough to elect. Moreover, when crimes are not investigated and prosecuted fairly, nonselectively, with a reasonable sense of proportion, the President pays the cost in political damage to his administration. [That] result, of course, was precisely what the Founders had in mind when they provided that all executive powers would be exercised by a *single* Chief Executive. [The] President is directly dependent on the people, and since there is only *one* President, *he* is responsible. * * *

That is the system of justice the rest of us are entitled to, but what of that select class consisting of present or former high-level executive-branch officials? If an allegation is made against them of any violation of any federal criminal law (except Class B or C misdemeanors or infractions) the Attorney General must give it his attention. That in itself is not objectionable. But if, after a 90-day investigation without the benefit of normal investigatory tools, the Attorney General is unable to say that there are "no reasonable grounds to believe" that further investigation is warranted, a process is set in motion that is *not* in the full control of persons "dependent on the people," and whose flaws cannot be blamed on the President. An independent counsel is selected, and the scope of her authority prescribed, by a panel of judges. What if they are politically partisan, as judges have been known to be, and select a prosecutor antagonistic to the administration, or even to the particular individual who has been selected for this special treatment? There is no remedy for that, not even a political one. Judges, after all, have life tenure, and appointing a sure-fire enthusiastic prosecutor could hardly be considered an impeachable offense. So if there is anything wrong with the selection, there is effectively no one to blame. * * * What would be the reaction if, in an area not covered by this statute, the Justice Department posted a public notice inviting applicants to assist in an investigation and possible prosecution of a certain prominent person? Does this not invite what Justice Jackson described as "picking the man and then searching the law books, or putting investigators to work, to pin some offense on him"? To be sure, the investigation must relate to the area of criminal offense specified by the life-tenured judges. But that has often been (and nothing prevents it from being) very broad—and should the independent counsel or her staff come up with something beyond that scope, nothing prevents her from asking the judges to expand her authority or, if that does not work, referring it to the Attorney General, whereupon the whole process would recommence and, if there was "reasonable basis to believe" that further investigation was warranted, that new offense would be referred to the Special Tribunal, which would in all likelihood assign it to the same independent counsel. It seems to me not conducive to fairness. But even if it were entirely evident that unfairness was in fact the result—the judges hostile to the administration, the independent counsel an old foe of the President, the staff refugees from the recently defeated administration—*there would be no one accountable to the public to whom the blame could be assigned.*

I do not mean to suggest that anything of this sort (other than the inevitable self-selection of the prosecutory staff) occurred in the present case. [But] the fairness of a process must be adjudged on the basis of what it permits to happen, not what it produced in a particular case. It is true, of course, that a similar list of horribles could be attributed to an ordinary Justice Department prosecution—a vindictive prosecutor, an antagonistic staff, etc. But the difference is the difference that the Founders envisioned when they established a single Chief

Executive accountable to the people: the blame can be assigned to someone who can be punished. * * *

It is [an] additional advantage of the unitary Executive that it can achieve a more uniform application of the law. Perhaps that is not always achieved, but the mechanism to achieve it is there. The mini-Executive that is the independent counsel, however, operating in an area where so little is law and so much is discretion, is intentionally cut off from the unifying influence of the Justice Department, and from the perspective that multiple responsibilities provide. What would normally be regarded as a technical violation (there are no rules defining such things), may in her small world assume the proportions of an indictable offense. What would normally be regarded as an investigation that has reached the level of pursuing such picayune matters that it should be concluded, may to her be an investigation that ought to go on for another year. How frightening it must be to have your own independent counsel and staff appointed, with nothing else to do but to investigate you until investigation is no longer worthwhile—with whether it is worthwhile not depending upon what such judgments usually hinge on, competing responsibilities. And to have that counsel and staff decide, with no basis for comparison, whether what you have done is bad enough, willful enough, and provable enough, to warrant an indictment. How admirable the constitutional system that provides the means to avoid such a distortion. And how unfortunate the judicial decision that has permitted it.

* * *

The notion that every violation of law should be prosecuted, including—indeed, *especially*—every violation by those in high places, is an attractive one, and it would be risky to argue in an election campaign that that is not an absolutely overriding value. [The] reality is, however, that it is not an absolutely overriding value, and it was with the hope that we would be able to acknowledge and apply such realities that the Constitution spared us, by life tenure, the necessity of election campaigns. I cannot imagine that there are not many thoughtful men and women in Congress who realize that the benefits of this legislation are far outweighed by its harmful effect upon our system of government, and even upon the nature of justice received by those men and women who agree to serve in the Executive Branch. But it is difficult to vote not to enact, and even more difficult to vote to repeal, a statute called, appropriately enough, the Ethics in Government Act. If Congress is controlled by the party other than the one to which the President belongs, it has little incentive to repeal it; if it is controlled by the same party, it dare not. By its short-sighted action today, I fear the Court has permanently encumbered the Republic with an institution that will do it great harm.

Worse than what it has done, however, is the manner in which it has done it. A government of laws means a government of rules. Today's decision on the basic issue of fragmentation of executive power is ungoverned by rule, and hence ungoverned by law. It extends into the very heart of our most significant constitutional function the "totality of the circumstances" mode of analysis that this Court has in recent years become fond of. Taking all things into account, we conclude that the power taken away from the President here is not really *too* much. The next time executive power is assigned to someone other than the President we may conclude, taking all things into account, that it *is* too much. That opinion, like this one, will not be confined by any rule. We will describe, as we have today (though I hope more accurately) the effects of the provision in question, and will authoritatively announce: "The President's need to control the exercise of the [subject officer's] discretion *is* so central to the functioning of the Executive Branch as to require complete control." This is not analysis; it is ad hoc judgment. And it fails to explain why it is not true that—as the text of the Constitution seems to require, as the Founders seemed to expect, and as our past cases have uniformly assumed—all purely executive power must be under the control of the President.

The ad hoc approach to constitutional adjudication has real attraction, even apart from its work-saving potential. It is guaranteed to produce a result, in every case, that will make a majority of the Court happy with the law. The law is, by definition, precisely what the majority thinks, taking all things into account, it *ought* to be. I prefer to rely upon the judgment of the wise men who constructed our system, and of the people who approved it, and of two centuries of history that have shown it to be sound. Like it or not, that judgment says, quite plainly, that "[t]he executive Power shall be vested in a President of the United States."

CONGRESSIONAL CONTROL OVER EXECUTIVE ACTION THROUGH REMOVAL POWER [NEW PART]

CON LAW: P. 214, before Part III

AMER CON: P. 170, before Sec. 3

BOWSHER v. SYNAR

478 U.S. 714, 106 S.Ct. 3181, 92 L.Ed.2d 583 (1986).

CHIEF JUSTICE BURGER delivered the opinion of the Court.

The question presented by these appeals is whether the assignment by Congress to the Comptroller General of the United States of certain functions under the Balanced Budget and Emergency Deficit Control Act of 1985 [Gramm-Rudman Act] violates the doctrine of separation of powers.

I

[The] purpose of the Act is to eliminate the federal budget deficit. To that end, the Act sets a "maximum deficit amount" for federal spending for each of fiscal years 1986 through 1991. The size of that maximum deficit amount progressively reduces to zero in fiscal year 1991. If in any fiscal year the federal budget deficit exceeds the maximum deficit amount by more than a specified sum, the Act requires across-the-board cuts in federal spending to reach the targeted deficit level, with half of the cuts made to defense programs and the other half made to non-defense programs. The Act exempts certain priority programs from these cuts.

These "automatic" reductions are accomplished through a rather complicated procedure, spelled out in § 251, the so-called "reporting provisions" of the Act. Each year, the Directors of the Office of Management and Budget (OMB) and the Congressional Budget Office (CBO) independently estimate the amount of the federal budget deficit for the upcoming fiscal year. If that deficit exceeds the maximum targeted deficit amount for that fiscal year by more than a specified amount, the Directors of OMB and CBO independently calculate, on a program-by-program basis, the budget reductions necessary to ensure that the deficit does not exceed the maximum deficit amount. The Act then requires the Directors to report jointly their deficit estimates and budget reduction calculations to the Comptroller General.

The Comptroller General, after reviewing the Directors' reports, then reports his conclusions to the President. The President in turn must issue a "sequestration" order mandating the spending reductions specified by the Comptroller General. There follows a period during which Congress may by legislation reduce spending to obviate, in whole or in part, the need for the sequestration order. If such reductions are not enacted, the sequestration order becomes effective and the spending reductions included in that order are made.

Anticipating constitutional challenge to these procedures, the Act also contains a "fallback" deficit reduction process to take effect "[i]n the event that any of the reporting procedures described in section 251 are invalidated." Under these provisions, the report prepared by the Directors of OMB and the CBO is submitted directly to a specially-created Temporary Joint Committee on Deficit Reduction, which must report in five days to both Houses a joint resolution setting forth the content of the Directors' report. Congress then must vote on the resolution under special rules, which render amendments out of order. If the resolution is passed and signed by the President, it then serves as the basis for a Presidential sequestration order.

[A three-judge federal court held the reporting provisions invalid. The Court affirmed.[a]]

III

[In] light of these precedents [*Myers* and *Humphrey's Executor*] we conclude that Congress cannot reserve for itself the power of removal of an officer charged with the execution of the laws except by impeachment. To permit the execution of the laws to be vested in an officer answerable only to Congress would, in practical terms, reserve in Congress control over the execution of the laws. As the District Court observed, "Once an officer is appointed, it is only the authority that can remove him, and not the authority that appointed him, that he must fear and, in the performance of his functions, obey." The structure of the Constitution does not permit Congress to execute the laws; it follows that Congress cannot grant to an officer under its control what it does not possess.

Our decision in *Chadha* supports this conclusion. [To] permit an officer controlled by Congress to execute the laws would be, in essence, to permit a congressional veto. Congress could simply remove, or threaten to remove, an officer for executing the laws in any fashion found to be unsatisfactory to Congress. This kind of congressional control over the execution of the laws, *Chadha* makes clear, is constitutionally impermissible.

The dangers of congressional usurpation of Executive Branch functions have long been recognized. [*Chadha*.] With these principles in mind, we turn to consideration of whether the Comptroller General is controlled by Congress.

IV

Appellants urge that the Comptroller General performs his duties independently and is not subservient to Congress. We agree with the District Court that this contention does not bear close scrutiny.

The critical factor lies in the provisions of the statute defining the Comptroller General's office relating to removability. Although the Comptroller General is nominated by the President from a list of three individuals recommended by the Speaker of the House of Representatives and the President pro tempore of the Senate, and confirmed by the Senate, he is removable only at the initiative of

a. Ruling that injury to a federal employee, a party to the actions, provided standing, the Court did not consider other claimed bases for standing (members of Congress and federal employees' union).

Congress. He may be removed not only by impeachment but also by Joint Resolution of Congress "at any time" resting on any one of the following bases:

"(i) permanent disability;

"(ii) inefficiency;

"(iii) neglect of duty;

"(iv) malfeasance; or

"(v) a felony or conduct involving moral turpitude." [7]

This provision was included, as one Congressman explained in urging passage of the Act, because Congress "felt that [the Comptroller General] should be brought under the sole control of Congress, so that Congress at the moment when it found he was inefficient and was not carrying on the duties of his office as he should and as the Congress expected, could remove him without the long, tedious process of a trial by impeachment." * * *

Justice White contends that "[t]he statute does not permit anyone to remove the Comptroller at will; removal is permitted only for specified cause, with the existence of cause to be determined by Congress following a hearing. Any removal under the statute would presumably be subject to post-termination judicial review to ensure that a hearing had in fact been held and the finding of cause for removal was not arbitrary."

[The] dissent's assessment of the statute fails to recognize the breadth of the grounds for removal. The statute permits removal for "inefficiency," "neglect of duty," or "malfeasance." These terms are very broad and, as interpreted by Congress, could sustain removal of a Comptroller General for any number of actual or perceived transgressions of the legislative will. The Constitutional Convention chose to permit impeachment of executive officers only for "Treason, Bribery, or other high Crimes and Misdemeanors." It rejected language that would have permitted impeachment for "maladministration," with Madison arguing that "[s]o vague a term will be equivalent to a tenure during pleasure of the Senate."

We need not decide whether that "inefficiency" or "malfeasance" are terms as broad as "maladministration" in order to reject the dissent's position that removing the Comptroller General requires "a feat of bipartisanship more difficult than that required to impeach and convict." (White, J., dissenting). * * *

Justice White, however, assures us that "[r]ealistic consideration" of the "practical result of the removal provision" reveals that the Comptroller General is unlikely to be removed by Congress. The separated powers of our government cannot be permitted to turn on judicial assessment of whether an officer exercising executive power is on good terms with Congress. The Framers recognized that, in the long term, structural protections against abuse of power were critical to preserving liberty. In constitutional terms, the removal powers over the Comptroller General's office dictate that he will be subservient to Congress.

This much said, we must also add that the dissent is simply in error to suggest that the political realities reveal that the Comptroller General is free from influence by Congress. The Comptroller General heads the General Accounting Office, "an instrumentality of the United States Government indepen-

---

7. Although the President could veto such a joint resolution, the veto could be overridden by a two-thirds vote of both Houses of Congress. Thus, the Comptroller General could be removed in the face of Presidential opposition. Like the District Court, we therefore read the removal provision as authorizing removal by Congress alone.

dent of the executive departments," which was created by Congress in 1921 as part of the Budget and Accounting Act of 1921. Congress created the office because it believed that it "needed an officer, responsible to it alone, to check upon the application of public funds in accordance with appropriations." Mansfield, *The Comptroller General* 65 (1939).

It is clear that Congress has consistently viewed the Comptroller General as an officer of the Legislative Branch. The Reorganization Acts of 1945 and 1949, for example, both stated that the Comptroller General and the GAO are "a part of the legislative branch of the Government." Similarly, in the Accounting and Auditing Act of 1950, Congress required the Comptroller General to conduct audits "as an agent of the Congress."

Over the years, the Comptrollers General have also viewed themselves as part of the Legislative Branch. * * *

Against this background, we see no escape from the conclusion that, because Congress had retained removal authority over the Comptroller General, he may not be entrusted with executive powers. The remaining question is whether the Comptroller General has been assigned such powers in the Balanced Budget and Emergency Deficit Control Act of 1985.

V

The primary responsibility of the Comptroller General under the instant Act is the preparation of a "report." This report must contain detailed estimates of projected federal revenues and expenditures. The report must also specify the reductions, if any, necessary to reduce the deficit to the target for the appropriate fiscal year. The reductions must be set forth on a program-by-program basis.

In preparing the report, the Comptroller General is to have "due regard" for the estimates and reductions set forth in a joint report submitted to him by the Director of CBO and the Director of OMB, the President's fiscal and budgetary advisor. However, the Act plainly contemplates that the Comptroller General will exercise his independent judgment and evaluation with respect to those estimates. The Act also provides that the Comptroller General's report "shall explain fully any differences between the contents of such report and the report of the Directors."

Appellants suggest that the duties assigned to the Comptroller General in the Act are essentially ministerial and mechanical so that their performance does not constitute "execution of the law" in a meaningful sense. On the contrary, we view these functions as plainly entailing execution of the law in constitutional terms. Interpreting a law enacted by Congress to implement the legislative mandate is the very essence of "execution" of the law. Under § 251, the Comptroller General must exercise judgment concerning facts that affect the application of the Act. He must also interpret the provisions of the Act to determine precisely what budgetary calculations are required. Decisions of that kind are typically made by officers charged with executing a statute.

The executive nature of the Comptroller General's functions under the Act is revealed in § 252(a)(3) which gives the Comptroller General the ultimate authority to determine the budget cuts to be made. Indeed, the Comptroller General commands the President himself to carry out, without the slightest variation (with exceptions not relevant to the constitutional issues presented), the directive of the Comptroller General as to the budget reductions: "The [Presidential] order *must provide* for reductions in the manner specified in section 251(a)(3), *must incorporate* the provisions of the [Comptroller General's] report submitted under section 251(b), and *must be consistent with such report in all respects.* The President *may not modify or recalculate any of the estimates, determinations, specifications, bases, amounts, or percentages* set forth in the report submitted under section 251(b) in determining the reductions to be specified in the order with respect to programs, projects, and activities, or with respect to budget activities, within an account." (emphasis added).

Congress of course initially determined the content of the Balanced Budget and Emergency Deficit Control Act; and undoubtedly the content of the Act determines the nature of the executive duty. However, as *Chadha* makes clear, once Congress makes its choice in enacting legislation, its participation ends. Congress can thereafter control the execution of its enactment only indirectly—by passing new legislation. By placing the responsibility for execution of the Balanced Budget and Emergency Deficit Control Act in the hands of an officer who is subject to removal only by itself, Congress in effect has retained control over the execution of the Act and has intruded into the executive function. The Constitution does not permit such intrusion.

VI

We now turn to the final issue of remedy. Appellants urge that rather than striking down § 251 and invalidating the significant power Congress vested in the Comptroller General to meet a national fiscal emergency, we should take the lesser course of nullifying the statutory provisions of the 1921 Act that authorizes Congress to remove the Comptroller General. At oral argument, counsel for the Comptroller General suggested that this might make the Comptroller General removable by the President. All appellants urge that Congress would prefer invalidation of the removal provisions rather than invalidation of § 251 of the Balanced Budget and Emergency Deficit Control Act.

Severance at this late date of the removal provisions enacted 65 years ago would significantly alter the Comptroller General's office, possibly by making him subservient to the Executive Branch. Recasting the Comptroller General as an officer of the Executive Branch would accordingly alter the balance that Congress had in mind in drafting the Budget and Accounting Act of 1921 and the Balanced Budget and Emergency Deficit Control Act, to say nothing of the wide array of other tasks and duties Congress has assigned the Comptroller General in other statutes. Thus appellant's argument would require this Court to undertake a weighing of the importance Congress attached to the removal provisions in the Budget and Accounting Act of 1921 as well as in other subsequent enactments against the importance it placed on the Balanced Budget and Emergency Deficit Control Act of 1985.

Fortunately this is a thicket we need not enter. The language of the Balanced Budget and Emergency Deficit Control Act itself settles the issue. In § 274(f), Congress has explicitly provided "fallback" provisions in the Act that take effect "[i]n the event [*any*] of the reporting procedures described in section 251 are invalidated." [Assuming] that appellants are correct in urging that this matter must be resolved on the basis of congressional intent, the intent appears to have been for § 274(f) to be given effect in this situation. Indeed, striking the removal provisions would lead to a statute that Congress would probably have refused to adopt.

* * * Accordingly, rather than perform the type of creative and imaginative statutory surgery urged by appellants, our holding simply permits the fallback provisions to come into play. * * * [b]

b. Stevens, J., joined by Marshall, J., concurred in the judgment but expressly dissented from "labeling the function assigned to the Comptroller General as 'executive powers' ":

JUSTICE WHITE, dissenting.

I

[Twice] in the past four years I have expressed my view that the Court's recent efforts to police the separation of powers have rested on untenable constitutional propositions leading to regrettable results. See *Northern Pipeline Construction Co. v. Marathon Pipe Line Co.*, 458 U.S. 50, 92–118, 102 S.Ct. 2858, 2882–2895, 73 L.Ed.2d 598, 629 (1982) (White, J., dissenting); *Chadha* (White, J., dissenting). Today's result is even more misguided. As I will explain, the Court's decision rests on a feature of the legislative scheme that is of minimal practical significance and that presents no substantial threat to the basic scheme of separation of powers. In attaching dispositive significance to what should be regarded as a triviality, the Court neglects what has in the past been recognized as a fundamental principle governing consideration of disputes over separation of powers: "The actual art of governing under our Constitution does not and cannot conform to judicial definitions of the power of any of its branches based on isolated clauses or even single Articles torn from context. While the Constitution diffuses power the better to secure liberty, it also contemplates that practice will integrate the dispersed powers into a workable government." *Youngstown* (Jackson, J., concurring). * * *

It is evident (and nothing in the Court's opinion is to the contrary) that the powers exercised by the Comptroller General under the Gramm-Rudman Act are not such that vesting them in an officer not subject to removal at will by the President would in itself improperly interfere with Presidential powers. Determining the level of spending by the Federal Government is not by nature a function central either to the exercise of the President's enumerated powers or to his general duty to ensure execution of the laws; rather, appropriating funds is a peculiarly legislative function, and one expressly committed to Congress by Art. I, § 9. [In] enacting Gramm-Rudman, Congress has chosen to exercise this legislative power to establish the level of federal spending by providing a detailed set of criteria for reducing expenditures below the level of appropriations in the event that certain conditions are met. Delegating the execution of this legislation—that is, the power to apply the Act's criteria and make the required calculations—to an officer independent of the President's will does not deprive the President of any power that he would otherwise have or that is essential to the performance of the duties of his office. Rather, the result of such a delegation, from the standpoint of the President, is no different from the result of more traditional forms of appropriation: under either system, the level of funds available to the Executive branch to carry out its duties is not within the President's discretionary control. * * *

"I am convinced that the Comptroller General must be characterized as an agent of Congress because of his longstanding statutory responsibilities; that the powers assigned to him under the Gramm-Rudman-Hollings Act require him to make policy that will bind the Nation; and that, when Congress, or a component or an agent of Congress, seeks to make policy that will bind the Nation, it must follow the procedures mandated by Article I of the Constitution—through passage by both Houses and presentment to the President. In short, Congress may not exercise its fundamental power to formulate national policy by delegating that power to one of its two Houses, to a legislative committee, or to an individual agent of the Congress such as the Speaker of the House of Representatives, the Sergeant at Arms of the Senate, or the Director of the Congressional Budget Office. *Chadha*. That principle, I believe, is applicable to the Comptroller General."

II

If, as the Court seems to agree, the assignment of "executive" powers under Gramm-Rudman to an officer not removable at will by the President would not in itself represent a violation of the constitutional scheme of separated powers, the question remains whether, as the Court concludes, the fact that the officer to whom Congress has delegated the authority to implement the Act is removable by a joint resolution of Congress should require invalidation of the Act.

* * * Today's majority concludes that the same concerns that underlay *Chadha* indicate the invalidity of a statutory provision allowing the removal by joint resolution for specified cause of any officer performing executive functions. Such removal power, the Court contends, constitutes a "congressional veto" analogous to that struck down in *Chadha,* for it permits Congress to "remove, or threaten to remove, an officer for executing the laws in any fashion found to be unsatisfactory." The Court concludes that it is "[t]his kind of congressional control over the execution of the laws" that *Chadha* condemns. * * *

[T]he Court overlooks or deliberately ignores the decisive difference between the congressional removal provision and the legislative veto struck down in *Chadha:* under the Budget and Accounting Act, Congress may remove the Comptroller only through a joint resolution, which by definition must be passed by both Houses and signed by the President. In other words, a removal of the Comptroller under the statute *satisfies the requirements of bicameralism and presentment laid down in Chadha.* The majority's citation of *Chadha* for the proposition that Congress may only control the acts of officers of the United States "by passing new legislation," in no sense casts doubt on the legitimacy of the removal provision, for that provision allows Congress to effect removal only through action that constitutes legislation as defined in *Chadha.*

To the extent that it has any bearing on the problem now before us, *Chadha* would seem to suggest the legitimacy of the statutory provision making the Comptroller removable through joint resolution, for the Court's opinion in *Chadha* reflects the view that the bicameralism and presentment requirements of Art. I represent the principal assurances that Congress will remain within its legislative role in the constitutionally prescribed scheme of separated powers. * * *

More importantly, the substantial role played by the President in the process of removal through joint resolution reduces to utter insignificance the possibility that the threat of removal will induce subservience to the Congress. [The] requirement of presidential approval obviates the possibility that the Comptroller will perceive himself as so completely at the mercy of Congress that he will function as its tool. If the Comptroller's conduct in office is not so unsatisfactory to the President as to convince the latter that removal is required under the statutory standard, Congress will have no independent power to coerce the Comptroller unless it can muster a two-thirds majority in both Houses—a feat of bipartisanship more difficult than that required to impeach and convict. The incremental in terrorem effect of the possibility of congressional removal in the face of a presidential veto is therefore exceedingly unlikely to have any discernible impact on the extent of congressional influence over the Comptroller.

The practical result of the removal provision is not to render the Comptroller unduly dependent upon or subservient to Congress, but to render him one of the most independent officers in the entire federal establishment. Those who have studied the office agree that the procedural and substantive limits on the power of Congress and the President to remove the Comptroller make dislodging him against his will practically impossible. As one scholar put it nearly fifty years ago, "Under the statute the Comptroller General, once confirmed, is safe so long as he avoids a public exhibition of personal immorality, dishonesty, or failing mentality." Mansfield, *The Comptroller General* 75–76 (1939). The passage of time has done little to cast doubt on this view: of the six Comptrollers who have served since 1921, none has been threatened with, much less subjected to, removal. Recent students of the office concur that "[b]arring resignation, death, physical or mental incapacity, or extremely bad behavior, the Comptroller General is assured his tenure if he wants it, and not a day more." Mosher, *The GAO* 242 (1979). The threat of "here-and-now subservience" is obviously remote indeed.

Realistic consideration of the nature of the Comptroller General's relation to Congress thus reveals that the threat to separation of powers conjured up by the majority is wholly chimerical. * * *

The majority's contrary conclusion rests on the rigid dogma that, outside of the impeachment process, any "direct congressional role in the removal of officers charged with the execution of the laws [is] inconsistent with separation of powers." Reliance on such an unyielding principle to strike down a statute posing no real danger of aggrandizement of congressional power is extremely misguided and insensitive to our constitutional role.[c] * * *

CON LAW P. 219, before Section 3

AMER COH P. 219

NEW SECTION: DELEGATION OF EXECUTIVE AND QUASI-LEGISLATIVE FUNCTIONS TO JUDICIARY

MISTRETTA v. UNITED STATES,

___ U.S. ___, 109 S.Ct. 647, 102 L.Ed.2d 714 (1989).

BLACKMUN, J., delivered the opinion of the Court.

[The Sentence Reform Act of 1984 created the U.S. Sentencing Commission "as an independent commission in the Judicial Branch" with seven bipartisan voting members to be appointed by the President, three of whom were to be federal judges.

[The Act's objectives were to escape (1) the great disparity in sentences imposed on similarly situated offenders due to the "almost unfettered" discretion of federal judges within wide ranges prescribed by Congress under the indeterminate sentence structure, and (2) the great uncertainty as to the time those

---

c. BLACKMUN, J., separately dissenting, agreed with White, J., that it was "unrealistic" to claim that the removal powers makes the Comptroller General "subservient to Congress." But to the extent removal power was found incompatible with constitutional separation of powers, he would "cure" it by refusing to allow Congressional removal "—if it ever is attempted—and not by striking down the central provisions of the Deficit Control Act. However wise or foolish it may be, that statute unquestionably ranks among the most important federal enactments of the past several decades. I cannot see the sense of invalidating legislation of this magnitude in order to preserve a cumbersome, 65-year-old remov-

al power that has never been exercised and appears to have been all but forgotten until this litigation. * * *

"I do not claim that the 1921 removal provision is a piece of statutory deadwood utterly without contemporary significance. But it comes close. Rarely if ever invoked even for symbolic purposes, the removal provision certainly pales in importance beside the legislative scheme the Court strikes down today—an extraordinarily far-reaching response to a deficit problem of unprecedented proportions. Because I believe that the constitutional defect found by the Court cannot justify the remedy it has imposed, I respectfully dissent."

sentenced would spend in prison in view of the judge's wide discretion to suspend sentences and grant probation, and the independent parole power of the executive-based Parole Commission applying its own guidelines.

[The Commission was to devise guidelines for federal sentencing that would establish, within the limits of existing law, ranges of determinate sentences for categories of offenses and defendants according to specified factors, "among others". The maximum of each range could not exceed its minimum by more than 25% or six months. All federal judges must sentence within the applicable range, except for deviations due to aggravating or mitigating factors not considered by the Commission in formulating the guidelines. The Parole Commission was abolished.

[After the Commission had adopted its guidelines, their constitutionality was challenged in many U.S. District Courts. In Mistretti the Court granted a petition for certiorari for a direct review of the denial of such a challenge, noting the "imperative public importance" of the issue. The Court rejected all challenges 8 to 1.]

III

DELEGATION OF POWER

[We] harbor no doubt that Congress' delegation of authority to the Sentencing Commission is sufficiently specific and detailed to meet constitutional requirements.[b] * * *

Developing proportionate penalties for hundreds of different crimes by a virtually limitless array of offenders is precisely the sort of intricate, labor-intensive task for which delegation to an expert body is especially appropriate. Although Congress has delegated significant discretion to the Commission to draw judgments from its analysis of existing sentencing practice and alternative sentencing models, "Congress is not confined to that method of executing its policy which involves the least possible delegation of discretion to administrative officers." *Yakus*. We have no doubt that in the hands of the Commission "the criteria which Congress has supplied are wholly adequate for carrying out the general policy and purpose" of the Act. *Sunshine Coal Co. v. Adkins*, 310 U.S. 381, 398 (1940).

IV

SEPARATION OF POWERS

Having determined that Congress has set forth sufficient standards for the exercise of the Commission's delegated authority, we turn to Mistretta's claim that the Act violates the constitutional principle of separation of powers. * * *

In applying the principle of separate powers in our jurisprudence, we have sought to give life to Madison's view of the appropriate relationship among the three coequal Branches. [Madison,] defending the Constitution against charges that it established insufficiently separate branches, addressed the point directly. Separation of powers, he wrote, "d[oes] not mean that these [three] departments ought to have no *partial agency* in, or no *control* over the acts of each other," but

---

b. The opinion spelled out in some detail the goals that Congress had specified for the commission, the factors it was to consider in fixing the grades of offenses and the categories of offenders. It invoked the authority of the cases that had approved delegation of legislative power to regulatory agencies and officers under much broader standards. See e.g. *Yakus*, note 4, Section 1, supra.

rather "that where the *whole* power of one department is exercised by the same hands which possess the *whole* power of another department, the fundamental principles of a free constitution, are subverted." The Federalist No. 47, pp. 325–326 (J. Cooke ed. 1961) (emphasis in original). See *Nixon v. Administrator of General Services*, 433 U.S., at 442, n. 5. Madison recognized that our constitutional system imposes upon the Branches a degree of overlapping responsibility, a duty of interdependence as well as independence the absence of which "would preclude the establishment of a Nation capable of governing itself effectively." *Buckley v. Valeo*, 424 U.S. 1, 121 (1976). In a passage now commonplace in our cases, Justice Jackson summarized the pragmatic, flexible view of differentiated governmental power to which we are heir:

> "While the Constitution diffuses power the better to secure liberty, it also contemplates that practice will integrate the dispersed powers into a workable government. It enjoins upon its branches separateness but interdependence, autonomy but reciprocity."

In adopting this flexible understanding of separation of powers, we simply have recognized Madison's teaching that the greatest security against tyranny—the accumulation of excessive authority in a single branch—lies not in a hermetic division between the Branches, but in a carefully crafted system of checked and balanced power within each Branch. * * *

[In] cases specifically involving the Judicial Branch, we have expressed our vigilance against two dangers: first, that the Judicial Branch neither be assigned nor allowed "tasks that are more appropriately accomplished by [other] branches," *Morrison* v. *Olson,* * * * and, second, that no provision of law "impermissibly threatens the institutional integrity of the Judicial Branch." *Commodity Futures Trading Comm'n v. Schor*, 478 U.S. 833, 871 (1986).

[Petitioner] claims that in delegating to an independent agency within the Judicial Branch the power to promulgate sentencing guidelines, Congress unconstitutionally has required the Branch, and individual Article III judges, to exercise not only their judicial authority, but legislative authority—the making of sentencing policy—as well. Such rulemaking authority, petitioner contends, may be exercised by Congress, or delegated by Congress to the Executive, but may not be delegated to or exercised by the Judiciary.

At the same time, petitioner asserts, Congress unconstitutionally eroded the integrity and independence of the Judiciary by requiring Article III judges to sit on the Commission, by requiring that those judges share their rulemaking authority with nonjudges, and by subjecting the Commission's members to appointment and removal by the President. According to petitioner, Congress, consistent with the separation of powers, may not upset the balance among the Branches by co-opting federal judges into the quintessentially political work of establishing sentencing guidelines, by subjecting those judges to the political whims of the Chief Executive, and by forcing judges to share their power with nonjudges.

A

LOCATION OF THE COMMISSION

The Sentencing Commission unquestionably is a peculiar institution within the framework of our Government. Although placed by the Act in the Judicial Branch, it is not a court and does not exercise judicial power

[Congress'] decision to create an independent rulemaking body to promulgate sentencing guidelines and to locate that body within the Judicial Branch is not unconstitutional unless Congress has vested in the Commission powers that are more appropriately performed by the other Branches or that undermine the integrity of the Judiciary. [As] a general principle, we stated as recently as last Term that " 'executive or administrative duties of a nonjudicial nature may not be imposed on judges holding office under Article III of the Constitution.' " *Morrison v. Olson.*

Nonetheless, we have recognized significant exceptions to this general rule and have approved the assumption of some nonadjudicatory activities by the Judicial Branch. In keeping with Justice Jackson's *Youngstown* admonition that the separation of powers contemplates the integration of dispersed powers into a workable government, we have recognized the constitutionality of a "twilight area" in which the activities of the separate Branches merge. In his dissent in *Myers v. United States*, 272 U.S. 52 (1926), Justice Brandeis explained that the separation of powers "left to each [Branch] power to exercise, in some respects, functions in their nature executive, legislative and judicial."

That judicial rulemaking, at least with respect to some subjects, falls within this twilight area is no longer an issue for dispute. None of our cases indicate that rulemaking *per se* is a function that may not be performed by an entity within the Judicial Branch, either because rulemaking is inherently nonjudicial or because it is a function exclusively committed to the Executive Branch. On the contrary, we specifically have held that Congress, in some circumstances, may confer rulemaking authority on the Judicial Branch. In *Sibbach v. Wilson & Co.*, 312 U.S. 1 (1941), we upheld a challenge to certain rules promulgated under the Rules Enabling Act of 1934 which conferred upon the Judiciary the power to promulgate federal rules of civil procedure. [Though] not the subject of constitutional challenge, by established practice we have recognized Congress' power to create the Judicial Conference of the United States, and the Rules Advisory Committees that it oversees, and the Administrative Office of the United States Courts whose myriad responsibilities include the administration of the entire probation service. These entities, some of which are comprised of judges, others of judges and nonjudges, still others of nonjudges only, do not exercise judicial power in the constitutional sense of deciding cases and controversies, but they share the common purpose of providing for the fair and efficient fulfillment of responsibilities that are properly the province of the Judiciary. Thus, although the judicial power of the United States is limited by express provision of Article III to "Cases" and "Controversies," we have never held, and have clearly disavowed in practice, that the Constitution prohibits Congress from assigning to courts or auxiliary bodies within the Judicial Branch administrative or rulemaking duties that, in the words of Chief Justice Marshall, are "necessary and proper, * * * for carrying into execution all the judgments which the judicial department has the power to pronounce." *Wayman v. Southard*, 10 Wheat., at 21. Because of their close relation to the central mission of the Judicial Branch, such extrajudicial activities are consonant with the integrity of the Branch and are not more appropriate for another Branch.

In light of this precedent and practice, we can discern no separation-of-powers impediment to the placement of the Sentencing Commission within the Judicial Branch. As we described at the outset, the sentencing function long has been a peculiarly shared responsibility among the Branches of government and has never been thought of as the exclusive constitutional province of any one Branch. See, e.g., *United States v. Addonizio*, 442 U.S. 178, 188–189 (1979). For more than a century, federal judges have enjoyed wide discretion to determine the appropriate sentence in individual cases and have exercised special authority to determine the sentencing factors to be applied in any given case. Indeed, the legislative history of the Act makes clear that Congress' decision to place the Commission within the Judicial Branch reflected Congress' "strong feeling" that sentencing has been and should remain "primarily a judicial function." Report, at 159. That Congress should vest such rulemaking in the Judicial Branch, far from being "incongruous" or vesting within the Judiciary responsibilities that more appropriately belong to another Branch, simply acknowledges the role that the Judiciary always has played, and continues to play, in sentencing.

Given the consistent responsibility of federal judges to pronounce sentence within the statutory range established by Congress, we find that the role of the Commission in promulgating guidelines for the exercise of that judicial function bears considerable similarity to the role of this Court in establishing rules of procedure under the various enabling acts. Such guidelines, like the Federal Rules of Criminal and Civil Procedure, are court rules—rules, to paraphrase Chief Justice Marshall's language in *Wayman*, for carrying into execution judgments that the judiciary has the power to pronounce. Just as the rules of procedure bind judges and courts in the proper management of the cases before them, so the Guidelines bind judges and courts in the exercise of their uncontested responsibility to pass sentence in criminal cases. In other words, the Commission's functions, like this Court's function in promulgating procedural rules, are clearly attendant to a central element of the historically acknowledged mission of the Judicial Branch.

[The] degree of political judgment about crime and criminality exercised by the Commission and the scope of the substantive effects of its work does to some extent set its rulemaking powers apart from prior judicial rulemaking. [We] do not believe, however, that the significantly political nature of the Commission's work renders unconstitutional its placement within the Judicial Branch. Our separation-of-powers analysis does not turn on the labelling of an activity as "substantive" as opposed to "procedural," or "political" as opposed to "judicial." See *Bowsher v. Synar*, ("[G]overnmental power cannot always be readily characterized with only one ∗ ∗ ∗ labe[l]") (opinion concurring in judgment). Rather, our inquiry is focused on the "unique aspects of the congressional plan at issue and its practical consequences in light of the larger concerns that underlie Article III." *Commodity Futures Trading Comm'n v. Schor*. In this case, the "practical consequences" of locating the Commission within the Judicial Branch pose no threat of undermining the integrity of the Judicial Branch or of expanding the powers of the Judiciary beyond the constitutional bounds by uniting within the Branch the political or quasi-legislative power of the Commission with the judicial power of the courts.

First, although the Commission is located in the Judicial Branch, its powers are not united with the powers of the Judiciary in a way that has meaning for separation-of-powers analysis. Whatever constitutional problems might arise if the powers of the Commission were vested in a court, the Commission is not a court, does not exercise judicial power, and is not controlled by or accountable to members of the Judicial Branch. The Commission, on which members of the Judiciary may be a minority, is an independent agency in every relevant sense. In contrast to a court's exercising judicial power, the Commission is fully accountable to Congress, which can revoke or amend any or all of the Guidelines as it sees fit. [In] contrast to a court, the Commission's members are subject to the President's limited powers of removal. In contrast to a court, its rulemaking is subject to the notice and comment requirements of the Administrative Procedure Act. [Because] Congress vested the power to promulgate sentencing guidelines in an independent agency, not a court, there can be no serious argument that Congress combined legislative and judicial power within the Judicial Branch.

Second, although the Commission wields rulemaking power and not the adjudicatory power exercised by individual judges when passing sentence, the placement of the Sentencing Commission in the Judicial Branch has not increased the Branch's authority. Prior to the passage of the Act, the Judicial Branch, as an aggregate, decided precisely the questions assigned to the Commission: what sentence is appropriate to what criminal conduct under what circumstances. It was the everyday business of judges, taken collectively, to evaluate and weigh the various aims of sentencing and to apply those aims to the individual cases that came before them. The Sentencing Commission does no more than this, albeit basically through the methodology of sentencing guidelines, rather than entirely individualized sentencing determinations. Accordingly, in placing the Commission in the Judicial Branch, Congress cannot be said to have aggrandized the authority of that Branch or to have deprived the Executive Branch of a power it once possessed. Indeed, because the Guidelines have the effect of promoting sentencing within a narrower range than was previously applied, the power of the Judicial Branch is, if anything, somewhat diminished by the Act.

B

COMPOSITION OF THE COMMISSION

We now turn to petitioner's claim that Congress' decision to require at least three federal judges to serve on the Commission and to require those judges to share their authority with nonjudges undermines the integrity of the Judicial Branch.

The text of the Constitution contains no prohibition against the service of active federal judges on independent commissions such as that established by the Act. * * *

Our inferential reading that the Constitution does not prohibit Article III judges from undertaking extrajudicial duties finds support in the historical practice of the Founders after ratification.[c] * * *

In light of the foregoing history and precedent, we conclude that the principle of separation of powers does not absolutely prohibit Article III judges from serving on commissions such as that created by the Act. The judges serve on the Sentencing Commission not pursuant to their status and authority as Article III judges, but solely because of their appointment by the President as the Act directs. Such power as these judges wield as Commissioners is not judicial power; it is administrative power derived from the enabling legislation. Just as the nonjudicial members of the Commission act as administrators, bringing their experience and wisdom to bear on the problems of sentencing disparity, so too the judges, uniquely qualified on the subject of sentencing, assume a wholly administrative role upon entering into the deliberations of the Commission. In other words, the Constitution, at least as a *per se* matter, does not forbid judges from wearing two hats; it merely forbids them from wearing both hats at the same time.

This is not to suggest, of course, that every kind of extrajudicial service under every circumstance necessarily accords with the Constitution. That the

c. The Court noted many instances in which federal justices and judges had served in other public offices and public commissions, though not always without controversy.

Constitution does not absolutely prohibit a federal judge from assuming extrajudicial duties does not mean that every extrajudicial service would be compatible with, or appropriate to, continuing service on the bench; nor does it mean that Congress may require a federal judge to assume extrajudicial duties as long as the judge is assigned those duties in an individual, not judicial, capacity. The ultimate inquiry remains whether a particular extrajudicial assignment undermines the integrity of the Judicial Branch.

[The Court asserted that judicial service on the Commission posed no threat to the independence of the judiciary, since service is voluntary, would not result in widespread judicial recusals, and would not affect the ability of those on the Commission or other judges "impartially to adjudicate sentencing issues."]

Although it is a judgment that is not without difficulty, we conclude that the participation of federal judges on the Sentencing Commission does not threaten, either in fact or in appearance, the impartiality of the Judicial Branch. We are drawn to this conclusion by one paramount consideration: that the Sentencing Commission is devoted exclusively to the development of rules to rationalize a process that has been and will continue to be performed exclusively by the Judicial Branch. In our view, this is an essentially neutral endeavor and one in which judicial participation is peculiarly appropriate. Judicial contribution to the enterprise of creating rules to limit the discretion of sentencing judges does not enlist the resources or reputation of the Judicial Branch in either the legislative business of determining what conduct should be criminalized or the executive business of enforcing the law. Rather, judicial participation on the Commission ensures that judicial experience and expertise will inform the promulgation of rules for the exercise of the Judicial Branch's own business—that of passing sentence on every criminal defendant. To this end, Congress has provided, not inappropriately, for a significant judicial voice on the Commission.

Justice Jackson underscored in *Youngstown* that the Constitution anticipates "reciprocity" among the Branches. 343 U.S., at 635. As part of that reciprocity and as part of the integration of dispersed powers into a workable government, Congress may enlist the assistance of judges in the creation of rules to govern the Judicial Branch. Our principle of separation of powers anticipates that the coordinate Branches will converse with each other on matters of vital common interest. While we have some reservation that Congress required such a dialogue in this case, the Constitution does not prohibit Congress from enlisting federal judges to present a uniquely judicial view on the uniquely judicial subject of sentencing. In this case, at least, where the subject lies so close to the heart of the judicial function and where purposes of the Commission are not inherently partisan, such enlistment is not coercion or co-optation, but merely assurance of judicial participation.[d]

d. Justice Scalia dissented "because I can find no place within our constitutional system for an agency created by Congress to exercise no other power than the making of laws." He would uphold "delegation of legislative authority" under "congressionally prescribed standards" only "in conjunction with lawful exercises of executive or judicial power."

"[The] whole theory of *lawful* Congressional 'delegation' is [that] a certain degree of discretion, and thus of lawmaking, *inheres* in most executive or judicial action, and it is up to Congress, by the relative specificity or generality of its statutory commands, to determine—up to a point—how small or how large that degree shall be." But in his view, the "lawmaking function of the Sentencing Commission is completely divorced from any responsibility for execution of the law or adjudication of private rights under the law. [The] only governmental power the Commission possesses is the power to make law; and it is not the Congress." (emphasis in original)

4. *Extraterritorial effect.* HEALY v. THE BEER INSTITUTE, ___ U.S. ___, 109 S.Ct. 2491, ___ L.Ed.2d ___ (1989), per BLACKMUN, J., pulled together into a "guiding principle" the Court's earlier disapprovals of state legislation with extraterritorial effect. At issue was the validity of a Connecticut statute aimed at eliminating the incentive for Connecticut residents to go into border states to buy beer at lower prices. Connecticut had no in-state brewers. The statute required that each month, on the sixth day, out-of-state shippers post their wholesale beer prices for the next month and affirm that they were no higher than those being charged in the border states at the moment of affirmation:

"The principles guiding this assessment [of the statute] reflect the Constitution's special concern both with the maintenance of a national economic union unfettered by state-imposed limitations on interstate commerce and with the autonomy of the individual States within their respective spheres.[13] Taken together, our cases concerning the extraterritorial effects of state economic regulation stand at a minimum for the following propositions: First, the 'Commerce Clause . . . precludes the application of a state statute to commerce that takes place wholly outside of the State's borders, whether or not the commerce has effects within the State,' *Edgar v. Mite Corp.* (plurality opinion); see also *Brown-Forman*, 476 U.S., at 581–583; and, specifically, a State may not adopt legislation that has the practical effect of establishing 'a scale of prices for use in other states.' *Baldwin v. Seelig.* Second, a statute that directly controls commerce occurring wholly outside the boundaries of a State exceeds the inherent limits of the enacting State's authority and is invalid regardless of whether the statute's extraterritorial reach was intended by the legislature. The critical inquiry is whether the practical effect of the regulation is to control conduct beyond the boundaries of the State. *Brown-Forman.* Third, the practical effect of the statute must be evaluated not only by considering the consequences of the statute itself, but also by considering how the challenged statute may interact with the legitimate regulatory regimes of other States and what effect would arise if not one, but many or every State adopted similar legislation. Generally speaking, the Commerce Clause protects against inconsistent legislation arising from the projection of one state regulatory regime into the jurisdiction of another State. Cf. *CTS Corp. v. Dynamics Corp. of America.* And, specifically, the Commerce Clause dictates that no State may force an out-of-state merchant to seek regulatory approval in one State before undertaking a transaction in another. *Brown-Forman.*[14]

"When these principles are applied to Connecticut's contemporaneous price-affirmation statute, the result is clear. The Court of Appeals correctly concluded that the Connecticut statute has the undeniable effect of controlling commercial activity occurring wholly outside the boundary of the State. Moreover, the practical effect of this affirmation law, in conjunction with the many other beer pricing and affirmation laws that have been or might be enacted throughout the

---

13. The plurality in *Edgar v. Mite Corp.* noted: "The limits on a State's power to enact substantive legislation are similar to the limits on the jurisdiction of state courts. In either case, 'any attempt "directly" to assert extraterritorial jurisdiction over persons or property would offend sister States and exceed the inherent limits of the State's power.'" 457 U.S. at 643, quoting *Shaffer v. Heitner,* 433 U.S. at 197.

14. [We] further recognized in *Brown-Forman* that the critical consideration in determining whether the extraterritorial reach of a statute violates the Commerce Clause is the overall effect of the statute on both local and interstate commerce. Our distillation of principles from prior cases involving extraterritoriality is meant as nothing more than a restatement of those specific concerns that have shaped this inquiry.

country, is to create just the kind of competing and interlocking local economic regulation that the Commerce Clause was meant to preclude.

"First, as explained by the Court of Appeals, the interaction of the Connecticut affirmation statute with the Massachusetts beer-pricing statute (which does not link domestic prices with out-of-state prices) has the practical effect of controlling Massachusetts prices. Massachusetts requires brewers to post their prices on the first day of the month to become effective on the first day of the following month. See Mass.Gen.Laws § 138:25B (1987). Five days later, however, those same brewers, in order to sell beer in Connecticut, must affirm that their Connecticut prices for the following month will be no higher than the lowest price that they are charging in any border State. Accordingly, on January 1, when a brewer posts his February prices for Massachusetts, that brewer must take account of the price he hopes to charge in Connecticut during the month of March. Not only will the January posting in Massachusetts establish a ceiling price for the brewer's March prices in Connecticut, but also, under the requirements of the Massachusetts law, the brewer will be locked into his Massachusetts price for the entire month of February (absent administrative leave) even though the Connecticut posting will have occurred on February 6. Thus, as a practical matter, Connecticut's nominally 'contemporaneous' affirmation statute 'prospectively' precludes the alteration of out-of-state prices after the moment of affirmation. More generally, the end result of the Connecticut statute's incorporation of out-of-state prices, as the Court of Appeals concluded, is that '[a] brewer can . . . undertake competitive pricing based on the market realities of either Massachusetts or Connecticut, but not both, because the Connecticut statute ties pricing to the regulatory schemes of the border states.' 849 F.2d, at 759. In other words, the Connecticut statute has the extraterritorial effect, condemned in *Brown-Forman*, of preventing brewers from undertaking competitive pricing in Massachusetts based on prevailing market conditions.

"Second, because New York law requires that promotional discounts remain in effect for 180 days, and the Connecticut statute treats promotional discounts as a reduction in price, the interaction of the New York and Connecticut laws is such that brewers may offer promotional discounts in New York only at the cost of locking in their discounted New York price as the ceiling for their Connecticut prices for the full 180 days of the New York promotional discount.

"Third, because volume discounts are permitted in Massachusetts, New York, and Rhode Island, but not in Connecticut, the effect of Connecticut's affirmation scheme is to deter volume discounts in each of these other States, because the lowest of the volume-discounted prices would have to be offered as the regular price for an entire month in Connecticut. See 849 F.2d, at 760.

"With respect to both promotional and volume discounts, then, the effect of the Connecticut statute is essentially indistinguishable from the extraterritorial effect found unconstitutional in *Brown-Forman*. The Connecticut statute, like the New York law struck down in *Brown-Forman*, requires out-of-state shippers to forgo the implementation of competitive-pricing schemes in out-of-state markets because those pricing decisions are imported by statute into the Connecticut market regardless of local competitive conditions. As we specifically reaffirmed in *Brown-Forman*, States may not deprive businesses and consumers in other States of 'whatever competitive advantages they may possess' based on the conditions of the local market. The Connecticut statute does precisely this.

"The Commerce Clause problem with the Connecticut statute appears in even starker relief when it is recalled that if Connecticut may enact a contemporaneous affirmation statute, so may each of the border States and, indeed, so may every other State in the Nation. Suppose, for example, that the border States each enacted statutes essentially identical to Connecticut's. Under those circumstances, in January, when a brewer posts his February prices in Connecticut and the border States, he must determine those prices knowing that the lowest bottle, can, or case price in any State would become the maximum bottle, can, or case price the brewer would be permitted to charge throughout the region for the month of March. This is true because in February, when the brewer posts his March prices in each State, he will have to affirm that no bottle, can, or case price is higher than the lowest bottle, can, or case price in the region—and these 'current' prices would have been determined by the January posting. Put differently, unless a beer supplier declined to sell in one of the States for an entire month, the maximum price in each State would be capped by previous prices in the other State. This maximum price would almost surely be the minimum price as well, since any reduction in either State would permanently lower the ceiling in both. Nor would such 'price gridlock' be limited to individual regions. The short-circuiting of normal pricing decisions based on local conditions would be carried to a national scale if and when a significant group of States enacted contemporaneous affirmation statutes that linked in-state prices to the lowest price in any State in the country. This kind of potential regional and even national regulation of the pricing mechanism for goods is reserved by the Commerce Clause to the Federal Government and may not be accomplished piecemeal through the extraterritorial reach of individual state statutes.

IV

"The Connecticut statute, moreover, violates the Commerce Clause in a second respect: On its face, the statute discriminates against brewers and shippers of beer engaged in interstate commerce. [By] its plain terms, the Connecticut affirmation statute applies solely to interstate brewers or shippers of beer, that is, either Connecticut brewers who sell both in Connecticut *and* in at least one border State or out-of-state shippers who sell both in Connecticut and in at least one border State. Under the statute, a manufacturer or shipper of beer is free to charge wholesalers within Connecticut whatever price it might choose so long as that manufacturer or shipper does not sell its beer in a border State. This discriminatory treatment establishes a substantial disincentive from companies doing business in Connecticut to engage in interstate commerce, essentially penalizing Connecticut brewers if they seek border-state markets and out-of-state shippers if they choose to sell both in Connecticut and in a border State. We perceive no neutral justification for this patent discrimination."

SCALIA, J., joined in the judgment and Part IV of the opinion: "I would refrain [from] applying the more expansive analysis which finds the law unconstitutional because it regulates or controls beer pricing in the surrounding States. [This] rationale is not only unnecessary but also questionable, resting as it does upon the mere economic reality that the challenged law will require sellers in New York, Massachusetts, and Rhode Island to take account of the price that they must post and charge in Connecticut when setting their prices in those other States. The difficulty with this is that innumerable valid state laws affect pricing decisions in other States—even so rudimentary a law as a maximum price regulation."

REHNQUIST, C.J., joined by STEVENS and O'CONNOR, JJ. dissented:

"The Connecticut statute here is markedly different from the New York statute condemned in *Baldwin*. Connecticut has no motive to favor local brewers over out-of-state brewers, because there *are* no local brewers. Its motive—unchallenged here—is to obtain from out-of-state brewers prices for Connecticut retailers and Connecticut beer drinkers as low as those charged by the brewers in neighboring States. Connecticut does not seek to erect any sort of tariff barrier to exclude out-of-state beer; its residents will drink out-of-state beer if they drink beer at all, and the State simply wishes its inhabitants to be treated as favorably as those of neighboring States by the brewers who sell interstate. There is no 'tariff wall' between Connecticut and other States; there is only a maximum price regulation with which the interstate brewer would rather not have to bother. But that is not a sufficient reason for saying that such a regulation violates the Commerce Clause.

"Neither the parties nor the Court point to any concrete evidence that the Connecticut regulation will have any effect on the beer prices charged in other States, much less a constitutionally impermissible one. It is merely assumed that consumers in the neighboring States possess 'competitive advantages' over Connecticut consumers. But it is equally possible that Connecticut's affirmation laws, a response to a history of unusually high beer prices in that State, see *United States Brewers Assn., Inc. v. Healy*, 692 F.2d 275, 276 (1982), may be justifiable as a remedy for some market imperfection that permits supracompetitive prices to be charged Connecticut consumers. The Court expresses the view that these regulations will affect the prices of beer in other States and goes on to say that such an effect constitutes 'regulating' or 'controlling' beer sales beyond its borders. But this view is simply the Court's personal forecast about the business strategies that distributors may use to set their prices in light of regulatory obligations in various States. Certainly a distributor that considers the Connecticut affirmation law when setting its prices in Massachusetts, or offering a discount in New York, is under no legal obligation to do so. * * *

"I am no more convinced by the Court's alternative rationale, that the Connecticut statute 'facially discriminates' against brewers and shippers of beer engaged in interstate commerce in favor of brewers and shippers who do business wholly [within] Connecticut. As the Court acknowledges, there are no Connecticut brewers, and the Court has not pointed to any evidence of shippers doing business in Connecticut but not in its border States. Consequently, the Court strikes down Connecticut's statute because it facially discriminates in favor of entities that apparently do not exist. [It] is not a proper exercise of our constitutional power to invalidate state legislation as facially discriminatory just because it has not taken into account every hypothetical circumstance that might develop in the market. * * *"

Chapter

STATE POWER TO REGULATE

SECTION: IN THE ABSENCE OF
FEDERAL REGULATION

EVOLUTION OF STANDARDS

CON LAW: P. 257, add to footnote c

AMER CON: P. 198, add to footnote c

For Justice Scalia's endorsement of these views relating to balancing, see his concurring opinion in *CTS Corp. v. Dynamics Corp.*, p. 55 of this Supplement.

REGULATION OF TRADE

INCOMING COMMERCE

CON LAW: P. 269, before note 2

AMER CON: P. 209, before note 2

Projecting legislation into other states to protect local consumers. New York required liquor distillers who sell at wholesale in New York to file a price schedule monthly, to sell in New York at those prices, and to sell at the lowest price the distiller charged wholesale in any other state for the same monthly period. BROWN–FOREMAN DISTILLERS CORP. v. NEW YORK LIQUOR AUTH., 476 U.S. 573, 106 S.Ct. 2080, 90 L.Ed.2d 552 (1986), per MARSHALL, J., held the "lowest price" provision violated the commerce clause:

"While a state may seek lower prices for its consumers, it may not insist that producers or consumers in other states surrender whatever competitive advantages they may possess. *Baldwin.* Economic protectionism is not limited to attempts to convey advantages to local merchants; it may include attempts to give local consumers an advantage over consumers in other states.

"[A] 'prospective' statute such as [New York's liquor statute] regulates out-of-state transactions in violation of the Commerce Clause. Once a distiller has posted prices in New York, it is not free to change its price elsewhere in the United States during the relevant month. [While] New York may regulate the sale of liquor within its borders [it] may not 'project its legislation into [other States] by regulating the price to be paid' for liquor in those states. *Edgar v. MITE Corp.* [p. 59 of this Supplement]. [New York] has 'project[ed] its legisla-

54

tion' into other States, and directly regulated commerce therein, in violation of *Baldwin*." [a]

OUTGOING COMMERCE

CON LAW: P. 283, before Part IV

AMER CON: P. 220, before Part IV

State takeover laws. An Indiana statute provided that a purchaser who acquired "control shares"[b] in an Indiana corporation would acquire voting rights only to the extent approved by a majority vote of the pre-existing disinterested stockholders. CTS CORP. v. DYNAMICS CORP., 481 U.S. 69, 107 S.Ct. 1637, 95 L.Ed.2d 67 (1987), per POWELL, J., upheld the statute, reversing a U.S. Court of Appeals ruling that it violated the commerce clause:[c]

"III

"A

"The principal objects of dormant Commerce Clause scrutiny are statutes that discriminate against interstate commerce. See, e.g., *Lewis v. BT Investment Managers, Inc.*, 447 U.S. 27, 36–37, 100 S.Ct. 2009, 64 L.Ed.2d 702 (1980); *Philadelphia v. New Jersey*. See, generally, Regan, *The Supreme Court and State Protectionism: Making Sense of the Dormant Commerce Clause*, 84 Mich.L.Rev. 1091 (1986). The Indiana Act is not such a statute. It has the same effects on tender offers whether or not the offeror is a domiciliary or resident of Indiana. Thus, it 'visits its effects equally upon both interstate and local business.'" [Because] nothing in the Indiana Act imposes a greater burden on out-of-state offerors than it does on similarly situated Indiana offerors, we reject the contention that the Act discriminates against interstate commerce.

"B

"This Court's recent Commerce Clause cases also have invalidated statutes that adversely may affect interstate commerce by subjecting activities to inconsistent regulations. E.g., *Brown–Forman Distillers Corp. v. New York State Liquor Authority; Edgar v. MITE Corp.*, 457 U.S. 604, 102 S.Ct. 1629, 73 L.Ed.2d 268 (1982) (plurality opinion of White, J.); *Kassel* (plurality opinion of Powell, J.). See *Southern Pacific Co. v. Arizona* (noting the 'confusion and difficulty' that would attend the 'unsatisfied need for uniformity' in setting maximum limits on train lengths); *Cooley v. Board of Wardens* (stating that the Commerce Clause prohibits States from regulating subjects that 'are in their nature national, or admit only of one uniform system, or plan of regulation'). The Indiana Act poses no such problem. So long as each State regulates voting rights only in the corporations it has created, each corporation will be subject to the law of only one State. No principle of corporation law and practice is more firmly established than a State's authority to regulate domestic corporations, including the authority to define the voting rights of [shareholders.]"

---

a. Stevens, J., joined by White, J. and Rehnquist, C.J. dissented, contending that "[in] lieu of evidence about the actual impact of the New York statute, the Court speculates that the [it] prevents price competition in transactions [in] other States." Brennan, J., did not participate.

b. "Control shares" are reached when the acquired shares would bring the purchaser's voting power to 20, 33⅓ or 50% but for the operation of the Act.

c. The Court also ruled that the federal anti-takeover Williams Act did not preempt the Indiana law.

"C

"The Court of Appeals did not find the Act unconstitutional for either of these threshold reasons. Rather, its decision rested on its view of the Act's potential to hinder tender offers. We think the Court of Appeals failed to appreciate the significance for Commerce Clause analysis of the fact that state regulation of corporate governance is regulation of entities whose very existence and attributes are a product of state [law.] By prohibiting certain transactions, and regulating others, such laws necessarily affect certain aspects of interstate [commerce.] Large corporations that are listed on national exchanges, or even regional exchanges, will have shareholders in many States and shares that are traded frequently. The markets that facilitate this national and international participation in ownership of corporations are essential for providing capital not only for new enterprises but also for established companies that need to expand their businesses. This beneficial free market system depends at its core upon the fact that a corporation—except in the rarest situations—is organized under, and governed by, the law of a single jurisdiction, traditionally the corporate law of the State of its incorporation.

"These regulatory laws may affect directly a variety of corporate transactions. Mergers are a typical example. In view of the substantial effect that a merger may have on the shareholders' interests in a corporation, many States require supermajority votes to approve [mergers.] By requiring a greater vote for mergers than is required for other transactions, these laws make it more difficult for corporations to merge. State laws also may provide for 'dissenters' rights' under which minority shareholders who disagree with corporate decisions to take particular actions are entitled to sell their shares to the corporation at fair market value.

"[A] State has an interest in promoting stable relationships among parties involved in the corporations it charters, as well as in ensuring that investors in such corporations have an effective voice in corporate affairs. There can be no doubt that the Act reflects these concerns. The primary purpose of the Act is to protect the shareholders of Indiana corporations. It does this by affording shareholders, when a takeover offer is made, an opportunity to decide collectively whether the resulting change in voting control of the corporation, as they perceive it, would be desirable. A change of management may have important effects on the shareholders' interests; it is well within the State's role as overseer of corporate governance to offer this opportunity. The autonomy provided by allowing shareholders collectively to determine whether the takeover is advantageous to their interests may be especially beneficial where a hostile tender offer may coerce shareholders into tendering their shares.

"Appellee Dynamics responds to this concern by arguing that the prospect of coercive tender offers is illusory, and that tender offers generally should be favored because they reallocate corporate assets into the hands of management who can use them most effectively.[13] See generally Easterbrook and Fischel, *The Proper Role of a Target's Management in Responding to a Tender Offer*, 94

13. It is appropriate to note when discussing the merits and demerits of tender offers that generalizations usually require qualification. No one doubts that some successful tender offers will provide more effective management or other benefits such as needed diversification. But there is no reason to *assume* that the type of conglomerate corporation that may result from repetitive takeovers necessarily will result is more effective management or otherwise be beneficial to shareholders. The divergent views in the literature—and even now being debated in the Congress—reflect the reality that the type and utility of tender offers vary widely. Of course, in many situations the offer to shareholders is simply a cash price substantially higher than the market price prior to the offer.

Harv.L.Rev. 1161 (1981). [Indiana's] concern with tender offers is not groundless. Indeed, the potentially coercive aspects of tender offers have been recognized by the Securities and Exchange Commission, see SEC Release No. 21079, p. 86,916, and by a number of scholarly commentators, see, e.g., Bradley & Rosenzweig, *Defensive Stock Repurchases*, 99 Harv.L.Rev. 1377, 1412–1413 (1986); Macey & McChesney, *A Theoretical Analysis of Corporate Greenmail*, 95 Yale L.J. 13, 20–22 (1985); Lowenstein, *Pruning Deadwood in Hostile Takeovers: A Proposal for Legislation*, 83 Colum.L.Rev. 249, 307–309 (1983). The Constitution does not require the States to subscribe to any particular economic theory. We are not inclined 'to second-guess the empirical judgments of lawmakers concerning the utility of legislation,' *Kassel* (BRENNAN, J., concurring). In our view, the possibility of coercion in some takeover bids offers additional justification for Indiana's decision to promote the autonomy of independent shareholders.

"Dynamics argues in any event that the State has ' "no legitimate interest in protecting the nonresident shareholders." ' (*MITE Corp.*). Dynamics relies heavily on the statement by the *MITE* Court that '[i]nsofar as the * * * law burdens out-of-state transactions, there is nothing to be weighed in the balance to sustain the law.' But that comment was made in reference to an Illinois law that applied as well to out-of-state corporations as to in-state corporations. We agree that Indiana has no interest in protecting nonresident shareholders *of nonresident corporations*. But this Act applies only to corporations incorporated in Indiana. We reject the contention that Indiana has no interest in providing for the shareholders of its corporations the voting autonomy granted by the Act. Indiana has a substantial interest in preventing the corporate form from becoming a shield for unfair business dealing. Moreover, unlike the Illinois statute invalidated in *MITE*, the Indiana Act applies only to corporations that have a substantial number of shareholders in Indiana. Thus, every application of the Indiana Act will affect a substantial number of Indiana residents, whom Indiana indisputably has an interest in protecting.

"D

"Dynamics' argument that the Act is unconstitutional ultimately rests on its contention that the Act will limit the number of successful tender offers. There is little evidence that this will occur. But even if true, this result would not substantially affect our Commerce Clause analysis. We reiterate that this Act does not prohibit any entity—resident or nonresident—from offering to purchase, or from purchasing, shares in Indiana corporations, or from attempting thereby to gain control. It only provides regulatory procedures designed for the better protection of the corporations' shareholders. We have rejected the 'notion that the Commerce Clause protects the particular structure or methods of operation in [a] market.' *Exxon*. The very commodity that is traded in the securities market is one whose characteristics are defined by state law. Similarly, the very commodity that is traded in the 'market for corporate control'—the corporation—is one that owes its existence and attributes to state law. Indiana need not define these commodities as other States do; it need only provide that residents and nonresidents have equal access to them. This Indiana has done. Accordingly, even if the Act should decrease the number of successful tender offers for Indiana corporations, this would not offend the Commerce Clause."

SCALIA, J., concurring in part and in the judgment, rejected the usual balancing approach to state legislation that neither discriminates against interstate commerce nor creates an impermissible risk of inconsistent state regulations: "While it has become standard practice at least since *Pike* to consider, in addition to these factors, whether the burden on commerce imposed by a state statute 'is clearly excessive in relation to the putative local benefits,' such an inquiry is ill suited to the judicial function and should be undertaken rarely if at all. This case is a good illustration of the point. Whether the control shares statute 'protects shareholders of Indiana corporations,' or protects incumbent management seems to me a highly debatable question, but it is extraordinary to think that the constitutionality of the Act should depend on the answer. Nothing in the Constitution says that the protection of entrenched management is any less important a 'putative local benefit' than the protection of entrenched shareholders, and I do not know what qualifies us to make that judgment—or the related judgment as to how effective the present statute is in achieving one or the other objective—or the ultimate (and most ineffable) judgment as to whether, given importance-level x, and effectiveness-level y, the worth of the statute is 'outweighed' by impact-on-commerce z.

"One commentator has suggested that, at least much of the time, we do not in fact mean what we say when we declare that statutes which neither discriminate against commerce nor present a threat of multiple and inconsistent burdens might nonetheless be unconstitutional under a 'balancing' test. See Regan, *The Supreme Court and State Protectionism: Making Sense of the Dormant Commerce Clause,* 84 Mich.L.Rev. 1091 (1986). If he is not correct, he ought to be. As long as a State's corporation law governs only its own corporations and does not discriminate against out-of-state interests, it should survive this Court's scrutiny under the Commerce Clause, whether it promotes shareholder welfare or industrial stagnation. Beyond that, it is for Congress to prescribe its invalidity."

WHITE, J., joined by Blackmun and Stevens, JJ., dissented:

"Given the impact of the Control Share Acquisitions Chapter, it is clear that Indiana is directly regulating the purchase and sale of shares of stock in interstate commerce. Appellant CTS's stock is traded on the New York Stock Exchange, and people from all over the country buy and sell CTS's shares daily. Yet, under Indiana's scheme, any prospective purchaser will be effectively precluded from purchasing CTS's shares if the purchaser crosses one of the Chapter's threshold ownership levels and a majority of CTS's shareholders refuse to give the purchaser voting rights. This Court should not countenance such a restraint on interstate trade.

"The United States, as *amicus curiae,* argues that Indiana's Control Share Acquisitions Chapter 'is written as a restraint on the *transferability* of voting rights in specified transactions, and it could not be written in any other way without changing its meaning. Since the restraint on the transfer of voting rights is a restraint on the transfer of shares, the Indiana Chapter, like the Illinois Act [in *MITE*], restrains "transfers of stock by stockholders to a third party." ' I agree. The majority ignores the practical impact of the Chapter in concluding that the Chapter does not violate the Commerce Clause. The Chapter is characterized as merely defining 'the attributes of shares in its corporations.' The majority sees the trees but not the forest.

"The Commerce Clause was included in our Constitution by the Framers to prevent the very type of economic protectionism Indiana's Control Share Chapter [represents].

"[A] state law which permits a majority of an Indiana corporation's stockholders to prevent individual investors, including out-of-state stockholders, from selling their stock to an out-of-state tender offeror and thereby frustrate any transfer of corporate control, is the archetype of the kind of state law that the Commerce Clause forbids.

"Unlike state blue sky laws, Indiana's Control Share Acquisitions Chapter regulates the purchase and sale of stock of Indiana corporations in interstate commerce. Indeed, as noted above, the Chapter will inevitably be used to block interstate transactions in such stock. Because the Commerce Clause protects the 'interstate market' in such securities, *Exxon,* and because the Control Share Chapter substantially interferes with this interstate market, the Chapter clearly conflicts with the Commerce Clause."

Notes and Questions

1. In EDGAR v. MITE CORP., 457 U.S. 624, 102 S.Ct. 2629, 73 L.Ed.2d 269 (1982), Illinois authorized its Secretary of State to hold hearings on and adjudicate the substantive fairness of tender offers and to deny the required registration if he concluded an offer was inequitable or would tend to work a fraud or deceit on the offerees. This applied to all corporations 10% of whose shares were owned by Illinois residents, or which had its principal office in Illinois.

Justice White's plurality opinion found the statute violated the commerce clause: "It is a direct restraint on interstate commerce and [has] an extraterritorial effect." by controlling "conduct beyond the boundary of the state." Further, applying the *Pike* test, the opinion found harmful effects on interstate commerce by preventing shareholders from selling their shares at a premium, "hindering the reallocation of economic resources to their highest-valued use," and by reducing the incentive "the tender offer mechanism provides incumbent management to perform well." Justice White could see "nothing to be weighed in the balance to sustain the law," at least "insofar as the Illinois law burdens out-of-state transactions" of nonresident shareholders.

2. *"Direct restraint on interstate trade."* Was it Justice White's view in *MITE* and *CTS* that "direct restraint" on the purchase of shares in the interstate market alone sufficed for a dormant commerce clause violation? Would such a view be consistent with the precedents? Sound? Did the Indiana law "restrain" the transfer of shares in the same sense as the Illinois law in *MITE*? Should the potential restraining impact of the Indiana law be viewed as only an "incidental" burden for which *Pike* would invoke a balancing judgment?

3. *"Balancing."* Apart from Justice Scalia's partial dissent, do the *CTS* opinions provide support for those who would jettison the *Pike* balancing formula for dormant commerce clause issues? Cf. Regan, *Siamese Essays: (I) CTS Corp. v. Dynamics Corp. of America and Dormant Commerce Clause Doctrine; (II) Extraterritorial State Legislation,* 85 Mich.L.Rev. 865, 1866–68 (1987). Did the Powell or White opinions apply *Pike* balancing considerations in *CTS*?

PROTECTING THE ENVIRONMENT AND NATURAL RESOURCES

CON LAW: P. 292, before Part VI

AMER CON: P. 227, before Part VI

NEW ENERGY CO. OF IND. v. LIMBACH, 486 U.S. 269, 108 S.Ct. 1803, 100 L.Ed.2d 302 (1988). In the early 1970's ethanol, usually made from corn, was mixed with gasoline to produce gasohol to lessen the fuel shortage and provide a market for surplus corn. Thereafter, its use continued with emphasis shifted to ethanol's environmental advantages as a substitute for lead to enhance fuel octane. Since gasohol is more costly to produce than leaded gasoline, many grain-producing states enacted ethanol subsidies or tax credits or exemptions to encourage its production and use.

Ohio granted a tax credit against its motor vehicle fuel tax for each gallon of ethanol used in gasohol, limited to ethanol produced in Ohio or in a state that granted reciprocal tax reduction from its motor vehicle fuel tax for Ohio-produced ethanol. Instead of a tax reduction, Indiana granted a direct subsidy to ethanol producers. Hence, ethanol produced in Indiana by New Energy Co. was ineligible for the Ohio tax credit. The Court, per SCALIA, J., unanimously held that application of the tax without the credit to New Energy's Indiana-produced ethanol discriminated in violation of the commerce clause:

"The Ohio provision at issue here explicitly deprives certain products of generally available beneficial tax treatment because they are made in certain other States, and thus on its face appears to violate the cardinal requirement of nondiscrimination. Appellees argue, however, that the availability of the tax credit to some out-of-state manufacturers (those in States that give tax advantages to Ohio-produced ethanol) shows that the Ohio provision, far from discriminating against interstate commerce, is likely to promote it, by encouraging other States to enact similar tax advantages that will spur the interstate sale of ethanol. We rejected a similar contention in an earlier 'reciprocity' case, *Great Atlantic & Pacific Tea Co. v. Cottrell*. The regulation at issue there permitted milk from out of State to be sold in Mississippi only if the State of origin accepted Mississippi milk on a reciprocal basis. Mississippi put forward, among other arguments, the assertion that 'the reciprocity requirement is in effect a free-trade provision, advancing the identical national interest that is served by the Commerce Clause.' In response, we said that 'Mississippi may not use the threat of economic isolation as a weapon to force sister States to enter into even a desirable reciprocity agreement.' More recently, we characterized a Nebraska reciprocity requirement for the export of ground water from the State as 'facially discriminatory legislation' which merited 'strictest scrutiny.' *Sporhase*.

"It is true that in *Cottrell* and *Sporhase* the effect of a State's refusal to accept the offered reciprocity was total elimination of all transport of the subject product into or out of the offering State; whereas in the present case the only effect of refusal is that the out-of-state product is placed at a substantial commercial disadvantage through discriminatory tax treatment. That makes no difference for purposes of Commerce Clause analysis. [In] *Hunt v. Washington Apple Advertising Comm'n*, we found invalid under the Commerce Clause a North Carolina statute that did not exclude apples from other States, but merely imposed additional costs upon Washington sellers and deprived them of the commercial advantage of their distinctive grading system. The present law likewise imposes an economic disadvantage upon out-of-state sellers; and the promise to remove that if reciprocity is accepted no more justifies disparity of treatment than it would justify categorical exclusion. * * *

"It has not escaped our notice that the appellant here, which is eligible to receive a cash subsidy under Indiana's program for in-state ethanol producers, is the potential beneficiary of a scheme no less discriminatory than the one that it attacks, and no less effective in conferring a commercial advantage over out-of-state competitors. To believe the Indiana scheme is valid, however, is not to believe that the Ohio scheme must be valid as well. The Commerce Clause does not prohibit all state action designed to give its residents an advantage in the marketplace, but only action of that description *in connection with the State's regulation of interstate commerce*. Direct subsidization of domestic industry does not ordinarily run afoul of that prohibition; discriminatory taxation of out-of-state manufactures does. Of course, even if the Indiana subsidy were invalid, retaliatory violation of the Commerce Clause by Ohio would not be acceptable. See *Cottrell*.

"Our cases leave open the possibility that a State may validate a statute that discriminates against interstate commerce by showing that it advances a legitimate local purpose that cannot be adequately served by reasonable nondiscriminatory alternatives. See, e.g., *Maine* v. *Taylor*, 477 U.S. 131, at 138, 151 (1986); *Sporhase*; *Hughes* v. *Oklahoma*; *Dean Milk*. This is perhaps just another way of saying that what may appear to be a 'discriminatory' provision in the constitutionally prohibited sense—that is, a protectionist enactment—may on closer analysis not be so. However it be put, the standards for such justification are high. Cf. *Philadelphia* v. *New Jersey* ('[W]here simple economic protectionism is effected by state legislation, a virtually *per se* rule of invalidity has been erected'); *Hughes* v. *Oklahoma* ('Facial discrimination by itself may be a fatal defect' and '[a]t a minimum * * * invokes the strictest scrutiny').

"Appellees advance two justifications for the clear discrimination in the present case: health and commerce. As to the first, they argue that the provision encourages use of ethanol (in replacement of lead as a gasoline octane-enhancer) to reduce harmful exhaust emissions, both in Ohio itself and in surrounding States whose polluted atmosphere may reach Ohio. Certainly the protection of health is a legitimate state goal, and we assume for purposes of this argument that use of ethanol generally furthers it. [But as] far as ethanol use in Ohio itself is concerned, there is no reason to suppose that ethanol produced in a State that does not offer tax advantages to ethanol produced in Ohio is less healthy, and thus should have its importation into Ohio suppressed by denial of the otherwise standard tax credit. And as far as ethanol use outside Ohio is concerned, surely that is just as effectively fostered by other States' subsidizing ethanol production or sale in some fashion other than giving a tax credit to Ohio-produced ethanol; but these helpful expedients do not qualify for the tax credit. It could not be clearer that health is not the purpose of the provision, but is merely an occasional and accidental effect of achieving what is its purpose, favorable tax treatment for *Ohio*-produced ethanol. Essentially the same reasoning also responds to appellees' second (and related) justification for the discrimination, that the reciprocity requirement is designed to increase commerce in ethanol by encouraging other States to enact ethanol subsidies. What is encouraged is not ethanol subsidies in general, but only favorable treatment for Ohio-produced ethanol. In sum, appellees' health and commerce justifications amount to no more than implausible speculation, which does not suffice to validate this plain discrimination against products of out-of-state manufacture."

Local environmental interest may validate apparent economic protectionism. Following the *Hughes* dicta, *Maine v. Taylor*, 477 U.S. 131, 106 S.Ct. 2440, 91 L.Ed.2d 110 (1986), per BLACKMUN, J., upheld 8 to 1 a Maine law that prohibited importation into Maine of live baitfish that competed with Maine's native baitfish industry. The Court relied on two trial court findings: (1) "Maine 'clearly has a legitimate and substantive purpose in prohibiting the importation of live baitfish' because 'substantive uncertainties' surrounded the effects baitfish parasites would have on the State's unique population of wild fish," and the "unpredictable [consequences] of introducing non-native species." (2) Less discriminatory means of protecting against these threats were currently "unavailable" despite the "abstract possibility" of developing acceptable testing procedures in the future. The Court added:

"A State must make reasonable efforts to avoid restraining the free flow of commerce across its borders, but it is not required to develop new and unproven means of protection at an uncertain cost. Appellee, of course, is free to work on his own or in conjunction with other bait dealers to develop scientifically acceptable sampling and inspection procedures for golden shiners; if and when such procedures are developed, Maine no longer may be able to justify its import ban. The State need not join in those efforts, however, and it need not pretend they already have succeeded." [a]

The balancing test—again questioned but followed. BENDIX AUTOLITE CORP. v. MIDWESCO ENTERPRISES, INC., ___ U.S. ___, 108 S.Ct. 2218, 100 L.Ed.2d 896 (1988), per KENNEDY, J., applied the commerce clause balancing test to invalidate an Ohio statute that tolled the state statute of limitations for any period that a "person" was not "present" in the state. To be "present" and avoid tolling, a corporation must appoint an agent for service of process as consent to general jurisdiction of the Ohio courts, even though, as in this case, Ohio's "long arm" statute made general jurisdiction available against the Illinois defendant under its contract to deliver and install a boiler in Ohio:

"The Ohio statute before us might have been held to be a discrimination that invalidates without extended inquiry. We choose, however, to assess the interests of the State, to demonstrate that its legitimate sphere of regulation is not much advanced by the statute while interstate commerce is subject to substantial restraints. We find that the burden imposed on interstate commerce by the tolling statute exceeds any local interest that the state might advance.

"[The] Ohio statutory scheme [forces] a foreign corporation to choose between exposure to the general jurisdiction of Ohio courts or forfeiture of the limitations defense, remaining subject to suit in Ohio in perpetuity. Requiring a foreign corporation to appoint an agent for service in all cases and to defend itself with reference to all transactions, including those in which it did not have the minimum contacts necessary for supporting personal jurisdiction, is a significant burden."

[Statute of limitations defenses] are an integral part of the legal system and are relied upon to project the liabilities of persons and corporations active in the commercial sphere. The State may not withdraw such defenses on conditions repugnant to the Commerce Clause. Where a State denies ordinary legal defenses or like privileges to out-of-state persons or corporations engaged in commerce, the State law will be reviewed under the Commerce Clause to determine whether the denial is discriminatory on its face or an impermissible burden on commerce. * * *

"In the particular case before us, the Ohio tolling statute must fall under the Commerce Clause. Ohio cannot justify its statute as a means of protecting its residents from corporations who become liable for acts done within the State but later withdraw from the jurisdiction, for it is conceded by all parties that the Ohio long arm statute would have permitted service on Midwesco throughout the period of limitations. The Ohio statute of limitations is tolled only for those foreign corporations that do not subject themselves to the general jurisdiction of Ohio courts. In this manner the Ohio statute imposes a greater burden on out-of-state companies than it does on Ohio companies, subjecting the activities of foreign and domestic corporations to inconsistent regulations. *CTS Corp.* v. *Dynamics Corp. of America.*"

a. Stevens, J., dissented, contending that "uncertainty" and "ambiguity about dangers and alternatives should actually defeat, rather than sustain, the discriminatory measure."

SCALIA, J., concurred in the judgment:

"I cannot confidently assess whether the Court's evaluation and balancing of interests in this case is right or wrong. Although the Court labels the effect of exposure to the general jurisdiction of Ohio's courts 'a significant burden' on commerce, I am not sure why that is. In precise terms, it is the burden of defending in Ohio (rather than some other forum) any lawsuit having all of the following features: (1) the plaintiff desires to bring it in Ohio, (2) it has so little connection to Ohio that service could not otherwise be made under Ohio's long-arm statute, and (3) it has a great enough connection to Ohio it is not subject to dismissal on *forum non conveniens* grounds. The record before us supplies no indication as to how many suits fit this description (even the present suit is not an example since appellee was subject to long-arm service), and frankly I have no idea how one would go about estimating the number. It may well be 'significant,' but for all we know it is 'negligible.'

"A person or firm that takes the other alternative, by declining to appoint a general agent for service, will remain theoretically subject to suit in Ohio (as the Court says) 'in perpetuity'—at least as far as the statute of limitations is concerned. But again, I do not know how we assess how significant a burden this is, unless anything that is theoretically perpetual must be significant. It seems very unlikely that anyone would intentionally wait to sue later rather than sooner—not only because the prospective defendant may die or dissolve, but also because prejudgment interest is normally not awarded, and the staleness of evidence generally harms the party with the burden of proof. The likelihood of an unintentionally delayed suit brought under this provision that could not be brought without it seems not enormously large. Moreover, whatever the likelihood is, it does not seem terribly plausible that any real-world deterrent effect on interstate transactions will be produced by the incremental cost of having to defend a *delayed* suit rather than a *timely* suit. But the point is, it seems to me we can do no more than speculate.

"On the other side of the scale, the Court considers the benefit of the Ohio scheme to local interests. These are, presumably, to enable the preservation of claims against defendants who have placed themselves beyond the personal jurisdiction of Ohio Courts, and (by encouraging appointment of an agent) to facilitate service upon out-of-state defendants who might otherwise be difficult to locate. [We] have no way of knowing how often these ends are in fact achieved, and the Court thus says little about them except to call them 'an important factor to consider.'

"Having evaluated the interests on both sides as roughly as this, the Court then proceeds to judge which is more important. This process is ordinarily called 'balancing,' *Pike,* but the scale analogy is not really appropriate, since the interests on both sides are incommensurate. It is more like judging whether a particular line is longer than a particular rock is heavy. All I am really persuaded of by the Court's opinion is that the burdens the Court labels 'significant' are more determinative of its decision than the benefits it labels 'important.' Were it not for the brief implication that there is here a discrimination unjustified by *any* state interest, I suggest an opinion could as persuasively have been written coming out the opposite way. We sometimes make similar 'balancing' judgments in determining how far the needs of the State can intrude upon the liberties of the individual, but that is of the essence of the courts' function as the nonpolitical branch. Weighing the governmental interests of a State against the needs of interstate commerce is, by contrast, a task squarely within the responsibility of Congress, see U.S. Const., Art. I, § 8, cl. 3, and 'ill suited to the judicial function.' *CTS Corp. v. Dynamics Corp. of America* (Scalia, J., concurring in part and concurring in judgment).

"I would therefore abandon the 'balancing' approach to these negative commerce clause cases, first explicitly adopted 18 years ago in *Pike,* and leave essentially legislative judgments to the Congress. Issues already decided I would leave untouched, but would adopt for the future an analysis more appropriate to our role and our abilities. This does no damage to the interests protected by the doctrine of *stare decisis.* Since the outcome of any particular still-undecided issue under the current methodology is in my view not predictable—except within the broad range that would in any event come out the same way under the test I would apply—no expectations can possibly be upset. To the contrary, the ultimate objective of the rule of *stare decisis* will be furthered. Because the outcome of the test I would apply is considerably more clear, confident expectations will more readily be able to be entertained.

"In my view, a state statute is invalid under the Commerce Clause if, and only if, it accords discriminatory treatment to interstate commerce in a respect not required to achieve a lawful state purpose. When such a validating purpose exists, it is for Congress and not us to determine it is not significant enough to justify the burden on commerce. The Ohio tolling statute is on its face discriminatory because it applies only to out-of-state corporations. That facial discrimination cannot be justified on the basis that 'it advances a legitimate local purpose that cannot be adequately served by reasonable nondiscriminatory alternatives,' *New Energy Co. of Indiana v. Limbach.* A tolling statute that operated only against persons beyond the reach of Ohio's long-arm statute, or against all persons that could not be found for mail service, would be narrowly tailored to advance the legitimate purpose of preserving claims; but the present statute extends the time for suit even against corporations which (like appellee) are fully suable within Ohio, and readily reachable through the mails.

"Because the present statute discriminates against interstate commerce by applying a disadvantageous rule against nonresidents for no valid state purpose that requires such a rule, I concur in the judgment that the Ohio statute violates the Commerce Clause." [a]

a. Rehnquist, C.J., dissented.

Chapter

STATE POWER TO TAX

SECTION: THE LAW AFTER *COMPLETE AUTO*: THE "PRACTICAL EFFECT" "FOUR–PART TEST"

DISCRIMINATION

CON LAW: P. 331, before note 7

Armco reaffirmed over Scalia, J.'s, strong dissent to the "internal consistency" test and to the negative implications of commerce clause. TYLER PIPE INDUSTRIES INC. v. WASHINGTON STATE DEPT. OF REVENUE, 483 U.S. 232, 107 S.Ct. 2810, 97 L.Ed.2d 199 (1987), reaffirmed the *Armco* ruling in an opinion reasserting basically the same reasoning in a similar situation. There Justice SCALIA, joined by Chief Justice Rehnquist, in dissent protested both the "internal consistency" requirement and, more broadly, the "doctrine of the negative Commerce Clause":

"Prior to *Armco*, the internal consistency test was applied only in cases involving apportionment of the net income of businesses that more than one state could tax. That was the issue in *Container Corp.* the only case cited by *Armco* in support of an internal consistency rule, and there is no reason automatically to require internal consistency in other contexts. A business can of course earn net income in more than one State, but the total amount of income is a unitary figure. Hence, when more than one State has taxing jurisdiction over a multistate enterprise, an inconsistent apportionment scheme could result in taxation of more than 100 percent of that firm's net income. Where, however, tax is assessed not on unitary income but on discrete events such as sale, manufacture, and delivery, which can occur in a single State, or in different States, that apportionment principle is not applicable; there is simply no unitary figure or event to apportion.

"It seems to me that we should adhere to our long tradition of judging State taxes on their own terms, and that there is even less justification for striking them down on the basis of assumptions as to what other States *might* do than there is for striking them down on the basis of what other States *in fact* do. Washington's B & O tax is plainly lawful on its own. It may well be that other States will impose similar taxes that will increase the burden on businesses operating interstate—just as it may well be that they will impose *dis*similar taxes that have the same effect. That is why the Framers gave Congress the power to regulate interstate commerce. Evaluating each State's taxing scheme on its own gives this Court the power to eliminate evident discrimination, while

65

at the same time leaving the States an appropriate degree of freedom to structure their revenue measures. Finer tuning than this is for the Congress.

II

"I think it particularly inappropriate to leap to a restrictive 'internal consistency' rule, since the platform from which we launch that leap is such an unstable structure. It takes no more than our opinions this term, and the number of prior decisions they explicitly or implicitly overrule, to demonstrate that the practical results we have deduced from the so-called 'negative' Commerce Clause form not a rock but a 'quagmire,' *Northwestern States.*

"[That] uncertainty in application has been attributable in no small part to the lack of any clear theoretical underpinning for judicial 'enforcement' of the Commerce Clause. The text of the Clause states that 'Congress shall have Power [To] regulate Commerce with foreign Nations, and among the several States, and with the Indian Tribes.' On its face, this is a charter for Congress, not the courts, to ensure 'an area of trade free from interference by the States.' *Boston Stock Exchange.* The pre-emption of state legislation would automatically follow, of course, if the grant of power to Congress to regulate interstate commerce were exclusive, as Charles Pinckney's draft constitution would have provided, see Abel, *The Commerce Clause in the Constitutional Convention and in Contemporary Comment,* 25 Minn.L.Rev. 432, 434 (1941), and as John Marshall at one point seemed to believe it was. See *Gibbons v. Odgen.* However, unlike the District Clause, which empowers Congress 'To exercise exclusive Legislation,' Art. I, § 8, cl. 17, the language of the Commerce Clause gives no indication of exclusivity. See *License Cases* (1847) (opinion of Taney, C.J.). Nor can one assume generally that Congress' Article I powers are exclusive; many of them plainly coexist with concurrent authority in the States. See *Kewanee Oil Co. v. Bicron Corp.,* 416 U.S. 470, 94 S.Ct. 1879, 40 L.Ed.2d 315 (1974) (patent power); *Goldstein v. California,* 412 U.S. 546, 93 S.Ct. 2303, 37 L.Ed.2d 163 (1973) (copyright power); *Houston v. Moore,* 5 Wheat. 1, 18 U.S. 1, 5 L.Ed. 19 (1820) (court martial jurisdiction over the militia); *Sturges v. Crowninshield,* 4 Wheat. 122, 17 U.S. 122, 4 L.Ed. 529 (1819) (bankruptcy power). Furthermore, there is no correlative denial of power over commerce to the States in Art. I, § 10, as there is, for example, with the power to coin money or make treaties. And both the States and Congress assumed from the date of ratification that at least some state laws regulating commerce were valid. See *License Cases.* The exclusivity rationale is infinitely less attractive today than it was in 1847. Now that we know interstate commerce embraces such activities as growing wheat for home consumption, *Wickard,* and local loan sharking, *Perez v. United States,* it is more difficult to imagine what state activity would survive an exclusive Commerce Clause than to imagine what would be precluded. * * *

"The least plausible theoretical justification of all is the idea that in enforcing the negative Commerce Clause the Court is not applying a constitutional command at all, but is merely interpreting the will of Congress, whose silence in certain fields of interstate commerce (but not in others) is to be taken as a prohibition of regulation. There is no conceivable reason why congressional inaction under the Commerce Clause should be deemed to have the same pre-emptive effect elsewhere accorded only to congressional action. There, as elsewhere, 'Congress' silence is just that—silence * * *.' *Alaska Airlines, Inc. v. Brock,* ___ U.S. ___, 107 S.Ct. 1476, 94 L.Ed.2d 661 (1987). * * *

"The historical record provides no grounds for reading the Commerce Clause to be other than what it says—an authorization for Congress to regulate commerce. The strongest evidence in favor of a negative Commerce Clause—that version of it which renders federal authority over interstate commerce exclusive—is Madison's comment during the Convention that 'Whether the States are now restrained from laying tonnage duties depends on the extent of the power "to regulate commerce." These terms are vague but seem to exclude this power of the States.' 2 M. Farrand, *Records of the Federal Convention of 1787*, p. 625 (1937). This comment, however, came during discussion of what became Art. I, § 10, cl. 3: 'No State shall, without the Consent of Congress, lay any Duty of Tonnage * * *.' The fact that it is difficult to conceive how the power to regulate commerce would *not* include the power to impose duties; and the fact that, despite this apparent coverage, the Convention went on to adopt a provision prohibiting States from levying duties on tonnage without congressional approval; suggest that Madison's assumption of exclusivity of the federal commerce power was ill considered and not generally shared.

"Against this mere shadow of historical support there is the overwhelming reality that the Commerce Clause, in its broad outlines, was not a major subject of controversy, neither during the constitutional debates nor in the ratifying conventions. Instead, there was 'nearly universal agreement that the federal government should be given the power of regulating commerce,' Abel, at 443–444, in much the form provided. 'The records disclose no constructive criticisms by the states of the commerce clause as proposed to them.' F. Frankfurter, *The Commerce Clause under Marshall, Taney and Waite* 12 (1937). In *The Federalist*, Madison and Hamilton wrote numerous discourses on the virtues of free trade and the need for uniformity and national control of commercial regulation, but said little of substance specifically about the Commerce Clause—and that little was addressed primarily to foreign and Indian trade. See generally Abel, at 470–474. Madison does not seem to have exaggerated when he described the Commerce Clause as an addition to the powers of the national government 'which few oppose and from which no apprehensions are entertained.' I think it beyond question that many 'apprehensions' would have been 'entertained' if supporters of the Constitution had hinted that the Commerce Clause, despite its language, gave this Court the power it has since assumed. As Justice Frankfurter pungently put it: 'the doctrine that state authority must be subject to such limitations as the Court finds it necessary to apply for the protection of the national community [is] an audacious doctrine, which, one may be sure, would hardly have been publicly avowed in support of the adoption of the Constitution.' Frankfurter, at 19.

"In sum, to the extent that we have gone beyond guarding against rank discrimination against citizens of other States—which is regulated not by the Commerce Clause but by the Privileges and Immunities Clause, U.S.Const., Art. IV, § 2, cl. 1 ('The Citizens of each State shall be entitled to all Privileges and Immunities of Citizens in the several States')—the Court for over a century has engaged in an enterprise that it has been unable to justify by textual support or even coherent nontextual theory, that it was almost certainly not intended to undertake, and that it has not undertaken very well. It is astonishing that we should be expanding our beachhead in this impoverished territory, rather than being satisfied with what we have already acquired by a sort of intellectual adverse possession."

FAIR APPORTIONMENT

CON LAW: P. 361, after note 4

Apportionment of gross receipts from wholesale sales. TYLER PIPE INDUS-TRIES v. WASHINGTON DEP'T OF REVENUE, supra, per STEVENS, J., also upheld the Washington tax on wholesaling measured by gross receipts as applied to total receipts on all sales to Washington buyers by an out-of-state manufactur-er working through a sales agent in Washington:

"Tyler [asserts] that the B & O tax does not fairly apportion the tax burden between its activities in Washington and its activities in other States. See *Complete Auto.* Washington taxes the full value of receipts from in-state wholesaling or manufacturing; thus, an out-of-state manufacturer selling in Washington is subject to an unapportioned wholesale tax even though the value of the wholesale transaction is partly attributable to manufacturing activity carried on in another State that plainly has jurisdiction to tax that activity. This apportionment argument rests on the erroneous assumption that through the B & O tax, Washington is taxing the unitary activity of manufacturing and wholesaling. We have already determined, however, that the manufacturing tax and wholesaling tax are not compensating taxes for substantially equivalent events in invalidating the multiple activities exemption. Thus, the activity of wholesaling—whether by an in-state or an out-of-state manufacturer—must be viewed as a separate activity conducted wholly within Washington that no other State has jurisdiction to tax. See *Moorman Mfg. Co. v. Bair* (gross receipts tax on sales to customers within state would be 'plainly valid'); *Standard Pressed Steel Co. v. Washington Revenue Dept.* (selling tax measured by gross proceeds of sales is 'apportioned exactly to the activities taxed')."

Does this provide an adequate explanation for *General Motors* and *Standard Steel* considered pp. 338–41?

CON LAW P. 361, before Part IV

5. *Internal and external consistency.* GOLDBERG v. SWEET, ___ U.S. ___, 109 S.Ct. 582, 102 L.Ed.2d 607 (1989), per MARSHALL, J., unanimously upheld an Illinois tax of 5% of the gross charge on all interstate telecommunications that originated or terminated in Illinois, and were charged to an Illinois service address, regardless where the call was billed or paid.[a]

I

A

"This case comes to us against a backdrop of massive technological and legal changes in the telecommunications industry. Years ago, all interstate telephone calls were relayed through electric wires and transferred by human operators working switchboards. Those days are past. Today, a computerized network of electronic paths transmits thousands of electronic signals per minute through a complex system of microwave radios, fiber optics, satellites and cables. When fully connected, this network offers billions of paths from one point to another. When a direct path is full or not working efficiently, the computer system instantly activates another path. Signals may even change paths in the middle of a telephone call without perceptible interruption. Thus, the path taken by the electronic signals is often indirect and typically bears no relation to state

a. An identical tax was imposed on intra-state telecommunications.

boundaries.[2] The number of possible paths, the nature of the electronic signals, and the system of computerized switching make it virtually impossible to trace and record the actual paths taken by the electronic signals which create an individual telephone call. * * *

II

B

"[Appellants] argue that the telecommunications tax is not fairly apportioned because Illinois taxes the gross charge of each telephone call. They interpret our prior cases [to] require Illinois to tax only a fraction of the gross charge of each telephone call based on the miles which the electronic signals traveled within Illinois as a portion of the total miles traveled.

"[The] central purpose behind the apportionment requirement is to ensure that each State taxes only its fair share of an interstate transaction. But 'we have long held that the Constitution imposes no single [apportionment] formula on the States,' and therefore have declined to undertake the essentially legislative task of establishing a 'single constitutionally mandated method of taxation.' *Container Corp.; Moorman Mfg. Co.* Instead, we determine whether a tax is fairly apportioned by examining whether it is internally and externally consistent. *Armco Inc.; Container Corp.*

"To be internally consistent, a tax must be structured so that if every State were to impose an identical tax, no multiple taxation would result. Thus, the internal consistency test focuses on the text of the challenged statute and hypothesizes a situation where other States have passed an identical statute. We conclude that the Tax Act is internally consistent, for if every State taxed only those interstate phone calls which are charged to an in-state service address, only one State would tax each interstate telephone call.

"Appellant Sprint [contends] that, under *Armco*, a court evaluating the internal consistency of a challenged tax must also compare the tax to the similar, but not identical, taxes imposed by other States. Sprint misreads *Armco*. If we were to determine the internal consistency of one State's tax by comparing it with slightly different taxes imposed by other States, the validity of state taxes would turn solely on 'the shifting complexities of the tax codes of 49 other States.' *Armco*. In any event, to the extent that other States have passed tax statutes which create a risk of multiple taxation, we reach that issue under the external consistency test, to which we now turn.

"The external consistency test asks whether the State has taxed only that portion of the revenues from the interstate activity which reasonably reflects the in-state component of the activity being taxed. *Container Corp.* We thus examine the in-state business activity which triggers the taxable event and the practical or economic effect of the tax on that interstate activity. Appellants first contend that any tax assessed on the gross charge of an interstate activity cannot reasonably reflect in-state business activity and therefore must be unapportioned. The Director argues that, because the Tax Act has the same economic effect as a sales tax, it can be based on the gross charge of the telephone call. See, e.g., *McGoldrick v. Berwind-White Coal Mining Co.*, 309 U.S. 33, 58 (1940) (sales tax). * * *

---

2. A signal traveling from one microwave tower to another may pass through a State but never touch anything in it. A satellite transmission may leave a caller's building, travel to outer space and remain there until it is received by a satellite dish at the building housing the receiving party.

"We believe that the Director has the better of this argument. The tax at issue has many of the characteristics of a sales tax. It is assessed on the individual consumer, collected by the retailer, and accompanies the retail purchase of an interstate telephone call. Even though such a retail purchase is not a purely local event since it triggers simultaneous activity in several States, cf. *McGoldrick,* the Tax Act reasonably reflects the way that consumers purchase interstate telephone calls.

"The Director further contends that the Illinois telecommunications tax is fairly apportioned because the Tax Act reaches only those interstate calls which are (1) originated or terminated in Illinois and (2) charged to an Illinois service address. Appellants Goldberg and McTigue, by contrast, raise the spectre of many States assessing a tax on the gross charge of an interstate telephone call. Appellants have exaggerated the extent to which the Tax Act creates a risk of multiple taxation. We doubt that States through which the telephone call's electronic signals merely pass have a sufficient nexus to tax that call. See *United Air Lines, Inc. v. Mahin,* 410 U.S. 623, 631 (1973) (State has no nexus to tax an airplane based solely on its flight over the State). We also doubt that termination of an interstate telephone call, by itself, provides a substantial enough nexus for a State to tax a call. See *National Bellas Hess, Inc. v. Department of Revenue of Illinois,* 386 U.S. 753 (1967) (receipt of mail provides insufficient nexus).

"We believe that only two States have a nexus substantial enough to tax a consumer's purchase of an interstate telephone call. The first is a State like Illinois which taxes the origination or termination of an interstate telephone call charged to a service address within that State. The second is a State which taxes the origination or termination of an interstate telephone call billed or paid within that State.

"We recognize that, if the service address and billing location of a taxpayer are in different States, some interstate telephone calls could be subject to multiple taxation. This limited possibility of multiple taxation, however, is not sufficient to invalidate the Illinois statutory scheme. To the extent that other States' telecommunications taxes pose a risk of multiple taxation, the credit provision contained in the Tax Act operates to avoid actual multiple taxation.[b]

* * *

"It should not be overlooked, moreover, that the external consistency test is essentially a practical inquiry. In previous cases we have endorsed apportionment formulas based upon the miles a bus, train, or truck traveled within the taxing State. But those cases all dealt with the movement of large physical objects over identifiable routes, where it was practicable to keep track of the distance actually traveled within the taxing State. [This] case, by contrast, involves the more intangible movement of electronic impulses through computerized networks. An apportionment formula based on mileage or some other geographic division of individual telephone calls would produce insurmountable administrative and technological barriers. [We] thus find it significant that Illinois' method of taxation is a realistic legislative solution to the technology of the present-day telecommunications industry.

b. The law provides a credit to any taxpayer who paid a tax on the same telephone call that triggered the Illinois tax.

"In sum, we hold that the Tax Act is fairly apportioned. Its economic effect is like a sales tax, the risk of multiple taxation is low, and actual multiple taxation is precluded by the credit provision." ∗ ∗ ∗[c]

Note

For an excellent critical discussion of the "internal consistence" rule see Walter Hellerstein, *Is "Internal Consistency" Foolish?: Reflections on an Emerging Commerce Clause Restraint on State Taxation,* 87 Mich.L.Rev. 138 (1988)

SECTION: SPECIAL CONSIDERATIONS FOR FOREIGN COMMERCE

CON LAW: P. 371, end of note 2

Should the import-export clause bar a state nondiscriminatory ad valorem property tax on imported tobacco held in a customs bonded warehouse by a tobacco manufacturing company for a two-year aging period after which, upon payment of customs duties, it would be processed in the company's local plant? Consider *R.J. Reynolds Tobacco Co. v. Durham County,* 479 U.S. 130, 107 S.Ct. 499, 93 L.Ed.2d 449 (1986).

c. The Court also held the tax valid under the "substantial nexus," "discrimination," and "fairly related" prongs of *Complete Auto.*

Justice Stevens and O'Connor concurred in the result and the opinion in part. Justice Scalia concurred in the judgment, reasserting his view that "only taxes that facially discriminate against interstate commerce violate the negative commerce clause."

Chapter

SUBSTANTIVE PROTECTION OF
ECONOMIC INTERESTS

SECTION: "TAKING" OF PROPERTY INTERESTS

"TAKING" THROUGH REGULATION

CON LAW: P. 419, end of note 6

AMER CON: P. 278, end of note 4

RTS & LIB: P. 91, end of note 4

Some time after cable television operators attached their cables to Florida Power Company's poles at agreed annual rents of $5.50 to $7.15 per pole, the operaters sought and obtained an FCC order under the Federal Pole Attachment Act, setting the rental at $1.79 per pole. FCC v. FLORIDA POWER CORP., 480 U.S. 245, 107 S.Ct. 1107, 94 L.Ed.2d 282 (1987), per MARSHALL, J., unanimously rejected the contention that under *Loretta* the order was a per se taking. Unlike *Loretta*, "nothing in the [Act as interpreted] gives cable companies any right to occupy space on utility poles." [6]

"[Respondents contend], in essence, that it is a taking under *Loretta* for a tenant invited to lease at a rent of $7.15 to remain at a regulated rent of $1.79. But it is the invitation, not the rent, that makes the difference. The line which separates these cases from *Loretta* is the unambiguous distinction between a commercial lessee and an interloper with a government license." [a]

CON LAW: P. 419, before note 7

AMER CON: P. 278, before Sec. 5

RTS & LIB: P. 91, before Sec. 5

Regulating harmful activities: Pennsylvania Mining revisited. KEYSTONE BITUMINOUS COAL ASS'N v. DeBENEDICTIS, 480 U.S. 470, 107 S.Ct. 1232, 94 L.Ed.2d 472 (1987), per STEVENS, J., upheld 5 to 4 [b] Pennsylvania's Subsidence Act (§ 4) that forbade mining bituminous coal "so as to cause damage as a result of the caving in, collapse or subsidence of" public buildings, human dwellings, cemeteries, perennial streams, impounds of water, acquifers supplying

6. [We] do not decide today what the application of *Loretta* would be if the FCC in a future case required utilities, over objection, to enter into, renew, or refrain from terminating pole attachment agreements.

a. The Court found the $1.79 rate not confiscatory.

b. Brennan, White, Marshall, and Blackmun, JJ., joined the Stevens opinion.

public water systems, and coal refuse disposal areas, unless the current owner of the structure consents and the resulting damage is fully repaired or compensated.[c] Pursuant to the statute, the Pennsylvania Dept. of Environmental Resources (DER) applied a formula that required 50% of the coal under protected structures to be kept in place to provide surface support. The lower federal courts denied an injunction against enforcement of the Act, distinguishing *Pennsylvania Coal*, and the Court affirmed:

"Unlike the Kohler Act, which was passed upon in *Pennsylvania Coal*, the Subsidence Act does not merely involve a balancing of the private economic interests of coal companies against the private interests of the surface owners. The Pennsylvania Legislature specifically found that important public interests are served by enforcing a policy that is designed to minimize subsidence in certain areas. Section 2 of the Subsidence Act provides: 'This act shall be deemed to be an exercise of the police powers of the Commonwealth for the protection of the health, safety and general welfare of the people of the Commonwealth, by providing for the conservation of surface land areas which may be affected in the mining of bituminous [coal], to aid in the protection of the safety of the public, to enhance the value of such lands for taxation, to aid in the preservation of surface water drainage and public water supplies and generally to improve the use and enjoyment of such [lands].'

"None of the indicia of a statute enacted solely for the benefit of private parties identified in Justice Holmes' opinion are present here. First, Justice Holmes explained that the Kohler Act was a 'private benefit' statute since it 'ordinarily does not apply to land when the surface is owned by the owner of the coal.' The Subsidence Act, by contrast, has no such exception. The current surface owner may only waive the protection of the Act if the DER consents. Moreover, the Court was forced to reject the Commonwealth's safety justification for the Kohler Act because it found that the Commonwealth's interest in safety could as easily have been accomplished through a notice requirement to landowners. The Subsidence Act, by contrast, is designed to accomplish a number of widely varying interests, with reference to which petitioners have not suggested alternative methods through which the Commonwealth could proceed. * * *

"Thus, the Subsidence Act differs from the Kohler Act in critical and dispositive respects. With regard to the Kohler Act, the Court believed that the Commonwealth had acted only to ensure against damage to some private landowners' homes. Justice Holmes stated that if the private individuals needed support for their structures, they should not have 'take[n] the risk of acquiring only surface rights.' Here, by contrast, the Commonwealth is acting to protect the public interest in health, the environment, and the fiscal integrity of the area. That private individuals erred in taking a risk cannot estop the State from exercising its police power to abate activity akin to a public nuisance. The Subsidence Act is a prime example that 'circumstances may so change in time [as] to clothe with such a [public] interest what at other times * * * would be a matter of purely private concern.' *Block v. Hirsh.* * * *

"The Court's hesitance to find a taking when the state merely restrains uses of property that are tantamount to public nuisances is consistent with the notion of 'reciprocity of advantage' that Justice Holmes referred to in *Pennsylvania Coal*. Under our system of government, one of the state's primary ways of preserving the public weal is restricting the uses individuals can make of their

c. The full text of the statute is set out in fn. 6 of the *Keystone* opinion.

property. While each of us is burdened somewhat by such restrictions, we, in turn, benefit greatly from the restrictions that are placed on others.[21] * * *

[The] public interest in preventing activities similar to public nuisances is a substantial one, which in many instances has not required compensation. The Subsidence Act, unlike the Kohler Act, plainly seeks to further such an interest. Nonetheless, we need not rest our decision on this factor alone, because petitioners have also failed to make a showing of diminution of value sufficient to satisfy the test set forth in *Pennsylvania Coal* and our other regulatory takings cases.

"Diminution of Value and Investment-Backed Expectations

"The second factor that distinguishes this case from *Pennsylvania Coal* is the finding in that case that the Kohler Act made mining of 'certain coal' commercially impracticable. In this case, by contrast, petitioners have not shown any deprivation significant enough to satisfy the heavy burden placed upon one alleging a regulatory taking. For this reason, their takings claim must fail.

"In addressing petitioners' claim we must not disregard the posture in which this case comes before us. The District Court granted summary judgment to respondents only on the facial challenge to the Subsidence Act. [The] posture of the case is critical because we have recognized an important distinction between a claim that the mere enactment of a statute constitutes a taking and a claim that the particular impact of government action on a specific piece of property requires the payment of just compensation. '[The] test to be applied in considering this facial challenge is fairly straightforward. A statute regulating the uses that can be made of property effects a taking if it "denies an owner economically viable use of his land * * *."' [c] Petitioners thus face an uphill battle in making a facial attack on the Act as a taking.

"The hill is made especially steep because petitioners have not claimed, at this stage, that the Act makes it commercially impracticable for them to continue mining their bituminous coal interests in western Pennsylvania. Indeed, petitioners have not even pointed to a single mine that can no longer be mined for profit. The only evidence available on the effect that the Subsidence Act has had on petitioners' mining operations comes from petitioners' answers to respondents' interrogatories. [The] total coal in [petitioners'] 13 mines amounts to over 1.46 billion tons. [Section] 4 requires them to leave less than 2% of their coal in place. But, as we have indicated, nowhere near all of the underground coal is extractable even aside from the Subsidence Act. The categories of coal that must be left for § 4 purposes and other purposes are not necessarily distinct sets, and there is no information in the record as to how much coal is actually left in the ground *solely* because of § 4. We do know, however, that petitioners have never claimed that their mining operations, or even any specific mines, have been unprofitable since the Subsidence Act was passed. Nor is there evidence that mining in any specific location affected by the 50% rule has been unprofitable. * * *

---

21. The Takings Clause has never been read to require the States or the courts to calculate whether a specific individual has suffered burdens under this generic rule in excess of the benefits received. Not every individual gets a full dollar return in benefits for the taxes he or she pays; yet, no one suggests that an individual has a right to compensation for the difference between taxes paid and the dollar value of benefits received.

c. The opinion quoted from *Hodel v. Virginia Surface Mining and Reclamation Assn., Inc.*

"The Coal in Place

"The parties have stipulated that enforcement of the DER's 50% rule will require petitioners to leave approximately 27 million tons of coal in place. Because they own that coal but cannot mine it, they contend that Pennsylvania has appropriated it for the public purposes described in the Subsidence Act.

"This argument fails for the reason explained in *Penn Central* and *Andrus*. The 27 million tons of coal do not constitute a separate segment of property for takings law purposes. Many zoning ordinances place limits on the property owner's right to make profitable use of some segments of his property. A requirement that a building occupy no more than a specified percentage of the lot on which it is located could be characterized as a taking of the vacant area as readily as the requirement that coal pillars be left in place. Similarly, under petitioners' theory one could always argue that a set-back ordinance requiring that no structure be built within a certain distance from the property line constitutes a taking because the footage represents a distinct segment of property for takings law purposes. There is no basis for treating the less than 2% of petitioners' coal as a separate parcel of [property.]

"When the coal that must remain beneath the ground is viewed in the context of any reasonable unit of petitioners' coal mining operations and financial-backed expectations, it is plain that the petitioners have not come close to satisfying their burden of proving that they have been denied the economically viable use of that property. The record indicates that only about 75% of petitioners' underground coal can be profitably mined in any event, and there is no showing that petitioners' reasonable 'investment-backed expectations' have been materially affected by the additional duty to retain the small percentage that must be used to support the structures protected by § 4." [d]

REHNQUIST, C.J., dissenting, joined by Powell, O'Connor and Scalia, JJ., noted that the Kohler Act invalidated in *Pennsylvania Coal*, like the Subsidence Act, was intended to serve "public interests," quoting the reference in the Kohler preamble to "wrecked and dangerous streets and highways, collapsed public buildings, churches, schools, factories, and private dwellings, broken gas, water and sewer systems, the loss of human life." But the dissent contended that, despite such public interest, these acts were not within the "nuisance exception" to the takings compensation requirement: " 'The nuisance exception to the taking guarantee [is] not coterminous with the police power itself.' *Penn Central* (Rehnquist, J. dissenting), is but a narrow exception to prevent a 'misuse or illegal use.' *Curtin v. Benson*, 222 U.S. 78, 32 S.Ct. 31, 56 L.Ed. 102 (1911). It is not intended to allow 'the prevention of a legal and essential use, an attribute of its ownership.' Id.

"The narrow nature of this exception is compelled by the concerns underlying the Fifth Amendment. [A] broad exception to the operation of the Just Compensation Clause based on the exercise of multifaceted health, welfare, and safety regulations would surely allow government much greater authority than we have recognized to impose societal burdens on individual landowners, for

d. The Court also ruled that the "bundle of rights" concept applied to the taking claim despite Pennsylvania's "unique" property law that regarded the "support estate" as an interest in land separate from the mineral estate and surface estate. Likewise, it rejected the contention that the Subsidence Act violated the contract clause by not allowing the owners of the mining interest to hold the surface owners to their contractual waiver of liability for surface damage. The Court invoked the "strong public interest in preventing this type of harm, the environmental effect of which transcends any private agreement between private parties." See Section 5, infra.

nearly every action the government takes is intended to secure for the public an extra measure of 'health, safety and welfare.'

"Thus, our cases applying the 'nuisance' rationale have involved at least two narrowing principles. First, nuisance regulations exempted from the Fifth Amendment have rested on discrete and narrow purposes. See *Goldblatt; Hadacheck; Mugler.* The Subsidence Act, however, is much more than a nuisance statute. The central purposes of the Act, though including public safety, reflect a concern for preservation of buildings, economic development, and maintenance of property values to sustain the Commonwealth's tax base. We should hesitate to allow a regulation based on essentially economic concerns to be insulated from the dictates of the Fifth Amendment by labeling it nuisance regulation.

"Second, and more significantly, our cases have never applied the nuisance exception to allow complete extinction of the value of a parcel of property. Though nuisance regulations have been sustained despite a substantial reduction in value, we have not accepted the proposition that the State may completely extinguish a property interest or prohibit all use without providing [compensation.]

"Here, petitioners' interests in particular coal deposits have been completely destroyed. By requiring that defined seams of coal remain in the ground § 4 of the Subsidence Act has extinguished any interest one might want to acquire in this property, for ' "the right to coal consists in the right to mine it." ' *Pennsylvania Coal.* Application of the nuisance exception in these circumstances would allow the State not merely to forbid one 'particular use' of property with many uses but to extinguish *all* beneficial use of petitioners' property.

"Though suggesting that the purposes alone are sufficient to uphold the Act, the Court avoids reliance on the nuisance exception by finding that the Subsidence Act does not impair petitioners' investment backed expectations or ability to profitably operate their businesses. This conclusion follows mainly from the Court's broad definition of the 'relevant mass of property,' which allows it to ascribe to the Subsidence Act a less pernicious effect on the interests of the property owner. The need to consider the effect of regulation on some identifiable segment of property makes all important the admittedly difficult task of defining the relevant parcel.

"[The] Court's refusal to recognize the coal in the ground as a separate segment of property for takings purposes is based on the fact that the alleged taking is 'regulatory,' rather than a physical intrusion. On the facts of this case, I cannot see how the label placed on the government's action is relevant to consideration of its impact on property rights.

"Our decisions establish that governmental action short of physical invasion may constitute a taking because such regulatory action might result in 'as complete [a loss] as if the [government] had entered upon the surface of the land and taken exclusive possession of it.' *United States v. Causby.* [We] have recognized that regulations—unlike physical invasions—do not typically extinguish the 'full bundle' of rights in a particular piece of property. *Andrus.* [This] characteristic of regulations frequently makes unclear the breadth of their impact on identifiable segments of property, and has required that we evaluate the effects in light of the 'several factors' enumerated in *Penn Central*: '[t]he economic impact of the regulation on the claimant, * * * the extent to which the regulation has interfered with investment-backed expectations, [and] the character of the governmental action.'

"No one, however, would find any need to employ these analytical tools where the government has physically taken an identifiable segment of property. Physical appropriation by the government leaves no doubt that it has in fact deprived the owner of all uses of the land. Similarly, there is no need for further analysis where the government by regulation extinguishes the whole bundle of rights in an identifiable segment of property, for the effect of this action on the holder of the property is indistinguishable from the effect of a physical taking. Thus, it is clear our decision in *Andrus* would have been different if the government had confiscated the avian artifacts. In my view, a different result would also follow if the government simply prohibited every use of that [property].

"In this case, enforcement of the Subsidence Act and its regulations will require petitioners to leave approximately 27 million tons of coal in place. There is no question that this coal is an identifiable and separable property interest. Unlike many property interests, the 'bundle' of rights in this coal is sparse. ' "For practical purposes, the right to coal consists in the right to mine it." ' *Pennsylvania Coal.* From the relevant perspective—that of the property owners—this interest has been destroyed every bit as much as if the government had proceeded to mine the coal for its own use. The regulation, then, does not merely inhibit one strand in the bundle, cf. *Andrus*, but instead destroys completely any interest in a segment of property. In these circumstances, I think it unnecessary to consider whether petitioners may operate individual mines or their overall mining operations profitably, for they have been denied all use of 27 million tons of coal." [e]

NOLLAN v. CALIFORNIA COASTAL COMMISSION
483 U.S. 825, 107 S.Ct. 3141, 97 L.Ed.2d 677 (1987).

JUSTICE SCALIA delivered the opinion of the Court.

[James and Marilyn Nollan owned a Pacific beachfront lot one-fourth mile south of Faria County Park, a public beach, and 1800 feet north of the Cove, another public beach area. The lot's oceanside boundary was the historic mean high tide line, about 10 feet seaward from Nollans' eight-foot high concrete seawall. The Coastal Commission conditioned replacement of Nollans' delapidated 521 square foot cottage with a two-story residence covering 2464 square feet of the lot in keeping with the rest of the neighborhood upon Nollans' allowing the public an easement to pass laterally across their property on the strip between the mean high tide line and the seawall. After a public hearing the Coastal Commission had found that the new house would increase blockage of the view of the ocean, thus contributing to "a 'wall' of residential structures" that would prevent the public "psychologically * * * from realizing a stretch of coastline exists nearby that they have every right to visit," would increase private use of the shorefront, and along with other area development would cumulatively "burden the public's ability to traverse to and along the shorefront." The Commission had similarly conditioned 43 of the 57 shorefront property development permits in the same tract of land. The remaining 14 had been approved before administrative regulations allowed imposition of the condi-

---

e. Rehnquist, C.J.'s opinion also dissented from the Court's rejection of the petitioners' claim based on the "support estate" as a sepa- rate interest in land. The dissent did not consider the contract clause claim.

tion. The California Court of Appeals upheld the condition over a takings clause claim. The United States Supreme Court reversed.]

Had California simply required the Nollans to make an easement across their beachfront available to the public on a permanent basis in order to increase public access to the beach, rather than conditioning their permit to rebuild their house on their agreeing to do so, we have no doubt there would have been a taking. To say that the appropriation of a public easement across a landowner's premises does not constitute the taking of a property interest but rather, (as Justice Brennan contends) "a mere restriction on its use" is to use words in a manner that deprives them of all their ordinary meaning. Indeed, one of the principal uses of the eminent domain power is to assure that the government be able to require conveyance of just such interests, so long as it pays for them. J. Sackman, 1 *Nichols on Eminent Domain* § 2.1[1] (Rev. 3d ed. 1985). Perhaps because the point is so obvious, we have never been confronted with a controversy that required us to rule upon it, but our cases' analysis of the effect of other governmental action leads to the same conclusion. We have repeatedly held that, as to property reserved by its owner for private use, "the right to exclude [others is] 'one of the most essential sticks in the bundle of rights that are commonly characterized as property.'" *Loretto*. In *Loretto* we observed that where governmental action results in "[a] permanent physical occupation" of the property, by the government itself or by others "our cases uniformly have found a taking to the extent of the occupation, without regard to whether the action achieves an important public benefit or has only minimal economic impact on the owner." We think a "permanent physical occupation" has occurred, for purposes of that rule, where individuals are given a permanent and continuous right to pass to and fro, so that the real property may continuously be traversed, even though no particular individual is permitted to station himself permanently upon the premises. * * *

Given [that] requiring uncompensated conveyance of the easement outright would violate the Fourteenth Amendment, the question becomes whether requiring it to be conveyed as a condition for issuing a land use permit alters the outcome. We have long recognized that land use regulation does not effect a taking if it "substantially advance[s] legitimate state interests" and does not "den[y] an owner economically viable use of his land." See *Penn Central* ("a use restriction may constitute a 'taking' if not reasonably necessary to the effectuation of a substantial government purpose"). Our cases have not elaborated on the standards for determining what constitutes a "legitimate state interest" or what type of connection between the regulation and the state interest satisfies the requirement that the former "substantially advance" the latter. They have made clear, however, that a broad range of governmental purposes and regulations satisfies these requirements. See Agins v. Tiburon, 447 U.S. 255, 100 S.Ct. 2138, 65 L.Ed.2d 106 (1980) (scenic zoning); *Penn Central* (landmark preservation); *Euclid v. Ambler Realty Co.* (residential zoning); Laitos and Westfall, *Government Interference with Private Interests in Public Resources*, 11 Harv.Envtl.L.Rev. 1, 66 (1987). The Commission argues that among these permissible purposes are protecting the public's ability to see the beach, assisting the public in overcoming the "psychological barrier" to using the beach created by a developed shorefront, and preventing congestion on the public beaches. We assume, without deciding, that this is so—in which case the Commission unquestionably would be able to deny the Nollans their permit outright if their new house (alone, or by reason of the cumulative impact produced in conjunction with other construction) would substantially impede these purposes, unless the denial would interfere so drastically with the Nollans' use of their property as to constitute a taking. See *Penn Central.*

The Commission argues that a permit condition that serves the same legitimate police-power purpose as a refusal to issue the permit should not be found to be a taking if the refusal to issue the permit would not constitute a taking. We agree. Thus, if the Commission attached to the permit some condition that would have protected the public's ability to see the beach notwithstanding construction of the new house—for example, a height limitation, a width restriction, or a ban on fences—so long as the Commission could have exercised its police power (as we have assumed it could) to forbid construction of the house altogether, imposition of the condition would also be constitutional. Moreover (and here we come closer to the facts of the present case), the condition would be constitutional even if it consisted of the requirement that the Nollans provide a viewing spot on their property for passersby with whose sighting of the ocean their new house would interfere. Although such a requirement, constituting a permanent grant of continuous access to the property, would have to be considered a taking if it were not attached to a development permit, the Commission's assumed power to forbid construction of the house in order to protect the public's view of the beach must surely include the power to condition construction upon some concession by the owner, even a concession of property rights, that serves the same end. If a prohibition designed to accomplish that purpose would be a legitimate exercise of the police power rather than a taking, it would be strange to conclude that providing the owner an alternative to that prohibition which accomplishes the same purpose is not.

The evident constitutional propriety disappears, however, if the condition substituted for the prohibition utterly fails to further the end advanced as the justification for the prohibition. [The] lack of nexus between the condition and the original purpose of the building restriction converts that purpose to something other than what it was. The purpose then becomes, quite simply, the obtaining of an easement to serve some valid governmental purpose, but without payment of compensation. Whatever may be the outer limits of "legitimate state interests" in the takings and land use context, this is not one of them. In short, unless the permit condition serves the same govermental purpose as the development ban, the building restriction is not a valid regulation of land use but "an out-and-out plan of extortion." *J.E.D. Associates, Inc. v. Atkinson*, 121 N.H. 581, 584, 432 A.2d 12, 14–15 (1981). See also *Loretto* fn. 17.

The Commission claims that it concedes as much, and that we may sustain the condition at issue here by finding that it is reasonably related to the public need or burden that the Nollans' new house creates or to which it contributes. We can accept, for purposes of discussion, the Commission's proposed test as to how close a "fit" between the condition and the burden is required, because we find that this case does not meet even the most untailored standards. The Commission's principal contention to the contrary essentially turns on a play on the word "access." The Nollans' new house, the Commission found, will interfere with "visual access" to the beach. That in turn (along with other shorefront development) will interfere with the desire of people who drive past the Nollans' house to use the beach, thus creating a "psychological barrier" to "access." The Nollans' new house will also, by a process not altogether clear from the Commission's opinion but presumably potent enough to more than offset the effects of the psychological barrier, increase the use of the public beaches, thus creating the need for more "access." These burdens on "access" would be alleviated by a requirement that the Nollans provide "lateral access" to the beach.

Rewriting the argument to eliminate the play on words makes clear that there is nothing to it. It is quite impossible to understand how a requirement that people already on the public beaches be able to walk across the Nollans' property reduces any obstacles to viewing the beach created by the new house. It is also impossible to understand how it lowers any "psychological barrier" to using the public beaches, or how it helps to remedy any additional congestion on them caused by construction of the Nollans' new house. We therefore find that the Commission's imposition of the permit condition cannot be treated as an exercise of its land use power for any of these purposes. Our conclusion on this point is consistent with the approach taken by every other court that has considered the question, with the exception of the California state courts [citing over 20 cases].

Justice Brennan argues that imposition of the access requirement is not irrational. In his version of the Commission's argument, the reason for the requirement is that in its absence, a person looking toward the beach from the road will see a street of residential structures including the Nollans' new home and conclude that there is no public beach nearby. If, however, that person sees people passing and repassing along the dry sand behind the Nollans' home, he will realize that there is a public beach somewhere in the vicinity. The Commission's action, however, was based on the opposite factual finding that the wall of houses completely blocked the view of the beach and that a person looking from the road would not be able to see it at all.

Even if the Commission had made the finding that Justice Brennan purposes, however, it is not certain that it would suffice. We do not share Justice Brennan's confidence that the Commission "should have little difficulty in the future in utilizing its expertise to demonstrate a specific connection between provisions for access and burdens on access," that will avoid the effect of today's decision. We view the Fifth Amendment's property clause to be more than a pleading requirement, and compliance with it to be more than an exercise in cleverness and imagination. As indicated earlier, our cases describe the condition for abridgement of property rights through the police power as a "*substantial* advanc[ing]" of a legitimate State interest. We are inclined to be particularly careful about the adjective where the actual conveyance of property is made a condition to the lifting of a land use restriction, since in that context there is heightened risk that the purpose is avoidance of the compensation requirement, rather than the stated police power objective.

We are left, then, with the Commission's justification for the access requirement unrelated to land use regulation: "[The] access required as a condition of this permit is part of a comprehensive program to provide continuous public access along Faria Beach as the lots undergo development or redevelopment."

That is simply an expression of the Commission's belief that the public interest will be served by a continuous strip of publicly accessible beach along the coast. The Commission may well be right that it is a good idea, but that does not establish that the Nollans (and other coastal residents) alone can be compelled to contribute to its realization. Rather, California is free to advance its "comprehensive program," if it wishes, by using its power of eminent domain for this "public purpose", see U.S.Const. Amend. V; but if it wants an easement across the Nollans' property, it must pay for it. * * *

JUSTICE BRENNAN, with whom JUSTICE MARSHALL joins, dissenting.

Appellants in this case sought to construct a new dwelling on their beach lot that would both diminish visual access to the beach and move private development closer to the public tidelands. The Commission reasonably concluded that such "buildout," both individually and cumulatively, threatens public access to the shore. It sought to offset this encroachment by obtaining assurance that the public may walk along the shoreline in order to gain access to the ocean. The Court finds this an illegitimate exercise of the police power, because it maintains that there is no reasonable relationship between the effect of the development and the condition imposed.

The first problem with this conclusion is that the Court imposes a standard of precision for the exercise of a State's police power that has been discredited for the better part of this century. Furthermore, even under the Court's cramped standard, the permit condition imposed in this case directly responds to the specific type of burden on access created by appellants' development. Finally, a review of those factors deemed most significant in takings analysis makes clear that the Commission's action implicates none of the concerns underlying the Takings Clause. The Court has thus struck down the Commission's reasonable effort to respond to intensified development along the California coast, on behalf of landowners who can make no claim that their reasonable expectations have been disrupted. The Court has, in short, given appellants a windfall at the expense of the public. * * *

The Commission is charged by both the state constitution and legislature to preserve overall public access to the California coastline. Furthermore, by virtue of its participation in the Coastal Zone Management Act program, the State must "exercise effectively [its] responsibilities in the coastal zone through the development and implementation of management programs to achieve wise use of the land and water resources of the coastal zone," 16 U.S.C. § 1452(2), so as to provide for, *inter alia,* "public access to the coas[t] for recreation purposes." § 1452(2)(D). The Commission has sought to discharge its responsibilities in a flexible manner. It has sought to balance private and public interests and to accept tradeoffs: to permit development that reduces access in some ways as long as other means of access are enhanced. In this case, it has determined that the Nollans' burden on access would be offset by a deed restriction that formalizes the public's right to pass along the shore. In its informed judgment, such a tradeoff would preserve the net amount of public access to the coastline. The Court's insistence on a precise fit between the forms of burden and condition on each individual parcel along the California coast would penalize the Commission for its flexibility, hampering the ability to fulfill its public trust mandate.

Even if we accept the Court's unusual demand for a precise match between the condition imposed and the specific type of burden on access created by the appellants, the State's action easily satisfies this requirement. First, the lateral access condition serves to dissipate the impression that the beach that lies behind the wall of homes along the shore is for private use only. It requires no exceptional imaginative powers to find plausible the Commission's point that the average person passing along the road in front of a phalanx of imposing permanent residences, including the appellants' new home, is likely to conclude that this particular portion of the shore is not open to the public. If, however, that person can see that numerous people are passing and repassing along the dry sand, this conveys the message that the beach is in fact open for use by the public. Furthermore, those persons who go down to the public beach a quarter-mile away will be able to look down the coastline and see that persons have continuous access to the tidelands, and will observe signs that proclaim the public's right of access over the dry sand. The burden produced by the diminution in visual access—the impression that the beach is not open to the public—is thus directly alleviated by the provision for public access over the dry sand. The Court therefore has an unrealistically limited conception of what measures could reasonably be chosen to mitigate the burden produced by a diminution of visual access.   *   *   *

In reviewing a Takings Clause claim, we have regarded as particularly significant the nature of the governmental action and the economic impact of regulation, especially the extent to which regulation interferes with investment-backed expectations. *Penn Central.* The character of the government action in this case is the imposition of a condition on permit approval, which allows the public to continue to have access to the coast. The physical intrusion permitted by the deed restriction is minimal. The public is permitted the right to pass and re-pass along the coast in an area from the seawall to the mean high tide mark. This area is at its *widest* 10 feet, which means that *even without the permit condition*, the public's right of access permits it to pass on average within a few feet of the seawall. Passage closer to the 8-foot high rocky seawall will make the appellants even less visible to the public than passage along the high tide area farther out on the beach. The intrusiveness of such passage is even less than the intrusion resulting from the required dedication of a sidewalk in front of private residences, exactions which are commonplace conditions on approval of development.   *   *   *

Examination of the economic impact of the Commission's action reinforces the conclusion that no taking has occurred. Allowing appellants to intensify development along the coast in exchange for ensuring public access to the ocean is a classic instance of government action that produces a "reciprocity of advantage." *Pennsylvania Coal.* Appellants have been allowed to replace a one-story 521-square-foot beach home with a two-story 1,674-square-foot residence and an attached two-car garage, resulting in development covering 2,464 square feet of the lot. Such development obviously significantly increases the value of appellants' property; appellants make no contention that this increase is offset by any diminution in value resulting from the deed restriction, much less that the restriction made the property less valuable than it would have been without the new construction. Furthermore, appellants gain an additional benefit from the Commission's permit condition program. They are able to walk along the beach beyond the confines of their own property only because the Commission has required deed restrictions as a condition of approving other new beach developments. Thus, appellants benefit both as private landowners and as members of the public from the fact that new development permit requests are conditioned on preservation of public access.   *   *   *

With respect to the permit condition program in general, the Commission should have little difficulty in the future in utilizing its expertise to demonstrate a specific connection between provisions for access and burdens on access produced by new development. Neither the Commission in its report nor the State in its briefs and at argument highlighted the particular threat to lateral access created by appellants' development project. In defending its action, the State emphasized the general point that *overall* access to the beach had been preserved, since the diminution of access created by the project had been offset by the gain in lateral access. This approach is understandable, given that the State relied on the reasonable assumption that its action was justified under the normal standard of review for determining legitimate exercises of a State's police power. In the future, alerted to the Court's apparently more demanding requirement, it need only make clear that a provision for public access directly responds to a particular type of burden on access created by a new development. Even if I did not believe that the record in this case satisfies this requirement, I would have to acknowledge that the record's documentation of the impact of coastal development indicates that the Commission should have little problem presenting its findings in a way that avoids a takings problem. * * *

JUSTICE BLACKMUN, dissenting.

[I disagree] with the Court's rigid interpretation of the necessary correlation between a burden created by development and a condition imposed pursuant to the State's police power to mitigate that burden. The land-use problems this country faces require creative solutions. These are not advanced by an "eye for an eye" mentality. The close nexus between benefits and burdens that the Court now imposes on permit conditions creates an anomaly in the ordinary requirement that a State's exercise of its police power need be no more than rationally based. In my view, the easement exacted from appellants and the problems their development created are adequately related to the governmental interest in providing public access to the beach. Coastal development by its very nature makes public access to the shore generally more difficult. Appellants' structure is part of that general development and, in particular, it diminishes the public's visual access to the ocean and decreases the public's sense that it may have physical access to the beach. These losses in access can be counteracted, at least in part, by the condition on appellants' construction permitting public passage that ensures access along the beach.

Traditional takings analysis compels the conclusion that there is no taking here. The governmental action is a valid exercise of the police power, and, so far as the record reveals, has a nonexistent economic effect on the value of appellants' property. No investment-backed expectations were diminished. * * *[a]

———

PENNELL v. CITY OF SAN JOSE, 485 U.S 1, 108 S.Ct. 849, 99 L.Ed.2d 1 (1988), per REHNQUIST, C.J., declined to decide, as "premature," a claim that San Jose's rent control ordinance facially violated the taking clause by requiring that in determining a reasonable rent consideration be given to "economic and financial hardship on the present tenant," as well as six other factors all bearing on the costs of providing an adequate rental unit or the condition of the rental market. The Court viewed it "particularly important" not to decide taking cases "except in an actual factual setting," but it did rule that the ordinance was not facially invalid under the due process or equal protection clauses, being a "rational attempt to accomodate conflicting interests."

SCALIA, J., joined by O'CONNOR, J., concurred in the latter ruling but viewed the taking issue as not premature and the tenant hardship factor as facially invalid under the taking clause:

"Once the other six factors of the ordinance have been applied to a landlord's property, so that he is receiving only a reasonable return, he can no longer be regarded as a 'cause' of exorbitantly priced housing; nor is he any longer reaping distinctively high profits from the housing shortage. The seventh factor, the 'hardship' provision, is invoked to meet a quite different social problem: the existence of some renters who are too poor to afford even reasonably priced housing. But *that* problem is no more caused or exploited by

a. Stevens, J., joined by Blackmun, J., also dissented.

landlords than it is by the grocers who sell needy renters their food, or the department stores that sell them their clothes, or the employers who pay them their wages, or the citizens of San Jose holding the higher-paying jobs from which they are excluded. And even if the neediness of renters could be regarded as a problem distinctively attributable to landlords in general, it is not remotely attributable to the *particular* landlords that the ordinance singles out—namely, those who happen to have a 'hardship' tenant at the present time, or who may happen to rent to a 'hardship' tenant in the future, or whose current or future affluent tenants may happen to decline into the 'hardship' category.

"The traditional manner in which American government has met the problem of those who cannot pay reasonable prices for privately sold necessities—a problem caused by the society at large—has been the distribution to such persons of funds raised from the public at large through taxes, either in cash (welfare payments) or in goods (public housing, publicly subsidized housing, and food stamps). Unless we are to abandon the guiding principle of the Takings Clause that 'public burdens * * * should be borne by the public as a whole,' *Armstrong,* this is the only manner that our Constitution permits. The fact that government acts through the landlord-tenant relationship does not magically transform general public welfare, which must be supported by all the public, into mere 'economic regulation,' which can disproportionately burden particular individuals. Here the City is not 'regulating' rents in the relevant sense of preventing rents that are excessive; rather, it is using the occasion of rent regulation (accomplished by the rest of the Ordinance) to establish a welfare program privately funded by those landlords who happen to have 'hardship' tenants.

"Of course all economic regulation effects wealth transfer. When excessive rents are forbidden, for example, landlords as a class become poorer and tenants as a class (or at least incumbent tenants as a class) become richer. Singling out landlords to be the transferors may be within our traditional constitutional notions of fairness, because they can plausibly be regarded as the source or the beneficiary of the high-rent problem. Once such a connection is no longer required, however, there is no end to the social transformations that can be accomplished by so-called 'regulation,' at great expense to the democratic process.

"The politically attractive feature of regulation is not that it permits wealth transfers to be achieved that could not be achieved otherwise; but rather that it permits them to be achieved 'off budget,' with relative invisibility and thus relative immunity from normal democatic processes. San Jose might, for example, have accomplished something like the result here by simply raising the real estate tax upon rental properties and using the additional revenues thus acquired to pay part of the rents of 'hardship' tenants. It seems to me doubtful, however, whether the citizens of San Jose would allow funds in the municipal treasury, from wherever derived, to be distributed to a family of four with income as high as $32,400 a year—the generous maximum necessary to qualify automatically as a 'hardship' tenant under the rental ordinance. The voters might well see other, more pressing, social priorities. And of course what $32,400-a-year renters can acquire through spurious 'regulation,' other groups can acquire as well. Once the door is opened it is not unreasonable to expect price regulations requiring private businesses to give special discounts to senior citizens (no matter how affluent), or to students, the handicapped, or war veterans. Subsidies for these groups may well be a good idea, but because of the operation of the Takings Clause our governmental system has required them to be applied, in general, through the process of taxing and spending, where both economic effects and competing priorities are more evident."

CON LAW: P. 419, after note 7

Inverse Condemnation. Justice Brennan's dissent in *San Diego Gas & Electric Co.* became the law in FIRST ENGLISH LUTHERAN CHURCH v. COUNTY OF LOS ANGELES, 482 U.S. 304, 107 S.Ct. 2378, 96 L.Ed.2d 250 (1986). There the Court, per REHNQUIST, C.J., reversed the California courts' dismissal of a complaint seeking only damages in which the church alleged that it was denied "all use of" its recreation property by an "interim ordinance" for "the immediate protection of public health and safety" that prohibited construction of any building in an "interim flood protection area" that included the church's property:

"In this case the California Court of Appeal held that a landowner who claims that his property has been 'taken' by a land-use regulation may not recover damages for the time before it is finally determined that the regulation constitutes a 'taking' of his property. We disagree, and conclude that in these circumstances the Fifth and Fourteenth Amendments to the United States Constitution would require compensation for that period. * * *

"We reject appellee's suggestion that, regardless of the state court's treatment of the question, we must independently evaluate the adequacy of the complaint and resolve the takings claim on the merits before we can reach the remedial question. However 'cryptic'—to use appellee's description—the allegations with respect to the taking were, the California courts deemed them sufficient to present the issue. We accordingly have no occasion to decide whether the ordinance at issue actually denied appellant all use of its property or whether the county might avoid the conclusion that a compensable taking had occurred by establishing that the denial of all use was insulated as a part of the State's authority to enact safety regulations. These questions, of course, remain open for decision on the remand we direct today. We now turn to the question of whether the Just Compensation Clause requires the government to pay for 'temporary' regulatory takings. * * *

"We have recognized that a landowner is entitled to bring an action in inverse condemnation as a result of ' "the self-executing character of the constitutional provision with respect to compensation * * *." ' As noted in Justice Brennan's dissent in *San Diego Gas & Electric Co.*, it has been established that at least since *Jacobs v. United States*, 290 U.S. 13, 54 S.Ct. 26, 78 L.Ed. 142 (1933), that claims for just compensation are grounded in the Constitution itself:

" 'The suits were based on the right to recover just compensation for property taken by the United States for public use in the exercise of its power of eminent domain. *That right was guaranteed by the Constitution.* The fact that condemnation proceedings were not instituted and that the right was asserted in suits by the owners did not change the essential nature of the claim. The form of the remedy did not qualify the right. It rested upon the Fifth Amendment. Statutory recognition was not necessary. A promise to pay was not necessary. Such a promise was implied because of the duty imposed by the Amendment. *The suits were thus founded upon the Constitution of the United States.*' Id. at 16. (Emphasis added.)

"[The] Court has recognized in more than one case that the government may elect to abandon its intrusion or discontinue regulations. Similarly, a governmental body may acquiesce in a judicial declaration that one of its ordinances has affected an unconstitutional taking of property; the landowner has no right under the Just Compensation Clause to insist that a 'temporary' taking be deemed a permanent taking. But we have not resolved whether abandonment by the government requires payment of compensation for the period of time during which regulations deny a landowner all use of his land.

"In considering this question, we find substantial guidance in cases where the government has only temporarily exercised its right to use private property. In *United States v. Dow,* 357 U.S. 17, 78 S.Ct. 1039, 2 L.Ed.2d 1109 (1958) though rejecting a claim that the Government may not abandon condemnation proceedings, the Court observed that abandonment 'results in an alteration in the property interest taken—from [one of] full ownership to one of temporary use and occupation * * *. In such cases compensation would be measured by the principles normally governing the taking of a right to use property temporarily.' Each of the cases cited by the *Dow* Court involved appropriation of private property by the United States for use during World War II. Though the takings were in fact 'temporary', there was no question that compensation would be required for the Government's interference with the use of the property; the Court was concerned in each case with determining the proper measure of the monetary relief to which the property holders were entitled.

"These cases reflect the fact that 'temporary' takings which, as here, deny a landowner all use of his property, are not different in kind from permanent takings, for which the Constitution clearly requires compensation. [In] the present case the interim ordinance was adopted by the county of Los Angeles in January 1979, and became effective immediately. Appellant filed suit within a month after the effective date of the ordinance and yet when the Supreme Court of California denied a hearing in the case on October 17, 1985, the merits of appellant's claim had yet to be determined. The United States has been required to pay compensation for leasehold interests of shorter duration than this. The value of a leasehold interest in property for a period of years may be substantial, and the burden on the property owner in extinguishing such an interest for a period of years may be great indeed. Where this burden results from governmental action that amounted to a taking, the Just Compensation Clause of the Fifth Amendment requires that the government pay the landowner for the value of the use of the land during this period. Cf. *United States v. Causby* ('It is the owner's loss, not the taker's gain, which is the measure of the value of the property taken'). Invalidation of the ordinance or its successor ordinance after this period of time, though converting the taking into a 'temporary' one, is not a sufficient remedy to meet the demands of the Just Compensation Clause. * * *

"Nothing we say today is intended to abrogate the principle that the decision to exercise the power of eminent domain is a legislative function, ' "for Congress and Congress alone to determine." ' *Hawaii Housing Authority v. Midkiff.* Once a court determines that a taking has occurred, the government retains the whole range of options already available—amendment of the regulation, withdrawal of the invalidated regulation, or exercise of eminent domain. Thus we do not, as the Solicitor General suggests, 'permit a court, at the behest of a private person, to require [the] Government to exercise the power of eminent domain * * *.' We merely hold that where the government's activities have already worked a taking of all use of property, no subsequent action by the government can relieve it of the duty to provide compensation for the period during which the taking was effective.

"We also point out that the allegation of the complaint which we treat as true for purposes of our decision was that the ordinance in question denied appellant all use of its property. We limit our holding to the facts presented, and of course do not deal with the quite different questions that would arise in the case of normal delays in obtaining building permits, changes in zoning ordinances, variances, and the like which are not before us. We realize that even our present holding will undoubtedly lessen to some extent the freedom and flexibility of land-use planners and governing bodies of municipal corporations when enacting land-use regulations. But such consequences necessarily flow from any decision upholding a claim of constitutional right; many of the provisions of the Constitution are designed to limit the flexibility and freedom of governmental authorities and the Just Compensation Clause of the Fifth Amendment is one of them."

STEVENS, J., dissented: "There may be some situations in which even the temporary existence of a regulation has such severe consequences that invalidation or repeal will not mitigate the damage enough to remove the 'taking' label. This hypothetical situation is what the Court calls a 'temporary taking.' But, contrary to the Court's implications, the fact that a regulation would constitute a taking if allowed to remain in effect permanently is by no means dispositive of the question whether the effect that the regulation has already had on the property is so severe that a taking occurred during the period before the regulation was invalidated.

"A temporary interference with an owner's use of his property may constitute a taking for which the Constitution requires that compensation be paid. At least with respect to physical takings, the Court has so held. Thus, if the Government appropriates a leasehold interest and uses it for a public purpose, the return of the premises at the expiration of the lease would obviously not erase the fact of the Government's temporary occupation. * * *

"[But] our cases also make it clear that regulatory takings and physical takings are very different in this, as well as other, respects. While virtually all physical invasions are deemed takings, see e.g., *Loretto*; *Causby*, a regulatory program that adversely affects property values does not constitute a taking unless it destroys a major portion of the property's value. See *Keystone Bituminous; Hodel v. Virginia Surface Mining & Reclamation Ass'n*. This diminution of value inquiry is unique to regulatory takings. Unlike physical invasions, which are relatively rare and easily identifiable without making any economic analysis, regulatory programs constantly affect property values in countless ways, and only the most extreme regulations can constitute takings. Some dividing line must be established between everyday regulatory inconveniences and those so severe that they constitute takings. The diminution of value inquiry has long been used in identifying that line. As Justice Holmes put it: "Government hardly could go on if to some extent values incident to property could not be diminished without paying for every such change in the general law." *Pennsylvania Coal*. It is this basic distinction between regulatory and physical takings that the Court ignores today.

"Regulations are three dimensional; they have depth, width, and length. As for depth, regulations define the extent to which the owner may not use the property in question. With respect to width, regulations define the amount of property encompassed by the restrictions. Finally, and for purposes of this case, essentially, regulations set forth the duration of the restrictions. It is obvious that no one of these elements can be analyzed alone to evaluate the impact of a regulation, and hence to determine whether a taking has occurred. For example, in *Keystone Bituminous* we declined to focus in on any discrete segment of the coal in the petitioners' mines, but rather looked to the effect that the restriction had on their entire mining project. Similarly, in *Penn Central,* the Court concluded that it was error to focus on the nature of the uses which were prohibited without also examining the many profitable uses to which the property could still be put. Both of these factors are essential to a meaningful analysis of the economic effect that regulations have on the value of property and on an owner's reasonable investment-based expectations with respect to the property.

"Just as it would be senseless to ignore these first two factors in assessing the economic effect of a regulation, one cannot conduct the inquiry without considering the duration of the restriction. See generally, Williams, Smith, Siemon, Mandelker, & Babcock, *The White River Junction Manifesto,* 9 Vt.L.Rev. 193, 215–218 (1984). For example, while I agreed with the Chief Justice's view that the permanent restriction on building involved in *Penn Central* constituted a taking, I assume that no one would have suggested that a temporary freeze on building would have also constituted a taking. Similarly, I am confident that even the dissenters in *Keystone Bituminous* would not have concluded that the restriction on bituminous coal mining would have constituted a taking had it simply required the mining companies to delay their operations until an appropriate safety inspection could be made.

"On the other hand, I am willing to assume that some cases may arise in which a property owner can show that prospective invalidation of the regulation cannot cure the taking—that the temporary operation of a regulation has caused such a significant diminution in the property's value that compensation must be afforded for the taking that has already occurred. For this ever to happen, the restriction on the use of the property would not only have to be a substantial one, but it would have to remain in effect for a significant percentage of the property's useful life. In such a case an application of our test for regulatory takings would obviously require an inquiry into the duration of the restriction, as well as its scope and severity. See *Williamson Planning Comm'n v. Hamilton Bank,* 473 U.S. 172, 105 S.Ct. 3108, 87 L.Ed.2d 126 (1985) (refusing to evaluate taking claim when the long-term economic effects were uncertain because it was not clear that restrictions would remain in effect permanently).

"The cases that the Court relies upon for the proposition that there is no distinction between temporary and permanent takings, are inapposite, for they all deal with physical takings—where the diminution of value test is inapplicable. None of those cases is controversial; the state certainly may not occupy an individual's home for a month and then escape compensation by leaving and declaring the occupation 'temporary.' But what does that have to do with the proper inquiry for regulatory takings? Why should there be a constitutional distinction between a permanent restriction that only reduces the economic value of the property by a fraction—perhaps one-third—and a restriction that merely postpones the development of a property for a fraction of its useful life—presumably far less than a third? In the former instance, no taking has occurred; in the latter case, the Court now proclaims that compensation for a taking must be provided. The Court makes no effort to explain these irreconcilable results. Instead, without any attempt to fit its proclamation into our regulatory takings cases, the Court boldly announces that once a property owner makes out a claim that a regulation would constitute a taking if allowed to stand, then he or she is entitled to damages for the period of time between its enactment and its invalidation. * * *

"The policy implications of today's decision are obvious and, I fear, far reaching. Cautious local officials and land-use planners may avoid taking any action that might later be challenged and thus give rise to a damage action. Much important regulation will never be enacted, even perhaps in the health and safety area. Were this result mandated by the Constitution, these serious implications would have to be ignored. But the loose cannon the Court fires today is not only unattached to the Constitution, but it also takes aim at a long line of precedents in the regulatory takings area. It would be the better part of valor simply to decide the case at hand instead of igniting the kind of litigation explosion that this decision will undoubtedly touch off." [a]

SECTION: CONTRACT CLAUSE

CON LAW: P. 430, after note 4

AMER CON: P. 285, after note 4

RTS & LIB: P. 98, after note 4

5. *Legislation increasing employer's liability to fund pension benefits.* (a) Contrast *Spannaus* with CONNOLLY v. PENSION BENEFIT GUARANTY CORP., 475 U.S. 211, 106 S.Ct. 1018, 89 L.Ed.2d 166 (1986), involving the federal Multiemployer Pension Plan Amendments Act (MPPAA) of 1980, implementing ERISA's [a] 1978 objective to protect anticipated retirement benefits on termination of pension plans. At issue was the requirement that an employer withdrawing from a multiemployer pension plan pay into that plan's fund the withdrawing employer's "proportionate share" [b] of the plan's "unfunded vested benefits," calculated as the difference between the plan's vested benefits and the current value of its assets at the time of withdrawal. The 1960 trust agreement creating the multiemployer Operating Engineers Pension Plan provided that no individual employer under the plan "has any liability to provide the benefits established by this Plan beyond [its] obligation" to make the contributions specified in the applicable collective bargaining agreement, even though the Pension Fund "does not have the assets to make the benefit payments." The Court, per WHITE, J., rejected the claim that this statutory "withdrawal liability" was a "taking" in violation of the withdrawing employers' property rights under the trust agreement:

"[H]ere, the United States has taken nothing for its own use, and only has nullified a contractual provision limiting liability by imposing an additional obligation that is otherwise within the power of Congress to impose. That the statutory withdrawal liability will operate in this manner and will redound to the benefit of pension trusts does not justify a holding that the provision violates the Taking Clause and is invalid on its face.

"[O]ur prior Taking Clause [cases] have identified three factors which have 'particular significance': (1) 'the economic impact of the regulation on the claimant'; (2) 'the extent to which the regulation has interfered with distinct investment-backed expectations'; and (3) 'the character of the governmental

---

a. While not joining the foregoing portions of the Stevens dissent, Blackmun and O'Connor, JJ., joined Parts I and III of the dissent, which argued (I) that the complaint did not sufficiently allege an unconstitutional taking, and (III) that the church should have been required to exhaust its remedies in the state courts by "demanding invalidation of the ordinance prior to seeking this Court's review of California procedures."

a. Employees' Retirement Income Security Act of 1980, 29 U.S.C. §§ 1381–1453.

b. O'Connor, J., joined by Powell, J., separately concurred to express concerns about issues not decided.

action.' *Penn Central*. Examining the MPPAA in light of these factors reinforces our belief that the imposition of withdrawal liability does not constitute a compensable taking under the Fifth Amendment.

"First, with respect to the nature of the governmental action, [the] Government does not physically invade or permanently appropriate any of the employer's assets for its own use. Instead, the Act safeguards the participants in multiemployer pension plans by requiring a withdrawing employer to fund its share of the plan obligations incurred during its association with the plan. This interference with the property rights of an employer arises from a public program that adjusts the benefits and burdens of economic life to promote the common good and, under our cases, does not constitute a taking requiring Government compensation.

"Next, as to the severity of the economic impact of the MPPAA, there is no doubt that the Act completely deprives an employer of whatever amount of money it is obligated to pay to fulfill its statutory liability. The assessment of withdrawal liability is not made in a vacuum, however, but directly depends on the relationship between the employer and the plan to which it had made contributions. * * *

"The final inquiry [is] whether the MPPAA has interfered with reasonable investment-backed expectations. Appellants argue that the only monetary obligations incurred by each employer involved in the Operating Engineers Pension Plan arose from the specific terms of the Plan and Trust Agreement between the employers and the union, and that the imposition of withdrawal liability upsets those reasonable expectations. Pension plans, however, were the objects of legislative concern long before the passage of ERISA in 1974, and surely as of that time, it was clear that if the PBGC exercised its discretion to pay benefits upon the termination of a multiemployer pension plan, employers who had contributed to the plan during the preceding five years were liable for their proportionate share of the plan's contributions during that period. It was also plain enough that the purpose of imposing withdrawal liability was to ensure that employees would receive the benefits promised them. When it became evident that ERISA fell short of achieving this end, Congress adopted the 1980 amendments. Prudent employers then had more than sufficient notice not only that pension plans were currently regulated, but also that withdrawal itself might trigger additional financial obligations. Those who do business in the regulated field cannot object if the legislative scheme is buttressed by subsequent amendments to achieve the legislative end.'

"[We] are far from persuaded that fairness and justice require the public, rather than the withdrawing employers and other parties to pension plan agreements, to shoulder the responsibility for rescuing plans that are in financial trouble. The employers in the present litigation voluntarily negotiated and maintained a pension plan which was determined to be within the strictures of ERISA. We do not know, as a fact, whether this plan was underfunded, but Congress determined that unregulated withdrawals from multiemployer plans could endanger their financial vitality and deprive workers of the vested rights they were entitled to anticipate would be theirs upon retirement. For this reason, Congress imposed withdrawal liability as one part of an overall statutory scheme to safeguard the solvency of private pension plans. We see no constitutionally compelled reason to require the Treasury to assume the financial burden of attaining this goal."

(b) Had the withdrawal liability been based on state legislation attacked under the contracts clause would the Court have reached the same result? How might the reasoning have differed? What are the likely similarities? Are there distinctive roles for each clause?

Chapter

PROTECTION OF INDIVIDUAL RIGHTS: DUE PROCESS, THE BILL OF RIGHTS, AND NONTEXTUAL CONSTITUTIONAL RIGHTS

SECTION: NATURE AND SCOPE OF FOURTEENTH AMENDMENT DUE PROCESS; APPLICABILITY OF THE BILL OF RIGHTS TO THE STATES

LEADING CRIMINAL PROCEDURE DECISIONS AND THE RETROACTIVE EFFECT OF A HOLDING OF UNCONSTITUTIONALITY

CON LAW: Pp. 450–51, add to fn. h

AMER CON: Pp. 305–06, add to fn. h

RTS & LIB: Pp. 118–19, add to fn. h

The "clear break" exception to the retroactive application of new rules recognized in *Johnson* (under which a new constitutional rule was not applied retroactively even to cases on direct review if the new rule explicit-ly overruled a past Supreme Court precedent or disapproved a practice the Court had sanctioned in prior cases) was rejected in *Griffith v. Kentucky,* 479 U.S. 314, 107 S.Ct. 708, 93 L.Ed.2d 649 (1987).

CON LAW: P. 452, add to fn. l

AMER CON: P. 307, add to fn. l

RTS & LIB: P. 120, add to fn. l

There were two parts to Justice Harlan's approach to retroactivity. He believed that new rulings should always be applied retroactively to cases on *direct* review (a view adopted in *Shea*), but that generally new rulings should not be applied retroactively to cases on *collateral* review. In *Teague v. Lane,* ___ U.S. ___, 109 S.Ct. 1060, 103 L.Ed.2d 334 (1989), seven Justices adopted Justice Harlan's basic position with respect to retroactivity on collateral review. There was, however, no clear majority as to what the exceptions to this general approach should be.

A four-Justice plurality, per O'Connor, J. (joined by Rehnquist, C.J., and Scalia and Kennedy, JJ.), identified two exceptions: A new ruling should be applied retroactively to cases on collateral review only (1) if it "places 'certain kinds of primary, private individual conduct beyond the power of the criminal law-making authority to proscribe'" or (2) if it mandates "new procedures without which the likelihood of an accurate conviction is serious-ly diminished." The latter exception is "'best illustrated by recalling the classic grounds for the issuance of a writ of habeas corpus—that the proceeding was dominated by mob violence; that the prosecutor knowingly made use of perjured testimony; or that the conviction was based on a confession extorted from the defendant by brutal methods.'"

A fifth member of the Court, concurring Justice White, characterized the plurality's view as "an acceptable application in collateral proceedings of the theories embraced by the Court in dealing with direct review." Two other members of the Court, concurring Justice Stevens, joined by Blackmun, J., agreed that "the Court should adopt Justice Harlan's analysis of retroactivity for habeas corpus cases as well as for cases still on direct review," but disagreed with the plurality about the exceptions to such a general approach.

SECTION: THE RIGHT OF "PRIVACY" (OR "AUTONOMY" OR "PERSONHOOD")

ROE v. WADE AND THE DEBATE IT STIRRED OVER "INTERPRETIVIST"/"NONINTERPRETIVIST" CONSTITUTIONAL DECISIONMAKING

CON LAW: P. 508, after line 4

AMER CON: P. 345, after note 6

RTS & LIB: P. 176, after line 4

Consider also the exchange between Justices Stevens, and White, in *Thornburgh v. American College of Obstetricians & Gynecologists,* set forth below; the exchange between Justices White and Blackmun in *Bowers v. Hardwick,* p. 139 of this Supplement; and the differing views of Justices Blackmun and Scalia in *Webster v. Reproductive Health Services,* p. 112 of this Supplement.

Consider, too, Justice Antonin Scalia's remarks, before ascending to the Supreme Court, in *An Imperial Judiciary: Fact or Myth* 35 (1979) (American Enterprise Institute forum): "Where do I draw the line [between a policy decision and a legitimate area within which the Supreme Court may operate]? In the area of constitutional rights, I draw the line at the point where the Court plucks out of the air a principle of action that is not now considered necessary by a majority of the people in the country, nor was ever considered necessary at any time in our history. An example would be the Court's decision on capital punishment. There is simply no historical justification for that, nor could the Court claim to be expressing a consensus of modern society. It is just not true. The same could be said about the abortion decision. It is very hard to tell you where the line between a proper and an improper decision should be drawn. It would fall short of making fundamental, social determinations that ought to be made through the democratic process, but that the society has not yet made."

JUSTICE O'CONNOR'S BROAD ATTACK ON, BUT THE COURT'S REAFFIRMATION OF, *ROE*'S ANALYSIS

CON LAW: P. 527, after note 3

AMER CON: P. 361, after note 2

RTS & LIB: P. 195, after note 3

THORNBURGH v. AMERICAN COLLEGE OF OBSTETRICIANS AND GYNECOLOGISTS

476 U.S. 747, 106 S.Ct. 2169, 90 L.Ed.2d 779 (1986).

JUSTICE BLACKMUN delivered the opinion of the Court. * * *

[Appellees challenged the constitutionality of various provisions of the Pennsylvania Abortion Control Act of 1982. The district court ruled that, with one exception (it held invalid and enjoined preliminarily the requirement of

§ 3205 that at least 24 hours must elapse between a woman's receipt of specified information and the performance of her abortion), appellees had failed to establish a likelihood of success on the merits and thus were not entitled to preliminary injunctive relief.

[The Third Circuit enjoined enforcement of the entire Act, holding unconstitutional, on the basis of the intervening decisions in *Akron, Ashcroft* and *Simopoulos,* the following provisions of the Act: (1) the portions of § 3205 ("informed consent") that, with respect to the requirement that the woman give her "informed consent" to an abortion, require her, inter alia, to be informed of the name of the physician who will perform the abortion, the "particular medical risks" of the abortion procedure to be used, the facts that there may be "detrimental physical and psychological effects," that medical assistance benefits may be available for prenatal care, childbirth, and neonatal care, and the availability of printed materials from the state that describe the fetus and list agencies offering alternatives to abortion; (2) § 3208 ("printed information"), requiring such printed materials to include a statement that there are agencies willing to help the mother carry her child to term and to assist her afterwards and a description of the probable anatomical and physiological characteristics of an unborn child at "two-week gestational increments"; (3) portions of § 3214 (reporting requirements), that require the physician to report, inter alia, the identity of the performing and referring physicians, information as to the woman's residence, age, race, marital status, and number of prior pregnancies, and the basis for any judgment that a medical emergency existed or for any determination of nonviability, and further provide that such reports shall not be deemed public records, but shall be available for public inspection and copying in a form that will not disclose the identity of any person filing a report; (4) § 3211(a) (determination of viability), requiring the physician, after the first trimester, to report the basis for his determination that a fetus is not viable; (5) § 3210(b) (requisite care in postviability abortions), requiring a physician performing a postviability abortion to use the abortion technique providing the best opportunity for the unborn child to be aborted alive unless it would present a "significantly greater medical risk" to the woman's life or health; and (6) § 3210(c) (second-physician provision), requiring a second physician to be present when viability is possible, such physician to take all reasonable measures to preserve the child's life and health.

[The Third Circuit held that the validity of other challenged provisions of the Act might depend on evidence adduced at the trial and accordingly remanded these features of the case to the district court.]

Less than three years ago, this Court, in *Akron, Ashcroft,* and *Simopoulos,* reviewed challenges to state and municipal legislation regulating the performance of abortions. In *Akron,* the Court specifically reaffirmed *Roe.* Again today, we reaffirm the general principles laid down in *Roe* and in *Akron.*

In the years [since] *Roe,* States and municipalities have adopted a number of measures seemingly designed to prevent a woman, with the advice of her physician, from exercising her freedom of choice. [But] the constitutional principles that led this Court to its decisions in 1973 still provide the compelling reason for recognizing the constitutional dimensions of a woman's right to decide whether to end her pregnancy. [The] States are not free, under the guise of protecting maternal health or potential life, to intimidate women into continuing pregnancies. Appellants claim that the statutory provisions before us today further legitimate compelling interests of the Commonwealth. Close analysis of those provisions, however, shows that they wholly subordinate constitutional privacy interests and concerns with maternal health in an effort to deter a woman from making a decision that, with her physician, is hers to make.

* * *

[The Court then examined various statutory provisions and found them constitutionally defective. As was true of the informational requirements in the Akron ordinance, Pennsylvania's "informed consent" and "printed information" provisions were "designed not to inform the woman's consent but rather to persuade her to withhold it altogether" and they "intrude upon the discretion of the pregnant woman's physician and thereby impose the 'undesired and uncomfortable strait jacket' with which the Court in *Danforth* was concerned." That Pennsylvania "does not, and surely would not, compel similar disclosure of every possible peril of necessary surgery or of simple vaccination, reveals the anti-abortion character of the statute and its real purpose."

[As for the reporting requirements, "a woman and her physician will necessarily be more reluctant to choose an abortion if there exists a possibility the her decision and her identity will become known publicly. Although the statute does not specifically require the reporting of the woman's name, the amount of information about her and the circumstances under which she had an abortion are so detailed that identification is likely. Identification is the obvious purpose of these extreme reporting requirements. [They] raise the spectre of public exposure and harassment of women who choose to exercise their personal, intensely private right, with their physician, to end a pregnancy. Thus, they pose an unacceptable danger of deterring the exercise of that right * * *."

[The provision concerning the standard of care for postviability abortions requires a "trade-off" between the woman's health and fetal survival, and fails to require that maternal health be the physician's paramount consideration. Finally, unlike the provision in *Ashcroft*, the requirement that a second physician be present during an abortion performed when viability is possible cannot be construed to contain an exception for those emergency situations where the health of the mother would be endangered by delay in the arrival of the second physician.]

Our cases long have recognized that the Constitution embodies a promise that a certain private sphere of individual liberty will be kept largely beyond the reach of government. That promise extends to women as well as to men. Few decisions are more personal and intimate, more properly private, or more basic to individual dignity and autonomy, than a woman's decision—with the guidance of her physician and within the limits specified in *Roe*—whether to end her pregnancy. A woman's right to make that choice freely is fundamental. Any other result, in our view, would protect inadequately a central part of the sphere of liberty that our law guarantees equally to all. * * *

JUSTICE STEVENS, concurring.

[T]he aspect of liberty at stake in this case is the freedom from unwarranted governmental intrusion into individual decisions in matters of childbearing. As Justice White explained in *Griswold*, that aspect of liberty comes to this Court with a momentum for respect that is lacking when appeal is made to liberties which derive merely from shifting economic arrangements.

Like the birth control statutes involved in *Griswold* and *Baird*, the abortion statutes involved in *Roe* and in the case before us today apply equally to decisions made by married persons and by unmarried persons. Consistently with his views in those cases, Justice White agrees that "a woman's ability to choose an abortion is a species of 'liberty' that is subject to the general protections of the Due Process Clause." His agreement with that "indisputable" proposition is not qualified or limited to decisions made by pregnant women who are married and, indeed, it would be a strange form of liberty if it were so limited.

Up to this point in Justice White's analysis, his opinion is fully consistent with the accepted teachings of the Court and with the major premises of *Roe.* For reasons that are not entirely clear, however, Justice White abruptly announces that the interest in "liberty" that is implicated by a decision not to bear a child that is made a few days after conception is *less* fundamental than a comparable decision made before conception. There may, of course, be a significant difference in the strength of the countervailing state interest, but I fail to see how a decision on child-bearing becomes *less* important the day after conception than the day before. Indeed, if one decision is more "fundamental" to the individual's freedom than the other, surely it is the post-conception decision that is the more serious. Thus, it is difficult for me to understand how Justice White reaches the conclusion that restraints upon this aspect of a woman's liberty do not "call into play anything more than the most minimal judicial scrutiny." [4]

If Justice White were correct in regarding the post-conception decision of the question whether to bear a child as a relatively unimportant, second-class sort of interest, I might agree with his view that the individual should be required to conform her decision to the will of the majority. But if that decision commands the respect that is traditionally associated with the "sensitive areas of liberty" protected by the Constitution, as Justice White characterized reproductive decisions in *Griswold,* no individual should be compelled to surrender the freedom to make that decision for herself simply because her "value preferences" are not shared by the majority. In a sense, the basic question is whether the "abortion decision" should be made by the individual or by the majority "in the unrestrained imposition of its own, extraconstitutional value preferences." But surely Justice White is quite wrong in suggesting that the Court is imposing value preferences on anyone else.[6]

4. At times Justice White's rhetoric conflicts with his own analysis. For instance, his emphasis on the lack of a decision by "the people [in] 1787, 1791, 1868, or any time since", stands in sharp contrast to his earlier, forthright rejection of "the simplistic view that constitutional interpretation can possibly be limited to 'the plain meaning' of the Constitution's text or to the subjective intention of the Framers." Similarly, his statement that an abortion decision should be subject to "the will of the people" does not take us very far in determining *which* people—the majorities in state legislatures or the individuals confronted with unwanted pregnancies. In view of his agreement that the decision about abortion is "a species of liberty" protected by the Constitution, moreover, and in view of the fact that "liberty" plays a rather prominent role in our Constitution, his suggestion that the Court's evaluation of that interest represents the imposition of "extraconstitutional value preferences" seems to me inexplicable. This characterization of the Court's analysis as "extraconstitutional" also does not reflect Justice White's simultaneous recognition that "[t]he Constitution [is] a document announcing fundamental principles in value-laden terms that leave ample scope for the exercise of normative judgment by those charged with interpreting and applying it." Finally, I fail to see how the fact that "men and women of good will and high commitment to constitutional government" are on both sides of the abortion issue helps to resolve the difficult constitutional question before us; I take it that the disputants in most constitutional controversies in our free society can be similarly characterized.

6. Justice White's characterization of the governmental interest as "protecting those who will be citizens if their lives are not ended in the womb" reveals that his opinion may be influenced as much by his own value preferences as by his view about the proper allocation of decisionmaking responsibilities between the individual and the State. For if federal judges must allow the State to make the abortion decision, presumably the State is free to decide that a woman may *never* abort, may *sometimes* abort, or, as in the People's

Justice White is also surely wrong in suggesting that the governmental interest in protecting fetal life is equally compelling during the entire period from the moment of conception until the moment of birth. Again, I recognize that a powerful theological argument can be made for that position, but I believe our jurisdiction is limited to the evaluation of secular state interests.[7] I should think it obvious that the state's interest in the protection of an embryo—even if that interest is defined as "protecting those who will be citizens"—increases progressively and dramatically as the organism's capacity to feel pain, to experience pleasure, to survive, and to react to its surroundings increases day by day. The development of a fetus—and pregnancy itself—are not static conditions, and the assertion that the government's interest is static simply ignores this reality.

Nor is it an answer to argue that life itself is not a static condition, and that "there is no nonarbitrary line separating a fetus from a child, or indeed, an adult human being." For, unless the religious view that a fetus is a "person" is adopted—a view Justice White refuses to embrace—there is a fundamental and well-recognized difference between a fetus and a human being; indeed, if there is not such a difference, the permissibility of terminating the life of a fetus could scarcely be left to the will of the state legislatures.[8] And if distinctions may be drawn between a fetus and a human being in terms of the state interest in their protection—even though the fetus represents one of "those who will be citizens"—it seems to me quite odd to argue that distinctions may not also be drawn between the state interest in protecting the freshly fertilized egg and the state interest in protecting the 9-month-gestated, fully sentient fetus on the eve of birth. Recognition of this distinction is supported not only by logic, but also by history and by our shared experiences.

Turning to Justice White's comments on *stare decisis,* he is of course correct in pointing out that the Court "has not hesitated to overrule decisions, or even whole lines of cases, where experience, scholarship, and reflection demonstrated that their fundamental premises were not to be found in the Constitution." But Justice White has not disavowed the "fundamental premises" on which the decision in *Roe* rests. He has not disavowed the Court's prior approach to the interpretation of the word "liberty" or, more narrowly, the line of cases that culminated in the unequivocal holding, applied to unmarried persons and married persons alike, "that the Constitution protects individual decisions in matters of childbearing from unjustified intrusion by the State." *Carey* (White, J., concurring in pertinent part).

Nor does the fact that the doctrine of stare decisis is not an absolute bar to the reexamination of past interpretations of the Constitution mean that the values underlying that doctrine may be summarily put to one side. There is a strong public interest in stability, and in the orderly conduct of our affairs, that is served by a consistent course of constitutional adjudication. Acceptance of the fundamental premises that underlie the decision in *Roe,* as well as the application of those premises in that case, places the primary responsibility for decision

Republic of China, must *always* abort if her family is already too large. In contrast, our cases represent a consistent view that the individual is primarily responsible for reproductive decisions, whether the State seeks to prohibit reproduction, *Skinner,* or to require it, *Roe.*

7. The responsibility for nurturing the soul of the newly born, as well as the unborn, rests

with individual parents, not with the State. No matter how important a sacrament such as baptism may be, a State surely could not punish a mother for refusing to baptize her child.

8. No member of this Court has ever suggested that a fetus is a "person" within the meaning of the Fourteenth Amendment.

in matters of childbearing squarely in the private sector of our society. The majority remains free to preach the evils of birth control and abortion and to persuade others to make correct decisions while the individual faced with the reality of a difficult choice having serious and personal consequences of major importance to her own future—perhaps to the salvation of her own immortal soul—remains free to seek and to obtain sympathetic guidance from those who share her own value preferences.

In the final analysis, the holding in *Roe* presumes that it is far better to permit some individuals to make incorrect decisions than to deny all individuals the right to make decisions that have a profound effect upon their destiny. Arguably a very primitive society would have been protected from evil by a rule against eating apples; a majority familiar with Adam's experience might favor such a rule. But the lawmakers who placed a special premium on the protection of individual liberty have recognized that certain values are more important than the will of a transient majority.

CHIEF JUSTICE BURGER, dissenting.

I agree with much of Justice White's and Justice O'Connor's dissents.

* * *

I based my concurring statements in *Roe* and *Maher* on the principle expressed in the Court's opinion in *Roe* that the right to an abortion "is not unqualified and must be considered against important state interests in regulation." [E]very member of the *Roe* Court rejected the idea of abortion on demand. The Court's opinion today, however, plainly undermines that important principle, and I regretfully conclude that some of the concerns of the dissenting Justices in *Roe*, as well as the concerns I expressed in my separate opinion, have now been realized. * * *

The Court's opinion today is but the most recent indication of the distance traveled since *Roe*. Perhaps the first important road marker was the Court's holding in *Danforth*, in which the Court held (over the dissent of Justice White joined by Justice Rehnquist and myself) that the State may not require that minors seeking an abortion first obtain parental consent. Parents, not judges or social workers, have the inherent right and responsibility to advise their children in matters of this sensitivity and consequence. Can one imagine a surgeon performing an amputation or even an appendectomy on a 14-year-old girl without the consent of a parent or guardian except in an emergency situation?

Yet today the Court goes beyond *Danforth* by remanding for further consideration of the provisions of Pennsylvania's statute requiring that a minor seeking an abortion without parental consent petition the appropriate court for authorization. Even if I were to agree that the Constitution requires that the States may not provide that a minor receive parental consent before undergoing an abortion, I would certainly hold that judicial approval may be required. This is in keeping with the longstanding common law principle that courts may function in *loco parentis* when parents are unavailable or neglectful. [In] my view, no remand is necessary on this point because the statutory provision in question is constitutional.

In discovering constitutional infirmities in state regulations of abortion that are in accord with our history and tradition, we may have lured judges into "roaming at large in the constitutional field." *Griswold* (Harlan, J., concurring). The soundness of our holdings must be tested by the decisions that purport to follow them. If *Danforth* and today's holding really mean what they seem to say, I agree we should reexamine *Roe*.

JUSTICE WHITE, with whom JUSTICE REHNQUIST joins, dissenting.

Today the Court carries forward the "difficult and continuing venture in substantive due process," *Danforth* (White, J., dissenting), that began with the decision in *Roe* and has led the Court further and further afield in the 13 years since that decision was handed down. I was in dissent in *Roe* and am in dissent today. In Part I below, I state why I continue to believe that this venture has been fundamentally misguided since its inception. In Part II, I submit that even accepting *Roe,* the concerns underlying that decision by no means command or justify the results reached today. Indeed, in my view, our precedents in this area, applied in a manner consistent with sound principles of constitutional adjudication, require reversal of the Court of Appeals on the ground that the provisions before us are facially constitutional.

I. [Because] the Constitution itself is ordained and established by the people of the United States, constitutional adjudication by this Court does not, in theory at any rate, frustrate the authority of the people to govern themselves through institutions of their own devising and in accordance with principles of their own choosing. But decisions that find in the Constitution principles or values that cannot fairly be read into that document usurp the people's authority, for such decisions represent choices that the people have never made and that they cannot disavow through corrective legislation. For this reason, it is essential that this Court maintain the power to restore authority to its proper possessors by correcting constitutional decisions that, on reconsideration, are found to be mistaken.

* * * Stare decisis did not stand in the way of the Justices who, in the late 1930s, swept away constitutional doctrines that had placed unwarranted restrictions on the power of the State and Federal Governments to enact social and economic legislation. Nor did stare decisis deter a different set of Justices, some fifteen years later, from rejecting the theretofore prevailing view that the Fourteenth Amendment permitted the States to maintain the system of racial segregation. *Brown v. Board of Education.* In both instances, history has been far kinder to those who departed from precedent than to those who would have blindly followed the rule of stare decisis. * * *

In my view, the time has come to recognize that [*Roe*] "departs from a proper understanding" of the Constitution and to overrule it. I do not claim that the arguments in support of this proposition are new ones or that they were not considered by the Court in *Roe* or in the cases that succeeded it. But if an argument that a constitutional decision is erroneous must be novel in order to justify overruling that precedent, the Court's decisions in *Lochner* and *Plessy* would remain the law, for the doctrines announced in those decisions were nowhere more eloquently or incisively criticized than in the dissenting opinions of Justices Holmes (in *Lochner*) and Harlan (in both cases). That the flaws in an opinion were evident at the time it was handed down is hardly a reason for adhering to it.

Roe posits that a woman has a fundamental right to terminate her pregnancy, and that this right may be restricted only in the service of two compelling state interests: the interest in maternal health (which becomes compelling only at the stage in pregnancy at which an abortion becomes more hazardous than carrying the pregnancy to term) and the interest in protecting the life of the fetus (which becomes compelling only at the point of viability). A reader of the Constitution might be surprised to find that it encompassed these detailed rules, for the text obviously contains no references to abortion, nor, indeed, to pregnancy or reproduction generally; and, of course, it is highly doubtful that the authors of any of the provisions of the Constitution believed that they were giving protection to abortion. As its prior cases clearly show, however, this Court does not subscribe to the simplistic view that constitutional interpretation can possibly be limited to the "plain meaning" of the Constitution's text or to the subjective intention of the Framers. The Constitution is not a deed setting forth the precise metes and bounds of its subject matter; rather, it is a document announcing fundamental principles in value-laden terms that leave ample scope for the exercise of normative judgment by those charged with interpreting and applying it. In particular, the Due Process Clause of the Fourteenth Amendment, has been read by the majority of the Court to be broad enough to provide substantive protection against State infringement of a broad range of individual interests.

In most instances, the substantive protection afforded the liberty or property of an individual by the Fourteenth Amendment is extremely limited: State action impinging on individual interests need only be rational to survive scrutiny under the Due Process Clause, and the determination of rationality is to be made with a heavy dose of deference to the policy choices of the legislature. Only "fundamental" rights are entitled to the added protection provided by strict judicial scrutiny of legislation that impinges upon them. I can certainly agree with the proposition—which I deem indisputable—that a woman's ability to choose an abortion is a species of "liberty" that is subject to the general protections of the Due Process Clause. I cannot agree, however, that this liberty is so "fundamental" that restrictions upon it call into play anything more than the most minimal judicial scrutiny.

Fundamental liberties and interests are most clearly present when the Constitution provides specific textual recognition of their existence and importance. Thus, the Court is on relatively firm ground when it deems certain of the liberties set forth in the Bill of Rights to be fundamental and therefore finds them incorporated in the Fourteenth Amendment's guarantee that no State may deprive any person of liberty without due process of law. When the Court ventures further and defines as "fundamental" liberties that are nowhere mentioned in the Constitution (or that are present only in the so-called "penumbras" of specifically enumerated rights), it must, of necessity, act with more caution, lest it open itself to the accusation that, in the name of identifying constitutional principles to which the people have consented in framing their Constitution, the Court has done nothing more than impose its own controversial choices of value upon the people. * * *

The Court has justified the recognition of a woman's fundamental right to terminate her pregnancy by invoking decisions upholding claims of personal autonomy in connection with the conduct of family life, the rearing of children, marital privacy and the use of contraceptives, and the preservation of the individual's capacity to procreate. Even if each of these cases was correctly decided and could be properly grounded in rights that are "implicit in the concept of ordered liberty" or "deeply rooted in this Nation's history and tradition," the issues in the cases cited differ from those at stake where abortion is concerned. As the Court appropriately recognized in *Roe*, "[t]he pregnant woman cannot be isolated in her privacy"; the termination of a pregnancy typically involves the destruction of another entity: the fetus. However one answers the metaphysical or theological question whether the fetus is a "human being" or the legal question whether it is a "person" as that term is used in the Constitution, one must at least recognize, first, that the fetus is an entity that bears in its cells all the genetic information that characterizes a member of the species homo sapiens and distinguishes an individual member of that species from all others, and second, that there is no nonarbitrary line separating a fetus from a child or, indeed, an adult human being. Given that the continued existence and development—that is to say, the *life*—of such an entity are so directly at stake in the woman's decision whether or not to terminate her pregnancy, that decision must be recognized as sui generis, different in kind from the others that the Court has protected under the rubric of personal or family privacy and autonomy.[2] Accordingly, the decisions cited by the Court both in *Roe* and in its opinion today as precedent for the fundamental nature of the liberty to choose abortion do not, even if all are accepted as valid, dictate the Court's classification.

If the woman's liberty to choose an abortion is fundamental, then, it is not because any of our precedents (aside from *Roe* itself) commands or justifies that result; it can only be because protection for this unique choice is itself "implicit in the concept of ordered liberty" or, perhaps, "deeply rooted in this Nation's history and tradition." It seems clear to me that it is neither. The Court's opinion in *Roe* itself convincingly refutes the notion that the abortion liberty is deeply rooted in the history or tradition of our people, as does the continuing and deep division of the people themselves over the question of abortion. As for the notion that choice in the matter of abortion is implicit in the concept of ordered liberty, it seems apparent to me that a free, egalitarian, and democratic society does not presuppose any particular rule or set of rules with respect to abortion. And again, the fact that many men and women of good will and high commitment to constitutional government place themselves on both sides of the abortion controversy strengthens my own conviction that the values animating the Constitution do not compel recognition of the abortion liberty as fundamental. In so denominating that liberty, the Court engages not in constitutional interpretation, but in the unrestrained imposition of its own, extraconstitutional value preferences.[3]

2. That the abortion decision, like the decisions protected in *Griswold, Eisenstadt,* and *Carey,* concerns childbearing (or, more generally, family life) in no sense necessitates a holding that the liberty to choose abortion is "fundamental." That the decision involves the destruction of the fetus renders it different in kind from the decision not to conceive in the first place. This difference does not go merely to the weight of the state interest in regulating abortion; it affects as well the characterization of the liberty interest itself. For if the liberty to make certain decisions with respect to contraception without governmental constraint is "fundamental," it is not only because those decisions are "serious" and "important" to the individual (Stevens, J., concurring), but also because some value of privacy or individual autonomy that is somehow implicit in the scheme of ordered liberties established by the Constitution supports a judgment that such decisions are none of government's business. The same cannot be said where, as here, the individual is not "isolated in her privacy."

My point can be illustrated by drawing on a related area in which fundamental liberty interests have been found: childrearing. The Court's decisions in *Moore v. East Cleveland, Pierce,* and *Meyer* can be read for the proposition that parents have a fundamental liberty to make decisions with respect to the upbringing of their children. But no one would suggest that this fundamental liberty extends to assaults committed upon children by their parents. It is not the case that parents have a fundamental liberty to engage in such activities and that the State may intrude to prevent them only because it has a compelling interest in the well-being of children; rather, such activities, by their very nature, should be viewed as outside the scope of the fundamental liberty interest.

3. Justice Stevens asserts that I am "quite wrong in suggesting that the Court is imposing value preferences on anyone else" when it denominates the liberty to choose abortion as "fundamental" (in contradistinction to such other, nonfundamental liberties as the liberty to use dangerous drugs or to operate a business without governmental interference) and thereby disempowers state electoral majorities from legislating in this area. I can only respond that I cannot conceive of a definition of

A second, equally basic error infects the Court's decision in *Roe*. The detailed set of rules governing state restrictions on abortion that the Court first articulated in *Roe* and has since refined and elaborated presupposes not only that the woman's liberty to choose an abortion is fundamental, but also that the state's countervailing interest in protecting fetal life (or, as the Court would have it, "potential human life") becomes "compelling" only at the point at which the fetus is viable. As Justice O'Connor pointed out three years ago in her dissent in *Akron,* the Court's choice of viability as the point at which the state's interest becomes compelling is entirely arbitrary. The Court's "explanation" for the line it has drawn is that the state's interest becomes compelling at viability "because the fetus then presumably has the capacity of meaningful life outside the mother's womb." As one critic of *Roe* has observed, this argument "mistakes a definition for a syllogism." Ely, *The Wages of Crying Wolf,* 82 Yale L.J. 920, 924 (1973).

The governmental interest at issue is in protecting those who will be citizens if their lives are not ended in the womb. The substantiality of this interest is in no way dependent on the probability that the fetus may be capable of surviving outside the womb at any given point in its development, as the possibility of fetal survival is contingent on the state of medical practice and technology, factors that are in essence morally and constitutionally irrelevant. The State's interest is in the fetus as an entity in itself, and the character of this entity does not change at the point of viability under conventional medical wisdom. Accordingly, the State's interest, if compelling after viability, is equally compelling before viability.[4]

Both the characterization of the abortion liberty as fundamental and the denigration of the State's interest in preserving the lives of nonviable fetuses are

the phrase "imposing value preferences" that does not encompass the Court's action.

Justice Stevens also suggests that it is the legislative majority that has engaged in "the unrestrained imposition of its own, extraconstitutional value choices" when a state legislature restricts the availability of abortion. But a legislature, unlike a court, has the inherent power to do so unless its choices are constitutionally *forbidden,* which, in my view, is not the case here.

4. Contrary to Justice Stevens' suggestion, this is no more a "theological" position than is the Court's own judgment that viability is the point at which the state interest becomes compelling. (Interestingly, Justice Stevens omits any real effort to defend this judgment.) The point is that the specific interest the Court has recognized as compelling after the point of viability—that is, the interest in protecting "potential human life"—is present as well before viability, and the point of viability seems to bear no discernible relationship to the strength of that interest. Thus, there is no basis for concluding that the essential character of the state interest becomes transformed at the point of viability.

Further, it is self-evident that neither the legislative decision to assert a state interest in fetal life before viability nor the judicial decision to recognize that interest as compelling constitutes an impermissible "religious" deci-

sion merely because it coincides with the belief of one or more religions. Certainly the fact that the prohibition of murder coincides with one of the Ten Commandments does not render a State's interest in its murder statutes less than compelling, nor are legislative and judicial decisions concerning the use of the death penalty tainted by their correspondence to varying religious views on that subject. The simple, and perhaps unfortunate, fact of the matter is that in determining whether to assert an interest in fetal life, a State cannot avoid taking a position that will correspond to some religious beliefs and contradict others. The same is true to some extent with respect to the choice this Court faces in characterizing an asserted state interest in fetal life, for denying that such an interest is a "compelling" one necessarily entails a negative resolution of the "religious" issue of the humanity of the fetus, whereas accepting the State's interest as compelling reflects at least tolerance for a state decision that is congruent with the equally "religious" position that human life begins at conception. Faced with such a decision, the most appropriate course of action for the Court is to defer to a legislative resolution of the issue: in other words, if a state legislature asserts an interest in protecting fetal life, I can see no satisfactory basis for *denying* that it is compelling.

essential to the detailed set of constitutional rules devised by the Court to limit the States' power to regulate abortion. If either or both of these facets of *Roe* were rejected, a broad range of limitations on abortion (including outright prohibition) that are now unavailable to the States would again become constitutional possibilities.

In my view, such a state of affairs would be highly desirable from the standpoint of the Constitution. Abortion is a hotly contested moral and political issue. Such issues, in our society, are to be resolved by the will of the people, either as expressed through legislation or through the general principles they have already incorporated into the Constitution they have adopted.[5] *Roe* implies that the people have already resolved the debate by weaving into the Constitution the values and principles that answer the issue. As I have argued, I believe it is clear that the people have never not in 1787, 1791, 1868, or at any time since—done any such thing. I would return the issue to the people by overruling *Roe.*

II. [P]recisely because *Roe* is not premised on the notion that abortion is itself desirable (either as a matter of constitutional entitlement or of social policy), the decision does not command the States to fund or encourage abortion, or even to approve of it. Rather, we have recognized that the States may legitimately adopt a policy of encouraging normal childbirth rather than abortion so long as the measures through which that policy is implemented do not amount to direct compulsion of the woman's choice regarding abortion. *McRae, Maher, Beal.* The provisions before the Court today quite obviously represent the State's effort to implement such a policy.

The majority's opinion evinces no deference toward the State's legitimate policy. Rather, the majority makes it clear from the outset that it simply disapproves of any attempt by Pennsylvania to legislate in this area. * * *

[The *Roe* Court] conceded that the State's interest in preserving the life of a viable fetus is a compelling one, and the Court has never disavowed that concession. The Court now holds that this compelling interest cannot justify *any* regulation that imposes a quantifiable medical risk upon the pregnant woman who seeks to abort a viable fetus: if attempting to save the fetus imposes any additional risk of injury to the woman, she must be permitted to kill it. This

---

5. Justice Stevens, fn. 4, finds a contradiction between my recognition that constitutional analysis requires more than mere textual analysis or a search for the specific intent of the Framers and my assertion that it is ultimately the will of the people that is the source of whatever values are incorporated in the Constitution. The fallacy of Justice Stevens' argument is glaring. The rejection of what has been characterized as "clause-bound" interpretivism does not necessarily carry with it a rejection of the notion that constitutional adjudication is a search for values and principles that are implicit (and explicit) in the structure of rights and institutions that the people have themselves created. The implications of those values for the resolution of particular issues will in many if not most cases not have been explicitly considered when the values themselves were chosen—indeed, there will be some cases in which those who framed the provisions incorporating certain principles into the Constitution will be found to have been incorrect in their assessment of the consequences of their decision. See, e.g., *Brown v. Board of Education.* Nonetheless, the hallmark of a correct decision of constitutional law is that it rests on principles selected by the people through their Constitution, and not merely on the personal philosophies, be they libertarian or authoritarian, of the judges of the majority. While constitutional adjudication involves judgments of value, it remains the case that some values are indeed "extraconstitutional," in that they have no roots in the Constitution that the people have chosen. The Court's decision in *Lochner* was wrong because it rested on the Court's belief that the liberty to engage in a trade or occupation without governmental regulation was somehow fundamental—an assessment of value that was unsupported by the Constitution. I believe that *Roe*—and today's decision as well—rests on similarly extraconstitutional assessments of the value of the liberty to choose an abortion.

holding hardly accords with the usual understanding of the term "compelling interest," which we have used to describe those governmental interests that are so weighty as to justify substantial and ordinarily impermissible impositions on the individual—impositions that, I had thought, could include the infliction of some degree of risk of physical harm. * * *

The Court's ruling today that any trade-off between the woman's health and fetal survival is impermissible is not only inconsistent with *Roe*'s recognition of a compelling state interest in viable fetal life; it directly contradicts one of the essential holdings of *Roe*—that is, that the State may forbid *all* post-viability abortions except when *necessary* to protect the life or health of the pregnant woman. As is evident, this holding itself involves a trade-off between maternal health and protection of the fetus, for it plainly permits the State to forbid a postviability abortion even when such an abortion may be statistically safer than carrying the pregnancy to term, provided that the abortion is not medically necessary. The trade-off contained in the Pennsylvania statute, even as interpreted by the majority, is no different in kind: the State has simply required that when an abortion of some kind is medically necessary, it shall be conducted so as to spare the fetus (to the greatest degree possible) unless a method less protective of the fetus is itself to some degree medically necessary for the woman. That this choice may involve the imposition of some risk on the woman undergoing the abortion should be no more troublesome than that a prohibition on nonnecessary postviability abortions may involve the imposition of some risk on women who are thereby forced to continue their pregnancies to term; yet for some reason, the Court concludes that whereas the trade-offs it devises are compelled by the Constitution, the essentially indistinguishable trade-off the State has attempted is foreclosed. This cannot be the law. * * *

III. The decision today appears symptomatic of the Court's own insecurity over its handiwork in *Roe* and the cases following that decision. Aware that in *Roe* it essentially created something out of nothing and that there are many in this country who hold that decision to be basically illegitimate, the Court responds defensively. Perceiving, in a statute implementing the State's legitimate policy of preferring childbirth to abortion, a threat to or criticism of the decision in *Roe*, the majority indiscriminately strikes down statutory provisions that in no way contravene the right recognized in *Roe*. I do not share the warped point of view of the majority, nor can I follow the tortuous path the majority treads in proceeding to strike down the statute before us. * * *

JUSTICE O'CONNOR, with whom JUSTICE REHNQUIST joins, dissenting.

This Court's abortion decisions have already worked a major distortion in the Court's constitutional jurisprudence. See *Akron* (O'Connor, J., dissenting). Today's decision goes further, and makes it painfully clear that no legal rule or doctrine is safe from ad hoc nullification by this Court when an occasion for its application arises in a case involving state regulation of abortion. The permissible scope of abortion regulation is not the only constitutional issue on which this Court is divided, but—except when it comes to abortion—the Court has generally refused to let such disagreements, however longstanding or deeply felt, prevent it from evenhandedly applying uncontroversial legal doctrines to cases that come before it. That the Court's unworkable scheme for constitutionalizing the regulation of abortion has had this institutionally debilitating effect should not be surprising, however, since the Court is not suited to the expansive role it has claimed for itself in the series of cases that began with *Roe*.

[In affirming the Third Circuit's invalidation of various provisions of the Pennsylvania Act], the Court prematurely decides serious constitutional questions on an inadequate record, in contravention of settled principles of constitutional adjudication and procedural fairness. The constitutionality of the challenged provisions was not properly before the Court of Appeals, and is not properly before this Court. There has been no trial on the merits, and appellants have had no opportunity to develop facts that might have a bearing on the constitutionality of the statute. The only question properly before the Court is whether or not a preliminary injunction should have been issued to restrain enforcement of the challenged provisions pending trial on the merits. This Court's decisions in *Akron, Ashcroft,* and *Simopoulos* do not establish a likelihood that appellees would succeed on the merits of their constitutional claims sufficient to warrant overturning the District Court's denial of a preliminary injunction. Under the approach to abortion regulation outlined in my dissenting opinion in *Akron,* to which I adhere, it is even clearer that no preliminary injunction should have issued. I therefore dissent.

[B]ecause Pennsylvania has not asked the Court to reconsider or overrule *Roe,* I do not address that question.

I do, however, remain of the views expressed in my dissent in *Akron.* The State has compelling interests in ensuring maternal health and in protecting potential human life, and these interests exist "throughout pregnancy." Under this Court's fundamental-rights jurisprudence, judicial scrutiny of state regulation of abortion should be limited to whether the state law bears a rational relationship to legitimate purposes such as the advancement of these compelling interests, with heightened scrutiny reserved for instances in which the State has imposed an "undue burden" on the abortion decision. An undue burden will generally be found "in situations involving absolute obstacles or severe limitations on the abortion decision," not wherever a state regulation "may 'inhibit' abortions to some degree." And if a state law does interfere with the abortion decision to an extent that is unduly burdensome, so that it becomes "necessary to apply an exacting standard of review," the possibility remains that the statute will withstand the stricter scrutiny.

These principles for evaluating state regulation of abortion were not newly minted in my dissenting opinion in *Akron.* Apart from *Roe*'s outmoded trimester framework, the "unduly burdensome" standard had been articulated and applied with fair consistency by this Court in cases such as *McRae, Maher, Beal,* and *Bellotti I.* In *Akron* and *Ashcroft* the Court, in my view, distorted and misapplied this standard, but made no clean break with precedent and indeed "follow[ed] this approach" in assessing some of the regulations before it in those cases.

The Court today goes well beyond mere distortion of the "unduly burdensome" standard. By holding that each of the challenged provisions is facially unconstitutional as a matter of law, and that no conceivable facts appellants might offer could alter this result, the Court appears to adopt as its new test a *per se* rule under which any regulation touching on abortion must be invalidated if it poses "an unacceptable danger of deterring the exercise of that right." Under this prophylactic test, it seems that the mere possibility that some women will be less likely to choose to have an abortion by virtue of the presence of a particular state regulation suffices to invalidate it. Simultaneously, the Court strains to discover "the anti-abortion character of the statute," and, as Justice White points out, invents an unprecedented canon of construction under which "in cases involving abortion, a permissible reading of a statute is to be avoided at all costs." I shall not belabor the dangerous extravagance of this dual approach, because I hope it represents merely a temporary aberration rather than a portent of lasting change in settled principles of constitutional law. Suffice it to say that I dispute not only the wisdom but the legitimacy of the Court's attempt to discredit and preempt state abortion regulation regardless of the interests it serves and the impact it has. * * *

In my view, today's decision makes bad constitutional law and bad procedural law. The "'undesired and uncomfortable straitjacket'" in this case, is not the one the Court purports to discover in Pennsylvania's statute; it is the one the Court has tailored for the 50 States. * * *

FURTHER ATTACK ON *ROE*

ORAL ARGUMENTS IN *WEBSTER**

* * *

Charles Fried [special assistant to the U.S. Attorney General] [We] are not asking the Court to unravel the fabric [of] privacy rights which this Court has woven in cases like *Meyer* and *Pierce* and *Moore* and *Griswold*. Rather, we are asking the Court to pull this one thread. And the reason is well stated in *Harris v. McRae*: Abortion is different.

It involves the purposeful termination, as the Court said, of potential life. And I would only add that in the minds of many legislators who pass abortion regulation, it is not merely potential life but actual human life. And though we do not believe that the 14th Amendment takes any position on that question, we think it is an utter non sequitur to say that, therefore, the organized community must also take no position in legislation and may not use such a position as a premise for regulation.

Justice Kennedy Your position, Mr. Fried, then is that *Griswold* is correct and should be retained?

Mr. Fried Exactly, Your Honor.

Justice Kennedy Is that because there is a fundamental right involved in that case?

Mr. Fried In *Griswold* there was a right which was well established in a whole fabric of quite concrete matters, quite concrete.

It involved not an abstraction such as the right to control one's body, an abstraction such as the right to be let alone, it involved quite concrete intrusions into the details of marital intimacy. And that was emphasized by the Court and is a very important aspect of the Court's decision.

Justice Kennedy Does the case stand for the proposition that there is a right to determine whether to procreate?

Mr. Fried *Griswold* surely does not stand for that proposition. * * *

Justice Kennedy What is the right involved in *Griswold*?

Mr. Fried The right involved in *Griswold*, as the Court clearly stated, was the right not to have the state intrude into, in a very violent way, into the details, inquire into the details of marital intimacy. There was a great deal of talk about inquiry into the marital bedroom, and I think that is a very different story from what we have here.

* These extracts are taken from the transcript of the oral arguments published in the New York Times, April 27, 1989, pp. 14–16.

Justice O'Connor Do you say there is no fundamental right to decide whether to have a child or not? * * *

Do you deny that the Constitution protects [the right to procreate]?

Mr. Fried I would hesitate to formulate the right in such abstract terms, and I think the Court prior to *Roe* quite prudently also avoided such sweeping generalities. That was the wisdom of *Griswold.*

Justice O'Connor Do you think that the state has the right to, if in a future century we had a serious overpopulation problem, has a right to require women to have abortions after so many children?

Mr. Fried I surely do not. That would be quite a different matter.

Justice O'Connor What do you rest that on?

Mr. Fried Because unlike abortion, which involves the purposeful termination of future life, that would involve not preventing an operation by violently taking hands on, laying hands on a woman and submitting her to an operation and a whole constellation—

Justice O'Connor And you would rest that on substantive due process protection?

Mr. Fried Absolutely.

Justice Kennedy How do you define the liberty interests of the woman in that connection?

Mr. Fried The liberty interest against a seizure would be involved. That is how the Court analyzed the matter in *Griswold.* That is how Justice Harlan analyzed the matter in his dissent in *Poe v. Ullman*, which is, in some sense, the root of this area of law.

Justice Kennedy How do you define the interest, the liberty interest, of a woman in an abortion case?

Mr. Fried Well, I would think that there are liberty interests involved in terms perhaps of the contraceptive interest, but there is an interest at all points, however the interest of the woman is defined, at all points it is an interest which is matched by the state's interest in potential life.

Justice Kennedy I understand it is matched, but I want to know how you define it.

Mr. Fried I would define it in terms of the concrete impositions on the woman which so offended the Court in *Griswold* and which are not present in the *Roe* situation.

Finally, I would like to make quite clear that in our view, if *Roe* were overruled, this Court would have to continue to police the far outer boundaries of abortion regulation under a due process rational basis test and that that test is muscular enough, as Chief Justice Rehnquist said in his dissent in *Roe*, to strike down any regulation which did not make adequate provision—

Justice William J. Brennan, Jr. Mr. Fried, do I correctly read what your brief says * * *, that *Griswold* is a Fourth Amendment case?

Mr. Fried It is a case which draws on the Fourth Amendment. It is not itself a Fourth Amendment case, it is a 14th Amendment case. But I would like to emphasize that the Court would have ample power under our submission to strike down any regulation which did not make proper provision for cases where the life of the mother was at risk.

I think the important thing to realize is that when *Roe* was decided, it swept off the table regulations in the majority of American jurisdictions, including regulations recently promulgated by the American Law Institute, and declared a principle which said that it was unfair and unreasonable to regulate abortion in ways that most Western countries still do regulate abortion.

We are not here today suggesting that the Court would, therefore, allow extreme and extravagant and bloodthirsty regulations and that it would lack the power to strike those down if they were presented to it. But it is a mistake to think that alone, among government institutions—

Justice Stevens Mr. Fried, is there a difference between the court's power in the case of an abortion that would be life threatening to the woman and an abortion that would merely cause her severe and prolonged disease? Is there a constitutional difference?

Mr. Fried I think that is a matter of degree, and it is perfectly clear that severe health effects shade over into a threat to the life. I cannot promise the Court that our submission would dispense the Federal courts from considering matters like that, but I also very much doubt that the Court would be presented with many such situations.

What is necessary is for the Court to return to legislatures an opportunity in some substantial way to express their preference, which the Court says they may express, for normal childbirth over abortion, and *Roe* stands as a significant barrier to that.

Justice Byron R. White Does your submission suggest that a public hospital, in a state that permits abortion, could not allow abortions?

Mr. Fried It is quite clear that a public hospital may, under this Court's decision in *Maher* and in *McRae*, may do as Missouri has here done and say that public funds cannot be expended.

Justice White Suppose there is a state that permits abortions and they are done in public hospitals. Do you think that is a—you say that there is human life involved, that is destroyed in abortions? Is there some problem about the state permitting abortions?

Mr. Fried Oh, no, I think there is not. As I have indicated, I think the Constitution takes no position on this point. There is a certain logic in some of the provisions which say that there should be, that there should be protection further back. But the country's experience and the Court's experience under the constitutionalization of that issue has been so regrettable that I could not in conscience recommend that it be constitutionalized in some other way at another point in the spectrum.

Now, if the Court does not in this case in its prudence decide to reconsider *Roe*, I would ask at least that it say nothing here that would further entrench this decision as a secure premise for reasoning in future cases. * * *

Frank Susman [attorney for Reproductive Health Services] [I think Mr. Fried's submission] is somewhat disingenuous when he suggests to this Court that he does not seek to unravel the whole cloth of procreational rights but merely to pull a thread. It has always been my personal experience that when I pull a thread, my sleeve falls off. There is no stopping.

It is not a thread he is after. It is the full range of procreational rights and choices that constitute the fundamental right that has been recognized by this Court. For better or for worse, there no longer exists any bright line between the fundamental right that was established in *Griswold* and the fundamental right of abortion that was established in *Roe*. These two rights, because of advances in medicine and science, now overlap. The coalesce and merge and they are not distinct.

Justice Scalia Excuse me, you find it hard to draw a line between those two but easy to draw a line between first, second and third trimester.

Mr. Susman I do not find it difficult—

Justice Scalia I don't see why a court that can draw that line can't separate abortion from birth control quite readily.

Mr. Susman If I may suggest the reasons in response to your question, Justice Scalia. The most common forms of what we generically in common parlance call contraception today, IUD's, low-dose birth control pills, which are the safest type of birth control pills available, act as abortifacients. They are correctly labeled as both.

Under this statute, which defines fertilization as the point of beginning, those forms of contraception are also abortifacients. Science and medicine refers to them as both. We are not still dealing with the common barrier methods of *Griswold*. We are no longer just talking about condoms and diaphragms.

Things have changed. The bright line, if there ever was one, has now been extinguished. That's why I suggest to this Court that we need to deal with one right, the right to procreate. We are no longer talking about two rights.

Justice Kennedy Do you agree that the state can forbid abortions save to preserve the life of the mother after the fetus is, say, eight months old?

Mr. Susman If I understand the question, Justice Kennedy, I think the health rights of the woman always are supreme at any stage of pregnancy.

Justice Kennedy Suppose the health rights of the mother are not involved? The life or health of the mother is not involved, can the state prohibit an abortion after the fetus is eight months old?

Mr. Susman Yes. I am willing to recognize the compelling interest granted in *Roe* of the state in potential fetal life after the point of viability.

Justice Kennedy But that is a line-drawing, isn't it?

Mr. Susman Yes, it is. But that is a line that is more easily drawn. I think there are many cogent reasons for picking the point of viability, which is what we have today under *Roe*.

First of all, historically, both at common law and in early statutes, this was always the line chosen. Whether it was called quickening or viability, there is little difference time-wise.

Justice O'Connor Well, there is a difference, is there not, in those two?

Mr. Susman Technically, between those two definitions, Justice O'Connor, yes. Quickening had less of a medical significance. It was [when] the woman could first detect movement.

Justice O'Connor When the fetus was first felt by the mother?

Mr. Susman A kick, yes, absolutely, approximately two or three weeks before what we would consider viability today. The second good reason, I think, for remaining with viability as our dividing line in this context, Justice Kennedy, is that it is one that the physician can determine on a case-by-case basis without periodic recourse to the courts.

Thirdly, it is a point in time that the physician can determine with or without the assistance of the woman. It is a medical judgment, I agree, and not a medical fact. One cannot pinpoint viability to a day or to an hour or to a second.

I would suggest again, as I indicated, that the line has now been erased. It is interesting also to note at the same time that the definition of conception or fertilization chosen by this statute does not even comport with the medical definition. The definition of conception promulgated, for example, by the American College of Obstetricians and Gynecologists, starts a week later than the definition that this section has chosen to use.

It is at all stages of procreation, whether before or after conception, that the standards of what constitute fundamental liberty are amply satisfied. Procreational interests are, indeed, implicit in the concept of ordered liberty, and neither liberty nor justice would exist without them.

It is truly a liberty whose exercise is deeply rooted in this nation's history and tradition. * * *

Thirty percent of pregnancies in this country today terminate in abortion. It is a high rate. It is a rate that sometimes astounds people, but it is a rate that has not changed one whit from the time the Constitution was enacted through the 1800's and through the 1900's. That has always been the rate.

It is significantly less than the worldwide rate. Worldwide, 40 percent of all pregnancies terminate in abortion. Abortion today is the most common surgical procedure in the United States with the possible exception of contraception.

It remains today, as it was in the days of *Roe*, 17 times safer than childbirth, 100 times safer than appendectomy, a safe procedure, minor surgery.

I suggest that there can be no ordered liberty for women without control over their education, their employment, their health, their childbearing and their personal aspirations. There does, in fact, exist a deeply rooted tradition that the government steer clear of decisions affecting the bedroom, childbearing and the doctor-patient relationship as it pertains to these concerns.

Chief Justice Rehnquist It is a deeply rooted tradition, but surely abortion was regulated by the states in the 19th century and in the 20th century?

Mr. Susman Yes, but I think it is necessary to go back and examine, as the historical brief does and other works, as to the reasons those regulations were enacted. Similarly, they were not done to protect the fetus. Those were not the purposes. If you look, for example—

Chief Justice Rehnquist If you say there is a deeply rooted tradition of freedom in this area, that suggests that there had been no legislative intervention to me. What you are, that simply is not the fact.

Mr. Susman I think we can look to a deeply rooted tradition as opposed to black and white issues, as opposed to slavery, and yet we have much legislation. In fact, following this Court's opinion in *Brown* in 1954, almost every Southern state without exception passed legislation directly in conflict with that opinion. So the fact that legislation has been enacted does not in my mind—

Chief Justice Rehnquist I am not talking about legislation post-*Roe*. I am talking about legislative regulation of abortion in the 19th century and the 20th century before *Roe*. * * * I don't see how you can argue that there was a deeply rooted tradition of no regulation.

Mr. Susman Because I think you have to examine the period before the regulations came into effect. Every state adopted anti-abortion legislation in the 1820's and the 1830's and the 1840's. But before that time it went without regulation.

It was accepted, it was not a crime at common law, as *Roe* and other works have recognized.

Justice Scalia That certainly is not uncontested. You mention the historical brief. There is more than one historical brief here, and one filed by the Association for Public Justice just simply contradicts your history and quotes authorities back to Blackstone and Cook saying that at common law abortion was unlawful.

Mr. Susman I think—

Justice Scalia And also contradicting your contention that the whole purpose was to protect the mother and not to protect the fetus. * * *

Mr. Susman Justice Scalia, I would not submit that the briefs do not disagree with each other. I do not dispute that. You or I or others might dispute as to whether the facts disagree, but the fact that different parties put different slants or different perspectives or interpretations on those facts certainly, I could not disagree with.

Justice Scalia Let me inquire—I can see deriving a fundamental right from either a long tradition that this, the right to abort, has always been protected. I don't see that tradition. But I suppose you could also derive a fundamental right just simply from the text of the Constitution plus the logic of the matter or whatever.

How can—can you derive it that way here without making a determination as to whether the fetus is a human life or not? It is very hard to say it just is a matter of basic principle that it must be a fundamental right unless you make the determination that the organism that is destroyed is not a human life. Can—can you as a matter of logic or principle make that determination otherwise?

Mr. Susman I think the basic question, and of course it goes to one of the specific provisions of the statute as to whether this is a human life or whether human life begins at conception, is not something that is verifiable as a fact. It is a question verifiable only by reliance upon faith.

It is a question of labels. Neither side in this issue and debate would ever disagree on the physiological facts. Both sides would agree as to when a heartbeat can first be detected. Both sides would agree as to when brain waves can be first detected. But when you come to try to place the emotional labels on what you call that collection of physiological facts, that is where people part company.

Justice Scalia I agree with you entirely, but what conclusion does that lead you to? That, therefore, there must be a fundamental right on the part of the woman to destroy this thing that we don't know what it is or, rather, that whether there is or isn't is a matter that you vote upon; since we don't now the answer, people have to make up their minds the best they can.

Mr. Susman The conclusion to which it leads me is that when you have an issue that is so divisive and so emotional and so personal and so intimate, that it must be left as a fundamental right to the individual to make that choice under her then attendant circumstances, her religious beliefs, her moral beliefs and in consultation with her physician. The very debate that went on outside this morning outside this building, and has gone on in various towns and communities across our nation, is the same debate that every woman who becomes pregnant and doesn't wish to be pregnant has with herself. * * *

WEBSTER v. REPRODUCTIVE HEALTH SERVICES

—— U.S. ——, 109 S.Ct. ——, —— L.Ed.2d —— (1989).

CHIEF JUSTICE REHNQUIST announced the judgment of the Court and delivered the opinion of the Court with respect to Parts I, II–A, II–B, and II–C, and an opinion with respect to Parts II–D, and III, in which JUSTICE WHITE and JUSTICE KENNEDY join.

This appeal concerns the constitutionality of a [1986] Missouri statute regulating the performance of abortions. The United States Court of Appeals for the Eighth Circuit struck down several provisions of the statute on the ground that they violated this Court's decision in *Roe v. Wade* and cases following it. We * * * now reverse.

I * * *

[The challenged statute contains] 20 provisions, 5 of which are now before the Court. The first provision, or preamble, contains "findings" by the state legislature that "[t]he life of each human being begins at conception," and that "unborn children have protectable interests in life, health, and well-being." §§ 1.205.1(1), (2) (1986). The Act further requires that all Missouri laws be interpreted to provide unborn children with the same rights enjoyed by other persons, subject to the Federal Constitution and this Court's precedents. § 1.205.2. Among its other provisions, the Act requires that, prior to performing an abortion on any woman whom a physician has reason to believe is 20 or more weeks pregnant, the physician ascertain whether the fetus is viable by performing "such medical examinations and tests as are necessary to make a finding of the gestational age, weight, and lung maturity of the unborn child." § 188.029. The Act also prohibits the use of public employees and facilities to perform or assist abortions not necessary to save the mother's life, and it prohibits the use of public funds, employees, or facilities for the purpose of "encouraging or counseling" a woman to have an abortion not necessary to save her life. §§ 188.205, 188.210, 188.215.

In July 1986, five health professional employed by the State [three physicians, a nurse and a social worker] and two nonprofit corporations brought this class action [in federal court]. Plaintiffs, appellees in this Court, sought declaratory and injunctive relief on the ground that certain statutory provisions violated the First, Fourth, Ninth, and Fourteenth Amendments to the Federal Constitution.

* * * The two nonprofit corporations are Reproductive Health Services, which offers family planning and gynecological services to the public, including abortion services up to 22 weeks "gestational age," [2] and Planned Parenthood of Kansas City, which provides abortion services up to 14 weeks gestational age. [The] individual plaintiffs, within the scope of their public employment, encourage and counsel pregnant women to have nontherapeutic abortions. Two of the physicians perform abortions.

[T]he District Court declared seven provisions of the Act unconstitutional and enjoined their enforcement. These provisions included the preamble, § 1.205; the "informed consent" provision, which required physicians to inform the pregnant woman of certain facts before performing an abortion, § 188.039; the requirement that post-16-week abortions be performed only in hospitals,

---

2. The Act defines "gestational age" as the "length of pregnancy as measured from the first day of the woman's last menstrual period."

§ 188.025; the mandated tests to determine viability, § 188.029; and the prohibition on the use of public funds, employees, and facilities to perform or assist nontherapeutic abortions, and the restrictions on the use of public funds, employees, and facilities to encourage or counsel women to have such abortions, §§ 188.205, 188.210, 188.215. The Court of Appeals for the Eighth Circuit affirmed, with one exception not relevant to this appeal. * * *

II

Decision of this case requires us to address four sections of the Missouri Act: (a) the preamble; (b) the prohibition on the use of public facilities or employees to perform abortions; (c) the prohibition on public funding of abortion counseling; and (d) the requirement that physicians conduct viability tests prior to performing abortions. We address these seriatim.

A

The Act's preamble sets forth "findings" by the Missouri legislature that "[t]he life of each human being begins at conception," and that "[u]nborn children have protectable interests in life, health, and well-being." §§ 1.205.1(1), (2). The Act then mandates that state laws be interpreted to provide unborn children with "all the rights, privileges, and immunities available to other persons, citizens, and residents of this state," subject to the Constitution and this Court's precedents. § 1.205.2.[4] In invalidating the preamble, the Court of Appeals relied on his Court's dictum that " 'a State may not adopt one theory of when life begins to justify its regulation of abortions.' " [quoting *Akron*]. It rejected Missouri's claim that the preamble was "abortion-neutral," and "merely determine[d] when life begins in a nonabortion context, a traditional state prerogative." The court thought that "[t]he only plausible inference" from the fact that "every remaining section of the bill save one regulates the performance of abortions" was that "the stated intended its abortion regulations to be understood against the backdrop of its theory of life." * * *

In our view, the Court of Appeals misconceived the meaning of the *Akron* dictum, which was only that a State could not "justify" an abortion regulation otherwise invalid under *Roe* on the ground that it embodied the State's view about when life begins. Certainly the preamble does not by its terms regulate abortion or any other aspect of appellees' medical practice. The Court has emphasized that *Roe* "implies no limitation on the authority of a State to make a value judgment favoring childbirth over abortion." *Maher*. The preamble can be read simply to express that sort of value judgment.

4. Section 1.205 provides in full:

"1. The general assembly of this state finds that:

"(1) The life of each human being begins at conception;

"(2) Unborn children have protectable interests in life, health, and well-being;

"(3) The natural parents of unborn children have protectable interests in the life, health, and well-being of their unborn child.

"2. Effective January 1, 1988, the laws of this state shall be interpreted and construed to acknowledge on behalf of the unborn child at every stage of development, all the rights, privileges, and immunities available to other persons, citizens, and residents of this state, subject only to the Constitution of the United States, and decisional interpretations thereof by the United States Supreme Court and specific provisions to the contrary in the statutes and constitution of this state.

"3. As used in this section, the term 'unborn children' or 'unborn child' shall include all unborn child or *[sic]* children or the offspring of human beings from the moment of conception until birth at every stage of biological development.

"4. Nothing in this section shall be interpreted as creating a cause of action against a woman for indirectly harming her unborn child by failing to properly care for herself or by failing to follow any particular program of prenatal care."

We think the extent to which the preamble's language might be used to interpret other state statutes or regulations is something that only the courts of Missouri can definitively decide. State law has offered protections to unborn children in tort and probate law and [the preamble] can be interpreted to do no more than that. * * * It will be time enough for federal courts to address the meaning of the preamble should it be applied to restrict the activities of appellees in some concrete way. Until then, this Court "is not empowered to decide . . . abstract propositions, or to declare, for the government of future cases, principles or rules of law which cannot affect the result as to the thing in issue in the case before it." We therefore need not pass on the constitutionality of the Act's preamble.

B

Section 188.210 provides that "[i]t shall be unlawful for any public employee within the scope of his employment to perform or assist in an abortion, not necessary to save the life of the mother," while § 188.215 makes it "unlawful for any public facility to be used for the purpose of performing or assisting an abortion not necessary to save the life of the mother." [We uphold these provisions.]

As we said earlier this Term, "our cases have recognized that the Due Process Clauses generally confer no affirmative right to governmental aid, even where such aid may be necessary to secure life, liberty, or property interests of which the government itself may not deprive the individual." [*Maher*] upheld a Connecticut welfare regulation under which Medicaid recipients received payments for medical services related to childbirth, but not for nontherapeutic abortions. The Court rejected the claim that this unequal subsidization of childbirth and abortion was impermissible under *Roe*. * * *

More recently, in *Harris v. McRae*, the Court upheld "the most restrictive version of the Hyde Amendment," which withheld from States federal funds under the Medicaid program to reimburse the costs of abortions, " 'except where the life of the mother would be endangered if the fetus were carried to term.' " As in *Maher* and *Poelker*, the Court required only a showing that Congress' authorization of "reimbursement for medically necessary services generally, but not for certain medically necessary abortions" was rationally related to the legitimate governmental goal of encouraging childbirth.

* * * Just as Congress' refusal to fund abortions in *McRae* left "an indigent woman with at least the same range of choice in deciding whether to obtain a medically necessary abortion as she would have had if Congress had chosen to subsidize no health care costs at all," Missouri's refusal to allow public employees to perform abortions in public hospitals leaves a pregnant woman with the same choices as if the State had chosen not to operate any public hospitals at all. The challenged provisions only restrict a woman's ability to obtain an abortion to the extent that she chooses to use a physician affiliated with a public hospital. This circumstance is more easily remedied, and thus considerably less burdensome, than indigency, which "may make it difficult— and in some cases, perhaps, impossible—for some women to have abortions" without public funding. *Maher*. Having held that the State's refusal to fund abortions does not violate *Roe*, it strains logic to reach a contrary result for the use of public facilities and employees. If the State may "make a value judgment favoring childbirth over abortion [and] implement that judgment by the allocation of public funds," *Maher*, surely it may do so through the allocation of other public resources, such as hospitals and medical staff. * * *

"Constitutional concerns are greatest," we said in *Maher*, "when the State attempts to impose its will by the force of law; the State's power to encourage actions deemed to be in the public interest is necessarily far broader." Nothing in the Constitution requires States to enter or remain in the business of performing abortions. Nor, as appellees suggest, do private physicians and their patients have some kind of constitutional right of access to public facilities for the performance of abortions. Indeed, if the State does recoup all of its costs in performing abortions, and no state subsidy, direct or indirect, is available, it is difficult to see how any procreational choice is burdened by the State's ban on the use of its facilities or employees for performing abortions.[8]

Maher, Poelker, and *McRae* all support the view that the State need not commit any resources to facilitating abortions, even if it can turn a profit by doing so. * * *

C

The Missouri Act contains three provisions relating to "encouraging or counseling a woman to have an abortion not necessary to save her life." Section 188.205 states that no public funds can be used for this purpose; § 188.210 states that public employees cannot, within the scope of their employment, engage in public speech; and § 188.215 forbids such speech in public facilities. [The Court of Appeals] held that all three of these provisions were unconstitutionally vague, and that "the ban on using public funds, employees, and facilities to encourage or counsel a woman to have an abortion is an unacceptable infringement of the woman's fourteenth amendment right to choose an abortion after receiving the medical information necessary to exercise the right knowingly and intelligently."

Missouri has chosen only to appeal the Court of Appeals' invalidation of the public funding provision, § 188.205. * * * We accept, for purposes of decision, the State's claim that [this provision] "is not directed at the conduct of any physician or health care provider, private or public," but "is directed solely at those persons responsible for expending public funds."

Appellees contend that they are not "adversely" affected under the State's interpretation of § 188.205, and therefore that there is no longer a case or controversy before us on this question. Plaintiffs are masters of their complaints and remain so at the appellate stage of a litigation. A majority of the Court agrees with appellees that the controversy over § 188.205 is now moot, because appellees' argument amounts to a decision to no longer seek a declaratory judgment that § 188.205 is unconstitutional and accompanying declarative relief. * * *

D

Section 188.029 of the Missouri Act provides:

"Before a physician performs an abortion on a woman he has reason to believe is carrying an unborn child of twenty or more weeks gestational age, the physician shall first determine if the unborn child is viable by using and exercising that degree of care, skill, and proficiency commonly exercised by the ordinarily skillful, careful, and prudent physician engaged in similar practice under the same or similar conditions. In making this determina-

---

8. A different analysis might apply if a particular State had socialized medicine and all of its hospitals and physicians were publicly funded. This case might also be different if the State barred doctors who performed abortions in private facilities from the use of public facilities for any purpose.

tion of viability, the physician shall perform or cause to be performed such medical examinations and tests as are necessary to make a finding of the gestational age, weight, and lung maturity of the unborn child and shall enter such findings and determination of viabilty in the medical record of the mother."

As with the preamble, the parties disagree over the meaning of this statutory provision. The State emphasizes the language of the first sentence, which speaks in terms of the physician's determination of viability being made by the standards of ordinary skill in the medical profession. Appellees stress the language of the second sentence, which prescribes such "tests as are necessary" to make a finding of gestational age, fetal weight, and lung maturity.

The Court of Appeals read § 188.029 as requiring that after 20 weeks "doctors *must* perform tests to find gestational age, fetal weight and lung maturity." The court indicated that the tests needed to determine fetal weight at 20 weeks are "unreliable and inaccurate" and would add $125 to $250 to the cost of an abortion. It also stated that "amniocentesis, the only method available to determine lung maturity, is contrary to accepted medical practice until 28–30 weeks of gestation, expensive, and imposes significant health risks for both the pregnant woman and the fetus." * * *

We think the viability-testing provision makes sense only if the second sentence is read to require only those tests that are useful to making subsidiary findings as to viability. If we construe this provision to require a physician to perform those tests needed to make the three specified findings *in all circumstances*, including when the physician's reasonable professional judgment indicates that the tests would be irrelevant to determining viability or even dangerous to the mother and the fetus, the second sentence of § 188.029 would conflict with the first sentence's *requirement* that a physician apply his reasonable professional skill and judgment. It would also be incongruous to read this provision, especially the word "necessary" to require the performance of tests irrelevant to the expressed statutory purpose of determining viability. It thus seems clear to us that the Court of Appeals' construction of § 188.029 violates well-accepted canons of statutory interpretation used in the Missouri courts * * *.

The viability-testing provision of the Missouri Act is concerned with promoting the State's interest in potential human life rather than in maternal health. Section 188.029 creates what is essentially a presumption of viability at 20 weeks, which the physician must rebut with tests indicating that the fetus is not viable prior to performing an abortion. It also directs the physician's determination as to viability by specifying consideration, if feasible, of gestational age, fetal weight, and lung capacity. The District Court found that "the medical evidence is uncontradicted that a 20-week fetus is *not* viable," and that "23½ to 24 weeks gestation is the earliest point in pregnancy where a reasonable possibility of viability exists." But it also found that there may be a 4-week error in estimating gestational age, which supports testing at 20 weeks.

[*Roe*] recognized that the State has "important and legitimate" interests in protecting maternal health and in the potentiality of human life. During the second trimester, the State "may, if it chooses, regulate the abortion procedure in ways that are reasonably related to maternal health." After viability, when the State's interest in potential human life was held to become compelling, the State "may, if it chooses, regulate, and even proscribe, abortion except where it is necessary, in appropriate medical judgment, for the preservation of the life or health of the mother."

In *Colautti v. Franklin,* upon which appellees rely, the Court held that a Pennsylvania statute regulating the standard of care to be used by a physician performing an abortion of a possibly viable fetus was void for vagueness. But in the course of reaching that conclusion, the Court reaffirmed its earlier statement in *Danforth,* that " 'the determination of whether a particular fetus is viable is, and must be, a matter for the judgement of the responsible attending physician.' " The dissent ignores the statement in *Colautti* that "neither the legislature nor the courts may proclaim one of the elements entering into the ascertainment of viability—be it weeks of gestation or fetal weight or any other single factor—as the determinant of when the State has a compelling interest in the life or health of the fetus." To the extent that § 188.029 regulates the method for determining viability, it undoubtedly does superimpose state regulation on the medical determination of whether a particular fetus is viable. The [courts below] thought it unconstitutional for this reason. To the extent that the viability tests increase the cost of what are in fact second-trimester abortions, their validity may also be questioned under *Akron,* where the Court held that a requirement that second trimester abortions must be performed in hospitals was invalid because it substantially increased the expense of those procedures.

We think that the doubt cast upon the Missouri statute by these cases is not so much a flaw in the statute as it is a reflection of the fact that the rigid trimester analysis of the course of a pregnancy enunciated in *Roe* has resulted in subsequent cases like *Colautti* and *Akron* making constitutional law in this area a virtual Procrustean bed. Statutes specifying elements of informed consent to be provided abortion patients, for example, were invalidated if they were thought to "structur[e] [the] dialogue between the woman and her physician." *Thornburgh.* As the dissenters in *Thornburgh* pointed out, such a statute would have been sustained under any traditional standard of judicial review, or for any other surgical procedure except abortion.

Stare decisis is a cornerstone of our legal system, but it has less power in constitutional cases, where, save for constitutional amendments, this Court is the only body able to make needed changes. We have not refrained from reconsideration of a prior construction of the Constitution that has proved "unsound in principle and unworkable in practice." We think the *Roe* trimester framework falls into that category.

In the first place, the rigid *Roe* framework is hardly consistent with the notion of a Constitution cast in general terms, as ours is, and usually speaking in general principles, as ours does. The key elements of the *Roe* framework—trimesters and viability—are not found in the text of the Constitution or in any place else one would expect to find a constitutional principle. Since the bounds of the inquiry are essentially indeterminate, the result has been a web of legal rules that have become increasingly intricate, resembling a code of regulations rather than a body of constitutional doctrine.[15] As Justice White has put it, the

---

15. For example, the Court has held that a State may require that certain information be given to a woman by a physician or his assistant, *Akron,* but that it may not require that such information be furnished to her only by the physician himself. Likewise, a State may require that abortions in the second trimester be performed in clinics, *Simopoulos,* but it may not require that such abortions be performed only in hospitals. *Akron.* We do not think these distinctions are of any constitutional import in view of our abandonment of the trimester framework. The dissent's claim that the State goes too far, even under *Maher, Poelker* and *McRae,* by refusing to permit the use of public facilities, as defined in § 188.200, for the performance of abortions is another

trimester framework has left this Court to serve as the country's "*ex officio* medical board with powers to approve or disapprove medical and operative practices and standards throughout the United States." *Danforth* (opinion concurring in part and dissenting in part).

In the second place, we do not see why the State's interest in protecting potential human life should come into existence only at the point of viability, and that there should therefore be a rigid line allowing state regulation after viability but prohibiting it before viability. The dissenters in *Thornburgh,* writing in the context of the *Roe* trimester analysis, would have recognized this fact by positing against the "fundamental right" recognized in *Roe* the State's "compelling interest" in protecting potential human life throughout pregnancy. "[T]he State's interest, if compelling after viability, is equally compelling before viability." *Thornburgh* (White, J., dissenting); (O'Connor, J., dissenting) ("State has compelling interests in ensuring maternal health and in protecting potential human life, and these interests exist 'throughout pregnancy' ").

The tests that § 188.029 requires the physician to perform are designed to determine viability. The State here has chosen viability as the point at which its interest in potential human life must be safeguarded. * * * It is true that the tests in question increase the expense of abortion, and regulate the discretion of the physician in determining the viability of the fetus. Since the tests will undoubtedly show in many cases that the fetus is not viable, the tests will have been performed for what were in fact second-trimester abortions. But we are satisfied that the requirement of these tests permissibly furthers the State's interest in protecting potential human life, and we therefore believe § 188.029 to be constitutional.

The dissent takes us to task for our failure to join in a "great issues" debate as to whether the Constitution includes an "unenumerated" general right to privacy as recognized in cases such as *Griswold* and *Roe.* But *Griswold,* unlike *Roe,* did not purport to adopt a whole framework, complete with detailed rules and distinctions, to govern the cases in which the asserted liberty interest would apply. As such, it was far different from the opinion, if not the holding, of *Roe,* which sought to establish a constitutional framework for judging state regulation of abortion during the entire term of pregnancy. That framework sought to deal with areas of medical practice traditionally subject to state regulation, and it sought to balance once and for all by reference only to the calendar the claims of the State to protect the fetus as a form of human life against the claims of a woman to decide for herself whether or not to abort a fetus she was carrying. The experience of the Court in applying *Roe* in later cases, see n. 15, suggests to us that there is wisdom in not unnecessarily attempting to elaborate the abstract differences between a "fundamental right" to abortion, as the Court described it in *Akron,* a "limited fundamental constitutional right," which Justice Blackmun's dissent today treats *Roe* as having established, or a liberty interest protected by the Due Process Clause, which we believe it to be. The Missouri testing requirement here is reasonably designed to ensure that abortions are not performed where the fetus is viable—an end which all concede is legitimate—and that is sufficient to sustain its constitutionality.

The dissent also accuses us, inter alia, of cowardice and illegitimacy in dealing with "the most politically divisive domestic legal issue of our time." There is no doubt that our holding today will allow some governmental regula-

example of the fine distinctions endemic in
the *Roe* framework.

tion of abortion that would have been prohibited under the language of cases such as *Colautti* and *Akron*. But the goal of constitutional adjudication is surely not to remove inexorably "politically divisive" issues from the ambit of the legislative process, whereby the people through their elected representatives deal with matters of concern to them. The goal of constitutional adjudication is to hold true the balance between that which the Constitution puts beyond the reach of the democratic process and that which it does not. We think we have done that today. The dissent's suggestion that legislative bodies, in a Nation where more than half of our population is women, will treat our decision today as an invitation to enact abortion regulation reminiscent of the dark ages not only misreads our views but does scant justice to those who serve in such bodies and the people who elect them.

III

Both appellants and the United States as Amicus Curiae have urged that we overrule our decision in *Roe v. Wade*. The facts of the present case, however, differ from those at issue in *Roe*. Here, Missouri has determined that viability is the point at which its interest in potential human life must be safeguarded. In *Roe*, on the other hand, the Texas statute criminalized the performance of *all* abortions, except when the mother's life was at stake. This case therfore affords us no occasion to revisit the holding of *Roe*, which was that the Texas statute unconstitutionally infringed the right to an abortion derived from the Due Process Clause, and we leave it undisturbed. To the extent indicated in our opinion, we would modify and narrow *Roe* and succeeding cases. * * *

JUSTICE O'CONNOR, concurring in part and concurring in the judgment.

I concur in Parts I, II–A, II–B, and II–C of the Court's opinion.

I

Nothing in the record before us or the opinions below indicates that subsections 1(1) and 1(2) of the preamble to Missouri's abortion regulation statute will affect a woman's decision to have an abortion. Justice Stevens suggests that the preamble may also "interfere[ ] with contraceptive choices," because certain contraceptive devices act on a female ovum after it has been fertilized by a male sperm. The Missouri Act defines "conception" as "the fertilization of the ovum of a female by a sperm of a male" and invests "unborn children" with "protectable interests in life, health, and well-being" from "the moment of conception. . . ." Justice Stevens asserts that any possible interference with a woman's right to use such post-fertilization contraceptive devices would be unconstitutional under *Griswold* and our subsequent contraception cases. Similarly, certain amici suggests that the Missouri Act's preamble may prohibit the developing technology of *in vitro* fertilization, a technique used to aid couples otherwise unable to bear children in which a number of ova are removed from the woman and fertilized by male sperm. * * * It may be correct that the use of postfertilization contraceptive devices is constitutionally protected by *Griswold* and its progeny but, as with a woman's abortion decision, nothing in the record or the opinions below indicates that the preamble will affect a woman's decision to practice contraception. * * * Neither is there any indication of the possibility that the preamble might be applied to prohibit the performance of *in vitro* fertilization. I agree with the Court, therefore, that all of these intimations of unconstitutionality are simply too hypothetical to support the use of declaratory judgment procedures and injunctive remedies in this case.

Similarly, it seems to me to follow directly from our previous decisions concerning state or federal funding of abortions that appellees' facial challenge to the constitutionality of Missouri's ban on the utilization of public facilities and the participation of public employees in the performance of abortions not necessary to save the life of the mother cannot succeed. Given Missouri's definition of "public facility" as "any public institution, public facility, public equipment, or any physical asset owned, leased, or controlled by this state or any agency or political subdivisions thereof," § 188.200(2), there may be conceivable applications of the ban on the use of public facilities that would be unconstitutional. Appellees and *amici* suggest that the State could try to enforce the ban against private hospitals using public water and sewage lines, or against private hospitals leasing state-owned equipment or state land. Whether some or all of these or other applications of § 188.215 would be constitutional need not be decided here. *Maher, Poelker,* and *McRae* stand for the proposition that some quite straightforward applications of the Missouri ban on the use of public facilities for performing abortions would be constitutional and that is enough to defeat appellees' assertion that the ban is facially unconstitutional. * * *

I also agree with the Court that, under the interpretation of § 188.205 urged by the State and adopted by the Court, there is no longer a case or controversy before us over the constitutionality of that provision. I would note, however, that this interpretation of § 188.205 is not binding on the Supreme Court of Missouri which has the final word on the meaning of that State's statutes. * * *

II

In its interpretation of Missouri's "determination of viability" provision, § 188.029, the plurality has proceeded in a manner unnecessary to deciding the question at hand. I agree with the plurality that it was plain error for the Court of Appeals to interpret the second sentence of § 188.029 as meaning that "doctors *must* perform tests to find gestational age, fetal weight and lung maturity" (emphasis in original). When read together with the first sentence of § 188.029—which requires a physician to "determine if the unborn child is viable by using and exercising that degree of care, skill, and proficiency commonly exercised by the ordinary skillful, careful, and prudent physician engaged in similar practice under the same or similar conditions"—it would be contradictory nonsense to read the second sentence as requiring a physician to perform viability examinations and tests in situations where it would be careless and imprudent to do so. The plurality is quite correct: "the viability-testing provision makes sense only if the second sentence is read to require only those tests that are useful to making subsidiary findings as to viability," and, I would add, only those examinations and tests that it would not be imprudent or careless to perform in the particular medical situation before the physician.

Unlike the plurality, I do not understand these viability testing requirements to conflict with any of the Court's past decisions concerning state regulation of abortion. Therefore, there is no necessity to accept the State's invitation to reexamine the constitutional validity of *Roe.* Where there is no need to decide a constitutional question, it is a venerable principle of this Court's adjudicatory processes not to do so for "[t]he Court will not 'anticipate a question of constitutional law in advance of the necessity of deciding it.'" * * * Quite simply, "[i]t is not the habit of the court to decide questions of a constitutional nature unless absolutely necessary to a decision of the case." The Court today has accepted the State's every interpretation of its abortion statute and has upheld, under our existing precedents, every provision of that statute which is properly before us. Precisely for this reconsideration of *Roe* falls not into any "good-cause exception" to this "fundamental rule of judicial restraint . . . ." When the constitutional invalidity of a State's abortion statute actually turns on the constitutional validity of *Roe v. Wade,* there will be time enough to reexamine *Roe.* And to do so carefully.

In assessing § 188.029 it is especially important to recognize that appellees did not appeal the District Court's ruling that the first sentence of § 188.029 is constitutional. There is, accordingly, no dispute between the parties before us over the constitutionality of the "presumption of viability at 20 weeks," created by the first sentence of § 188.029. If anything might arguably conflict with the Court's previous decisions concerning the determination of viability, I would think it is the introduction of this presumption. * * * The 20-week presumption of viability in the first sentence of § 188.029, it could be argued (though, I would think, unsuccessfully), restricts "the judgment of the responsible attending physician," by imposing on that physician the burden of overcoming the presumption. This presumption may be a "superimpos[ition] [of] state regulation on the medical determination of whether a particular fetus is viable," but, if so, it is a restriction on the physician's judgment that is not before us. As the plurality properly interprets the second sentence of § 188.029, it does nothing more than delineate means by which the unchallenged 20-week presumption of viability may be overcome if those means are useful in doing so and can be prudently employed. Contrary to the plurality's suggestion, the District Court did not think the second sentence of § 188.029 unconstitutional for this reason. Rather, both the District Court and the Court of Appeals thought the second sentence to be unconstitutional precisely because they interpreted that sentence to impose state regulation on the determination of viability that it does not impose.

Appellees suggest that the interpretation of § 188.029 urged by the State may "virtually eliminat[e] the constitutional issue in this case." Appellees therefore propose that we should abstain from deciding that provision's constitutionality "in order to allow the state courts to render the saving construction the State has proposed." Where the lower court has so clearly fallen into error I do not think abstention is necessary or prudent. Accordingly, I consider the constitutionality of the second sentence of § 188.029, as interpreted by the State, to determine whether the constitutional issue is actually eliminated.

I do not think the second sentence of § 188.029, as interpreted by the Court, imposes a degree of state regulation on the medical determination of viability that in any way conflicts with prior decisions of this Court. As the plurality recognizes, the requirement that, where not imprudent, physicians perform examinations and tests useful to making subsidiary findings to determine viability "promot[es] the State's interest in potential human life rather than in maternal health." No decision of this Court has held that the State may not directly promote its interest in potential life when viability is possible. Quite the contrary. In *Thornburgh* the Court considered a constitutional challenge to a Pennsylvania statute requiring that a second physician be present during an abortion performed "when viability is possible." For guidance, the Court looked to the earlier decision in *Ashcroft,* upholding a Missouri statute requiring the presence of a second physician during an abortion performed after viability. The *Thornburgh* majority struck down the Pennsylvania statute merely because the statute had no exception for emergency situations and not because it found a constitutional difference between the State's promotion of its interest in potential life when viability is possible and when viability is certain. Despite the clear recognition by the *Thornburgh* majority that the Pennsylvania and Missouri statutes differed in this respect, there is no hint in the opinion of the *Thornburgh* Court that the State's interest in potential life differs depending whether it seeks to further that interest postviability or when viability is possible. Thus, all nine Members of the *Thornburgh* Court appear to have agreed that it is not constitutionally impermissible for the State to enact regulations designed to protect the State's interest in potential life when viability is possible. That is exactly what Missouri has done in § 188.029.

Similarly, the basis for reliance by the [courts below] on *Colautti* disappears when § 188.029 is properly interpreted. In *Colautti* the Court observed:

> "Because this point [of viability] may differ with each pregnancy, neither the legislature nor the courts may proclaim one of the elements entering into the ascertainment of viability—be it weeks of gestation or fetal weight or any other single factor—as the determinant of when the State has a compelling interest in the life or health of the fetus. Viability is the critical point."

The courts below, on the interpretation of § 188.029 rejected here, found the second sentence of that provision at odds with this passage from *Colautti*. On this Court's interpretation of § 188.029 it is clear that Missouri has not substituted any of the "elements entering into the ascertainment of viability" as "the determinant of when the State has a compelling interest in the life or health of the fetus." All the second sentence of § 188.029 does is to require, when not imprudent, the performance of "those tests that are useful to making *subsidiary* findings as to viability" (emphasis added). Thus, consistent with *Colautti*, viability remains the "critical point" under § 188.029.

Finally, and rather half-heartedly, the plurality suggests that the marginal increase in the cost of an abortion created by Missouri's viability testing provision may make § 188.029, even as interpreted, suspect under this Court's decision in *Akron*, striking down a second-trimester hospitalization requirement. I dissented [in] *Akron* because it was my view that, even apart from *Roe's* trimester framework which I continue to consider problematic, see *Thornburgh* (dissenting opinion), the *Akron* majority had distorted and misapplied its own standard for evaluating state regulation of abortion which the Court had applied with fair consistency in the past: that, previability, "a regulation imposed on a lawful abortion is not unconstitutional unless it unduly burdens the right to seek an abortion."

It is clear to me that requiring the performance of examinations and tests useful to determining whether a fetus is viable, when viability is possible, and when it would not be medically imprudent to do so, does not impose an undue burden on a woman's abortion decision. On this ground alone I would reject the suggestion that § 188.029 as interpreted is unconstitutional. More to the point, however, just as I see no conflict between § 188.029 and *Colautti* or any decision of this Court concerning a State's ability to give effect to its interest in potential life, I see no conflict between § 188.029 [and] *Akron*. The second-trimester hospitalization requirement struck down in *Akron* imposed, in the majority's view, "a heavy, and unnecessary, burden," more than doubling the cost of "women's access to a relatively inexpensive, otherwise accessible, and safe abortion procedure." By contrast, the cost of examinations and tests that could usefully and prudently be performed when a woman is 20–24 weeks pregnant to determine whether the fetus is viable would only marginally, if at all, increase the cost of an abortion. See Brief for American Association of Prolife Obstetricians and Gynecologists et al. as Amici Curiae 3 ("At twenty weeks gestation, an ultrasound examination to determine gestational age is standard medical practice. It is routinely provided by the plaintiff clinics. An ultrasound examination can effectively provide all three designated findings of sec. 188.029"); id., at 22 ("A finding of fetal weight can be obtained from the same ultrasound test used to determine gestational age"); id., at 25 ("There are a number of different methods in standard medical practice to determine fetal lung maturity at twenty or more weeks gestation. The most simple and most obvious is by inference. It is well known that fetal lungs do not mature until 33–34 weeks gestation. . . . If an assessment of the gestational age indicates that the child is less than thirty-three weeks, a general finding can be made that the fetal lungs are not mature. This finding can then be used by the physician in making his determination of viability under section 188.029") * * *.

Moreover, the examinations and tests required by § 188.029 are to be performed when viability is possible. This feature of § 188.029 distinguishes it from the second-trimester hospitalization requirement struck down by the *Akron* majority. As the court recognized in *Thornburgh* the State's compelling interest in potential life postviability renders its interest in determining the critical point of viability equally compelling. Under the Court's precedents, the same cannot be said for the *Akron* second-trimester hospitalization requirement. As I understand the Court's opinion in *Akron*, therefore, the plurality's suggestion today that *Akron* casts doubt on the validity of § 188.029, even as the Court has interpreted it, is without foundation and cannot provide a basis for reevaluating *Roe*. * * *

JUSTICE SCALIA, concurring in part and concurring in the judgment.

I join Parts I, II–A, II–B and II–C of the opinion of The Chief Justice. As to Part II–D, I share Justice Blackmun's view that it effectively would overrule *Roe*. I think that should be done, but would do it more explicitly. Since today we contrive to avoid doing it, and indeed to avoid almost any decision of national import, I need not set forth my reasons, some of which have been well recited in dissents of my colleagues in other cases. * * *

The outcome of today's case will doubtless be heralded as a triumph of judicial statesmanship. It is not that, unless it is statesmanlike needlessly to prolong this Court's self-awarded sovereignty over a field where it has little proper business since the answers to most of the cruel questions posed are political and not juridical—a sovereignty which therefore quite properly, but to the great damage of the Court, makes it the object of the sort of organized public pressure that political institutions in a democracy ought to receive.

Justice O'Connor's assertion, that a " 'fundamental rule of judicial restraint' " requires us to avoid reconsidering *Roe*, cannot be taken seriously. By finessing *Roe* we do not, as she suggests, adhere to the strict and venerable rule that we should avoid " 'decid[ing] questions of a constitutional nature.' " We have not disposed of this case on some statutory or procedural ground, but have decided, and could not avoid deciding, whether the Missouri statute meets the requirements of the United States Constitution. The only choice available is whether, in deciding that constitutional question, we should use *Roe* as the benchmark, or something else. What is involved, therefore, is not the rule of avoiding constitutional issues where possible, but the quite separate principle that we will not " 'formulate a rule of constitutional law broader than is required by the precise facts to which it is to be applied.' " The latter is a sound

general principle, but one often departed from when good reason exists.   *   *   *
I have not identified with certainty the first instance of our deciding a case on
broader constitutional grounds than absolutely necessary, but it is assuredly no
later than *Marbury v. Madison,* where we held that mandamus could constitutionally issue against the Secretary of State, although that was unnecessary
given our holding that the law authorizing issuance of the mandamus by this
Court was unconstitutional.

   *   *   * It would be wrong, in any decision, to ignore the reality that our
policy not to "formulate a rule of constitutional law broader than is required by
the precise facts" has a frequently applied good-cause exception.   But it seems
particularly perverse to convert the policy into an absolute in the present case,
in order to place beyond reach the inexpressibly "broader-than-was-required-by-
the-precise-facts" structure established by *Roe.*

   The real question, then, is whether there are valid reasons to go beyond the
most stingy possible holding today.   It seems to me there are not only valid but
compelling ones.   Ordinarily, speaking no more broadly than is absolutely
required avoids throwing settled law into confusion; doing so today preserves a
chaos that is evident to anyone who can read and count.   Alone sufficient to
justify a broad holding is the fact that our retaining control, through *Roe,* of
what I believe to be, and many of our citizens recognize to be, a political issue,
continuously distorts the public perception of the role of this Court.   We can now
look forward to at least another Term with carts full of mail from the public, and
streets full of demonstrators, urging us—their unelected and life-tenured judges
who have been awarded those extraordinary, undemocratic characteristics precisely in order that we might follow the law despite the popular will—to follow
the popular will.   Indeed, I expect we can look forward to even more of that than
before, given our indecisive decision today.   And if these reasons for taking the
unexceptional course of reaching a broader holding are not enough, then consider the nature of the constitutional question we avoid: In most cases, we do no
harm by not speaking more broadly than the decision requires.   Anyone affected
by the conduct that the avoided holding would have prohibited will be able to
challenge it himself, and have his day in court to make the argument.   Not so
with respect to the harm that many States believed, pre-*Roe,* and many may
continue to believe, is caused by largely unrestricted abortion.   That will
continue to occur if the States have the constitutional power to prohibit it, and
would do so, but we skillfully avoid telling them so.   Perhaps those abortions
cannot constitutionally be proscribed.   That is surely an arguable question, the
question that reconsideration of *Roe* entails.   But what is not at all arguable, it
seems to me, is that we should decide now and not insist that we be run into a
corner before we grudgingly yield up our judgment.   The only sound reason for
the latter course is to prevent a change in the law—but to think that desirable
begs the question to be decided.

   It was an arguable question today whether § 188.029 of the Missouri law
contravened this Court's understanding of *Roe,** and I would have examined *Roe*

---

* That question, compared with the question
whether we should reconsider and reverse
Roe, is hardly worth a footnote, but I think
Justice O'Connor answers that incorrectly as
well.   In *Roe* we said that "the physician [has
the right] to administer medical treatment
according to his professional judgment up to
the points where important state interests
provide compelling justifications for intervention."   We have subsequently made clear that
it is also a matter of medical judgment when
viability (one of those points) is reached.
"The time when viability is achieved may
vary with each pregnancy, and the determination of whether a particular fetus is viable is,
and must be, a matter for the judgment of the
responsible attending physician." *Danforth.*
Section 188.029 conflicts with the purpose and

rather than examining the contravention. Given the Court's newly contracted abstemiousness, what will it take, one must wonder, to permit us to reach that fundamental question? The result of our vote today is that we will not reconsider that prior opinion, even if most of the Justices think it is wrong, unless we have before us a statute that in fact contradicts it—and even then (under our newly discovered "no-broader-than-necessary" requirement) only minor problematical aspects of *Roe* will be reconsidered, unless one expects State legislatures to adopt provisions whose compliance with *Roe* cannot even be argued with a straight face. It thus appears that the mansion of constitutionalize abortion-law, constructed overnight in *Roe v. Wade*, must be disassembled door-jamb by door-jamb, and never entirely brought down, no matter how wrong it may be.

Of the four courses we might have chosen today—to reaffirm *Roe*, to overrule it explicitly, to overrule it sub silentio, or to avoid the question—the last is the least responsible. On the question of the constitutionality of § 188.029, I concur in the judgment of the Court and strongly dissent from the manner in which it has been reached.

JUSTICE BLACKMUN, with whom JUSTICE BRENNAN and JUSTICE MARSHALL join, concurring in part and dissenting in part.

Today, *Roe v. Wade*, and the fundamental constitutional right of women to decide whether to terminate a pregnancy, survive but are not secure. Although the Court extricates itself from this case without making a single, even incremental, change in the law of abortion, the plurality and Justice Scalia would overrule *Roe* (the first silently, the other explicitly) and would return to the States virtually unfettered authority to control the quintessentially intimate, personal, and life-directing decision whether to carry a fetus to term. Although today, no less than yesterday, the Constitution and the decisions of this Court prohibit a State from enacting laws that inhibit women from the meaningful exercise of that right, a plurality of this Court implicitly invites every state legislature to enact more and more restrictive abortion regulations in order to provoke more and more test cases, in the hope that sometime down the line the Court will return the law of procreative freedom to the severe limitations that generally prevailed in this country before January 22, 1973. Never in my

hence the fair import of this principle because it will sometimes require a physician to perform tests that he would not otherwise have performed to determine whether a fetus is viable. It is therefore a legislative imposition on the judgment of the physician, and one that increases the cost of an abortion.

Justice O'Connor would nevertheless uphold the law because it "does not impose an undue burden on a woman's abortion decision." This conclusion is supported by the observation that the required tests impose only a marginal cost on the abortion procedure, far less of an increase than the cost-doubling hospitalization requirement invalidated in *Akron*. The fact that the challenged regulation is less costly than what we struck down in *Akron* tells us only that we cannot decide the present case on the basis of that earlier decision. It does not tell us whether the present requirement is an "undue burden," and I know of no basis for determining that this particular burden (or any other for that matter) is "due." One could with equal justification conclude that it is not. To avoid the question of *Roe*'s validity, with the attendant costs that this will have for the Court and for the principles of self-governance, on the basis of a standard that offers "no guide but the Court's own discretion," merely adds to the irrationality of what we do today.

Similarly irrational is the new concept that Justice O'Connor introduces into the law in order to achieve her result, the notion of a State's "interest in potential life when viability is possible." Since "viability" means the mere *possibility* (not the certainty) of survivability outside the womb, "possible viability" must mean the possibility of a possibility of survivability outside the womb. Perhaps our next opinion will expand the third trimester into the second even further, by approving state action designed to take account of "the chance of possible viability."

memory has a plurality announced a judgment of this Court that so foments disregard for the law and for our standing decisions.

Nor in my memory has a plurality gone about its business in such a deceptive fashion. At every level of its review, from its effort to read the real meaning out of the Missouri statute, to its intended evisceration of precedents and its deafening silence about the constitutional protections that it would jettison, the plurality obscures the portent of its analysis. With feigned restraint, the plurality announces that its analysis leaves *Roe* "undisturbed," albeit "modif[ied] and narrow[ed]." But this disclaimer is totally meaningless. The plurality opinion is filled with winks, and nods, and knowing glances to those who would do away with *Roe* explicitly, but turns a stone face to anyone in search of what the plurality conceives as the scope of a woman's right under the Due Process Clause to terminate a pregnancy free from the coercive and brooding influence of the State. The simple truth is that *Roe* would not survive the plurality's analysis, and that the plurality provides no substitute for *Roe*'s protective umbrella.

I fear for the future. I fear for the liberty and equality of the millions of women who have lived and come of age in the 16 years since *Roe* was decided. I fear for the integrity of, and public esteem for, this Court.

I dissent.

I

The plurality parades through the four challenged sections of the Missouri statute seriatim. I shall not do this, but shall relegate most of my comments as to those sections to the margin.[1] Although I disagree with the plurality's

1. Contrary to the plurality (with whom Justice O'Connor on this point joins), I do not see how the preamble, § 1.205, realistically may be construed as "abortion-neutral." It declares that "[t]he life of each human being begins at conception" and that "[u]nborn children have protectable interests in life, health, and well-being." By the preamble's specific terms, these declarations apply to all of Missouri's laws which, in turn, are to be interpreted to protect the rights of the unborn to the fullest extent possible under the Constitution of the United States and the decisions of this Court. As the Court of Appeals concluded, the Missouri Legislature "intended its abortion regulations to be understood against the backdrop of its theory of life." I note the Solicitor General's acknowledgment that this backdrop places "a burden of uncertain scope on the performance of abortion by supplying a general principle that would fill in whatever interstices may be present in existing abortion precedents."

In my view, a State may not expand indefinitely the scope of its abortion regulations by creating interests in fetal life that are limited solely by reference to the decisional law of this Court. Such a statutory scheme, whose scope is dependent on the uncertain and disputed limits of our holdings, will have the unconstitutional effect of chilling the exercise of a woman's right to terminate a pregnancy and of burdening the freedom of health professionals to provide abortion services. In this case, moreover, because the preamble defines fetal life as beginning upon "the fertilization of the ovum of a female by a sperm of a male," § 188.015(3), the provision also unconstitutionally burdens the use of contraceptive devices, such as the IUD and the "morning after" pill, which may operate to prevent pregnancy only after conception as defined in the statute.

The plurality (again joined by Justice O'Connor) upholds §§ 188.210 and .215 on the ground that the constitutionality of these provisions follows from our holdings in *Maher, Poelker* and *Harris v. McRae*. There were strong dissents in all those cases.

Whatever one may think of *Maher, Poelker*, and *Harris*, however, they most certainly do not control this case, where the State not only has withdrawn from the business of abortion, but has taken affirmative steps to assure that abortions are not performed by *private* physicians in *private* institutions. Specifically, by defining "public facility" as "any public institution, public facility, public equipment, or any physical asset owned, leased, or controlled by this state or any agency or political subdivision thereof," § 188.200, the Missouri statute prohibits the performance of abortions in institutions that in all pertinent respects are private, yet are located on property owned, leased, or controlled by the government. Thus, under the statute, no abortion may be performed at Truman Medical Center in Kan-

consideration of §§ 1.205, 188.210, and 188.215, and am especially disturbed by its misapplication of our past decisions in upholding Missouri's ban on the performance of abortions at "public facilities," the plurality's discussion of these provisions is merely prologue to its consideration of the statute's viability-testing requirement, § 188.029—the only section of the Missouri statute that the plurality construes as implicating *Roe* itself. There, tucked away at the end of its opinion, the plurality suggests a radical reversal of the law of abortion; and there, primarily, I direct my attention.

In the plurality's view, the viability-testing provision imposes a burden on second-trimester abortions as a way of furthering the State's interest in protecting the potential life of the fetus. Since under the *Roe* framework, the State may not fully regulate abortion in the interest of potential life (as opposed to maternal health) until the third trimester, the plurality finds it necessary, in order to save the Missouri testing provision, to throw out *Roe*'s trimester framework. In flat contradiction to *Roe*, the plurality concludes that the State's interest in potential life is compelling before viability, and upholds the testing provision because it "permissibly furthers" that state interest.

A

At the outset, I note that in its haste to limit abortion rights, the plurality compounds the errors of its analysis by needlessly reaching out to address constitutional questions that are not actually presented. The conflict between sas City—where, in 1985, 97 percent of all Missouri hospital abortions at 16 weeks or later were performed—even though the Center is a private hospital, staffed primarily by private doctors, and administered by a private corporation: the Center is located on ground leased from a political subdivision of the State.

The sweeping scope of Missouri's "public facility" provision sharply distinguishes this case from *Maher, Poelker*, and *Harris*. * * * Missouri's public facility ban, by contrast, goes far beyond merely offering incentives in favor of childbirth (as in *Maher* and *Harris*), or a straightforward disassociation of state-owned institutions and personnel from abortion services (as in *Poelker*). Here, by defining as "public" every health-care institution with some connection to the State, no matter how attenuated, Missouri has brought to bear the full force of its economic power and control over essential facilities to discourage its citizens from exercising their constitutional rights, even where the State itself could never be understood as authorizing, supporting, or having any other positive association with the performance of an abortion. See R. Dworkin, *The Great Abortion Case*, New York Review of Books, June 29, 1989, p. 49.

The difference is critical. Even if the State may decline to subsidize or to participate in the exercise of a woman's right to terminate a pregnancy, and even if a State may pursue its own abortion policies in distributing public benefits, it may not affirmatively constrict the availability of abortions by defining as "public" that which in all meaningful respects is private. With the certain knowledge that a substantial percentage of private health-care providers will fall under the public facility ban, Missouri does not "leav[e] a pregnant woman with the same choices as if the State had not chosen to operate any public hospitals at all"; rather, the public facility ban leaves the pregnant woman with far fewer choices, or, for those too sick or too poor to travel, perhaps no choice at all. This aggressive and shameful infringement on the right of women to obtain abortions in consultation with their chosen physicians, unsupported by any state interest, much less a compelling one, violates the command of *Roe*.

Indeed, Justice O'Connor appears to recognize the constitutional difficulties presented by Missouri's "public facilities" ban, and rejects respondents' "facial" challenge to the provisions on the ground that a facial challenge cannot succeed where, as here, at least some applications of the challenged law are constitutional. While I disagree with this approach, Justice O'Connor's writing explicitly leaves open the possibility that some applications of the "public facilities" ban may be unconstitutional, regardless of *Maher, Poelker*, and *Harris*.

I concur in Part II–C of The Chief Justice's opinion, holding that respondents' challenge to § 188.205 is moot, although I note that the constitutionality of this provision might become the subject of relitigation between these parties should the Supreme Court of Missouri adopt an interpretation of the provision that differs from the one accepted here.

§ 188.029 and *Roe*'s trimester framework, which purportedly drives the plurality to reconsider our past decisions, is a contrived conflict: the product of an aggressive misreading of the viability-testing requirement and a needlessly wooden application of the *Roe* framework.

The plurality's reading of § 188.029 (also joined by Justice O'Connor) is irreconcilable with the plain language of the statute and is in derogation of this Court's settled view that "'district courts and courts of appeals are better schooled in and more able to interpret the laws of their respective States.'" Abruptly setting aside the construction of § 188.029 adopted by both the District Court and Court of Appeals as "plain error," the plurality reads the viability-testing provision as requiring only that before a physician may perform an abortion on a woman whom he believes to be carrying a fetus of 20 or more weeks gestational age, the doctor must determine whether the fetus is viable and, as part of that exercise, must, to the extent feasible and consistent with sound medical practice, conduct tests necessary to make findings of gestational age, weight, and lung maturity. But the plurality's reading of the provision, according to which the statute requires the physician to perform tests only in order to determine *viability*, ignores the statutory language explicitly directing that "the physician *shall* perform or cause to be performed such medical examinations and tests as are *necessary to make a finding of the gestational age, weight, and lung maturity* of the unborn child and *shall* enter such findings" in the mother's medical record. § 188.029 (emphasis added). The statute's plain language requires the physician to undertake whatever tests are necessary to determine gestational age, weight, and lung maturity, regardless of whether these tests are necessary to a finding of viability, and regardless of whether the tests subject the pregnant woman or the fetus to additional health risks or add substantially to the cost of an abortion.[2]

Had the plurality read the statute as written, it would have had no cause to reconsider the *Roe* framework. As properly construed, the viability-testing provision does not pass constitutional muster under even a rational-basis standard, the least restrictive level of review applied by this Court. By mandating tests to determine fetal weight and lung maturity for every fetus thought to be more than 20 weeks gestational age, the statute requires physicians to undertake procedures, such as amniocentesis, that, in the situation presented, have no medical justification, impose significant additional health risks on both the pregnant woman and the fetus, and bear no rational relation to the State's interest in protecting fetal life.[3] As written, § 188.029 is an arbitrary imposition of discomfort, risk, and expense, furthering no discernible interest except to make the procurement of an abortion as arduous and difficult as possible. Thus, were it not for the plurality's tortured effort to avoid the plain import of § 188.029, it could have struck down the testing provision as patently irrational irrespective of the *Roe* framework.[4]

---

2. I consider irrefutable Justice Stevens' discussion of this interpretive point.

3. The District Court found that "the only method to evaluate [fetal] lung maturity is by amniocentesis," a procedure that "imposes additional significant health risks for both the pregnant woman and the fetus." Yet the medical literature establishes that to require amniocentesis for all abortions after 20 weeks would be contrary to sound medical practice and, moreover, would be useless for the pur-

pose of determining lung maturity until no earlier than between 28 and 30 weeks gestational age. Thus, were § 188.029 read to require a finding of lung maturity, it would require physicians to perform a highly intrusive procedure of risk that would yield no result relevant to the question of viability.

4. I also agree with the Court of Appeals, 851 F.2d, at 1074–1075, that, as written, § 188.029 is contrary [to] *Colautti*.

The plurality eschews this straightforward resolution, in the hope of precipitating a constitutional crisis. Far from avoiding constitutional difficulty, the plurality attempts to engineer a dramatic retrenchment in our jurisprudence by exaggerating the conflict between its untenable construction of § 188.029 and the *Roe* trimester framework.

No one contests that under the *Roe* framework the State, in order to promote its interest in potential human life, may regulate and even proscribe non-therapeutic abortions once the fetus becomes viable. If, as the plurality appears to hold, the testing provision simply requires a physician to use appropriate and medically sound tests to determine whether the fetus is actually viable when the estimated gestational age is greater than 20 weeks (and therefore within what the District Court found to be the margin of error for viability), then I see little or no conflict with *Roe*.[5] Nothing in *Roe*, or any of its progeny, holds that a State may not effectuate its compelling interest in the potential life of a viable fetus by seeking to ensure that no viable fetus is mistakenly aborted because of the inherent lack of precision in estimates of gestational age. A requirement that a physician make a finding of viability, one way or the other, for every fetus that falls within the range of possible viability does no more than preserve the State's recognized authority. Although, as the plurality correctly points out, such a testing requirement would have the effect of imposing additional costs on second-trimester abortions where the tests indicated that the fetus was not viable, these costs would be merely incidental to, and a necessary accommodation of, the State's unquestioned right to prohibit non-therapeutic abortions after the point of viability. In short, the testing provision, as construed by the plurality is consistent with the *Roe* framework and could be upheld effortlessly under current doctrine.[6]

How ironic it is, then, and disingenuous, that the plurality scolds the Court of Appeals for adopting a construction of the statute that fails to avoid constitutional difficulties. By distorting the statute, the plurality manages to avoid invalidating the testing provision on what should have been noncontroversial constitutional grounds; having done so, however, the plurality rushes headlong

5. The plurality never states precisely its construction of § 188.029. I base my synopsis of the plurality's views mainly on its assertion that the entire provision must be read in light of its requirement that the physician act only in accordance with reasonable professional judgment, *ante*, at 18, and that the provision imposes no requirement that a physician perform irrelevant or dangerous tests. To the extent that the plurality may be reading the provision to require tests other than those that a doctor, exercising reasonable professional judgment, would deem necessary to a finding of viability, the provision bears no rational relation to a legitimate governmental interest, and cannot stand.

6. As convincingly demonstrated by Justice O'Connor, the cases cited by the plurality, are not to the contrary. As noted by the plurality, in both *Colautti* and *Danforth*, we stressed that the determination of viability is a matter for the judgment of the responsible attending physician. But § 188.029, at least as construed by the plurality, is consistent with this requirement. The provision does nothing to remove the determination of viability from the purview of the attending physician; it merely instructs the physician to make a finding of viability using tests to determine gestational age, weight, and lung maturity when such tests are feasible and medically appropriate.

I also see no conflict with the Court's holding in *Akron* that the State may not impose "a heavy, *and unnecessary*, burden on women's access to a relatively inexpensive, and otherwise accessible, and safe abortion procedure" (emphasis added). In *Akron*, we invalidated a city ordinance requiring that all second-trimester abortions be performed in acute-care hospitals on the ground that such a requirement was not medically necessary and would double the cost of abortions. By contrast, the viability determination at issue in this case (as read by the plurality), is necessary to the effectuation of the State's compelling interest in the potential human life of viable fetuses and applies not to all second-trimester abortions, but instead only to that small percentage of abortions performed on fetuses estimated to be of more than 20 weeks gestational age.

into a much deeper constitutional thicket, brushing past an obvious basis for upholding § 188.029 in search of a pretext for scuttling the trimester framework. Evidently, from the plurality's perspective, the real problem with the Court of Appeals' construction of § 188.029 is not that it raised a constitutional difficulty, but that it raised the wrong constitutional difficulty—one not implicating *Roe*. The plurality has remedied that, traditional canons of construction and judicial forbearance notwithstanding.

B

Having set up the conflict between § 188.029 and the *Roe* trimester framework, the plurality summarily discards *Roe*'s analytic core as " 'unsound in principle and unworkable in practice.' " This is so, the plurality claims, because the key elements of the framework do not appear in the text of the Constitution, because the framework more closely resembles a regulatory code than a body of constitutional doctrine, and because under the framework the State's interest in potential human life is considered compelling only after viability, when, in fact, that interest is equally compelling throughout pregnancy. The plurality does not bother to explain these alleged flaws in *Roe*. Bald assertion masquerades as reasoning. The object, quite clearly, is not to persuade, but to prevail.

1. The plurality opinion is far more remarkable for the arguments that it does not advance than for those that it does. The plurality does not even mention, must less join, the true jurisprudential debate underlying this case: whether the Constitution includes an "unenumerated" general right to privacy as recognized in many of our decisions, most notably *Griswold* and *Roe*, and, more specifically, whether and to what extent such a right to privacy extends to matters of childbearing and family life, including abortion. See, e.g., *Eisenstadt* (contraception); *Loving* (marriage); *Skinner* (procreation); *Pierce* (childrearing).[7] These are questions of unsurpassed significance in this Court's interpretation of the Constitution, and mark the battleground upon which this case was fought * * *. On these grounds, abandoned by the plurality, the Court should decide this case.

But rather than arguing that the text of the Constitution makes no mention of the right to privacy, the plurality complains that the critical elements of the *Roe* framework—trimesters and viability—do not appear in the Constitution and are, therefore, somehow inconsistent with a Constitution cast in general terms. Were this a true concern, we would have to abandon most of our constitutional jurisprudence. As the plurality well knows, or should know, the "critical elements" of countless constitutional doctrines nowhere appear in the Constitu-

---

7. The plurality, ignoring all of the aforementioned cases except *Griswold*, responds that this case does not require consideration of the "great issues" underlying this case because *Griswold*, "unlike *Roe*, did not purport to adopt a whole framework [to] govern the cases in which the asserted liberty interest would apply." This distinction is highly ironic. [*Roe*] adopted the framework of which the plurality complains as a mechanism necessary to give effect both to the constitutional rights of the pregnant woman and to the State's significant interests in maternal health and potential life. Concededly, *Griswold* does not adopt a framework for determining the permissible scope of state regulation of contraception. The reason is simple: in *Griswold* (and

Eisenstadt), the Court held that the challenged statute, regulating the use of medically safe contraception, did not properly serve *any* significant state interest. Accordingly, the Court had no occasion to fashion a framework to accommodate a State's interests in regulating contraception. Surely, the plurality is not suggesting that it would find *Roe* unobjectionable if the Court had forgone the framework and, as in the contraception decisions, had left the State with little or no regulatory authority. The plurality's focus on the framework is merely an excuse for avoiding the real issues embedded in this case and a mask for its hostility to the constitutional rights that *Roe* recognized.

tion's text. The Constitution makes no mention, for example, of the First Amendment's "actual malice" standard for proving certain libels or of the standard for determining when speech is obscene. Similarly, the Constitution makes no mention of the rational-basis test, or the specific verbal formulations of intermediate and strict scrutiny by which this Court evaluates claims under the Equal Protection Clause. The reason is simple. Like the *Roe* framework, these tests or standards are not, and do not purport to be, rights protected by the Constitution. Rather, they are judge-made methods for evaluating and measuring the strength and scope of constitutional rights or for balancing the constitutional rights of individuals against the competing interests of government.

With respect to the *Roe* framework, the general constitutional principle, indeed the fundamental constitutional right, for which it was developed is the right to privacy, a species of "liberty" protected by the Due Process Clause, which under our past decisions safeguards the right of women to exercise some control over their own role in procreation. As we recently reaffirmed in *Thornburgh*, few decisions are "more basic to individual dignity and autonomy" or more appropriate to that "certain private sphere of individual liberty" that the Constitution reserves from the intrusive reach of government than the right to make the uniquely personal, intimate, and self-defining decision whether to end a pregnancy. It is this general principle, the " 'moral fact that a person belongs to himself and not others nor to society as a whole,' " that is found in the Constitution. The trimester framework simply defines and limits that right to privacy in the abortion context to accommodate, not destroy, a State's legitimate interest in protecting the health of pregnant women and in preserving potential human life. Fashioning such accommodations between individual rights and the legitimate interests of government, establishing benchmarks and standards with which to evaluate the competing claims of individuals and government, lies at the very heart of constitutional adjudication. To the extent that the trimester framework is useful in this enterprise, it is not only consistent with constitutional interpretation, but necessary to the wise and just exercise of this Court's paramount authority to define the scope of constitutional rights.

2. The plurality next alleges that the result of the trimester framework has "been a web of legal rules that have become increasingly intricate, resembling a code of regulations rather than a body of constitutional doctrine." Again, if this were a true and genuine concern, we would have to abandon vast areas of our constitutional jurisprudence. Are [the distinctions that have been drawn in the abortion area] any finer, or more "regulatory," than the distinctions we have often drawn in our First Amendment jurisprudence, where, for example, we have held that a "release time" program permitting public-school students to leave school grounds during school hours to receive religious instruction does not violate the Establishment Clause, even though a release-time program permitting religious instruction on school grounds does violate the Clause? Our Fourth Amendment jurisprudence recognizes factual distinctions no less intricate.

* * *

That numerous constitutional doctrines result in narrow differentiations between similar circumstances does not mean that this Court has abandoned adjudication in favor of regulation. Rather, these careful distinctions reflect the process of constitutional adjudication itself, which is often highly fact-specific, requiring such determinations as whether state laws are "unduly burdensome" or "reasonable" or bear a "rational" or "necessary" relation to asserted state interests. * * *

["Differences of degree" have been said to be characteristic of civilized law and these "differences"] fully account for our holdings in *Simopoulos*, and *Akron*. Those decisions rest on this Court's reasoned and accurate judgment that hospitalization and doctor-counselling requirements unduly burdened the right of women to terminate a pregnancy and were not rationally related to the State's asserted interest in the health of pregnant women, while Virginia's *substantially less restrictive* regulations were not unduly burdensome and did rationally serve the State's interest. That the Court exercised its best judgment in evaluating these markedly different statutory schemes no more established the Court as an "'*ex officio* medical board'" than our decisions involving religion in the public schools establish the Court as a national school board, or our decisions concerning prison regulations establish the Court as a bureau of prisons. * * * If, in delicate and complicated areas of constitutional law, our legal judgments "have become increasingly intricate," it is not, as the plurality contends, because we have overstepped our judicial role. Quite the opposite: the rules are intricate because we have remained conscientious in our duty to do justice carefully, especially when fundamental rights rise or fall with our decisions.

3. Finally, the plurality asserts that the trimester framework cannot stand because the State's interest in potential life is compelling throughout pregnancy, not merely after viability. The opinion contains not one word of rationale for its view of the State's interest. This "it-is-so-because-we-say-so" jurisprudence constitutes nothing other than an attempted exercise of brute force; reason, much less persuasion, has no place.

In answering the plurality's claim that the State's interest in the fetus is uniform and compelling throughout pregnancy, I cannot improve upon what Justice Stevens has written [quoting at length from Justice Stevens' concurring opinion in *Thornburgh*, p. 97 of this Supplement, lines 5 to 26.]

For my own part, I remain convinced, as six other Members of this Court 16 years ago were convinced, that the *Roe* framework, and the viability standard in particular, fairly, sensibly, and effectively functions to safeguard the constitutional liberties of pregnant women while recognizing and accommodating the State's interest in potential human life. The viability line reflects the biological facts and truths of fetal development; it marks that threshold moment prior to which a fetus cannot survive separate from the woman and cannot reasonably and objectively be regarded as a subject of rights or interests distinct from, or paramount to, those of the pregnant woman. At the same time, the viability standard takes account of the undeniable fact that as the fetus evolves into its postnatal form, and as it loses its dependence on the uterine environment, the State's interest in the fetus' potential human life, and in fostering a regard for human life in general, becomes compelling. As a practical matter, because viability follows "quickening"—the point at which a woman feels movement in her womb—and because viability occurs no earlier than 23 weeks gestational age, it establishes an easily applicable standard for regulating abortion while providing a pregnant woman ample time to exercise her fundamental right with her responsible physician to terminate her pregnancy.[9] Although I have stated

9. Notably, neither the plurality nor Justice O'Connor advance the now-familiar catchphrase criticism of the *Roe* framework that because the point of viability will recede with advances in medical technology, *Roe* "is clearly on a collision course with itself." This critique has no medical foundation. As the medical literature and the amicus briefs filed in this case conclusively demonstrate, "there is an 'anatomic threshold' for fetal viability of about 23–24 weeks gestation." Prior to that time, the crucial organs are not sufficiently mature to provide the mutually sustaining functions that are prerequisite to extrauterine

previously for a majority of this Court that "[c]onstitutional rights do not always have easily ascertainable boundaries," to seek and establish those boundaries remains the special responsibility of this Court. *Thornburgh.* In *Roe,* we discharged that responsibility as logic and science compelled. The plurality today advances not one reasonable argument as to why our judgment in that case was wrong and should be abandoned.

C

Having contrived an opportunity to reconsider the *Roe* framework, and then having discarded that framework, the plurality finds the testing provision unobjectionable because it "permissibly furthers the State's interest in protecting potential human life." This newly minted standard is circular and totally meaningless. Whether a challenged abortion regulation "permissibly furthers" a legitimate state interest is the *question* that courts must answer in abortion cases, not the standard for courts to apply. In keeping with the rest of its opinion, the plurality makes no attempt to explain or to justify its new standard, either in the abstract or as applied in this case. Nor could it. The "permissibly furthers" standard has no independent meaning, and consists of nothing other than what a majority of this Court may believe at any given moment in any given case. The plurality's novel test appears to be nothing more than a dressed-up version of rational-basis review, this Court's most lenient level of scrutiny. One thing is clear, however: were the plurality's "permissibly furthers" standard adopted by the Court, for all practical purposes, *Roe* would be overruled.

The "permissibly furthers" standard completely disregards the irreducible minimum of *Roe*: the Court's recognition that a woman has a limited fundamental constitutional right to decide whether to terminate a pregnancy. That right receives no meaningful recognition in the plurality's written opinion. Since, in the plurality's view, the State's interest in potential life is compelling as of the moment of conception, and is therefore served only if abortion is abolished, every hindrance to a woman's ability to obtain an abortion must be "permissible." Indeed, the more severe the hindrance, the more effectively (and permissibly) the State's interest would be furthered. A tax on abortions or a criminal prohibition would both satisfy the plurality's standard. So, for that matter, would a requirement that a pregnant woman memorize and recite today's plurality opinion before seeking an abortion.

The plurality pretends that *Roe* survives, explaining that the facts of this case differ from those in *Roe*: here, Missouri has chosen to assert its interest in potential life only at the point of viability, whereas, in *Roe,* Texas had asserted that interest from the point of conception, criminalizing all abortions, except where the life of the mother was at stake. This, of course, is a distinction without a difference. The plurality repudiates every principle for which *Roe* stands; in good conscience, it cannot possibly believe that *Roe* lies "undisturbed" merely because this case does not call upon the Court to reconsider the Texas statute, or one like it. If the Constitution permits a State to enact any statute that reasonably furthers its interest in potential life, and if that interest arises

---

survival, or viability. Moreover, "no technology exists to bridge the development gap between the three-day embryo culture and the 24th week of gestation." Nor does the medical community believe that the development of any such technology is possible in the foreseeable future. In other words, the threshold of fetal viability is, and will remain, no different from what it was at the time *Roe* was decided. Predictions to the contrary are pure science fiction. See Brief for A Group of American Law Professors as Amici Curiae 23–25.

as of conception, why would the Texas statute fail to pass muster? One suspects that the plurality agrees. It is impossible to read the plurality opinion and especially its final paragraph, without recognizing its implicit invitation to every State to enact more and more restrictive abortion laws, and to assert their interest in potential life as of the moment of conception. All these laws will satisfy the plurality's non-scrutiny, until sometime, a new regime of old dissenters and new appointees will declare what the plurality intends: that *Roe* is no longer good law.[11]

D

Thus, "not with a bang, but a whimper," the plurality discards a landmark case of the last generation, and casts into darkness the hopes and visions of every woman in this country who had come to believe that the Constitution guaranteed her the right to exercise some control over her unique ability to bear children. The plurality does so either oblivious or insensitive to the fact that millions of women, and their families, have ordered their lives around the right to reproductive choice, and that this right has become vital to the full participation of women in the economic and political walks of American life. The plurality would clear the way once again for government to force upon women the physical labor and specific and direct medical and psychological harms that may accompany carrying a fetus to term. The plurality would clear the way again for the State to conscript a woman's body and to force upon her a "distressful life and future." *Roe*.

The result, as we know from experience, would be that every year hundreds of thousands of women, in desperation, would defy the law, and place their health and safety in the unclean and unsympathetic hands of back-alley abortionists, or they would attempt to perform abortions upon themselves, with disastrous results. Every year, many women, especially poor and minority women, would die or suffer debilitating physical trauma, all in the name of enforced morality or religious dictates or lack of compassion, as it may be.

Of the aspirations and settled understandings of American women, of the inevitable and brutal consequences of what it is doing, the tough-approach plurality utters not a word. This silence is callous. It is also profoundly destructive of this Court as an institution. To overturn a constitutional decision is a rare and grave undertaking. To overturn a constitutional decision that secured a fundamental personal liberty to millions of persons would be unprece-

---

11. The plurality claims that its treatment of *Roe*, and a woman's right to decide whether to terminate a pregnancy, "hold[s] true the balance between that which the Constitution puts beyond the reach of the democratic process and that which it does not." This is unadulterated nonsense. The plurality's balance matches a lead weight (the State's allegedly compelling interest in fetal life as of the moment of conception) against a feather (a "liberty interest" of the pregnant woman that the plurality barely mentions, much less describes). The plurality's balance—no balance at all—places nothing, or virtually nothing, beyond the reach of the democratic process.

Justice Scalia candidly argues that this is all for the best. I cannot agree. "The very purpose of a Bill of Rights was to withdraw certain subjects from the vicissitudes of politi-

cal controversy, to place them beyond the reach of majorities and officials and to establish them as legal principles to be applied by the Courts. * * *." *West Virginia Board of Education v. Barnette*, 319 U.S. 624, 638, 63 S.Ct. 1178, 87 L.Ed. 1628 (1943). In a Nation that cherishes liberty, the ability of a woman to control the biological operation of her body and to determine with her responsible physician whether or not to carry a fetus to term, must fall within that limited sphere of individual autonomy that lies beyond the will or the power of any transient majority. This Court stands as the ultimate guarantor of that zone of privacy, regardless of the bitter disputes to which our decisions may give rise. In *Roe*, and our numerous cases reaffirming *Roe*, we did no more than discharge our constitutional duty.

dented in our 200 years of constitutional history. Although the doctrine of *stare decisis* applies with somewhat diminished force in constitutional cases generally, even in ordinary constitutional cases "any departure from *stare decisis* demands special justification." [This] requirement of justification applies with unique force where, as here, the Court's abrogation of precedent would destroy people's firm belief, based on past decisions of this Court, that they possess an unabridge-able right to undertake certain conduct.

[T]he plurality makes no serious attempt to carry "the heavy burden of persuading [that] changes in society or in the law dictate" the abandonment of *Roe* and its numerous progeny, much less the greater burden of explaining the abrogation of a fundamental personal freedom. Instead, the plurality pretends that it leaves *Roe* standing, and refuses even to discuss the real issue underlying this case: whether the Constitution includes an unenumerated right to privacy that encompasses a woman's right to decide whether to terminate a pregnancy. To the extent that the plurality does criticize the *Roe* framework, these criticisms are pure ipse dixit.

This comes at a cost. The doctrine of *stare decisis* "permits society to presume that bedrock principles are founded in the law rather than in the proclivities of individuals, and thereby contributes to the integrity of our constitutional system of government, both in appearance and in fact." Today's decision involves the most politically divisive domestic legal issue of our time. By refusing to explain or to justify its proposed revolutionary revision in the law of abortion, and by refusing to abide not only by our precedents, but also by our canons for reconsidering those precedents, the plurality invites charges of cowardice and illegitimacy to our door. I cannot say that these would be undeserved.

II

For today, at least, the law of abortion stands undisturbed. For today, the women of this Nation still retain the liberty to control their destinies. But the signs are evident and very ominous, and a chill wind blows. * * *

JUSTICE STEVENS, concurring in part and dissenting in part.

Having joined Part II–C of the Court's opinion, I shall not comment on § 188.205 of the Missouri statute. With respect to the challenged portions of §§ 188.210 and 188.215, I agree with Justice Blackmun that the record identifies a sufficient number of unconstitutional applications to support the Court of Appeals' judgment invalidating those provisions. The reasons why I would also affirm that court's invalidation of § 188.029, the viability testing provision, and § 1.205.1(1), (2) of the preamble,[1] require separate explanation.

I

It seems to me that in Part II–D of its opinion, the plurality strains to place a construction on § 188.029 that enables it to conclude, "[W]e would modify and narrow *Roe* and succeeding cases." That statement is ill-advised because there is no need to modify even slightly the holdings of prior cases in order to uphold § 188.029. For the most plausible nonliteral construction, as both Justice

---

1. The State prefers to refer to subsections (1) and (2) of § 1.205 as "prefatory statements with no substantive effect." It is true that § 1.205 is codified in Chapter 1, Laws in Force and Construction of Statutes, [while] all other provisions at issue are codified in Chapter 188, Regulation of Abortions * * *. But because § 1.205 appeared at the beginning of House Bill No. 1596, it is entirely appropriate to consider it as a preamble relevant to those regulations.

Blackmun [and] Justice O'Connor have demonstrated, is constitutional and entirely consistent with our precedents.

I am unable to accept Justice O'Connor's construction of the second sentence in § 188.029, however, because I believe it is foreclosed by two controlling principles of statutory interpretation. First, it is our settled practice to accept "the interpretation of state law in which the District Court and the Court of Appeals have concurred even if an examination of the state-law issue without such guidance might have justified a different conclusion." Second, "[t]he fact that a particular application of the clear terms of a statute might be unconstitutional does not provide us with a justification for ignoring the plain meaning of the statute." In this case, I agree with the [courts below] that the meaning of the second sentence of § 188.029 is too plain to be ignored. The sentence twice uses the mandatory term "shall," and contains no qualifying language. If it is implicitly limited to tests that are useful in determining viability, it adds nothing to the requirement imposed by the preceding sentence.

My interpretation of the plain language is supported by the structure of the statute as a whole, particularly the preamble, which "finds" that life "begins at conception" and further commands that state laws shall be construed to provide the maximum protection to "the unborn child at every stage of development." I agree with the District Court that "[o]bviously, the purpose of this law is to protect the potential life of the fetus, rather than to safeguard maternal health." A literal reading of the statute tends to accomplish that goal. Thus it is not "incongruous" to assume that the Missouri Legislature was trying to protect the potential human life of nonviable fetuses by making the abortion decision more costly. On the contrary, I am satisfied that the [courts below] correctly concluded that the Missouri Legislature meant exactly what it said in the second sentence of § 188.029. I am also satisfied, for the reasons stated by Justice Blackmun, that the testing provision is manifestly unconstitutional * * * "irrespective of the *Roe* [*v. Wade*, 410 U.S. 113 (1973),] framework."

II

The Missouri statute defines "conception" as "the fertilization of the ovum of a female by a sperm of a male," even though standard medical texts equate "conception" with implantation in the uterus, occurring about six days after fertilization. Missouri's declaration therefore implies regulation not only of previability abortions, but also of common forms of contraception such as the IUD and the morning-after pill.[7] Because the preamble, read in context, threatens serious encroachments upon the liberty of the pregnant woman and the health professional, I am persuaded that these plaintiffs, appellees before us, have standing to challenge its constitutionality.

To the extent that the Missouri statute interferes with contraceptive choices, I have no doubt that it is unconstitutional under the Court's holdings in *Griswold, Eisenstadt* and *Carey* * * *.

[Justice Stevens then quotes at length from Justice Stewart's concurring opinion in *Roe*, where Justice Stewart viewed *Griswold* as one of a long line of cases "decided under the doctrine of substantive due process," and "accept[ed] it

---

7. An intrauterine device, commonly called an IUD, "works primarily by preventing a fertilized egg from implanting." Other contraceptive methods that may prevent implantation include "morning-after pills," high-dose estrogen pills taken after intercourse, particularly in cases of rape, ARHP Brief 33, and the French RU 486, a pill that works "during the indeterminate period between contraception and abortion." Low-level estrogen "combined" pills—a version of the ordinary, daily ingested birth control pill—also may prevent the fertilized egg from reaching the uterine wall and implanting.

as such," and concluded that "the Court today is correct in holding that the right asserted by Jane Roe is embraced within the personal liberty protected by the Due Process Clause of the Fourteenth Amendment."] [8]

One might argue that the *Griswold* holding applies to devices "preventing conception"—that is, fertilization—but not to those preventing implantation, and therefore, that *Griswold* does not protect a woman's choice to use an IUD or take a morning-after pill. There is unquestionably a theological basis for such an argument,[9] just as there was unquestionably a theological basis for the Connecticut statute that the Court invalidated in *Griswold*. Our jurisprudence, however, has consistently required a secular basis for valid legislation. Because I am not aware of any secular basis for differentiating between contraceptive procedures that are effective immediately before and those that are effective immediately after fertilization, I believe it inescapably follows that the preamble to the Missouri statute is invalid under *Griswold* and its progeny.

Indeed, I am persuaded that the absence of any secular purpose for the legislative declarations that life begins at conception and that conception occurs at fertilization makes the relevant portion of the preamble invalid under the Establishment Clause of the First Amendment to the Federal Constitution. This conclusion does not, and could not, rest on the fact that the statement happens to coincide with the tenets of certain religions or on the fact that the legislators who voted to enact it may have been motivated by religious considerations. Rather, it rests on the fact that the preamble, an unequivocal endorsement of a religious tenet of some but by no means all Christian faiths, serves no identifiable secular purpose. That fact alone compels a conclusion that the statute violates the Establishment Clause.[12]

My concern can best be explained by reference to the position on this issue that was endorsed by St. Thomas Aquinas and widely accepted by the leaders of the Roman Catholic Church for many years [the view that the soul was not present until the formation of the fetus 40 or 80 days after conception, for males and females respectively].

If the views of St. Thomas were held as widely today as they were in the Middle Ages, and if a state legislature were to enact a statute prefaced with a "finding" that female life begins 80 days after conception and male life begins 40 days after conception, I have no doubt that this Court would promptly conclude that such an endorsement of a particular religious tenet is violative of the Establishment Clause.

In my opinion the difference between that hypothetical statute and Missouri's preamble reflects nothing more than a difference in theological doctrine. The preamble to the Missouri statute endorses the theological position that there is the same secular interest in preserving the life of a fetus during the first 40 or 80 days of pregnancy as there is after viability—indeed, after the time when the

8. The contrast between Justice Stewart's careful explication that our abortion precedent flowed naturally from a stream of substantive due process cases and Justice Scalia's notion that our abortion law was "constructed overnight in *Roe v. Wade*" is remarkable.

9. Several *amici* state that the "sanctity of human life from conception and opposition to abortion are, in fact, sincere and deeply held religious beliefs" * * *.

12. Pointing to the lack of consensus about life's onset among experts in medicine, philosophy, and theology, the *Roe* Court established that the Constitution does not permit a State to adopt a theory of life that overrides a pregnant woman's rights. [The] constitutional violation is doubly grave if, as here, the only basis for the State's "finding" is nonsecular.

fetus has become a "person" with legal rights protected by the Constitution.[13] To sustain that position as a matter of law, I believe Missouri has the burden of identifying the secular interests that differentiate the first 40 days of pregnancy from the period immediately before or after fertilization when, as *Griswold* and related cases establish, the Constitution allows the use of contraceptive procedures to prevent potential life from developing into full personhood. Focusing our attention on the first several weeks of pregnancy is especially appropriate because that is the period when the vast majority of abortions are actually performed.

As a secular matter, there is an obvious difference between the state interest in protecting the freshly fertilized egg and the state interest in protecting a 9-month-gestated, fully sentient fetus on the eve of birth. There can be no interest in protecting the newly fertilized egg from physical pain or mental anguish, because the capacity for such suffering does not yet exist; respecting a developed fetus, however, that interest is valid. In fact, if one prescinds the theological concept of ensoulment—or one accepts St. Thomas Aquinas' view that ensoulment does not occur for at least 40 days, a State has no greater secular interest in protecting the potential life of an embryo that is still "seed" than in protecting the potential life of a sperm or an unfertilized ovum.

There have been times in history when military and economic interests would have been served by an increase in population. No one argues today, however, that Missouri can assert a societal interest in increasing its population as its secular reason for fostering potential life. Indeed, our national policy, as reflected in legislation the Court upheld last Term, is to prevent the potential life that is produced by "pregnancy and childbirth among unmarried adolescents." *Bowen v. Kendrick* [p. 309 of this Supplement]. If the secular analysis were based on a strict balancing of fiscal costs and benefits, the economic costs of unlimited childbearing would outweigh those of abortion. There is, of course, an important and unquestionably valid secular interest in "protecting a young pregnant woman from the consequences of an incorrect decision," *Danforth* (Stevens, J., concurring in part and dissenting in part). Although that interest is served by a requirement that the woman receive medical and, in appropriate circumstances, parental advice, it does not justify the state legislature's official endorsement of the theological tenet embodied in §§ 1.205.1(1), (2).

The State's suggestion that the "finding" in the preamble to its abortion statute is, in effect, an amendment to its tort, property, and criminal laws is not persuasive. The Court of Appeals concluded that the preamble "is simply an impermissible state adoption of a theory of when life begins to justify its abortion regulations." [N]one of the tort, property, or criminal law cases cited by the State was either based on or buttressed by a theological answer to the question of when life begins. Rather, the Missouri courts, as well as a number of other state courts, had already concluded that a "fetus is a 'person,' 'minor,' or 'minor child' within the meaning of their particular wrongful death statutes."

Bolstering my conclusion that the preamble violates the First Amendment is the fact that the intensely divisive character of much of the national debate over the abortion issue reflects the deeply held religious convictions of many participants in the debate. The Missouri Legislature may not inject its endorsement of

---

13. No Member of this Court has ever questioned the holding in *Roe* that a fetus is not a "person" within the meaning of the Fourteenth Amendment. Even the dissenters in *Roe* implicitly endorsed that holding by arguing that state legislatures should decide whether to prohibit or to authorize abortions. [By] characterizing the basic question as "a political issue," Justice Scalia likewise implicitly accepts this holding.

a particular religious tradition into this debate, for "[t]he Establishment Clause does not allow public bodies to foment such disagreement." See *Allegheny County v. Greater Pittsburgh ACLU* [p. 312 of this Supplement] (Stevens, J., concurring in part and dissenting in part).

In my opinion the preamble to the Missouri statute is unconstitutional for two reasons. To the extent that it has substantive impact on the freedom to use contraceptive procedures, it is inconsistent with the central holding in *Griswold*. To the extent that it merely makes "legislative findings without operative effect," as the State argues, it violates the Establishment Clause of the First Amendment. Contrary to the theological "finding" of the Missouri Legislature, a woman's constitutionally protected liberty encompasses the right to act on her own belief that—to paraphrase St. Thomas Aquinas—until a seed has acquired the powers of sensation and movement, the life of a human being has not yet begun.

FAMILY LIVING ARRANGEMENTS, PARENTAL RIGHTS, AND THE "RIGHT TO MARRY"

CON LAW: P. 531, add to fn. b

AMER CON: P. 363, add to fn. b

RTS & LIB: P. 199, add to fn. b

See also the Court's discussion of "the freedom to enter into and carry on certain intimate or private relationships" in *Board of Directors of Rotary International v. Rotary Club of Duarte*, p. 280 of this Supplement.

SEXUAL CONDUCT, "LIFESTYLES," THE RIGHTS OF THE INVOLUNTARILY COMMITTED MENTALLY RETARDED, AND THE "RIGHT TO DIE"

CONSENSUAL ADULT HOMOSEXUAL CONDUCT

CON LAW: P. 542, substitute for *Dronenburg*

AMER CON: P. 367, substitute for *Dronenburg*

RTS & LIB: P. 210, substitute for *Dronenburg*

BOWERS v. HARDWICK

478 U.S. 186, 106 S.Ct. 2841, 92 L.Ed.2d 140 (1986).

JUSTICE WHITE delivered the opinion of the Court.

In August 1982, respondent was charged with violating the Georgia statute criminalizing sodomy [1] by committing that act with another adult male in the bedroom of respondent's home. After a preliminary hearing, the District Attorney decided not to present the matter to the grand jury unless further evidence developed.

Respondent then brought suit in the Federal District Court, challenging the constitutionality of the statute insofar as it criminalized consensual sodomy.[2]

1. Ga.Code Ann. § 16–6–2 (1984) provides, in pertinent part, as follows:

"(a) A person commits the offense of sodomy when he performs or submits to any sexual act involving the sex organs of one person and the mouth or anus of [another].

"(b) A person convicted of the offense of sodomy shall be punished by imprisonment for not less than one nor more than 20 [years]."

2. John and Mary Doe were also plaintiffs in the action. They alleged that they wished

He asserted that he was a practicing homosexual, that the Georgia statute, as administered by the defendants, placed him in imminent danger of arrest, and that the statute [violated the Constitution]. The District Court granted the defendant's motion to dismiss for failure to state a claim. [The U.S. Court of Appeals for the Eleventh Circuit reversed, holding] that the Georgia statute violated respondent's fundamental rights because his homosexual activity is a private and intimate association that is beyond the reach of state regulation by reason of the Ninth Amendment and the Due Process Clause * * *. We agree with the State that the Court of Appeals erred, and hence we reverse its judgment.

This case does not require a judgment on whether laws against sodomy between consenting adults in general, or between homosexuals in particular, are wise or desirable. It raises no question about the right or propriety of state legislative decisions to repeal their laws that criminalize homosexual sodomy, or of state court decisions invalidating those laws on state constitutional grounds. The issue presented is whether the Federal Constitution confers a fundamental right upon homosexuals to engage in sodomy and hence invalidates the laws of the many States that still make such conduct illegal and have done so for a very long time. The case also calls for some judgment about the limits of the Court's role in carrying out its constitutional mandate.

We first register our disagreement with the Court of Appeals [that] the Court's prior cases have construed the Constitution to confer a right of privacy that extends to homosexual sodomy and for all intents and purposes have decided this case. The reach of this line of cases was sketched in *Carey*. *Pierce* and *Meyer* were described as dealing with child rearing and education; *Prince* with family relationships; *Skinner* with procreation; *Loving v. Virginia*[a] with marriage; *Griswold* and *Eisenstadt* with contraception; and *Roe* with abortion. The latter three cases were interpreted as construing the Due Process Clause of the Fourteenth Amendment to confer a fundamental individual right to decide whether or not to beget or bear a child.

Accepting the decisions in these cases and the above description of them, we think it evident that none of the rights announced in those cases bears any resemblance to the claimed constitutional right of homosexuals to engage in acts of sodomy that is asserted in this case. No connection between family, marriage, or procreation on the one hand and homosexual activity on the other has been [demonstrated]. Moreover, any claim that these cases nevertheless stand for the proposition that any kind of private sexual conduct between consenting adults is constitutionally insulated from state proscription is unsupportable. Indeed, the Court's opinion in *Carey* twice asserted that the privacy right [did] not reach so far.

to engage in sexual activity proscribed by § 16–6–2 in the privacy of their home, and that they had been "chilled and deterred" from engaging in such activity by both the existence of the statute and Hardwick's arrest. The District Court held, however, that because they had neither sustained, nor were in immediate danger of sustaining, any direct injury from the enforcement of the statute, they did not have proper standing to maintain the action. The Court of Appeals affirmed the District Court's judgment dismissing the Does'

claim for lack of standing, and the Does do not challenge that holding in this Court.

The only claim properly before the Court, therefore, is Hardwick's challenge to the Georgia statute as applied to consensual homosexual sodomy. We express no opinion on the constitutionality of the Georgia statute as applied to other acts of sodomy.

a. *Loving* [CON LAW p. 1166, AMER CON p. 900, RTS & LIB p. 832] is discussed in fn. b and fn. 5 to Blackmun, J.'s dissent, *infra*.

Precedent aside, however, respondent would have us announce [a] fundamental right to engage in homosexual sodomy. This we are quite unwilling to do. * * *

Striving to assure itself and the public that announcing rights not readily identifiable in the Constitution's text involves much more than the imposition of the Justices' own choice of values on the States and the Federal Government, the Court has sought to identify the nature of the rights qualifying for heightened judicial protection. In *Palko* it was said that this category includes those fundamental liberties that are "implicit in the concept of ordered liberty," such that "neither liberty nor justice would exist if [they] were sacrificed." A different description of fundamental liberties appeared in *Moore v. East Cleveland* (opinion of Powell, J.), where they are characterized as those liberties that are "deeply rooted in this Nation's history and tradition."

It is obvious to us that neither of these formulations would extend a fundamental right to homosexuals to engage in acts of consensual sodomy. Proscriptions against that conduct have ancient roots. Sodomy was a criminal offense at common law and was forbidden by the laws of the original thirteen States when they ratified the Bill of Rights. In 1868, when the Fourteenth Amendment was ratified, all but 5 of the 37 States in the Union had criminal sodomy laws. In fact, until 1961, all 50 States outlawed sodomy, and today, 24 States and the District of Columbia continue to provide criminal penalties for sodomy performed in private and between consenting adults. Against this background, to claim that a right to engage in such conduct is "deeply rooted in this Nation's history and tradition" or "implicit in the concept of ordered liberty" is, at best, facetious.

Nor are we inclined to take a more expansive view of our authority to discover new fundamental rights imbedded in the Due Process Clause. The Court is most vulnerable and comes nearest to illegitimacy when it deals with judge-made constitutional law having little or no cognizable roots in the language or design of the Constitution. That this is so was painfully demonstrated by the face-off between the Executive and the Court in the 1930's, which resulted in the repudiation of much of the substantive gloss that the Court had placed on the Due Process Clause of the Fifth and Fourteenth Amendments. There should be, therefore, great resistance to expand the substantive reach of those Clauses, particularly if it requires redefining the category of rights deemed to be fundamental. Otherwise, the Judiciary necessarily takes to itself further authority to govern the country without express constitutional authority. The claimed right pressed on us today falls far short of overcoming this resistance.

Respondent, however, asserts that the result should be different where the homosexual conduct occurs in the privacy of the home. He relies on *Stanley v. Georgia* [CON LAW p. 722, AMER CON p. 500, RTS & LIB p. 389], where the Court held that the First Amendment prevents conviction for possessing and reading obscene material in the privacy of [one's home].

Stanley did protect conduct that would not have been protected outside the home, and it partially prevented the enforcement of state obscenity laws; but the decision was firmly grounded in the First Amendment. The right pressed upon us here has no similar support in the text of the Constitution, and it does not qualify for recognition under the prevailing principles for construing the Fourteenth Amendment. Its limits are also difficult to discern. Plainly enough, otherwise illegal conduct is not always immunized whenever it occurs in the home. Victimless crimes, such as the possession and use of illegal drugs do not escape the law where they are committed at home. *Stanley* itself recognized that its holding offered no protection for the possession in the home of drugs, firearms, or stolen goods. And if respondent's submission is limited to the voluntary sexual conduct between consenting adults, it would be difficult, except by fiat, to limit the claimed right to homosexual conduct while leaving exposed to prosecution adultery, incest, and other sexual crimes even though they are committed in the home. We are unwilling to start down that road.

Even if the conduct at issue here is not a fundamental right, respondent asserts that there must be a rational basis for the law and that there is none in this case other than the presumed belief of a majority of the electorate in Georgia that homosexual sodomy is immoral and unacceptable. This is said to be an inadequate rationale to support the law. The law, however, is constantly based on notions of morality, and if all laws representing essentially moral choices are to be invalidated under the Due Process Clause, the courts will be very busy indeed. Even respondent makes no such claim, but insists that majority sentiments about the morality of homosexuality should be declared inadequate. We do not agree, and are unpersuaded that the sodomy laws of some 25 States should be invalidated on this basis.[8] * * *

CHIEF JUSTICE BURGER, concurring.

I join the Court's opinion, but I write separately to underscore my view that in constitutional terms there is no such thing as a fundamental right to commit homosexual sodomy. [To] hold that the act of homosexual sodomy is somehow protected as a fundamental right would be to cast aside millennia of moral teaching.

This is essentially not a question of personal "preferences" but rather of the legislative authority of the State. I find nothing in the Constitution depriving a State of the power to enact the statute challenged here.

JUSTICE POWELL, concurring.

I join the opinion of the Court. I agree with the Court that there is no fundamental right—i.e., no substantive right under the Due Process Clause— such as that claimed by respondent, and found to exist by the Court of Appeals. This is not to suggest, however, that respondent may not be protected by the Eighth Amendment of the Constitution. The Georgia statute at issue in this case authorizes a court to imprison a person for up to 20 years for a single private, consensual act of sodomy. In my view, a prison sentence for such conduct—certainly a sentence of long duration—would create a serious Eighth Amendment issue. Under the Georgia statute a single act of sodomy, even in the private setting of a home, is a felony comparable in terms of the possible sentence imposed to serious felonies such as aggravated battery, first degree arson, and robbery.

In this case, however, respondent has not been tried, much less convicted and sentenced.[2] Moreover, respondent has not raised the Eighth Amendment issue below. For these reasons this constitutional argument is not before us.

---

8. Respondent does not defend the judgment below based on the Ninth Amendment, the Equal Protection Clause or the Eighth Amendment.

2. It was conceded at oral argument that, prior to the complaint against respondent Hardwick, there had been no reported decision involving prosecution for private homosexual sodomy under this statute for several decades. Moreover, the State has declined to present the criminal charge against Hardwick to a grand jury, and this is a suit for declaratory judgment brought by respondents challenging the validity of the statute. The history of nonenforcement suggests the moribund character today of laws criminalizing this type of private, consensual conduct. Some 26 states have repealed similar statutes. But the

JUSTICE BLACKMUN, with whom JUSTICE BRENNAN, JUSTICE MARSHALL, and JUSTICE STEVENS join, dissenting.

This case is no more about "a fundamental right to engage in homosexual sodomy," as the Court purports to declare, than *Stanley* was about a fundamental right to watch obscene movies, or *Katz v. United States*, 389 U.S. 347, 88 S.Ct. 507, 19 L.Ed.2d 576 (1967), was about a fundamental right to place interstate bets from a telephone booth.[a] Rather, this case is about "the most comprehensive of rights and the right most valued by civilized men," namely, "the right to be let alone." *Olmstead v. United States*, 277 U.S. 438, 478, 48 S.Ct. 564, 572, 72 L.Ed. 944 (1928) (Brandeis, J., dissenting).

The statute at issue denies individuals the right to decide for themselves whether to engage in particular forms of private, consensual sexual activity. [T]he fact that the moral judgments expressed by statutes like § 16–6–2 may be "natural and familiar [should not] conclude our judgment upon the question whether statutes embodying them conflict with the Constitution of the United States." *Roe,* quoting *Lochner* (Holmes, J., dissenting). Like Justice Holmes, I believe that "[i]t is revolting to have no better reason for a rule of law than that so it was laid down in the time of Henry IV. It is still more revolting if the grounds upon which it was laid down have vanished long since, and the rule simply persists from blind imitation of the past." I believe we must analyze respondent's claim in the light of the values that underlie the constitutional right to privacy. If that right means anything, it means that, before Georgia can prosecute its citizens for making choices about the most intimate aspects of their lives, it must do more than assert that the choice they have made is an "'abominable crime not fit to be named among Christians.'" * * *

[T]he Court's almost obsessive focus on homosexual activity is particularly hard to justify in light of the broad language Georgia has used. Unlike the Court, the Georgia Legislature has not proceeded on the assumption that homosexuals are so different from other citizens that their lives may be controlled in a way that would not be tolerated if it limited the choices of those other citizens. Rather, Georgia has provided that "[a] person commits the offense of sodomy when he performs or submits to any sexual act involving the sex organs of one person and the mouth or anus of another." The sex or status of the persons who engage in the act is irrelevant as a matter of state law. In fact, to the extent I can discern a legislative purpose for Georgia's 1968 enactment, that purpose seems to have been to broaden the coverage of the law to reach heterosexual as well as homosexual activity. I therefore see no basis for the Court's decision to treat this case as an "as applied" challenge to § 16–6–2, see n. 2, or for Georgia's attempt, both in its brief and at oral argument, to defend § 16–6–2 solely on the grounds that it prohibits homosexual activity. Michael Hardwick's standing may rest in significant part on Georgia's apparent willingness to enforce against homosexuals a law it seems not to have any desire to enforce against heterosexuals. But his claim that § 16–6–2 involves an unconstitutional intrusion into his privacy and his right of intimate association does not depend in any way on his sexual orientation.

constitutional validity of the Georgia statute was put in issue by respondents, and for the reasons stated by the Court, I cannot say that conduct condemned for hundreds of years has now become a fundamental right.

a. *Katz* held that electronic surveillance of defendant violated the privacy upon which he justifiably relied when using a telephone booth and thus constituted a "search and seizure" within the meaning of the Fourth Amendment, even though the challenged surveillance technique involved no physical penetration of the phone booth from which defendant placed his calls.

Second, I disagree with the Court's refusal to consider whether § 16–6–2 runs afoul of the Eighth or Ninth Amendments or the Equal Protection Clause of the Fourteenth Amendment. [See] n. 8. Respondent's complaint expressly invoked the Ninth Amendment, and he relied heavily before this Court on *Griswold,* which identifies that Amendment as one of the specific constitutional provisions giving "life and substance" to our understanding of privacy. More importantly, the procedural posture of the case requires that we affirm the Court of Appeals' judgment if there is *any* ground on which respondent may be entitled to relief. This case is before us on petitioner's motion to dismiss for failure to state a claim. [Thus,] even if respondent did not advance claims based on the Eighth or Ninth Amendments, or on the Equal Protection Clause, his complaint should not be dismissed if any of those provisions could entitle him to relief. I need not reach either the Eighth Amendment or the Equal Protection Clause issues because I believe that Hardwick has stated a cognizable claim that § 16–6–2 interferes with constitutionally protected interests in privacy and freedom of intimate association. But neither the Eighth Amendment nor the Equal Protection Clause is so clearly irrelevant that a claim resting on either provision should be peremptorily dismissed. The Court's cramped reading of the issue before it makes for a short opinion, but it does little to make for a persuasive one.

"Our cases long have recognized that the Constitution embodies a promise that a certain private sphere of individual liberty will be kept largely beyond the reach of government." *Thornburgh* [p. 93 of this Supplement]. In construing the right to privacy, the Court has proceeded along two somewhat distinct, albeit complementary, lines. First, it has recognized a privacy interest with reference to certain *decisions* that are properly for the individual to make. E.g., *Roe, Pierce.* Second, it has recognized a privacy interest with reference to certain *places* without regard for the particular activities in which the individuals who occupy them are engaged. The case before us implicates both the decisional and the spatial aspects of the right to privacy.

The Court concludes today that none of our prior cases dealing with various decisions that individuals are entitled to make free of governmental interference "bears any resemblance to the claimed constitutional right of homosexuals to engage in acts of sodomy that is asserted in this case." While it is true that these cases may be characterized by their connection to protection of the family, the Court's conclusion that they extend no further than this boundary ignores the warning in *Moore* (plurality opinion), against "clos[ing] our eyes to the basic reasons why certain rights associated with the family have been accorded shelter under the Fourteenth Amendment's Due Process Clause." We protect those rights not because they contribute, in some direct and material way, to the general public welfare, but because they form so central a part of an individual's life. "[T]he concept of privacy embodies the 'moral fact that a person belongs to himself and not others nor to society as a whole.'" *Thornburgh* (Stevens, J., concurring). And so we protect the decision whether to marry precisely because marriage "is an association that promotes a way of life, not causes; a harmony in living, not political faiths; a bilateral loyalty, not commercial or social projects." *Griswold.* We protect the decision whether to have a child because parenthood alters so dramatically an individual's self-definition, not because of demographic considerations or the Bible's command to be fruitful and multiply. Cf. *Thornburgh* (Stevens, J., concurring). And we protect the family because it contributes so powerfully to the happiness of individuals, not because of a preference for stereotypical households. Cf. *Moore* (plurality opinion). * * *

Only the most willful blindness could obscure the fact that sexual intimacy is "a sensitive, key relationship of human existence, central to family life, community welfare, and the development of human personality." The fact that individuals define themselves in a significant way through their intimate sexual relationships with others suggests, in a Nation as diverse as ours, that there may be many "right" ways of conducting those relationships, and that much of the richness of a relationship will come from the freedom an individual has to *choose* the form and nature of these intensely personal bonds. See Karst, *The Freedom of Intimate Association,* 89 Yale L.J. 624, 637 (1980).

In a variety of circumstances we have recognized that a necessary corollary of giving individuals freedom to choose how to conduct their lives is acceptance of the fact that different individuals will make different choices. For example, in holding that the clearly important state interest in public education should give way to a competing claim by the Amish to the effect that extended formal schooling threatened their way of life, the Court declared: "There can be no assumption that today's majority is 'right' and the Amish and others like them are 'wrong.' A way of life that is odd or even erratic but interferes with no rights or interests of others is not to be condemned because it is different." *Wisconsin v. Yoder* [CON LAW p. 1103, AMER CON p. 849, RTS & LIB p. 770]. The Court claims that its decision today merely refuses to recognize a fundamental right to engage in homosexual sodomy; what the Court really has refused to recognize is the fundamental interest all individuals have in controlling the nature of their intimate associations with others.

The behavior for which Hardwick faces prosecution occurred in his own home, a place to which the Fourth Amendment attaches special significance. The Court's treatment of this aspect of the case is symptomatic of its overall refusal to consider the broad principles that have informed our treatment of privacy in specific cases. Just as the right to privacy is more than the mere aggregation of a number of entitlements to engage in specific behavior, so too, protecting the physical integrity of the home is more than merely a means of protecting specific activities that often take place there. ∗ ∗ ∗

The Court's interpretation of the pivotal case of *Stanley v. Georgia* is entirely unconvincing. *Stanley* held that Georgia's undoubted power to punish the public distribution of constitutionally unprotected, obscene material did not permit the State to punish the private possession of such material. According to the majority here, *Stanley* relied entirely on the First Amendment, and thus, it is claimed, sheds no light on cases not involving printed materials. But that is not what *Stanley* said. Rather, the *Stanley* Court anchored its holding in the Fourth Amendment's special protection for the individual in his home ∗ ∗ ∗.

The central place that *Stanley* gives Justice Brandeis' dissent in *Olmstead,* a case raising *no* First Amendment claim, shows that *Stanley* rested as much on the Court's understanding of the Fourth Amendment as it did on the First. Indeed, in *Paris Adult Theatre* [CON LAW p. 724, AMER CON p. 502, RTS & LIB p. 391] the Court suggested that reliance on the Fourth Amendment not only supported the Court's outcome in *Stanley* but actually was *necessary* to it: "If obscene material unprotected by the First Amendment in itself carried with it a 'penumbra' of constitutionally protected privacy, this Court would not have found it necessary to decide *Stanley* on the narrow basis of the 'privacy of the home,' which was hardly more than a reaffirmation that 'a man's home is his castle.' " "The right of the people to be secure in [their] houses," expressly guaranteed by the Fourth Amendment, is perhaps the most "textual" of the various constitutional provisions that inform our understanding of the right to privacy, and thus I cannot agree with the Court's statement that "[t]he right pressed upon us here has [no] support in the text of the Constitution." Indeed, the right of an individual to conduct intimate relationships in the intimacy of his or her own home seems to me to be the heart of the Constitution's protection of privacy.

The Court's failure to comprehend the magnitude of the liberty interests at stake in this case leads it to slight the question whether [petitioner] has justified Georgia's infringement on these interests. I believe that neither of the two general justifications for § 16–6–2 that petitioner has advanced warrants dismissing respondent's challenge for failure to state a claim.

First, petitioner asserts that the acts made criminal by the statute may have serious adverse consequences for "the general public health and welfare," such as spreading communicable diseases or fostering other criminal activity. Inasmuch as this case was dismissed by the District Court on the pleadings, it is not surprising that the record before us is barren of any evidence to support petitioner's claim. In light of the state of the record, I see no justification for the Court's attempt to equate the private, consensual sexual activity at issue here with the "possession in the home of drugs, firearms, or stolen goods," to which *Stanley* refused to extend its protection. None of the behavior so mentioned in *Stanley* can properly be viewed as "[v]ictimless," drugs and weapons are inherently dangerous, and for property to be "stolen," someone must have been wrongfully deprived of it. Nothing in the record before the Court provides any justification for finding the activity forbidden by § 16–6–2 to be physically dangerous, either to the persons engaged in it or to others.[4]

The core of petitioner's defense of § 16–6–2, however, is that respondent and others who engage in the conduct prohibited by § 16–6–2 interfere with Georgia's exercise of the " 'right of the Nation and of the States to maintain a decent society,' " *Paris Adult Theatre*. Essentially, petitioner argues, and the Court agrees, that the fact that the acts described in § 16–6–2 "for hundreds of years, if not thousands, have been uniformly condemned as immoral" is a sufficient reason to permit a State to ban them today.

I cannot agree that either the length of time a majority has held its convictions or the passions with which it defends them can withdraw legislation from this Court's scrutiny. See, e.g., *Roe; Loving;* [b] *Brown v. Board of Educa-*

---

4. Although I do not think it necessary to decide today issues that are not even remotely before us, it does seem to me that a court could find simple, analytically sound distinctions between certain private, consensual sexual conduct, on the one hand, and adultery and incest (the only two vaguely specific "sexual crimes" to which the majority points), on the other. For example, marriage, in addition to its spiritual aspects, is a civil contract that entitles the contracting parties to a variety of governmentally provided benefits. A State might define the contractual commitment necessary to become eligible for these benefits to include a commitment of fidelity and then punish individuals for breaching that contract. Moreover, a State might conclude that adultery is likely to injure third persons, in particular, spouses and children of persons who engage in extramarital affairs. With respect to incest, a court might well agree with respondent that the nature of familial rela-

tionships renders true consent to incestuous activity sufficiently problematical that a blanket prohibition of such activity is warranted. Notably, the Court makes no effort to explain why it has chosen to group private, consensual homosexual activity with adultery and incest rather than with private, consensual heterosexual activity by unmarried persons or, indeed, with oral or anal sex within marriage.

b. *Loving* struck down a Virginia antimiscegenation statute, concluding: "There is patently no legitimate overriding purpose independent of invidious racial discrimination which justifies this classification. [There] can be no doubt that restricting the freedom to marry solely because of racial classifications violates the central meaning of the Equal Protection Clause." The Court also held that denying so "fundamental" a "freedom" as marriage "on so unsupportable a basis as the racial classifications in these statutes" constition.[5] As Justice Jackson wrote so eloquently for the Court in *West Virginia State Bd. of Educ. v. Barnette* [CON LAW p. 1096, AMER CON p. 843, RTS & LIB 763]. "[F]reedom to differ is not limited to things that do not matter much. That would be a mere shadow of freedom. The test of its substance is the right to differ as to things that touch the heart of the existing order." It is precisely because the issue raised by this case touches the heart of what makes individuals what they are that we should be especially sensitive to the rights of those whose choices upset the majority.

The assertion that "traditional Judeo-Christian values proscribe" the conduct involved cannot provide an adequate justification for § 16–6–2. That certain, but by no means all, religious groups condemn the behavior at issue gives the State no license to impose their judgments on the entire citizenry. The legitimacy of secular legislation depends instead on whether the State can advance some justification for its law beyond its conformity to religious doctrine.[6] A State can no more punish private behavior because of religious intolerance than it can punish such behavior because of racial animus. * * *

Nor can § 16–6–2 be justified as a "morally neutral" exercise of Georgia's power to "protect the public environment," *Paris Adult Theatre*. * * * Petitioner and the Court fail to see the difference between laws that protect public sensibilities and those that enforce private morality. Statutes banning public sexual activity are entirely consistent with protecting the individual's liberty interest in decisions concerning sexual relations: the same recognition that those decisions are intensely private which justifies protecting them from governmental interference can justify protecting individuals from unwilling exposure to the sexual activities of others. But the mere fact that intimate behavior may be punished when it takes place in public cannot dictate how States can regulate intimate behavior that occurs in intimate places.[7]

This case involves no real interference with the rights of others, for the mere knowledge that other individuals do not adhere to one's value system

---

tuted a denial of due process. At the time *Loving* was decided, 16 states prohibited and punished marriages on the basis of racial classifications.

  5. The parallel between *Loving* and this case is almost uncanny. There, too, the State relied on a religious justification for its law. [There], too, defenders of the challenged statute relied heavily on the fact that when the Fourteenth Amendment was ratified, most of the States had similar prohibitions. There, too, at the time the case came before the Court, many of the States still had criminal statutes concerning the conduct at issue. [Yet] the Court held, not only that the individious racism of Virginia's law violated the Equal Protection Clause, but also that the law deprived the Lovings of due process by denying them the "freedom of choice to marry" that had "long been recognized as one of the vital personal rights essential to the orderly pursuit of happiness by free men."

  6. The theological nature of the origin of Anglo-American antisodomy statutes is patent. It was not until 1533 that sodomy was made a secular offense in England. Until that time, the offense was, in Sir James Stephen's words, "merely ecclesiastical." [The]

transfer of jurisdiction over prosecutions for sodomy to the secular courts seems primarily due to the alteration of ecclesiastical jurisdiction attendant on England's break with the Roman Catholic Church, rather than to any new understanding of the sovereign's interest in preventing or punishing the behavior involved.

  7. At oral argument a suggestion appeared that, while the Fourth Amendment's special protection of the home might prevent the State from enforcing § 16–6–2 against individuals who engage in consensual sexual activity there, that protection would not make the statute invalid. The suggestion misses the point entirely. If the law is not invalid, then the police *can* invade the home to enforce it, provided, of course, that they obtain a determination of probable cause from a neutral magistrate. One of the reasons for the Court's holding in *Griswold* was precisely the possibility, and repugnancy, of permitting searches to obtain evidence regarding the use of contraceptives. Permitting the kinds of searches that might be necessary to obtain evidence of the sexual activity banned by § 16–6–2 seems no less intrusive, or repugnant.

cannot be a legally cognizable interest, let alone an interest that can justify invading the houses, hearts, and minds of citizens who choose to live their lives differently. * * *

JUSTICE STEVENS, with whom JUSTICE BRENNAN and JUSTICE MARSHALL join, dissenting.

Like the statute that is challenged in this case, the rationale of the Court's opinion applies equally to the prohibited conduct regardless of whether the parties who engage in it are married or unmarried, or are of the same or different sexes.[2] Sodomy was condemned as an odious and sinful type of behavior during the formative period of the common law. That condemnation was equally damning for heterosexual and homosexual sodomy. Moreover, it provided no special exemption for married couples. The license to cohabit and to produce legitimate offspring simply did not include any permission to engage in sexual conduct that was considered a "crime against nature."

The history of the Georgia statute before us clearly reveals this traditional prohibition of heterosexual, as well as homosexual, sodomy.[6] Indeed, at one point in the 20th century, Georgia's law was construed to permit certain sexual conduct between homosexual women even though such conduct was prohibited between heterosexuals. The history of the statutes cited by the majority as proof for the proposition that sodomy is not constitutionally protected similarly reveals a prohibition on heterosexual, as well as homosexual, sodomy.[8]

Because the Georgia statute expresses the traditional view that sodomy is an immoral kind of conduct regardless of the identity of the persons who engage in it, I believe that a proper analysis of its constitutionality requires consideration of two questions: First, may a State totally prohibit the described conduct by means of a neutral law applying without exception to all persons subject to its jurisdiction? If not, may the State save the statute by announcing that it will only enforce the law against homosexuals? The two questions merit separate discussion.

Our prior cases make two propositions abundantly clear. First, the fact that the governing majority in a State has traditionally viewed a particular practice as immoral is not a sufficient reason for upholding a law prohibiting the practice; neither history nor tradition could save a law prohibiting miscegenation from constitutional attack.[9] Second, individual decisions by married persons, concerning the intimacies of their physical relationship, even when not intended to produce offspring, are a form of "liberty" protected by the Due Process Clause of the Fourteenth Amendment. *Griswold.* Moreover, this protection extends to intimate choices by unmarried as well as married persons. *Carey; Eisenstadt.* * * *

2. The Court states that the "issue presented is whether the Federal Constitution confers a fundamental right upon homosexuals to engage in sodomy and hence invalidates the laws of the many States that still make such conduct illegal and have done so for a very long time." In reality, however, it is the indiscriminate prohibition of sodomy, heterosexual as well as homosexual, that has been present "for a very long time." Moreover, the reasoning the Court employs would provide the same support for the statute as it is written as it does for the statute as it is narrowly construed by the Court.

6. The predecessor of the current Georgia statute provided, "Sodomy is the carnal knowledge and connection against the order of nature, by man with man, or in the same unnatural manner with woman." * * *

8. A review of the statutes cited by the majority discloses that, in 1791, in 1868, and today, the vast majority of sodomy statutes do not differentiate between homosexual and heterosexual sodomy.

9. See *Loving.* Interestingly, miscegenation was once treated as a crime similar to sodomy.

Society has every right to encourage its individual members to follow particular traditions in expressing affection for one another and in gratifying their personal desires. It, of course, may prohibit an individual from imposing his will on another to satisfy his own selfish interests. It also may prevent an individual from interfering with, or violating, a legally sanctioned and protected relationship, such as marriage. And it may explain the relative advantages and disadvantages of different forms of intimate expression. But when individual married couples are isolated from observation by others, the way in which they voluntarily choose to conduct their intimate relations is a matter for them—not the State—to decide.[10] The essential "liberty" that animated the development of the law in cases like *Griswold, Eisenstadt,* and *Carey* surely embraces the right to engage in nonreproductive, sexual conduct that others may consider offensive or immoral.

Paradoxical as it may seem, our prior cases thus establish that a State may not prohibit sodomy within "the sacred precincts of marital bedrooms," *Griswold,* or, indeed, between unmarried heterosexual adults. *Eisenstadt.* In all events, it is perfectly clear that the State of Georgia may not totally prohibit the conduct proscribed by § 16–6–2 of the Georgia Criminal Code.

If the Georgia statute cannot be enforced as it is written—if the conduct it seeks to prohibit is a protected form of liberty for the vast majority of Georgia's citizens—the State must assume the burden of justifying a selective application of its law. Either the persons to whom Georgia seeks to apply its statute do not have the same interest in "liberty" that others have, or there must be a reason why the State may be permitted to apply a generally applicable law to certain persons that it does not apply to others.

The first possibility is plainly unacceptable. Although the meaning of the principle that "all men are created equal" is not always clear, it surely must mean that every free citizen has the same interest in "liberty" that the members of the majority share. From the standpoint of the individual, the homosexual and the heterosexual have the same interest in deciding how he will live his own life, and, more narrowly, how he will conduct himself in his personal and voluntary associations with his companions. State intrusion into the private conduct of either is equally burdensome.

The second possibility is similarly unacceptable. A policy of selective application must be supported by a neutral and legitimate interest—something more substantial than a habitual dislike for, or ignorance about, the disfavored group. Neither the State nor the Court has identified any such interest in this case. The Court has posited as a justification for the Georgia statute "the presumed belief of a majority of the electorate in Georgia that homosexual sodomy is immoral and unacceptable." But the Georgia electorate has expressed no such belief—instead, its representatives enacted a law that presumably reflects the belief that *all sodomy* is immoral and unacceptable. Unless the Court is prepared to conclude that such a law is constitutional, it may not rely on the work product of the Georgia Legislature to support its holding. For the Georgia statute does not single out homosexuals as a separate class meriting special disfavored treatment.

Nor, indeed, does the Georgia prosecutor even believe that all homosexuals who violate this statute should be punished. This conclusion is evident from the

10. Indeed, the Georgia Attorney General concedes that Georgia's statute would be unconstitutional if applied to a married couple. ∗ ∗ ∗ Significantly, Georgia passed the current statute three years after the Court's decision in *Griswold.*

fact that the respondent in this very case has formally acknowledged in his complaint and in court that he has engaged, and intends to continue to engage, in the prohibited conduct, yet the State has elected not to process criminal charges against him. As Justice Powell points out, moreover, Georgia's prohibition on private, consensual sodomy has not been enforced for decades. The record of nonenforcement, in this case and in the last several decades, belies the Attorney General's representations about the importance of the State's selective application of its generally applicable law.[12]

Both the Georgia statute and the Georgia prosecutor thus completely fail to provide the Court with any support for the conclusion that homosexual sodomy, *simpliciter,* is considered unacceptable conduct in that State, and that the burden of justifying a selective application of the generally applicable law has been met.

The Court orders the dismissal of respondent's complaint even though the State's statute prohibits all sodomy; even though that prohibition is concededly unconstitutional with respect to heterosexuals; and even though the State's post hoc explanations for selective application are belied by the State's own actions. At the very least, I think it clear at this early stage of the litigation that respondent has alleged a constitutional claim sufficient to withstand a motion to dismiss.[13]   *   *   *

SECTION: THE DEATH PENALTY AND RELATED PROBLEMS: CRUEL AND UNUSUAL PUNISHMENT

IS THE DEATH PENALTY ALWAYS—OR EVER—"CRUEL AND UNUSUAL"?

CON LAW: P. 567, add to fn. c

AMER CON: P. 385, add to fn. c

RTS & LIB: P. 235, add to fn. c

In *Maynard v. Cartwright,* ___ U.S. ___, 108 S.Ct. 1853, 100 L.Ed.2d 372 (1988), the Court held, without a dissent, that the language of one of Oklahoma's statutory aggravating circumstances, that the murder was "especially heinous, atrocious, or cruel," gave no more guidance to the jury than the language held unconstitutional in *Godfrey.*

12. It is, of course, possible to argue that a statute has a purely symbolic role. [Since] the Georgia Attorney General does not even defend the statute as written, however, the State cannot possibly rest on the notion that the statute may be defended for its symbolic message.

13. Indeed, at this stage, it appears that the statute indiscriminately authorizes a policy of selective prosecution that is neither limited to the class of homosexual persons nor embraces all persons in that class, but rather applies to those who may be arbitrarily selected by the prosecutor for reasons that are not revealed either in the record of this case or in the text of the statute. If that is true, although the text of the statute is clear enough, its true meaning may be "so intolerably vague that evenhanded enforcement of the law is a virtual impossibility."

MANDATORY DEATH SENTENCES

CON LAW: P. 581, after note 2

AMER CON: P. 394, after note 2

RTS & LIB: P. 249, after note 2

3. In *Woodson*, the Court reserved judgment on the constitutionality of a mandatory death penalty statute "limited to an extremely narrow category of homicide, such as murder by a prisoner serving a life sentence." A decade later, in SUMNER v. SHUMAN, 483 U.S. 66, 107 S.Ct. 2716, 97 L.Ed.2d 56 (1987), a 6–3 majority, per BLACKMUN, J., held that "a departure from the individualized capital-sentencing doctrine is not justified" even in such a case:

"Not only do the two elements that are incorporated in the [now-repealed Nevada statute, (a) that defendant had been convicted of murder while in prison, and (b) that he had been convicted of an earlier crime which yielded a sentence of life imprisonment without possibility of parole,] serve as incomplete indicators of the circumstances surrounding the murder and of the defendant's criminal record, but they say nothing of the 'circumstances such as the youth of the offender, [the] influence of drugs, alcohol, or extreme emotional disturbance, and even the existence of circumstances which the offender reasonably believed provided a moral justification for his conduct.' * * *

"The force of the deterrent argument for the mandatory statute is weakened considerably by the fact that every prison system in the country is currently operating without the threat of a mandatory death penalty for life-term inmates. The fact that the Nevada legislature saw fit to repeal the specific statute at issue here a decade ago seriously undermines [the] contention that such a statute is required as a deterrent. * * *

"We also reject the proposition that a mandatory death penalty for life-term inmates convicted of murder is justified because of the State's retribution interests. [T]here are other sanctions less severe than execution that can be imposed even on a life-term inmate. [His] confinement can be limited further, such as through a transfer to a more restrictive custody or correctional facility or deprivation of privileges of work or socialization. In any event, even the retribution interests of the State cannot be characterized according to a category of offense because '[s]ociety's legitimate desire for retribution is less strong with respect to a defendant who played a minor role in the murder for which he was convicted.' Although a sentencing authority may decide that a sanction less than death is not appropriate in a particular case, the fundamental respect for humanity underlying the Eighth Amendment requires that the defendant be able to present any relevant mitigating evidence that could justify a lesser sentence."

Dissenting Justice WHITE, joined by Rehnquist, C.J., and Scalia, J., maintained that "the Constitution does not bar a state legislature from determining, in this limited class of cases, that, as a matter of law, no amount of mitigating evidence could ever be sufficient to outweigh the aggravating factors that characterize a first-degree murder committed by one who is already incarcerated for committing a previous murder and serving a life sentence. * * * An inmate serving a life sentence who is convicted of capital murder and who is *legally* responsible for his action, that is, one who does not have a meritorious defense recognized as relieving the inmate of such responsibility, has, in my view, no constitutional right to persuade the sentencer to impose essentially no punishment at all for taking the life of another, whether guard or inmate."

OTHER CONSTITUTIONAL CHALLENGES

CON LAW: P. 584, add to note 7

AMER CON: P. 396, end of section

RTS & LIB: P. 252, add to note 7

Distinguishing *Enmund*, a 5–4 majority held in TISON v. ARIZONA, 481 U.S. 137, 107 S.Ct. 1676, 95 L.Ed.2d 127 (1987), that the Eighth Amendment proportionality requirement does not bar the death penalty in the case of a defendant who neither intended to kill the victim nor inflicted the fatal wounds, but whose participation in the felony resulting in murder "is major and whose mental state is one of reckless indifference to the value of human life." Petitioner brothers planned and effected the prison escape of their father and another convicted murderer. After leaving the prison, petitioners helped to abduct, detain and rob a family of four. They then watched their father and the other convict murder the members of that family. Although both petitioners maintained that they were surprised by the shooting, neither made any effort to help the victims, but drove away in the victims' car with the rest of the escape party. Petitioners were convicted of capital murder and sentenced to death on the basis of a state felony-murder rule providing that a killing occurring during the perpetration of robbery or kidnapping is capital murder and that each participant in the kidnapping or robbery is legally responsible for the acts of his accomplices. Observed the Court, per O'CONNOR, J.:

"A narrow focus on the question of whether or not a given defendant 'intended to kill' [is] a highly unsatisfactory means of definitively distinguishing the most culpable and dangerous of murderers. [T]he reckless disregard for human life implicit in knowingly engaging in criminal activities known to carry a grave risk of death represents a highly culpable mental state, [one] that may be taken into account in making a capital sentencing judgment when that conduct causes its natural, though also not inevitable, lethal result.

"The petitioners' own personal involvement in the crimes was not minor, [but] 'substantial.' Far from merely sitting in a car away from the actual scene of the murders acting as the getaway driver to a robbery, each petitioner was actively involved in every element of the kidnapping-robbery and was physically present during the entire sequence of criminal activity culminating in the murder of [the] family and the subsequent flight. * * *

"Only a small minority of those jurisdictions imposing capital punishment for felony murder have rejected the possibility of a capital sentence absent an intent to kill and we do not find this minority position constitutionally required. [We] hold that major participation in the felony committed, combined with reckless indifference to human life, is sufficient to satisfy the *Enmund* culpability requirement."

BRENNAN J., joined by Marshall, Blackmun and Stevens, JJ., dissented: "The Court's decision today to approve the death penalty for accomplices who [have not in fact killed, attempted to kill, or intended that a killing take place or that lethal force be used] is inconsistent with *Enmund* and with the only justifications this Court has put forth for imposing the death penalty in any case.

"[The Tisons] are similarly situated with Earl Enmund in every respect that mattered to the decision in *Enmund*. * * * Like Enmund, the Tisons have been sentenced to death for the intentional acts of others which the Tisons did not expect, which were not essential to the felony, and over which they had no control. Unlike Enmund, however, the Tisons will be the first individuals in over 30 years to be executed for such behavior.

" * * * So rarely does any State (let alone any Western country other than our own) ever execute a person who neither killed nor intended to kill that 'these death sentences are cruel and unusual in the same way that being struck by lightening is cruel and unusual.' *Furman* (Stewart, J., concurring). This case thus demonstrates, as *Furman* also did, that we have yet to achieve a system capable of 'distinguishing the few cases in which the [death penalty] is imposed from the many cases in which it is not.' (White, J., concurring)."

CON LAW: P. 586, after note 3

AMER CON: P. 396, end of section

RTS & LIB: P. 254, after note 3

4. *Execution of juveniles.* In THOMPSON v. OKLAHOMA, ___ U.S. ___, 108 S.Ct. 2687, 101 L.Ed.2d 702 (1988), a 5–3 majority (Kennedy, J., not participating) ruled that the Eighth and Fourteenth Amendments prohibit the execution of a person who was under 16 years of age at the time of his or her offense. The principal opinion was written by STEVENS, J., joined by Brennan, Marshall, and Blackmun, JJ., whose review of relevant legislative enactments[a] and jury determinations[b]—"indicators of contemporary standards of decency"—led to the conclusion that "the imposition of the death penalty on a 15-year-old offender is now generally abhorrent to the conscience of the community."

Retribution and deterrence of capital crimes are said to be the two principal purposes of the death penalty. "Given the lesser culpability of the juvenile offender, [his or her] capacity for growth, and society's fiduciary obligations to its children, [the retributive purpose] is simply inapplicable to the execution of a 15-year-old offender."

The deterrence rationale "is equally unacceptable." For "[t]he likelihood that the teenage offender has made the kind of cost-benefit analysis that attaches any weight to the possibilities of execution is so remote as to be virtually nonexistent. And even if one posits such a cold-blooded calculation by a 15-year-old, it is fanciful to believe that he would be deterred by the knowledge that a small number of persons his age have been executed during the 20th century."

Thus, the four-Justice plurality was "not persuaded that the imposition of the death penalty for offenses committed by persons under 16 years of age has made, or can be expected to make, any measurable contribution to the goals that capital punishment is intended to achieve. It is, therefore, 'nothing more than

---

a. Nineteen of the 37 States that authorize capital punishment do not explicitly set any minimum age. "When we confine our attention to the 18 States that have expressly established a minimum age in their death-penalty statutes, we find that all of them require that the defendant have attained at least the age of 16 at the time of the capital offense." Moreover, observed Justice Stevens, "[t]he conclusion that it would offend civilized standards of decency to execute a person who was less than 16 years old at the time of his or her offense is consistent with the views that have

been expressed by professional organizations [such as the American Bar Association and the American Law Institute], by other nations that share our Anglo-American heritage, and by the leading members of the Western European community."

b. Of the 1,393 persons sentenced to death for willful homicide during the years 1982–86, only five, including petitioner in this case, were less than 16 years old at the time of the offense. No execution of a person under 16 has taken place since 1948.

the purposeless and needless imposition of pain and suffering,' *Coker*, and thus an unconstitutional punishment."

JUSTICE O'CONNOR, whose vote was pivotal, concurred in the judgment:

"Although I believe that a national consensus forbidding the execution of any person for a crime committed before the age of 16 very likely does exist, I am reluctant to adopt this conclusion as a matter of constitutional law without better evidence than we now possess. Because I conclude that the sentence in this case can and should be set aside on narrower grounds than those adopted by the plurality, and because the grounds on which I rest should allow us to face the more general question when better evidence is available, I concur only in the judgment of the Court.

"[T]here is no indication that any legislative body in this country has rendered a considered judgment approving the imposition of capital punishment on juveniles who were below the age of 16 at the time of the offense. It nonetheless is true, although I think the dissent has overstated its significance, that the Federal Government and 19 States have adopted statutes that appear to have the legal effect of rendering some of these juveniles death-eligible. That fact is a real obstacle in the way of concluding that a national consensus forbids this practice.

"[The] plurality emphasizes that four decades have gone by since the last execution of a defendant who was younger than 16 at the time of the offense, and that only 5 out of 1,393 death sentences during a recent 5-year period involved such defendants. Like the statistics about the behavior of legislatures, these execution and sentencing statistics support the inference of a national consensus opposing the death penalty for 15-year-olds, but they are not dispositive. * * *

"Under the Eighth Amendment, the death penalty has been treated differently from all other punishments. [The] Court [has] imposed a series of unique substantive and procedural restrictions designed to ensure that capital punishment is not imposed without the serious and calm reflection that ought to precede any decision of such gravity and finality.

"[The] case before us today raises some of the same concerns that have led us to erect barriers to the imposition of capital punishment in other contexts. Oklahoma has enacted a statute that authorizes capital punishment for murder, without setting any minimum age at which the commission of murder may lead to the imposition of that penalty. The State has also, but quite separately, provided that 15-year-old murder defendants may be treated as adults in some circumstances. Because it proceeded in this manner, there is a considerable risk that the Oklahoma legislature either did not realize that its actions would have the effect of rendering 15-year-old defendants death-eligible or did not give the question the serious consideration that would have been reflected in the explicit choice of some minimum age for death-eligibility. Were it clear that no national consensus forbids the imposition of capital punishment for crimes committed before the age of 16, the implicit nature of the Oklahoma legislature's decision would not be constitutionally problematic. In the peculiar circumstances we face today, however, the Oklahoma statutes have presented this Court with a result that is of very dubious constitutionality, and they have done so without the earmarks of careful consideration that we have required for other kinds of decisions leading to the death penalty. In this unique situation, I am prepared to conclude that petitioner and others who were below the age of 16 at the time of their offense may not be executed under the authority of a capital punishment statute that specifies no minimum age at which the commission of a capital crime can lead to the offender's execution." *

Dissenting JUSTICE SCALIA, joined by Rehnquist, C.J., and White, J., emphasized that the question presented was not whether an automatic death penalty could be applied to individuals younger than 16 when they commit certain crimes or whether such individuals can be deprived of the benefit of a rebuttable presumption that he or she is not responsible enough to be punished as an adult, but "whether there is a national consensus that no criminal so much as one day under 16, after individualized consideration of his circumstances, including the overcoming of a presumption that he should not be tried as an adult, can possibly be deemed mature and responsible enough to be punished with death for any crime." He saw "no plausible basis for answering [this] question in the affirmative."

The plurality had focused on the 18 States establishing a minimum age for capital punishment. But the dissent failed to see why an accurate analysis would not include the 19 States that have determined that no minimum age for capital punishment is appropriate, "leaving that to be governed by their general rules for the age at which juveniles can be criminally responsible."

As for the statistics of executions relied on by the plurality, they "demonstrate nothing except the fact that our society has always agreed that executions of 15-year-old criminals should be rare, and in more modern times has agreed that they (like all other executions) should be even rarer still. There is no rational basis for discerning in that a societal judgment that no one so much as a day under 16 can *ever* be mature and morally responsible enough to deserve that penalty; and there is no justification except our own predilection for converting a statistical rarity of occurrence into an absolute constitutional ban. * * * One could readily run the same statistical argument with respect to other classes of defendants. Between 1930 and 1955, for example, 30 women were executed in the United States. Only 3 were executed between then and 1986—and none in the 22-year period between 1962 and 1984. Proportionately, the drop is as impressive as that which the plurality points to in the 15-year-old executions. * * * Surely the conclusion is not that it is unconstitutional to impose capital punishment upon a woman."

Nor were the dissenters impressed with Justice O'Connor's approach. As they understood her separate concurrence, "it agrees (1) that we have no constitutional authority to set aside this death penalty unless we can find it contrary to a firm national consensus that persons younger than 16 at the time of their crime cannot be executed, and (2) that we cannot make such a finding. It does not, however, reach the seemingly inevitable conclusion that (3) we therefore have no constitutional authority to set aside this death penalty."

---

* Contrary to the dissent's suggestion, the conclusion I have reached in this case does not imply that I would reach a similar conclusion in cases involving "those of extremely low intelligence, or those over 75, or any number of other appealing groups as to which the existence of a national consensus regarding capital punishment may be in doubt [because] they are not specifically named in the capital statutes." In this case, there is significant affirmative evidence of a national consensus forbidding the execution of defendants who were below the age of 16 at the time of the offense. The evidence includes 18 state stat- utes setting a minimum age of 16 or more, and it is such evidence—not the mere failure of Oklahoma to specify a minimum age or the "appealing" nature of the group to which petitioner belongs—that leaves me unwilling to conclude that petitioner may constitutionally be executed. Cases in which similarly persuasive evidence was lacking would in my view not be analogous to the case before us today. The dissent is mistaken both when it reads into my discussion a contrary implication and when it suggests that there are ulterior reasons behind the implication it has incorrectly drawn.

The concurrence, maintained the dissenters, "hoists on to the deck of our Eighth Amendment jurisprudence the loose cannon of a brand new principle. If the concurrence's view were adopted, henceforth a finding of national consensus would no longer be required to invalidate state action in the area of capital punishment. All that would be needed is uncertainty regarding the existence of a national consensus, whereupon various protective requirements could be imposed, even to the point of specifying the process of legislation. If 15-year-olds must be explicitly named in capital statutes, why not those of extremely low intelligence, or those over 75, or any number of other appealing groups as to which the existence of a national consensus regarding capital punishment may be in doubt for the same reason the concurrence finds it in doubt here, *viz.*, because they are not specifically named in the capital statutes? [The] concurrence's approach is a solomonic solution to the problem of how to prevent execution in the present case while at the same time not holding that the execution of those under 16 when they commit murder is categorically unconstitutional. Solomon, however, was not subject to the constitutional constraints of the judicial department of a national government in a federal, democratic system."

———

A year later, however, in the consolidated cases of STANFORD v. KENTUCKY and WILKINS v. MISSOURI, ___ U.S. ___, 109 S.Ct. 2969, ___ L.Ed.2d ___ (1989), "discern[ing] neither an historical nor a modern societal consensus forbidding the imposition of capital punishment on any person who murders at 16 or 17 years of age," a 5–4 majority, per SCALIA, J., held that such punishment does not violate the Eighth Amendment:

" '[F]irst' among the 'objective indicia that reflect the public attitude toward a given sanction' are statutes passed by society's elected representatives, *McCleskey v. Kemp* [p. 159 of this Supplement]. Of the 37 states whose laws permit capital punishment, 15 decline to impose it upon 16-year-old offenders and 12 decline to impose it on 17-year-old offenders. This does not establish the degree of national consensus this Court has previously thought sufficient to label a particular punishment cruel and unusual. [Even if there were no national consensus in *favor* of capital punishment for 16- or 17-year-olds, it] is not the burden of Kentucky and Missouri [to] establish a national consensus approving what their citizens have voted to do; rather, it is the 'heavy burden' of petitioners to establish a national consensus *against* it. As far as the most reliable indication of consensus is concerned—the pattern of enacted laws—petitioners have failed to carry that burden."

The Court also rejected the argument that even if the laws themselves did not establish a settled consensus against the execution of juveniles, such a consensus was established by "the application of the laws" [e.g. the reluctance of juries to impose, and prosecutors to seek, the death penalty for 16- and 17-year-old offenders]:

"Petitioners are quite correct that a far smaller number of offenders under 18 than over 18 have been sentenced to death in this country. * * * These statistics, however, carry little significance. Given the undisputed fact that a far smaller percentage of capital crimes is committed by persons under 18 than over 18, the discrepancy in treatment is much less than might seem. Granted, however, that a substantial discrepancy exists, that does not establish the requisite proposition that the death sentence for offenders under 18 is categorically unacceptable to prosecutors and juries. To the contrary, it is not only possible but overwhelmingly probable that the very considerations which induce petitioners and their supporters to believe that death should *never* be imposed on offenders under 18 cause prosecutors and juries to believe that it should *rarely* be imposed."

Dissenting Justice BRENNAN, joined by Marshall, Blackmun and Stevens, JJ., contended that the Court had given "a distorted view" of the evidence of contemporary standards provided by legislative determinations: When one includes the 15 jurisdictions (including the District of Columbia) "in which capital punishment is not authorized at all, it appears that the governments in fully 27 of the States have concluded that no one under 18 should face the death penalty. A further 3 states refuse to authorize sentences of death for those who committed their offense when under 17, making a total of 30 States that would not tolerate the execution of petitioner Wilkins."

Moreover, "[f]urther indicators of contemporary standards of decency that should inform our consideration of the Eighth Amendment question are the opinions of respected organizations. [There] is no dearth of opinion from such groups that the state-sanctioned killing of minors is unjustified [mentioning the American Bar Association, the American Law Institute, the National Council of Juvenile and Family Court Judges and the National Commission on Reform of the Federal Criminal Laws].

Also revelant to Eighth Amendment analysis, wrote Justice Brennan, is legislation in other countries. "Many countries, of course—over 50, including nearly all in Western Europe—have formally abolished the death penalty, or have limited its use to exceptional crimes such as treason. Twenty-seven others do not in practice impose the death penalty. Of the nations that retain capital punishment, a majority—65—prohibit the execution of juveniles."

"Together," concluded Justice Brennan, "the rejection of the death penalty for juveniles by a majority of the States, the rarity of the sentence for juveniles, both as an absolute and a comparative matter, the decisions of respected organizations in relevant fields that this punishment is unacceptable, and its rejection generally throughout the world, provide to my mind a strong grounding for the view that it is not constitutionally tolerable that certain states persist in authorizing the execution of adolescent offenders. It is unnecessary, however, to rest a view that the Eighth Amendment prohibits the execution of minors solely upon a judgment as to the meaning to be attached to the evidence of contemporary values outlined above, for the execution of juveniles fails to satisfy two well-established and independent Eighth Amendment requirements—that a punishment not be disproportionate, and that it make a contribution to acceptable goals of punishment."

5. *Execution of the mentally retarded.* In PENRY v. LYNAUGH, ___ U.S. ___, 109 S.Ct. 2934, ___ L.Ed.2d ___ (1989), the Court held that the Eighth Amendment does not categorically forbid the execution of mentally retarded people.[a] This case involved a 22-year-old defendant who had an IQ between 50 and 63, which indicates mild to moderate retardation. A psychologist testified that he had the "mental age" of a 6½ year old and the social maturity, or ability

---

a. However, the Court overturned Penry's death sentence on another ground: The failure, under the Texas capital sentencing proceeding, to inform the jury that it could consider and give effect to the mitigating evidence of Penry's mental retardation and abused background by declining to impose the death penalty deprived him of his right to have a jury consider all mitigating evidence that he presented before sentencing him to die.

to function in the world, of a 9 or 10 year old. A 5–4 majority, per O'Connor, J. observed:

"The common law prohibition against punishing 'idiots' for their crimes suggests that it may indeed be 'cruel and unusual' punishment to execute persons who are profoundly or severely retarded and wholly lacking the capacity to appreciate the wrongfulness of their actions. Because of the protections afforded by the insanity defenses today, such a person is not likely to be convicted or face the prospect of punishment. [Moreover, persons] 'unaware of the punishment they are about to suffer and why they are to suffer it' cannot be executed.

"Such a case is not before us today. Penry was found competent to stand trial. [In] addition, the jury rejected his insanity defense, which reflected their conclusion that Penry knew that his conduct was wrong and was capable of conforming his conduct to the requirements of the law.

"Penry argues, however that there is objective evidence today of an emerging national consensus against executions of the mentally retarded * * *. Only one State, however, explicitly bans execution of retarded persons who have been found guilty of a capital offense. * * *

"Penry does not offer any evidence of the general behavior of juries with respect to sentencing mentally retarded defendants, nor of decisions of prosecutors. He points instead to several public opinion surveys that indicate strong public opposition to execution of the retarded. [In] addition, the American Association on Mental Retardation (AAMR), the country's oldest and largest association of professionals working with the mentally retarded, [has opposed, by resolution,] the execution of persons who are mentally retarded. [The] public sentiment expressed [in] polls and resolutions may ultimately find expression in legislation, which is an objective indicator of contemporary values upon which we can rely. But at present, there is insufficient evidence of a national consensus against executing mentally retarded people convicted of capital offenses for us to conclude that it is categorically prohibited by the Eighth Amendment."

Dissenting on this issue, Justice BRENNAN, joined by Marshall, J., maintained:

"The impairment of a mentally retarded offender's reasoning abilities, control over impressive behavior, and moral development * * * limits her culpability so that [the] ultimate penalty of death is always and necessarily disproportionate to her blameworthiness and hence is unconstitutional. * * *

"[Moreover,] killing mentally retarded offenders does not measurably further the penal goals of either retribution or deterrence. [Since] mentally retarded offenders as a class lack the culpability that is a prerequisite to the proportionate imposition of the death penalty, it follows that execution can never be the 'just dessert' of a retarded offender and that the punishment does not serve the retributive goal. [And] the very factors that make it disproportionate and unjust to execute the mentally retarded also make the death penalty of the most minimal deterrent effect so far as retarded potential offenders are concerned." [b]

b. In a separate opinion, Justice Stevens, joined by Blackmun, J., also concluded that execution of the mentally retarded is unconstitutional.

CON LAW: P. 590, before *Spaziano*

AMER CON: P. 396, end of section

RTS & LIB: P. 258, before *Spaziano*

McCLESKEY v. KEMP

481 U.S. 279, 107 S.Ct. 1756, 95 L.Ed.2d 262 (1987).

[Petitioner, a black man, was convicted in a Georgia trial court of armed robbery and the murder of a white police officer in the course of the robbery and sentenced to death. He sought federal habeas corpus relief, contending that the Georgia capital sentencing process was administered in a racially discriminatory manner in violation of the Eighth Amendment and the Equal Protection Clause of the Fourteenth Amendment.[a] In support of his claim, petitioner proffered a statistical study, Baldus, Pulaski & Woodworth, *Comparative Review of Death Sentences: An Empirical Study of the Georgia Experience,* 74 J.Crim.L. & C. 661 (1983) (the Baldus study).

[This study examined over 2,000 murder cases that occurred in Georgia during the 1970s and concluded that, even after taking account of many nonracial variables, defendants charged with killing white victims were 4.3 times as likely to receive a death sentence as those charged with killing blacks. Moreover, according to this study, black defendants were 1.1 times as likely to receive a death sentence as other defendants. Thus, the study indicates that black defendants, such as petitioner, who kill whites have the greatest likelihood of being sentenced to death.

[The federal district court ruled that the Baldus study "failed to contribute anything of value" to petitioner's claim and denied relief. The U.S. Court of Appeals for the Eleventh Circuit assumed that the Baldus study "showed that systematic and substantial disparities existed in the penalties imposed upon homicide victims in Georgia based on race of the homicide victim, that the disparities existed at a less substantial rate in death sentencing based on race of defendants and that [these factors] were at work in [the county in which petitioner was tried]." Even assuming the validity of the study, however, the Court of Appeals found the statistics "insufficient to demonstrate discriminatory intent or unconstitutional discrimination in the Fourteenth Amendment context [and] insufficient to show irrationality, arbitrariness and capriciousness under any kind of Eighth Amendment analysis." Thus, it affirmed the district court's denial of habeas corpus relief.]

JUSTICE POWELL delivered the opinion of the Court. * * *

[McCleskey argues, inter alia,] that the Baldus study demonstrates that the Georgia capital sentencing system violates the Eighth Amendment.[b] * * *

[O]ur decisions since *Furman* have identified a constitutionally permissible range of discretion in imposing the death penalty. First, there is a required threshold below which the death penalty cannot be imposed. In this context, the

---

a. For discussion of the portion of Justice Powell's opinion for the Court rejecting petitioner's equal protection claim, see p. 271 of this Supplement.

b. The Court noted [fn. 7]: "As did the Court of Appeals, we assume the [Baldus] study is valid statistically without reviewing the factual findings of the District Court. Our assumption that the Baldus study is statistically valid does not include the assumption that the study shows that racial considerations actually enter into any sentencing decisions in Georgia. Even a sophisticated multiple regression analysis such as the Baldus study can only demonstrate a *risk* that the factor of race entered into some capital sentencing decisions and a necessarily lesser risk that race entered into any particular sentencing decision."

State must establish rational criteria that narrow the decisionmaker's judgment as to whether the circumstances of a particular defendant's case meet the threshold. Moreover, a societal consensus that the death penalty is disproportionate to a particular offense prevents a State from imposing the death penalty for that offense. Second, States cannot limit the sentencer's consideration of any relevant circumstance that could cause it to decline to impose the penalty. In this respect, the State cannot channel the sentencer's discretion, but must allow it to consider any relevant information offered by the defendant.

In light of our precedents under the Eighth Amendment, McCleskey cannot argue successfully that his sentence is "disproportionate to the crime in the traditional sense." See *Pulley v. Harris.* He does not deny that he committed a murder in the course of a planned robbery, a crime for which this Court has determined that the death penalty constitutionally may be imposed. [He argues, rather,] that the sentence in his case is disproportionate to the sentences in other murder cases.

On the one hand, he cannot base a constitutional claim on an argument that his case differs from other cases in which defendants *did* receive the death penalty. On automatic appeal, the Georgia Supreme Court found that McCleskey's death sentence was not disproportionate to other death sentences imposed in the State. * * * Moreover, where the statutory procedures adequately channel the sentencer's discretion, such proportionality review is not constitutionally required.

On the other hand, absent a showing that the Georgia capital punishment system operates in an arbitrary and capricious manner, McCleskey cannot prove a constitutional violation by demonstrating that other defendants who may be similarly situated did *not* receive the death penalty. In *Gregg*, the Court confronted the argument that "the opportunities for discretionary action that are inherent in the processing of any murder case under Georgia law," specifically the opportunities for discretionary leniency, rendered the capital sentences imposed arbitrary and capricious. We rejected this contention. * * *

Because McCleskey's sentence was imposed under Georgia sentencing procedures that focus discretion "on the particularized nature of the crime and the particularized characteristics of the individual defendant," we lawfully may presume that McCleskey's death sentence was not "wantonly and freakishly" imposed and thus that the sentence is not disproportionate within any recognized meaning under the Eighth Amendment.

Although our decision in *Gregg* as to the facial validity of the Georgia capital punishment statute appears to foreclose McCleskey's disproportionality argument, he further contends that the Georgia capital punishment system is arbitrary and capricious in *application*, and therefore his sentence is excessive, because racial considerations may influence capital sentencing decisions in Georgia. We now address this claim.

To evaluate McCleskey's challenge, we must examine exactly what the Baldus study may show. Even Professor Baldus does not contend that his statistics *prove* that race enters into any capital sentencing decisions or that race was a factor in McCleskey's particular case. Statistics at most may show only a likelihood that a particular factor entered into some decisions. There is, of course, some risk of racial prejudice influencing a jury's decision in a criminal case. There are similar risks that other kinds of prejudice will influence other criminal trials. The question "is at what point that risk becomes constitutionally unacceptable." McCleskey asks us to accept the likelihood allegedly shown by the Baldus study as the constitutional measure of an unacceptable risk of racial prejudice influencing capital sentencing decisions. This we decline to do.

∗ ∗ ∗

McCleskey's argument that the Constitution condemns the discretion allowed decisionmakers in the Georgia capital sentencing system is antithetical to the fundamental role of discretion in our criminal justice system. Discretion in the criminal justice system offers substantial benefits to the criminal defendant. Not only can a jury decline to impose the death sentence, it can decline to convict, or choose to convict of a lesser offense. ∗ ∗ ∗ Similarly, the capacity of prosecutorial discretion to provide individualized justice is "firmly entrenched in American law." ∗ ∗ ∗ Of course, "the power to be lenient [also] is the power to discriminate," but a capital-punishment system that did not allow for discretionary acts of leniency "would be totally alien to our notions of criminal justice." *Gregg.*

At most, the Baldus study indicates a discrepancy that appears to correlate with race. Apparent disparities in sentencing are an inevitable part of our criminal justice system. The discrepancy indicated by the Baldus study is "a far cry from the major systemic defects identified in *Furman,*" *Pulley v. Harris.* As this Court has recognized, any mode for determining guilt or punishment "has its weaknesses and the potential for misuse." Despite these imperfections, our consistent rule has been that constitutional guarantees are met when "the mode [for determining guilt or punishment] itself has been surrounded with safeguards to make it as fair as possible." Where the discretion that is fundamental to our criminal process is involved, we decline to assume that what is unexplained is invidious. In light of the safeguards designed to minimize racial bias in the process, the fundamental value of jury trial in our criminal justice system, and the benefits that discretion provides to criminal defendants, we hold that the Baldus study does not demonstrate a constitutionally significant risk of racial bias affecting the Georgia capital-sentencing process.[37]

37. Justice Brennan's eloquent dissent of course reflects his often repeated opposition to the death sentence. His views, that also are shared by Justice Marshall, are principled and entitled to respect. Nevertheless, since *Gregg* was decided in 1976, seven members of this Court consistently have upheld sentences of death under *Gregg*-type statutes providing for meticulous review of each sentence in both state and federal courts. The ultimate thrust of Justice Brennan's dissent is that *Gregg* and its progeny should be overruled. He does not, however, expressly call for the overruling of any prior decision. Rather, relying on the Baldus study, Justice Brennan, joined by Justices Marshall, Blackmun and Stevens, questions the very heart of our criminal justice system: the traditional discretion that prosecutors and juries necessarily must have.

We have held that discretion in a capital punishment system is necessary to satisfy the Constitution. *Woodson.* Yet, the dissent now claims that the "discretion afforded prosecutors and jurors in the Georgia capital sentencing system" violates the Constitution by creating "opportunities for racial considerations to influence criminal proceedings." The dissent contends that in Georgia "[n]o guidelines gov-

ern prosecutorial decisions [and] that Georgia provides juries with no list of aggravating and mitigating factors, nor any standard for balancing them against one another." Prosecutorial decisions necessarily involve both judgmental and factual decisions that vary from case to case. Thus, it is difficult to imagine guidelines that would produce the predictability sought by the dissent without sacrificing the discretion essential to a humane and fair system of criminal justice. Indeed, the dissent suggests no such guidelines for prosecutorial discretion.

The reference to the failure to provide juries with the list of aggravating and mitigating factors is curious. The aggravating circumstances are set forth in detail in the Georgia statute. The jury is not provided with a list of aggravating circumstances because not all of them are relevant to any particular crime. Instead, the prosecutor must choose the relevant circumstances and the State must prove to the jury that at least one exists beyond a reasonable doubt before the jury can even consider imposing the death sentence. It would be improper and often prejudicial to allow jurors to speculate as to aggravating

Two additional concerns inform our decision in this case. First, McCleskey's claim, taken to its logical conclusion, throws into serious question the principles that underlie our entire criminal justice system. The Eighth Amendment is not limited in application to capital punishment, but applies to all penalties. Thus, if we accepted McCleskey's claim that racial bias has impermissibly tainted the capital sentencing decision, we could soon be faced with similar claims as to other types of penalty. Moreover, the claim that his sentence rests on the irrelevant factor of race easily could be extended to apply to claims based on unexplained discrepancies that correlate to membership in other minority groups, and even to gender. Similarly, since McCleskey's claim relates to the race of his victim, other claims could apply with equally logical force to statistical disparities that correlate with the race or sex of other actors in the criminal justice system, such as defense attorneys, or judges. Also, there is no logical reason that such a claim need be limited to racial or sexual bias. If arbitrary and capricious punishment is the touchstone under the Eighth Amendment, such a claim could—at least in theory—be based upon any arbitrary variable, such as the defendant's facial characteristics, or the physical attractiveness of the defendant or the victim, that some statistical study indicates may be influential in jury decisionmaking. As these examples illustrate, there is no limiting principle to the type of challenge brought by McCleskey.[45] The Consti-

circumstances wholly without support in the evidence.

The dissent's argument that a list of mitigating factors is required is particularly anomalous. We have held that the Constitution requires that juries be allowed to consider "any relevant mitigating factor," even if it is not included in a statutory list. The dissent does not attempt to harmonize its criticism with this constitutional principle. The dissent also does not suggest any standard, much less a workable one, for balancing aggravating and mitigating factors. If capital defendants are to be treated as "uniquely individual human beings," Woodson, then discretion to evaluate and weigh the circumstances relevant to the particular defendant and the crime he committed is essential.

The dissent repeatedly emphasizes the need for "a uniquely high degree of rationality in imposing the death penalty." Again, no suggestion is made as to how greater "rationality" could be achieved under any type of statute that authorizes capital punishment. The Gregg-type statute imposes unprecedented safeguards in the special context of capital punishment. These include: (i) a bifurcated sentencing proceeding; (ii) the threshold requirement of one or more aggravating circumstances; and (iii) mandatory state Supreme Court review. All of these are administered pursuant to this Court's decisions interpreting the limits of the Eighth Amendment on the imposition of the death penalty, and all are subject to ultimate review by this Court. These ensure a degree of care in the imposition of the sentence of death that can be described only as unique. Given these safeguards already inherent in the imposition and review of capital sentences, the dissent's call

for greater rationality is no less than a claim that a capital-punishment system cannot be administered in accord with the Constitution. As we reiterate, the requirement of heightened rationality in the imposition of capital punishment does not "plac[e] totally unrealistic conditions on its use." Gregg.

45. Justice Stevens, who would not overrule Gregg, suggests in his dissent that the infirmities alleged by McCleskey could be remedied by narrowing the class of death-eligible defendants to categories identified by the Baldus study where "prosecutors consistently seek, and juries consistently impose, the death penalty without regard to the race of the victim or the race of the offender." This proposed solution is unconvincing. First, "consistently" is a relative term, and narrowing the category of death-eligible defendants would simply shift the borderline between those defendants who received the death penalty and those who did not. A borderline area would continue to exist and vary in its boundaries. Moreover, because the discrepancy between borderline cases would be difficult to explain, the system would likely remain open to challenge on the basis that the lack of explanation rendered the sentencing decisions unconstitutionally arbitrary.

Second, even assuming that a category with theoretically consistent results could be identified, it is difficult to imagine how Justice Stevens' proposal would or could operate on a case-by-case basis. Whenever a victim is white and the defendant is a member of a different race, what steps would a prosecutor be required to take—in addition to weighing the customary prosecutorial considerations—before concluding in the particular case that he lawfully could prosecute? In the absence

tution does not require that a State eliminate any demonstrable disparity that correlates with a potentially irrelevant factor in order to operate a criminal justice system that includes capital punishment. * * *

Second, McCleskey's arguments are best presented to the legislative bodies. It is not the responsibility—or indeed even the right—of this Court to determine the appropriate punishment for particular crimes. It is the legislatures, the elected representatives of the people, that are "constituted to respond to the will and consequently the moral values of the people." Legislatures also are better qualified to weigh and "evaluate the results of statistical studies in terms of their own local conditions and with a flexibility of approach that is not available to the courts," *Gregg.* Capital punishment is now the law in more than two thirds of our States. It is the ultimate duty of courts to determine on a case-by-case basis whether these laws are applied consistently with the Constitution. Despite McCleskey's wide ranging arguments that basically challenge the validity of capital punishment in our multi-racial society, the only question before us is whether in his case, the law of Georgia was properly applied. We agree with the [courts below] that this was carefully and correctly done in this case. * * *

JUSTICE BRENNAN, with whom JUSTICE MARSHALL joins, and with whom JUSTICE BLACKMUN and JUSTICE STEVENS join in all but Part I, dissenting.

I. Adhering to my view that the death penalty is in all circumstances cruel and unusual punishment forbidden by the Eighth and Fourteenth Amendments, I would vacate the decision below insofar as it left undisturbed the death sentence imposed in this case. The Court observes that "[t]he *Gregg* -type statute imposes unprecedented safeguards in the special context of capital punishment," which "ensure a degree of care in the imposition of the death penalty that can be described only as unique." Notwithstanding these efforts, murder defendants in Georgia with white victims are more than four times as likely to receive the death sentence as are defendants with black victims. Nothing could convey more powerfully the intractable reality of the death penalty: "that the effort to eliminate arbitrariness in the infliction of that ultimate sanction is so plainly doomed to failure that it—and the death penalty—must be abandoned altogether." *Godfrey v. Georgia* (Marshall, J., concurring).

Even if I did not hold this position, however, I would reverse [for] petitioner McCleskey has clearly demonstrated that his death sentence was imposed in violation of the Eighth and Fourteenth Amendments. While I join [the parts] of Justice Blackmun's dissenting opinion discussing petitioner's Fourteenth Amendment claim,[c] I write separately to emphasize how conclusively McCleskey has also demonstrated precisely the type of risk of irrationality in sentencing that we have consistently condemned in our Eighth Amendment jurisprudence.

of a current, Baldus-type study focused particularly on the community in which the crime was committed, where would he find a standard? Would the prosecutor have to review the prior decisions of community prosecutors and determine the types of cases in which juries in his jurisdiction "consistently" had imposed the death penalty when the victim was white and the defendant was of a different race? And must he rely solely on statistics? Even if such a study were feasible, would it be unlawful for the prosecutor, in making his final decision in a particular case, to consider the evidence of guilt and the presence of aggravating and mitigating factors? However conscientiously a prosecutor might attempt to identify death-eligible defendants under the dissent's suggestion, it would be a wholly speculative task at best, likely to result in less rather than more fairness and consistency in the imposition of the death penalty.

c. Justice Blackmun's dissenting opinion is discussed at p. 329 of this Supplement.

II. At some point in this case, Warren McCleskey doubtless asked his lawyer whether a jury was likely to sentence him to die. A candid reply to this question would have been disturbing. First, counsel would have to tell McCleskey that few of the details of the crime or of McCleskey's past criminal conduct were more important than the fact that his victim was white. Furthermore, counsel would feel bound to tell McCleskey that defendants charged with killing white victims in Georgia are 4.3 times as likely to be sentenced to death as defendants charged with killing blacks. In addition, frankness would compel the disclosure that it was morely likely than not that the race of McCleskey's victim would determine whether he received a death sentence: 6 of every 11 defendants convicted of killing a white person would not have received the death penalty if their victims had been black, while, among defendants with aggravating and mitigating factors comparable to McCleskey, 20 of every 34 would not have been sentenced to die if their victims had been black. Finally, the assessment would not be complete without the information that cases involving black defendants and white victims are more likely to result in a death sentence than cases featuring any other racial combination of defendant and victim. The story could be told in a variety of ways, but McCleskey could not fail to grasp its essential narrative line: there was a significant chance that race would play a prominent role in determining if he lived or died.

The Court today holds that Warren McCleskey's sentence was constitutionally imposed. It finds no fault in a system in which lawyers must tell their clients that race casts a large shadow on the capital sentencing process. The Court arrives at this conclusion by stating that the Baldus study cannot "*prove* that race enters into any capital sentencing decisions or that race was a factor in McCleskey's particular case." Since, according to Professor Baldus, we cannot say "to a moral certainty" that race influenced a decision, we can identify only "a likelihood that a particular factor entered into some decisions" and "a discrepancy that appears to correlate with race." This "likelihood" and "discrepancy," holds the Court, is insufficient to establish a constitutional violation. The Court reaches this conclusion by placing four factors on the scales opposite McCleskey's evidence: the desire to encourage sentencing discretion, the existence of "statutory safeguards" in the Georgia scheme, the fear of encouraging widespread challenges to other sentencing decisions, and the limits of the judicial role. The Court's evaluation of the significance of petitioner's evidence is fundamentally at odds with our consistent concern for rationality in capital sentencing, and the considerations that the majority invokes to discount that evidence cannot justify ignoring its force.

III. It is important to emphasize at the outset that the Court's observation that McCleskey cannot prove the influence of race on any particular sentencing decision is irrelevant in evaluating his Eighth Amendment claim. Since *Furman*, the Court has been concerned with the *risk* of the imposition of an arbitrary sentence, rather than the proven fact of one. * * * This emphasis on risk acknowledges the difficulty of divining the jury's motivation in an individual case. In addition, it reflects the fact that concern for arbitrariness focuses on the rationality of the system as a whole, and that a system that features a significant probability that sentencing decisions are influenced by impermissible considerations cannot be regarded as rational.[1] As we said in *Gregg*, "the

---

1. Once we can identify a pattern of arbitrary sentencing outcomes, we can say that a defendant runs a risk of being sentenced arbitrarily. It is thus immaterial whether the operation of an impermissible influence such as race is intentional. While the Equal Protection Clause forbids racial discrimination, and intent may be critical in a successful

petitioner looks to the sentencing system as a whole (as the Court did in *Furman* and we do today)": a constitutional violation is established if a plaintiff demonstrates a "*pattern* of arbitrary and capricious sentencing" (emphasis added).

* * *

Defendants challenging their death sentences thus never have had to prove that impermissible considerations have actually infected sentencing decisions. We have required instead that they establish that the system under which they were sentenced posed a significant risk of such an occurrence. McCleskey's claim does differ, however, in one respect from these earlier cases: it is the first to base a challenge not on speculation about how a system *might* operate, but on empirical documentation of how it *does* operate.

The Court assumes the statistical validity of the Baldus study, and acknowledges that McCleskey has demonstrated a risk that racial prejudice plays a role in capital sentencing in Georgia. Nonetheless, it finds the probability of prejudice insufficient to create constitutional concern. Close analysis of the Baldus study, however, in light of both statistical principles and human experience, reveals that the risk that race influenced McCleskey's sentence is intolerable by any imaginable standard.

The Baldus study indicates that, after taking into account some 230 nonracial factors that might legitimately influence a sentencer, the jury *more likely than not* would have spared McCleskey's life had his victim been black. The study distinguishes between those cases in which (1) the jury exercises virtually no discretion because the strength or weakness of aggravating factors usually suggests that only one outcome is appropriate; and (2) cases reflecting an "intermediate" level of aggravation, in which the jury has considerable discretion in choosing a sentence. McCleskey's case falls into the intermediate range. In such cases, death is imposed in 34% of white-victim crimes and 14% of black-victim crimes, a difference of 139% in the rate of imposition of the death penalty. In other words, just under 59%—almost 6 in 10—defendants comparable to McCleskey would not have received the death penalty if their victims had been black.

Furthermore, even examination of the sentencing system as a whole, factoring in those cases in which the jury exercises little discretion, indicates the influence of race on capital sentencing. For the Georgia system as a whole, race accounts for a six percentage point difference in the rate at which capital punishment is imposed. Since death is imposed in 11% of all white-victim cases, the rate in comparably aggravated black-victim cases is 5%. The rate of capital sentencing in a white-victim case is thus 120% greater than the rate in a black-victim case. Put another way, over half—55%—of defendants in white-victim crimes in Georgia would not have been sentenced to die if their victims had been black. Of the more than 200 variables potentially relevant to a sentencing decision, race of the victim is a powerful explanation for variation in death sentence rates—as powerful as nonracial aggravating factors such as a prior murder conviction or acting as the principal planner of the homicide.

claim under that provision, the Eighth Amendment has its own distinct focus: whether punishment comports with social standards of rationality and decency. It may be, as in this case, that on occasion an influence that makes punishment arbitrary is also proscribed under another constitutional provision. That does not mean, however, that the standard for determining an Eighth Amendment violation is superceded by the standard for determining a violation under this other provision. Thus, the fact that McCleskey presents a viable Equal Protection claim does not require that he demonstrate intentional racial discrimination to establish his Eighth Amendment claim.

These adjusted figures are only the most conservative indication of the risk that race will influence the death sentences of defendants in Georgia. Data unadjusted for the mitigating or aggravating effect of other factors show an even more pronounced disparity by race. The capital sentencing rate for all white-victim cases was almost *11 times* greater than the rate for black-victim cases. Furthermore, blacks who kill whites are sentenced to death at nearly *22 times* the rate of blacks who kill blacks, and more than *7 times* the rate of whites who kill blacks. In addition, prosecutors seek the death penalty for 70% of black defendants with white victims, but for only 15% of black defendants with black victims, and only 19% of white defendants with black victims. Since our decision upholding the Georgia capital-sentencing system in *Gregg*, the State has executed 7 persons. All of the 7 were convicted of killing whites, and 6 of the 7 executed were black. Such execution figures are especially striking in light of the fact that, during the period encompassed by the Baldus study, only 9.2% of Georgia homicides involved black defendants and white victims, while 60.7% involved black victims.

McCleskey's statistics have particular force because most of them are the product of sophisticated multiple-regression analysis. Such analysis is designed precisely to identify patterns in the aggregate, even though we may not be able to reconstitute with certainty any individual decision that goes to make up that pattern. Multiple-regression analysis is particularly well-suited to identify the influence of impermissible considerations in sentencing, since it is able to control for permissible factors that may explain an apparent arbitrary pattern. While the decision-making process of a body such as a jury may be complex, the Baldus study provides a massive compilation of the details that are most relevant to that decision. * * *

The statistical evidence in this case thus relentlessly documents the risk that McCleskey's sentence was influenced by racial considerations. This evidence shows that there is a better than even chance in Georgia that race will influence the decision to impose the death penalty: a majority of defendants in white-victim crimes would not have been sentenced to die if their victims had been black. In determining whether this risk is acceptable, our judgment must be shaped by the awareness that "[t]he risk of racial prejudice infecting a capital sentencing proceeding is especially serious in light of the complete finality of the death sentence" [and] that "[i]t is of vital importance to the defendant and to the community that any decision to impose the death sentence be, and appear to be, based on reason rather than caprice or emotion." In determining the guilt of a defendant, a state must prove its case beyond a reasonable doubt. That is, we refuse to convict if the chance of error is simply less likely than not. Surely, we should not be willing to take a person's life if the chance that his death sentence was irrationally imposed is *more* likely than not. In light of the gravity of the interest at stake, petitioner's statistics on their face are a powerful demonstration of the type of risk that our Eighth Amendment jurisprudence has consistently condemned.

Evaluation of McCleskey's evidence cannot rest solely on the numbers themselves. We must also ask whether the conclusion suggested by those numbers is consonant with our understanding of history and human experience. Georgia's legacy of a race-conscious criminal justice system, as well as this Court's own recognition of the persistent danger that racial attitudes may affect criminal proceedings, indicate that McCleskey's claim is not a fanciful product of mere statistical artifice. * * *

This historical review of Georgia criminal law is not intended as a bill of indictment calling the State to account for past transgressions. Citation of past practices does not justify the automatic condemnation of current ones. But it would be unrealistic to ignore the influence of history in assessing the plausible implications of McCleskey's evidence. "[A]mericans share a historical experience that has resulted in individuals within the culture ubiquitously attaching a significance to race that is irrational and often outside their awareness." Lawrence, *The Id, The Ego, and Equal Protection: Reckoning With Unconscious Racism*, 39 Stan.L.Rev. 327 (1987).

* * * Our cases reflect a realization of the myriad of opportunities for racial considerations to influence criminal proceedings: in the exercise of peremptory challenges; in the selection of the grand jury; in the selection of the petit jury; in the exercise of prosecutorial discretion; in the conduct of argument; and in the conscious or unconscious bias of jurors.

The discretion afforded prosecutors and jurors in the Georgia capital-sentencing system creates such opportunities. No guidelines govern prosecutorial decisions to seek the death penalty, and Georgia provides juries with no list of aggravating and mitigating factors, nor any standard for balancing them against one another. Once a jury identifies one aggravating factor, it has complete discretion in choosing life or death, and need not articulate its basis for selecting life imprisonment. The Georgia sentencing system therefore provides considerable opportunity for racial considerations, however subtle and unconscious, to influence charging and sentencing decisions.

History and its continuing legacy thus buttress the probative force of McCleskey's statistics. Formal dual criminal laws may no longer be in effect, and intentional discrimination may no longer be prominent. Nonetheless, as we acknowledged in *Turner v. Murray*, 476 U.S. 28, 106 S.Ct. 1683, 90 L.Ed.2d 27 (1986), "subtle, less consciously held racial attitudes" continue to be of concern, and the Georgia system gives such attitudes considerable room to operate. The conclusions drawn from McCleskey's statistical evidence are therefore consistent with the lessons of social experience.

The majority thus misreads our Eighth Amendment jurisprudence in concluding that McCleskey has not demonstrated a degree of risk sufficient to raise constitutional concern. The determination of the significance of his evidence is at its core an exercise in human moral judgment, not a mechanical statistical analysis. It must first and foremost be informed by awareness of the fact that death is irrevocable, and that as a result "the qualitative difference of death from all other punishments requires a greater degree of scrutiny of the capital sentencing determination." For this reason, we have demanded a uniquely high degree of rationality in imposing the death penalty. A capital-sentencing system in which race more likely than not plays a role does not meet this standard. It is true that every nuance of decision cannot be statistically captured, nor can any individual judgment be plumbed with absolute certainty. Yet the fact that we must always act without the illumination of complete knowledge cannot induce paralysis when we confront what is literally an issue of life and death. Sentencing data, history, and experience all counsel that Georgia has provided insufficient assurance of the heightened rationality we have required in order to take a human life.

IV. The Court cites four reasons for shrinking from the implications of McCleskey's evidence: the desirability of discretion for actors in the criminal-justice system, the existence of statutory safeguards against abuse of that discretion, the potential consequences for broader challenges to criminal sentencing, and an understanding of the contours of the judicial role. While these concerns underscore the need for sober deliberation, they do not justify rejecting evidence as convincing as McCleskey has presented.

The Court maintains that petitioner's claim "is antithetical to the fundamental role of discretion in our criminal justice system." It states that "[w]here the discretion that is fundamental to our criminal process is involved, we decline to assume that what is unexplained is invidious." Reliance on race in imposing capital punishment, however, is antithetical to the very rationale for granting sentencing discretion. Discretion is a means, not an end. * * *

Considering the race of a defendant or victim in deciding if the death penalty should be imposed is completely at odds with [the] concern that an individual be evaluated as a unique human being. Decisions influenced by race rest in part on a categorical assessment of the worth of human beings according to color, insensitive to whatever qualities the individuals in question may possess. Enhanced willingness to impose the death sentence on black defendants, or diminished willingness to render such a sentence when blacks are victims, reflects a devaluation of the lives of black persons. When confronted with evidence that race more likely than not plays such a role in a capital-sentencing system, it is plainly insufficient to say that the importance of discretion demands that the risk be higher before we will act—for in such a case the very end that discretion is designed to serve is being undermined. * * *

The Court also declines to find McCleskey's evidence sufficient in view of "the safeguards designed to minimize racial bias in the [capital sentencing] process." * * * It is clear that *Gregg* bestowed no permanent approval on the Georgia system. It simply held that the State's statutory safeguards were assumed sufficient to channel discretion without evidence otherwise.

It has now been over 13 years since Georgia adopted the provisions upheld in *Gregg*. Professor Baldus and his colleagues have compiled data on almost 2500 homicides committed during the period 1973–1979. They have taken into account the influence of 230 nonracial variables, using a multitude of data from the State itself, and have produced striking evidence that the odds of being sentenced to death are significantly greater than average if a defendant is black or his or her victim is white. The challenge to the Georgia system is not speculative or theoretical; it is empirical. As a result, the Court cannot rely on the statutory safeguards in discounting McCleskey's evidence, for it is the very effectiveness of those safeguards that such evidence calls into question. * * *

The Court next states that its unwillingness to regard the petitioner's evidence as sufficient is based in part on the fear that recognition of McCleskey's claim would open the door to widespread challenges to all aspects of criminal sentencing. Taken on its face, such a statement seems to suggest a fear of too much justice. Yet surely the majority would acknowledge that if striking evidence indicated that other minority groups, or women, or even persons with blond hair, were disproportionately sentenced to death, such a state of affairs would be repugnant to deeply rooted conceptions of fairness. The prospect that there may be more widespread abuse than McCleskey documents may be dismaying, but it does not justify complete abdication of our judicial role. * * *

In fairness, the Court's fear that McCleskey's claim is an invitation to descend a slippery slope also rests on the realization that any humanly imposed system of penalties will exhibit some imperfection. Yet to reject McCleskey's powerful evidence on this basis is to ignore both the qualitatively different character of the death penalty and the particular repugnance of racial discrimination, considerations which may properly be taken into account in determining whether various punishments are "cruel and unusual." Furthermore, it fails to take account of the unprecedented refinement and strength of the Baldus study.

* * *

The Court also maintains that accepting McCleskey's claim would pose a threat to all sentencing because of the prospect that a correlation might be demonstrated between sentencing outcomes and other personal characteristics. Again, such a view is indifferent to the considerations that enter into a determination of whether punishment is "cruel and unusual." Race is a consideration whose influence is expressly constitutionally proscribed. We have expressed a moral commitment, as embodied in our fundamental law, that this specific characteristic should not be the basis for allotting burdens and benefits.

* * *

Certainly, a factor that we would regard as morally irrelevant, such as hair color, at least theoretically could be associated with sentencing results to such an extent that we would regard as arbitrary a system in which that factor played a significant role. [However,] the evaluation of evidence suggesting such a correlation must be informed not merely by statistics, but by history and experience. One could hardly contend that this nation has on the basis of hair color inflicted upon persons deprivation comparable to that imposed on the basis of race. Recognition of this fact would necessarily influence the evaluation of data suggesting the influence of hair color on sentencing, and would require evidence of statistical correlation even more powerful than that presented by the Baldus study. * * *

Finally, the Court justifies its rejection of McCleskey's claim by cautioning against usurpation of the legislatures' role in devising and monitoring criminal punishment. The Court is, of course, correct to emphasize the gravity of constitutional intervention and the importance that it be sparingly employed. The fact that "[c]apital punishment is now the law in more than two thirds of our States," however, does not diminish the fact that capital punishment is the most awesome act that a State can perform. The judiciary's role in this society counts for little if the use of governmental power to extinguish life does not elicit close scrutiny. [The Court] fulfills, rather than disrupts, the scheme of separation of powers by closely scrutinizing the imposition of the death penalty, for no decision of a society is more deserving of the "sober second thought." * * *

The Court's decision today will not change what attorneys in Georgia tell other Warren McCleskeys about their chances of execution. Nothing will soften the harsh message they must convey, nor alter the prospect that race undoubtedly will continue to be a topic of discussion. McCleskey's evidence will not have obtained judicial acceptance, but that will not affect what is said on death row. However many criticisms of today's decision may be rendered, these painful conversations will serve as the most eloquent dissents of all.[d]

---

d. In a separate dissent, Justice Blackmun, with whom Marshall and Stevens, JJ., joined and with whom Brennan, J., joined in all but Part IV–B (maintaining that acceptance of petitioner's claim would not eliminate capital punishment in Georgia because "in extremely aggravated murders the risk of discriminatory enforcement of the death penalty is minimized"), concluded that if one assumes that the data presented by petitioner is valid, "as we must in light of the Court of Appeals' assumption, there exists in the Georgia capital-sentencing scheme a risk of racially based discrimination that is so acute that it violates the Eighth Amendment." But the great bulk of Justice Blackmun's opinion was devoted to

For strong criticism of *McCleskey*, see S. Gross & R. Mauro, *Death & Discrimination: Racial Disparities in Capital Sentencing*, chs. 10 & 11 (1988); Burt, *Disorder in the Court: The Death Penalty and the Constitution*, 85 Mich.L. Rev. 1741, 1795–1800 (1987); Carter, *When Victims Happen to Be Black*, 97 Yale L.J. 420, 440–47 (1988); R. Kennedy, *Race, Reform, and Retrenchment: Transformation and Legitimation in Antidiscrimination Law*, 101 Harv.L.Rev. 1388 (1988); V. Berger, Book Review, 87 Colum.L.Rev. 1301, 1320–24 (1987); *Developments in the Law—Race and the Criminal Process*, 101 Harv.L.Rev. 1472, 1603–26 (1988); Notes, 101 Harv.L.Rev. 119, 158 (1987), 62 Notre Dame L.Rev. 688 (1987). But see Scheidegger, *Capital Punishment in 1987: The Puzzle Nears Completion*, 15 W. State U. L.Rev. 95, 121–25 (1987).

"The harsh criticism directed at the Supreme Court's decision," observes Professor Kennedy, supra at 1389 n. 11, "is, to a large extent, a reprise of the excoriating commentary that greeted the lower courts' handling of the case." In this connection, see, e.g., W. White, *The Death Penalty in the Eighties: An Examination of the Modern System of Capital Punishment* 129–35 (1987); Gross, *Race and Death: The Judicial Evaluation of Evidence of Discrimination in Capital Sentencing*, 18 U.C. Davis L.Rev. 1275 (1985); Comment, 41 U. Miami L.Rev. 295 (1986).

CON LAW: P. 591, end of section

AMER CON: P. 396, end of section

RTS & LIB: P. 259, end of section

In BOOTH v. MARYLAND, 482 U.S. 496, 107 S.Ct. 2529, 96 L.Ed.2d 440 (1987), a 5–4 majority, per POWELL, J., held that the Eighth Amendment prohibits a capital sentencing jury from considering a "victim impact statement." Defendant had robbed and murdered an elderly couple, the Bronsteins. After he had been convicted of murder, the jury considered a victim impact statement (VIS), describing the effect of the crime on the Bronsteins and their family, before sentencing defendant to death. Many of the relatives' comments emphasized the Bronsteins' outstanding personal qualities and how deeply they would be missed. Other parts of the VIS described the emotional trauma suffered by members of

a discussion of why he believed the Georgia capital punishment system violates the Equal Protection Clause. See p. 329 of this Supplement.

In a third dissenting opinion, Justice Stevens, joined by Blackmun, J., maintained that the studies supporting McCleskey's claim "demonstrate a strong probability that [his] sentencing jury * * * was influenced by the fact that McCleskey is black and his victim was white, and that [the jury's sense that a defendant has lost his moral entitlement to live] would not have been generated if he had killed a member of his own race. This sort of disparity is constitutionally intolerable."

Justice Stevens called the majority's evident fear "that the acceptance of McCleskey's claim would sound the death knell for capital punishment in Georgia" "unfounded": "One of the lessons of the Baldus study is that there exist certain categories of extremely serious crimes for which proecutors consistently seek, and juries consistently impose, the death penalty without regard to the race of the victim or the race of the offender. If Georgia were to narrow the class of death-eligible defendants to those categories, the danger of arbitrary and discriminatory imposition of the death penalty would be significantly decreased, if not eradicated."

Although Justice Stevens would reverse, he believed that further proceedings were needed to determine whether McCleskey's death sentence should be set aside: "First, the Court of Appeals must decide whether the Baldus study is valid. I am persuaded that it is, but orderly procedure requires that the Court of Appeals address this issue before we actually decide the question. Second, it is necessary for the District Court to determine whether the particular facts of McCleskey's crime and his background place this case within the range of cases that present an unacceptable risk that race played a decisive role in McCleskey's sentencing."

the family and the personal problems they had faced as a result of the crimes. The Court ruled that such factors could not be taken into account in deciding whether a person should receive the death penalty:

"When carrying out [its] task, the [capital sentencing jury] is required to focus on the defendant as a 'uniquely individual human being.' The focus of a VIS, however, is not on the defendant, but on the character and reputation of the victim and the effect on his family. These factors may be wholly unrelated to the blameworthiness of a particular defendant. [This] evidence thus could divert the jury's attention away from the defendant's background and record, and the circumstances of the crime. * * *

"As evidenced by [the] VIS in this case, the family members were articulate and persuasive in expressing their grief and the extent of their loss. But in some cases the victim will not leave behind a family, or the family members may be less articulate in describing their feelings even though their sense of loss is equally severe. The fact that the imposition of the death sentence may turn on such distinctions illustrates the danger of allowing juries to consider this information. Certainly the degree to which a family is willing and able to express its grief is irrelevant to the decision whether a defendant, who may merit the death penalty, should live or die. * * *

"We also note that it would be difficult—if not impossible—to provide a fair opportunity to rebut such evidence without shifting the focus of the sentencing hearing away from the defendant. A threshold problem is that victim impact information is not easily susceptible to rebuttal. * * * Putting aside the strategic risks of attacking the victim's character before the jury, in appropriate cases the defendant presumably would be permitted to put on evidence that the victim was of dubious moral character, was unpopular, or was ostracized from his family. The prospect of a 'mini-trial' on the victim's character is more than simply unappealing; it could well distract the sentencing jury from its constitutionally required task—determining whether the death penalty is appropriate in light of the background and record of the accused and the particular circumstances of the crime. We thus reject the contention that the presence or absence of emotional distress of the victim's family, or the victim's personal characteristics, are proper sentencing considerations in a capital case.

"The second type of information presented to the jury in the VIS was the family members' opinions and characterizations of the crimes. The Bronsteins' son, for example, stated that his parents were 'butchered like animals' * * *.

"One can understand the grief and anger of the family caused by the brutal murders in this case, and there is no doubt that jurors are generally aware of these feelings. But the formal presentation of this information by the State can serve no other purpose than to inflame the jury and divert it from deciding the case on the relevant evidence concerning the crime and the defendant. [A]ny decision to impose the death sentence must 'be, and appear to be, based on reason rather than caprice or emotion.' " [a]

Dissenting JUSTICE WHITE, joined by Rehnquist, C.J., and O'Connor and Scalia, JJ., could not see "anything 'cruel or unusual' or otherwise unconstitu-

---

a. The Court pointed out that its decision "is guided by the fact that death is a 'punishment different from all other sanctions.'" After noting that "[a]t least 36 States permit the use of victim impact statements in some contexts, reflecting a legislative judgment that the effect of the crime on victims should have a place in the criminal justice system" and that "Congress also has provided for victim participation in federal criminal cases," the Court added: "We imply no opinion as to the use of these statements in non-capital cases."

tional about the legislature's decision to use victim impact statements in capital sentencing hearings":

"[The judgment of the Maryland legislature] is entitled to particular deference; determinations of appropriate sentencing considerations are 'peculiarly questions of legislative policy' and the Court should recognize that '[i]n a democratic society legislatures, not courts, are constituted to respond to the will and consequently the moral values of the people' (quoting *Furman*, Burger, C.J., dissenting).

"* * * I fail to see why the State cannot, if it chooses, include as a sentencing consideration the particularized harm that an individual's murder causes to the rest of society and in particular to his family. To the extent that the Court is concerned that sentencing juries might be moved by victim impact statements to rely on impermissible factors such as the race of the victim, there is no showing that the statements in this case encouraged this, nor should we lightly presume such misconduct on the jury's part.

"The Court's reliance on the alleged arbitrariness that can result from the differing ability of victims' families to articulate their sense of loss is a makeweight consideration: No two prosecutors have exactly the same ability to present their arguments to the jury; no two witnesses have exactly the same ability to communicate the facts; but there is no requirement in capital cases that the evidence and argument be reduced to the lowest common denominator.

"The supposed problems arising from a defendant's rebuttal of victim impact statements are speculative and unconnected to the facts of this case. No doubt a capital defendant must be allowed to introduce relevant evidence in rebuttal to a victim impact statement, but Maryland has in no wise limited the right of defendants in this regard. Petitioner introduced no such rebuttal evidence, probably because he considered, wisely, that it was not in his best interest to do so. At bottom, the Court's view seems to be that it is somehow unfair to confront a defendant with an account of the loss his deliberate act has caused the victim's family and society. I do not share that view, but even if I did I would be unwilling to impose it on States that see matters differently."

In a separate dissent, JUSTICE SCALIA, joined by Rehnquist, C.J., and White and O'Connor, JJ., observed:

"The Court's opinion does not explain why a defendant's *eligibility* for the death sentence can (*and always does*) turn upon considerations not relevant to his moral guilt. If a bank robber aims his gun at a guard, pulls the trigger, and kills his target, he may be put to death. If the gun unexpectedly misfires, he may not. His moral guilt in both cases is identical, but his responsibility in the former is greater. Less than two months ago, we held that two brothers who planned and assisted in their father's escape from prison could be sentenced to death because in the course of the escape their father and an accomplice murdered a married couple and two children. *Tison* [p. 152 of this Supplement]. Had their father allowed the victims to live, the brothers could not be put to death; but because he decided to kill, the brothers may. The difference between life and death for these two defendants was thus a matter 'wholly unrelated to the[ir] blameworthiness.' But it was related to their personal responsibility, i.e., to the degree of harm that they had caused. In sum, the principle upon which the Court's opinion rests—that the imposition of capital punishment is to be determined solely on the basis of moral guilt—does not exist, neither in the text of the Constitution, nor in the historic practices of our society, nor even in the opinions of this Court. * * *

"To require, as we have, that all mitigating factors which render capital punishment a harsh penalty in the particular case be placed before the sentencing authority, while simultaneously requiring, as we do today, that evidence of much of the human suffering the defendant has inflicted be suppressed, is in effect to prescribe a debate on the appropriateness of the capital penalty with one side muted." [b]

SECTION: PROCEDURAL DUE PROCESS IN NON–CRIMINAL CASES

WHAT KIND OF HEARING—AND WHEN?

CON LAW: P. 619, after *Goss*

AMER CON: P. 413, at end

RTS & LIB: P. 287, after *Goss*

In BETHEL SCHOOL DIST. v. FRASER, p. 237 of this Supplement, speaking at a school-sponsored assembly attended by 600 students, many of whom were 14–year olds, respondent gave a speech nominating a fellow student for student government office. During his speech, respondent referred to his candidate, as the Court described it, "in terms of an elaborate, graphic and explicit sexual metaphor." Some students hooted and yelled; some simulated the sexual activities alluded to in respondent's speech. The morning after the assembly, a school official notified respondent that the school considered his speech a violation of the school's "disruptive conduct rule" published in the school handbook, which prohibited "conduct [that] materially and substantially interferes with the educational process," "including the use of obscene, profane language or gestures." Respondent was given a chance to explain his conduct, and he admitted that he had deliberately used sexual innuendo in the speech. He was then suspended for three days. (He served two days of his suspension, but was allowed to return to school on the third day.)

Respondent sought review of this disciplinary action through the school district's grievance procedure. A hearing officer concluded that the speech fell within the ordinary meaning of "obscene," as used in the disruptive-conduct rule and affirmed the discipline. The Court, per BURGER, C.J., rejected respondent's contention that his suspension violated due process because he had no way of knowing that his speech would subject him to disciplinary sanctions: "Given the school's need to be able to impose disciplinary sanctions for a wide range of unanticipated conduct disruptive of the educational process, the school disciplinary rules need not be as detailed as a criminal code which imposes criminal sanctions. Cf. *Arnett*. Two days' suspension from school does not rise to the level of a penal sanction calling for the full panoply of procedural due process protections applicable to a criminal prosecution. Cf. *Goss*. The school disciplinary rule proscribing 'obscene' language and the prespeech admonition of teachers gave adequate warning to Fraser that his lewd speech could subject him to sanctions."

STEVENS, J., dissenting, maintained that the discipline imposed on Fraser "was sufficiently serious to justify invocation of the School District's grievance procedure. See *Goss*. Stevens, J., considered and rejected three possible theo-

---

b. See also *South Carolina v. Gathers*, ___ U.S. ___, 109 S.Ct. 2207, ___ L.Ed.2d ___ (1989), applying *Booth* to prohibit prosecutor's comments on personal qualities of murder victim.

ries for concluding that Fraser should have known that he would be punished for giving the speech: (1) The evidence in the record, as interpreted by the lower federal courts, "makes it perfectly clear that respondent's speech was not 'conduct' prohibited by the disciplinary rule"; (2) the three teachers' responses, when respondent reviewed the text of his speech with them before he gave it, "certainly did not give him any better notice of the likelihood of discipline than did the student handbook itself"; (3) it could hardly be said that the impropriety was "so obvious that no specific notice was required."

Chapter

FREEDOM OF EXPRESSION AND ASSOCIATION

SECTION: WHAT SPEECH SHOULD BE PROTECTED AND HOW MUCH PROTECTION SHOULD IT GET?

ADVOCACY OF ILLEGAL ACTION

A MODERN "RESTATEMENT"

CON LAW: P. 674, addition to fn. a

AMER CON: P. 459, addition to fn. a

RTS & LIB: P. 342, addition to fn. a

See *Rankin v. McPherson*, p. 214 of this Supplement.

REPUTATION AND PRIVACY

PUBLIC OFFICIALS AND SEDITIOUS LIBEL

CON LAW: P. 682, add to fn. a

AMER CON: P. 467, add to fn. a

RTS & LIB: P. 350, add to fn. a

ANDERSON v. LIBERTY LOBBY, INC., 477 U.S. 242, 106 S.Ct. 2505, 91 L.Ed.2d 202 (1986), per WHITE, J., held that the convincing clarity requirement must be considered by a federal court in ruling on a motion for summary judgment under Federal Rule of Civil Procedure 56. That is, " 'giving full play to the right of the jury to determine credibility, weigh the evidence, and draw justifiable inferences of fact,' " the judge is to determine whether the evidence presented is of sufficient quantum and quality that "a reasonable jury might find that actual malice had been shown with convincing clarity." BRENNAN, J., dis-senting, and REHNQUIST, J., joined by Burger, C.J., dissenting, argued that the convincing clarity requirement was not relevant to a summary judgment motion because a judge could not apply it without impermissibly weighing evidence, drawing inferences, or determining credibility.

For insight into the difficulties of applying an "independent judgment" standard, see *Harte–Hanks Communications v. Connaughton*, ___ U.S. ___, 109 S.Ct. 2678, ___ L.Ed.2d ___ (1989).

PRIVATE INDIVIDUALS AND PUBLIC FIGURES

CON LAW: P. 699, after note 1

AMER CON: P. 484, after note 1

RTS & LIB: P. 367, after note 1

PHILADELPHIA NEWSPAPERS, INC. v. HEPPS, 475 U.S. 767, 106 S.Ct. 1558, 89 L.Ed.2d 783 (1986), per O'CONNOR, J., held that "at least when a newspaper publishes speech of public concern," a private-figure plaintiff alleging defamation has the burden of proving falsity. The Court noted that it had "no occasion to consider the quantity of proof of falsity that a private-figure plaintiff must present to recover damages. Nor need we consider what standards would apply if the plaintiff sues a nonmedia defendant,[a] or if a State were to provide a plaintiff with the opportunity to obtain a judgment that declared the speech at issue to be false but did not give rise to liability for damages."

STEVENS, J., joined by Burger, C.J., and White and Rehnquist, JJ., dissented, noting that since the plaintiff under *Gertz* was already required to show at least fault, "the only litigants [who] will benefit from today's decision are those who act negligently or maliciously. [A]s long as publishers are protected by the requirement that the plaintiff has the burden of proving fault, there can be little, if any, basis for a concern that a significant amount of true speech will be deterred unless the private person victimized by a malicious libel can also carry the burden of proving falsity. The Court's decision trades on the good names of private individuals with little First Amendment coin to show for it."

CON LAW: P. 700, after note 5

AMER CON: P. 485, after note 5

RTS & LIB: P. 368, after note 5

BORK, J.—CONCURRING IN *OLLMAN v. EVANS*

SCALIA, J.—DISSENTING IN *OLLMAN v. EVANS*

Ollman v. Evans, 750 F.2d 970 (D.C.Cir.1984) (en banc) addressed the difficult question of what standards should guide lower courts in separating "fact" from "opinion" in the libel context. The particular question discussed by the many opinions in the case was whether the following statement about a prominent Marxist political scientist [a] by columnists Evans and Novak was fact or opinion: "[Ollman's] pamphleteering is hooted at by one political scientist in a major eastern university, whose scholarship and reputation as a liberal are well known. *'Ollman has no status within the profession,* but is a pure and simple activist,' he said." (Emphasis added.) The majority opinion by Starr, J., determined that the statement was one of opinion, not of fact, after examining the common usage of the specific language, the extent to which the statement was capable of being verified objectively as true or false, the full context of the statement in the column, and the broader social context in which the statement appeared. Beyond the fact-opinion issue, of general interest is the exchange between concurring Judge (now Supreme Court nominee) Bork and dissenting

---

a. Brennan, J., concurring, joined by Blackmun, J., wrote separately to note that he would not distinguish between media and nonmedia defendants.

a. A letter of Ollman's counsel demanding retraction by Evans and Novak stated that "a poll of 317 leading and representative political scientists" ranked him "10th in the entire field of all political scientists in terms of occupational prestige."

Judge (now Justice) Scalia about defamation, the first amendment and the role of the judiciary.

BORK, J., concurring, argued that "the functional meaning of the challenged statement as shown by its context and its qualities [was] 'recognizable political hyperbole.'" He noted that "Ollman, by his own actions, entered a political arena in which heated discourse was to be expected and must be protected; the 'fact' proposed to be tried is in truth wholly unsuitable for trial, which further imperils free discussion; the statement is not of the kind that would usually be accepted as one of hard fact and appeared in a context that further indicated it was rhetorical hyperbole." More broadly, he maintained that defamation law imposed no "sharp dichotomy" between opinion and fact and certainly was not to be controlled by "grammatical analysis": "If placing the bare assertion in question into one of two compartments labelled 'opinion' and 'fact' were the only issue we were allowed to consider, I would join the dissent. But I do not think these simple categories, semantically defined, with their flat and barren descriptive nature, their utter lack of subtlety and resonance, are nearly sufficient to encompass the rich variety of factors that should go into analysis when there is a sense, which I certainly have here, that values meant to be protected by the first amendment are threatened.

"The temptation to adhere to sharply-defined categories is understandable. Judges generalize, they articulate concepts, they enunciate such things as four-factor frame-works, three-pronged tests, and two-tiered analyses in an effort, laudable by and large, to bring order to a universe of unruly happenings and to give guidance for the future to themselves and to others. But it is certain that life will bring up cases whose facts simply cannot be handled by purely verbal formulas, or at least not handled with any sophistication and feeling for the underlying values at stake. When such a case appears and a court attempts nevertheless to force the old construct upon the new situation, the result is mechanical jurisprudence. Here we face such a case, and it seems to me better to revert to first principles than to employ categories which, in these circumstances, inadequately enforce the first amendment's design.

"Viewed from that perspective, the statement challenged in this lawsuit, in terms of the policies of the first amendment, is functionally more like an 'opinion' than a 'fact' and should not be actionable. [U]nless we continue to develop doctrine to fit first amendment concerns, we are remitted to old categories which, applied woodenly, do not address modern problems. * * *

"The American press is extraordinarily free and vigorous, as it should be. It should be, not because it is free of inaccuracy, oversimplification, and bias, but because the alternative to that freedom is worse than those failings. Yet the area in which legal doctrine is currently least adequate to preserve press freedom is the area of defamation law, the area in which this action lies. We are said to have in the first amendment 'a profound national commitment to the principle that debate on public issues should be uninhibited, robust, and wide-open.' *New York Times.* That principle has resulted in the almost total abolition of prior restraints on publication; *New York Times Co. v. United States* [Casebooks, Sec. 2]; *Nebraska Press Ass'n v. Stuart* [Casebooks, Sec. 3] the curtailment of the possibility of criminal sanctions; *Garrison;* and, in *New York Times* itself, the construction of serious obstacles to private defamation actions by government officials. The cases that came afterward deployed similar obstacles to defamation actions by 'public figures,' *Butts; Rosenbloom; Gertz.* Thus, we have a judicial tradition of a continuing evolution of doctrine to serve the central purpose of the first amendment.

"Judge Scalia's dissent implies that the idea of evolving constitutional doctrine should be anathema to judges who adhere to a philosophy of judicial restraint. But most doctrine is merely the judge-made superstructure that implements basic constitutional principles. There is not at issue here the question of creating new constitutional rights or principles, a question which would divide members of this court along other lines than that of the division in this case. When there is a known principle to be explicated the evolution of doctrine is inevitable. Judges given stewardship of a constitutional provision— such as the first amendment—whose core is known but whose outer reach and contours are ill-defined, face the never-ending task of discerning the meaning of the provision from one case to the next. There would be little need for judges— and certainly no office for a philosophy of judging—if the boundaries of every constitutional provision were self-evident. They are not. In a case like this, it is the task of the judge in this generation to discern how the framers' values, defined in the context of the world they knew, apply to the world we know. The world changes in which unchanging values find their application. The fourth amendment was framed by men who did not foresee electronic surveillance. But that does not make it wrong for judges to apply the central value of that amendment to electronic invasions of personal privacy. The commerce power was established by men who did not foresee the scope and intricate interdependence of today's economic activities. But that does not make it wrong for judges to forbid states the power to impose burdensome regulations on the interstate movement of trailer trucks. The first amendment's guarantee of freedom of the press was written by men who had not the remotest idea of modern forms of communication. But that does not make it wrong for a judge to find the values of the first amendment relevant to radio and television broadcasting.

"So it is with defamation actions. We know very little of the precise intentions of the framers and ratifiers of the speech and press clauses of the first amendment. But we do know that they gave into our keeping the value of preserving free expression and, in particular, the preservation of political expression, which is commonly conceded to be the value at the core of those clauses. Perhaps the framers did not envision libel actions as a major threat to that freedom. I may grant that, for the sake of the point to be made. But if, over time, the libel action becomes a threat to the central meaning of the first amendment, why should not judges adapt their doctrines? Why is it different to refine and evolve doctrine here, so long as one is faithful to the basic meaning of the amendment, than it is to adapt the fourth amendment to take account of electronic surveillance, the commerce clause to adjust to interstate motor carriage, or the first amendment to encompass the electronic media? I do not believe there is a difference. To say that such matters must be left to the legislature is to say that changes in circumstances must be permitted to render constitutional guarantees meaningless. It is to say that not merely the particular rules but the entire enterprise of the Supreme Court in *New York Times* was illegitimate.

"We must never hesitate to apply old values to new circumstances, whether those circumstances are changes in technology or changes in the impact of traditional common law actions. *Sullivan* was an instance of the Supreme Court doing precisely this, as *Brown v. Board of Education* was more generally an example of the Court applying an old principle according to a new understanding of a social situation. The important thing, the ultimate consideration, is the constitutional freedom that is given into our keeping. A judge who refuses to see new threats to an established constitutional value, and hence provides a crabbed interpretation that robs a provision of its full, fair and reasonable meaning, fails in his judicial duty. That duty, I repeat, is to ensure that the powers and freedoms the framers specified are made effective in today's circumstances. The evolution of doctrine to accomplish that end contravenes no postulate of judicial restraint. The evolution I suggest does not constitute a major change in doctrine but is, as will be shown, entirely consistent with the implications of Supreme Court precedents.

"We now face a need similar to that which courts have met in the past. *New York Times,* for reasons that need not detain us here, seems not to have provided in full measure the protection for the marketplace of ideas that it was designed to do. Instead, in the past few years a remarkable upsurge in libel actions, accompanied by a startling inflation of damage awards, has threatened to impose a self-censorship on the press which can as effectively inhibit debate and criticism as would overt governmental regulation that the first amendment most certainly would not permit. *See* Lewis, *New York Times v. Sullivan Reconsidered: Time to Return to 'The Central Meaning of the First Amendment,'* 83 Colum.L.Rev. 603 (1983).[1] It is not merely the size of damage awards but an entire shift in the application of libel laws that raises problems for press freedom. *See* Smolla, *Let the Author Beware: The Rejuvenation of the American Law of Libel,* 132 U.Pa.L.Rev. 1 (1983).[2] Taking such matters into account is not, as one dissent suggests, to engage in sociological jurisprudence, at least not in any improper sense. Doing what I suggest here does not require courts to take account of social conditions or practical considerations to any greater extent than the Supreme Court has routinely done in such cases as *New York Times.* Nor does analysis here even approach the degree to which the Supreme Court quite properly took such matters into account in *Brown.* Matters such as the relaxation of legal rules about permissible recovery, the changes in tort law to

1. Lewis makes clear that, unlike some journalists, he is not given to reflexive perceptions of approaching tyranny in every decision that goes against the press; nevertheless he writes:

"This is an appropriate time to think again about that great case [*New York Times*]. It is a time of growing libel litigation, of enormous judgments and enormous costs. The press and its lawyers are deeply worried; the protection that they thought was won for free expression in *New York Times v. Sullivan* seems to them to be crumbling. Some would say that libel actions are a more serious threat than ever. Now the American press is addicted to self-pity. Although it is the freest in the world, and freer now than it ever has been, it often cries that doom is at hand. But this time even someone as skeptical of press claims as I am must admit that there is something to the concern."

2. Smolla refers to "a dramatic proliferation of highly publicized libel actions brought by well-known figures who seek, and often receive, staggering sums of money." He suggests some interesting reasons why libel litigation has so suddenly been reinvigorated:

"I contend that there are four contributing causes to the recent rejuvenation of American libel law. [The] first factor is a new legal and cultural seriousness about the inner self.

Tort law has undergone a relaxation of rules that formerly prohibited recovery for purely emotional or psychic injury, a doctrinal evolution that parallels the growth of the 'me-generation.' A second factor is the infiltration into the law of defamation of many of the attitudes that have produced a trend in tort law over the past twenty years favoring compensation and risk-spreading goals over fault principles in the selection of liability rules. A third cause of the new era in libel is the increasing difficulty in distinguishing between the informing and entertaining functions of the media. The blurring of this line between entertainment and information has affected the method and substance of communications in important ways and highlights the inadequacies of the current legal standards governing defamation actions. The final factor is doctrinal confusion, caused in large part by a pervasive failure to accommodate constitutional and common law values in a coherent set of standards that is responsive to the realities of modern communications. That doctrinal confusion is particularly telling in an environment where cultural trends, such as a heightened concern for the inner self, and legal trends, such as the trend in tort law in favor of strict liability, both work against the ideals of free expression."

favor compensation, and the existence of doctrinal confusion, *see* Smolla, *supra*, are matters that courts know well. Indeed, courts are responsible for these developments.

"The only solution to the problem libel actions pose would appear to be close judicial scrutiny to ensure that cases about types of speech and writing essential to a vigorous first amendment do not reach the jury.[3] *See Bose Corp. v. Consumers Union.* This requires a consideration of the totality of the circumstances that provide the context in which the statement occurs and which determine both its meaning and the extent to which making it actionable would burden freedom of speech or press. That, it must be confessed, is a balancing test and risks admitting into the law an element of judicial subjectivity. To that objection there are various answers. A balancing test is better than no protection at all. Given the appellate process, moreover, the subjective judgment of no single judge will be controlling. Over time, as reasons are given, the element of subjectivity will be reduced. There is, in any event, at this stage of the law's evolution, no satisfactory alternative. Hard categories and sharply-defined principles are admirable, if they are available, but usually, in the world in which we live, they share the problem of absolutes, of which they are a subgenre: they do not stand up when put to the test of hard cases."

SCALIA, J., dissenting, characterized the disparagement of Ollman's reputation as a "classic and cooly crafted libel." He observed that the statement at issue was "put in the mouth of one whom [Evans and Novak] describe as (1) an expert on the subject of status in the political science profession, and (2) a political *liberal*, i.e., one whose view of Ollman would *not* be distorted on the basis of greatly differing political opinion. They were saying, in effect, 'This is not merely our prejudiced view; it is the conclusion of an impartial and indeed sympathetic expert.' Try as they may, however, to convey to the world the *fact* that Ollman is poorly regarded in his profession, [Bork, J.'s] concurrence insists upon calling it an opinion. It will not do."

In addition, Scalia, J., sharply objected to a second thread of argument he believed to be "subtly woven" through Bork, J.'s concurring opinion, i.e., "In the field of political polemics, even statements that *are* fact rather than opinion must be excused because the reader 'is most unlikely to regard [them] as to be *trusted* automatically.' Bork (emphasis added). Once the reader is alert[ed] that he is in the context of controversy and politics, and that what he reads does not even purport to be as balanced, objective, and fair-minded [as] what is contained [in] news columns, he can expect libelous factual statements to be 'more of the same,' id. And since he would be a fool to *believe* them, they are not actionable. I am not prepared to accept this novel view that since political debate is always discounted, a decent amount of defamation in that context is protected by the first amendment. Besides the fact that it is unprecedented, it is impracticable. Whereas there are some rational limits (if only vague ones) upon what sorts of statements can be considered opinion and hence nondefamatory—limits which are plainly exceeded here—there is really no mechanism to gauge how much defamation is a decent amount.

"It is *this* 'risk of judicial subjectivity' rather than that which inheres in the unavoidable need in all libel cases to balance the 'totality of the circumstances,' which troubles me. Beyond that, I may add, I distrust the more general risk of

---

3. Since most libel plaintiffs demand a jury, as Ollman did, I discuss the problem in the context of jury trials. I doubt the problem would be greatly mitigated if the factfinder were a judge.

judicial subjectivity presented by the concurrence's creative approach to first amendment jurisprudence. It is an approach which embraces 'a continuing evolution of doctrine,' not merely as a consequence of thoughtful perception that old cases were decided wrongly at the time they were rendered (see, e.g., *Brown*); and not even in response to a demonstrable, authoritatively expressed development of public values (see, e.g., *Roberts v. Louisiana*, 428 U.S. 325, 336, 96 S.Ct. 3001, 3007, 49 L.Ed.2d 974 (1976) (plurality opinion)); but rather in reaction to judicially perceived 'modern problems,' which require 'evolution of the law in accordance with the deepest rationale of the first amendment.' [2] It seems to me that the identification of 'modern problems' to be remedied is quintessentially legislative rather than judicial business—largely because it is such a subjective judgment; and that the remedies are to be sought through democratic change rather than through judicial pronouncement that the Constitution now prohibits what it did not prohibit before. The concurrence perceives a 'modern problem' consisting of a 'freshening stream of libel actions, [which]—may threaten the public and constitutional interest in free, and frequently rough, discussion,' and of claims for damages that are 'quite capable of silencing political commentators forever.' Perhaps that perception is correct, though it is hard to square with the explosion of communications in general, and political commentary in particular, in this 'Media Age.' But then again, perhaps those are right who discern a distressing tendency for our political commentary to descend from discussion of public issues to destruction of private reputations; who believe that, by putting some brake upon that tendency, defamation liability under existing standards not only does not impair but fosters the type of discussion the first amendment is most concerned to protect; and who view high libel judgments as no more than an accurate reflection of the vastly expanded damage that can be caused by media that are capable of holding individuals up to public obloquy from coast to coast and that reap financial rewards commensurate with that power. I do not know the answers to these questions, but I do know that it is frightening to think that the existence or nonexistence of a *constitutional* rule (the willfully false disparagement of professional reputation in the context of political commentary cannot be actionable) is to depend upon our ongoing personal assessments of such sociological factors. And not only is our cloistered capacity to identify 'modern problems' suspect, but our ability to provide condign solutions through the rude means of constitutional prohibition is nonexistent. What a strange notion that the problem of excessive libel awards should be solved by permitting, in political debate, intentional destruction of reputation—rather than by placing a legislative limit upon the amount of libel recovery. It has not often been thought, by the way, that the press is among the least effective of legislative lobbyists."

2. In opposing such unguided "evolution" I am not in need of the concurrence's reminder that the fourth amendment must be applied to modern electronic surveillance, the commerce clause to trucks and the first amendment to broadcasting. The application of existing principles to new phenomena—either new because they have not existed before or new because they have never been presented to a court before, see *New York Times*—is what I would call not "evolution" but merely routine elaboration of the law. What is under discussion here is not application of preexisting principles to new phenomena, but rather *alteration* of preexisting principles in their application to preexisting phenomena on the basis of judicial perception of changed social circumstances. The principle that the first amendment does not protect the deliberate impugning of character or reputation, in its application to the preexisting phenomenon of political controversy, is to be revised to permit "bumping" of some imprecisable degree because we perceive that libel suits are now too common and too successful.

PRIVACY

CON LAW: P. 702, after note 1

AMER CON: P. 487, after note 1

RTS & LIB: P. 370, after note 1

HUSTLER MAGAZINE v. FALWELL, 485 U.S. 46, 108 S.Ct. 876, 99 L.Ed.2d 41 (1988), per REHNQUIST, C.J., held that public figures and public officials offended by a mass media parody could not recover for the tort of intentional infliction of emotional distress without a showing of *New York Times* malice. Parodying a series of liquor advertisements in which celebrities speak about their "first time" the editors of *Hustler* chose plaintiff Jerry Falwell (a nationally famous minister, host of a nationally syndicated television show, and founder of the Moral Majority political organization) "as the featured celebrity and drafted an alleged 'interview' with him in which he states that his 'first time' was during a drunken incestuous rendezvous with his mother in an outhouse. The *Hustler* parody portrays [Falwell] and his mother [a] 'as drunk and immoral,' and suggests that [Falwell] is a hypocrite who preaches only when he is drunk. In small print at the bottom of the page, the ad contains the disclaimer, 'ad parody—not to be taken seriously.' The magazine's table of contents also lists the ad as 'Fiction; Ad and Personality Parody.' * * *

"This case presents us with a novel question involving First Amendment limitations upon a State's authority to protect its citizens from the intentional infliction of emotional distress.[3] We must decide whether a public figure may recover damages for emotional harm caused by the publication of an ad parody offensive to him, and doubtless gross and repugnant in the eyes of most. [Falwell] would have us find that a State's interest in protecting public figures from emotional distress is sufficient to deny First Amendment protection to speech that is patently offensive and is intended to inflict emotional injury, even when that speech could not reasonably have been interpreted as stating actual facts about the public figure involved. * * *

"In [Falwell's] view, [so] long as the utterance was intended to inflict emotional distress, was outrageous, and did in fact inflict serious emotional distress, it is of no constitutional import whether the statement was a fact or an opinion, or whether it was true or false. It is the intent to cause injury that is the gravamen of the tort, and the State's interest in preventing emotional harm simply outweighs whatever interest a speaker may have in speech of this type.

"Generally speaking the law does not regard the intent to inflict emotional distress as one which should receive much solicitude, and it is quite understandable that most if not all jurisdictions have chosen to make it civilly culpable where the conduct in question is sufficiently 'outrageous.' But in the world of debate about public affairs, many things done with motives that are less than admirable are protected by the First Amendment. '[Debate] on public issues will not be uninhibited if the speaker must run the risk that it will be proved in court that he spoke out of hatred; even if he did speak out of hatred, utterances honestly believed contribute to the free interchange of ideas and the ascertainment of truth.' *Garrison.* Thus while such a bad motive may be deemed

---

a. Falwell's mother was not a plaintiff. What result if she were?

3. Under Virginia law, in an action for intentional infliction of emotional distress a plaintiff must show that the defendant's con-

duct (1) is intentional or reckless; (2) offends generally accepted standards of decency or morality; (3) is causally connected with the plaintiff's emotional distress; and (4) caused emotional distress that was severe.

controlling for purposes of tort liability in other areas of the law, we think the First Amendment prohibits such a result in the area of public debate about public figures.

"Were we to hold otherwise, there can be little doubt that political cartoonists and satirists would be subjected to damage awards without any showing that their work falsely defamed its subject. * * *

"[Falwell] contends, however, that the caricature in question here was so 'outrageous' as to distinguish it from more traditional political cartoons. There is no doubt that the caricature of [Falwell] and his mother published in Hustler is at best a distant cousin of [traditional] political cartoons * * * and a rather poor relation at that. If it were possible by laying down a principled standard to separate the one from the other, public discourse would probably suffer little or no harm. But we doubt that there is any such standard, and we are quite sure that the pejorative description 'outrageous' does not supply one. 'Outrageousness' in the area of political and social discourse has an inherent subjectiveness about it which would allow a jury to impose liability on the basis of the jurors' tastes or views, or perhaps on the basis of their dislike of a particular expression.

"We conclude that public figures and public officials may not recover for the tort of intentional infliction of emotional distress by reason of publications such as the one here at issue without showing in addition that the publication contains a false statement of fact which was made with 'actual malice,' i.e., with knowledge that the statement was false or with reckless disregard as to whether or not it was true." [b]

CON LAW: P. 703, after note 3

AMER CON: P. 488, after note 3

RTS & LIB: P. 371, after note 3

FLORIDA STAR v. B.J.F.

— U.S. —, 109 S.Ct. 2603, — L.Ed.2d — (1989).

JUSTICE MARSHALL delivered the opinion of the Court.

Florida Stat. § 794.03 (1987) makes it unlawful to "print, publish, or broadcast . . . . in any instrument of mass communication" the name of the victim of a sexual offense. Pursuant to this statute, appellant The Florida Star was found civilly liable for publishing the name of a rape victim which it had obtained from a publicly released police report. The issue presented here is whether this result comports with the First Amendment. We hold that it does not. * * *

[B.J.F.] testified that she had suffered emotional distress from the publication of her name. She stated that she had heard about the article from fellow workers and acquaintances; that her mother had received several threatening phone calls from a man who stated that he would rape B.J.F. again; and that these events had forced B.J.F. to change her phone number and residence, to seek police protection, and to obtain mental health counseling. * * *

The jury awarded B.J.F. $75,000 in compensatory damages and $25,000 in punitive damages. * * *

[We do not] accept appellant's invitation to hold broadly that truthful publication may never be punished consistent with the First Amendment. Our cases have carefully eschewed reaching this ultimate question, mindful that the

---

b. White, J., concurred, but stated that *New York Times* was irrelevant because of the jury's finding that the parody contained no assertion of fact. Kennedy, J., took no part.

future may bring scenarios which prudence counsels our not resolving anticipatorily. See, e.g., *Near v. Minnesota*, [Casebooks, Section 2] (hypothesizing "publication of the sailing dates of transports or the number and location of troops"); see also *Garrison v. Louisiana* (endorsing absolute defense of truth "where discussion of public affairs is concerned," but leaving unsettled the constitutional implications of truthfulness "in the discrete area of purely private libels"). Indeed, in *Cox Broadcasting*, we pointedly refused to answer even the less sweeping question "whether truthful publications may ever be subjected to civil or criminal liability" for invading "an area of privacy" defined by the State. [We] continue to believe that the sensitivity and significance of the interests presented in clashes between First Amendment and privacy rights counsel relying on limited principles that sweep no more broadly than the appropriate context of the instant case.

In our view, this case is appropriately analyzed with reference to such a limited First Amendment principle. It is the one, in fact, which we articulated in *Smith v. Daily Mail Pub. Co.*, [Casebooks, Section 3] in our synthesis of prior cases involving attempts to punish truthful publication: "[I]f a newspaper lawfully obtains truthful information about a matter of public significance then state officials may not constitutionally punish publication of the information, absent a need to further a state interest of the highest order." * * *

Applied to the instant case, the *Daily Mail* principle clearly commands reversal. The first inquiry is whether the newspaper "lawfully obtain[ed] truthful information about a matter of public significance." It is undisputed that the news article describing the assault on B.J.F. was accurate. In addition, appellant lawfully obtained B.J.F.'s name. Appellee's argument to the contrary is based on the fact that under Florida law, police reports which reveal the identity of the victim of a sexual offense are not among the matters of "public record" which the public, by law, is entitled to inspect. But the fact that state officials are not required to disclose such reports does not make it unlawful for a newspaper to receive them when furnished by the government. Nor does the fact that the Department apparently failed to fulfill its obligation under § 794.03 not to "cause or allow to be . . . published" the name of a sexual offense victim make the newspaper's ensuing receipt of this information unlawful. Even assuming the Constitution permitted a State to proscribe *receipt* of information, Florida has not taken this step. It is, clear, furthermore, that the news article concerned "a matter of public significance[.]" That is, the article generally, as opposed to the specific identity contained within it, involved a matter of paramount public import: the commission, and investigation, of a violent crime which had been reported to authorities.

The second inquiry is whether imposing liability on appellant pursuant to § 794.03 serves "a need to further a state interest of the highest order." Appellee argues that a rule punishing publication furthers three closely related interests: the privacy of victims of sexual offenses; the physical safety of such victims, who may be targeted for retaliation if their names become known to their assailants; and the goal of encouraging victims of such crimes to report these offenses without fear of exposure.

At a time in which we are daily reminded of the tragic reality of rape, it is undeniable that these are highly significant interests, a fact underscored by the Florida Legislature's explicit attempt to protect these interests by enacting a criminal statute prohibiting much dissemination of victim identities. We accordingly do not rule out the possibility that, in a proper case, imposing civil sanctions for publication of the name of a rape victim might be so overwhelmingly necessary to advance these interests as to satisfy the *Daily Mail* standard. For three independent reasons, however, imposing liability for publication under the circumstances of this case is too precipitous a means of advancing these interests to convince us that there is a "need" within the meaning of the *Daily Mail* formulation for Florida to take this extreme step.

First is the manner in which appellant obtained the identifying information in question. [B.J.F.'s] identity would never have come to light were it not for the erroneous, if inadvertent, inclusion by the Department of her full name in an incident report made available in a press room open to the public. Florida's policy against disclosure of rape victims' identities, reflected in § 794.03, was undercut by the Department's failure to abide by this policy. Where, as here, the government has failed to police itself in disseminating information, it is clear [that] the imposition of damages against the press for its subsequent publication can hardly be said to be a narrowly tailored means of safeguarding anonymity.

That appellant gained access to the information in question through a government news release makes it especially likely that, if liability were to be imposed, self-censorship would result. Reliance on a news release is a paradigmatically "routine newspaper reporting techniqu[e]." The government's issuance of such a release, without qualification, can only convey to recipients that the government considered dissemination lawful, and indeed expected the recipients to disseminate the information further. Had appellant merely reproduced the news release prepared and released by the Department, imposing civil damages would surely violate the First Amendment. The fact that appellant converted the police report into a news story by adding the linguistic connecting tissue necessary to transform the report's facts into full sentences cannot change this result.

A second problem with Florida's imposition of liability for publication is the broad sweep of the negligence *per se* standard applied under the civil cause of action implied from § 794.03. Unlike claims based on the common law tort of invasion of privacy, civil actions based on § 794.03 require no case-by-case findings that the disclosure of a fact about a person's private life was one that a reasonable person would find highly offensive. On the contrary, under the *per se* theory of negligence adopted by the courts below, liability follows automatically from publication. This is so regardless of whether the identity of the victim is already known throughout the community; whether the victim has voluntarily called public attention to the offense; or whether the identity of the victim has otherwise become a reasonable subject of public concern—because, perhaps, questions have arisen whether the victim fabricated an assault by a particular person. Nor is there a scienter requirement of any kind under § 794.03, engendering the perverse result that truthful publications challenged pursuant to this cause of action are less protected by the First Amendment than even the least protected defamatory falsehoods: those involving purely private figures, where liability is evaluated under a standard, usually applied by a jury, of ordinary negligence. See *Gertz.* * * *

Third, and finally, the facial underinclusiveness of § 794.03 raises serious doubts about whether Florida is, in fact, serving, with this statute, the significant interests which appellee invokes in support of affirmance. Section 794.03 prohibits the publication of identifying information only if this information appears in an "instrument of mass communication," a term the statute does not define. Section 794.03 does not prohibit the spread by other means of the identities of victims of sexual offenses. An individual who maliciously spreads word of the identity of a rape victim is thus not covered, despite the fact that the communication of such information to persons who live near, or work with, the victim may have consequences equally devastating as the exposure of her name to large numbers of strangers.

When a State attempts the extraordinary measure of punishing truthful publication in the name of privacy, it must demonstrate its commitment to advancing this interest by applying its prohibition evenhandedly, to the small-time disseminator as well as the media giant. Where important First Amendment interests are at stake, the mass scope of disclosure is not an acceptable surrogate for injury. Without more careful and inclusive precautions against alternative forms of dissemination, we cannot conclude that Florida's selective ban on publication by the mass media satisfactorily accomplishes its stated purpose.

Our holding today is limited. We do not hold that truthful publication is automatically constitutionally protected, or that there is no zone of personal privacy within which the State may protect the individual from intrusion by the press, or even that a State may never punish publication of the name of a victim of a sexual offense. We hold only that where a newspaper publishes truthful information which it has lawfully obtained, punishment may lawfully be imposed, if at all, only when narrowly tailored to a state interest of the highest order, and that no such interest is satisfactorily served by imposing liability under § 794.03 to appellant under the facts of this case. * * *

JUSTICE SCALIA, concurring in part and concurring in the judgment.

I think it sufficient to decide this case to rely upon the third ground set forth in the Court's opinion: that a law cannot be regarded as protecting an interest "of the highest order" and thus as justifying a restriction upon truthful speech, when it leaves appreciable damage to that supposedly vital interest unprohibited. In the present case, I would anticipate that the rape victim's discomfort at the dissemination of news of her misfortune among friends and acquaintances would be at least as great as her discomfort at its publication by the media to people to whom she is only a name. Yet the law in question does not prohibit the former in either oral or written form. Nor is it at all clear, as I think it must be to validate this statute, that Florida's general privacy law would prohibit such gossip. Nor, finally, is it credible that the interest meant to be served by the statute is the protection of the victim against a rapist still at large—an interest that arguably would extend only to mass publication. There would be little reason to limit a statute with that objective to rape alone; or to extend it to all rapes, whether or not the felon has been apprehended and confined. In any case, the instructions here did not require the jury to find that the rapist was at large.

This law has every appearance of a prohibition that society is prepared to impose upon the press but not upon itself. Such a prohibition does not protect an interest "of the highest order." For that reason, I agree that the judgment of the court below must be reversed.

JUSTICE WHITE, with whom THE CHIEF JUSTICE and JUSTICE O'CONNOR join, dissenting.

"Short of homicide, [rape] is the 'ultimate violation of self.' " *Coker v. Georgia*, [CON LAW p. 581, AMER CON p. 394, RTS & LIB p. 832] (opinion of White, J.). For B.J.F., however, the violation she suffered at a rapist's knifepoint marked only the beginning of her ordeal. A week later, while her assailant was still at large, an account of this assault—identifying by name B.J.F. as the victim—was published by The Florida Star. As a result, B.J.F.

received harassing phone calls, required mental health counseling, was forced to move from her home, and was even threatened with being raped again. Yet today, the Court holds that a jury award of $75,000 to compensate B.J.F. for the harm she suffered due to the Star's negligence is at odds with the First Amendment. I do not accept this result.

[T]he three "independent reasons" the Court cites for reversing the judgment for B.J.F. [do not] support its result.

The first of these reasons [is] the fact "appellant gained access to [B.J.F.'s name] through a government news release." "The government's issuance of such a release, without qualification, can only convey to recipients that the government considered dissemination lawful," the Court suggests. [But the] "release" of information provided by the government was not, as the Court says, "without qualification." As the Star's own reporter conceded at trial, the crime incident report that inadvertently included B.J.F.'s name was posted in a room that contained signs making it clear that the names of rape victims were not matters of public record, and were not to be published. The Star's reporter indicated that she understood that she "[was not] allowed to take down that information" (i.e., B.J.F.'s name) and that she "[was] not supposed to take the information from the police department." Thus, by her own admission the posting of the incident report did not convey to the Star's reporter the idea that "the government considered dissemination lawful"; the Court's suggestion to the contrary is inapt. * * *

Unfortunately, as this case illustrates, mistakes happen: even when States take measures to "avoid" disclosure, sometimes rape victim's names are found out. As I see it, it is not too much to ask the press, in instances such as this, to respect simple standards of decency and refrain from publishing a victim's name, address, and/or phone number.

Second, the Court complains that appellant was judged here under too strict a liability standard. The Court contends that a newspaper might be found liable under the Florida courts' negligence *per se* theory without regard to a newspaper's scienter or degree of fault. The short answer to this complaint is that whatever merit the Court's argument might have, it is wholly inapposite here, where the jury found that appellant acted with "reckless indifference towards the rights of others," a standard far higher than the *Gertz* standard the Court urges as a constitutional minimum today. B.J.F. proved the Star's negligence at trial—and, actually, far more than simple negligence; the Court's concerns about damages resting on a strict liability or mere causation basis are irrelevant to the validity of the judgment for appellee.

But even taking the Court's concerns in the abstract, they miss the mark. Permitting liability under a negligence *per se* theory does not mean that defendants will be held liable without a showing of negligence, but rather, that the standard of care has been set by the legislature, instead of the courts. The Court says that negligence *per se* permits a plaintiff to hold a defendant liable without a showing that the disclosure was "of a fact about a person's private life [that] a reasonable person would find highly offensive." But the point here is that the legislature—reflecting popular sentiment—has determined that disclosure of the fact that a person was raped is categorically a revelation that reasonable people find offensive. And as for the Court's suggestion that the Florida courts' theory permits liability without regard for whether the victim's identity is already known, or whether she herself has made it known—these are facts that would surely enter into the calculation of damages in such a case. In any event, none of these mitigating factors was present here; whatever the force of these arguments generally, they do not justify the Court's ruling against B.J.F. in this case.

Third, the Court faults the Florida criminal statute for being underinclusive: § 794.03 covers disclosure of rape victim's names in "instrument[s] of mass communication," but not other means of distribution, the Court observes. But our cases which have struck down laws that limit or burden the press due to their underinclusiveness have involved situations where a legislature has singled out one segment of the news media or press for adverse treatment. Here, the Florida law evenhandedly covers all "instrument[s] of mass communication" no matter their form, media, content, nature or purpose. It excludes neighborhood gossips because presumably the Florida Legislature has determined that neighborhood gossips do not pose the danger and intrusion to rape victims that "instrument[s] of mass communication" do. Simply put: Florida wanted to prevent the widespread distribution of rape victim's names, and therefore enacted a statute tailored almost as precisely as possible to achieving that end.

* * *

At issue in this case is whether there is any information about people, which—though true—may not be published in the press. By holding that only "a state interest of the highest order" permits the State to penalize the publication of truthful information, and by holding that protecting a rape victim's right to privacy is not among those state interests of the highest order, the Court accepts appellant's invitation to obliterate one of the most note-worthy legal inventions of the 20th-Century: the tort of the publication of private facts. W. Prosser, J. Wade, & V. Schwartz, *Torts* 951–952 (8th ed. 1988). Even if the Court's opinion does not say as much today, such obliteration will follow inevitably from the Court's conclusion here. * * *

I do not suggest that the Court's decision today is radical departure from a previously charted course. The Court's ruling has been foreshadowed. In *Time, Inc. v. Hill*, we observed that—after a brief period early in this century where Brandeis' view was ascendant—the trend in "modern" jurisprudence has been to eclipse an individual's right to maintain private any truthful information that the press wished to publish. More recently, in *Cox Broadcasting*, we acknowledged the possibility that the First Amendment may prevent a State from ever subjecting the publication of truthful but private information to civil liability. Today, we hit the bottom of the slippery slope.

I would find a place to draw the line higher on the hillside: a spot high enough to protect B.J.F.'s desire for privacy and peace-of-mind in the wake of a horrible personal tragedy. There is no public interest in publishing the names, addresses, and phone numbers of persons who are the victims of crime—and no public interest in immunizing the press from liability in the rare cases where a State's efforts to protect a victim's privacy have failed. Consequently, I respectfully dissent.[5]

---

5. The Court does not address the distinct constitutional questions raised by the award of punitive damages in this case. Consequently, I do not do so either. That award is more troublesome than the compensatory award discussed above. Cf. Note, *Punitive Damages and Libel Law*, 98 Harv.L.Rev. 847 (1985).

OWNERSHIP OF SPEECH

CON LAW: P. 708, addition to note 1

RTS & LIB: P. 708, addition to note 1

See also *San Francisco Arts and Athletics, Inc. v. United States Olympic Comm.*, pp. 205, 365 of this Supplement.

OBSCENITY

THE SEARCH FOR A RATIONALE

CON LAW: P. 725, add to fn. b

AMER CON: P. 504, add to fn. b

RTS & LIB: P. 393, add to fn. b

For the declaration that *Stanley*'s "privacy of the home" principle is "firmly grounded" in the first amendment while resisting the principle's expansion to protect consensual adult homosexual sodomy in the home, see *Bowers v. Hardwick,* p. 139 of this Supplement. But see Blackmun, J., joined by Brennan, Marshall, and Stevens, JJ., dissenting in *Bowers* ("*Stanley* rested as much on the Court's understanding of the Fourth Amendment as it did on the First").

A REVISED STANDARD

CON LAW: P. 731, addition to fn. e

AMER CON: P. 510, addition to fn. e

RTS & LIB: P. 399, addition to fn. e

Consider SABLE COMMUNICATIONS v. FCC, ___ U.S. ___, 109 S.Ct. 2829, ___ L.Ed.2d ___ (1989) (upholding congressional ban on obscene interstate commercial telephone messages): "There is no constitutional barrier under *Miller* to prohibiting communications that are obscene in some communities under local standards even though they are not obscene in others. If a ["dial-a-porn" company's] audience is comprised of different communities with different local standards, [the company] ultimately bears the burden of complying with the prohibition on obscene messages." The Court invalidated a ban on "indecent" interstate commercial telephone messages. See p. 277 of this Supplement.

CON LAW: P. 736, after note 1

AMER CON: P. 515, after note 1

RTS & LIB: P. 404, after note 1

POPE v. ILLINOIS, 481 U.S. 497, 107 S.Ct. 1918, 95 L.Ed.2d 439 (1987), per WHITE, J., held that the question of whether purportedly obscene material lacked serious literary, artistic, political, or scientific value was to be judged by what a "reasonable person" would find, not by "community standards": "In *Miller* itself, the Court was careful to point out that '[t]he First Amendment protects works which, taken as a whole, have serious literary, artistic, political, or scientific value, regardless of whether the government or a majority of the people approve of the ideas these works represent.' Just as the ideas a work represents need not obtain majority approval to merit protection, neither, insofar as the First Amendment is concerned, does the value of the work vary from community to community based on the degree of local acceptance it has won. The proper inquiry is not whether an ordinary member of any given community would find serious literary, artistic, political, or scientific value in allegedly obscene material, but whether a reasonable person would find such value in the material, taken as a whole." [a]

SCALIA, J., concurred: "I join the Court's opinion with regard to an 'objective' or 'reasonable person' test of 'serious literary, artistic, political, or scientific value' because I think that [is] the most faithful assessment of what *Miller* intended, and because we have not been asked to reconsider *Miller* in the present case. I must note, however, that in my view it is quite impossible to come to an objective assessment of (at least) literary or artistic value, there being many accomplished people who have found literature in Dada, and art in the replication of a soup can. Since ratiocination has little to do with esthetics, the fabled 'reasonable man' is of little help in the inquiry, and would have to be replaced with, perhaps, the 'man of tolerably good taste'—a description that betrays the lack of an ascertainable standard. If evenhanded and accurate decisionmaking is not always impossible under such a regime, it is at least impossible in the cases that matter. I think we would be better advised to adopt as a legal maxim what has long been the wisdom of mankind: De gustibus non est disputandum. Just as there is no use arguing about taste, there is no use litigating about it. For the law courts to decide 'What is Beauty' is a novelty even by today's standards.

"The approach proposed by Part II of [Stevens, J.'s] dissent does not eliminate this difficulty, but arguably aggravates it. It is refined enough judgment to estimate whether a reasonable person would find literary or artistic value in a particular publication; it carries refinement to the point of meaninglessness to ask whether he could do so. Taste being, as I have said, unpredictable, the answer to the question must always be 'yes'—so that there is little practical difference between that proposal and Part III of [his] dissent, which asserts more forthrightly that 'government may not constitutionally criminalize mere possession or sale of obscene literature, absent some connection to minors, or obtrusive display to unconsenting adults.'

"All of today's opinions, I suggest, display the need for reexamination of *Miller*."

STEVENS, J., joined by Marshall, J., and in large part [b] by Brennan, J., dissented: "[The Court's formulation] assumes that all reasonable persons would resolve the value inquiry in the same way. In fact, there are many cases in which some reasonable people would find that specific sexually oriented materials have serious artistic, political, literary, or scientific value, while other reasonable people would conclude that they have no such value. The Court's formulation does not tell the jury how to decide such cases.

a. The Court remanded to the lower court to determine whether the instructions below (calling upon jurors to determine how the material would be viewed by ordinary adults in the State of Illinois) were harmless error. Blackmun, J., concurring in part and dissenting in part, agreed with the Court's rendition of the *Miller* test, but denied that the error below could appropriately be deemed harmless. Brennan, J., dissenting, adhered to his view that state interference with distribution of obscene material to consenting adults is unconstitutional.

b. Brennan, J., joined Stevens, J., in concluding that the remand to search for harmless error was inappropriate, that the Court's *Miller* formulation was deficient, and that criminalizing the sale of obscene materials to consenting adults is unconstitutional. He refused, however, to accept Stevens, J.'s contention that states should retain substantial leeway in civil regulation of sexually explicit material.

"In my judgment, communicative material of this sort is entitled to the protection of the First Amendment if some reasonable persons could consider it as having serious literary artistic, political, or scientific value. * * *

"The purpose of the third element of the *Miller* test is to ensure that the obscenity laws not be allowed to 'level the available reading matter to the majority or lowest common denominator of the population. * * * It is obvious that neither Ulysses nor Lady Chatterley's Lover would have literary appeal to the majority of the population.' F. Schauer, *The Law of Obscenity* 144 (1976). A juror asked to create 'a reasonable person' in order to apply the standard that the Court announces today, might well believe that the majority of the population who find no value in such a book are more reasonable than the minority who do find value. First Amendment protection surely must not be contingent on this type of subjective determination."

CON LAW: P. 737, after note 2

AMER CON: P. 515, after note 2

RTS & LIB: P. 405, after note 2

3. *Chilling Or Confiscating Protected Speech.* Does *Miller* unduly threaten protected non-obscene speech? In upholding "stiff" RICO penalties against those who commit multiple violations of obscenity laws and who are accordingly defined to be "racketeers," FORT WAYNE BOOKS, INC. v. INDIANA, ___ U.S. ___, 109 S.Ct. 916, 103 L.Ed.2d 34 (1989), per WHITE, J., conceded that "perhaps . . . some cautious booksellers will practice self-censorship and remove First Amendment protected material from their shelves. But deterrence of the sale of obscene materials is a legitimate end of state obscenity laws, and our cases have long recognized the practical reality that 'any form of criminal obscenity statute applicable to a bookseller will induce some tendency to self-censorship and have some inhibitory effect on the dissemination of material not obscene.' *Smith v. California.*[a] The mere assertion of some possible self-censorship resulting from a statute is not enough to render an anti-obscenity law unconstitutional under our precedents."

Although the Court upheld substantial jail sentences and fines, it did not reach the question whether Indiana, as punishment for the crime, could constitutionally accomplish forfeiture of all the defendant's real and personal property used or acquired in the course of committing the offenses (including all the books in Fort Wayne's three bookstores, obscene or not).[b] STEVENS, J., joined by Brennan and Marshall, JJ., dissenting, reached the issue: "The most realistic interpretation of the Indiana Legislature's intent in making obscenity a RICO predicate offense is to expand beyond traditional prosecution of legally obscene materials into restriction of materials that, though constitutionally protected, have the same undesired effect on the community's morals as those that are actually obscene. Fulfillment of that intent would surely overflow the boundaries imposed by the Constitution."

a. *Smith* concluded that the ordinance before it had "such a tendency to inhibit constitutionally protected expression that it cannot stand under the Constitution."

b. The Court held that pretrial seizure of non-obscene expressive materials was invalid. Seizure of allegedly obscene materials for evidentiary purposes is permissible on a showing of probable cause, but "the publication may not be taken out of circulation completely until there has been a determination of obscenity after an adversary hearing." O'Connor, J., concurred with the Court's disposition of the Fort Wayne case, but advanced a jurisdictional objection to the Court's entertaining the companion case. Stevens, J., joined by Brennan and Marshall, JJ., concurred in the invalidation of the pretrial seizure.

"FIGHTING WORDS," OFFENSIVE WORDS AND HOSTILE AUDIENCES

OFFENSIVE LANGUAGE: A STATE CONSTITUTIONAL PERSPECTIVE

CON LAW: P. 754, addition to note 3

AMER CON: P. 532, addition to note 3

RTS & LIB: P. 422, addition to note 3

Without questioning the power of states or municipalities to proscribe fighting words, or the failure to disperse in response to a valid police order, or the physical obstruction of an officer's investigation, or disorderly conduct, HOUSTON v. HILL, 482 U.S. 451, 107 S.Ct. 2502, 96 L.Ed.2d 398 (1987), per BRENNAN, J., invalidated as overbroad a Houston ordinance forbidding speech that in any manner interrupts a police officer in the performance of his or her duties: "The ordinance's plain language is admittedly violated scores of times daily, [yet] only some individuals—those chosen by the police in their unguided discretion—are arrested." [a]

POWELL, J., concurring in part and dissenting in part, argued that if the state were to construe the ordinance to require proof of intent to interfere with an officer's duties, overbreadth and vagueness difficulties might be overcome. In order to narrow the focus of the constitutional question, he would have certified the state law question to the appropriate Texas court.[b] Bowing to the Court's determination to consider the ordinance without such a narrowing construction, he concluded that the ordinance was unconstitutionally vague.[c]

NEW CATEGORIES

HARM TO CHILDREN AND THE OVERBREADTH DOCTRINE

CON LAW: P. 759, after note 2

AMER CON: P. 538, after note 2

RTS & LIB: P. 427, after note 2

3. *Overbreadth without a chilling effect?* Massachusetts prohibited adults from posing or exhibiting nude children for purposes of photographs, publications, or pictures, moving or otherwise. Bona fide scientific or medical purposes were excepted as were educational or cultural purposes for a bona fide school, museum, or library. Douglas Oakes was prosecuted for taking 10 color photographs of his 14-year-old stepdaughter in a state of nudity covered by the statute. The Massachusetts Supreme Judicial Court declared the statute overbroad. After certiorari was granted in MASSACHUSETTS v. OAKES, ___ U.S. ___, 109 S.Ct. 2637, ___ L.Ed.2d ___ (1989), Massachusetts added a "lascivious intent" requirement to the statute and eliminated the exemptions. O'CONNOR, joined by Rehnquist, C.J., and White and Kennedy, JJ., accordingly refused to entertain

a. Blackmun, J., concurring, joined the Court's opinion, but reaffirmed his view that *Gooding* and *Lewis* were wrongly decided.

b. O'Connor, J., and Rehnquist, C.J., joined this portion of Powell, J.'s opinion.

c. Scalia, J., joined with Powell, J., on the vagueness issue and on some procedural is-

sues, but thought the ordinance was properly before the Court. Rehnquist, C.J., dissenting, stated that he did not agree that the ordinance "in the absence of an authoritative construction by the Texas courts, is unconstitutional."

the overbreadth challenge and voted to remand the case for determination of the statute's constitutionality as applied: "Because it has been repealed, the former version of [the Massachusetts law] cannot chill protected speech."

SCALIA, J., joined by Blackmun, Brennan, Marshall, and Stevens, JJ., disagreed:[a] "It seems to me strange judicial theory that a conviction initially invalid can be resuscitated by postconviction alteration of the statute under which it was obtained. [Even as a policy matter, the] overbreadth doctrine serves to protect constitutionally legitimate speech not merely *ex post*, that is, after the offending statute is enacted, but also *ex ante*, that is, when the legislature is contemplating what sort of statute to enact. If the promulgation of overbroad laws affecting speech was cost free[,] if *no* conviction of constitutionally proscribable conduct would be lost, so long as the offending statute was narrowed before the final appeal—then legislatures would have significantly reduced incentive to stay within constitutional bounds in the first place. [More] fundamentally, however, [it] seems to me that we are only free to pursue policy objectives through the modes of action traditionally followed by the courts and by the law. [I] have heard of a voidable contract, but never of a voidable law. The notion is bizarre."

4. *How substantial is substantial overbreadth?* Five justices addressed the overbreadth question in *Oakes*, supra, but the substantive issue was not resolved. BRENNAN, J., joined by Marshall and Stevens, JJ., objected that the statute would make it criminal for parents "to photograph their infant children or toddlers in the bath or romping naked on the beach." More generally, he argued that the first amendment "blocks the prohibition of nude posing by minors in connection with the production of works of art not depicting lewd behavior. * * * Many of the world's great artists—Degas, Renoir, Donatello, to name but a few—have worked from models under 18 years of age, and many acclaimed photographs have included nude or partially clad minors."

SCALIA, J., joined by Blackmun, J., disagreed: "[G]iven the known extent of the kiddie-porn industry[,] I would estimate that the legitimate scope [of the statute] vastly exceeds the illegitimate. * * * Even assuming that proscribing artistic depictions of preadolescent genitals and postadolescent breasts is impermissible,[2] the body of material that would be covered is, as far as I am aware, insignificant compared with the lawful scope of the statute. That leaves the family photos. [Assuming] that it is unconstitutional (as opposed to merely foolish) to prohibit such photography, I do not think it so common as to make the statute *substantially* overbroad. [My] perception differs, for example, from Justice Brennan's belief that there is an 'abundance of baby and child photographs taken every day' depicting genitals."

a. Although these five justices agreed that the overbreadth challenge should be entertained, they divided on the merits of the challenge. Scalia, J., joined by Blackmun, J., found no merit in the overbreadth claim (see note 4 infra) and voted to reverse and to remand for determination of the statute's constitutionality as applied. The three remaining justices (see note 4 infra) agreed with the overbreadth challenge and voted to affirm the judgment below. O'Connor, J.'s opinion, therefore, became the plurality opinion, and the Court's judgment was to vacate the judgment below and to remand. In the end, six justices voted against the overbreadth challenge: four because it was moot; two because it did not meet the requirement of substantial overbreadth.

2. [Most] adults, I expect, would not hire themselves out as nude models, whatever the intention of the photographer or artist, and however unerotic the pose. There is no cause to think children are less sensitive. It is not unreasonable, therefore, for a State to regard parents' using (or permitting the use) of their children as nude models, or other adults' use of consenting minors, as a form of child exploitation.

HARM TO WOMEN: FEMINISM AND PORNOGRAPHY

CON LAW: P. 765, after note 5

AMER CON: P. 544, after note 5

RTS & LIB: P. 433, after note 5

The Indianapolis version of the anti-pornography civil rights ordinance was struck down in AMERICAN BOOKSELLERS ASS'N v. HUDNUT, 771 F.2d 323 (7th Cir.1985), aff'd, 475 U.S. 1001, 106 S.Ct. 1172, 89 L.Ed.2d 291 (1986). The Seventh Circuit, per EASTERBROOK, J., ruled that the definition of pornography infected the entire ordinance (including provisions against trafficking, coercion into pornography, forcing pornography on a person, and assault or physical attack due to pornography) because it impermissibly discriminated on the basis of point of view: "Indianapolis enacted an ordinance defining 'pornography' as a practice that discriminates against women. * * *

" 'Pornography' under the ordinance is 'the graphic sexually explicit subordination of women, whether in pictures or in words, that also includes one or more of the following: (1) Women are presented as sexual objects who enjoy pain or humiliation; or (2) Women are presented as sexual objects who experience sexual pleasure in being raped; or (3) Women are presented as sexual objects tied up or cut up or mutilated or bruised or physically hurt, or as dismembered or truncated or fragmented or severed into body parts; or (4) Women are presented as being penetrated by objects or animals; or (5) Women are presented in scenarios of degradation, injury, abasement, torture, shown as filthy or inferior, bleeding, bruised, or hurt in a context that makes these conditions sexual; or (6) Women are presented as sexual objects for domination, conquest, violation, exploitation, possession, or use, or through postures or positions of servility or submission or display.'

"The statute provides that the 'use of men, children, or transsexuals in the place of women in paragraphs (1) through (6) above shall also constitute pornography under this section.' The ordinance as passed in April 1984 defined 'sexually explicit' to mean actual or simulated intercourse or the uncovered exhibition of the genitals, buttocks or anus. An amendment in June 1984 deleted this provision, leaving the term undefined.

"The Indianapolis ordinance does not refer to the prurient interest, to offensiveness, or to the standards of the community. It demands attention to particular depictions, not to the work judged as a whole. It is irrelevant under the ordinance whether the work has literary, artistic, political, or scientific value. The City and many amici point to these omissions as virtues. They maintain that pornography influences attitudes, and the statute is a way to alter the socialization of men and women rather than to vindicate community standards of offensiveness. And as one of the principal drafters of the ordinance has asserted, 'if a woman is subjected, why should it matter that the work has other value?' MacKinnon, *Pornography, Civil Rights, and Speech,* 20 Harv.Civ.Rts.—Civ.Lib.L.Rev. 1, 21 (1985).

"Civil rights groups and feminists have entered this case as amici on both sides. Those supporting the ordinance say that it will play an important role in reducing the tendency of men to view women as sexual objects, a tendency that leads to both unacceptable attitudes and discrimination in the workplace and violence away from it. Those opposing the ordinance point out that much radical feminist literature is explicit and depicts women in ways forbidden by the ordinance and that the ordinance would reopen old battles. It is unclear

how Indianapolis would treat works from James Joyce's *Ulysses* to Homer's *Iliad;* both depict women as submissive objects for conquest and domination.

"We do not try to balance the arguments for and against an ordinance such as this. The ordinance discriminates on the ground of the content of the speech. Speech treating women in the approved way—in sexual encounters 'premised on equality' (MacKinnon, supra, at 22)—is lawful no matter how sexually explicit. Speech treating women in the disapproved way—as submissive in matters sexual or as enjoying humiliation—is unlawful no matter how significant the literary, artistic, or political qualities of the work taken as a whole. The state may not ordain preferred viewpoints in this way. The Constitution forbids the state to declare one perspective right and silence opponents. * * *

author's pt of view

" 'If there is any fixed star in our constitutional constellation, it is that no official, high or petty, can prescribe what shall be orthodox in politics, nationalism, religion, or other matters of opinion or force citizens to confess by word or act their faith therein.' *West Virginia State Bd. of Educ. v. Barnette.* Under the First Amendment the government must leave to the people the evaluation of ideas. Bald or subtle, an idea is as powerful as the audience allows it to be. A belief may be pernicious—the beliefs of Nazis led to the death of millions, those of the Klan to the repression of millions. A pernicious belief may prevail. Totalitarian governments today rule much of the planet, practicing suppression of billions and spreading dogma that may enslave others. One of the things that separates our society from theirs is our absolute right to propagate opinions that the government finds wrong or even hateful. * * *

"Under the ordinance graphic sexually explicit speech is 'pornography' or not depending on the perspective the author adopts. Speech that 'subordinates' women and also, for example, presents women as enjoying pain, humiliation, or rape, or even simply presents women in 'positions of servility or submission or display' is forbidden, no matter how great the literary or political value of the work taken as a whole. Speech that portrays women in positions of equality is lawful, no matter how graphic the sexual content. This is thought control. It establishes an 'approved' view of women, of how they may react to sexual encounters, of how the sexes may relate to each other. Those who espouse the approved view may use sexual images; those who do not, may not.

thought control.

"Indianapolis justifies the ordinance on the ground that pornography affects thoughts. Men who see women depicted as subordinate are more likely to treat them so. Pornography is an aspect of dominance.[1] It does not persuade people so much as change them. It works by socializing, by establishing the expected

---

1. "Pornography constructs what a woman is in terms of its view of what men want sexually. * * * Pornography's world of equality is a harmonious and balanced place. Men and women are perfectly complementary and perfectly bipolar. [All] the ways men love to take and violate women, women love to be taken and violated. [What] pornography *does* goes beyond its content: It eroticizes hierarchy, it sexualizes inequality. It makes dominance and submission sex. Inequality is its central dynamic; the illusion of freedom coming together with the reality of force is central to its working. [P]ornography is neither harmless fantasy nor a corrupt and confused misrepresentation of an otherwise neutral and healthy sexual situation. It institutionalizes the sexuality of male supremacy, fusing the erotization of dominance and submission with the social construction of male and female. * * * Men treat women as who they see women as being. Pornography constructs who that is. Men's power over women means that the way men see women defines who women can be. Pornography [is] a sexual reality." MacKinnon, supra, at 17–18 (note omitted, emphasis in original). See also Dworkin, *Pornography: Men Possessing Women* (1981). A national commission in Canada recently adopted a similar rationale for controlling pornography. Special Commission on Pornography and Prostitution, 1 *Pornography and Prostitution in Canada* 49–59 (1985).

and the permissible. In this view pornography is not an idea; pornography is the injury.

"There is much to this perspective. Beliefs are also facts. People often act in accordance with the images and patterns they find around them. People raised in a religion tend to accept the tenets of that religion, often without independent examination. People taught from birth that black people are fit only for slavery rarely rebelled against that creed; beliefs coupled with the self-interest of the masters established a social structure that inflicted great harm while enduring for centuries. Words and images act at the level of the subconscious before they persuade at the level of the conscious. Even the truth has little chance unless a statement fits within the framework of beliefs that may never have been subjected to rational study.

"Therefore we accept the premises of this legislation. Depictions of subordination tend to perpetuate subordination. The subordinate status of women in turn leads to affront and lower pay at work, insult and injury at home, battery and rape on the streets.[2] In the language of the legislature, '[p]ornography is central in creating and maintaining sex as a basis of discrimination. Pornography is a systematic practice of exploitation and subordination based on sex which differentially harms women. The bigotry and contempt it produces, with the acts of aggression it fosters, harm women's opportunities for equality and rights [of all kinds].'

"Yet this simply demonstrates the power of pornography as speech. All of these unhappy effects depend on mental intermediation. Pornography affects how people see the world, their fellows, and social relations. If pornography is what pornography does, so is other speech. Hitler's orations affected how some Germans saw Jews. Communism is a world view, not simply a *Manifesto* by Marx and Engels or a set of speeches. Efforts to suppress communist speech in the United States were based on the belief that the public acceptability of such ideas would increase the likelihood of totalitarian government. [Many] people believe that the existence of television, apart from the content of specific programs, leads to intellectual laziness, to a penchant for violence, to many other ills. The Alien and Sedition Acts passed during the administration of John Adams rested on a sincerely held belief that disrespect for the government leads to social collapse and revolution—a belief with support in the history of many nations. Most governments of the world act on this empirical regularity, suppressing critical speech. In the United States, however, the strength of the support for this belief is irrelevant. Seditious libel is protected speech unless the danger is not only grave but also imminent. See *New York Times v. Sullivan;* cf. *Brandenburg v. Ohio.*

2. MacKinnon's article collects empirical work that supports this proposition. The social science studies are very difficult to interpret, however, and they conflict. Because much of the effect of speech comes through a process of socialization, it is difficult to measure incremental benefits and injuries caused by particular speech. Several psychologists have found, for example, that those who see violent, sexually explicit films tend to have more violent thoughts. But how often does this lead to actual violence? National commissions on obscenity here, in the United Kingdom, and in Canada have found that it is not possible to demonstrate a direct link between obscenity and rape or exhibitionism. The several opinions in *Miller v. California* discuss the U.S. commission. See also *Report of the Committee on Obscenity and Film Censorship* 61–95 (Home Office, Her Majesty's Stationery Office, 1979); 1 *Pornography and Prostitution in Canada* 71–73, 95–103. In saying that we accept the finding that pornography as the ordinance defines it leads to unhappy consequences, we mean only that there is evidence to this effect, that this evidence is consistent with much human experience, and that as judges we must accept the legislative resolution of such disputed empirical questions.

"Racial bigotry, anti-semitism, violence on television, reporters' biases—these and many more influence the culture and shape our socialization. None is directly answerable by more speech, unless that speech too finds its place in the popular culture. Yet all is protected as speech, however insidious. Any other answer leaves the government in control of all of the institutions of culture, the great censor and director of which thoughts are good for us.

"Sexual responses often are unthinking responses, and the association of sexual arousal with the subordination of women therefore may have a substantial effect. But almost all cultural stimuli provoke unconscious responses. Religious ceremonies condition their participants. Teachers convey messages by selecting what not to cover; the implicit message about what is off limits or unthinkable may be more powerful than the messages for which they present rational argument. Television scripts contain unarticulated assumptions. People may be conditioned in subtle ways. If the fact that speech plays a role in a process of conditioning were enough to permit governmental regulation, that would be the end of freedom of speech. * * *

"Much of Indianapolis's argument rests on the belief that when speech is 'unanswerable,' and the metaphor that there is a 'marketplace of ideas' does not apply, the First Amendment does not apply either. The metaphor is honored; Milton's *Aeropagitica* and John Stewart Mill's *On Liberty* defend freedom of speech on the ground that the truth will prevail, and many of the most important cases under the First Amendment recite this position. The Framers undoubtedly believed it. As a general matter it is true. But the Constitution does not make the dominance of truth a necessary condition of freedom of speech. To say that it does would be to confuse an outcome of free speech with a necessary condition for the application of the amendment.

"A power to limit speech on the ground that truth has not yet prevailed and is not likely to prevail implies the power to declare truth. At some point the government must be able to say (as Indianapolis has said): 'We know what the truth is, yet a free exchange of speech has not driven out falsity, so that we must now prohibit falsity.' If the government may declare the truth, why wait for the failure of speech? Under the First Amendment, however, there is no such thing as a false idea, *Gertz v. Robert Welch, Inc.,* so the government may not restrict speech on the ground that in a free exchange truth is not yet dominant. * * *

"We come, finally, to the argument that pornography is 'low value' speech, that it is enough like obscenity that Indianapolis may prohibit it. Some cases hold that speech far removed from politics and other subjects at the core of the Framers' concerns may be subjected to special regulation. E.g., *FCC v. Pacifica Foundation; Young v. American Mini Theatres, Inc.* (plurality opinion); *Chaplinsky v. New Hampshire.* These cases do not sustain statutes that select among viewpoints, however. In *Pacifica* the FCC sought to keep vile language off the air during certain times. The Court held that it may; but the Court would not have sustained a regulation prohibiting scatological descriptions of Republicans but not scatological descriptions of Democrats, or any other form of selection among viewpoints.

"At all events, pornography is not low value speech within the meaning of these cases. Indianapolis seeks to prohibit certain speech because it believes this speech influences social relations and politics on a grand scale, that it controls attitudes at home and in the legislature. This precludes a characterization of the speech as low value. True, pornography and obscenity have sex in common. But Indianapolis left out of its definition any reference to literary, artistic, political, or scientific value. The ordinance applies to graphic sexually explicit subordination in works great and small.[3] The Court sometimes balances the value of speech against the costs of its restriction, but it does this by category of speech and not by the content of particular works. See Ely, *Flag Desecration: A Case Study in the Roles of Categorization and Balancing in First Amendment Analysis,* 88 Harv.L.Rev. 1482 (1975); Stone, *Restrictions of Speech Because of its Content: The Strange Case of Subject-Matter Restrictions,* 46 U.Chi.L.Rev. 81 (1978). Indianapolis has created an approved point of view and so loses the support of these cases.

"Any rationale we could imagine in support of this ordinance could not be limited to sex discrimination. Free speech has been on balance an ally of those seeking change. Governments that want stasis start by restricting speech. Culture is a powerful force of continuity; Indianapolis paints pornography as a part of the culture of power. Change in any complex system ultimately depends on the ability of outsiders to challenge accepted views and the reigning institutions. Without a strong guarantee of freedom of speech, there is no effective right to challenge what is." [a]

IS SOME PROTECTED SPEECH LESS EQUAL THAN OTHER PROTECTED SPEECH?

NEAR OBSCENE SPEECH

CON LAW: P. 767, before *Erznoznik*

AMER LAW: P. 545, before *Erznoznik*

RTS & LIB: P. 435, before *Erznoznik*

Note on Organization

The *Renton, Newport,* and *DeBartolo* cases, infra, have been edited with an eye to the possibility that many, if not most, teachers will now wish to discuss the cases in Sec. 4 before proceeding to the study of Near Obscene Speech, Commercial Speech, Private Speech, and Labor Speech.

CON LAW: P. 775, before Notes and Questions

AMER CON: P. 553, before Notes and Questions

RTS & LIB: P. 443, before Notes and Questions

RENTON v. PLAYTIME THEATRES, INC., 475 U.S. 41, 106 S.Ct. 925, 89 L.Ed.2d 29 (1986), per REHNQUIST, J., upheld a zoning ordinance that prohibited

3. Indianapolis briefly argues that *Beauharnais v. Illinois,* which allowed a state to penalize "group libel," supports the ordinance. In *Collin v. Smith,* we concluded that cases such as *New York Times v. Sullivan* had so washed away the foundations of *Beauharnais* that it could not be considered authoritative. If we are wrong in this, however, the case still does not support the ordinance. It is not clear that depicting women as subordinate in sexually explicit ways, even combined with a depiction of pleasure in rape, would fit within the definition of a group libel. The well received film *Swept Away* used explicit sex, plus taking pleasure in rape, to make a political statement, not to defame. Work must be an insult or slur for its own sake to come within the ambit of *Beauharnais,* and a work need not be scurrilous at all to be pornography under the ordinance.

a. The balance of the opinion suggested ways that parts of the ordinance might be salvaged, if redrafted. It suggested, for example, that the city might forbid coerced participation in any film or in "any film containing explicit sex." If the latter were adopted, would it make a difference if the section applied to persons coerced into participation in such films without regard to whether they were forced into explicit sex scenes? Swygert, J., concurring, joined part of Easterbrook, J.'s opinion for the court, but objected both to the "questionable and broad assertions regarding how human behavior can be conditioned" and to the "advisory" opinion on how parts of the ordinance might be redrafted.

adult motion picture theaters from locating within 1,000 feet of any residential zone, church, park, or school. The effect was to exclude such theaters from approximately 94% of the land in the city. Of the remaining 520 acres, a substantial part was occupied by a sewage disposal and treatment plant, a horse racing track and environs, a warehouse and manufacturing facilities, a Mobil Oil tank farm, and a fully-developed shopping center: "[T]he resolution of this case is largely dictated by our decision in *Young*. There, although five Members of the Court did not agree on a single rationale for the decision, we held that the city of Detroit's zoning ordinance, which prohibited locating an adult theater within 1,000 feet of any two other 'regulated uses' or within 500 feet of any residential zone, did not violate the First and Fourteenth Amendments. The Renton ordinance, like the one in *Young*, does not ban adult theaters altogether, but merely provides that such theaters may not be located within 1,000 feet of any residential zone, single- or multiple-family dwelling, church, park, or school. The ordinance is therefore properly analyzed as a form of time, place, and manner regulation.

"Describing the ordinance as a time, place, and manner regulation is, of course, only the first step in our inquiry. This Court has long held that regulations enacted for the purpose of restraining speech on the basis of its content presumptively violate the First Amendment. See *Chicago Police Dept. v. Mosley*, [Casebooks, Sec. 5, I, B]. On the other hand, so-called 'content-neutral' time, place, and manner regulations are acceptable so long as they are designed to serve a substantial governmental interest and do not unreasonably limit alternative avenues of communication.

"At first glance, the Renton ordinance, like the ordinance in *Young*, does not appear to fit neatly into either the 'content-based' or the 'content-neutral' category. To be sure, the ordinance treats theaters that specialize in adult films differently from other kinds of theaters. Nevertheless, [the] City Council's '*predominate* concerns' were with the secondary effects of adult theaters, and not with the content of adult films themselves. * * *

"[This] finding as to 'predominate' intent is more than adequate to establish that the city's pursuit of its zoning interests here was unrelated to the suppression of free expression.ª The ordinance by its terms is designed to prevent crime, protect the city's retail trade, maintain property values, and generally 'protec[t] and preserv[e] the quality of [the city's] neighborhoods, commercial districts, and the quality of urban life,' not to suppress the expression of unpopular views. As Justice Powell observed in *Young*, '[i]f [the city] had been concerned with restricting the message purveyed by adult theaters, it would have tried to close them or restrict their number rather than circumscribe their choice as to location.'

"In short, the [ordinance] does not contravene the fundamental principle that underlies our concern about 'content-based' speech regulations: that 'gov-

---

a. The court of appeals had held that a finding of predominate intent was inadequate, and would have remanded for the district court to determine whether a "motivating factor" to restrict the exercise of first amendment rights was present. In response, the Court interpreted the court of appeals opinion to require the invalidation of the ordinance if such a motive were found to be present "apparently no matter how small a part this motivating factor may have played in the City Council's decision." This view of the law, the Court continued, "was rejected in *United States v. O'Brien* [Casebooks, Sec. 4]: 'It is a familiar principle of constitutional law that this Court will not strike down an otherwise constitutional statute on the basis of an alleged illicit legislative motive. [What] motivates one legislator to make a speech about a statute is not necessarily what motivates scores of others to enact it, and the stakes are sufficiently high for us to eschew guess-work.'"

ernment may not grant the use of a forum to people whose views it finds acceptable, but deny use to those wishing to express less favored or more controversial views.' *Mosley.*

"It was with this understanding in mind that, in *Young,* a majority of this Court decided that, at least with respect to businesses that purvey sexually explicit materials,[2] zoning ordinances designed to combat the undesirable secondary effects of such businesses are to be reviewed under the standards applicable to 'content-neutral' time, place, and manner regulations.

"The appropriate inquiry in this case, then, is whether the Renton ordinance is designed to serve a substantial governmental interest and allows for reasonable alternative avenues of communication."

After concluding that the ordinance was designed to serve substantial government interests, the Court ruled that the Renton ordinance allowed "for reasonable alternative avenues of communication": "[W]e note that the ordinance leaves some 520 acres, or more than five percent of the entire land area of Renton, open to use as adult theater sites. [Respondents] argue, however, that some of the land in question is already occupied by existing businesses, that 'practically none' of the undeveloped land is currently for sale or lease, and that in general there are no 'commercially viable' adult theater sites within the 520 acres left open by the Renton ordinance. The Court of Appeals accepted these arguments, concluded that the 520 acres was not truly 'available' land, and therefore held that the Renton ordinance 'would result in a substantial restriction' on speech.

"We disagree with both the reasoning and the conclusion of the Court of Appeals. That respondents must fend for themselves in the real estate market, on an equal footing with other prospective purchasers and lessees, does not give rise to a First Amendment violation. And although we have cautioned against the enactment of zoning regulations that have 'the effect of suppressing, or greatly restricting access to, lawful speech,' *Young,* fn. 35 (plurality opinion), we have never suggested that the First Amendment compels the Government to ensure that adult theaters, or any other kinds of speech-related businesses for that matter, will be able to obtain sites at bargain prices. [T]he First Amendment requires only that Renton refrain from effectively denying respondents a reasonable opportunity to open and operate an adult theater within the city, and the ordinance before us easily meets this requirement. * * *[4]" [b]

BRENNAN, J., joined by Marshall, J., dissented: "The fact that adult movie theaters may cause harmful 'secondary' land use effects may arguably give Renton a compelling reason to regulate such establishments; it does not mean, however, that such regulations are content-neutral. * * *

"The ordinance discriminates on its face against certain forms of speech based on content. Movie theaters specializing in 'adult motion pictures' may not be located within 1,000 feet of any residential zone, single- or multiple-family

2. See *Young* (plurality opinion) ("[I]t is manifest that society's interest in protecting this type of expression is of a wholly different, and lesser, magnitude than the interest in untrammeled political debate * * *.").

4. * * * We reject respondents' "vagueness" argument for the same reasons that led us to reject a similar challenge in *Young.* There, the Detroit ordinance applied to theaters "used to present material distinguished or characterized by an emphasis on [sexually ex-

plicit matter]." We held that "even if there may be some uncertainty about the effect of the ordinances on other litigants, they are unquestionably applicable to these respondents." We also held that the Detroit ordinance created no "significant deterrent effect" that might justify invocation of the First Amendment "overbreadth" doctrine.

b. Blackmun, J., concurred in the result without opinion.

dwelling, church, park, or school. Other motion picture theaters, and other forms of 'adult entertainment,' such as bars, massage parlors, and adult bookstores, are not subject to the same restrictions. This selective treatment strongly suggests that Renton was interested not in controlling the 'secondary effects' associated with adult businesses, but in discriminating against adult theaters based on the content of the films they exhibit. [Moreover,] many of the City Council's 'findings' do not relate to legitimate land use concerns. As the Court of Appeals observed, '[b]oth the magistrate and the district court recognized that many of the stated reasons for the ordinance were no more than expressions of dislike for the subject matter.'[3] That some residents may be offended by the *content* of the films shown at adult movie theaters cannot form the basis for state regulation of speech. See *Terminiello v. Chicago.*

"Some of the 'findings' [do] relate to supposed 'secondary effects' associated with adult movie theaters[4] [but they were added by the City Council only after this law suit was filed and the Court should not] accept these post-hoc statements at face value. [As] the Court of Appeals concluded, '[t]he record presented by Renton to support its asserted interest in enacting the zoning ordinance is very thin.' * * *[5] * * *[7]

"Even assuming that the ordinance should be treated like a content-neutral time, place, and manner restriction, I would still find it unconstitutional. [T]he ordinance is invalid because it does not provide for reasonable alternative avenues of communication.[c] The District Court found that the ordinance left 520 acres in Renton available for adult theater sites, an area comprising about

3. For example, "finding" number 2 states that "[l]ocation of adult entertainment land uses on the main commercial thoroughfares of the City gives an impression of legitimacy to, and causes a loss of sensitivity to the adverse effect of pornography upon children, established family relations, respect for marital relationship and for the sanctity of marriage relations of others, and the concept of non-aggressive, consensual sexual relations."

"Finding" number 6 states that "[l]ocation of adult land uses in close proximity to residential uses, churches, parks, and other public facilities, and schools, will cause a degradation of the community standard of morality. Pornographic material has a degrading effect upon the relationship between spouses."

4. For example, "finding" number 12 states that "[l]ocation of adult entertainment land uses in proximity to residential uses, churches, parks and other public facilities, and schools, may lead to increased levels of criminal activities, including prostitution, rape, incest and assaults in the vicinity of such adult entertainment land uses."

5. As part of the amendment passed after this lawsuit commenced, the City Council added a statement that it had intended to rely on the Washington Supreme Court's opinion in *Northend Cinema, Inc. v. Seattle,* 90 Wash.2d 709, 585 P.2d 1153 (1978), cert. denied, 441 U.S. 946, 99 S.Ct. 2166, 60 L.Ed.2d 1048 (1979), which upheld Seattle's zoning regulations against constitutional attack. Again, despite the suspicious coincidental timing of the

amendment, the Court holds that "Renton was entitled to rely [on] the 'detailed findings' summarized in [the] *Northend Cinema* opinion." In *Northend Cinema,* the court noted that "[t]he record is replete with testimony regarding the effects of adult movie theater locations on residential neighborhoods." The opinion however, does not explain the evidence it purports to summarize, and provided no basis for determining whether Seattle's experience is relevant to Renton's.

7. As one commentator has noted: "[A]nyone with any knowledge of human nature should naturally assume that the decision to adopt almost any content-based restriction might have been affected by an antipathy on the part of at least some legislators to the ideas or information being suppressed. The logical assumption, in other words, is not that there is not improper motivation but, rather, because legislators are only human, that there is a substantial risk that an impermissible consideration has in fact colored the deliberative process." Stone, *Restrictions on Speech Because of its Content: The Peculiar Case of Subject-Matter Restrictions,* 46 U.Chi.L.Rev. 81, 106 (1978).

c. Brennan, J., argued that the ordinance also failed as an acceptable time, place, and manner restriction because it was not narrowly tailored to serve a significant governmental interest. *Heffron v. International Soc. for Krishna Consciousness* [Casebooks, Sec. 5, I, A].

five percent of the city. However, the Court of Appeals found that because much of this land was already occupied, '[l]imiting adult theater uses to these areas is a substantial restriction on speech.' Many 'available' sites are also largely unsuited for use by movie theaters. [T]hese facts serve to distinguish this case from *Young*, where there was no indication that the Detroit zoning ordinance seriously limited the locations available for adult businesses. See *Young*, fn. 35 (plurality opinion) ('The situation would be quite different if the ordinance had the effect of * * * greatly restricting access to, lawful speech').

"Despite the evidence in the record, the Court reasons that the fact 'that respondents must fend for themselves in the real estate market, on an equal footing with other prospective purchasers and lessees, does not give rise to a First Amendment violation.' However, respondents are not on equal footing with other prospective purchasers and lessees, but must conduct business under severe restrictions not imposed upon other establishments. The Court also argues that the First Amendment does not compel 'the government to ensure that adult theatres, or any other kinds of speech-related businesses for that matter, will be able to obtain sites at bargain prices.' However, respondents do not ask Renton to guarantee low-price sites for their businesses, but seek, only a reasonable opportunity to operate adult theaters in the city. By denying them this opportunity, Renton can effectively ban a form of protected speech from its borders. The ordinance 'greatly restrict[s] access to, lawful speech,' *Young* (plurality opinion), and is plainly unconstitutional."

The distinction between secondary effects of adult theaters and the content of adult films was addressed by several justices in the context of considering a District of Columbia ordinance banning the display of any sign within 500 feet of a foreign embassy that would tend to bring the embassy into "public odium" or "public disrepute." In BOOS v. BARRY, p. 255 of this Supplement, city officials argued that the ordinance was primarily concerned with a secondary effect, in particular the obligation under international law to protect the dignity of foreign diplomats. O'CONNOR, J., joined by Stevens and Scalia, JJ., disagreed: "We think this [argument] misreads *Renton*. We spoke in that decision only of *secondary* effects of speech, referring to regulations that apply to a particular category of speech because the regulatory targets happen to be associated with that type of speech. So long as the justifications for regulation have nothing to do with content, i.e., the desire to suppress crime has nothing to do with the actual films being shown inside adult movie theatres, we concluded that the regulation was properly analyzed as content-neutral.

"Regulations that focus on the direct impact of speech on its audience present a different situation. Listeners' reactions to speech are not the type of 'secondary effects' we referred to in *Renton*. To take an example factually close to *Renton*, if the ordinance there was justified by the city's desire to prevent the psychological damage it felt was associated with viewing adult movies, then analysis of the measure as a content-based statute would have been appropriate. The hypothetical regulation targets the direct impact of a particular category of speech, not a secondary feature that happens to be associated with that type of speech.

"Applying these principles to the case at hand leads readily to the conclusion that the display clause is content-based. The clause is justified *only* by reference to the content of speech. Respondents and the United States do not point to the 'secondary effects' of picket signs in front of embassies. They do not point to congestion, to interference with ingress or egress, to visual clutter, or to the need to protect the security of embassies. Rather, they rely on the need to protect the dignity of foreign diplomatic personnel by shielding them from speech that is critical of their governments. This justification focuses *only* on the content of the speech and the direct impact that speech has on its listeners. The emotive impact of speech on its audience is not a 'secondary effect.' Because the display clause regulates speech due to its potential primary impact, we conclude it must be considered content-based." [a]

BRENNAN, J., joined by Marshall, J., agreed with the conclusion that the ordinance was content-based, but objected to O'Connor, J.'s "assumption that the *Renton* analysis applies not only outside the context of businesses purveying sexually explicit materials but even to political speech.

"The dangers and difficulties posed by the *Renton* analysis are extensive. Although in this case it is easy enough to determine that the display clause does not aim at a 'secondary effect' of speech, future litigants are unlikely to be so bold or so forthright as to defend a restriction on speech with the argument that the restriction aims to protect listeners from the indignity of hearing speech that criticizes them. Rather, they are likely to defend content-based restrictions by pointing to secondary effects like 'congestion, * * * visual clutter, or * * * security * * *.' But such secondary effects offer countless excuses for content-based suppression of political speech. No doubt a plausible argument could be made that the political gatherings of some parties are more likely than others to attract large crowds causing congestion, that picketing for certain causes is more likely than other picketing to cause visual clutter, or that speakers delivering a particular message are more likely than others to attract an unruly audience. [The] *Renton* analysis [creates] a possible avenue for governmental censorship whenever censors can concoct 'secondary' rationalizations for regulating the content of political speech. * * *" [b]

CON LAW: P. 776, addition to note 3

AMER CON: P. 554, addition to note 3

RTS & LIB: P. 443, addition to note 3

NEWPORT v. IACOBUCCI, 479 U.S. 92, 107 S.Ct. 383, 93 L.Ed.2d 334 (1986), per curiam, held that an ordinance prohibiting nude or nearly nude dancing in local establishments licensed to sell liquor for consumption on the premises [a] was

a. In an earlier passage O'Connor, J., responded to the argument that the ordinance was not content-based on the theory that the government was not selecting between viewpoints. The argument was instead that "the permissible message on a picket sign is determined solely by the policies of a foreign government. We reject this contention, although we agree the provision is not viewpoint-based. The display clause determines which viewpoint is acceptable in a neutral fashion by looking to the policies of foreign governments. While this prevents the display clause from being directly viewpoint-based, a label with potential First Amendment ramifications of its own, it does not render the statute content-neutral. Rather, we have held that a regulation that 'does not favor either side of a political controversy' is nonetheless impermissible because the 'First Amendment's hostility to

content-based regulation extends * * * to prohibition of public discussion of an entire topic.' Here the government has determined that an entire category of speech—signs or displays critical of foreign governments—is not to be permitted."

b. Rehnquist, J., joined by White and Blackmun, JJ., voted to uphold the ordinance on the basis of Bork, J's opinion below in *Finzer v. Barry,* 798 F.2d 1450 (D.C.Cir.1986). Bork, J., stated that the need to adhere to principles of international law might constitute a secondary effect under *Renton* but was not "entirely sure" whether *Renton* alone could dictate that result and did not resolve the issue. Id. at 1469–70 n. 15.

a. The Newport ordinance provided that, "It shall be unlawful for and a person is guilty of performing nude or nearly nude activity

within the state's constitutional power under the twenty-first amendment: "The Newport City Commission, in the preamble to the ordinance determined that nude dancing in establishments serving liquor was 'injurious to the citizens' of the city. It found the ordinance necessary to a range of purposes, including, 'prevent[ing] blight and the deterioration of the City's neighborhoods' and 'decreasing the incidence of crime, disorderly conduct and juvenile delinquency.' Given the 'added presumption in favor of the validity of the * * * regulation [that] the Twenty-first Amendment requires,' *California v. LaRue*, 409 U.S. 109, 93 S.Ct. 390, 34 L.Ed.2d 342 (1972), it is plain, as in *New York State Liquor Authority v. Bellanca*, 452 U.S. 714, 101 S.Ct. 2599, 69 L.Ed.2d 357 (1981) (per curiam), that [the] interest in maintaining order outweighs the interest in free expression by dancing nude." [b]

STEVENS, J., joined by Marshall, J., dissented: "There are dimensions to this case that the Court's opinion completely ignores. To begin with, the Newport ordinance is not limited to nude dancing, 'gross sexuality,' or barrooms.[4] On the contrary, the ordinance applies to every business establishment that requires a liquor license, and, even then, its prohibition is not limited to nudity or to dancing.[5] The State's power to regulate the sale of alcoholic beverages extends to a host of business establishments other than ordinary bars. For example, a theatre cannot sell champagne during an intermission without a liquor license. It is surely strange to suggest that a dramatic production like 'Hair' would lose its First Amendment protection because alcoholic beverages might be served in the lobby during intermission.

"Perhaps the Court would disavow its rationale if a city sought to apply its ordinance to the performers in a play like 'Hair' or to a production of 'Romeo and Juliet' containing a scene that violates Newport's ordinance. But such a disavowel would, I submit, merely confirm my view that the Twenty-first Amendment really has no bearing whatsoever on the question whether the State's interest in maintaining order in licensed premises outweighs the interest in free expression that is protected by the First Amendment—whether that interest is asserted by a dancer, an actor, or merely an unpopular customer.

when that person appears on a business establishment's premises in such manner or attire as to expose to view any portion of the pubic area, anus, vulva or genitals, or any simulation thereof, or when any female appears on a business establishment's premises in such manner or attire as to expose to view [a] portion of the breast referred to as the areola, nipple, or simulation thereof."

b. In an earlier footnote, the Court quoted approvingly from Stewart, J.'s opinion in *LaRue:* "This is not to say that the Twenty-first Amendment empowers a State to act with total irrationality or invidious discrimination in controlling the distribution and dispensation of liquor within its borders. And it most assuredly is not to say that the Twenty-first Amendment necessarily overrides in its allotted area any other relevant provision of the Constitution."

Marshall, J., dissented from the summary fashion with which the Court had treated the case, noting, for example, that the parties had not been given an opportunity to file briefs on

the merits. Scalia, J., separately stated that he would grant the petition for certiorari and set the case for oral argument.

4. This is not to say that an ordinance limited to barrooms would necessarily be valid. [A] barroom might be the most appropriate forum for this type of entertainment since the patrons of such establishments generally know what to expect when they enter and they are free to leave if they disapprove of what they see or hear. This case is wholly unlike those in which we have recognized the legitimate interest in keeping pigs out of the parlor. Cf. *FCC v. Pacifica Foundation*, Casebooks, Sec. 8, II. As long as people who like pigs keep them in secluded barnyards, they do not offend the sensibilities of the general public.

5. The ordinance makes it a crime for any female to appear on a licensed business establishment's premises "in such manner or attire as to expose to view any portion of the breast referred to as the areola, nipple, or simulation thereof."

"Similarly, I recognize that the Court's attention in this case is focused on the spectre of unregulated nudity, particularly sexually suggestive dancing. But if there is any integrity to the Court's reasoning on the State's power under the Twenty-first Amendment, it must also embrace other forms of expressive conduct or attire that might be offensive to the majority, or perhaps likely to stimulate violent reactions, but would nevertheless ordinarily be entitled to First Amendment protection. For example, liquor cannot be sold in an athletic stadium, hotel, restaurant, or sidewalk cafe without a liquor license. According to the Court's rationale any restriction on speech—be it content-based or neutral—in any of these places enjoys a presumption of validity. It is a strange doctrine indeed that implies that Paul Robert Cohen had a constitutional right to wear his vulgar jacket in a courtroom, but could be sent to jail for wearing it in Yankee Stadium. * * *

"I continue to believe that the Court is quite wrong in proceeding as if the Twenty-first Amendment repealed not only the Eighteenth Amendment, but some undefined portion of the First Amendment as well." [c]

COMMERCIAL SPEECH

CON LAW: P. 786, after note 1

AMER CON: P. 564, after note 1

RTS & LIB: P. 454, after note 1

SHAPERO v. KENTUCKY BAR ASS'N, ___ U.S. ___, 108 S.Ct. 1916, 100 L.Ed.2d 475 (1988), per BRENNAN, J., held that a state could not prohibit attorneys from sending personal letters soliciting business from persons known to face particular legal problems. Shapero's letter in part stated that "It has come to my attention that your home is being foreclosed on. [Call] NOW, don't wait. It may surprise you what I may be able to do for you." In response to the contention that this case was "*Ohralik* in writing," Brennan, J., stated: "In assessing the potential for overreaching and undue influence, the mode of communication makes all the difference. * * * A letter like a printed advertisement (but unlike a lawyer), can readily be put in a drawer to be considered later, ignored, or discarded." [a]

CON LAW: P. 791, addition to note 3

AMER CON: P. 569, addition to note 3

RTS & LIB: P. 459, addition to note 3

The Amateur Sports Act of 1978, 36 U.S.C. §§ 371–96 authorizes the United States Olympic Committee to prohibit certain commercial and promotional uses of the word "Olympic." Can a non-profit corporation constitutionally be prevented from selling T-shirts, buttons, bumper stickers, and other items, all

c. Stevens, J., also argued that the weight given by the Court to the twenty-first amendment could not be reconciled with its failure to give the amendment similar force in other contexts. See *Larkin v. Grendel's Den, Inc.*, Casebooks, infra (freedom of religion); *Craig v. Boren*, Casebooks, infra (gender equality).

a. Brennan, J., observed that the state could regulate potential abuses by requiring attorneys to file solicitation letters with supporting materials to a supervising agency. White, J., joined by Stevens, J., concurred, but declined to reach the merits of the particular letter at issue until the state courts had considered the question.

O'Connor, J., joined by Rehnquist, C.J., and Scalia, J., dissenting, would reconsider *Bates* in light of the "defective analogy between professional services and standardized consumer products" and would "return to the States the legislative function that has so inappropriately been taken from them in the context of attorney advertising."

emblazoned with the title "Gay Olympic Games"? From uses of the word for athletic or theatrical events? Does it matter if admission is charged? See *San Francisco Arts & Athletics, Inc. v. United States Olympic Comm.*, pp. 189, 365 of this Supplement (no first amendment right for others to "appropriate" the value given to the word Olympic by the efforts of the United States Olympic Committee).

BOARD OF TRUSTEES v. FOX, ___ U.S. ___, 109 S.Ct. 3028, ___ L.Ed.2d ___ (1989), per SCALIA, J., confronted a challenge to a State University of New York ("SUNY") regulation that barred a substantial amount of commercial activity on SUNY campuses (including the dormitories), but allowing various exceptions for food, laundry, dry cleaning, legal beverages, banking, the campus bookstore, etc. The challenge was initially brought by students involved in housewares sales.[a] Citing *Bolger*, the Court rejected the proposition that housewares sales presentations (given in the dorms at so-called "Tupperware" parties) could fall outside the commercial speech category even though they informed students on matters of financial responsibility and how to run an efficient home. Moreover, it concluded that SUNY's regulation implicated substantial interests including the promotion of an educational rather than a commercial atmosphere on campus, the promotion of safety and security, the prevention of commercial exploitation of students, and the preservation of "residential tranquility." Nonetheless, it remanded for a determination of whether these goals were furthered by the scheme in compliance with commercial speech doctrine.

It declined to determine whether the regulation was overbroad. The regulation, for example, would have foreclosed attorneys, guidance counselors, or tutors from dispensing advice (so long as they charged a fee) even at a student's invitation in the student's dormitory room. The Court stated that such speech would not be commercial speech because it did not propose a commercial transaction and reaffirmed that the existence of a profit motive is insufficient to make speech commercial. But, it maintained that the as applied challenge should be addressed before the overbreadth challenge: "Where an overbreadth attack is successful, the statute is obviously invalid in *all* its applications, since every person to whom it is applied can defend on the basis of the same overbreadth. A successful attack upon a commercial-speech restriction on narrow tailoring grounds, by contrast, does not assure a defense to those whose own commercial solicitation *can* be constitutionally proscribed—though obviously the rationale of the narrow-tailoring holding may be so broad as to render the statute effectively unenforceable. * * *

"It is not the usual judicial practice, however, nor do we consider it generally desirable, to proceed to an overbreadth issue unnecessarily—that is, before it is determined that the statute would be valid as applied. Such a course would convert use of the overbreadth doctrine from a necessary means of vindicating the plaintiff's own right not to be bound by a statute that is unconstitutional into a means of mounting gratuitous wholesale attacks upon state and federal laws."

BLACKMUN, J., joined by Brennan and Marshall, JJ., dissenting, maintained that the regulation was clearly overbroad: "I, therefore, would hold [it] unconstitutional on its face now, in order to avoid chilling protected speech during the pendency of the proceedings on remand."

a. The students objected that they could not host or attend "Tupperware" parties and that the SUNY regulations prevented them from having discussions with commercial invitees in their rooms.

CON LAW: P. 791, after note 3

AMER CON: P. 569, after note 3

RTS & LIB: P. 459, after note 3

Puerto Rico permits advertising for several forms of gambling, including horse racing, cockfighting, and the lottery. Advertising of casino gambling, however, is subject to a complicated body of regulations enforced by the Tourism Company of Puerto Rico (a public company with regulatory powers). These regulations allow casino advertising designed to attract tourists; they prohibit casino advertising aimed at Puerto Rican residents. For example, casino advertising is permitted when distributed in airports or on docks where cruise ships arrive and is permitted in media that primarily reach tourists rather than residents, e.g., *The New York Times,* trade magazines, even advertisements on network television (that reaches Puerto Rico via cable). Advertising of the hotels containing the casinos is permitted in the local Puerto Rican media "when the trade name of the hotel is used even though it may contain a reference to the casino provided that the word casino is never used alone nor specified." But advertisements designed to attract residents of Puerto Rico to the casinos are expressly prohibited.

POSADAS DE PUERTO RICO ASSOCIATES v. TOURISM COMPANY, 478 U.S. 328, 106 S.Ct. 2968, 92 L.Ed.2d 266 (1986), per REHNQUIST, J., upheld the advertising restrictions: "The particular kind of commercial speech at issue here, namely, advertising of casino gambling aimed at the residents of Puerto Rico, concerns a lawful activity and is not misleading or fraudulent, at least in the abstract. We must therefore proceed to the three remaining steps of the *Central Hudson* analysis in order to determine whether Puerto Rico's advertising restrictions run afoul of the First Amendment. The first of these three steps involves an assessment of the strength of the government's interest in restricting the speech. The interest at stake in this case, as determined by the Superior Court, is the reduction of demand for casino gambling by the residents of Puerto Rico. Appellant acknowledged the existence of this interest in [a] letter to the Tourism Company. ('The legislators wanted the tourists to flock to the casinos to gamble, but not our own people'). The Tourism Company's brief before this Court explains the legislature's belief that '[e]xcessive casino gambling among local residents—[would] produce serious harmful effects on the health, safety and welfare of the Puerto Rican citizens, such as the disruption of moral and cultural patterns, the increase in local crime, the fostering of prostitution, the development of corruption, and the infiltration of organized crime.' These are some of the very same concerns, of course, that have motivated the vast majority of the 50 States to prohibit casino gambling. We have no difficulty in concluding that the Puerto Rico Legislature's interest in the health, safety, and welfare of its citizens constitutes a 'substantial' governmental interest. Cf. *Renton.*

"The last two steps of the *Central Hudson* analysis basically involve a consideration of the 'fit' between the legislature's ends and the means chosen to accomplish those ends. Step three asks the question whether the challenged restrictions on commercial speech 'directly advance' the government's asserted interest. In the instant case, the answer to this question is clearly 'yes.' The Puerto Rico Legislature obviously believed, when it enacted the advertising restrictions at issue here, that advertising of casino gambling aimed at the residents of Puerto Rico would serve to increase the demand for the product advertised. We think the legislature's belief is a reasonable one, and the fact that appellant has chosen to litigate this case all the way to this Court indicates that appellant shares the legislature's view. See *Central Hudson* ('There is an immediate connection between advertising and demand for electricity. Central Hudson would not contest the advertising ban unless it believed that promotion would increase its sales'); cf. *Metromedia, Inc. v. San Diego* [Casebooks, Section 7] (plurality opinion of White, J.) (finding third prong of *Central Hudson* test satisfied where legislative judgment 'not manifestly unreasonable').

"Appellant argues, however, that the challenged advertising restrictions are underinclusive because other kinds of gambling such as horse racing, cockfighting, and the lottery may be advertised to the residents of Puerto Rico. Appellant's argument is misplaced for two reasons. First, whether other kinds of gambling are advertised in Puerto Rico or not, the restrictions on advertising of casino gambling 'directly advance' the legislature's interest in reducing demand for games of chance. Second, the legislature's interest, as previously identified, is not necessarily to reduce demand for all games of chance, but to reduce demand for casino gambling. According to the Superior Court, horse racing, cockfighting, 'picas,' or small games of chance at fiestas, and the lottery 'have been traditionally part of the Puerto Rican's roots,' so that 'the legislator could have been more flexible than in authorizing more sophisticated games which are not so widely sponsored by the people.' In other words, the legislature felt that for Puerto Ricans the risks associated with casino gambling were significantly greater than those associated with the more traditional kinds of gambling in Puerto Rico. In our view, the legislature's separate classification of casino gambling, for purposes of the advertising ban, satisfies the third step of the *Central Hudson* analysis.

"We also think it clear beyond peradventure that the challenged statute and regulations satisfy the fourth and last step of the *Central Hudson* analysis, namely, whether the restrictions on commercial speech are no more extensive than necessary to serve the government's interest. The narrowing constructions of the advertising restrictions announced by the Superior Court ensure that the restrictions will not affect advertising of casino gambling aimed at tourists, but will apply only to such advertising when aimed at the residents of Puerto Rico. Appellant contends, however, that the First Amendment requires the Puerto Rico Legislature to reduce demand for casino gambling among the residents of Puerto Rico not by suppressing commercial speech that might *encourage* such gambling, but by promulgating additional speech designed to *discourage* it. We reject this contention. We think it is up to the legislature to decide whether or not such a 'counterspeech' policy would be as effective in reducing the demand for casino gambling as a restriction on advertising. The legislature could conclude, as it apparently did here, that residents of Puerto Rico are already aware of the risks of casino gambling, yet would nevertheless be induced by widespread advertising to engage in such potentially harmful conduct.

"In short, we conclude that the statute and regulations at issue in this case, as construed by the Superior Court, pass muster under each prong of the *Central Hudson* test. We therefore hold that the Supreme Court of Puerto Rico properly rejected appellant's First Amendment claim.[9]

9. It should be apparent from our discussion of the First Amendment issue, and particularly the third and fourth prongs of the *Central Hudson* test, that appellant can fare no better under the equal protection guarantee of the Constitution. Cf. *Renton*. If there is a sufficient "fit" between the legislature's means and ends to satisfy the concerns of the First Amendment, the same "fit" is surely adequate under the applicable "rational basis" equal protection analysis.

Justice Stevens, in dissent, asserts the additional equal protection claim, not raised by appellant either below or in this Court, that the Puerto Rico statute and regulations imper-

"Appellant argues, however, that the challenged advertising restrictions are constitutionally defective under our decisions in *Carey* and *Bigelow.* In *Carey*, this Court struck down a ban on any 'advertisement or display' of contraceptives, and in *Bigelow*, we reversed a criminal conviction based on the advertisement of an abortion clinic. We think appellant's argument ignores a crucial distinction between the *Carey* and *Bigelow* decisions and the instant case. In *Carey* and *Bigelow*, the underlying conduct that was the subject of the advertising restrictions was constitutionally protected and could not have been prohibited by the State. Here, on the other hand, the Puerto Rico Legislature surely could have prohibited casino gambling by the residents of Puerto Rico altogether. In our view, the greater power to completely ban casino gambling necessarily includes the lesser power to ban advertising of casino gambling, and *Carey* and *Bigelow* are hence inapposite.

"Appellant also makes the related argument that, having chosen to legalize casino gambling for residents of Puerto Rico, the First Amendment prohibits the legislature from using restrictions on advertising to accomplish its goal of reducing demand for such gambling. We disagree. In our view, appellant has the argument backwards. As we noted in the preceding paragraph, it is precisely *because* the government could have enacted a wholesale prohibition of the underlying conduct that it is permissible for the government to take the less intrusive step of allowing the conduct, but reducing the demand through restrictions on advertising. It would surely be a Pyrrhic victory for casino owners such as appellant to gain recognition of a First Amendment right to advertise their casinos to the residents of Puerto Rico, only to thereby force the legislature into banning casino gambling by residents altogether. It would just as surely be a strange constitutional doctrine which would concede to the legislature the authority to totally ban a product or activity, but deny to the legislature the authority to forbid the stimulation of demand for the product or activity through advertising on behalf of those who would profit from such increased demand. Legislative regulation of products or activities deemed harmful, such as cigarettes, alcoholic beverages, and prostitution, has varied from outright prohibition on the one hand, see, e.g., Cal.Penal Code (prohibiting soliciting or engaging in act of prostitution), to legalization of the product or activity with restrictions on stimulation of its demand on the other hand, see e.g., Nev.Rev.Stat. (authorizing licensing of houses of prostitution except in counties with more than 250,000 population), (prohibiting advertising of houses of prostitution '[i]n any public theater, on the public streets of any city or town, or on any public highway,' or 'in [a] place of business'). To rule out the latter, intermediate kind of response would require more than we find in the First Amendment.[11]"

missibly discriminate between different kinds of publications. Justice Stevens misunderstands the nature of the Superior Court's limiting construction of the statute and regulations. According to the Superior Court, "[i]f the object of [an] advertisement is the tourist, it passes legal scrutiny." It is clear from the court's opinion that this basic test applies *regardless of whether the advertisement appears in a local or non-local publication.* Of course, the likelihood that a casino advertisement appearing in *The New York Times* will be primarily addressed to tourists, and not Puerto Rico residents, is far greater than would be the case for a similar advertisement appearing in the *San Juan Star.* But it is simply the demographics of the two newspapers' readerships, and not any form of "discrimination" on the part of the Puerto Rico Legislature or the Superior Court, which produces this result.

11. Justice Stevens claims that the Superior Court's narrowing construction creates an impermissible "prior restraint" on protected speech, because that court required the submission of certain casino advertising to appellee for its prior approval. This argument was not raised by appellant, either below or in this Court, and we therefore express no view on the constitutionality of the particular portion

BRENNAN, J., joined by Marshall and Blackmun, JJ., dissented: "[W]hile the First Amendment ordinarily prohibits regulation of speech based on the content of the communicated message, the government may regulate the content of commercial speech in order to prevent the dissemination of information that is false, deceptive, or misleading, see *Zauderer; Friedman; Ohralik,* or that proposes an illegal transaction, see *Pittsburgh Press.* We have, however, consistently invalidated restrictions designed to deprive consumers of accurate information about products and services legally offered for sale.

"[N]o differences between commercial and other kinds of speech justify protecting commercial speech less extensively where, as here, the government seeks to manipulate private behavior by depriving citizens of truthful information concerning lawful activities. [Accordingly,] I believe that where the government seeks to suppress the dissemination of nonmisleading commercial speech relating to legal activities, for fear that recipients will act on the information provided, such regulation should be subject to strict judicial scrutiny.

"The Court, rather than applying strict scrutiny, evaluates Puerto Rico's advertising ban under the relaxed standards normally used to test government regulation of commercial speech. Even under these standards, however, I do not believe that Puerto Rico constitutionally may suppress all casino advertising directed to its residents. [Neither] the statute on its face nor the legislative history indicates that the Puerto Rico Legislature thought that serious harm would result if residents were allowed to engage in casino gambling;[2] indeed, the available evidence suggests exactly the opposite. Puerto Rico has legalized gambling casinos, and permits its residents to patronize them. Thus, the Puerto Rico legislature has determined that permitting residents to engage in casino gambling will not produce the 'serious harmful effects' that have led a majority of States to ban such activity. Residents of Puerto Rico are also permitted to engage in a variety of other gambling activities—including horse racing, 'picas', dog racing, cockfighting, and the Puerto Rico lottery—all of which are allowed to advertise freely to residents.[3] Indeed, it is surely not far-fetched to suppose that the legislature chose to restrict casino advertising not because of the 'evils' of casino gambling, but because it preferred that Puerto Ricans spend their gambling dollars on the Puerto Rico lottery. In any event, in light of the legislature's determination that serious harm will *not* result if residents are permitted

of the Superior Court's narrowing construction cited by Justice Stevens.

2. The Act's Statement of Motives says only that: "The purpose of this Act is to contribute to the development of tourism by means of the authorization of certain games of chance—[and] by the establishment of regulations for and the strict surveillance of said games by the government, in order to ensure for tourists the best possible safeguards, while at the same time opening for the Treasurer of Puerto Rico an additional source of income." There is no suggestion that discouraging residents from patronizing gambling casinos would further Puerto Rico's interests in developing tourism, ensuring safeguards for tourists, or producing additional revenue.

3. The Court seeks to justify Puerto Rico's selective prohibition of casino advertising by asserting that "the legislature felt that for Puerto Ricans the risks associated with casino

gambling were significantly greater than those associated with the more traditional kinds of gambling in Puerto Rico." Nothing in the record suggests that the legislature believed this to be the case. Appellee has failed to show that casino gambling presents risks different from those associated with other gambling activities, such that Puerto Rico might, consistently with the First Amendment, choose to suppress only casino advertising directed to its residents. For this reason, I believe that Puerto Rico's selective advertising ban also violates appellant's rights under the Equal Protection Clause. In rejecting appellant's equal protection claim, the Court erroneously uses a "rational basis" analysis, thereby ignoring the important First Amendment interests implicated by this case. Cf. *Chicago Police Dept. v. Mosley,* [Casebooks, Section 5, I, B].

and *encouraged* to gamble, I do not see how Puerto Rico's interest in discouraging its residents from engaging in casino gambling can be characterized as 'substantial,' even if the legislature had actually asserted such an interest which, of course, it has not.

"The Court nevertheless sustains Puerto Rico's advertising ban because the legislature *could* have determined that casino gambling would seriously harm the health, safety, and welfare of the Puerto Rican citizens.[4] This reasoning is contrary to this Court's long established First Amendment jurisprudence. When the government seeks to place restrictions upon commercial speech, a court may not, as the Court implies today, simply speculate about valid reasons that the government might have for enacting such restrictions. [A]ppellees have failed to show that a substantial government interest supports Puerto Rico's ban on protected expression.

"[E]ven assuming that an advertising ban would effectively reduce residents' patronage of gambling casinos,[5] it is not clear how it would directly advance Puerto Rico's interest in controlling the 'serious harmful effects' the Court associates with casino gambling. In particular, it is unclear whether banning casino advertising aimed at residents would affect local crime, prostitution, the development of corruption, or the infiltration of organized crime. Because Puerto Rico actively promotes its casinos to tourists, these problems are likely to persist whether or not residents are also encouraged to gamble. Absent some showing that a ban on advertising aimed only at residents will directly advance Puerto Rico's interest in controlling the harmful effects allegedly associated with casino gambling, Puerto Rico may not constitutionally restrict protected expression in that way.

"Finally, appellee has failed to show that Puerto Rico's interest in controlling the harmful effects allegedly associated with casino gambling 'cannot be protected adequately by more limited regulation of appellant's commercial expression.' *Central Hudson.* Rather than suppressing constitutionally protected expression, Puerto Rico could seek directly to address the specific harms thought to be associated with casino gambling. Thus, Puerto Rico could continue carefully to monitor casino operations to guard against 'the development of corruption, and the infiltration of organized crime.' It could vigorously enforce its criminal statutes to combat 'the increase in local crime [and] the fostering of prostitution.' It could establish limits on the level of permissible betting, or promulgate additional speech designed to discourage casino gambling among

4. The Court reasons that because Puerto Rico could legitimately decide to prohibit casino gambling entirely, it may also take the "less intrusive step" of legalizing casino gambling but restricting speech. According to the Court, it would "surely be a strange constitutional doctrine which would concede to the legislature the authority to totally ban [casino gambling] but deny to the legislature the authority to forbid the stimulation of demand for [casino gambling]" by banning advertising. I do not agree that a ban on casino advertising is "less intrusive" than an outright prohibition of such activity. A majority of States have chosen not to legalize casino gambling, and we have never suggested that this might be unconstitutional. However, having decided to legalize casino gambling, Puerto Rico's decision to ban truthful speech concerning entirely lawful activity raises serious First Amendment problems. Thus, the "constitutional doctrine" which bans Puerto Rico from banning advertisements concerning lawful casino gambling is not so strange a restraint—it is called the First Amendment.

5. Unlike the Court, I do not read the fact that appellant has chosen to litigate the case here necessarily to indicate the appellant itself believes that Puerto Rico residents would respond to casino advertising. In light of appellee's arbitrary and capricious application of § 8, appellant could justifiably have believed that, notwithstanding the Superior Court's "narrowing" construction, its First Amendment rights could be safeguarded effectively only if the Act was invalidated on its face.

residents, in order to avoid the 'disruption of moral and cultural patterns,' that might result if residents were to engage in excessive casino gambling. Such measures would directly address the problems appellee associates with casino gambling, while avoiding the First Amendment problems raised where the government seeks to ban constitutionally protected speech.

"[I]t is incumbent upon the government to *prove* that more limited means are not sufficient to protect its interests, and for a *court* to decide whether or not the government has sustained this burden. See *Central Hudson.* In this case, nothing suggests that the Puerto Rico Legislature ever considered the efficacy of measures other than suppressing protected expression. More importantly, there has been no showing that alternative measures would inadequately safeguard the Commonwealth's interest in controlling the harmful effects allegedly associated with casino gambling. Under these circumstances, Puerto Rico's ban on advertising clearly violates the First Amendment.[4]"

STEVENS, J., joined by Marshall and Blackmun, JJ., also dissented: "The Court concludes that 'the greater power to completely ban casino gambling necessarily includes the lesser power to ban advertising of casino gambling.' Whether a State may ban all advertising of an activity that it permits but could prohibit—such as gambling, prostitution, or the consumption of marijuana or liquor—is an elegant question of constitutional law. It is not, however, appropriate to address that question in this case because Puerto Rico's rather bizarre restraints on speech are so plainly forbidden by the First Amendment. * * *

"With respect to the publisher, in stark, unabashed language, the Superior Court's construction favors certain identifiable publications and disfavors others. If the publication (or medium) is from outside Puerto Rico, it is very favored indeed. [If] the publication is native to Puerto Rico, however—the *San Juan Star,* for instance—it is subject to a far more rigid system of restraints and controls regarding the manner in which a certain form of speech (casino ads) may be carried in its pages. Unless the Court is prepared to uphold an Illinois regulation of speech that subjects *The New York Times* to one standard and *The Chicago Tribune* to another, I do not understand why it is willing to uphold a Puerto Rico regulation that applies one standard to *The New York Times* and another to the *San Juan Star.*

"With respect to the audience, the newly construed regulations plainly discriminate in terms of the intended listener or reader. [The] regulation thus poses what might be viewed as a reverse Privileges and Immunities problem: Puerto Rico's residents are singled out for disfavored treatment in comparison to all other Americans. But nothing so fancy is required to recognize the obvious First Amendment problem in this kind of audience discrimination. I cannot imagine that this Court would uphold an Illinois regulation that forbade advertising 'addressed' to Illinois residents while allowing the same advertiser to communicate his message to visitors and commuters; we should be no more willing to uphold a Puerto Rico regulation that forbids advertising 'addressed' to Puerto Rico residents.

"With respect to the message, the regulations now take one word of the English language—'casino'—and give it a special opprobrium. Use of that suspicious six letter word is permitted only 'where the trade name of the hotel is

---

4. The Court seeks to buttress its holding by noting that some States have regulated other "harmful" products, such as cigarettes, alcoholic beverages, and legalized prostitution, by restricting advertising. While I believe that Puerto Rico may not prohibit all casino advertising directed to its residents, I reserve judgment as to the constitutionality of the variety of advertising restrictions adopted by other jurisdictions.

used even though it may contain a reference to the casino.' The regulations explicitly include an important provision—'that the word casino is never used alone nor specified.' (The meaning of 'specified'—perhaps italicization, or bold-face, or all capital letters—is presumably left to subsequent case-by-case adjudication). Singling out the use of a particular word for official sanctions raises grave First Amendment concerns, and Puerto Rico has utterly failed to justify the disfavor in which that particular six-letter word is held. * * *

"The general proposition advanced by the majority today—that a State may prohibit the advertising of permitted conduct if it may prohibit the conduct altogether—bears little resemblance to the grotesquely flawed regulation of speech advanced by Puerto Rico in this case.[2] The First Amendment surely does not permit Puerto Rico's frank discrimination among publications, audiences, and words. Nor should sanctions for speech be as unpredictable and haphazardous as the role of dice in a casino."

Notes and Questions

1. *Virginia Pharmacy compared.* Suppose Virginia reasons that because it could "totally ban a product or activity," e.g., drugs, it has the authority "to forbid the stimulation of the demand for the product or activity through [price] advertising on behalf of those who would profit from such increased demand?" Constitutional? Was this argument raised in *Virginia Pharmacy*?

2. *Central Hudson compared. Central Hudson* insisted that the Commission "demonstrat[e] that its interest in conservation cannot be protected adequately by more limited regulation of appellant's commercial expression." Moreover, it listed a number of alternatives the Commission might consider. *Posadas* settled for the conclusion that the legislature "could" conclude as it "apparently did" that a suggested alternative would be ineffective. Should the legislature have been forced to demonstrate that the suggested alternative would be ineffective?

BOARD OF TRUSTEES v. FOX, p. 206 of this Supplement, per Scalia, J., held that the *Central Hudson* test does not require government to foreclose the possibility of all less restrictive alternatives. It is enough if the fit between means and ends is "reasonable." It need not be "perfect." Like time, place, and manner regulations, however, the relationship between means and end must be "narrowly tailored to achieve the desired objective." Under that standard, as interpreted (see p. 206 of this Supplement), government may not " 'burden substantially more speech than is necessary to further the government's legitimate interest,' " [a] but need not foreclose "all conceivable alternatives." Scalia, J., argued that to have a more demanding test in commercial speech than that used for time, place, and manner regulations would be inappropriate because time, place, and manner regulations can apply to political speech.[b]

2. Moreover, the Court has relied on an inappropriate major premise. The fact that Puerto Rico might prohibit all casino gambling does not necessarily mean that it could prohibit residents from patronizing casinos that are open to tourists. Even under the Court's reasoning, discriminatory censorship cannot be justified as a less restrictive form of economic regulation unless discriminatory regulation is itself permissible.

a. Quoting *Ward v. Rock Against Racism*, p. 254 of this Supplement.

b. Blackmun, J., joined by Brennan and Marshall, JJ., dissenting, did not reach this issue. See p. 206 of this Supplement.

PRIVATE SPEECH

CON LAW: P. 797, after note 1

AMER CON: P. 575, after note 1

RTS & LIB: P. 465, after note 1

RANKIN v. McPHERSON

483 U.S. 378, 107 S.Ct. 2891, 97 L.Ed.2d 315 (1987).

JUSTICE MARSHALL delivered the opinion of the Court.

The issue in this case is whether a clerical employee in a county constable's office was properly discharged for remarking, after hearing of an attempt on the life of the President, "If they go for him again, I hope they get him."

I

On January 12, 1981, respondent Ardith McPherson was appointed a deputy in the office of the constable of Harris County, Texas. The constable is an elected official who functions as a law enforcement officer. At the time of her appointment, McPherson, a black woman, was 19 years old and had attended college for a year, studying secretarial science. Her appointment was conditional for a 90-day probationary period.

Although McPherson's title was "deputy constable," this was the case only because all employees of the constable's office, regardless of job function, were deputy constables. She was not a commissioned peace officer, did not wear a uniform, and was not authorized to make arrests or permitted to carry a gun. McPherson's duties were purely clerical. Her work station was a desk at which there was no telephone, in a room to which the public did not have ready access. Her job was to type data from court papers into a computer that maintained an automated record of the status of civil process in the county. Her training consisted of two days of instruction in the operation of her computer terminal.

On March 30, 1981, McPherson and some fellow employees heard on an office radio that there had been an attempt to assassinate the President of the United States. Upon hearing that report, McPherson engaged a co-worker, Lawrence Jackson, who was apparently her boyfriend, in a brief conversation, which according to McPherson's uncontroverted testimony went as follows:

"Q: What did you say?

"A: I said I felt that that would happen sooner or later.

"Q: Okay. And what did Lawrence say?

"A: Lawrence said, yeah, agreeing with me.

"Q: Okay. Now, when you—after Lawrence spoke, then what was your next comment?

"A: Well, we were talking—it's a wonder why they did that. I felt like it would be a black person that did that, because I feel like most of my kind is on welfare and CETA, and they use medicaid, and at the time, I was thinking that's what it was.

"* * * But then after I said that, and then Lawrence said, yeah, he's cutting back medicaid and food stamps. And I said, yeah, welfare and CETA. I said, shoot, if they go for him again, I hope they get him."

McPherson's last remark was overheard by another deputy constable, who, unbeknownst to McPherson, was in the room at the time. The remark was reported to Constable Rankin, who summoned McPherson. McPherson readily admitted that she had made the statement, but testified that she told Rankin, upon being asked if she made the statement, "Yes, but I didn't mean anything by it." After their discussion, Rankin fired McPherson.

McPherson brought suit in the United States District Court for the Southern District of Texas under 42 U.S.C. § 1983, alleging that petitioner Rankin, in discharging her, had violated her constitutional rights under color of state law.

* * *

II

It is clearly established that a State may not discharge an employee on a basis that infringes that employee's constitutionally protected interest in freedom of speech. [The] determination whether a public employer has properly discharged an employee for engaging in speech requires "a balance between the interests of the [employee], as a citizen, in commenting upon matters of public concern and the interest of the State, as an employer, in promoting the efficiency of the public services it performs through its employees." *Pickering; Connick.* This balancing is necessary in order to accommodate the dual role of the public employer as a provider of public services and as a government entity operating under the constraints of the First Amendment. On one hand, public employers are *employers*, concerned with the efficient function of their operations; review of every personnel decision made by a public employer could, in the long run, hamper the performance of public functions. On the other hand, "the threat of dismissal from public employment is * * * a potent means of inhibiting speech." *Pickering.* * * *

A

The threshold question in applying this balancing test is whether McPherson's speech may be "fairly characterized as constituting speech on a matter of public concern." *Connick.*[7] The District Court apparently found that McPherson's speech did not address a matter of public concern.[8] The Court of Appeals rejected this conclusion, finding that "the life and death of the President are obviously matters of public concern." Our view of these determinations of the courts below is limited in this context by our constitutional obligation to assure that the record supports this conclusion: " 'we are compelled to examine for ourselves the statements in issue and the circumstances under which they [were] made to see whether or not they * * * are of a character which the principles of the First Amendment, as adopted by the Due Process Clause of the Fourteenth Amendment, protect.' " *Connick.*

Considering the statement in context, as *Connick* requires, discloses that it plainly dealt with a matter of public concern. The statement was made in the course of a conversation addressing the policies of the President's administration. It came on the heels of a news bulletin regarding what is certainly a matter of heightened public attention: an attempt on the life of the President.

---

7. Even where a public employee's speech does not touch upon a matter of public concern, that speech is not "totally beyond the protection of the First Amendment," *Connick*, but "absent the most unusual circumstances a federal court is not the appropriate forum in which to review the wisdom of a personnel decision taken by a public agency allegedly in reaction to the employee's behavior."

8. The District Court, after its second hearing in this case, delivered its opinion from the bench and did not explicitly address the elements of the required balancing test. It did, however, state that the case was "not like the *Myers* case where Ms. Myers was trying to comment upon the internal affairs of the office, or matters upon public concern. I don't think it is a matter of public concern to approve even more to the second attempt at assassination." * * *

While a statement that amounted to a threat to kill the President would not be protected by the First Amendment, the District Court concluded, and we agree, that McPherson's statement did not amount to a threat punishable under 18 U.S.C. § 871(a) or 18 U.S.C. § 2385, or, indeed, that could properly be criminalized at all. ⁂

[The] inappropriate or controversial character of a statement is irrelevant to the question whether it deals with a matter of public concern. ⁂

B

Because McPherson's statement addressed a matter of public concern, *Pickering* next requires that we balance McPherson's interest in making her statement against "the interest of the State, as an employer, in promoting the efficiency of the public services it performs through its employees."[13] The State bears a burden of justifying the discharge on legitimate grounds. *Connick*.

In performing the balancing, the statement will not be considered in a vacuum; the manner, time, and place of the employee's expression are relevant, as is the context in which the dispute arose. See *Connick*. [While] McPherson's statement was made at the workplace, there is no evidence that it interfered with the efficient functioning of the office. The Constable was evidently not afraid that McPherson had disturbed or interrupted other employees—he did not inquire to whom respondent had made the remark and testified that he "was not concerned who she had made it to." In fact, Constable Rankin testified that the possibility of interference with the functions of the Constable's office had *not* been a consideration in his discharge of respondent and that he did not even inquire whether the remark had disrupted the work of the office.

Nor was there any danger that McPherson had discredited the office by making her statement in public. McPherson's speech took place in an area to which there was ordinarily no public access; her remark was evidently made in a private conversation with another employee. There is no suggestion that any member of the general public was present or heard McPherson's statement. Nor is there any evidence that employees other than Jackson who worked in the room even heard the remark. Not only was McPherson's discharge unrelated to the functioning of the office, it was not based on any assessment by the constable that the remark demonstrated a character trait that made respondent unfit to perform her work.

[Evidently] because McPherson had made the statement, and because the constable believed that she "meant it," he decided that she was not a suitable employee to have in a law enforcement agency. But in weighing the State's interest in discharging an employee based on any claim that the content of a statement made by the employee somehow undermines the mission of the public employer, some attention must be paid to the responsibilities of the employee within the agency. The burden of caution employees bear with respect to the words they speak will vary with the extent of authority and public accountability the employee's role entails. Where, as here, an employee serves no confidential, policymaking, or public contact role, the danger to the agency's successful function from that employee's private speech is minimal. We cannot believe that every employee in Constable Rankin's office, whether computer operator, electrician, or file clerk, is equally required, on pain of discharge, to avoid any statement susceptible of being interpreted by the Constable as an indication that

13. We agree with Justice Powell that a purely private statement on a matter of public concern will rarely, if ever, justify discharge of a public employee. ⁂

the employee may be unworthy of employment in his law enforcement agency.[17] At some point, such concerns are so removed from the effective function of the public employer that they cannot prevail over the free speech rights of the public employee.[18]

This is such a case.

JUSTICE POWELL, concurring.

It is not easy to understand how this case has assumed constitutional dimensions and reached the Supreme Court of the United States. The fact that the case is here, however, illustrates the uniqueness of our Constitution and our system of judicial review: courts at all levels are available and receptive to claims of injustice, large and small, by any and every citizen of this country.

* * *

There is no dispute that McPherson's comment was made during a private conversation with a co-worker who happened also to be her boyfriend. She had no intention or expectation that it would be overheard or acted on by others. Given this, I think it is unnecessary to engage in the extensive analysis normally required by *Connick* and *Pickering*. If a statement is on a matter of public concern, as it was here, it will be an unusual case where the employer's legitimate interests will be so great as to justify punishing an employee for this type of private speech that routinely takes place at all levels in the workplace. The risk that a single, offhand comment directed to only one other worker will lower morale, disrupt the work force, or otherwise undermine the mission of the office borders on the fanciful. To the extent that the full constitutional analysis of the competing interests is required, I generally agree with the Court's opinion.

* * *

In my view, however, the case is hardly as complex as might be expected in a dispute that now has been considered five separate times by three different federal courts. The undisputed evidence shows that McPherson made an ill-considered—but protected—comment during a private conversation, and the Constable made an instinctive, but intemperate, employment decision on the basis of this speech. I agree that on these facts, McPherson's private speech is protected by the First Amendment.

I join the opinion of the Court.

17. We therefore reject the notion, expressed by petitioner's counsel at oral argument, that the fact that an employee was deputized meant, regardless of that employee's job responsibility, that the Constable could discharge the employee for any expression inconsistent with the goals of a law enforcement agency.

"MR. LEE [counsel for petitioner]: The man who sweeps the floor in the constable's office is not employed by the constable. He's employed by commissioners' court who takes care of all of the courthouses."

"QUESTION: I guess it's a lucky thing then that the constable is not himself responsible for keeping the courthouse clean, which could have been the case. I mean, you—

"MR. LEE: Which could have been the case, yes, sir. That is right, because he would then—

"QUESTION: Then your argument would indeed extend to the man who swept the floor; right? * * *

"QUESTION: And you would be making the same argument here—

"MR. LEE: Yes, sir.

"QUESTION: —because that man had the name of deputy?

"MR. LEE: That's right."

18. This is not to say that clerical employees are insulated from discharge where their speech, taking the acknowledged factors into account, truly injures the public interest in the effective functioning of the public employer. Compare *McMullen v. Carson*, 754 F.2d 936 (11th Cir. 1985) (clerical employee in sheriff's office properly discharged for stating on television news that he was an employee for the sheriff's office and a recruiter for the Ku Klux Klan).

JUSTICE SCALIA, with whom THE CHIEF JUSTICE, JUSTICE WHITE, and JUSTICE O'CONNOR join, dissenting.

I agree with the proposition, felicitously put by Constable Rankin's counsel, that no law enforcement agency is required by the First Amendment to permit one of its employees to "ride with the cops and cheer for the robbers." * * *

That McPherson's statement does not constitute speech on a matter of "public concern" is demonstrated by comparing it with statements that have been found to fit that description in prior decisions involving public employees. McPherson's statement is a far cry from the question by the assistant district attorney in *Connick* whether her co-workers "ever [felt] pressured to work in political campaigns," *Connick*; from the letter written by the public school teacher in *Pickering* criticizing the board of education's proposals for financing school construction, *Pickering*; from the legislative testimony of a state college teacher in *Perry v. Sindermann* advocating that a particular college be elevated to 4-year status; from the memorandum given by a teacher to a radio station in *Mt. Healthy City Board of Ed. v. Doyle* dealing with teacher dress and appearance; and from the complaints about school board policies and practices at issue in *Givhan v. Western Line Consolidated School Dist.*

McPherson's statement is indeed so different from those that it is only one step removed from statements that we have previously held entitled to no First Amendment protection, even in the nonemployment context—including assassination threats against the President (which are illegal under 18 U.S.C. § 871), see *Frohwerk*; "'fighting' words," *Chaplinsky*; epithets or personal abuse, *Cantwell v. Connecticut*; and advocacy of force or violence, *Harisiades v. Shaughnessy*, 342 U.S. 580, 72 S.Ct. 512, 96 L.Ed. 586 (1952). A statement lying so near the category of completely unprotected speech cannot fairly be viewed as lying within the "heart" of the First Amendment's protection; it lies within that category of speech that can neither be characterized as speech on matters of public concern nor properly subject to criminal penalties. Once McPherson stopped explicitly criticizing the President's policies and expressed a desire that he be assassinated, she crossed the line. * * *

I cannot respond to the Court's progression of reasoning except to say I do not understand it. Surely the Court does not mean to adopt the reasoning of the court below, which was that McPherson's statement was "addressed to a matter of public concern" within the meaning of *Connick* because the public would obviously be "concerned" about the assassination of the President. That is obviously untenable: The public would be "concerned" about a statement threatening to blow up the local federal building or demanding a $1 million extortion payment, yet that kind of "public concern" does not entitle such a statement to any First Amendment protection at all.

Even if I agreed that McPherson's statement was speech on a matter of "public concern," I would still find it unprotected. It is important to be clear on what the issue is in this part of the case. It is not, as the Court suggests, whether "Rankin's interest *in discharging [McPherson]* outweighed her rights under the First Amendment." Rather, it is whether his interest *in preventing the expression of such statements in his agency* outweighed her First Amendment interest in making the statement. We are not deliberating, in other words, (or at least should not be) about whether the sanction of dismissal was, as the concurrence puts it, "an * * * intemperat[e] employment decision." It may well have been—and personally I think it was. But we are not sitting as a panel to develop sound principles of proportionality for adverse actions in the state civil service. We are asked to determine whether, given the interests of this law enforcement office, McPherson had a *right* to say what she did—so that she could not only not be fired for it but could not be formally reprimanded for it, or even prevented from repeating it endlessly into the future. It boggles the mind to think that she has such a right.

The Constable testified that he "was very concerned that this remark was made." Rightly so. As a law enforcement officer, the Constable obviously has a strong interest in preventing statements by any of his employees approving, or expressing a desire for, serious, violent crimes—regardless of whether the statements actually interfere with office operations at the time they are made or demonstrate character traits that make the speaker unsuitable for law enforcement work. ＊ ＊ ＊

Statements by the Constable's employees to the effect that "if they go for the President again, I hope they get him" might also, to put it mildly, undermine public confidence in the Constable's office. A public employer has a strong interest in preserving its reputation with the public. We know—from undisputed testimony—that McPherson had or might have had some occasion to deal with the public while carrying out her duties.

The Court's sweeping assertion (and apparent holding) that where an employee "serves no confidential, policymaking, or public contact role, the danger to the agency's successful function from that employee's private speech is minimal" is simply contrary to reason and experience. Nonpolicymaking employees (the assistant district attorney in *Connick* for example) can hurt working relationships and undermine public confidence in an organization every bit as much as policymaking employees. I, for one, do not look forward to the new First Amendment world the Court creates, in which nonpolicymaking employees of the Equal Employment Opportunity Commission must be permitted to make remarks on the job approving of racial discrimination, nonpolicymaking employees of the Selective Service System to advocate noncompliance with the draft laws, and (since it is really quite difficult to contemplate anything more absurd than the present case itself), nonpolicymaking constable's deputies to express approval for the assassination of the President. ＊ ＊ ＊

CON LAW: P. 803, after note 3

AMER CON: P. 582, after note 3

RTS & LIB: P. 471, after note 3

Missouri prohibits communications between prison inmates in different prisons unless the correspondence concerns "legal matters" or is with immediate family members, or is otherwise specially approved. Should the public/private distinction make a difference in this context? What if the communication concerns presidential politics? Prisoners' rights? See generally *Turner v. Safley*, 482 U.S. 78, 107 S.Ct. 2254, 96 L.Ed.2d 64 (1987) (upholding the Missouri scheme).

LABOR SPEECH [NEW PART]

CON LAW: P. 803, after note 3

RTS & LIB: P. 471, after note 3

DEBARTOLO CORP. v. FLORIDA GULF TRADES COUNCIL
485 U.S. 568, 108 S.Ct. 1392, 99 L.Ed.2d 645 (1988).

JUSTICE WHITE delivered the opinion of the Court.

This case centers around the respondent union's peaceful handbilling of the businesses operating in a shopping mall in Tampa, Florida, owned by petitioner, the Edward J. DeBartolo Corporation (DeBartolo). The union's primary labor dispute was with H. J. High Construction Company (High) over alleged substandard wages and fringe benefits. High was retained by the H. J. Wilson Company (Wilson) to construct a department store in the mall, and neither DeBartolo nor any of the other 85 or so mall tenants had any contractual right to influence the selection of contractors.

The union, however, sought to obtain their influence upon Wilson and High by distributing handbills asking mall customers not to shop at any of the stores in the mall "until the Mall's owner publicly promises that all construction at the Mall will be done using contractors who pay their employees fair wages and fringe benefits." The handbills' message was that "[t]he payment of substandard wages not only diminishes the working person's ability to purchase with earned, rather than borrowed, dollars, but it also undercuts the wage standard of the entire community." The handbills made clear that the union was seeking only a consumer boycott against the other mall tenants, not a secondary strike by their employees. At all four entrances to the mall for about three weeks in December 1979, the union peacefully distributed the handbills without any accompanying picketing or patrolling.

[DeBartolo] [filed] a complaint with the National Labor Relations Board (Board), charging the union with engaging in unfair labor practices under § 8(b)(4) of the National Labor Relations Act (NLRA), 61 Stat. 141, as amended, 29 U.S.C. § 158(b)(4).[2] [T]he Board held that the union's handbilling was proscribed by § 8(b)(4)(ii)(B).

---

2. That section provides in pertinent part: "§ 158. Unfair labor practices * * *

"(b) Unfair labor practices by labor organization It shall be an unfair labor practice for a labor organization or its agents—* * *

"(4)(i) to engage in, or to induce or encourage any individual employed by any person engaged in commerce or in an industry affecting commerce to engage in, a strike or a refusal in the course of his employment to use, manufacture, process, transport, or otherwise handle or work on any goods, articles, materials, or commodities or to perform any services; or (ii) to threaten, coerce, or restrain any person engaged in commerce or in an industry affecting commerce, where in either case an object thereof is—* * *

"(B) forcing or requiring any person to cease using, selling, handling, transporting, or otherwise dealing in the products of any other producer, processor, or manufacturer, or to cease doing business with any other person, or forcing or requiring any other employer to recognize or bargain with a labor organization as the representative of his employees unless such labor organization has been certified as the representative of such employees under the provisions of section 159 of this title: *Provided*, That nothing contained in this clause (B) shall be construed to make unlawful, where not otherwise unlawful, any primary strike or primary picketing; * * *

"*Provided further*, [the 'publicity proviso'] That for the purposes of this paragraph (4) only, nothing contained in such paragraph shall be construed to prohibit publicity, other than picketing, for the purpose of truthfully advising the public, including consumers and members of a labor organization, that a product or products are produced by an employer with whom the labor organization has a primary dispute and are distributed by another employer, as long as such publicity does not have an effect of inducing any individual employed by any person other than the primary employer in the course of his employment to

[T]he Board has construed § 8(b)(4) of the Act to cover handbilling at a mall entrance urging potential customers not to trade with any retailers in the mall, in order to exert pressure on the proprietor of the mall to influence a particular mall tenant not to do business with a nonunion construction contractor. [T]he Board's construction of the statute, as applied in this case, poses serious questions of the validity of § 8(b)(4) under the First Amendment. The handbills involved here truthfully revealed the existence of a labor dispute and urged potential customers of the mall to follow a wholly legal course of action, namely, not to patronize the retailers doing business in the mall. The handbilling was peaceful. No picketing or patrolling was involved. On its face, this was expressive activity arguing that substandard wages should be opposed by abstaining from shopping in a mall where such wages were paid. Had the union simply been leafletting the public generally, including those entering every shopping mall in town, pursuant to an annual educational effort against substandard pay, there is little doubt that legislative proscription of such leaflets would pose a substantial issue of validity under the First Amendment. The same may well be true in this case, although here the handbills called attention to a specific situation in the mall allegedly involving the payment of unacceptably low wages by a construction contractor.

That a labor union is the leafletter and that a labor dispute was involved does not foreclose this analysis. We do not suggest that communications by labor unions are never of the commercial speech variety and thereby entitled to a lesser degree of constutitional protection. The handbills involved here, however, do not appear to be typical commercial speech such as advertising the price of a product or arguing its merits, for they pressed the benefits of unionism to the community and the dangers of inadequate wages to the economy and the standard of living of the populace. Of course, commercial speech itself is protected by the First Amendment, *Virginia Pharmacy*, and however these handbills are to be classified, [we] must independently inquire whether there is another interpretation, not raising these serious constitutional concerns, that may fairly be ascribed to § 8(b)(4)(ii). * * *

The case turns on whether handbilling such as involved here must be held to "threaten, coerce, or restrain any person" to cease doing business with another, within the meaning of § 8(b)(4)(ii)(B). We note first that "induc[ing] or encourag[ing]" employees of the secondary employer to strike is proscribed by § 8(b)(4)(i). But more than mere persuasion is necessary to prove a violation of § 8(b)(4)(ii): that section requires a showing of threats, coercion, or restraints. Those words, we have said, are "nonspecific, indeed vague," and should be interpreted with "caution" and not given a "broad sweep"; and in applying § 8 (b)(1)(A) they were not to be construed to reach peaceful recognitional picketing. Neither is there any necessity to construe such language to reach the handbills involved in this case. There is no suggestion that the leaflets had any coercive effect on customers of the mall. There was no violence, picketing, or patrolling and only an attempt to persuade customers not to shop in the mall.

The Board nevertheless found that the handbilling "coerced" mall tenants and explained in a footnote that "[a]ppealing to the public not to patronize secondary employers is an attempt to inflict economic harm on the secondary employers by causing them to lose business. [S]uch appeals constitute 'economic retaliation' and are therefore a form of coercion." Our decision in *NLRB v.*

refuse to pick up, deliver, or transport any goods, or not to perform any services, at the establishment of the employer engaged in such distribution."

Fruit and Vegetable Packers, Local 760, 377 U.S. 58, 84 S.Ct. 1063, 12 L.Ed.2d 129 (1964) (*Tree Fruits*),[a] however, makes untenable the notion that *any* kind of handbilling, picketing, or other appeals to a secondary employer to cease doing business with the employer involved in the labor dispute is "coercion" within the meaning of § 8(b)(4)(ii)(B) if it has some economic impact on the neutral. In that case, the union picketed a secondary employer, a retailer, asking the public not to buy a product produced by the primary employer. We held that the impact of this picketing was not coercion within the meaning of § 8(b)(4) even though, if the appeal succeeded, the retailer would lose revenue.[4]

NLRB v. Retail Store Employees Local 1001, 447 U.S. 607, 100 S.Ct. 2372, 65 L.Ed.2d 377 (1980) (*Safeco*), in turn, held that consumer picketing urging a general boycott of a secondary employer aimed at causing him to sever relations with the union's real antagonist was coercive and forbidden by § 8(b)(4).[b] It is urged that *Safeco* rules this case because the union sought a general boycott of all tenants in the mall. But "picketing is qualitatively 'different from other modes of communication,'" and *Safeco* noted that the picketing there actually threatened the neutral with ruin or substantial loss. As Justice Stevens pointed out in his concurrence in *Safeco*, picketing is "a mixture of conduct and communication" and the conduct element "often provides the most persuasive deterrent to third persons about to enter a business establishment." Handbills containing the same message, he observed, are "much less effective than labor picketing" because they "depend entirely on the persuasive force of the idea."[c] Similarly, the Court stated in *Hughes v. Superior Court*, 339 U.S. 460, 70 S.Ct. 718, 94 L.Ed. 985 (1950): "Publication in a newspaper, or by distribution of circulars, may convey the same information or make the same charge as do those patrolling a picket line. But the very purpose of a picket line is to exert influences, and it produces consequences, different from other modes of communication."[d]

a. *Tree Fruits* involved union picketing and handbilling urging consumers not to buy Washington apples from Safeway markets. The union's dispute was with those who supplied apples to Safeway, not with Safeway. In finding no violation, the Court observed that if the union's appeal succeeds, "the secondary employers' purchases from the struck firms are decreased only because the public has diminished its purchases of the struck product. On the other hand, when consumer picketing is employed to persuade customers not to trade at all with the secondary employer, the latter stops buying the struck product, not because of a falling demand, but in response to pressure designed to inflict injury on his business generally. In such case, the union does more than merely follow the struck product; it creates a separate dispute with the secondary employer."

4. The Board points out that *Tree Fruits* indicates urging customer boycotts can be coercion within the meaning of § 8(b)(4). But the Court was there talking about picketing and not mere handbilling.

b. *Safeco* involved union picketing (and handbilling that was not challenged) urging consumers to cancel their Safeco insurance policies. The union's dispute was with Safeco, not with the title companies, but 90% of the title companies' income was derived from the sale of Safeco insurance.

c. The *Safeco* plurality, per Powell, J., argued that legislative prohibition of the concededly truthful picketing was justified because such picketing "spreads labor discord by coercing a neutral party to join the fray." The prohibition of picketing in pursuit of such "unlawful objectives" was said to impose "no impermissible restrictions upon constitutionally protected speech." See St. Antoine, *Free Speech or Economic Weapon? The Persisting Problem of Picketing*, 16 Suffolk U.L.Rev. 883, 901 (1982): "[*Safeco*] was the first time the Supreme Court had ever clearly sustained a ban on peaceful and orderly picketing addressed to, and calling for seemingly lawful responses by, individual consumers acting on their own." Contrast *Claiborne Hardware*, Casebooks, Sec. 9, I.

d. *Hughes* involved picketing of a grocery store with placards reading "Lucky Won't Hire Negro Clerks in Proportion to Negro Trade—Don't Patronize." California enjoined the picketing on the ground that the picketing was for an unlawful purpose, i.e., it encouraged racial discrimination: if the picketing were permitted, "then other races, white, yellow, brown, and red, would have equal rights to demand discriminatory hiring on a

In *Tree Fruits*, we could not discern with the "requisite clarity" that Congress intended to proscribe all peaceful consumer picketing at secondary sites. There is even less reason to find in the language of § 8(b)(4)(ii), standing alone, any clear indication that handbilling, without picketing, "coerces" secondary employers. The loss of customers because they read a handbill urging them not to patronize a business, and not because they are intimidated by a line of picketers, is the result of mere persuasion, and the neutral who reacts is doing no more than what its customers honestly want it to do. * * *

The Board's reading of § 8(b)(4) would make an unfair labor practice out of any kind of publicity or communication to the public urging a consumer boycott of employers other than those the [publicity] proviso specifically deals with.[e] On the facts of this case, newspaper, radio, and television appeals not to patronize the mall would be prohibited; and it would be an unfair labor practice for unions in their own meetings to urge their members not to shop in the mall. * * *

In our view, interpreting § 8(b)(4) as not reaching the handbilling involved in this case is not foreclosed either by the language of the section or its legislative history. That construction makes unnecessary passing on the serious constitutional questions that would be raised by the Board's understanding of the statute. * * *[f]

Notes and Questions

1. *The problem of categorization.* What is the relationship between labor publicity handbilling and commercial speech? Public speech? Private speech? Should it be separately categorized?[g] Should there be different categories for speech by employers and speech by employees? Consider *NLRB v. Gissel Packing Co.*, 395 U.S. 575, 89 S.Ct. 1918, 23 L.Ed.2d 547 (1969) (discussing anti-union statements by employer during union organizational drive): "Any assessment of the precise scope of employer expression [must] be made in the context of its labor relations setting. Thus, an employer's rights cannot outweigh the equal right of the employees to associate [freely]. And any balancing of those rights must take into account the economic dependence of the employees on their employers, and the necessary tendency of the former, because of that

racial basis." Concurring with California's assessment that the picketers' objective was unlawful (even though an employer could "voluntarily" have adopted racial quotas without violating any law), the Court, per Frankfurter, J., stated that "The Constitution does not demand that the element of communication in picketing prevail over the mischief furthered by its use in these situations." Moreover, picketing was declared to be "more than free speech, since it involves patrol and [the] loyalties and responses evoked and exacted by picket lines are unlike those flowing from appeals by printed word." Finally, Frankfurter, J., referred to the "compulsive features in picketing, beyond the aspect of mere communication as an appeal to [reason]."

e. Earlier in the litigation, the Court held (*DeBartolo Corp. v. NLRB*, 463 U.S. 147, 103 S.Ct. 2926, 77 L.Ed.2d 535 (1983)), that the publicity proviso did not protect the union's handbilling because the proviso is limited to publicity "intended to inform the public that

the primary employer's product is 'distributed by' the secondary employer" and the cotenants did not distribute any product produced by High.

f. O'Connor and Scalia, JJ., concurred in the judgment without opinion; Kennedy, J., took no part.

g. See Cox, *Foreword: Freedom of Expression in the Burger Court*, 94 Harv.L.Rev. 1 (1980); Getman, *Labor Speech and Free Speech: The Curious Policy of Limited Expression*, 43 Md.L.Rev. 4 (1984); Goldman, The First Amendment and Nonpicketing Labor Publicity, 36 Vand.L.Rev. 1469 (1983); Harper, fn. h, infra; Pope, *Labor and the Constitution: From Abolition to Deindustrialization*, 65 Texas L.Rev. 1071 (1987); Pope, fn.h infra; St. Antoine, fn.c supra; Tribe, note 2 infra; Note, *Labor Picketing and Commercial Speech: Free Enterprise Values in the Doctrine of Free Speech*, 91 Yale L.J. 938 (1982); Note, *Peaceful Labor Picketing and the First Amendment*, 82 Colum.L.Rev. 1469 (1982).

relationship, to pick up intended implications of the latter that might be more readily dismissed by a more disinterested ear. Stating these obvious principles is but another way of recognizing that what is basically at stake is the establishment of a nonpermanent, limited relationship between the employer, his economically dependent employee, and his union agent, not the election of legislators or the enactment of legislation whereby that relationship is ultimately defined and where the independent voter may be freer to listen more objectively and employers as a class freer to talk. Compare *New York Times Co. v. Sullivan*."

2. *The speech-conduct distinction.* Does the Court's speech-conduct distinction adequately distinguish handbilling from picketing? Consider L. Tribe, *Constitutional Choices* 200 (1985): "In a significant number of labor cases, the speech-conduct distinction has been employed to justify restrictions directed specifically at the communicative impact of expressive activity. [As] articulated by Justice Stevens in [*Safeco*], the 'signal' doctrine mandates a lowered level of protection for expression 'that calls for an automatic response to a signal, rather than a reasoned response to an idea.' Though generally mentioned in the same breath as coercion, the idea of a signal by itself does not carry any implication of physical or economic coercion. The idea appears to be rather that by triggering deeply held sentiments, picketing bypasses viewers' faculties of reason and, thus, in a sense brainwashes them into compliance with the boycott.[h]

"Yet this aspect of labor picketing is common to other kinds of picketing, to most effective political communication, and to virtually all advertising—political or commercial—carried in the electronic media.[i] Thus, the speech-conduct distinction, with or without the 'signal' wrinkle, adds nothing to the underlying logic of the cases but does provide another superficially neutral facade to cover the Court's consistent denial of protection to labor picketing."

3. *The determination of truth.* The Court notes that the handbills "truthfully revealed the existence of a labor dispute." What if the existence of a labor dispute were concealed? Consider *Hospital & Service Employees Union Local 399 v. NLRB*, 743 F.2d 1417 (1984). The union distributed handbills and published advertisements in labor newspapers urging a boycott of Delta Airlines and detailing facts about Delta's safety record. The union opined that, "It takes

h. In an influential article, Professor Cox had employed the signal concept somewhat differently. Signal picketing was characterized as that directed primarily, if not exclusively to union members, not the general public. Picketing was the "signal" by which the discipline and organized economic power of unions was invoked. Picketing directed primarily to the general public ("publicity picketing"), he argued, depended upon the persuasiveness of the message rather than the sanctions inherent in the discipline and power of unions. See Cox, *Strikes, Picketing and the Constitution*, 4 Vand.L.Rev. 574, 592–602 (1951). See Harper, *The Consumer's Emerging Right to Boycott*, 93 Yale L.J. 409, 442 (1984) (Stevens' *Safeco* opinion "distorted" Cox's distinction; but recommending a distinction between consumer boycotts and producer boycotts). Compare Pope, *The Three Systems Ladder of First Amendment Values*, 11 Hastings Con.L.Q. 189, 243–45 (criticizing Harp-

er's distinction as unreasonably denying labor the use of employee boycotts) with Gregory, *Constitutional Limitations on the Regulation of Union and Employer Conduct*, 49 Mich. L.Rev. 191, 206–07 (1950) (criticizing Cox's distinction as recommending judicial favoritism for labor) ("All picketing is obviously intended to coerce.") and Jones, *Picketing and Coercion: A Jurisprudence of Epithets*, 39 Va.L.Rev. 1023, 1050–52 (1953) (distinguishing between coercion and causing economic loss for picketed business).

i. See also St. Antoine, supra fn.c, at 902: "To the extent that Justice Stevens' emphasis is on an automatic response to a cryptic 'unfair,' as distinct from a reasoned response to a long list of particularized grievances, I can only restate my belief that a political party's two-word bumper sticker is as much protected by the first amendment as the elaborate platform adopted at its national convention."

more than money to fly Delta. It takes nerve. Let's look at the accident record."

Although the NLRB did not question the underlying facts about Delta's safety record, it maintained that the union materials were not true, but misleading in that they did not reveal the primary dispute.[j] The NLRB sought to prohibit not only the handbills, but also the ads. What result? What if the facts about safety were inaccurate? Should the NLRB be able to sanction the making of false and misleading statements in union representation elections? To set such elections aside because of materially misleading statements? See *Midland Nat'l Life Ins.*, 263 N.L.R.B. No. 24, 1982–83 NLRB Dec. (CCH) ¶ 15,072 (1982).

SECTION: PRIOR RESTRAINTS

CON LAW: P. 806, after note 2

AMER CON: P 584, after note 2

RTS & LIB: P. 473, after note 2

By city ordinance, Lakewood, Ohio gives the Mayor power (subject to whatever conditions the Mayor deems necessary and reasonable) to grant or deny applications for annual permits to place newsracks on public property.[a] The ordinance provides no standards to bind or guide the Mayor's discretion, but requires the Mayor to state reasons for any permit denial. The Plain Dealer Publishing Company declined to apply for a permit and challenged the ordinance on its face. LAKEWOOD v. PLAIN DEALER PUBLISHING CO., ___ U.S. ___, 108 S.Ct. 2138, 100 L.Ed.2d 771 (1988), per BRENNAN, J., declared the ordinance's conferral of mayoral discretion [b] unconstitutional: "At the outset, we confront the issue whether the Newspaper may bring a facial challenge to the City's ordinance. [W]e have previously identified two major First Amendment risks associated with unbridled licensing schemes: self-censorship by speakers in order to avoid being denied a license to speak; and the difficulty of effectively detecting, reviewing, and correcting content-based censorship 'as applied' without standards by which to measure the licensor's action. It is when statutes threaten these risks to a significant degree that courts must entertain an immediate facial attack on the law. Therefore, a facial challenge lies whenever a licensing law gives a government official or agency substantial power to discriminate based on the content or viewpoint of speech by suppressing disfavored speech or disliked speakers. This is not to say that the press or a speaker may challenge as censorship any law involving discretion to which it is subject. The law must have a close enough nexus to expression, or to conduct commonly associated with expression, to pose a real and substantial threat of the identified censorship risks.

"The regulatory scheme in the present case contains two features which, at least in combination, justify the allowance of a facial challenge. First, Lakewood's ordinance requires that the Newspaper apply annually for newsrack licenses. Thus, it is the sort of system in which an individual must apply for multiple licenses over time, or periodically renew a license. When such a system

---

j. Other handbills discussed the primary dispute along with the safety record. The NLRB also sought to prohibit these as "coercive." Constitutional?

a. In addition, the ordinance required architectural approval of the newsrack design, an agreement to indemnify the city against any liability arising from the newsrack, and a $100,000 public liability insurance policy.

b. The Court did not pass on other aspects of the ordinance, remanding instead for a determination of whether the mayoral discretion aspect of the ordinance was severable from the rest.

is applied to speech, or to conduct commonly associated with speech, the licensor does not necessarily view the text of the words about to be spoken, but can measure their probable content or viewpoint by speech already uttered. A speaker in this position is under no illusion regarding the effect of the 'licensed' speech on the ability to continue speaking in the future. Yet demonstrating the link between 'licensed' expression and the denial of a later license might well prove impossible. While perhaps not as direct a threat to speech as a regulation allowing a licensor to view the actual content of the speech to be licensed or permitted, a multiple or periodic licensing requirement is sufficiently threatening to invite judicial concern.

② "A second feature of the licensing system at issue here is that it is directed narrowly and specifically at expression or conduct commonly associated with expression: the circulation of newspapers. Such a framework creates an agency or establishes an official charged particularly with reviewing speech, or conduct commonly associated with it, breeding an 'expertise' tending to favor censorship over speech. [Here] again, without standards to bound the licensor, speakers denied a license will have no way of proving that the decision was unconstitutionally motivated, and, faced with that prospect, they will be pressured to conform their speech to the licensor's unreviewable preference.

ordinance must be content and viewpoint neutral. "Because of these features in the regulatory system at issue here, we think that a facial challenge is appropriate, and that standards controlling the Mayor's discretion must be required. Of course, the City may require periodic licensing, and may even have special licensing procedures for conduct commonly associated with expression; but the Constitution requires that the City establish neutral criteria to insure that the licensing decision is not based on the content or viewpoint of the speech being considered.

"In contrast to the type of law at issue in this case, laws of general application that are not aimed at conduct commonly associated with expression and do not permit licensing determinations to be made on the basis of ongoing expression or the words about to be spoken, carry with them little danger of censorship. For example, a law requiring building permits is rarely effective as a means of censorship. To be sure, on rare occasion an opportunity for censorship will exist, such as when an unpopular newspaper seeks to build a new plant. But such laws provide too blunt a censorship instrument to warrant judicial intervention prior to an allegation of actual misuse. And if such charges are made, the general application of the statute to areas unrelated to expression will provide the courts a yardstick with which to measure the licensor's occasional speech-related decision.

news vs. soda "The foregoing discussion explains why the dissent's analogy between newspapers and soda vendors is inapposite. Newspapers are in the business of expression, while soda vendors are in the business of selling soft drinks. Even if the soda vendor engages in speech, that speech is not related to the soda; therefore preventing it from installing its machines may penalize unrelated speech, but will not directly prevent that speech from occurring. In sum, a law giving the Mayor unbridled discretion to decide which soda vendors may place their machines on public property does not vest him with frequent opportunities to exercise substantial power over the content or viewpoint of the vendor's speech by suppressing the speech or directly controlling the vendor's ability to speak. * * *

"Having concluded that the Newspaper may facially challenge the Lakewood ordinance, we turn to the merits. Section 901.181, Codified Ordinances,

City of Lakewood, provides: 'The Mayor shall either deny the application [for a permit], stating the reasons for such denial or grant said permit subject to the following terms ∗ ∗ ∗.' Section 901.181(c) sets out some of those terms, including: '(7) such other terms and conditions deemed necessary and reasonable by the Mayor.' It is apparent that the face of the ordinance itself contains no explicit limits on the Mayor's discretion. Indeed, nothing in the law as written requires the Mayor to do more than make the statement 'it is not in the public interest' when denying a permit application. Similarly, the Mayor could grant the application, but require the newsrack to be placed in an inaccessible location without providing any explanation whatever. To allow these illusory 'constraints' to constitute the standards necessary to bound a licensor's discretion renders the guaranty against censorship little more than a high-sounding ideal.

"The City asks us to presume that the Mayor will deny a permit application only for reasons related to the health, safety, or welfare of Lakewood citizens, and that additional terms and conditions will be imposed only for similar reasons. This presumes the Mayor will act in good faith and adhere to standards absent from the statute's face. But this is the very presumption that the doctrine forbidding unbridled discretion disallows. The doctrine requires that the limits the City claims are implicit in its law be made explicit by textual incorporation, binding judicial or administrative construction, or well-established practice. This Court will not write nonbinding limits into a silent state statute.[11]"

WHITE, J., joined by Stevens and O'Connor, JJ., dissented: "The Court has historically been reluctant to entertain facial attacks on statutes, i.e., claims that a statute is invalid in all of its applications. Our normal approach has been to determine whether a law is unconstitutional as applied in the particular case before the Court. This rule is also the usual approach we follow when reviewing laws that require licenses or permits to engage in business or other activities. ∗ ∗ ∗

"There are, however, a few well-established contexts in which the Court has departed from its insistence on as-applied approach to constitutional adjudication. One of them is where a permit or license is required to engage in expressive activities protected by the First Amendment, and official discretion to grant or deny is not suitably confined. ∗ ∗ ∗

"The prevailing feature of these exceptional cases, however, is that each of them involved a law that required a license to engage in activity protected by the First Amendment. In each of the cases, the expressive conduct which a city sought to license was an activity which the locality could not prohibit altogether.

---

11. Some have argued, unpersuasively, that pre-enforcement challenges, like this one, unfairly deprive the City of the chance to obtain a constitutional state court construction or to establish a local practice. It is true that when a state law has been authoritatively construed so as to render it constitutional, or a well-understood and uniformly applied practice has developed that has virtually the force of a judicial construction, the state law is read in light of those limits. That rule applies even if the face of the statute might not otherwise suggest the limits imposed. Further, this Court will presume any narrowing construction or practice to which the law is "fairly susceptible." But we have never held

that a federal litigant must await a state-court construction or the development of an establish practice before bringing the federal suit.

Once it is agreed that a facial challenge is permissible to attack a law imposing censorship, nothing is gained by requiring one actually denied a license to bring the action. Facial attacks, by their nature, are not dependent on the facts surrounding any particular permit denial. Thus, waiting for an alleged abuse before considering a facial challenge would achieve nothing except to allow the law to exist temporarily in a limbo of uncertainly and to risk censorship of free expression during the interim.

Streets, sidewalks, and parks are traditional public fora; leafletting, pamphletting, and speaking in such places may be regulated, but they may not be entirely forbidden.

"[*Lovell*] would be applicable here if the City of Lakewood sought to license the distribution of all newspapers in the City, or if it required licenses for all stores which sold newspapers. These are obviously newspaper circulation activities which a municipality cannot prohibit and therefore, any licensing scheme of this scope would have to pass muster under the [*Lovell*] doctrine. But—and this is critical—Lakewood has not cast so wide a net. Instead, it has sought to license only the placement of newsracks (and other like devices) on City property. As I read our precedents, [*Lovell*] is applicable here only if the Plain Dealer has a constitutional right to distribute its papers by means of dispensing devices or newsboxes, affixed to the public sidewalks. * * *

"[But] the First Amendment does not create a right of newspaper publishers to take a portion of city property to erect a structure to distribute their papers. There is no constitutional right to place newsracks on city sidewalks over the objections of the city. * * *

"Because the Lakewood Ordinance does not directly regulate an activity protected by the First Amendment, we should instead take the traditional, as-applied approach to adjudication. Appellee's facial challenge to the Mayor's discretion [should] therefore be rejected. * * *

"But if, for example, a Lakewood ordinance provided for the issuance of newsrack licenses to only those newspapers owned by persons of a particular race, or only to members of a select political party, such a law would be clearly violative of the First Amendment (or some other provision of the Constitution), and would be facially invalid. And if the Mayor of Lakewood granted or refused license applications for similar improper reasons, his exercise of the power provided him under § 901.181(c)(7) would be susceptible to constitutional attack. Thus, I do not embrace the 'greater-includes-the-lesser' syllogism—one that this Court abandoned long ago. Cf. *Hague v. C. I. O.*

"Instead, my view is simply this: where an activity that could be forbidden altogether (without running afoul of the First Amendment) is subjected to a local license requirement, the mere presence of administrative discretion in the licensing scheme will not render it invalid *per se*. In such a case—which does not involve the exercise of First Amendment protected freedoms—[*Lovell*] does not apply, and our usual rules concerning the permissibility of discretionary local licensing laws (and facial challenges to those laws) must prevail. * * *

"Seeking a way to limit its own expansive ruling, the Court provides two concrete examples of instances in which its newly crafted 'nexus to expression' rule will *not* strike down local ordinances that permit discretionary licensing decisions. First, we are told that a law granting unbridled discretion to a Mayor to grant licenses for soda machine placements passes constitutional muster because it does not give that official 'frequent opportunities to exercise substantial power over the content or viewpoint of the vendor's speech.' How the Court makes this empirical assessment, I do not know. It seems to me that the nature of a vendor's product—be it newspapers or soda pop—is not the measure of how potent a license law can be in the hands of local officials seeking to control or alter the vendor's speech. Of course, the newspaper vendor's speech is likely to be more public, more significant, and more widely known than the soda vendor's speech—and therefore more likely to incur the wrath of public officials. *But* in terms of the 'usefulness' of the license power to exert control over a licensee's speech, there is no difference whatsoever between the situation of the soda vendor and the newspaper vendor.[12]

"If the Court's treatment of the soda machine problem is not curious enough, it also 'assures' us that its ruling does not invalidate local laws requiring, for example, building permits—even as they apply to the construction of newspaper printing facilities. These laws, we are told, provide 'too blunt a censorship instrument to warrant judicial intervention.' Thus, local 'laws of general application that are not aimed at conduct commonly associated with expression' appear to survive the Court's decision today.

"But what if Lakewood, following this decision, repeals local ordinance § 901.181 (the detailed newsrack permit law) and simply left § 901.18 (the general ordinance concerning 'any * * * structure or device' on city property) on the books? That section vests absolute discretion (without any of the guidelines found in § 901.181) in the City Council to give or withhold permission for the erection of devices on city streets. Because this law is of 'general application,' it should survive scrutiny under the Court's opinion—even as applied to newsracks. If so, the Court's opinion takes on an odd 'the-greater-but-not-the-lesser' quality: the more activities that are subject to a discretionary licensing law, the more likely that law is to pass constitutional muster."

CON LAW: P. 820, after note 3

RTS & LIB: P. 488, after note 3

RILEY v. NATIONAL FEDERATION OF THE BLIND, __ U.S. __, 108 S.Ct. 2669, 101 L.Ed. 2667 (1988), per BRENNAN, J., invalidated a scheme for licensing professional fundraisers who were soliciting on behalf of charitable organizations: "[North Carolina's] provision requires professional fundraisers to await a determination regarding their license application before engaging in solicitation, while volunteer fundraisers, or those employed by the charity, may solicit immediately upon submitting an application. [It] is well settled that a speaker's rights are not lost merely because compensation is received; a speaker is no less a speaker because he or she is paid to speak. [Generally,] speakers need not obtain a license to speak. However, that rule is not absolute. For example, states may impose valid time, place, or manner restrictions. North Carolina seeks to come within the exception by alleging a heightened interest in regulating those who solicit money. Even assuming that the State's interest does justify requiring fundraisers to obtain a license before soliciting, such a regulation must provide that the licensor 'will, within a specified brief period, either issue a license or go to court.' *Freedman.* That requirement is not met here * * *. The statute on its face does not purport to require when a determination must be made, nor is there an administrative regulation or interpretation doing so."

REHNQUIST, C.J., joined by O'Connor, J., dissented: "It simply is not true that [fundraisers] are prevented from engaging in any protected speech on their own behalf by the State's licensing requirements; the requirements only restrict their ability to engage in the profession of 'solicitation' without a license. We do not view bar admission requirements as invalid because they restrict a prospec-

---

12. Indeed, in practical terms, if two businesses contemplated the prospect of standing before Lakewood's officials to seek vending machine permits—a sole proprietorship seeking a license for a soda machine that is the only source of the owner's income, and the Plain Dealer Publishing Co., seeking licenses for newsracks—I have little doubt about which applicant would be more likely to feel constrained to alter its expressive conduct in anticipation of the encounter.

tive lawyer's 'right' to be hired as an advocate by a client. So in this case we should not subject to strict scrutiny the State's attempt to license a business—professional fundraising—some of whose members might reasonably be thought to pose a risk of fraudulent activity." [a]

SECTION: FAIR ADMINISTRATION OF JUSTICE AND THE FIRST AMENDMENT AS SWORD

JUSTICE AND THE FIRST AMENDMENT AS SWORD

CON LAW: P. 844, before Notes and Questions

AMER CON: P. 618, before Notes and Questions

RTS & LIB: P. 511, before Notes and Questions

PRESS–ENTERPRISE CO. v. SUPERIOR COURT
478 U.S. 1, 106 S.Ct. 2735, 92 L.Ed.2d 1 (1986).

CHIEF JUSTICE BURGER delivered the opinion of the Court.

We granted certiorari to decide whether petitioner has a First Amendment right of access to transcripts of a preliminary hearing growing out of a criminal prosecution.

On December 23, 1981, the State of California filed a complaint in the Riverside County Municipal Court, charging Robert Diaz with 12 counts of murder and seeking the death penalty. The complaint alleged that Diaz, a nurse, murdered 12 patients by administering massive doses of the heart drug lidocaine. The preliminary hearing on the complaint commenced on July 6, 1982. Diaz moved to exclude the public from the proceedings under California Penal Code Ann. § 868 (West 1985), which requires such proceedings to be open unless "exclusion of the public is necessary in order to protect the defendant's right to a fair and impartial trial."[1] The Magistrate granted the unopposed motion, finding that closure was necessary because the case had attracted national publicity and "only one side may get reported in the media."

The preliminary hearing continued for 41 days. Most of the testimony and the evidence presented by the State was medical and scientific; the remainder consisted of testimony by personnel who worked with Diaz on the shifts when the 12 patients died. Diaz did not introduce any evidence, but his counsel subjected most of the witnesses to vigorous cross-examination. Diaz was held to answer on all charges. At the conclusion of the hearing, petitioner Press-Enterprise Company asked that the transcript of the proceedings be released. The Magistrate refused and sealed the record.

On January 21, 1983, the State moved in Superior Court to have the transcripts of the preliminary hearing released to the public; petitioner later joined in support of the motion. Diaz opposed the motion, contending that release of the transcripts would result in prejudicial pretrial publicity. The Superior Court found that the information in the transcript was "as factual as it

---

a. Stevens, J., also dissented from the Court's treatment of the licensing issue. For other aspects of the case, see p. 228 of this Supplement.

1. [Before] 1982, the statute gave the defendant the unqualified right to close the proceedings. After the California Supreme Court rejected a First Amendment attack on the old statute, the California Legislature amended the statute to include the present requirement that the hearing be closed only upon a finding by the Magistrate that closure is "necessary in order to protect the defendant's right to a fair trial."

could be," and that the facts were neither "inflammatory" nor "exciting" but there was, nonetheless, "a reasonable likelihood that release of all or any part of the transcript might prejudice defendant's right to a fair and impartial trial."

Petitioner then filed a peremptory writ of mandate with the Court of Appeal. That court originally denied the writ but, after being so ordered by the California Supreme Court, set the matter for a hearing. Meanwhile, Diaz waived his right to a jury trial and the Superior Court released the transcript. After holding that the controversy was not moot, the Court of Appeal denied the writ of mandate.

The California Supreme Court thereafter denied petitioner's peremptory writ of mandate, holding that there is no general First Amendment right of access to preliminary hearings. [Having] found no general First Amendment right of access, the court then considered the circumstances in which the closure would be proper under the California access statute. Under the statute, the court reasoned, if the defendant establishes a "reasonable likelihood of substantial prejudice" the burden shifts to the prosecution or the media to show by a preponderance of the evidence that there is no such reasonable probability of prejudice. * * *[a]

The right to an open public trial is a shared right of the accused and the public, the common concern being the assurance of fairness. Only recently, in *Waller v. Georgia,* for example, we considered whether the defendant's Sixth Amendment right to an open trial prevented the closure of a suppression hearing over the defendant's objection. We noted that the First Amendment right of access would in most instances attach to such proceedings and that "the explicit Sixth Amendment right of the accused is no less protective of a public trial than the implicit First Amendment right of the press and public." When the defendant objects to the closure of a suppression hearing, therefore, the hearing must be open unless the party seeking to close the hearing advances an overriding interest that is likely to be prejudiced.

Here, unlike *Waller,* the right asserted is not the defendant's Sixth Amendment right to a public trial since the defendant requested a *closed* preliminary hearing. Instead, the right asserted here is that of the public under the First Amendment. See *Gannett* (Powell, J., concurring). The California Supreme Court concluded that the First Amendment was not implicated because the proceeding was not a criminal trial, but a preliminary hearing. However, the First Amendment question cannot be resolved solely on the label we give the event, i.e., "trial" or otherwise, particularly where the preliminary hearing functions much like a full scale trial.

In cases dealing with the claim of a First Amendment right of access to criminal proceedings, our decisions have emphasized two complementary considerations. First, because a " 'tradition of accessibility implies the favorable judgment of experience' " *Globe Newspaper* (quoting *Richmond Newspapers* (Brennan, J., concurring)), we have considered whether the place and process has historically been open to the press and general public. * * *

Second, in this setting the Court has traditionally considered whether public access plays a significant positive role in the functioning of the particular process in question. *Globe Newspaper.* Although many governmental processes operate best under public scrutiny, it takes little imagination to recognize that

a. Noting that the transcript had long since been released to the press, the Court first disposed of the contention that the con-troversy was moot: the controversy is "capable of repetition, yet evading review."

there are some kinds of government operations that would be totally frustrated if conducted openly. A classic example is that "the proper functioning of our grand jury system depends upon the secrecy of grand jury proceedings." Other proceedings plainly require public access. In *Press-Enterprise I* [(1984), Casebooks infra], we summarized the holdings of prior cases, noting that openness in criminal trials, including the selection of jurors, "enhances both the basic fairness of the criminal trial and the appearance of fairness so essential to public confidence in the system." * * *

The considerations that led the Court to apply the First Amendment right of access to criminal trials in *Richmond Newspapers* and *Globe* and the selection of jurors in *Press Enterprise I* lead us to conclude that the right of access applies to preliminary hearings as conducted in California.

First, there has been a tradition of accessibility to preliminary hearings of the type conducted in California. Although grand jury proceedings have traditionally been closed to the public and the accused, preliminary hearings conducted before neutral and detached magistrates have been open to the public. Long ago in the celebrated trial of Aaron Burr for treason, for example, with Chief Justice Marshall sitting as trial judge, the probable cause hearing was held in the Hall of the House of Delegates in Virginia, the court room being too small to accommodate the crush of interested citizens. From *Burr* until the present day, the near uniform practice of state and federal courts has been to conduct preliminary hearings in open court. * * *

The second question is whether public access to preliminary hearings as they are conducted in California plays a particularly significant positive role in the actual functioning of the process. We have already determined in *Richmond Newspapers, Globe,* and *Press Enterprise I* that public access to criminal trials and the selection of jurors is essential to the proper functioning of the criminal justice system. California preliminary hearings are sufficiently like a trial to justify the same conclusion.

In California, to bring a felon to trial, the prosecutor has a choice of securing a grand jury indictment or a finding of probable cause following a preliminary hearing. Even when the accused has been indicted by a grand jury, however, he has an absolute right to an elaborate preliminary hearing before a neutral magistrate. *Hawkins v. Superior Court,* 22 Cal.3d 584, 150 Cal.Rptr. 435, 586 P.2d 916 (1978). The accused has the right to personally appear at the hearing, to be represented by counsel, to cross-examine hostile witnesses, to present exculpatory evidence, and to exclude illegally obtained evidence. If the magistrate determines that probable cause exists, the accused is bound over for trial; such a finding leads to a guilty plea in the majority of cases.

It is true that unlike a criminal trial, the California preliminary hearing cannot result in the conviction of the accused and the adjudication is before a magistrate or other judicial officer without a jury. But these features, standing alone, do not make public access any less essential to the proper functioning of the proceedings in the overall criminal justice process. Because of its extensive scope, the preliminary hearing is often the final and most important step in the criminal proceeding. As the California Supreme Court stated in *San Jose Mercury-News v. Municipal Court,* 30 Cal.3d 498, 511, 179 Cal.Rptr. 772, 779, 638 P.2d 655, 663 (1982), the preliminary hearing in many cases provides "the sole occasion for public observation of the criminal justice system."

Similarly, the absence of a jury, long recognized as "an inestimable safeguard against the corrupt or overzealous prosecutor and against the compliant, biased, or eccentric judge," *Duncan v. Louisiana,* makes the importance of public access to a preliminary hearing even more significant. "People in an open society do not demand infallability from their institutions, but it is difficult for them to accept what they are prohibited from observing." *Richmond Newspapers.*

Denying the transcripts of a 41-day preliminary hearing would frustrate what we have characterized as the "community therapeutic value" of openness. Id. Criminal acts, especially certain violent crimes, provoke public concern, outrage, and hostility. "When the public is aware that the law is being enforced and the criminal justice system is functioning, an outlet is provided for these understandable reactions and emotions." *Press Enterprise I.* * * *

We therefore conclude that the qualified First Amendment right of access to criminal proceedings applies to preliminary hearings as they are conducted in California.

Since a qualified First Amendment right of access attaches to preliminary hearings in California, [the] proceedings cannot be closed unless specific, on the record findings are made demonstrating that "closure is essential to preserve higher values and is narrowly tailored to serve that interest." *Press-Enterprise I.* If the interest asserted is the right of the accused to a fair trial, the preliminary hearing shall be closed only if specific findings are made demonstrating that first, there is a substantial probability that the defendant's right to a fair trial will be prejudiced by publicity that closure would prevent and, second, reasonable alternatives to closure cannot adequately protect the defendant's free trial rights.

The California Supreme Court, interpreting its access statute, concluded "that the magistrate shall close the preliminary hearing upon finding a reasonable likelihood of substantial prejudice." As the court itself acknowledged, the "reasonable likelihood" test places a lesser burden on the defendant than the "substantial probability" test which we hold is called for by the First Amendment. Moreover, that court failed to consider whether alternatives short of complete closure would have protected the interests of the accused.

In *Gannett* we observed that: "Publicity concerning pretrial suppression hearings such as the one involved in the present case poses special risks of unfairness. The whole purpose of such hearings is to screen out unreliable or illegally obtained evidence and insure that this evidence does not become known to the jury. Publicity concerning the proceedings at a pretrial hearing, however, could influence public opinion against a defendant and inform potential jurors of inculpatory information wholly inadmissible at the actual trial."

But this risk of prejudice does not automatically justify refusing public access to hearings on every motion to suppress. Through voir dire, cumbersome as it is in some circumstances, a court can identify those jurors whose prior knowledge of the case would disable them from rendering an impartial verdict. And even if closure were justified for the hearings on a motion to suppress, closure of an entire 41-day proceeding would rarely be warranted. The First Amendment right of access cannot be overcome by the conclusory assertion that publicity might deprive the defendant of that right. And any limitation " 'must be narrowly tailored to serve that interest.' " *Press Enterprise I.*

The standard applied by the California Supreme Court failed to consider the First Amendment right of access to criminal proceedings. Accordingly, the judgment of the California Supreme Court is reversed.

JUSTICE STEVENS, with whom JUSTICE REHNQUIST joins as to Part II, dissenting.

The constitutional question presented by this case is whether members of the public have a First Amendment right to insist upon access to the transcript of a preliminary hearing during the period before the public trial, even though the accused, the prosecutor, and the trial judge have all agreed to the sealing of the transcript in order to assure a fair trial.

The preliminary hearing transcript to which petitioner sought access consists of 4,239 pages of testimony by prosecution witnesses heard over 8 weeks. The testimony, contained in 47 volumes, accuses Mr. Robert Diaz, a nurse, of murdering 12 patients in the hospital in which he worked by injecting them with lethal doses of a heart drug. The transcript reveals that the defense put on no witnesses of its own.

Immediately after the Magistrate ordered the defendant bound over for trial, defense counsel moved that the transcript of the preliminary hearing be sealed to protect his client's right to a fair trial. The transcript, in the words of the Magistrate, revealed "only one side of the story." The transcript also contained the Magistrate's characterization of Mr. Diaz as "the most dangerous type of individual there is." The prosecutor did not oppose this motion, and the Magistrate, after hearing petitioner's objection, ordered the transcript sealed.

The Superior Court trial judge denied a motion to unseal the transcript. He found—and the finding is amply supported by the record—that "there is a reasonable likelihood that making all or any part of the transcripts public might prejudice the defendant's right to a fair and impartial trial." The Magistrate had earlier rejected less restrictive alternatives to sealing the transcript, concluding that "the only way to protect" the defendant's "[fair trial] right would be to seal the transcript." [1] * * *

In view of the above, the trial judge had an obvious and legitimate reason for refusing to make the transcript public any sooner than he did. His decision plainly did not violate the defendant's right to a public trial under the Sixth Amendment, for it was the defendant who objected to release of the transcript. See *Gannett*. In my opinion, the judge's decision did not violate the First Amendment either.

I. Although perhaps obvious, it bears emphasis that the First Amendment right asserted by petitioner is not a right to publish or otherwise communicate information lawfully or unlawfully acquired. That right, which lies at the core of the First Amendment and which erased the legacy of restraints on publication against which the drafters of that Amendment rebelled, may be overcome only by a governmental objective of the highest order attainable in no less intrusive way. The First Amendment right asserted by petitioner in this case, in contrast, is not the right to publicize information in its possession, but the right to acquire access thereto.

I have long believed that a proper construction of the First Amendment embraces a right of access to information about the conduct of public affairs. [Neither] our elected nor our appointed representatives may abridge the free flow of information simply to protect their own activities from public scrutiny.

---

1. In so ruling, the Magistrate recognized that he had "an affirmative constitutional duty to insure that a defendant has a fair trial," under *Gannett* ("To safeguard the due process rights of the accused, a trial judge has an affirmative constitutional duty to minimize the effects of prejudicial pretrial publicity. And because of the Constitution's pervasive concern for these due process rights, a trial judge may surely take protective measures even when they are not strictly and inescapably necessary").

An official policy of secrecy must be supported by some legitimate justification that serves the interest of the public office.[4]

But it has always been apparent that the freedom to obtain information that the Government has a legitimate interest in not disclosing is far narrower than the freedom to disseminate information, which is "virtually absolute" in most contexts, *Richmond Newspapers* (Stevens, J., concurring). In this case, the risk of prejudice to the defendant's right to a fair trial is perfectly obvious. For me, that risk is far more significant than the countervailing interest in publishing the transcript of the preliminary hearing sooner rather than later. The interest in prompt publication—in my view—is no greater than the interest in prompt publication of grand jury transcripts. As explained more fully below, we have always recognized the legitimacy of the governmental interest in the secrecy of grand jury proceedings, and I am unpersuaded that the difference between such proceedings and the rather elaborate procedure for determining probable cause that California has adopted strengthens the First Amendment claim to access asserted in this case.

II. [I]n our prior cases history mattered primarily for what it revealed about the intentions of the Framers and ratifiers of the First Amendment. In this case, however, it is uncontroverted that a common law right of access did not inhere in preliminary proceedings at the time the First Amendment was adopted, and that the Framers and ratifiers of that provision could not have intended such proceedings to remain open.[5] * * *

In the final analysis, the Court's lengthy historical disquisition demonstrates only that in many States preliminary proceedings are generally open to the public. In other States, numbering California and Michigan among them, such proceedings have been closed.[6] To paraphrase the Court's analysis in [a recent decision], "the fact that the States" have adopted different rules regarding the openness of preliminary proceedings "is merely a reflection of our federal system, which demands '[t]olerance for a spectrum of state procedures dealing with a common problem of law enforcement.' That [California's] particular

---

4. In *Houchins* I explained why I believed that the plaintiffs were entitled to put an end to the warden's policy of concealing prison conditions from the public. "Those conditions are wholly without claim to confidentiality. While prison officials have an interest in the time and manner of public acquisition of information about the institutions they administer, there is no legitimate penological justification for concealing from citizens the conditions in which their fellow citizens are being confined." It seemed clear that an "official prison policy of concealing such knowledge from the public by arbitrarily cutting off the flow of information at its source abridges the freedom of speech and of the press protected by the First and Fourteenth Amendments to the Constitution."

5. [The] Chief Justice pointed out in his concurring opinion in *Gannett* that "[a]t common law there was a very different presumption [i.e., in favor of closure] for proceedings which preceded the trial." "[N]o one ever suggested that there was any 'right' of the public to be present at such pretrial proceedings as were available in that time [that the Bill of Rights was adopted]."

6. Ironically, California and Michigan are both States in which preliminary proceedings are generally open to the public, and are thus—surprisingly—part of the recent common law trend in favor of openness relied on by the Court. It is only on the facts of record in this case that the California courts ordered the transcript sealed. Since many—if not most—of the state court decisions collected by the Court hold that the right to a public preliminary hearing is personal to the accused, or, more commonly, that it is overcome by a showing of potentially prejudicial publicity equivalent to or less than that required in California, courts in these States would presumably have also denied access if presented with the facts of this case. On this observation, and in view of the fact that the reasoning of the state courts is heavily dependent on this Court's cases granting access to criminal proceedings (even if they are ultimately grounded in state law), it is remarkable that the Court finds any historical basis for a public right of access to preliminary proceedings on a showing in excess of that required in California and met by the defendant in this case.

approach has been adopted in few other States does not render [its] choice unconstitutional." As Justice Stewart admonished: we must not "confus[e] the existence of a constitutional right with the common-law tradition of open * * * proceedings." *Gannett.* * * *

If the Court's historical evidence proves too little, the "value of openness" on which it relies proves too much, for this measure would open to public scrutiny far more than preliminary hearings "as they are conducted in California" (a comforting phrase invoked by the Court in one form or another more than 8 times in its opinion).[7] In brief, the Court's rationale for opening the "California preliminary hearing" is that it "is often the final and most important step in the criminal proceeding"; that it provides " 'the sole occasion for public observation of the criminal justice system' "; that it lacks the protective presence of a jury; and that closure denies an outlet for community catharis. The obvious defect in the Court's approach is that its reasoning applies to the traditionally secret grand jury with as much force as it applies to California preliminary hearings. A grand jury indictment is just as likely to be the "final step" in a criminal proceeding and the "sole occasion" for public scrutiny as is a preliminary hearing. Moreover, many critics of the grand jury maintain that the grand jury protects the accused less well than does a legally-knowledgable judge who personally presides over a preliminary hearing. See *Hawkins v. Superior Court* (holding deprivation of preliminary hearing to constitute a denial of equal protection under State Constitution in part because " 'the grand jury is the total captive of the prosecutor who, if he is candid, will concede that he can indict anybody, at any time, for almost anything, before any grand jury' " (quoting Campbell, *Eliminate the Grand Jury*, 64 J. Crim.L. & C. 174 (1973)). Finally, closure of grand juries denies an outlet for community rage. When the Court's explanatory veneer is stripped away, what emerges is the reality that the California preliminary hearing is functionally identical to the traditional grand jury. * * *

The Court's reasoning—if carried to its logical outcome—thus contravenes the "long-established policy that maintains the secrecy of the grand jury proceedings in the federal courts" and in the courts of 19 States.[8]

In fact, the logic of the Court's access right extends even beyond the confines of the criminal justice system to encompass proceedings held on the civil side of the docket as well. [Despite] the Court's valiant attempt to limit the logic of its holding, the ratio decidendi of today's decision knows no bounds.

---

7. Given the Court's focus on the history of preliminary proceedings in general, and its reliance on the broad values served by openness, I do not see the relevance of the facts that preliminary proceedings in California bear an outward resemblance to criminal trials. To the extent that it matters that in California "[t]he accused has the right to personally appear at the hearing, to be represented by counsel, to cross-examine hostile witnesses, to present exculpatory evidence, and to exclude illegally obtained evidence," it bears mention that many other States have reformed their grand juries to include one or more of these procedural reforms, see LaFave & Israel, *Criminal Procedure* § 15.2(b) (1984). After today's decision, one can only wonder whether the public enjoys a right of access to any or all of these proceedings as well.

8. Five reasons are commonly given for the policy of grand jury secrecy: "(1) To prevent the escape of those whose indictment may be contemplated; (2) to insure the utmost freedom to the grand jury in its deliberations, and to prevent persons subject to indictment or their friends from importuning the grand jurors; (3) to prevent subornation of perjury or tampering with the witnesses who may testify before [the] grand jury and later appear at the trial of those indicted by it; (4) to encourage free and untrammeled disclosures by persons who have information with respect to the commission of crimes; (5) to protect innocent accused who is exonerated from disclosure of the fact that he has been under investigation, and from the expense of standing trial where there was no probability of guilt."

By abjuring strict reliance on history and emphasizing the broad value of openness, the Court tacitly recognizes the importance of public access to government proceedings generally. Regrettably, the Court has taken seriously the stated requirement that the sealing of a transcript be justified by a "compelling" or "overriding" governmental interest and that the closure order be "narrowly tailored to serve that interest." [A] requirement of some legitimate reason for closure in this case requires an affirmance. The constitutionally-grounded fair trial interests of the accused if he is bound over for trial, and the reputational interests of the accused if he is not, provide a substantial reason for delaying access to the transcript for at least the short time before trial. * * *

SECTION: UNCONVENTIONAL FORMS OF COMMUNICATION

CON LAW: P. 861, after note 4

AMER CON: P. 635, after note 4

RTS & LIB: P. 528, after note 4

Matthew Fraser, a senior at Bethel High School, was suspended for three days and denied permission to speak at graduation for allegedly violating the school's disruptive conduct rule. The rule proscribed any conduct that "materially and substantially interferes with the educational [process,] including the use of obscene, profane language or gestures." The conduct at issue was a nominating speech for school office delivered by Fraser on behalf of a classmate at a school assembly called for the purpose of hearing nominating speeches. The full text of Fraser's speech is as follows: "I know a man who is firm—he's firm in his pants, he's firm in his shirt, his character is firm—but most of all, his belief in you, the students of Bethel is firm. Jeff Kuhlman is a man who takes his point and pounds it in. If necessary, he'll take an issue and nail it to the wall. He doesn't attack things in spurts—he drives hard, pushing and pushing until finally—he succeeds. Jeff is a man who will go to the very end—even the climax, for each and every one of you. So vote for Jeff for ASB vice-president—he'll never come between you and the best our high school can be."

Fraser brought a civil rights action challenging the school's disciplinary action and prevailed in the lower courts.[a] BETHEL SCHOOL DIST. v. FRASER, 478 U.S. 675, 106 S.Ct. 3159, 92 L.Ed.2d 549 (1986), per BURGER, C.J., held that the school district "acted entirely within its permissible authority in imposing sanctions upon Fraser in response to his offensively lewd and indecent speech": "The marked distinction between the political 'message' of the armbands in *Tinker* and the sexual content of respondent's speech in this case seems to have been given little weight by the Court of Appeals. In upholding the students' right to engage in a nondisruptive, passive expression of a political viewpoint in *Tinker,* this Court was careful to note that the case did 'not concern speech or action that intrudes upon the work of the schools or the rights of other students.'

a. The district court awarded damages and enjoined the school district from preventing Fraser from speaking at the commencement ceremonies. Fraser, who had been elected graduation speaker by a write-in vote of his classmates, in fact delivered a speech at the graduation exercises. Fraser served two days of his suspension and was permitted to return to school on the third day.

"It is against this background that we turn to consider the level of First Amendment protection accorded to Fraser's utterances and actions before an official high school assembly attended by 600 students.

"[The] undoubted freedom to advocate unpopular and controversial views in schools and classrooms must be balanced against the society's countervailing interest in teaching students the boundaries of socially appropriate behaviour. Even the most heated political discourse in a democratic society requires consideration for the personal sensibilities of the other participants and audiences.

"In our Nation's legislative halls, where some of the most vigorous political debates in our society are carried on, there are rules prohibiting the use of expressions offensive to other participants in the debate. The Manual of Parliamentary Practice, drafted by Thomas Jefferson and adopted by the House of Representatives to govern the proceedings in that body, prohibits the use of 'impertinent' speech during debate and likewise provides that '[n]o person is to use indecent language against the proceedings of the House.' The Rules of Debate applicable in the Senate likewise provide that a Senator may be called to order for imputing improper motives to another Senator or for referring offensively to any State. Senators have been censored for abusive language directed at other Senators. Can it be that what is proscribed in the halls of Congress is beyond the reach of school officials to regulate?

"The First Amendment guarantees wide freedom in matters of adult public discourse. A sharply divided Court upheld the right to express an antidraft viewpoint in a public place, albeit in terms highly offensive to most citizens. See *Cohen.* It does not follow, however, that simply because the use of an offensive form of expression may not be prohibited to adults making what the speaker considers a political point, that the same latitude must be permitted to children in a public school. [As] cogently expressed by Judge Newman, 'the First Amendment gives a high school student the classroom right to wear Tinker's armband, but not Cohen's jacket.' *Thomas v. Board of Education,* 607 F.2d 1043, 1057 (2d Cir.1979) (concurring).

"Surely it is a highly appropriate function of public school education to prohibit the use of vulgar and offensive terms in public discourse. Indeed, the 'fundamental values necessary to the maintenance of a democratic political system' disfavor the use of terms of debate highly offensive or highly threatening to others. Nothing in the Constitution prohibits the states from insisting that certain modes of expression are inappropriate and subject to sanctions. The inculcation of these values is truly the 'work of the schools.' The determination of what manner of speech in the classroom or in school assembly is inappropriate properly rests with the school board.

"[The] schools, as instruments of the state, may determine that the essential lessons of civil, mature conduct cannot be conveyed in a school that tolerates lewd, indecent, or offensive speech and conduct such as that indulged in by this confused boy.

"The pervasive sexual innuendo in Fraser's speech was plainly offensive to both teachers and students—indeed to any mature person. By glorifying male sexuality, and in its verbal content, the speech was acutely insulting to teenage girl students. The speech could well be seriously damaging to its less mature audience, many of whom were only 14 years old and on the threshold of awareness of human sexuality. Some students were reported as bewildered by the speech and the reaction of mimicry it provoked.

"This Court's First Amendment jurisprudence has acknowledged limitations on the otherwise absolute interest of the speaker in reaching an unlimited audience where the speech is sexually explicit and the audience may include children. In *Ginsberg v. New York,* this Court upheld a New York statute banning the sale of sexually oriented material to minors, even though the material in question was entitled to First Amendment protection with respect to adults. And in addressing the question whether the First Amendment places any limit on the authority of public schools to remove books from a public school library, all Members of the Court, otherwise sharply divided, acknowledged that the school board has the authority to remove books that are vulgar. *Board of Educ. v. Pico* [Casebooks, Sec. 6, II]. These cases recognize the obvious concern on the part of parents, and school authorities acting in loco parentis to protect children—especially in a captive audience—from exposure to sexually explicit, indecent, or lewd speech.

"We have also recognized an interest in protecting minors from exposure to vulgar and offensive spoken language. In *FCC v. Pacifica Foundation* [Casebooks, Sec. 8, II], we dealt with the power of the Federal Communications Commission to regulate a radio broadcast described as 'indecent but not obscene.' There the Court reviewed an administrative condemnation of the radio broadcast of a self-styled 'humorist' who described his own performance as being in 'the words you couldn't say on the public, ah, airwaves, um, the ones you definitely wouldn't say ever.' The Commission concluded that 'certain words depicted sexual and excretory activities in a patently offensive manner, [and] noted that they "were broadcast at a time when children were undoubtedly in the audience." ' [We] concluded that the broadcast was properly considered 'obscene, indecent, or profane' within the meaning of the statute. The plurality opinion went on to reject the radio station's assertion of a First Amendment right to broadcast vulgarity: 'These words offend for the same reasons that obscenity offends. Their place in the hierarchy of First Amendment values was aptly sketched by Mr. Justice Murphy when he said: "[S]uch utterances are no essential part of any exposition of ideas, and are of such slight social value as a step to truth that any benefit that may be derived from them is clearly outweighed by the social interest in order and morality." ' *Chaplinsky.*

"[A] high school assembly or classroom is no place for a sexually explicit monologue directed towards an unsuspecting audience of teenage students. Accordingly, it was perfectly appropriate for the school to disassociate itself to make the point to the pupils that vulgar speech and lewd conduct is wholly inconsistent with the 'fundamental values' of public school education."[b]

BRENNAN, J., concurred: "The Court, referring to [Fraser's] remarks as 'obscene,' 'vulgar,' 'lewd,' and 'offensively lewd,' concludes that school officials properly punished respondent for uttering the speech. Having read the full text of respondent's remarks, I find it difficult to believe that it is the same speech the Court describes. To my mind, the most that can be said about respondent's speech—and all that need be said—is that in light of the discretion school officials have to teach high school students how to conduct civil and effective public discourse, and to prevent disruption of school educational activities, it was not unconstitutional for school officials to conclude, under the circumstances of this case, that respondent's remarks exceeded permissible limits.

b. Blackmun, J., concurred without opinion.

"[If] respondent had given the same speech outside of the school environment, he could not have been penalized simply because government officials considered his language to be inappropriate, see *Cohen;* the Court's opinion does not suggest otherwise.[1] Moreover, despite the Court's characterizations, the language respondent used is far removed from the very narrow class of 'obscene' speech which the Court has held is not protected by the First Amendment. *Ginsberg; Roth.* It is true, however, that the State has interests in teaching high school students how to conduct civil and effective public discourse and in avoiding disruption of educational school activities. Thus, the Court holds that under certain circumstances, high school students may properly be reprimanded for giving a speech at a high school assembly which school officials conclude disrupted the school's educational mission.[2] Respondent's speech may well have been protected had he given it in school but under different circumstances, where the school's legitimate interest in teaching and maintaining civil public discourse were less weighty.

"[Under] the circumstances of this case, however, I believe that school officials did not violate the First Amendment in determining that respondent should be disciplined for the disruptive language he used while addressing a high school assembly.[3]

MARSHALL, J., dissented: "I agree with the principles that Justice Brennan sets out in his opinion concurring in the judgment. I dissent from the Court's decision, however, because in my view the school district failed to demonstrate that respondent's remarks were indeed disruptive. [I] recognize that the school administration must be given wide latitude to determine what forms of conduct are inconsistent with the school's educational mission; nevertheless, where speech is involved, we may not unquestioningly accept a teacher's or administrator's assertion that certain pure speech interfered with education. Here the board, despite a clear opportunity to do so, failed to bring in evidence sufficient to convince either of the two lower courts that education at Bethel School was disrupted by respondent's speech. I therefore see no reason to disturb the Court of Appeals' judgment."

STEVENS, J., also dissented: "Frankly, my dear, I don't give a damn.'

"When I was a high school student, the use of those words in a public forum shocked the Nation. Today Clark Gable's four-letter expletive is less offensive

1. In the course of its opinion, the Court makes certain remarks concerning the authority of school officials to regulate student language in public schools. For example, the Court notes that "[n]othing in the Constitution prohibits the states from insisting that certain modes of expression are inappropriate and subject to sanctions." These statements obviously do not, and indeed given our prior precedents could not, refer to the government's authority generally to regulate the language used in public debate outside of the school environment.

2. The Court speculates that the speech was "insulting" to female students, and "seriously damaging" to 14-year olds, so that school officials could legitimately suppress such expression in order to protect these groups. There is no evidence in the record that any students, male or female, found the speech "insulting." And while it was not unreasonable for school officials to conclude that respondent's remarks were inappropriate for a school-sponsored assembly, the language respondent used does not even approach the sexually explicit speech regulated in *Ginsberg,* or the indecent speech banned in *Pacifica Foundation.* Indeed, to my mind, respondent's speech was no more "obscene," "lewd," or "sexually explicit" than the bulk of programs currently appearing on prime time television or in the local cinema. Thus, I disagree with the Court's suggestion that school officials could punish respondent's speech out of a need to protect younger students.

3. Respondent served two days' suspension and had his name removed from the list of candidates for graduation speaker at the school's commencement exercises, although he was eventually permitted to speak at the graduation. While I find this punishment somewhat severe in light of the nature of respondent's transgression, I cannot conclude that school officials exceeded the bounds of their disciplinary authority.

than it was then.   Nevertheless, I assume that high school administrators may prohibit the use of that word in classroom discussion and even in extracurricular activities that are sponsored by the school and held on school premises.   For I believe a school faculty must regulate the content as well as the style of student speech in carrying out its educational mission.   It does seem to me, however, that if a student is to be punished for using offensive speech, he is entitled to fair notice of the scope of the prohibition and the consequences of its violation.   The interest in free speech protected by the First Amendment and the interest in fair procedure protected by the Due Process Clause of the Fourteenth Amendment combine to require this conclusion.

"This respondent was an outstanding young man with a fine academic record.   The fact that he was chosen by the student body to speak at the school's commencement exercises demonstrates that he was respected by his peers.   This fact is relevant for two reasons.   It confirms the conclusion that the discipline imposed on him—a three-day suspension and ineligibility to speak at the school's graduation exercises—was sufficiently serious to justify invocation of the School District's grievance procedures.   More importantly, it indicates that he was probably in a better position to determine whether an audience composed of 600 of his contemporaries would be offended by the use of a four-letter word—or a sexual metaphor—than is a group of judges who are at least two generations and 3,000 miles away from the scene of the crime.[2] * * *

"It seems fairly obvious that respondent's speech would be inappropriate in certain classroom and formal social settings.   On the other hand, in a locker room or perhaps in a school corridor the metaphor in the speech might be regarded as rather routine comment.   If this be true, and if respondent's audience consisted almost entirely of young people with whom he conversed on a daily basis, can we—at this distance—confidently assert that he must have known that the school administration would punish him for delivering it?

"For three reasons, I think not.   First, it seems highly unlikely that he would have decided to deliver the speech if he had known that it would result in his suspension and disqualification from delivering the school commencement address.   Second, I believe a strong presumption in favor of free expression should apply whenever an issue of this kind is arguable.   Third, because the Court has adopted the policy of applying contemporary community standards in evaluating expression with sexual connotations, this Court should defer to the views of the district judges who are in a much better position to evaluate this speech than we are."

CON LAW: P. 864, after *Spence*

AMER CON: P. 639, before note 1

RTS & LIB: P. 532, before note 1

TEXAS v. JOHNSON

___ U.S. ___, 109 S.Ct. 2533, ___ L.Ed.2d ___ (1989).

JUSTICE BRENNAN delivered the opinion of the Court.

After publicly burning an American flag as a means of political protest, Gregory Lee Johnson was convicted of desecrating a flag in violation of Texas law.   This case presents the question whether his conviction is consistent with the First Amendment.   We hold that it is not.

---

2.   As the Court of Appeals noted, there "is no evidence in the record indicating that any students found the speech to be offensive."

I

While the Republican National Convention was taking place in Dallas in 1984, respondent Johnson participated in a political demonstration dubbed the "Republican War Chest Tour." As explained in literature distributed by the demonstrators and in speeches made by them, the purpose of this event was to protest the policies of the Reagan administration and of certain Dallas-based corporations. The demonstrators marched through the Dallas streets, chanting political slogans and stopping at several corporate locations to stage "die-ins" intended to dramatize the consequences of nuclear war. On several occasions they spray-painted the walls of buildings and overturned potted plants, but Johnson himself took no part in such activities. He did, however, accept an American flag handed to him by a fellow protestor who had taken it from a flag pole outside one of the targeted buildings.

The demonstration ended in front of Dallas City Hall, where Johnson unfurled the American flag, doused it with kerosene, and set it on fire. While the flag burned, the protestors chanted, "America, the red, white, and blue, we spit on you." After the demonstrators dispersed, a witness to the flag-burning collected the flag's remains and buried them in his backyard. No one was physically injured or threatened with injury, though several witnesses testified that they had been seriously offended by the flag-burning.

Of the approximately 100 demonstrators, Johnson alone was charged with a crime. The only criminal offense with which he was charged was the desecration of a venerated object in violation of Tex.Penal Code Ann. § 42.09(a)(3) (1989).[1] * * *

II

Johnson was convicted of flag desecration for burning the flag rather than for uttering insulting words.[2] This fact somewhat complicates our consideration

1. Tex.Penal Code Ann. § 42.09 (1989) provides in full: "§ 42.09. Desecration of Venerated Object

"(a) A person commits an offense if he intentionally or knowingly desecrates:

"(1) a public monument;

"(2) a place of worship or burial; or

"(3) a state or national flag.

"(b) For purposes of this section, 'desecrate' means deface, damage, or otherwise physically mistreat in a way that the actor knows will seriously offend one or more persons likely to observe or discover his action.

"(c) An offense under this section is a Class A misdemeanor."

2. Because the prosecutor's closing argument observed that Johnson had led the protestors in chants denouncing the flag while it burned, Johnson suggests that he may have been convicted for uttering critical words rather than for burning the flag. He relies on *Street v. New York* in which we reversed a conviction obtained under a New York statute that prohibited publicly defying or casting contempt on the flag "either by words or act" because we were persuaded that the defendant may have been convicted for his words alone. Unlike the law we faced in *Street*, however, the Texas flag-desecration statute does not on its face permit conviction for remarks critical of the flag, as Johnson himself admits. Nor was the jury in this case told that it could convict Johnson of flag desecration if it found only that he had uttered words critical of the flag and its referents.

Johnson emphasizes, though, that the jury was instructed—according to Texas' law of parties—that "'a person is criminally responsible for an offense committed by the conduct of another if acting with intent to promote or assist the commission of the offense, he solicits, encourages, directs, aids, or attempts to aid the other person to commit the offense.'" The State offered this instruction because Johnson's defense was that he was not the person who had burned the flag. Johnson did not object to this instruction at trial, and although he challenged it on direct appeal, he did so only on the ground that there was insufficient evidence to support it. It is only in this Court that Johnson has argued that the law-of-parties instruction might have led the jury to convict him for his words alone. Even if we were to find that this argument is properly raised here, however, we would conclude that it has no merit in these circumstances. The instruction would not have permitted a conviction merely for the pejorative nature of Johnson's words, and those words themselves did not encourage the burning of

of his conviction under the First Amendment. We must first determine whether Johnson's burning of the flag constituted expressive conduct, permitting him to invoke the First Amendment in challenging his conviction. See, e.g., *Spence*. If his conduct was expressive, we next decide whether the State's regulation is related to the suppression of free expression. *O'Brien; Spence* n. 8. If the State's regulation is not related to expression, then the less stringent standard we announced in *O'Brien* for regulations of noncommunicative conduct controls. If it is, then we are outside of *O'Brien*'s test, and we must ask whether this interest justifies Johnson's conviction under a more demanding standard.[3] A third possibility is that the State's asserted interest is simply not implicated on these facts, and in that event the interest drops out of the picture. * * *

In deciding whether particular conduct possesses sufficient communicative elements to bring the First Amendment into play, we have asked whether "[a]n intent to convey a particularized message was present, and [whether] the likelihood was great that the message would be understood by those who viewed it." [*Spence*.] * * *

We have not automatically concluded, however, that any action taken with respect to our flag is expressive. Instead, in characterizing such action for First Amendment purposes, we have considered the context in which it occurred. In *Spence*, for example, we emphasized that Spence's taping of a peace sign to his flag was "roughly simultaneous with and concededly triggered by the Cambodian incursion and the Kent State tragedy." The State of Washington had conceded, in fact, that Spence's conduct was a form of communication, and we stated that "the State's concession is inevitable on this record."

The State of Texas conceded for purposes of its oral argument in this case that Johnson's conduct was expressive conduct and this concession seems to us as prudent as was Washington's in *Spence*. * * *

III

In order to decide whether *O'Brien*'s test applies here * * * we must decide whether Texas has asserted an interest in support of Johnson's conviction that is unrelated to the suppression of expression. [The] State offers two separate interests to justify this conviction: preventing breaches of the peace, and preserving the flag as a symbol of nationhood and national unity. We hold that the first interest is not implicated on this record and that the second is related to the suppression of expression.

the flag as the instruction seems to require. Given the additional fact that "the bulk of the State's argument was premised on Johnson's culpability as a sole actor," we find it too unlikely that the jury convicted Johnson on the basis of this alternative theory to consider reversing his conviction on this ground.

3. Although Johnson has raised a facial challenge to Texas' flag-desecration statute, we choose to resolve this case on the basis of his claim that the statute as applied to him violates the First Amendment. Section 42.09 regulates only physical conduct with respect to the flag, not the written or spoken word, and although one violates the statute only if one "knows" that one's physical treatment of the flag "will seriously offend one or more persons likely to observe or discover his ac-

tion," this fact does not necessarily mean that the statute applies only to *expressive* conduct protected by the First Amendment. A tired person might, for example, drag a flag through the mud, knowing that this conduct is likely to offend others, and yet have no thought of expressing any idea; neither the language nor the Texas courts' interpretations of the statute precludes the possibility that such a person would be prosecuted for flag desecration. Because the prosecution of a person who had not engaged in expressive conduct would pose a different case, and because we are capable of disposing of this case on narrower grounds, we address only Johnson's claim that § 42.09 as applied to political expression like his violates the First Amendment.

A

Texas claims that its interest in preventing breaches of the peace justifies Johnson's conviction for flag desecration.[4] However, no disturbance of the peace actually occurred or threatened to occur because of Johnson's burning of the flag. [The] only evidence offered by the State at trial to show the reaction to Johnson's actions was the testimony of several persons who had been seriously offended by the flag-burning.

The State's position, therefore, amounts to a claim that an audience that takes serious offense at particular expression is necessarily likely to disturb the peace and that the expression may be prohibited on this basis. [W]e have not permitted the Government to assume that every expression of a provocative idea will incite a riot, but have instead required careful consideration of the actual circumstances surrounding such expression, asking whether the expression "is directed to inciting or producing imminent lawless action and is likely to incite or produce such action." *Brandenburg.* To accept Texas' arguments that it need only demonstrate "the potential for a breach of the peace," and that every flag-burning necessarily possesses that potential, would be to eviscerate our holding in *Brandenburg.* This we decline to do.

Nor does Johnson's expressive conduct fall within that small class of "fighting words" that are "likely to provoke the average person to retaliation, and thereby cause a breach of the peace." *Chaplinsky.* No reasonable onlooker would have regarded Johnson's generalized expression of dissatisfaction with the policies of the Federal Government as a direct personal insult or an invitation to exchange fisticuffs.

We thus conclude that the State's interest in maintaining order is not implicated on these facts. * * *

B

The State also asserts an interest in preserving the flag as a symbol of nationhood and national unity. [The] State, apparently, is concerned that such conduct will lead people to believe either that the flag does not stand for nationhood and national unity, but instead reflects other, less positive concepts, or that the concepts reflected in the flag do not in fact exist, that is, we do not enjoy unity as a Nation. These concerns blossom only when a person's treatment of the flag communicates some message, and thus are related "to the suppression of free expression" within the meaning of *O'Brien.* We are thus outside of *O'Brien*'s test altogether.

IV

It remains to consider whether the State's interest in preserving the flag as a symbol of nationhood and national unity justifies Johnson's conviction. [If Johnson] had burned the flag as a means of disposing of it because it was dirty or torn, he would not have been convicted of flag desecration under this Texas law: federal law designates burning as the preferred means of disposing of a flag

4. Relying on our decision in *Boos v. Barry*, [p. __ of this Supplement], Johnson argues that this state interest is related to the suppression of free expression within the meaning of *O'Brien.* He reasons that the violent reaction to flag-burnings feared by Texas would be the result of the message conveyed by them, and that this fact connects the State's interest to the suppression of expression. This view has found some favor in the lower courts. Johnson's theory may overread *Boos* insofar as it suggests that a desire to prevent a violent audience reaction is "related to expression" in the same way that a desire to prevent an audience from being offended is "related to expression." Because we find that the State's interest in preventing breaches of the peace is not implicated on these facts, however, we need not venture further into this area.

"when it is in such condition that it is no longer a fitting emblem for display," 36 U.S.C. § 176(k), and Texas has no quarrel with this means of disposal. The Texas law is thus not aimed at protecting the physical integrity of the flag in all circumstances, but is designed instead to protect it only against impairments that would cause serious offense to others.[6] Texas concedes as much: "Section 42.09(b) reaches only those severe acts of physical abuse of the flag carried out in a way likely to be offensive. The statute mandates intentional or knowing abuse, that is, the kind of mistreatment that is not innocent, but rather is intentionally designed to seriously offend other individuals."

Whether Johnson's treatment of the flag violated Texas law thus depended on the likely communicative impact of his expressive conduct. Our decision in *Boos v. Barry* tells us that this restriction on Johnson's expression is content-based. In *Boos*, we considered the constitutionality of a law prohibiting "the display of any sign within 50 feet of a foreign embassy if that sign tends to bring that foreign government into 'public odium' or 'public disrepute.'" Rejecting the argument that the law was content-neutral because it was justified by "our international law obligation to shield diplomats from speech that offends their dignity," we held that a "[t]he emotive impact of speech on its audience is not a 'secondary effect'" unrelated to the content of the expression itself.

According to the principles announced in *Boos*, Johnson's political expression was restricted because of the content of the message he conveyed. We must therefore subject the State's asserted interest in preserving the special symbolic character of the flag to "the most exacting scrutiny." *Boos v. Barry*.[8] * * *

According to Texas, if one physically treats the flag in a way that would tend to cast doubt on either the idea that nationhood and national unity are the flag's referents or that national unity actually exists, the message conveyed thereby is a harmful one and therefore may be prohibited.

If there is a bedrock principle underlying the First Amendment, it is that the Government may not prohibit the expression of an idea simply because society finds the idea itself offensive or disagreeable. [We] have not recognized an exception to this principle even where our flag has been involved. [We] never before have held that the Government may ensure that a symbol be used to express only one view of that symbol or its referents. Indeed, in *Schacht v. United States*, we invalidated a federal statute permitting an actor portraying a member of one of our armed forces to "'wear the uniform of that armed force if the portrayal does not tend to discredit that armed force.'" This proviso, we held, "which leaves Americans free to praise the war in Vietnam but can send persons like Schacht to prison for opposing it, cannot survive in a country which has the First Amendment."

We perceive no basis on which to hold that the principle underlying our decision in *Schacht* does not apply to this case. To conclude that the Government may permit designated symbols to be used to communicate only a limited set of messages would be to enter territory having no discernible or defensible

---

6. *Cf. Smith v. Goguen* (Blackmun, J., dissenting) (emphasizing that lower court appeared to have construed state statute so as to protect physical integrity of the flag in all circumstances); *id.* (Rehnquist, J., dissenting) (same).

8. Our inquiry is, of course, bounded by the particular facts of this case and by the statute under which Johnson was convicted. There was no evidence that Johnson himself stole the flag he burned, nor did the prosecu-

tion or the arguments urged in support of it depend on the theory that the flag was stolen. Thus, our analysis does not rely on the way in which the flag was acquired, and nothing in our opinion should be taken to suggest that one is free to steal a flag so long as one later uses it to communicate an idea. We also emphasize that Johnson was prosecuted *only* for flag desecration—not for trespass, disorderly conduct, or arson.

boundaries. Could the Government, on this theory, prohibit the burning of state flags? Of copies of the Presidential seal? Of the Constitution? In evaluating these choices under the First Amendment, how would we decide which symbols were sufficiently special to warrant this unique status? To do so, we would be forced to consult our own political preferences, and impose them on the citizenry, in the very way that the First Amendment forbids us to do.

There is, moreover, no indication—either in the text of the Constitution or in our cases interpreting it—that a separate juridical category exists for the American flag alone. Indeed, we would not be surprised to learn that the persons who framed our Constitution and wrote the Amendment that we now construe were not known for their reverence for the Union Jack. The First Amendment does not guarantee that other concepts virtually sacred to our Nation as a whole—such as the principle that discrimination on the basis of race is odious and destructive—will go unquestioned in the marketplace of ideas. See *Brandenburg*. We decline, therefore, to create for the flag an exception to the joust of principles protected by the First Amendment.

It is not the State's ends, but it means, to which we object. It cannot be gainsaid that there is a special place reserved for the flag in this Nation, and thus we do not doubt that the Government has a legitimate interest in making efforts to "preserv[e] the national flag as an unalloyed symbol of our country." We reject the suggestion, urged at oral argument by counsel for Johnson, that the Government lacks "any state interest whatsoever" in regulating the manner in which the flag may be displayed. Congress has, for example, enacted precatory regulations describing the proper treatment of the flag, see 36 U.S.C. §§ 173–177, and we cast no doubt on the legitimacy of its interest in making such recommendations. To say that the Government has an interest in encouraging proper treatment of the flag, however, is not to say that it may criminally punish a person for burning a flag as a means of political protest. "National unity as an end which officials may foster by persuasion and example is not in question. The problem is whether under our Constitution compulsion as here employed is a permissible means for its achievement."

We are fortified in today's conclusion by our conviction that forbidding criminal punishment for conduct such as Johnson's will not endanger the special role played by our flag or the feelings it inspires. To paraphrase Justice Holmes, we submit that nobody can suppose that this one gesture of an unknown man will change our Nation's attitude towards its flag. See *Abrams* (Holmes, J., dissenting). Indeed, Texas' argument that the burning of an American flag " 'is an act having a high likelihood to cause a breach of the peace,' " and its statute's implicit assumption that physical mistreatment of the flag will lead to "serious offense," tend to confirm that the flag's special role is not in danger; if it were, no one would riot or take offense because a flag had been burned.

We are tempted to say, in fact, that the flag's deservedly cherished place in our community will be strengthened, not weakened, by our holding today. Our decision is a reaffirmation of the principles of freedom and inclusiveness that the flag best reflects, and of the conviction that our toleration of criticism such as Johnson's is a sign and source of our strength. Indeed, one of the proudest images of our flag, the one immortalized in our own national anthem, is of the bombardment it survived at Fort McHenry. It is the Nation's resilience, not its rigidity, that Texas sees reflected in the flag—and it is that resilience that we reassert today.

The way to preserve the flag's special role is not to punish those who feel differently about these matters. It is to persuade them that they are wrong. [And,] precisely because it is our flag that is involved, one's response to the flag-burner may exploit the uniquely persuasive power of the flag itself. We can imagine no more appropriate response to burning a flag than waving one's own, no better way to counter a flag-burner's message than by saluting the flag that burns, no surer means of preserving the dignity even of the flag that burned than by—as one witness here did—according its remains a respectful burial. We do not consecrate the flag by punishing its desecration, for in doing so we dilute the freedom that this cherished emblem represents. * * *

JUSTICE KENNEDY, concurring.

I write not to qualify the words Justice Brennan chooses so well, for he says with power all that is necessary to explain our ruling. I join his opinion without reservation, but with a keen sense that this case, like others before us from time to time, exacts its personal toll. * * *

Our colleagues in dissent advance powerful arguments why respondent may be convicted for his expression, reminding us that among those who will be dismayed by our holding will be some who have had the singular honor of carrying the flag in battle. And I agree that the flag holds a lonely place of honor in an age when absolutes are distrusted and simple truths are burdened by unneeded apologetics.

With all respect to those views, I do not believe the Constitution gives us the right to rule as the dissenting members of the Court urge, however painful this judgment is to announce. Though symbols often are what we ourselves make of them, the flag is constant in expressing beliefs Americans share, beliefs in law and peace and that freedom which sustains the human spirit. The case here today forces recognition of the costs to which those beliefs commit us. It is poignant but fundamental that the flag protects those who hold it in contempt.

For all the record shows, this respondent was not a philosopher and perhaps did not even possess the ability to comprehend how repellent his statements must be to the Republic itself. But whether or not he could appreciate the enormity of the offense he gave, the fact remains that his acts were speech, in both the technical and the fundamental meaning of the Constitution. So I agree with the Court that he must go free.

CHIEF JUSTICE REHNQUIST, with whom JUSTICE WHITE and JUSTICE O'CONNOR join, dissenting.

In holding this Texas statute unconstitutional, the Court ignores Justice Holmes' familiar aphorism that "a page of history is worth a volume of logic." *New York Trust Co. v. Eisner*, 256 U.S. 345, 41 S.Ct. 506, 65 L.Ed. 963 (1921). For more than 200 years, the American flag has occupied a unique position as the symbol of our Nation, a uniqueness that justifies a governmental prohibition against flag burning in the way respondent Johnson did here. * * * [a]

The American flag, then, throughout more than 200 years of our history, has come to be the visible symbol embodying our Nation. It does not represent the

---

a. Rehnquist, C.J., proceeded for some pages to invoke a legacy of prose, poetry, and law in honor of flags in general and the American flag in particular both in peace and in war, quoting poetry from, among others, Ralph Waldo Emerson and John Greenleaf Whittier. Emerson's poem referred to the Union Jack, but he did not always speak so warmly of the American flag. After passage of the Fugitive Slave Law Emerson wrote, "We sneak about with the infamy of crime in the streets, & cowardice in ourselves and frankly once for all the Union is sunk, the flag is hateful, and shall be hissed." *Emerson in His Journals* 421 (J. Porte ed. 1982).

views of any particular political party, and it does not represent any particular political philosophy. The flag is not simply another "idea" or "point of view" competing for recognition in the marketplace of ideas. Millions and millions of Americans regard it with an almost mystical reverence regardless of what sort of social, political, or philosophical beliefs they may have. I cannot agree that the First Amendment invalidates the Act of Congress, and the laws of 48 of the 50 States, which make criminal the public burning of the flag.

More than 80 years ago in *Halter v. Nebraska*, this Court upheld the constitutionality of a Nebraska statute that forbade the use of representations of the American flag for advertising purposes upon articles of merchandise. The Court there said: "For that flag every true American has not simply an appreciation but a deep affection. . . . Hence, it has often occurred that insults to a flag have been the cause of war, and indignities put upon it, in the presence of those who revere it, have often been resented and sometimes punished on the spot."

Only two Terms ago, in *San Francisco Arts & Athletics, Inc. v. United States Olympic Committee*, [p. 365 of this Supplement], the Court held that Congress could grant exclusive use of the word "Olympic" to the United States Olympic Committee. The Court thought that this "restrictio[n] on expressive speech properly [was] characterized as incidental to the primary congressional purpose of encouraging and rewarding the USOC's activities." As the Court stated, "when a word [or symbol] acquires value 'as the result of organization and the expenditure of labor, skill, and money' by an entity, that entity constitutionally may obtain a limited property right in the word [or symbol]." Surely Congress or the States may recognize a similar interest in the flag.[b]

But the Court insists that the Texas statute prohibiting the public burning of the American flag infringes on respondent Johnson's freedom of expression. Such freedom, of course, is not absolute. [T]he public burning of the American flag by Johnson was no essential part of any exposition of ideas, and at the same time it had a tendency to incite a breach of the peace. Johnson was free to make any verbal denunciation of the flag that he wished; indeed, he was free to burn the flag in private. He could publicly burn other symbols of the Government or effigies of political leaders. He did lead a march through the streets of Dallas, and conducted a rally in front of the Dallas City Hall. He engaged in a "die-in" to protest nuclear weapons. He shouted out various slogans during the march, including: "Reagan, Mondale which will it be? Either one means World War III"; "Ronald Reagan, killer of the hour, Perfect example of U.S. power"; and "red, white and blue, we spit on you, you stand for plunder, you will go under." For none of these acts was he arrested or prosecuted; it was only when he proceeded to burn publicly an American flag stolen from its rightful owner that he violated the Texas statute. * * * As with "fighting words," so with flag burning, for purposes of the First Amendment: It is "no essential part of any exposition of ideas, and [is] of such slight social value as a step to truth that any benefit that may be derived from [it] is clearly outweighed" by the public interest in avoiding a probable breach of the peace. * * *

b. In response, Brennan, J., observed that *Halter* was decided "nearly twenty years" before the first amendment was applied to the states and "[m]ore important" that *Halter* involved "purely commercial rather than political speech." Similarly, he stated that the authorization "to prohibit certain commercial and promotion uses of the word 'Olympic' [does not] even begin to tell us whether the Government may criminally punish physical conduct towards the flag engaged in as a means of political protest."

The result of the Texas statute is obviously to deny one in Johnson's frame of mind one of many means of "symbolic speech." Far from being a case of "one picture being worth a thousand words," flag burning is the equivalent of an inarticulate grunt or roar that, it seems fair to say, is most likely to be indulged in not to express any particular idea, but to antagonize others. [The] Texas statute deprived Johnson of only one rather inarticulate symbolic form of protest—a form of protest that was profoundly offensive to many—and left him with a full panoply of other symbols and every conceivable form of verbal expression to express his deep disapproval of national policy. Thus, in no way can it be said that Texas is punishing him because his hearers—or any other group of people—were profoundly opposed to the message that he sought to convey. Such opposition is no proper basis for restricting speech or expression under the First Amendment. It was Johnson's use of this particular symbol, and not the idea that he sought to convey by it or by his many other expressions, for which he was punished. * * *

The uniquely deep awe and respect for our flag felt by virtually all of us are bundled off under the rubric of "designated symbols," that the First Amendment prohibits the government from "establishing." But the government has not "established" this feeling; 200 years of history have done that. The government is simply recognizing as a fact the profound regard for the American flag created by that history when it enacts statutes prohibiting the disrespectful public burning of the flag.

The Court concludes its opinion with a regrettably patronizing civics lecture, presumably addressed to the Members of both Houses of Congress, the members of the 48 state legislatures that enacted prohibitions against flag burning, and the troops fighting under that flag in Vietnam who objected to its being burned: "The way to preserve the flag's special role is not to punish those who feel differently about these matters. It is to persuade them that they are wrong." The Court's role as the final expositor of the Constitution is well established, but its role as a platonic guardian admonishing those responsible to public opinion as if they were truant school children has no similar place in our system of government. The cry of "no taxation without representation" animated those who revolted against the English Crown to found our Nation—the idea that those who submitted to government should have some say as to what kind of laws would be passed. Surely one of the high purposes of a democratic society is to legislate against conduct that is regarded as evil and profoundly offensive to the majority of people—whether it be murder, embezzlement, pollution, or flag burning. * * *

Uncritical extension of constitutional protection to the burning of the flag risks the frustration of the very purpose for which organized governments are instituted. The Court decides that the American flag is just another symbol, about which not only must opinions pro and con be tolerated, but for which the most minimal public respect may not be enjoined. The government may conscript men into the Armed Forces where they must fight and perhaps die for the flag, but the government may not prohibit the public burning of the banner under which they fight. I would uphold the Texas statute as applied in this case.[2]

2. In holding that the Texas statute as applied to Johnson violates the First Amendment, the Court does not consider Johnson's claims that the statute is unconstitutionally vague or overbroad. I think those claims are without merit. [By] defining "desecrate" as "deface," "damage" or otherwise "physically mistreat" in a manner that the actor knows will "seriously offend" others, § 42.09 only prohibits flagrant acts of physical abuse and

JUSTICE STEVENS, dissenting. * * *

Even if flag burning could be considered just another species of symbolic speech under the logical application of the rules that the Court has developed in its interpretation of the First Amendment in other contexts, this case has an intangible dimension that makes those rules inapplicable.

A country's flag is a symbol of more than "nationhood and national unity." [T]he American flag * * * is more than a proud symbol of the courage, the determination, and the gifts of nature that transformed 13 fledgling Colonies into a world power. It is a symbol of freedom, of equal opportunity, of religious tolerance, and of goodwill for other peoples who share our aspirations. The symbol carries its message to dissidents both at home and abroad who may have no interest at all in our national unity or survival.

The value of the flag as a symbol cannot be measured. Even so, I have no doubt that the interest in preserving that value for the future is both significant and legitimate. Conceivably that value will be enhanced by the Court's conclusion that our national commitment to free expression is so strong that even the United States as ultimate guarantor of that freedom is without power to prohibit the desecration of its unique symbol. But I am unpersuaded. The creation of a federal right to post bulletin boards and graffiti on the Washington Monument might enlarge the market for free expression, but at a cost I would not pay. Similarly, in my considered judgment, sanctioning the public desecration of the flag will tarnish its value—both for those who cherish the ideas for which it waves and for those who desire to don the robes of martyrdom by burning it. That tarnish is not justified by the trivial burden on free expression occasioned by requiring that an available, alternative mode of expression—including uttering words critical of the flag be employed.

It is appropriate to emphasize certain propositions that are not implicated by this case. [The] statute does not compel any conduct or any profession of respect for any idea or any symbol. [Nor] does the statute violate "the government's paramount obligation of neutrality in its regulation of protected communication." The content of respondent's message has no relevance whatsoever to the case. The concept of "desecration" does not turn on the substance of the message the actor intends to convey, but rather on whether those who view the *act* will take serious offense. Accordingly, one intending to convey a message of respect for the flag by burning it in a public square might nonetheless be guilty of desecration if he knows that others—perhaps simply because they misperceive the intended message—will be seriously offended. Indeed, even if the actor knows that all possible witnesses will understand that he intends to send a message of respect, he might still be guilty of desecration if he also knows that this understanding does not lessen the offense taken by some of those witnesses. The case has nothing to do with "disagreeable ideas." It involves disagreeable conduct that, in my opinion, diminishes the value of an important national asset.

The Court is therefore quite wrong in blandly asserting that respondent "was prosecuted for his expression of dissatisfaction with the policies of this country, expression situated at the core of our First Amendment values." Respondent was prosecuted because of the method he chose to express his dissatisfaction with those policies. Had he chosen to spray paint—or perhaps

destruction of the flag of the sort at issue here—soaking a flag with lighter fluid and igniting it in public—and not any of the examples of improper flag etiquette cited in Respondent's brief.

convey with a motion picture projector—his message of dissatisfaction on the facade of the Lincoln Memorial, there would be no question about the power of the Government to prohibit his means of expression. The prohibition would be supported by the legitimate interest in preserving the quality of an important national asset. Though the asset at stake in this case is intangible, given its unique value, the same interest supports a prohibition on the desecration of the American flag.*

The ideas of liberty and equality have been an irresistible force in motivating leaders like Patrick Henry, Susan B. Anthony, and Abraham Lincoln, schoolteachers like Nathan Hale and Booker T. Washington, the Philippine Scouts who fought at Bataan, and the soldiers who scaled the bluff at Omaha Beach. If those ideas are worth fighting for—and our history demonstrates that they are—it cannot be true that the flag that uniquely symbolizes their power is not itself worthy of protection from unnecessary desecration.

I respectfully dissent.

Notes and Questions

1. *Was Johnson convicted for his speech?* Johnson defended at trial on the ground that he did *not* burn the flag. Two witnesses, who had been observers of the march for the American Civil Liberties Union, testified that Johnson did not burn the flag. One witness, a police officer, testified that he saw Johnson set the flag on fire. The jury was instructed (over Johnson's objection) that Johnson could be convicted *either* if he burned the flag himself or if he encouraged the flag burning (the "law of the parties" rule). In closing argument the prosecutor argued both theories to the jury. In particular, the prosecutor said: "[I]f you look at this evidence from start to finish, the participating in the beginning, the literature, the shirt [Johnson wore a shirt bearing the name of the Revolutionary Communist Youth Brigade], who he is, the chanting, the yelling, the megaphone, the encouragement . . . being there, wanting this to happen, there is no question he encouraged it all. He's guilty as sin as far as the law of parties is concerned."

Is Brennan, J., on solid ground in fn. 2 when he finds it unlikely that Johnson was convicted on the encouragement theory? Did the Court need to reach the flagburning issue? Was it wise to do so?

2. *The Flag's Physical Integrity.* Brennan, J., observes that the Texas law is "not aimed at protecting the physical integrity of the flag in all circumstances . . . ." What if it were? Consider Tribe, *Give Old Glory A Break: Protect It and Ideas*, N.Y. Times, July 3, 1989, at 18: "Properly understood, the Court's decision upheld no right to desecrate the flag, even in political protest, but

---

* The Court suggested that a prohibition against flag desecration is not content-neutral because this form of symbolic speech is only used by persons who are critical of the flag or the ideas it represents. In making this suggestion the Court does not pause to consider the far-reaching consequences of its introduction of disparate impact analysis into our First Amendment jurisprudence. It seems obvious that a prohibition against the desecration of a gravesite is content-neutral even if it denies some protesters the right to make a symbolic statement by extinguishing the flame in Arlington Cemetery where John F. Kennedy is buried while permitting others to salute the flame by bowing their heads. Few would doubt that a protester who extinguishes the flame has desecrated the gravesite, regardless of whether he prefaces that act with a speech explaining that his purpose is to express deep admiration or unmitigated scorn for the late President. Likewise, few would claim that the protester who bows his head has desecrated the gravesite, even if he makes clear that his purpose is to show disrespect. In such a case, as in a flag burning case, the prohibition against desecration has absolutely nothing to do with the content of the message the the symbolic speech is intended to convey.

merely required that Government protection of the flag be separated from Government suppression of detested views. . . . Thus, if a flag desecration law were written and enforced without regard to the presence or absence of any message, government could defend the values embodied in the flag without addressing the values expressed by its destruction. I believe the Court would uphold such a law."

Should it? Consider Tribe, id.: "Look at how people are rallying against the deliberate poisoning of the Treaty Oak in Austin, a landmark that took root before Columbus set sail for the New World. The point of punishing whoever was responsible for that tragedy need not be to censor the views he or she expressed. The point is simply to give force to the community's shared sense that the object is worthy of special protection." But consider, Hertzberg, *TRB From Washington: Flagellation*, 201 New Republic 4 (July 17 & 24, 1989): "[A]n important ontological point has been overlooked: you can't burn the flag. It can't be done. *A* flag, yes. *The* flag, no. *The* flag . . . exists (a) in the realm of Platonic ideals and (b) in the minds and hearts of people. [A]s long as it exists in human hearts, [the flag] is fireproof. * * *

"If flying the flag is symbolic speech, so is burning one; and speech, in this country, is supposed to be free."

3. *Alternative Sources of Outrage.* Assuming that flag desecration statutes or proposed amendments are motivated by a desire to suppress dissent that is perceived to go too far,[c] could the Johnsons of the world find alternative ways to communicate their outrage and, in turn, to outrage the public? Would a first amendment flag exception step down a slippery slope? Consider Kamisar, *Keeping Up With the Gregory Johnsons*, Baltimore Sun, July 22, 1989, at 9A: "[If the proposed amendment to make 'physical desecration" of the flag punishable were adopted, people like Johnson] could still strike at the emotional core of many Americans by displaying the flag and shouting insulting words at it. Or they could fly Old Glory *below* the Nicaraguan flag or fly it upside down or *tape* scurrilous words or defiant symbols on it. Or they could simply burn huge color photographs of the flag. None of these acts would impair the physical integrity of the flag but all would deeply offend tens of millions of Americans.

"Of course, such contemptuous forms of political protest might lead to a second constitutional amendment, one that placed the flag 'off limits' entirely, i.e., forbade any defilement or profane *use* of the flag (terms not easy to define or to apply). But even such an expansion of the original exception to the First Amendment's protection would not thwart people like Mr. Johnson for very long.

"They could build their street demonstrations around large replicas of another venerated national symbol, the Statue of Liberty. At the high point in their demonstrations (or should one say, low point?) they could melt down Miss Liberty—or smash her with sledgehammers. * * *

"Even if the Statue of Liberty, as well as the flag, were withdrawn from the roster of materials that could be used as a background for political protest, people like Gregory Johnson would not be at a loss. They could, for example, display copies of the U.S. Constitution (easily obtainable in pamphlet form from the government printing office or the Commission on the Bicentennial of the Constitution), then tear, trample upon or burn this precious document. Such conduct would be accompanied, no doubt, by vulgar, derisive songs or shouts.

---

c. Consider President George Bush, N.Y. Times, June 28, 1989, at B7: "As President, I will uphold our precious right to dissent, but burning the flag goes too far and I want to see that matter remedied."

Once again, a majority of Americans and even a larger majority of their representatives would maintain that this was 'going to far.'

"[I]f sufficiently aroused, the American people could conceivably strip *all* 'symbolic speech' of constitutional protection. Even such a significant contraction of the First Amendment, however, would not leave people like Johnson without other ways to offend.

"There are, after all, important *verbal* symbols of nationhood and unity, such as the national anthem and the pledge of allegiance. Dissidents could express opposition to their country's policies or attitudes by publicly parodying these revered verbal symbols. They could, for example, sing 'O'er the land of the pigs and the home of the wimps' or pledge allegiance to 'one nation under Satan.' It would be no surprise if such derisive treatment of our national symbols—what would surely be called assaults on the 'integrity' of these symbols—sparked outrage anew and led to still another campaign to carve out still another exception to the First Amendment." .

AMER CON: P. 640, at end of section

ARCARA v. CLOUD BOOKS, INC., p. 289 of this Supplement.

SECTION: GOVERNMENT PROPERTY AND THE PUBLIC FORUM

FOUNDATION CASES

MANDATORY ACCESS

CON LAW: P. 869, substitute for last sentence of note 5

AMER CON: P. 643, substitute for last sentence of note 5

RTS & LIB: P. 536, substitute for last sentence of note 5

But the test is differently stated in different cases. For example, *U.S. Postal Service v. Council of Greenburgh*, 453 U.S. 114, 101 S.Ct. 2676, 69 L.Ed.2d 517 (1981), speaks of "adequate" as opposed to "ample" alternative channels of communication, and *City of Renton v. Playtime Theatres, Inc.*, p. 198 of this Supplement, transcends the difference by requiring that the restriction not "unreasonably limit" alternative channels of communication. Beyond these differences, a number of cases state that the regulation must be "narrowly tailored" to serve a significant government interest as opposed to just serving a significant government interest. See, e.g., *Perry Educ. Ass'n v. Perry Local Educators' Ass'n; U.S. v. Grace*, Casebooks, Sec. 5.

City Council v. Taxpayers for Vincent, Casebooks, Sec. 7, joined the "narrowly tailored" version of the reasonable time, place, and manner test together with the *O'Brien* test—as if they were the same—and *Clark v. Community For Creative Non-Violence*, Casebooks, Sec. 4, explicitly stated that the standard applied to time, place, and manner restrictions is "little, if any, different" from the *O'Brien* test. This, among other things, despite the fact that the time, place, and manner test requires a showing of "ample" (*Clark*) or "adequate" (*Vincent*) alternative channels of communication and *O'Brien* by its terms, at least, does not.

Dean Stone, for one, argues that the time, place, and manner test and the *O'Brien* test are functionally similar in that when either test applies, the government regulation is upheld. Cf. Stone, *Content-Neutral Restrictions*, 54

U.Chi.L.Rev. 46, 52 (1987). This is a plausible, albeit contestable, reading of the small number of Supreme Court cases that have applied these tests, but Stone's conclusion does not hold in the lower courts (nor does he contend to the contrary). Not only have restrictions been struck down under both of the tests, but the lower courts have frequently struggled with the Court's different phrasings in an attempt to figure out which test to apply, often with the view that determining which test or version of the test to apply might matter. For a sample, see *Century Communications Corp. v. FCC*, 835 F.2d 292 (D.C.Cir.1987), *cert. denied*, 108 S.Ct. 2014 (1988); *Olivieri v. Ward*, 801 F.2d 602 (2d Cir.1986); *City of Watseka v. Illinois Pub. Action Council*, 796 F.2d 1547 (7th Cir.1986), *aff'd*, 479 U.S. 1048 (1987); *Wisconsin Action Coalition v. City of Kenosha*, 767 F.2d 1248 (7th Cir.1985); *Avalon Cinema Corp. v. Thompson*, 667 F.2d 659 (8th Cir.1981); *Women Strike For Peace v. Morton*, 472 F.2d 1273 (D.C.Cir.1972); *Breen v. Kahl*, 419 F.2d 1034 (7th Cir.1969), *cert. denied*, 398 U.S. 937 (1970).

WARD v. ROCK AGAINST RACISM, ___ U.S. ___, 109 S.Ct. 2746, ___ L.Ed.2d ___ (1989), per KENNEDY, J., observes that "[E]ven in a public forum the government may impose reasonable restrictions on the time, place, or manner of protected speech, provided the restrictions 'are justified without reference to the content of the regulated speech, that they are narrowly tailored to serve a significant governmental interest, and that they leave open ample alternative channels for communication of the information.'" The case reasserts that the *O'Brien* test is little different from the time, place, and manner test, and then states: "Lest any confusion on the point remain, we reaffirm today that a regulation of the time, place, or manner of protected speech must be narrowly tailored to serve the government's legitimate content-neutral interests but that it need not be the least-restrictive or least-intrusive means of doing so. Rather, the requirement of narrow tailoring is satisfied 'so long as [the] regulation promotes a substantial government interest that would be achieved less effectively absent the regulation.' To be sure, this standard does not mean that a time, place, or manner regulation may burden substantially more speech than is necessary to further the government's legitimate interests. Government may not regulate expression in such a manner that a substantial portion of the burden on speech does not serve to advance its goals."[7] MARSHALL, J., dissenting, joined by Brennan and Stevens, JJ., complains of the Court's "serious distortion of the narrowly tailoring requirement" and states that the Court's rejection of the less restrictive alternative test relies on "language in a few opinions . . . taken out of context."

Should the time, place, and manner test be different from the *O'Brien* test? Is there any difference between those tests and the approach employed in *Schneider*?

LIMITED PUBLIC FORUMS AND NONPUBLIC FORUMS

CON LAW: P. 884, after note 4

AMER CON: P. 658, after note 4

RTS & LIB: P. 551, after note 4

BOARD OF AIRPORT COMMISSIONERS v. JEWS FOR JESUS, INC., 482 U.S. 569, 107 S.Ct. 2568, 96 L.Ed.2d 500 (1987), per O'CONNOR, J., struck down a

---

7. A ban on handbilling, of course, would suppress a great quantity of speech that does not cause the evils that it seeks to eliminate, whether they be fraud, crime, litter, traffic congestion, or noise. For that reason, a complete ban on handbilling would be substantially broader than necessary to achieve the interests justifying it.

commission resolution banning all "First Amendment activities" at Los Angeles International Airport ("LAX"):

"The petitioners contend that LAX is neither a traditional public forum nor a public forum by government designation, and accordingly argue that the latter standard governing access to a nonpublic forum is appropriate. The respondents, in turn, argue that LAX is a public forum subject only to reasonable time, place or manner restrictions. Moreover, at least one commentator contends that *Perry* does not control a case such as this in which the respondents already have access to the airport, and therefore concludes that this case is analogous to *Tinker*. See Laycock, Equal Access and Moments of Silence: The Equal Status of Religious Speech by Private Speakers, 81 Nw.U.L.Rev. 1, 48 (1986). Because we conclude that the resolution is facially unconstitutional under the First Amendment overbreadth doctrine regardless of the proper standard, we need not decide whether LAX is indeed a public forum, or whether the *Perry* standard is applicable when access to a nonpublic forum is not restricted. * * *

"On its face, the resolution at issue in this case reaches the universe of expressive activity, and, by prohibiting *all* protected expression, purports to create a virtual 'First Amendment Free Zone' at LAX. The resolution does not merely regulate activity in the Central Terminal Area that might create problems such as congestion or the disruption of the activities of those who use LAX. Instead, the resolution expansively states that LAX 'is not open for First Amendment activities by any individual and/or [entity].' The resolution therefore does not merely reach the activity of respondents at LAX; it prohibits even talking and reading, or the wearing of campaign buttons or symbolic clothing. Under such a sweeping ban, virtually every individual who enters LAX may be found to violate the resolution by engaging in some 'First Amendment activit[y].' We think it obvious that such a ban cannot be justified even if LAX were a nonpublic forum because no conceivable governmental interest would justify such an absolute prohibition of speech.

"Additionally, we find no apparent saving construction of the resolution. [T]he resolution is not 'fairly subject to an interpretation which will render unnecessary or substantially modify the federal constitutional question.'

"[I]t is difficult to imagine that the resolution could be limited by anything less than a series of adjudications, and the chilling effect of the resolution on protected speech in the meantime would make such a case-by-case adjudication intolerable.

"The petitioners suggest that the resolution is not substantially overbroad because it is intended to reach only expressive activity unrelated to airport-related purposes. Such a limiting construction, however, is of little assistance in substantially reducing the overbreadth of the resolution. Much nondisruptive speech—such as the wearing of a T-Shirt or button that contains a political message—may not be 'airport related,' but is still protected speech even in a nonpublic forum. See *Cohen*.[a] Moreover, the vagueness of this suggested construction itself presents serious constitutional difficulty. The line between airport-related speech and nonairport-related speech is, at best, murky."

District of Columbia Code Section 22–1115 prohibits the *display* of any sign within 500 feet of a foreign embassy that tends to bring the foreign government

a. White J., joined by Rehnquist, J., joined the Court's opinion, but concurred to stress that the Court's opinion should not be understood to classify LAX as a traditional public forum and to state that the public forum issue should have been resolved.

into "public odium" or "public disrepute" or (as construed) the *congregation* of three or more persons within 500 feet of a foreign embassy when the police reasonably believe that a threat to the security or peace of the embassy is present. Is the display clause constitutional? The congregation clause? Is the street outside a foreign embassy a traditional public forum? Under international law, the United States is obligated to prevent any disturbance of the peace or the impairment of the dignity of foreign diplomatic personnel. Is protection of the dignity of foreign diplomatic personnel, therefore, a compelling governmental interest? See *Boos v. Barry,* 485 U.S. 312, 108 S.Ct. 1157, 99 L.Ed.2d 333 (1988) (striking down display clause; upholding congregation clause).

THE PUBLIC FORUM AND THE PRIVATE RESIDENCE
[NEW PART]

CON LAW: P. 884, after note 4

AMER CON: P. 658, after note 4

RTS & LIB: P. 551, after note 4

On a number of occasions between April 20, 1985 and May 20, 1985, Sandra Schultz, together with groups ranging from ten to more than forty, marched with anti-abortion pickets for one to one and a half hours on the street outside a doctor's home in Brookfield, Wisconsin. In response, the Town Board passed an ordinance prohibiting picketing "before or about" any residence. Schultz filed suit challenging the ordinance on its face.

FRISBY v. SCHULTZ, ___ U.S. ___, 108 S.Ct. 2495, 101 L.Ed.2d 420 (1988), per O'CONNOR, J., interpreted the ordinance to apply only to "focused picketing [a] taking place solely in front of [and directed at] a particular residence," not to "general marching through residential neighborhoods, or even walking a route in front of an entire block of houses." So construed,[b] the Court upheld the ordinance: "The antipicketing ordinance operates at the core of the First Amendment by prohibiting appellees from engaging in picketing on an issue of public concern. [Moreover,] a public street does not lose its status as a traditional public forum simply because it runs through a residential neighborhood. [The] residential character of those streets may well inform the application of the relevant test, but it does not lead to a different test; the antipicketing ordinance must be judged against the stringent standards we have established for restrictions on speech in traditional public fora * * *."

The Court ruled that the ordinance was content neutral and proceeded to inquire whether it was narrowly tailored to serve a significant government interest while leaving open ample alternative channels of communication:

"As appellants explain, the limited nature of the prohibition makes it virtually self-evident that ample alternatives remain: 'Protestors have not been barred from the residential neighborhoods. They may enter such neighborhoods, alone or in groups, even marching. * * * They may go door-to-door to proselytize their views. They may distribute literature in this manner * * * or through the mails. They may contact residents by telephone, short of harassment.'

a. The Court understood picketing to embrace posting or marching at a particular place—whether or not a sign was carried.

b. The lower courts understood the ordinance to ban all picketing in residential areas.

The Court adopted a narrowing construction "in order to avoid constitutional difficulties."

"We readily agree that the ordinance preserves ample alternative channels of communication and thus move on to inquire whether the ordinance serves a significant government interest. '[The] State's interest in protecting the well-being, tranquility, and privacy of the home is certainly of the highest order in a free and civilized society.' *Carey v. Brown.* [One] important aspect of residential privacy is protection of the unwilling listener. Although in many locations, we expect individuals simply to avoid speech they do not want to hear, cf. *Erznoznik, Cohen,* the home is different. [I]ndividuals are not required to welcome unwanted speech into their own homes and [the] government may protect this freedom.

"This principle is reflected even in prior decisions in which we have invalidated complete bans on expressive activity, including bans operating in residential areas. See, e.g., *Schneider* (handbilling); *Martin v. Struthers* (door-to-door solicitation). In all such cases, we have been careful to acknowledge that unwilling listeners may be protected when within their own homes. In *Schneider,* for example, in striking down a complete ban on handbilling, we spoke of a right to distribute literature only 'to one willing to receive it.' Similarly, when we invalidated a ban on door-to-door solicitation in *Martin,* we did so on the basis that the 'home owner could protect himself from such intrusion by an appropriate sign "that he is unwilling to be disturbed."' [There] simply is no right to force speech into the home of an unwilling listener.

"It remains to be considered, however, whether the Brookfield ordinance is narrowly tailored to protect only unwilling recipients of the communications. A statute is narrowly tailored if it targets and eliminates no more than the exact source of the 'evil' it seeks to remedy. [The] type of focused picketing prohibited by the Brookfield ordinance is fundamentally different from more generally directed means of communication that may not be completely banned in residential areas. [In] such cases 'the flow of information [is not] into * * * household[s], but to the public.' *Organization for a Better Austin v. Keefe,* 402 U.S. 415, 91 S.Ct. 1575, 29 L.Ed.2d 1 (1971).[c] Here, in contrast, the picketing is narrowly directed at the household, not the public. The type of picketers banned by the Brookfield ordinance generally do not seek to disseminate a message to the general public, but to intrude upon the targeted resident, and to do so in an especially offensive way. Moreover, even if some such picketers have a broader communicative purpose, their activity nonetheless inherently and offensively intrudes on residential privacy. * * *

"In this case, for example, appellees subjected the doctor and his family to the presence of a relatively large group of protestors on their doorstep in an attempt to force the doctor to cease performing abortions. But the actual size of the group is irrelevant; even a solitary picket can invade residential privacy. See *Carey* (Rehnquist, J., dissenting) ('Whether * * * alone or accompanied by others * * * there are few of us that would feel comfortable knowing that a stranger lurks outside our home'). The offensive and disturbing nature of the form of the communication banned by the Brookfield ordinance thus can scarcely be questioned.

c. *Keefe* involved the distribution of leaflets alleging that a real estate broker was involved in racial "blockbusting" and "panic peddling." The leaflets were distributed at a shopping center, at the broker's church, and at the doors of his neighbors. The Court, per Burger, C.J., stated: "The claim that the expressions were intended to exercise a coercive impact on [the broker] does not remove them from the reach of the First Amendment." Nor were the places of distribution deemed problematic.

"The First Amendment permits the government to prohibit offensive speech as intrusive when the 'captive' audience cannot avoid the objectionable speech. The target of the focused picketing banned by the Brookfield ordinance is just such a 'captive.' The resident is figuratively, and perhaps literally, trapped within the home, and because of the unique and subtle impact of such picketing is left with no ready means of avoiding the unwanted speech. Thus, the 'evil' of targeted residential picketing, 'the very presence of an unwelcome visitor at the home' is 'created by the medium of expression itself.' Accordingly, the Brookfield ordinance's complete ban of that particular medium of expression is narrowly tailored.

"Of course, this case presents only a facial challenge to the ordinance. Particular hypothetical applications of the ordinance—to, for example, a particular resident's use of his or her home as a place of business or public meeting, or to picketers present at a particular home by invitation of the resident—may present somewhat different questions. [S]ince our First Amendment analysis is grounded in protection of the unwilling residential listener, the constitutionality of applying the ordinance to such hypotheticals remains open to question. These are, however, questions we need not address today in order to dispose of appellees' facial challenge." [d]

BRENNAN, J., joined by Marshall, J., dissented: "Without question there are many aspects of residential picketing that, if unregulated, might easily become intrusive or unduly coercive. Indeed, some of these aspects are illustrated by this very case. As the District Court found, before the ordinance took effect up to 40 sign-carrying, slogan-shouting protesters regularly converged on Dr. Victoria's home and, in addition to protesting, warned young children not to go near the house because Dr. Victoria was a 'baby killer.' Further, the throng repeatedly trespassed onto the Victoria's property and at least once blocked the exits to their home. Surely it is within the government's power to enact regulations as necessary to prevent such intrusive and coercive abuses. Thus, for example, the government could constitutionally regulate the number of residential picketers, the hours during which a residential picket may take place, or the noise level of such a picket. In short, substantial regulation is permitted to neutralize the intrusive or unduly coercive aspects of picketing around the home. But to say that picketing may be substantially regulated is not to say that it may be prohibited in its entirety. Once size, time, volume, and the like have been controlled to ensure that the picket is no longer intrusive or coercive, only the speech itself remains, conveyed perhaps by a lone, silent individual, walking back and forth with a sign. Such speech, which no longer implicates the heightened government interest in residential privacy, is nevertheless banned by the Brookfield law. Therefore, the ordinance is not narrowly tailored.

"[The Court] conjures up images of a 'lurking' stranger, secreting himself or herself outside a residence like a thief in the night, threatening physical harm. This hardly seems an apt depiction of a solitary picket, especially at midafternoon, whose presence is objectionable because it is notorious. Contrary to the Court's declaration in this regard, it seems far more likely that a picketer who truly desires only to harass those inside a particular residence will find that goal

d. White, J., concurring, was unsure about the scope of the ordinance. He would sustain the ordinance as applied to the picketing at issue in this case and deny a facial challenge for the present. He stated that the ordinance would be unconstitutional on its face if it were ultimately construed to prohibit all picketing in residential neighborhoods, but not if it were confined to picketing before a single residence. Nonetheless, he suggested that single residence picketing by small groups might be constitutionally protected in some circumstances.

unachievable in the face of a narrowly tailored ordinance substantially limiting, for example, the size, time, and volume of the protest. If, on the other hand, the picketer intends to communicate generally, a carefully crafted ordinance will allow him or her to do so without intruding upon or unduly harassing the resident. Consequently, the discomfort to which the Court must refer is merely that of knowing there is a person outside who disagrees with someone inside. This may indeed be uncomfortable, but it does not implicate the Town's interest in residential privacy and therefore does not warrant silencing speech." [e]

STEVENS, J., also dissented: "'GET WELL CHARLIE—OUR TEAM NEEDS YOU.'"

"In Brookfield, Wisconsin, it is unlawful for a fifth grader to carry such a sign in front of a residence for the period of time necessary to convey its friendly message to its intended audience. * * *

"My hunch is that the town will probably not enforce its ban against friendly, innocuous, or even brief unfriendly picketing, and that the Court may be right in concluding that its legitimate sweep makes its overbreadth insubstantial. But there are two countervailing considerations that are persuasive to me. The scope of the ordinance gives the town officials far too much discretion in making enforcement decisions; while we sit by and await further developments, potential picketers must act at their peril. Second, it is a simple matter for the town to amend its ordinance and to limit the ban to conduct that unreasonably interferes with the privacy of the home and does not serve a reasonable communicative purpose."

SECTION: GOVERNMENT SUPPORT OF SPEECH

SUBSIDIES AND TAX EXPENDITURES

AMER CON: P. 662, after note 5

ARKANSAS WRITERS' PROJECT, INC. v. RAGLAND, p. 285 of this Supplement.

CON LAW: P. 888, after note 5

AMER CON: P. 662, after note 5

RTS & LIB: P. 555, after note 5

LAURENCE TRIBE—AMERICAN CONSTITUTIONAL LAW § 11–5, at 781–84 (2d ed. 1988).

§ 11–5. The Elusive Distinction Between Withholding a Subsidy and Imposing a Penalty

A problem pervading much of contemporary constitutional law is that of drawing a workable distinction between government's undoubtedly broad power to decide which activities to subsidize or otherwise encourage, and government's considerably narrower power to decide which activities to penalize or otherwise discourage, whether directly or by attaching conditions to various privileges or gratuities.

The notion that, whenever a privilege or benefit might be withheld altogether, it may be withheld on whatever conditions government chooses to impose, has been repeatedly repudiated since the mid-20th century. Independently

e. Like White, J., Brennan, J., was suspicious of the Court's single residence construction of the ordinance, but he accepted it for purposes of the dissent.

unconstitutional conditions—those that make enjoyment of a benefit contingent on sacrifice of an independent constitutional right—are invalid; whether a condition is unconstitutional depends on whether government may properly demand sacrifice of the alleged right in the particular context. That was the holding of *FCC v. League of Women Voters*[2] and of *Babbitt v. Planned Parenthood Federation.*[3]

But the fact that government *may not penalize* exercise of a right by withholding an otherwise discretionary benefit does not imply that government *must subsidize* exercise of the right. Thus, although *Planned Parenthood* makes it clear that those who undergo, perform or counsel abortion may not be required to cease those activities as a condition of receiving public funding for their other activities, it certainly does not follow that government must pay for abortions or abortion counseling. Indeed, the Supreme Court held in *Harris v. McRae* that the government is even free to influence an indigent pregnant woman's constitutionally protected reproductive choice by refusing public health funds for abortions while [subsidizing] medical care for childbirth within its comprehensive medical benefits program.

Even when the Constitution forbids government to interfere with an individual's choice between two alternatives—such as the choice between abortion and childbirth, or that between public and private education—it does not follow that

---

2. By a 5–4 vote, the Court invalidated a provision of the Public Broadcasting Act that prohibited any noncommercial educational station receiving public funds from endorsing candidates or editorializing. The stations were thus forced to give up their right to engage in quintessential first amendment expression if they wished to receive public subsidies for any of their programming. Writing for the Court, Justice Brennan concluded that the ban suppressed protected speech without being narrowly tailored to the goal of providing a balanced presentation of issues to the public. Upon close inspection of the statute, the Court rejected Justice Stevens' argument that the law was a legitimate way to preclude the insidious tendency that public funding might have to induce stations to skew their editorials in favor of the government, or their endorsements in favor of incumbents, in order to improve their prospects for continued benefits. In dissent, Justice Rehnquist, joined by Chief Justice Burger and Justice White, protested that all Congress had done was to attach to a discretionary subsidy a requirement that the managers of educational stations not promote their private views at public expense.

3. ___ U.S. ___, 107 S.Ct. 391, 93 L.Ed.2d 346 (1986), aff'g *Planned Parenthood of Central & Northern Arizona v. Arizona,* 789 F.2d 1348 (9th Cir.1986). An Arizona bill appropriating state funds to pay for family-planning services contained a provision forbidding the channeling of any such funds "to agencies or entities which offer abortions, abortion procedures, counseling for abortion procedures or abortion referrals." Planned Parenthood sued to enjoin enforcement of this prohibition. The state sought to defend the prohibition as a prophylactic measure designed to implement the state's right, under *Maher v. Roe* to withhold public funds from abortion-related services. The state argued that, because "it was impossible for the state to monitor use of the funds to prevent their use for abortion-related services," through a system of "ear-marking * * * [,] tracing [,] [and] auditing," the state's only way to prevent use of its funds for abortion-related activities was to keep organizations like Planned Parenthood from obtaining state family-planning funds for *any* purpose. The Ninth Circuit held that no such impossibility had been established and that, on the contrary, Planned Parenthood had "successfully segregated state funds from its abortion-related expenditures." The court flatly rejected any notion that such funding segregation is *inherently* illusory and that "*any* expenditure on abortion-related activities necessarily is derived from state funds" to the extent that those funds constitute a portion of the recipient's budget (emphasis in original). Although Chief Justice Rehnquist, Justice White, and Justice Scalia would have set the case for plenary briefing and argument rather than summarily affirming, it would be difficult to justify any result other than the one the Ninth Circuit reached without holding, in effect, that wholly speculative difficulties of segregating and monitoring public funds give the government a lever over all recipients of such funds whereby such recipients may be forced to choose between foregoing public subsidy and abandoning private activities in which the first and fourteenth amendments entitle those recipients to engage.

government may not put its thumb on the scale by subsidizing one alternative but not the other.   Were that not the case, the subsidy of public schooling would entail a constitutional duty to subsidize the private alternatives that, under *Pierce v. Society of Sisters*, the government must leave parents free to choose. "It cannot be that because government may not prohibit the use of contraceptives, or prevent parents from sending their child to a private school, government, therefore, has an affirmative obligation to ensure that all persons have the financial resources to obtain contraceptives or send their children to private schools."   *Harris v. McRae*.   Whatever one thinks of the validity of educational voucher plans, one surely cannot argue that the Constitution compels government to institute them.

There may well be settings, however, in which the very decision to subsidize one activity entails a decision to penalize another.   Thus, if government were to pay a bounty to those who agreed to vote for incumbents, it would necessarily be penalizing supporters of the opposing candidates, in clear violation of basic norms of equality inherent in the franchise.   Arguably, too, if government were to fund all who advocate freedom of abortion—but not those who advocate saving the fetus—it would in effect be penalizing the "pro-life" position.[9]   Or if government were to permit tax-deductible contributions to be used by pro-life advocates in their lobbying efforts while refusing "pro-choice" advocates the same privilege, it might be said to have penalized the latter.

This sort of argument may be made with some plausibility in any zero-sum situation, in which amplifying the vote or even the voice of one side is the same as muffling the vote or the voice of the other.   But the Court has been properly reluctant to regard selective subsidies of certain voices as automatically having such a viewpoint (or even a subject-matter) bias.   Note, for example, the unanimous conclusion of the Court in *Regan v. Taxation With Representation* (*TWR*) that a governmental decision to subsidize the political lobbying of veterans' organizations but of no other organizations, through rules permitting only the former to engage in such lobbying with tax-deductible contributions, is subject to no heightened first amendment scrutiny.[10]

Even when viewpoint bias is acknowledged, a complicating feature of the analysis arises from whatever special freedom government might be thought to enjoy when it acts less as a regulator of expression than as a participant in the marketplace of ideas.   When government adds its own voice to the dialogue, and perhaps also when it subsidizes the voices of its surrogates, it is not subject to the usual form or level of first amendment scrutiny.

A second complicating feature in the analysis arises because government's power to set the terms on which it offers a subsidy must be thought to include at least some power to restrict not only how that very subsidy is used but also certain other activities of the subsidized person or entity when those other activities bear a close enough relationship to use of the subsidy.   Hence, for example, the power to restrict use of public campaign funds has been held, in

---

9. Cf. *Arkansas Writers' Project, Inc. v. Ragland*, 481 U.S. 221, 107 S.Ct. 1722, 95 L.Ed.2d 209 (1987) (invalidating state tax on general-interest magazines that exempts newspapers and religious, professional, trade, and sports journals).

10. Subject only to a test for minimum rationality, the selective subsidy was upheld. Although government has long rewarded veterans with such things as special opportunities in public employment, see *Personnel Administrator of Massachusetts v. Feeney* (upholding over equal protection challenge a lifetime, absolute veterans' preference in state civil service employment), it seems problematic to reward military service not with preferred access to a privilege or with some other traditional form of benefit, but with the "currency" of a louder political voice.

Buckley v. Valeo, to include a power to cap even the private campaign expenditures of those who receive such public funds. Although the Court in the same case held campaign expenditure limits invalid under the first amendment in the absence of public funding, and although the Court has held that public funding does not permit imposition of a cap on independent expenditures made by others on behalf of the publicly-funded candidate,[14] it is understandable that the Court should have concluded, in *Buckley v. Valeo,* that a candidate may be forced to choose between running a campaign funded exclusively with a public grant and running a campaign funded solely with unlimited private spending.

A third complication arises whenever the government's authority to limit use of a public subsidy, and the recipient's right not to be penalized for independently protected activity, come together in the same case. Both features were involved in *Regan v. TWR,* inasmuch as the Court was unanimous in agreeing that government should be free not to subsidize political lobbying, but it also seemed clear that government could not penalize lobbying with private funds by one who received a public subsidy for other activities.[16] The structure of the Internal Revenue Code made it possible for both principles to be respected, since the Code permitted organizations eligible for tax-deductible contributions under § 501(c)(3) to retain that status while setting up financially independent but wholly controlled § 501(c)(4) lobbying arms that would conduct lobbying directed by their § 501(c)(3) affiliates but funded without benefit of any taxpayer-assisted dollars. This statutory scheme, which the majority noted and which the concurring opinion expressly deemed crucial, should be regarded as indispensable to the *Regan v. TWR* holding.[19]

Finally, cases might arise in which the option of setting up a separately funded lobbying arm poses serious independent difficulties. For example, telling broadcast licensees that they may engage in political editorializing without losing their public funding (as *FCC v. League of Women Voters* holds they must be permitted to do), but insisting that all of their political editorializing be cleanly separated from the rest of the programming—that there be a sharp division between culture and politics—would entail a problematic intrusion into those broadcasters' editorial discretion. Even more severe constitutional problems would be posed by telling churches that they may retain their tax-exempt status under § 501(c)(3) only if they conduct all of their lobbying efforts through separately funded affiliates rather than from the pulpit.

Whenever a problematic degree of governmental entanglement would be required to police such a division, the compromise solution approved in *Regan v. TWR* might be unavailable. A choice would then have to be made—a choice between (1) denying government the ability to restrict the use private recipients may make of public subsidies (thereby freeing some individuals or groups to lobby with public funds, for example), and (2) giving government that ability by denying recipients the opportunity to receive public subsidies without sacrificing their freedom to use private funds for exercise of private rights (thereby putting some to what would otherwise seem to be an unconstitutional choice).

See also *Lyng v. UAW,* p. 279 of this Supplement.

14. See *Federal Election Comm'n v. NCPAC,* 470 U.S 480, 493, 105 S.Ct. 1459, 1467, 84 L.Ed.2d 455 (1985).

16. For example, food stamp recipients surely could not be told they would be cut off and left to starve if they were to use other funds to try to influence the political process.

19. Cf. *Babbitt* discussed in fn. 3 supra.

GOVERNMENT AS EDUCATOR

CON LAW: P. 900, after note 3

AMER CON: P. 674, after note 3

RTS & LIB: P. 567, after note 3

HAZELWOOD SCHOOL DISTRICT v. KUHLMEIER

484 U.S. 260, 108 S.Ct. 562, 98 L.Ed.2d 592 (1988).

JUSTICE WHITE delivered the opinion of the Court.

This case concerns the extent to which educators may exercise editorial control over the contents of a high school newspaper produced as part of the school's journalism curriculum.

I

Petitioners are the Hazelwood School District in St. Louis County, Missouri; various school officials; Robert Eugene Reynolds, the principal of Hazelwood East High School, and Howard Emerson, a teacher in the school district. Respondents are three former Hazelwood East students who were staff members of Spectrum, the school newspaper. They contend that school officials violated their First Amendment rights by deleting two pages of articles from the May 13, 1983, issue of Spectrum.

Spectrum was written and edited by the Journalism II class at Hazelwood East. The newspaper was published every three weeks or so during the 1982–1983 school year. More than 4,500 copies of the newspaper were distributed during that year to students, school personnel, and members of the community.

The Board of Education allocated funds from its annual budget for the printing of Spectrum. [The] Journalism II course was taught by Robert Stergos for most of the 1982–1983 academic year. Stergos left Hazelwood East to take a job in private industry on April 29, 1983, when the May 13 edition of Spectrum was nearing completion, and petitioner Emerson took his place as newspaper adviser for the remaining weeks of the term.

The practice at Hazelwood East during the spring 1983 semester was for the journalism teacher to submit page proofs of each Spectrum issue to Principal Reynolds for his review prior to publication. On May 10, Emerson delivered the proofs of the May 13 edition to Reynolds, who objected to two of the articles scheduled to appear in that edition. One of the stories described three Hazelwood East students' experiences with pregnancy; the other discussed the impact of divorce on students at the school.

Reynolds was concerned that, although the pregnancy story used false names "to keep the identity of these girls a secret," the pregnant students still might be identifiable from the text. He also believed that the article's references to sexual activity and birth control were inappropriate for some of the younger students at the school. In addition, Reynolds was concerned that a student identified by name in the divorce story had complained that her father "wasn't spending enough time with my mom, my sister and I" prior to the divorce, "was always out of town on business or out late playing cards with the guys," and "always argued about everything" with her mother. Reynolds believed that the student's parents should have been given an opportunity to respond to these remarks or to consent to their publication. He was unaware that Emerson had deleted the student's name from the final version of the article.

Reynolds believed that there was no time to make the necessary changes in the stories before the scheduled press run and that the newspaper would not appear before the end of the school year if printing were delayed to any significant extent. He concluded that his only options under the circumstances were to publish a four-page newspaper instead of the planned six-page newspaper, eliminating the two pages on which the offending stories appeared, or to publish no newspaper at all. Accordingly, he directed Emerson to withhold from publication the two pages containing the stories on pregnancy and divorce.[1] He informed his superiors of the decision, and they concurred. * * *

II

Students in the public schools do not "shed their constitutional rights to freedom of speech or expression at the schoolhouse gate." *Tinker.* They cannot be punished merely for expressing their personal views on the school premises—whether "in the cafeteria, or on the playing field, or on the campus during the authorized hours"—unless school authorities have reason to believe that such expression will "substantially interfere with the work of the school or impinge upon the rights of other students." *Tinker.*

We have nonetheless recognized that the First Amendment rights of students in the public schools "are not automatically coextensive with the rights of adults in other settings," *Bethel School District No. 403 v. Fraser,* and must be "applied in light of the special characteristics of the school environment." *Tinker.* A school need not tolerate student speech that is inconsistent with its "basic educational mission," *Fraser,* even though the government could not censor similar speech outside the school. Accordingly, we held in *Fraser* that a student could be disciplined for having delivered a speech that was "sexually explicit" but not legally obscene at an official school assembly, because the school was entitled to "disassociate itself" from the speech in a manner that would demonstrate to others that such vulgarity is "wholly inconsistent with the 'fundamental values' of public school education." We thus recognized that "[t]he determination of what manner of speech in the classroom or in school assembly is inappropriate properly rests with the school board," rather than with the federal courts. It is in this context that respondents' First Amendment claims must be considered.

A

We deal first with the question whether Spectrum may appropriately be characterized as a forum for public expression. The public schools do not possess all of the attributes of streets, parks, and other traditional public forums that "time out of mind, have been used for purposes of assembly, communicating thoughts between citizens, and discussing public questions." *Hague v. CIO.* Hence, school facilities may be deemed to be public forums only if school authorities have "by policy or by practice" opened those facilities "for indiscriminate use by the general public" or by some segment of the public, such as student organizations. *Perry.* If the facilities have instead been reserved for other intended purposes, "communicative or otherwise," then no public forum has been created, and school officials may impose reasonable restrictions on the speech of students, teachers, and other members of the school community. *Perry.*

---

1. The two pages deleted from the newspaper also contained articles on teenage marriage, runaways, and juvenile delinquents, as well as a general article on teenage pregnancy. Reynolds testified that he had no objection to these articles and that they were deleted only because they appeared on the same pages as the two objectionable articles.

[T]he evidence relied upon by the Court of Appeals fails to demonstrate the "clear intent to create a public forum," *Cornelius,* that existed in cases in which we found public forums to have been created. School [officials] "reserve[d] the forum for its intended purpos[e]," *Perry,* as a supervised learning experience for journalism students. Accordingly, school officials were entitled to regulate the contents of Spectrum in any reasonable manner. It is this standard, rather than our decision in *Tinker,* that governs this case.

The question whether the First Amendment requires a school to tolerate particular student speech—the question that we addressed in *Tinker*—is different from the question whether the First Amendment requires a school affirmatively to promote particular student speech.[3]

[A] school may in its capacity as publisher of a school newspaper or producer of a school play "disassociate itself," *Fraser,* not only from speech that would "substantially interfere with [its] work * * * or impinge upon the rights of other students," *Tinker,* but also from speech that is, for example, ungrammatical, poorly written, inadequately researched, biased or prejudiced, vulgar or profane, or unsuitable for immature audiences.[4] A school must be able to set high standards for the student speech that is disseminated under its auspices—standards that may be higher than those demanded by some newspaper publishers or theatrical producers in the "real" world—and may refuse to disseminate student speech that does not meet those standards. [Otherwise,] the schools would be unduly constrained from fulfilling their role as "a principal instrument in awakening the child to cultural values, in preparing him for later professional training, and in helping him to adjust normally to his environment." *Brown* v. *Board of Education.*

Accordingly, we conclude that the standard articulated in *Tinker* for determining when a school may punish student expression need not also be the standard for determining when a school may refuse to lend its name and resources to the dissemination of student expression. Instead, we hold that educators do not offend the First Amendment by exercising editorial control over the style and content of student speech in school-sponsored expressive activities so long as their actions are reasonably related to legitimate pedagogical concerns. * * *

JUSTICE BRENNAN, with whom JUSTICE MARSHALL and JUSTICE BLACKMUN join, dissenting.

3. The distinction that we draw between speech that is sponsored by the school and speech that is not is fully consistent with *Papish* v. *Board of Curators* which involved an off-campus "underground" newspaper that school officials merely had allowed to be sold on a state university campus.

4. The dissent perceives no difference between the First Amendment analysis applied in *Tinker* and that applied in *Fraser.* We disagree. The decision in *Fraser* rested on the "vulgar," "lewd," and "plainly offensive" character of a speech delivered at an official school assembly rather than on any propensity of the speech to "materially disrupt[ ] classwork or involve[ ] substantial disorder or invasion of the rights of others." Indeed, the *Fraser* Court cited as "especially relevant" a portion of Justice Black's dissenting opinion in *Tinker* "disclaim[ing] any purpose * * *

to hold that the Federal Constitution compels the teachers, parents and elected school officials to surrender control of the American public school system to public school students." Of course, Justice Black's observations are equally relevant to the instant case.

a. White, J., concluded that Principal Reynolds acted reasonably in requiring deletion of the pages from the newspaper. In addition to concerns about privacy and failure to contact persons discussed in the stories, White, J., found that it was "not unreasonable for the principal to have concluded that [frank talk about sexual histories, albeit not graphic, with comments about use or nonuse of birth control] was inappropriate in a school-sponsored publication distributed to 14–year–old freshmen and presumably taken home to be read by students' even younger brothers and sisters."

* * *

The Court is certainly correct that the First Amendment permits educators "to assure that participants learn whatever lessons the activity is designed to teach. * * *" That is, however, the essence of the *Tinker* test, not an excuse to abandon it. Under *Tinker,* school officials may censor only such student speech as would "materially disrup[t]" a legitimate curricular function. Manifestly, student speech is more likely to disrupt a curricular function when it arises in the context of a curricular activity—one that "is designed to teach" something—than when it arises in the context of a noncurricular activity. Thus, under *Tinker,* the school may constitutionally punish the budding political orator if he disrupts calculus class but not if he holds his tongue for the cafeteria. That is not because some more stringent standard applies in the curricular context. (After all, this Court applied the same standard whether the Tinkers wore their armbands to the "classroom" or the "cafeteria.") It is because student speech in the noncurricular context is less likely to disrupt materially any legitimate pedagogical purpose.

I fully agree with the Court that the First Amendment should afford an educator the prerogative not to sponsor the publication of a newspaper article that is "ungrammatical, poorly written, inadequately researched, biased or prejudiced," or that falls short of the "high standards [for] student speech that is disseminated under [the school's] auspices * * *." But we need not abandon *Tinker* to reach that conclusion; we need only apply it. The enumerated criteria reflect the skills that the curricular newspaper "is designed to teach." The educator may, under *Tinker,* constitutionally "censor" poor grammar, writing, or research because to reward such expression would "materially disrup[t]" the newspaper's curricular purpose. * * *

The Court relies on bits of testimony to portray the principal's conduct as a pedagogical lesson to Journalism II students who "had not sufficiently mastered those portions of [the] curriculum that pertained to the treatment of controversial issues and personal attacks, the need to protect the privacy of individuals [and] 'the legal, moral, and ethical restrictions imposed upon journalists * * *.'" In that regard, the Court attempts to justify censorship of the article on teenage pregnancy on the basis of the principal's judgment that (1) "the [pregnant] students' anonymity was not adequately protected," despite the article's use of aliases; and (2) the judgment "that the article was not sufficiently sensitive to the privacy interests of the students' boyfriends and parents * * *." Similarly, the Court finds in the principal's decision to censor the divorce article a journalistic lesson that the author should have given the father of one student an "opportunity to defend himself" against her charge that (in the Court's words) he "chose 'playing cards with the guys' over home and family * * *."

But the principal never consulted the students before censoring their work. [T]hey learned of the deletions when the paper was released. [Further,] he explained the deletions only in the broadest of generalities. In one meeting called at the behest of seven protesting Spectrum staff members (presumably a fraction of the full class), he characterized the articles as "'too sensitive' for 'our immature audience of readers,'" and in a later meeting he deemed them simply "inappropriate, personal, sensitive and unsuitable for the newspaper." The Court's supposition that the principal intended (or the protesters understood) those generalities as a lesson on the nuances of journalistic responsibility is utterly incredible. If he did, a fact that neither the District Court nor the Court of Appeals found, the lesson was lost on all but the psychic Spectrum staffer.

The Court's second excuse for deviating from precedent is the school's interest in shielding an impressionable high school audience from material whose substance is "unsuitable for immature audiences." [*Tinker*] teaches us that the state educator's undeniable, and undeniably vital, mandate to inculcate moral and political values is not a general warrant to act as "thought police" stifling discussion of all but state-approved topics and advocacy of all but the official position.

[The] mere fact of school sponsorship does not, as the Court suggests, license such thought control in the high school, whether through school suppression of disfavored viewpoints or through official assessment of topic sensitivity. [Just] as a school board may not purge its state-funded library of all books that " 'offen[d] [its] social, political and moral tastes,' " *Pico,* school officials may not, out of like motivation, discriminatorily excise objectionable ideas from a student publication. The State's prerogative to dissolve the student newspaper entirely (or to limit its subject matter) no more entitles it to dictate which viewpoints students may express on its pages, than the State's prerogative to close down the schoolhouse entitles it to prohibit the nondisruptive expression of antiwar sentiment within its gates.

Official censorship of student speech on the ground that it addresses "potentially sensitive topics" is, for related reasons, equally impermissible. I would not begrudge an educator the authority to limit the substantive scope of a school-sponsored publication to a certain, objectively definable topic, such as literary criticism, school sports, or an overview of the school year. Unlike those determinate limitations, "potential topic sensitivity" is a vaporous nonstandard [that] invites manipulation to achieve ends that cannot permissibly be achieved through blatant viewpoint discrimination and chills student speech to which school officials might not object. * * * [b]

DISPARAGING SPEECH BY GOVERNMENT

CON LAW: P. 900, before part III

AMER CON: P. 674, before part III

RTS & LIB: P. 567, before part III

Keene, a citizen of California, an attorney, and a member of the California State Senate desired to exhibit three films produced by the National Film Board of Canada, namely, "If You Love This Planet," "Acid Heaven," and "Acid Rain: Requiem or Recovery." The Foreign Agents Registration Act requires "agents of a foreign principal" who disseminate "political propaganda" in the United States to file a registration statement with the Attorney General, to make various disclosures about the pattern of the materials' distribution, and to conspicuously mark such propaganda with an accurate statement revealing the relationship between the person transmitting the propaganda and such propaganda, and that the person distributing the propaganda was registered as an agent of a foreign principal with the Department of Justice, and that a registration statement is publicly available, and that registration with the Justice Department does not indicate approval of the distributed materials by the United States Government.

Under the Act, as interpreted, the National Film Board of Canada was the "agent of foreign principal," i.e., Canada. Accordingly, the National Film Board of Canada had registered with the Justice Department. In January, 1983, the

b. Brennan, J., further argued that the material deleted was not conceivably tortious and that less restrictive alternatives, such as more precise deletions, were readily available.

Justice Department determined that the films were "political propaganda" within the meaning of the Act, and informed the Film Board that if it were to distribute these films, it would need to file required statutory reports and conspicuously mark the film with the required disclosures. Subsequently, the Justice Department agreed to review the administrative decision that the films were "political propaganda."

As interpreted by the Justice Department, Keene was not an agent of a foreign principal, and he, therefore, could exhibit the film without registration and without labeling the film with the various disclosures. Nonetheless, Keene objected to the government's treatment of the films as "political propaganda," and indicated that he would "exhibit the three films periodically in the future, but only if the defendants are permanently enjoined from classifying the films as 'political propaganda.'" The federal district court granted an injunction holding that governmental use of the term "political propaganda" in conjunction with the films violated the first amendment.

Without reaching questions concerning the constitutionality of the underlying registration or labeling provisions of the Foreign Agents Registration Act, MEESE v. KEENE, 481 U.S. 465, 107 S.Ct. 1862, 95 L.Ed.2d 415 (1987), per STEVENS, J., held that the use of the term political propaganda, as defined in the Act, to designate those expressive materials that must comply with the Act's requirements did not violate the first amendment: "We begin our examination of the District Court's ruling on the First Amendment issue by noting that the term 'political propaganda' has two meanings. In popular parlance many people assume that propaganda is a form of slanted, misleading speech that does not merit serious attention and that proceeds from a concern for advancing the narrow interests of the speaker rather than from a devotion to the truth. Casualty reports of enemy belligerents, for example, are often dismissed as nothing more than 'propaganda.' As defined in the Act, the term political propaganda includes misleading advocacy of that kind. But it also includes advocacy materials that are completely accurate and merit the closest attention and the highest respect.[a] Standard reference works include both broad, neutral definitions of the word 'propaganda' that are consistent with the way the word is defined in this statute,[10] and also the narrower, pejorative definition.[11] * * *

"The District Court [found] that the basic purpose of the statute as a whole was 'to inform recipients of advocacy materials produced by or under the aegis of

a. The Act defines political propaganda to include: ". . . any oral, visual, graphic, written, pictorial, or other communication or expression by any person (1) which is reasonably adapted to, or which the person disseminating the same believes will, or which he intends to, prevail upon, indoctrinate, convert, induce, or in any other way influence a recipient or any section of the public within the United States with reference to the political or public interests, policies, or relations of a government of a foreign country or a foreign political party or with reference to the foreign policies of the United States or promote in the United States racial, religious, or social dissensions, or (2) which advocates, advises, instigates, or promotes any racial, social, political, or religious disorder, civil riot, or other conflict involving the use of force or violence in any other American republic or the overthrow of any government or political subdivision of any other

American republic by any means involving the use of force or violence." 22 U.S.C. § 611(j).

10. See, e.g., Webster's Third New International Dictionary 1817 (1981 ed.) ("doctrines, ideas, argument, facts, or allegations spread by deliberate effort through any medium of communication in order to further one's cause or to damage an opposing cause").

11 See, e.g., Webster's New World Dictionary, College Edition 1167 (1968) ("now often used disparagingly to connote deception or distortion."); The New Columbia Encyclopedia 2225 (1975) ("[A]lmost any attempt to influence public opinion, including lobbying, commercial advertising, and missionary work, can be broadly construed as propaganda. Generally, however, the term is restricted to the manipulation of political beliefs.")

a foreign government of the source of such materials' [and] that it could not be gainsaid that this kind of disclosure serves rather than disserves the First Amendment. The statute itself neither prohibits nor censors the dissemination of advocacy materials by agents of foreign principals.

"The argument that the District Court accepted rests not on what the statute actually says, requires, or prohibits, but rather upon a potential misunderstanding of its effect. Simply because the term 'political propaganda' is used in the text of the statute to define the regulated materials, the Court assumed that the public will attach an 'unsavory connotation' to the term and thus believe that the materials have been 'officially censured by the Government.' [According] to the District Court, the denigration of speech to which the label 'political propaganda' has been attached constitutes 'a conscious attempt to place a whole category of materials beyond the pale of legitimate discourse,' and is therefore an unconstitutional abridgement of that speech. We find this argument unpersuasive, indeed, untenable, for three reasons.

"First, the term 'political propaganda' does nothing to place regulated expressive materials 'beyond the pale of legitimate discourse.' [b] [To] the contrary, Congress simply required the disseminators of such material to make additional disclosures that would better enable the public to evaluate the import of the propaganda. The statute does not prohibit appellee from advising his audience that the films have not been officially censured in any way. Disseminators of propaganda may go beyond the disclosures required by statute and add any further information they think germane to the public's viewing of the materials. By compelling some disclosure of information and permitting more, the Act's approach recognizes that the best remedy for misleading or inaccurate speech contained within materials subject to the Act is fair, truthful, and accurate speech. * * *

"Ironically, it is the injunction entered by the District Court that withholds information from the public. The suppressed information is the fact that the films fall within the category of materials that Congress has judged to be 'political propaganda'. A similar paternalistic strategy of protecting the public from information was followed by the Virginia Assembly, which enacted a ban on the advertising of prescription drug prices by pharmacists. See *Virginia Pharmacy.*

"[T]he District Court in this case assumed that the reactions of the public to the label 'political propaganda' would be such that the label would interfere with freedom of speech. In *Virginia Pharmacy* we squarely held that a zeal to protect the public from 'too much information' could not withstand First Amendment scrutiny. * * *

"Second, the reasoning of the District Court is contradicted by history. The statutory definition of 'political propaganda' has been on the books for over four

b. The Court distinguished *Lamont v. Postmaster General,* Casebooks, Section 7, stating that the physical detention of mail, not its mere designation as "communist political propaganda" was the offending element of the statutory scheme. The Act set "administrative officials astride the flow of mail to inspect it, approve it, write the addressee about it, and await a response before dispatching the mail." By contrast, the Court argued that the Foreign Agents Registration Act posed no obstacle to Keene's access to the materials.

In response, Blackmun, J., dissenting, observed that the "communist political propaganda [detained in *Lamont*] and delivered only upon the addressee's request was defined by reference to the same 'neutral' definition of 'political propaganda' in the Act that is at issue here. Yet the Court examined the effects of the statutory requirements and had no trouble concluding that the need to request delivery of mail classified as 'communist political propaganda' was almost certain to have a deterrent effect upon debate."

decades. We should presume that the people who have a sufficient understanding of the law to know that the term 'political propaganda' is used to describe the regulated category also know that the definition is a broad, neutral one rather than a pejorative one. Given this long history, it seems obvious that if the fear of misunderstanding had actually interfered with the exhibition of a significant number of foreign-made films, that effect would be disclosed in the record.

"Third, Congress' use of the term 'political propaganda' does not lead us to suspend the respect we normally owe to the Legislature's power to define the terms that it uses in legislation. We have no occasion here to decide the permissible scope of Congress' 'right to speak'; we simply view this particular choice of language, statutorily defined in a neutral and evenhanded manner, as one that no constitutional provision prohibits the Congress from making. [If] the term 'political propaganda' is construed consistently with the neutral definition contained in the text of the statute itself, the constitutional concerns voiced by the District Court completely disappear." c

BLACKMUN, J., joined by Brennan and Marshall, JJ., dissented: "The Court's decision rests upon its conclusion that the term 'political propaganda' is neutral and without negative connotation. It reaches this conclusion by limiting its examination to the statutory definition of the term and by ignoring the realities of public reaction to the designation. But even given that confined view of its inquiry, it is difficult to understand how a statutory categorization which includes communication that 'instigates ＊   ＊   ＊ civil riot [or] the overthrow [of] government [by] any means involving the use of force or violence,' § 611(j)(2), can be regarded as wholly neutral. Indeed, the legislative history of the Act indicates that Congress fully intended to discourage communications by foreign agents.

"The Act grew out of the investigations of the House UnAmerican Activities Committee, formed in 1934 to investigate Nazi propaganda activities in the United States and the dissemination of subversive propaganda controlled by foreign countries attacking the American form of government. The Act mandated disclosure, not direct censorship, but the underlying goal was to control the spread of propaganda by foreign agents. This goal was stated unambiguously by the House Committee on the Judiciary: 'We believe that the spotlight of pitiless publicity will serve as a deterrent to the spread of pernicious propaganda.'
＊   ＊   ＊

"I can conclude only that the Court has asked, and has answered, the wrong question. Appellee does not argue that his speech is deterred by the statutory definition of 'propaganda.' He argues, instead, that his speech is deterred by the common perception that material so classified is unreliable and not to be trusted,

---

c. Scalia, J., took no part. In *Block v. Meese*, 793 F.2d 1303 (D.C.Cir.1986), however, then Circuit Judge Scalia ruled on the issue. "[E]ven if classification as 'propaganda' constituted an expression of official government disapproval of the ideas in question, neither precedent nor reason would justify us in finding such an expression *in itself* unlawful. [W]e know of no case in which the first amendment has been held to be implicated by governmental action consisting of no more than governmental criticism of the speech's content. [A] rule excluding official praise or criticism of ideas would lead to the strange conclusion that it is permissible for the government to prohibit racial discrimination, but not to criticize racial bias; to criminalize polygamy, but not to praise the monogamous family; to make war on Hitler's Germany, but not to denounce Nazism. [The] line of permissibility [falls] not between criticism of ideas in general and criticism of the ideas contained in specific books or expressed by specific persons; but between the disparagement of ideas general or specific and the suppression of ideas through the exercise or threat of state power. If the latter is rigorously prescribed, see *Bantam Books,* the former can hold no terror."

bolstered by the added weight and authority accorded any classification made by the all-pervasive Federal Government. Even if the statutory definition is neutral, it is the common understanding of the Government's action that determines the effect on discourse protected by the First Amendment. * * *

"The Court likens the injunction issued by the District Court to the state ban on advertising prices of prescription drugs struck down in *Virginia Pharmacy*. But there is a significant difference between the 'paternalistic strategy of protecting the public from information,' by way of a *ban* on information and a prohibition of the government disparagement at issue in this case. [Under] the District Court's ruling, opponents of the viewpoint expressed by the National Film Board of Canada remained completely free to point out the foreign source of the films. The difference was that dialogue on the value of the films and the viewpoints they express could occur in an atmosphere free of the constraint imposed by government condemnation. It is the Government's classification of those films as 'political propaganda' that is paternalistic. For that government action does more than simply provide additional information. It places the power of the Federal Government, with its authority, presumed neutrality, and assumed access to all the facts, behind an appellation *designed* to reduce the effectiveness of the speech in the eyes of the public.

"Appellants have not even attempted to articulate any justification for saddling the expression of would-be film exhibitors with the classification 'political propaganda.' [There] are two ways in which the purpose of the Act to inform the public is fulfilled. First, the Act requires films transmitted by foreign agents to be 'conspicuously marked' with the name and address of the agent and the foreign principal, and, second, the Act requires dissemination reports for the film and the agent's registration statement to be placed on file with the Department of Justice, available for public inspection. The public is able to learn of its opportunity to examine these files by reading the label affixed to the film.

"The purposes of the Act could be fulfilled by such a process without categorizing the films as 'political propaganda.' But the importance of conveying any of this information to the public is belied by the Government's position that the informative label can be removed by appellee. After the complaint in this case (which included a challenge to the labeling requirement) was filed in the District Court, the Department of Justice asserted that it 'has never construed the Act to apply to a peson in [appellee's] position, and thus has not, does not, and will not require [appellee] to attach the neutral statutory disclaimer to, or exhibit the disclaimer on said films if he obtains them.' The only reasonable interpretation of this statement is that any exhibitor would be 'a person in [appellee's] position' and thus exempt from the labeling requirements. But if the labeling requirements apply to the foreign agent only, and can be removed by recipients of the film, the information will never reach the public, its intended audience. This nullification of the primary purpose of the statute means that the classification of the films as 'political propaganda' places a purely gratuitous burden on a would-be exhibitor and serves no governmental interest at all, let alone a compelling one.

"Even if appellants could assert a compelling interest, the propaganda classification carries a derogatory meaning that is unnecessary to the asserted purpose of the Act. The Department of Justice admitted as much in a letter regarding proposed changes in the legislation:

'We believe Congress should *   *   * consider replacing the broad definition of "political propaganda," which currently defines materials that must be

labelled, with a more concise definition, more narrowly focused on the
United States political process. We would also support the use of a more
neutral term like political "advocacy" or "information" to denominate
information that must be labelled.' Letter, dated August 8, 1983, to the
Honorable Robert W. Kastenmeier, Chairman, Subcommittee on Courts,
Civil Liberties and the Administration of Justice, of the House Committee on
the Judiciary, from Edward C. Schmults, Deputy Attorney General, Department of Justice.

"Given that position, the Court errs in tolerating even the slightest infringement
of First Amendment rights by governmental use of a classification deemed
unnecessary by those who enforce it."

GOVERNMENT INVOLVEMENT WITH SPEECH AND
THE CAPTIVE AUDIENCE

CON LAW: P. 902, add to note 3

AMER CON: P. 676, add to note 3

RTS & LIB: P. 569, add to note 3

See THORNBURGH v. AMERICAN COLLEGE OF OBSTETRICIANS AND
GYNECOLOGISTS, p. 93 of this Supplement. Do the "informed consent"
provisions of the Pennsylvania statute raise first amendment captive audience
issues? Do women seeking abortions have a first amendment right not to be
"propagandized"? Is the line between "reasonable" disclosure requirements and
government propaganda "clear enough" for judicial administration? Without
referring to the first amendment, the Court, per BLACKMUN, J., objected that the
state-prescribed communications came "close to being, state medicine imposed
upon the woman, not the professional guidance she seeks, and it officially
structures—as it was intended to do—the dialogue between the woman and her
physician." A "decisive" objection was that much of the required information
was designed "not to inform the woman's consent but rather to persuade her to
withhold it altogether."

WHITE, J., joined by Rehnquist, J., dissented: "[I] fail to see how providing a
woman with accurate information—whether relevant or irrelevant—could ever
be deemed to impair *any* constitutionally protected interest (even if, as the
majority hypothesizes, the information may upset her)." See also p. 277 of this
Supplement.

SECTION: BROADCAST REGULATION AND
ACCESS TO THE MASS MEDIA

ACCESS TO THE MASS MEDIA

ACCESS BY STATUTE: THE FIRST AMENDMENT AS SHIELD

CON LAW: P. 929, add to note 8

AMER CON: P. 703, add to note 8

RTS & LIB: P. 596, add to note 8

LOS ANGELES v. PREFERRED COMMUNICATIONS, INC., 476 U.S. 488,
106 S.Ct. 2034, 90 L.Ed.2d 480 (1986): Cable television operators present news,
information, and entertainment to viewers of video screens by transmitting
electronic signals from a central location by means of cables attached to public

utility facilities. Los Angeles solicited bids for a cable television franchise in the south central area of the city. The solicitation indicated that only one franchise would be awarded and set forth various criteria to be used in the selection process including the capacity to provide 52 channels and two-way communication, the willingness to set aside channels for various public purposes and to provide public access facilities, the degree of local participation in management or ownership reflecting the ethnic and economic diversity of the franchise area, and the willingness to engage in creative and aggressive affirmative action. After a lengthy process, the franchise was awarded to A Community Cable Entertainment/Services System, Inc. Nonetheless, Preferred Communications, Inc. sought to lease space on utility poles under the city's control so that it too could provide cable television service to the south central area. Los Angeles refused access, observing that Preferred had not participated in the bidding process. In response, Preferred filed suit alleging that Los Angeles' refusal to lease space or otherwise permit access to the utility poles violated the first amendment. The city did not deny that there was enough physical capacity to accommodate more than one cable television system. It argued that its decision to restrict access to its facilities was justified by the limited economic demand for more than one cable company, by the disruptive effect that installing and maintaining another cable system would have on the public right-of-way, and by the potential alternative uses that might be made of the space on utility structures. It invoked the public forum line of cases in support of the contention that the complaint should be dismissed for failure to state a claim. The Court, per REHNQUIST, J., held that dismissal of the complaint was inappropriate:

"We agree with the Court of Appeals that respondent's complaint should not have been dismissed, and we therefore affirm the judgment of that court; but we do so on a narrower ground than the one taken by it.[a] The well pleaded facts in the complaint include allegations of sufficient excess physical capacity and economic demand for cable television operators in the area which respondent sought to serve.[2] The City, while admitting the existence of excess physical capacity on the utility poles, the rights-of-way, and the like, justifies the limit on franchises in terms of minimizing the demand that cable systems make for the use of public property. The City characterizes these uses as the stringing of nearly 700 miles of hanging and buried wire and other appliances necessary for the operation of its system. The City also characterizes them as a permanent visual blight, and adds that the process of installation and repair of such a system in effect subjects City facilities designed for other purposes to a servitude which will cause traffic delays and hazards and esthetic unsightliness. Respondent in its turn replies that the City does not provide anything more than speculations and assumptions, and that the City's legitimate concerns are easily satisfied without the need to limit the right to speak to a single speaker.

"We of course take the well-pleaded allegations of the complaint as true for the purpose of a motion to dismiss. Ordinarily such a motion frames a legal issue such as the one which the Court of Appeals undertook to decide in this case. But this case is different from a case between private litigants for two

---

a. As Rehnquist, J., put it, the Court of Appeals had "expressed the view that the facts alleged in the complaint brought respondent into the ambit of cases such as *Miami Herald* rather than of cases such as *Red Lion* [and] *Vincent*."

2. They also include allegations that the City imposes numerous other conditions upon

a successful applicant for a franchise. It is claimed that, entirely apart from the limitation of franchises to one in each area, these conditions violate respondent's First Amendment rights. The Court of Appeals did not reach these contentions, and neither do we.

reasons: first, it is an action of a municipal corporation taken pursuant to a city ordinance that is challenged here, and, second, the ordinance is challenged on colorable First Amendment grounds. The City has adduced essentially factual arguments to justify the restrictions on cable franchising imposed by its ordinance, but the factual assertions of the City are disputed at least in part by the respondent. We are unwilling to decide the legal questions posed by the parties without a more thoroughly developed record of proceedings in which the parties have an opportunity to prove those disputed factual assertions upon which they rely.

"We do think that the activities in which respondent allegedly seeks to engage plainly implicate First Amendment interests. Respondent alleges: 'The business of cable television, like that of newspapers and magazines, is to provide its subscribers with a mixture of news, information and entertainment. As do newspapers, cable television companies use a portion of their available space to reprint (or retransmit) the communications of others, while at the same time providing some original content.' Thus, through original programming or by exercising editorial discretion over which stations or programs to include in its repertoire, respondent seeks to communicate messages on a wide variety of topics and in a wide variety of formats. We recently noted that cable operators exercise 'a significant amount of editorial discretion regarding what their programming will include.' *FCC v. Midwest Video Corp.*, 440 U.S. 689, 707, 99 S.Ct. 1435, 1445, 59 L.Ed.2d 692 (1979). Cable television partakes of some of the aspects of speech and the communication of ideas as do the traditional enterprises of newspaper and book publishers, public speakers and pamphleteers. Respondent's proposed activities would seem to implicate First Amendment interests as do the activities of wireless broadcasters, which were found to fall within the ambit of the First Amendment in *Red Lion* even though the free speech aspects of the wireless broadcasters' claim were found to be outweighed by the government interests in regulating by reason of the scarcity of available frequencies.

"Of course, the conclusion that respondent's factual allegations implicate protected speech does not end the inquiry. 'Even protected speech is not equally permissible in all places and at all times.' *Cornelius v. NAACP Legal Defense & Educational Fund, Inc.* Moreover, where speech and conduct are joined in a single course of action, the First Amendment values must be balanced against competing societal interests. See, e.g., *Vincent; United States v. O'Brien.* We do not think, however, that it is desirable to express any more detailed views on the proper resolution of the First Amendment question raised by the respondent's complaint and the City's responses to it without a fuller development of the disputed issues in the case. We think that we may know more than we know now about how the constitutional issues should be resolved when we know more about the present uses of the public utility poles and rights-of-way and how respondent proposes to install and maintain its facilities on them."

BLACKMUN, J., joined by Marshall and O'Connor, JJ., concurring, underscored the narrow holding of the Court: "I join the Court's opinion on the understanding that it leaves open the question of the proper standard for judging First Amendment challenges to a municipality's restriction of access to cable facilities. Different communications media are treated differently for First Amendment purposes. Compare *Miami Herald* with *FCC v. League of Women Voters.* In assessing First Amendment claims concerning cable access, the Court must determine whether the characteristics of cable television make it sufficiently analogous to another medium to warrant application of an already existing standard or whether those characteristics require a new analysis. As this case arises out of a motion to dismiss, we lack factual information about the nature of cable television. Recognizing these considerations, the Court does not attempt to choose or justify any particular standard. It simply concludes that, in challenging Los Angeles' policy of exclusivity in cable franchising, respondent alleges a cognizable First Amendment claim."

ACCESS BY CONSTITUTIONAL RIGHT: THE FIRST AMENDMENT AS SWORD

CON LAW: P. 937, after note 3

AMER CON: P. 711, after note 3

RTS & LIB: P. 604, after note 3

FCC, [GENERAL] FAIRNESS DOCTRINE OBLIGATIONS OF BROADCAST LICENSEES, 102 F.C.C.2d 143 (1985): The FCC has concluded a 15 month administrative proceeding with an official denunciation of the fairness doctrine and has invited Congress to repeal it: "On the basis of the voluminous factual record compiled in this proceeding, our experience in administering the doctrine and our general expertise in broadcast regulation, we no longer believe that the fairness doctrine, as a matter of policy, serves the public interest. In making this determination, we do not question the interest of the listening and viewing public in obtaining access to diverse and antagonistic sources of information. Rather, we conclude that the fairness doctrine is no longer a necessary or appropriate means by which to effectuate this interest. We believe that the interest of the public in viewpoint diversity is fully served by the multiplicity of voices in the marketplace today and that the intrusion by government into the content of programming occasioned by the enforcement of the doctrine unnecessarily restricts the journalistic freedom of broadcasters. Furthermore, we find that the fairness doctrine, in operation, actually inhibits the presentation of controversial issues of public importance to the detriment of the public and in degradation of the editorial prerogatives of broadcast journalists.

"We believe that the same factors which demonstrate that the fairness doctrine is no longer appropriate as a matter of policy also suggest that the doctrine may no longer be permissible as a matter of constitutional law. We recognize that the United States Supreme Court, in *Red Lion* upheld the constitutionality of the fairness doctrine. But in the intervening sixteen years the information services marketplace has expanded markedly, thereby making it unnecessary to rely upon intrusive government regulation in order to assure that the public has access to the marketplace of ideas. In addition, the compelling evidence adduced in this proceeding demonstrates that the fairness doctrine, in operation, inhibits the presentation of controversial issues of public importance; this fact impels the dual conclusion that the doctrine impedes the public's access to the marketplace of ideas and poses an unwarranted intrusion upon the journalistic freedom of broadcasters.

"While we are firmly convinced that the fairness doctrine, as a matter of policy, disserves the public interest, the issue as to whether or not Congress has empowered us to eliminate the doctrine is not one which is easily resolved. The fairness doctrine evolved as an administrative policy promulgated by the Commission pursuant to congressionally delegated power. While we do not believe that the fairness doctrine is a necessary component of the general 'public interest' standard contained in the Communications Act, the question of whether or not Congress in amending Section 315 in 1959 codified the doctrine, thereby requiring us to retain it, is more problematic. In any event, the fairness doctrine has been a longstanding administrative policy and central tenet of broadcast regulation that Congress has chosen not to eliminate. Moreover, there are proposals pending before Congress to repeal the doctrine. As a consequence, we believe that it would be inappropriate at this time for us to either eliminate or significantly restrict the scope of the doctrine. Instead, we will afford Congress an opportunity to review the fairness doctrine in light of the evidence adduced in this proceeding."

Telecommunications Research and Action Center v. FCC, 801 F.2d 501 (D.C. Cir.1986), per Bork, J., joined by Scalia, J., held that the fairness doctrine had not been codified by Congress. In response to the *Telecommunications* decision, Congress passed legislation (S 742) designed to codify the fairness doctrine and to prevent the FCC from dispensing with the requirement. Congressional leaders argued that the scarcity of broadcast frequencies justified the fairness doctrine. On June 3, 1987, the legislation was sent to the White House for Presidential approval.

President Reagan vetoed the legislation on June 20, 1987: "The Supreme Court indicated in *Red Lion* a willingness to reconsider the appropriateness of the fairness doctrine if it reduced rather than enhanced broadcast coverage. In a later case, the Court acknowledged the changes in the technological and economic environment in which broadcasting operates. It may now fairly be concluded that the growth in the number of available media outlets does indeed outweigh whatever justification may have seemed to exist at the period during which the doctrine was developed. The FCC has itself concluded that the doctrine is an unnecessary and detrimental regulatory mechanism. [T]he FCC found that the doctrine in fact *inhibits* broadcasters from presenting controversial issues of public importance, and thus defeats its own purpose. [S 742] simply cannot be reconciled with the freedom of speech and the press secured by our Constitution. It is, in my judgment, unconstitutional."

Meredith Corp. v. FCC, 809 F.2d 863 (D.C. Cir.1987) stated that the FCC had cast "grave legal doubt on the fairness doctrine" in its 1985 Fairness Report and ruled that the agency acted improperly by attempting to enforce the fairness doctrine without responding to a broadcaster's constitutional objections to its enforcement.

On remand, in *Syracuse Peace Council*, 2 FCC Rcd 5043 (1987), the FCC concluded that "under the constitutional standard established by *Red Lion* and its progeny, the fairness doctrine contravenes the First Amendment and its enforcement is no longer in the public interest." On the next appellate round, the D.C. Circuit, *Syracuse Peace Council v. FCC*, 867 F.2d 654 (1989), affirmed the FCC's determination that the fairness doctrine no longer serves the public interest without reaching constitutional issues.

BROADCASTING AND CONTENT REGULATION: BEYOND THE FAIRNESS DOCTRINE

CON LAW: P. 952, after note 4

AMER CON: P. 726, after note 4

RTS & LIB: P. 619, after note 4

INDECENT SPEECH

5. *Telephonic "indecency" compared.* SABLE COMMUNICATIONS v. FCC, p. 189 of this Supplement, per WHITE, J., invalidated a congressional ban on "indecent" interstate commercial telephone messages, i.e., "dial-a-porn." [a] The Court thought *Pacifica* was "readily distinguishable from this case, most obviously because it did not involve a total ban on broadcasting indecent material. [Second,] there is no 'captive audience' problem; callers generally will not be unwilling listeners. [Third,] the congressional record contains no legislative findings that would justify us in concluding that there is no constitutionally acceptable less restrictive means, short of a total ban, to achieve the Government's interest in protecting minors."

indecent ≠ obscene

"PUBLIC" BROADCASTERS AND EDITORIALS

CON LAW: P. 952, add to fn. 11

RTS & LIB: P. 619, add to fn. 11

[*For a flurry of "signals,"* see pp. 275–276 of this Supplement]

SECTION: THE RIGHT NOT TO SPEAK, THE RIGHT TO ASSOCIATE, AND THE RIGHT NOT TO ASSOCIATE

THE RIGHT NOT TO BE ASSOCIATED WITH PARTICULAR IDEAS

CON LAW: P. 968, after note 5

AMER CON: P. 732, after note 5

RTS & LIB: P. 635, after note 5

THORNBURGH v. AMERICAN COLLEGE OF OBSTETRICIANS AND GYNECOLOGISTS, p. 93 of this Supplement, per BLACKMUN, J., invalidated Pennsylvania's attempt to force doctors to be the courier to their patients of an assortment of state-prescribed information as a prerequisite for consent to abortion. Without referring to the first amendment, the Court objected to the intrusion of the state's mandated speech upon the discretion of the physician and the "attempt to wedge the Commonwealth's message" into the "privacy of the informed-consent dialogue between the woman and her physician": "Even the listing of agencies in the printed Pennsylvania form presents serious problems;

a. The Court upheld a ban on "obscene" interstate commercial telephonic messages. See p. 189 of this Supplement. Scalia, J., concurring, noted: "[W]hile we hold the Constitution prevents Congress from banning indecent speech in this fashion, we do not hold that the Constitution requires public utilities to carry it." Brennan, J., joined by Marshall and Stevens, JJ., concurred on the indecency issue and dissented on the obscenity issue.

it contains names of agencies that well may be out of step with the needs of the particular woman and thus places the physician in an awkward position and infringes upon his or her professional responsibilities. Forcing the physician or counselor to present the materials and the list to the woman makes him or her in effect an agent of the State in treating the woman and places his or her imprimatur upon both the materials and the list. All this is, or comes close to being, state medicine imposed upon the woman, not the professional medical guidance she seeks, and it officially structures—as it obviously was intended to do—the dialogue between the woman and her physician."

O'CONNOR, J., dissenting, joined by Rehnquist, J., saw a potential first amendment problem but did not reach the issue: "I do not dismiss the possibility that requiring the physician or counselor to read aloud the State's printed materials if the woman wishes access to them but cannot read raises First Amendment concerns. Even the requirement that women who can read be informed of the availability of those materials, and furnished with them on request, may create some possibility that the physician or counselor is being required to 'communicate [the State's] ideology.' [S]ee *Wooley*. Since the Court of Appeals did not reach appellees' First Amendment claim, and since appellees do not raise it here, I need not decide whether this potential problem would be sufficiently serious to warrant issuance of a preliminary [injunction]." [a]

WHITE, J., joined by Rehnquist, J., dissenting, characterized any concern with doctor's rights as "nonsensical": "[N]othing in the Constitution indicates a preference for the liberty of doctors over that of lawyers, accountants, bakers, or brickmakers. Accordingly, if the State may not 'structure' the dialogue between doctor and patient, it should also follow that the State may not, for example, require attorneys to disclose to their clients information concerning the risks of representing the client in a particular proceeding. Of course, we upheld such disclosure requirements only last Term. See *Zauderer*."

RILEY v. NATIONAL FEDERATION OF THE BLIND, p. 229 of this Supplement, per BRENNAN, J., invalidated North Carolina's requirement that professional fundraisers disclose to potential donors (prior to any appeal for funds) the percentage of charitable contributions that had been turned over to charities in the previous 12 months: "It is not clear that a professional's speech is necessarily commercial whenever it relates to that person's financial motivation for speaking. But even assuming, without deciding, that such speech in the abstract is indeed merely 'commercial,' we do not believe that the speech retains its commercial character when it is inextricably intertwined with otherwise fully protected speech. * * *

"In contrast to the prophylactic, imprecise, and unduly burdensome rule the State has adopted to reduce its alleged donor misperception, more benign and narrowly tailored options are available.[b] For example, as a general rule, the

a. Are the first amendment interests of the patient more substantial than that of the doctor? See p. 272 of this Supplement.

b. In an earlier footnote, the Court stated that, "[N]othing in this opinion should be taken to suggest that the State may not require a fundraiser to disclose unambiguously his or her professional status. On the contrary, such a narrowly tailored requirement would withstand First Amendment scrutiny."

Stevens, J., concurred. Scalia, J., also concurred, but objected to the footnote: "[It] represents a departure from our traditional understanding [that] where the dissemination of ideas is concerned, it is safer to assume that the people are smart enough to get the information they need than to assume that the Government is wise or impartial enough to make the judgment for them."

State may itself publish the detailed financial disclosure forms it requires professional fundraisers to file. This procedure would communicate the desired information to the public without burdening a speaker with unwanted speech during the course of a solication. Alternatively, the State may vigorously enforce its antifraud laws to prohibit professional fundraisers from obtaining money on false pretenses or by making false statements. These more narrowly tailored rules are in keeping with the First Amendment directive that government not dictate the content of speech absent compelling necessity, and then, only by means precisely tailored."

REHNQUIST, C.J., joined by O'Connor, J., dissented:

"[Because the statute is aimed at the commercial aspect of the solicitation, and because the State's interests in enacting the disclosure requirements are sufficiently strong, I cannot conclude that the First Amendment prevents the State from imposing the type of disclosure requirement involved here, at least in the absence of a showing that the effect of the disclosure is to dramatically limit contributions or impede a charity's ability to disseminate ideas or information."

FREEDOM OF ASSOCIATION AND EMPLOYMENT

CON LAW: P. 973, after note 3

AMER CON: P. 737, after note 3

RTS & LIB: P. 640, after note 3

A 1981 amendment to the Food Stamp Act provides that no family shall become eligible to participate in the program during the time that any member of the household is on strike nor shall receive any increase in food stamp allotments by virtue of decreased income of the striking member. LYNG v. UAW, 481 U.S. 360, 108 S.Ct. 1184, 99 L.Ed.2d 380 (1988), per WHITE, J., stated that associational rights included the "combination of workers together in order better to assert their lawful rights" but found no interference with such association: "[The statute] does not 'order' appellees not to associate together for the purpose of conducting a strike, or for any other purpose, and it does not 'prevent' them from associating together or burden their ability to do so in any significant manner. [I]t seems 'exceedingly unlikely' that this statute will prevent individuals from continuing to associate together in unions to promote their lawful objectives.[a] [A] 'legislature's decision not to subsidize the exercise of a fundamental right does not infringe the right.' *Regan*."[b]

MARSHALL, J., joined by Brennan and Blackmun, JJ., dissenting, saw no need to reach the First Amendment issue (although he was "unconvinced" by the Court's treatment of the issue) because, he argued, the statute failed to meet even the most deferential scrutiny. In light of a variety of statutory benefits easing management's burden in labor disputes, he concluded: "Altering the backdrop of governmental support in this one-sided and devastating way amounts to a penalty on strikers, not neutrality."[c]

a. Should a penalty for the exercise of a right be unconstitutional even if it does not inhibit the exercise of that right?

b. How does one distinguish the mere failure to subsidize from a penalty? Is participation in a strike protected association?

c. The government had argued that the statute was justified by the interest of governmental neutrality in private labor disputes.

CON LAW: P. 977, after note 3

AMER CON: P. 741, after note 3

RTS & LIB: P. 644, after note 3

CHICAGO TEACHERS UNION v. HUDSON, 475 U.S. 292, 106 S.Ct. 1066, 89 L.Ed.2d 232 (1986), per STEVENS, J., held that first amendment requirements for "the Union's collection of agency fees [from non-members] include an adequate explanation of the basis for the fee, a reasonably prompt opportunity to challenge the amount of the fee before an impartial decisionmaker, and an escrow for the amounts reasonably in dispute while [challenges] are pending." WHITE, J., joined by Burger, C.J., concurring, joined the Court's opinion, but stressed that the issue of expenditures that were neither germane to collective bargaining nor in support of particular political or ideological endeavors had not been resolved and observed that the lower court's "questionable" [a] remarks on the issue were dicta. In addition, he expressed the view that a complaining non-member need not exhaust internal union hearing procedures before proceeding to arbitration, but might fairly be required to exhaust the arbitration procedure before turning to the courts.

INTIMATE ASSOCIATION AND EXPRESSIVE ASSOCIATION: THE RIGHT TO EXCLUDE MEMBERS

CON LAW: P. 982, after *Roberts*

AMER CON: P. 746, after *Roberts*

RTS & LIB: P. 649, after *Roberts*

BOARD OF DIRECTORS OF ROTARY INTERNATIONAL v. ROTARY CLUB OF DUARTE, 485 U.S. 537, 107 S.Ct. 1940, 95 L.Ed.2d 474 (1987), per POWELL, J., followed *Roberts* and held that Rotary International's policy of excluding women was not protected by the first amendment and also held that the local Duarte chapter had no first amendment right to exclude women.[a] Rotary International, "an association of thousands of local Rotary Clubs," could claim no constitutionally protected "right of private association." Similarly, the absence of an upper limit on local membership, the yearly ten percent turnover in membership, the business and professional purposes of the local, the policy of admitting all fully qualified prospective members, the policy of permitting numerous visitors to meetings, and the desire to publicize the meetings and activities in local newspapers supported the conclusion that the relationship among local Rotary Club members was not the kind of intimate or private relation that warranted constitutional protection.[b]

---

a. Posner, J., writing for a divided panel had argued that forced expenditures for non-germane-non-ideological activities violated a non-member's freedom of association. Compare *Communication Workers v. Beck*, ___ U.S. ___, 108 S.Ct. 2641, 101 L.Ed.2d 634 (1988) (no first amendment issue reached, but forced expenditures for purposes other than collective bargaining including non-germane-non-ideological activities violate National Labor Relations Act).

a. The Duarte chapter had no desire to exclude women, and in fact, was contesting Rotary International's right to impose its exclusionary policy on local chapters. The Duarte chapter argued that California law pre-

cluded it from engaging in gender discrimination, that California had acted within constitutional limits, and that Rotary International was, therefore, precluded from enforcing its policy on the local.

b. See also *New York State Club Ass'n v. New York*, ___ U.S. ___, 108 S.Ct. 2225, 101 L.Ed.2d 1 (1988) (upholding city ordinance against facial challenge that prohibits discrimination based on race, creed, or sex by institutions (except benevolent orders or religious corporations) with more than 400 members that provide regular meal service and receive payment from nonmembers for the furtherance of trade or business).

Finally, the Court concluded that California's gender discrimination prohibition did not unduly interfere with freedom of association for the purpose of engaging in protected speech or religious activities. Like the Minnesota law in *Roberts*, the California statute made no distinction on the basis of the organization's viewpoint. Although Rotary Clubs take no positions on "public questions," they were recognized "to engage in a variety of commendable service activities [protected] by the First Amendment." The California law, however, did not require the clubs to abandon or alter any activities.

Even if the California law worked "some slight infringement" on Rotary members' right of expressive association, that "infringement" was said to be "justified because it serves the State's compelling interest in eliminating discrimination against women." [c]

CON LAW: P. 983, after note 2

AMER CON: P. 747, after note 2

RTS & LIB: P. 650, after note 2

3. *Confining the Scope of Association.* DALLAS v. STANGLIN, ___ U.S. ___, 109 S.Ct. 1591, 104 L.Ed.2d 18 (1989), per REHNQUIST, C.J., held that an ordinance restricting admission to certain dance halls to persons between the ages of 14 and 18 implicated no first amendment rights: "The hundreds of teenagers who congregate each night at this particular dance hall are not members of any organized association; they are patrons of the same business establishment. Most are strangers to one another, and the dance hall admits all who are willing to pay the admission fee. There is no suggestion that these patrons 'take positions on public questions,' or perform any [other] similar activities. * * *

"The cases cited in *Roberts* recognize that 'freedom of speech' means more than simply the right to talk and to write. It is possible to find some kernel of expression in almost every activity a person undertakes—for example, walking down the street, or meeting one's friends at a shopping mall—but such a kernel is not sufficient to bring the activity within the protection of the First Amendment. We think the activity of these dance-hall patrons—coming together to engage in recreational dancing—is not protected by the First Amendment. Thus this activity qualifies neither as a form of 'intimate association' nor as a form of 'expressive association' as those terms were described in *Roberts*." [a]

c. In response to the claim that Rotary's international activities could be seriously impaired, the Court observed that the legal effect of the judgment below was limited to the State of California. Scalia, J., concurred in the judgment without opinion. Blackmun and O'Connor, JJ., took no part.

a. Stevens, J., joined by Blackmun, J., concurred, stating that the "opportunity to make friends and enjoy the company of other people—in a dance hall or elsewhere" involves substantive due process rights (which, he concluded, were not violated by the ordinance), but not any first amendment right of association.

INTIMATE ASSOCIATION AND EXPRESSIVE ASSOCIATION: THE RIGHT TO ASSOCIATE WITH NON–MEMBERS

CON LAW: P. 983, after note 2

AMER CON: P. 747, after note 2

RTS & LIB: P. 650, after note 2

The Connecticut Republican Party adopted a rule permitting registered independent voters to vote in Republican primaries for federal and statewide offices. Connecticut law, however, prohibited party non-members from voting in primary elections. Republicans, therefore, proposed an amendment of Connecticut law allowing independents to vote in primaries whenever permitted by Party rules. Both houses of the Connecticut legislature were then controlled by the Democratic party, and the proposed amendment was defeated in a vote substantially along party lines. Subsequently, the Republicans gained control of the Connecticut legislature and an amendment to the statute was passed only to be vetoed by the Democratic Governor.

TASHJIAN v. REPUBLICAN PARTY OF CONNECTICUT, 479 U.S. 208, 107 S.Ct. 544, 93 L.Ed.2d 514 (1986), per MARSHALL, J., held that the Connecticut statute impermissibly burdened the association rights of the Republican party and its members: "The Party's attempt to broaden the base of public participation in and support for its activities is conduct undeniably central to the exercise of the right of association. [The] freedom to join together in furtherance of common political beliefs 'necessarily presupposes the freedom to identify the people who constitute the association.' * * *

"The statute here places limits upon the group of registered voters whom the Party may invite to participate in the 'basic function' of selecting the Party's candidates. The State thus limits the Party's associational opportunities at the crucial juncture at which the appeal to common principles may be translated into concerted action, and hence to political power in the community.[7]

"[A]ppellant [the Connecticut Secretary of State] contends that [the Connecticut statute] furthers the State's compelling interest in protecting the integrity of the two-party system and the responsibility of party government. Appellant argues vigorously and at length that the closed primary system chosen by the state legislature promotes responsiveness by elected officials and strengthens the effectiveness of the political parties.

The relative merits of closed and open primaries have been the subject of substantial debate since the beginning of this century, and no consensus has as yet emerged. Appellant invokes a long and distinguished line of political

---

7. Appellant contends that any infringement of the associational right of the Party or its members is *de minimis,* because Connecticut law, as amended during the pendency of this litigation, provides that any previously unaffiliated voter may become eligible to vote in the Party's primary by enrolling as a Party member as late as noon on the last business day preceding the primary. * * *

This is not a satisfactory response to the Party's contentions for two reasons. First, as the Court of Appeals noted, the formal affiliation process is one which individual voters may employ in order to associate with the Party, but it provides no means by which the members of the Party may choose to broaden opportunities for joining the association by their own act, without any intervening action by potential voters. Second, and more importantly, the requirement of public affiliation with the Party in order to vote in the primary conditions the exercise of the associational right upon the making of a public statement of adherence to the Party which the State requires regardless of the actual beliefs of the individual voter. Cf. *Wooley; Barnette.*
* * *

scientists and public officials who have been supporters of the closed primary. But our role is not to decide whether the state legislature was acting wisely in enacting the closed primary system in 1955, or whether the Republican Party makes a mistake in seeking to depart from the practice of the past 30 years.[12]

"We have previously recognized the danger that 'splintered parties and unrestrained factionalism may do significant damage to the fabric of government.' *Storer v. Brown.* We upheld a California statute which denied access to the ballot to any independent candidate who had voted in a party primary or been registered as a member of a political party within one year prior to the immediately preceding primary election. * * *

"The statute in *Storer* was designed to protect the parties and the party system against the disorganizing effect of independent candidacies launched by unsuccessful putative party nominees. This protection [is] undertaken to prevent the disruption of the political parties from without, and not, as in this case, to prevent the parties from taking internal steps affecting their own process for the selection of candidates. The [regulation] upheld in *Storer* [imposed] certain burdens upon the protected First and Fourteenth Amendment interests of some individuals, both voters and potential candidates, in order to protect the interests of others. In the present case, the state statute is defended on the ground that it protects the integrity of the Party against the Party itself.

"Under these circumstances, the views of the State, which to some extent represent the views of the one political party transiently enjoying majority power, as to the optimum methods for preserving party integrity lose much of their force. The State argues that its statute is well designed to save the Republican Party from undertaking a course of conduct destructive of its own interests. But on this point 'even if the State were correct, a State, or a court, may not constitutionally substitute its own judgment for that of the Party.' [13]

"We conclude that the interests which the appellant adduces in support of the statute are insubstantial,[a] and accordingly the statute, as applied to the Party in this case, is unconstitutional." [b]

---

12. We note that appellant's direst predictions about destruction of the integrity of the election process and decay of responsible party government are not borne out by the experience of the 29 States which have chosen to permit more substantial openness in their primary systems than Connecticut has permitted heretofore.

13. Our holding today does not establish that state regulation of primary voting qualifications may never withstand challenge by a political party or its membership. A party seeking, for example, to open its primary to all voters, including members of other parties, would [threaten] other parties with the disorganization effects which the [statute] in *Storer* [was] designed to prevent. We have observed on several occasions that a State may adopt a "policy of confining each voter to a single nominating act," a policy decision which is not involved in the present case. * * *

a. The Court also concluded that the Connecticut statute could not be justified as a means to avoid administrative burdens ("[T]he possibility of future increases in the cost of administering the election system is not a

sufficient basis here for infringing appellees' First Amendment rights."); or as a means to avoid party raiding (a "raid on the Republican Party primary by independent voters" is a "curious concept" that, in any event, is not impeded by the statute); or as a means to avoid voter confusion ("[A]ppellant's concern that candidates selected under the Party rule will be the nominee of an 'amorphous' group using the Party's name is inconsistent with the facts" in part because under a statute not challenged in the case, a candidate could not appear on the primary ballot without obtaining at least 20% of the vote at a Party convention open only to Party members, a provision that "greatly attenuates the State's concern that the ultimate nominee will be wedded to the Party in nothing more than a marriage of convenience.").

b. The Court rejected the contention that implementation of the party rule would violate the Qualifications Clause of the Constitution, Art. I, § 2, cl. 1 and the Seventeenth Amendment. Stevens, J., joined by Scalia, J., dissented from that conclusion.

SCALIA, J., joined by Rehnquist, C.J., and O'Connor, J., dissented: "There is no question here of restricting the Republican Party's ability to recruit and enroll Party members by offering them the ability to select Party candidates; [Connecticut] permits an independent voter to join the Party as late as the day before the primary. Nor is there any question of restricting the ability of the Party's members to select whatever candidate they desire. Appellees' only complaint is that the Party cannot leave the selection of its candidate to persons who are *not* members of the Party, and are unwilling to become members. It seems to me fanciful to refer to this as an interest in freedom of association between the members of the Republican Party and the putative independent voters. The Connecticut voter who, while steadfastly refusing to register as a Republican, casts a vote in the Republican primary, forms no more meaningful an 'association' with the Party than does the independent or the registered Democrat who responds to questions by a Republican Party pollster. If the concept of freedom of association is extended to such casual contacts, it ceases to be of any analytic use. * * *

"The ability of the members of the Republican Party to select their own candidate, on the other hand, unquestionably implicates an associational freedom—but it can hardly be thought that that freedom is unconstitutionally impaired here. The Party is entirely free to put forward, if it wishes, that candidate who has the highest degree of support among Party members and independents combined. The State is under no obligation, however, to let its party primary be used, instead of a party-funded opinion poll, as the means by which the party identifies the relative popularity of its potential candidates among independents. Nor is there any reason apparent to me why the State cannot insist that this decision to support what might be called the independents' choice be taken *by the party membership in a democratic fashion,* rather than through a process that permits the members' votes to be diluted—and perhaps even absolutely outnumbered—by the votes of outsiders.

"The Court's opinion characterizes this, disparagingly, as an attempt to 'protec[t] the integrity of the Party against the Party itself.' There are two problems with this characterization. The first, and less important, is that it is not true. We have no way of knowing that a majority of the Party's members is in favor of allowing ultimate selection of its candidates for federal and statewide office to be determined by persons outside the Party. That decision was not made by democratic ballot, but by the Party's state convention—which, for all we know, may have been dominated by officeholders and office seekers whose evaluation of the merits of assuring election of the Party's candidates, vis-a-vis the merits of proposing candidates faithful to the Party's political philosophy, diverged significantly from the views of the Party's rank and file. I had always thought it was a major purpose of state-imposed party primary requirements to protect the general party membership against this sort of minority control. Second and more important, however, *even if* it were the fact that the majority of the Party's members wanted its candidates to be determined by outsiders, there is no reason why the State is bound to honor that desire—any more than it would be bound to honor a party's democratically expressed desire that its candidates henceforth be selected by convention rather than by primary, or by the party's executive committee in a smoke-filled room. In other words, the validity of the state-imposed primary requirement itself, which we have hitherto considered 'too plain for argument,' *American Party of Texas v. White,* presupposes that the State *has* the right 'to protect the Party against the Party itself.' Connecticut may lawfully require that significant elements of the democratic election process be democratic—whether the Party wants that or not. It is beyond my understanding why the Republican Party's delegation of its democratic choice to a Republican Convention can be proscribed, but its delegation of that choice to nonmembers of the Party cannot.

"In the case before us, Connecticut has said no more than this: Just as the Republican Party may, if it wishes, nominate the candidate recommended by the Party's executive committee, so long as its members select that candidate by name in a democratic vote; so also it may nominate the independents' choice, so long as its members select him by name in a democratic vote. That seems to me plainly and entirely constitutional."

GOVERNMENT MANDATED DISCLOSURES AND FREEDOM OF ASSOCIATION

POLITICAL ASSOCIATION

CON LAW: P. 988, after note 5

AMER CON: P. 758, after note 5

RTS & LIB: P. 655, after note 5

6. *A Party's Right to Disclose Its Electoral Preference.* EU v. SAN FRANCISCO COUNTY DEMOCRATIC CENTRAL COMMITTEE, __ U.S. __, 109 S.Ct. 1013, 103 L.Ed.2d 271 (1989), per MARSHALL, J., held that a California statute forbidding official governing bodies of political parties from endorsing or opposing candidates for partisan[a] office in primary elections violated protected speech and association rights.[b] The Court not only disputed California's contention that the political parties had consented to the statute, but also stated that: "[T]he State's focus on the parties' alleged consent ignores the independent First Amendment rights of the parties' members. It is wholly undemonstrated that the members authorized the parties to consent to infringements of members' rights."

BEYOND ASSOCIATION: THE CONSTITUTIONAL PLACE OF THE PRESS REVISITED

CON LAW: P. 1007, after *Minneapolis Star*

RTS & LIB: P. 674, after *Minneapolis Star*

Arkansas imposes a tax on the receipts from sales of tangible personal property. Many items are exempt from the sales tax including newspapers and "religious, professional, trade and sports journals and/or publications printed and published within this State * * * when sold through regular subscriptions." The regulations define a publication as "a pamphlet, magazine, journal, or periodical, other than a newspaper,[a] designed for the information or en-

---

a. California also bans such endorsements in nonpartisan elections, but the issue was not before the Court. But see Geary v. Renne, 708 F.Supp. 278 (N.D.Cal.1989) (invalidating the ban).

b. The Court also struck down various provisions regulating the structure of political parties, e.g., length of term for the party chair and a requirement that the chair rotate between residents of northern and southern California. None of the California provisions met the compelling state interest requirement. Stevens, J., concurred, but observed that the compelling state interest terminology was not a helpful test, but a prelude to an inevitable result. Rehnquist, C.J., did not participate.

a. A newspaper is defined in the regulation as "a publication in sheet form containing reports of current events and articles of general interest to the public, published regularly in short intervals such as daily, weekly,

tertainment of the general public or any segment thereof." The Arkansas Supreme Court ruled that in order to qualify for the "publication" exemption, a magazine had to be a "religious, professional, trade, or sports periodical." It, therefore, held that the Arkansas sales tax applied to the *Arkansas Times,* a general interest [b] monthly magazine published by the Arkansas Writers' Project, Inc., and that no first amendment problem was raised because publishers are not immune from "ordinary forms of taxation."

ARKANSAS WRITERS' PROJECT, INC. v. RAGLAND, 481 U.S. 221, 107 S.Ct. 1722, 95 L.Ed.2d 209 (1987), per MARSHALL, J., held that "a state sales tax scheme that taxes general interest magazines, but exempts newspaper and religious, professional, trade, and sports journals violates the First Amendment's guarantee of freedom of the press": "Our cases clearly establish that a discriminatory tax on the press burdens rights protected by the First Amendment.[3] See *Minneapolis Star & Tribune v. Minnesota Commissioner of Revenue,* 460 U.S. 575, 103 S.Ct. 1365, 75 L.Ed.2d 295 (1983); *Grosjean.* In *Minneapolis Star,* the discrimination took two distinct forms. First, in contrast to generally applicable economic regulations to which the press can legitimately be subject, the Minnesota use tax treated the press differently from other enterprises. Second, the tax targeted a small group of newspapers. This was due to the fact that the first $100,000 of paper and ink were exempt from the tax; thus 'only a handful of publishers pay any tax at all, and even fewer pay any significant amount of tax.'

"Both types of discrimination can be established even where, as here, there is no evidence of an improper censorial motive. [On] the facts of this case, the fundamental question is not whether the tax singles out the press as a whole, but whether it targets a small group within the press. While we indicated in *Minneapolis Star* that a genuinely nondiscriminatory tax on the receipts of newspapers would be constitutionally permissible, the Arkansas sales tax cannot be characterized as nondiscriminatory, because it is not evenly applied to all magazines. [Because] the Arkansas sales tax scheme treats some magazines less favorably than others, it suffers from the second type of discrimination identified in *Minneapolis Star.*

"Indeed, this case involves a more disturbing use of selective taxation than *Minneapolis Star,* because the basis on which Arkansas differentiates between magazines is particularly repugnant to First Amendment principles: a magazine's tax status depends entirely on its *content.* [If] articles in *Arkansas Times* were uniformly devoted to religion or sports, the magazine would be exempt from the sales tax. [In] order to determine whether a magazine is subject to sales tax, Arkansas' 'enforcement authorities must necessarily examine the content of the message that is conveyed * * *.' *FCC v. League of Women Voters of California.* Such official scrutiny of the content of publications as the basis for imposing a tax is entirely incompatible with the First Amendment's guarantee of freedom of the press. * * *

"The Commissioner [suggests] that the exemption of religious, professional, trade and sports journals was intended to encourage 'fledgling' publishers, who

or bi-weekly, and intended for general circulation."

b. Although the magazine published articles on a variety of subjects including religion and sports, the parties stipulated that *Arkansas Times* was not a religious, professional, trade, or sports journal. They also stipulated that *Arkansas Times* was not a newspaper.

3. Appellant's First Amendment claims are obviously intertwined with interests arising under the Equal Protection Clause. See *Mosley.* However, since Arkansas' sales-tax system directly implicates freedom of the press, we analyze it primarily in First Amendment terms. See *Minneapolis Star.*

have only limited audiences and therefore do not have access to the same volume of advertising revenues as general interest magazines such as *Arkansas Times*. Even assuming that an interest in encouraging fledgling publications might be a compelling one, we do not find the [exemption] narrowly tailored to achieve that end. To the contrary, the exemption is both overinclusive and underinclusive. The types of magazines enumerated [are] exempt, regardless of whether they are 'fledgling;' even the most lucrative and well-established religious, professional, trade and sports journals do not pay sales tax. By contrast, struggling general interest magazines and struggling specialty magazines on subjects other than those specified [are] ineligible for favorable tax treatment.

"[Because] we hold today that the State's selective application of its sales tax to magazines is unconstitutional and therefore invalid, our ruling eliminates the differential treatment of newspapers and magazines. Accordingly, we need not decide whether a distinction between different types of periodicals presents an additional basis for invalidating the sales tax, as applied to the press." [c]

SCALIA, J., joined by Rehnquist, C.J., dissented: "All government displays an enduring tendency to silence, or to facilitate silencing, those voices that it disapproves. In the case of the Judicial Branch of Government, the principal restraint upon that tendency, as upon other judicial error, is the requirement that judges write opinions providing logical reasons for treating one situation differently from another. I dissent from today's decision because it provides no rational basis for distinguishing the subsidy scheme here under challenge from many others that are common and unquestionably lawful. It thereby introduces into First Amendment law an element of arbitrariness that ultimately erodes rather than fosters the important freedoms at issue.

"[T]he Court's [application] of the 'strict scrutiny' test rests upon the premise that for First Amendment purposes denial of exemption from taxation is equivalent to regulation. That premise is demonstrably erroneous and cannot be consistently applied. Our opinions have long recognized—in First Amendment contexts as elsewhere—the reality that tax exemptions, credits, and deductions are 'a form of subsidy that is administered through the tax system,' and the general rule that 'a legislature's decision not to subsidize the exercise of a fundamental right does not infringe the right, and thus is not subject to strict scrutiny.' *Regan v. Taxation With Representation of Washington* (upholding denial of tax exemption for organization engaged in lobbying even though veterans' organizations received exemption regardless of lobbying activities). See also *Buckley v. Valeo* (declining to apply strict scrutiny to campaign finance law that excludes certain candidates); *Harris v. McRae* (declining to apply strict scrutiny to legislative decision not to subsidize abortions even though other medical procedures were subsidized); *Maher v. Roe* (same).

"The reason that denial of participation in a tax exemption or other subsidy scheme does not necessarily 'infringe' a fundamental right is that—unlike direct restriction or prohibition—such a denial does not, as a general rule, have any significant coercive effect. It may, of course, be manipulated so as to do so, in which case the courts will be available to provide relief. But that is not remotely the case here. It is implausible that the 4% sales tax, generally applicable to all sales in the State with the few enumerated exceptions, was meant to inhibit, or had the effect of inhibiting, this appellant's publication.

c. Stevens, J., concurred in part and concurred in the judgment.

"Perhaps a more stringent, prophylactic rule is appropriate, and can consistently be applied, when the subsidy pertains to the expression of a particular viewpoint on a matter of political concern—a tax exemption, for example, that is expressly available only to publications that take a particular point of view on a controversial issue of foreign policy. [There] is no need, however, and it is realistically quite impossible, to extend to all speech the same degree of protection against exclusion from a subsidy that one might think appropriate for opposing shades of political expression.

"By seeking to do so, the majority casts doubt upon a wide variety of tax preferences and subsidies that draw distinctions based upon subject-matter. The U.S. Postal Service, for example, grants a special bulk rate to written material disseminated by certain nonprofit organizations—religious, educational, scientific, philanthropic, agricultural, labor, veterans', and fraternal organizations. See Domestic Mail Manual § 623 (1985). Must this preference be justified by a 'compelling governmental need' because a nonprofit organization devoted to some other purpose—dissemination of information about boxing, for example—does not receive the special rate? The Kennedy Center, which is subsidized by the Federal Government in the amount of up to $23 million per year, see 20 U.S.C. § 76n(a), is authorized by statute to 'present classical and contemporary music, opera, drama, dance, and poetry.' § 76j. Is this subsidy subject to strict scrutiny because other kinds of expressive activity, such as learned lectures and political speeches, are excluded? Are government research grant programs or the funding activities of the Corporation for Public Broadcasting, see 47 U.S.C. § 396(g)(2), subject to strict scrutiny because they provide money for the study or exposition of some subjects but not others?

"Because there is no principled basis to distinguish the subsidization of speech in these areas—which we would surely uphold—from the subsidization that we strike down here, our decision today places the granting or denial of protection within our own idiosyncratic discretion. In my view, that threatens First Amendment rights infinitely more than the tax exemption at issue."

TEXAS MONTHLY, INC. v. BULLOCK, ___ U.S. ___, 109 S.Ct. 890, 103 L.Ed.2d 1 (1989) confronted a Texas statute exempting religious periodicals from sales and use tax provisions, but denying such an exemption for other periodicals. The Court held that the selective exemption violated the establishment clause (see page 308 of this Supplement), but did not resolve the free press issue. Five justices, however, argued that if the demands if the religion clauses were met, no press clause barrier would remain even if content discrimination were involved. SCALIA, J., joined by Rehnquist, C.J., and Kennedy, J., dissenting, argued that the goal of accommodating religion was consistent with establishment clause requirements and stated: "If the purpose of accommodating religion can support action that might otherwise violate the Establishment Clause, I see no reason why it does not also support action that might otherwise violate the Press Clause or the Speech Clause. [Just] as the Constitution sometimes *requires* accommodation of religious expression despite not only the Establishment Clause but also the Speech and Press Clauses, so also it sometimes *permits* accommodation despite all these clauses. Such accommodation is unavoidably content-based—because the Freedom of Religion clause is content-based."

BLACKMUN, J., joined by O'Connor, J., concurring, agreed for the most part with Scalia, J.'s analysis of the press clause issue. But he concluded that the Texas statute violated the Establishment Clause. If both religious and philosophical literature were exempted, however, press and religion clause objections would be resolved in his judgment: "Such a statute . . . should survive Press Clause scrutiny because its exemption would be narrowly tailored to meet the compelling interests that underlie both the Free Exercise and Establishment Clauses."

WHITE, J., concurring, thought the statute's content discrimination was "plainly forbidden by the Press Clause of the First Amendment" and did not reach the establishment clause issue.[a]

New York Public Health law authorizes the forced closure of a building for one year if it has been used for the purpose of "lewdness, assignation or prostitution." Pursuant to this statute, a civil complaint alleged that prostitution solicitation and sexual activities by patrons were occurring on the premises of an adult bookstore all within the observation of the proprietor. Accordingly, the complaint called for the closure of the building for one year. There was no claim that any books in the store were obscene. The New York Court of Appeals held that the closure remedy violated the first amendment because it was broader than necessary to achieve the restriction against illicit sexual activities. It reasoned that an injunction against the alleged sexual conduct could further the state interest without infringing on first amendment values.

ARCARA v. CLOUD BOOKS, INC., 478 U.S. 697, 106 S.Ct. 3172, 92 L.Ed.2d 568 (1986), per BURGER, C.J., reversed, holding that the closure remedy did not violate the first amendment; indeed, that the closure remedy did not require any first amendment scrutiny: "This Court has applied First Amendment scrutiny to a statute regulating conduct which has the incidental effect of burdening the expression of a particular political opinion. *United States v. O'Brien.* * * *

"We have also applied First Amendment scrutiny to some statutes which, although directed at activity with no expressive component, impose a disproportionate burden upon those engaged in protected First Amendment activities. In *Minneapolis Star,* we struck down a tax imposed on the sale of large quantities of newsprint and ink because the tax had the effect of singling out newspapers to shoulder its burden. We imposed a greater burden of justification on the State even though the tax was imposed upon a nonexpressive activity, since the burden of the tax inevitably fell disproportionately—in fact, almost exclusively— upon the shoulders of newspapers exercising the constitutionally protected freedom of the press. Even while striking down the tax in *Minneapolis Star,* we emphasized: 'Clearly, the First Amendment does not prohibit all regulation of the press. It is beyond dispute that the States and the Federal Government can subject newspapers to generally applicable economic regulations without creating constitutional problems.'

"The New York Court of Appeals held that the *O'Brien* test for permissible governmental regulation was applicable to this case because the closure order sought by petitioner would also impose an incidental burden upon respondents' bookselling activities. That court ignored a crucial distinction between the circumstances presented in *O'Brien* and the circumstances of this case: unlike the symbolic draft card burning in *O'Brien,* the sexual activity carried on in this case manifests absolutely no element of protected expression.[a] In *Paris Adult*

a. Brennan, J., joined by Marshall and Stevens, JJ., did not reach the press clause issue.

a. In an earlier section of the opinion, Burger, C.J., stated that, "petitioners in *O'Brien* had, as respondents here do not, at least the semblance of expressive activity in their claim that the otherwise unlawful burning of a draft card was to 'carry a message' of the actor's opposition to the draft."

Theatre, we underscored the fallacy of seeking to use the First Amendment as a cloak for obviously unlawful public sexual conduct by the diaphanous device of attributing protected expressive attributes to that conduct. First Amendment values may not be invoked by merely linking the words 'sex' and 'books.'

"Nor does the distinction drawn by the New York Public Health Law inevitably single out bookstores or others engaged in First Amendment protected activities for the imposition of its burden, as did the tax struck down in *Minneapolis Star*. As we noted in *Minneapolis Star*, neither the press nor booksellers may claim special protection from governmental regulations of general applicability simply by virtue of their First Amendment protected activities. If the city imposed closure penalties for demonstrated Fire Code violations or health hazards from inadequate sewage treatment, the First Amendment would not aid the owner of premises who had knowingly allowed such violations to persist.

"Nonetheless, respondents argue that the effect of the statutory closure remedy impermissibly burdens its First Amendment protected bookselling activities. The severity of this burden is dubious at best, and is mitigated by the fact that respondents remain free to sell the same materials at another location.[2] In any event, this argument proves too much, since every civil and criminal remedy imposes some conceivable burden on First Amendment protected activities. One liable for a civil damages award has less money to spend on paid political announcements or to contribute to political causes, yet no one would suggest that such liability gives rise to a valid First Amendment claim. * * *

"It is true that the closure order in this case would require respondents to move their bookselling business to another location. Yet we have not traditionally subjected every criminal and civil sanction imposed through legal process to 'least restrictive means' scrutiny simply because each particular remedy will have some effect on the First Amendment activities of those subject to sanction. Rather, we have subjected such restrictions to scrutiny only where it was conduct with a significant expressive element that drew the legal remedy in the first place, as in *O'Brien*, or where a statute based on a nonexpressive activity has the inevitable effect of singling out those engaged in expressive activity, as in *Minneapolis Star*. This case involves neither situation, and we conclude the First Amendment is not implicated by the enforcement of a public health regulation of general application against the physical premises in which respondents happen to sell books.[4]" b

2. For the same reason, we must reject the Court of Appeals' reasoning analogizing the closure order sought in this case to an unconstitutional prior restraint under *Near v. Minnesota*. The closure order sought in this case differs from a prior restraint in two significant respects. First, the order would impose no restraint at all on the dissemination of particular materials, since respondent is free to carry on his bookselling business at another location, even if such locations are difficult to find. Second, the closure order sought, would not be imposed on the basis of an advance determination that the distribution of particular materials is prohibited—indeed, the imposition of the closure order has nothing to do with any expressive conduct at all.

4. Respondents assert that closure of their premises is sought as a pretext for suppression of First Amendment protected expression. However, there is no suggestion on the record before us that the closure of respondents' bookstore was sought under the public health nuisance statute as a pretext for the suppression of First Amendment protected material. Were respondents able to establish the existence of such a speech suppressive motivation or policy on the part of the District Attorney, they might have a claim of selective prosecution. Respondents in this case made no such assertion before the trial court.

b. On remand, the New York Court of Appeals held that, in the absence of a showing that the state had chosen a course no broader than necessary to accomplish its purpose, any forced closure of the bookstore would unduly impair the bookseller's rights of free expression under the New York State constitution.

O'CONNOR, J., joined by Stevens, J., concurred: "I agree that the Court of Appeals erred in applying a First Amendment standard of review where, as here, the government is regulating neither speech nor an incidental, non-expressive effect of speech. Any other conclusion would lead to the absurd result that any government action that had some conceivable speech-inhibiting consequences, such as the arrest of a newscaster for a traffic violation, would require analysis under the First Amendment. If, however, a city were to use a nuisance statute as a pretext for closing down a book store because it sold indecent books or because of the perceived secondary effects of having a purveyor of such books in the neighborhood, the case would clearly implicate First Amendment concerns and require analysis under the appropriate First Amendment standard of review. Because there is no suggestion in the record or opinion below of such pretextual use of the New York nuisance provision in this case, I concur in the Court's opinion and judgment."

BLACKMUN, J., joined by Brennan and Marshall, JJ., dissented: "Despite the obvious role that commercial bookstores play in facilitating free expression, the Court today concludes that a closure order would raise no First Amendment concerns, apparently because it would be triggered, not by respondents' sale of books, but by the nonexpressive conduct of patrons. But the First Amendment, made applicable to the States by the Fourteenth Amendment, protects against all laws 'abridging the freedom of speech'—not just those specifically directed at expressive activity. Until today, this Court has never suggested that a State may suppress speech as much as it likes, without justification, so long as it does so through generally applicable regulations that have 'nothing to do with any expressive conduct.' * * *

"At some point, of course, the impact of state regulation on First Amendment rights become so attenuated that it is easily outweighed by the state interest. But when a State directly and substantially impairs First Amendment activities, such as by shutting down a bookstore, I believe that the State must show, at a minimum, that it has chosen the least restrictive means of pursuing its legitimate objectives. The closure of a bookstore can no more be compared to a traffic arrest of a reporter than the closure of a church could be compared to the traffic arrest of its clergyman.

"A State has a legitimate interest in forbidding sexual acts committed in public, including a bookstore. An obvious method of eliminating such acts is to arrest the patron committing them. But the statute in issue does not provide for that. Instead, it imposes absolute liability on the bookstore simply because the activity occurs on the premises. And the penalty—a mandatory 1-year closure— imposes an unnecessary burden on speech. Of course 'linking the words "sex" and "books"' is not enough to extend First Amendment protection to illegal sexual activity, but neither should it suffice to *remove* First Amendment protection from books situated near the site of such activity. The State's purpose in stopping public lewdness cannot justify such a substantial infringement of First Amendment rights. * * *

"Petitioner has not demonstrated that a less restrictive remedy would be inadequate to abate the nuisance. The Court improperly attempts to shift to the bookseller the responsibility for finding an alternative site. But surely the Court would not uphold a city ordinance banning all public debate on the theory

From New York's perspective, the question is not "who is aimed at but who is hit." See *People ex rel. Arcara v. Cloud Books, Inc.,* 68

N.Y.2d 553, 510 N.Y.S.2d 844, 503 N.E.2d 492 (1986).

that the residents could move somewhere else. [Because] the statute is not narrowly tailored to further the asserted governmental interest, it is unconstitutional as applied to respondents."[c]

SECTION: WEALTH AND THE POLITICAL PROCESS: CONCERNS FOR EQUALITY

CON LAW: P. 1025, after note 1

AMER CON: P. 789, after note 1

RTS & LIB: P. 692, after note 1

Colorado makes it a felony to pay persons to circulate initiative or referendum petitions. The purposes of the provision are to assure that a ballot measure has a sufficiently broad base of popular support to warrant its placement on the ballot and to eliminate an incentive to produce fraudulent signatures. Constitutional? See *Meyer v. Grant,* ___ U.S. ___, 108 S.Ct. 1886, 100 L.Ed.2d 425 (1988) (invalidating statute: "[T]he circulation of a petition involves the type of interactive communication concerning political change that is appropriately described as 'core political speech' ").

CON LAW: P. 1026, after note 6

AMER CON: P. 790, after note 6

RTS & LIB: P. 693, after note 6

FEC v. MASSACHUSETTS CITIZENS FOR LIFE, INC., 479 U.S. 238, 107 S.Ct. 616, 93 L.Ed.2d 539 (1986) per BRENNAN, J., held that 2 U.S.C. § 441b, prohibiting corporations from using their treasury funds for the purpose of influencing any election for federal office, was unconstitutional as applied to independent expenditures of a nonprofit, nonstock corporation. Massachusetts Citizens for Life, Inc. ("MCFL"), during the years 1973–78 periodically (three to eight times a year) distributed a newsletter to recipients ranging from approximately two to six thousand in number. In September, 1978, MCFL published a Special Election Edition. Nearly 6,000 copies were mailed to past contributors; 50,674 copies were mailed to people regarded by MCFL as sympathetic; and some 44,000 copies were apparently made available to other non-members. The publication listed the positions of some 400 state and federal candidates on three "pro-life" issues, urged voters to vote for "pro-life" candidates and provided photographs of the thirteen most favorably regarded candidates. Next to the exhortation to vote pro-life, the publication recited that "This special election edition does not represent an endorsement of any particular candidate." Unpersuaded by this disclaimer, the Court affirmed the Court of Appeals finding that the publication constituted an expenditure by MCFL for the purpose of influencing an election for federal office.

The Court rejected MCFL's contention that its Special Election Edition was a press publication within the meaning of the Federal Elections Campaign Act.[a]: "We need not decide whether the regular MCFL newsletter is exempt under [the press] provision, because, even assuming that it is, the 'Special Edition' cannot be considered comparable to any single issue of the newsletter. It was not pub-

---

c. Compare *Ft. Wayne Brooks, Inc. v. Indiana,* p. 191 of this Supplement.

a. 2 U.S.C. § 431(9)(B)(i) provides a press exemption for "any news story, commentary, or editorial distributed through the facilities of any ∗ ∗ ∗ newspaper, magazine, or other periodical publication, unless such facilities are owned or controlled by any political party, political committee, or candidate."

lished through the facilities of the regular newsletter, but by a staff which prepared no previous or subsequent newsletters. It was not distributed to the newsletter's regular audience, but to a group twenty times the size of that audience, most of whom were members of the public who had never received the newsletter. No characteristic of the Edition associated it in any way with the normal MCFL publication. The MCFL masthead did not appear on the flyer, and, despite an apparent belated attempt to make it appear otherwise, the Edition contained no volume and issue number identifying it as one in a continuing series of issues.

"MCFL protests that determining the scope of the press exemption by reference to such factors inappropriately focuses on superficial considerations of form. However, it is precisely such factors that in combination permit the distinction of campaign flyers from regular publications. We regard such an inquiry as essential, since we cannot accept the notion that the distribution of such flyers by entities that happen to publish newsletters automatically entitles such organizations to the press exemption. A contrary position would open the door for those corporations and unions with in-house publications to engage in unlimited spending directly from their treasuries to distribute campaign material to the general public, thereby eviscerating § 441b's prohibition.

"In sum, we hold that MCFL's publication and distribution of the Special Election Edition is in violation of § 441b. We therefore turn to the constitutionality of that provision as applied to appellee."

The Court held that § 441b as applied to the independent expenditures of MCFL infringed "protected speech without a compelling justification for such infringement": "The Commission [relies] on the long history of regulation of corporate political activity as support for the application of § 441b to MCFL. [We] have described that rationale in recent opinions as the need to restrict 'the influence of political war chests funneled through the corporate form;' to 'eliminate the effect of aggregated wealth on federal elections;' to curb the political influence of 'those who exercise control over large aggregations of capital;' and to regulate the 'substantial aggregations of wealth amassed by the special advantages which go with the corporate form of organization.'

"This concern over the corrosive influence of concentrated corporate wealth reflects the conviction that it is important to protect the integrity of the marketplace of political ideas. It acknowledges the wisdom of Justice Holmes' observation that 'the ultimate good desired is better reached by free trade in ideas—that the best test of truth is the power of the thought to get itself accepted in the competition of the [market].' Abrams.

"Direct corporate spending on political activity raises the prospect that resources amassed in the economic marketplace may be used to provide an unfair advantage in the political marketplace. Political 'free trade' does not necessarily require that all who participate in the political marketplace do so with exactly equal resources. See NCPAC (invalidating limits on independent spending by political committees); Buckley (striking down expenditure limits in 1971 Campaign Act). Relative availability of funds is after all a rough barometer of public support. The resources in the treasury of a business corporation, however, are not an indication of popular support for the corporation's political ideas. They reflect instead the economically motivated decisions of investors and customers. The availability of these resources may make a corporation a formidable political presence, even though the power of the corporation may be no reflection of the power of its ideas.

"By requiring that corporate independent expenditures be financed through a political committee expressly established to engage in campaign spending, § 441b seeks to prevent this threat to the political marketplace. [Regulation] of corporate political activity thus has reflected concern not about use of the corporate form *per se*, but about the potential for unfair deployment of wealth for political purposes.[12] Groups such as MCFL, however, do not pose that danger of corruption. MCFL was formed to disseminate political ideas, not to amass capital. The resources it has available are not a function of its success in the economic marketplace, but its popularity in the political marketplace.[b] * * *

"The Commission next argues in support of § 441b that it prevents an organization from using an individual's money for purposes that the individual may not support. We acknowledged the legitimacy of this concern as to the dissenting stockholder and union member in *National Right to Work*. But such persons, as noted, contribute investment funds or union dues for economic gain, and do not necessarily authorize the use of their money for political ends. Furthermore, because such individuals depend on the organization for income or for a job, it is not enough to tell them that any unhappiness with the use of their money can be redressed simply by leaving the corporation or the union. It was thus wholly reasonable for Congress to require the establishment of a separate political fund to which persons can make voluntary contributions.

"This rationale for regulation is not compelling with respect to independent expenditures by appellee. Individuals who contribute to appellee are fully aware of its political purposes, and in fact contribute precisely because they support those purposes. It is true that a contributor may not be aware of the exact use to which his or her money ultimately may be put, or the specific candidate that it may be used to support. However, individuals contribute to a political organization in part because they regard such a contribution as a more effective means of advocacy than spending the money under their own personal direction. Any contribution therefore necessarily involves at least some degree of delegation of authority to use such funds in a manner that best serves the shared political purposes of the organization and contributor. In addition, an individual desiring more direct control over the use of his or her money can simply earmark the contribution for a specific purpose, an option whose availability does not depend on the applicability of § 441b. Finally, a contributor dissatisfied with how funds are used can simply stop contributing.

"[We] acknowledge the legitimacy of Congress' concern that organizations that amass great wealth in the economic marketplace not gain unfair advantage in the political marketplace.

"Regardless of whether that concern is adequate to support application of § 441b to commercial enterprises, a question not before us, that justification does not extend uniformly to all corporations. Some corporations have features more akin to voluntary political associations than business firms, and therefore should not have to bear burdens on independent spending solely because of their incorporated status.

"In particular, MCFL has three features essential to our holding that it may not constitutionally be bound by § 441b's restriction on independent spending. *First*, it was formed for the express purpose of promoting political ideas, and

---

12. The regulation imposed as a result of this concern is of course distinguishable from the complete foreclosure of any opportunity for political speech that we invalidated in the state referendum context in *Bellotti*.

b. In distinguishing *National Right to Work*, the Court observed that "restrictions on contributions require less compelling justification than restrictions on independent spending."

cannot engage in business activities. If political fundraising events are expressly denominated as requests for contributions that will be used for political purposes, including direct expenditures, these events cannot be considered business activities. This ensures that political resources reflect political support. *Second,* it has no shareholders or other persons affiliated so as to have a claim on its assets or earnings. This ensures that persons connected with the organization will have no economic disincentive for disassociating with it if they disagree with its political activity.[13] *Third,* MCFL was not established by a business corporation or a labor union, and it is its policy not to accept contributions from such entities. This prevents such corporations from serving as conduits for the type of direct spending that creates a threat to the political marketplace." [c]

REHNQUIST, C.J., joined by White, Blackmun, and Stevens, JJ., concurred with the view that MCFL's Special Edition violated § 441b, but dissented on the constitutional issue: "I do not dispute that the threat from corporate political activity will vary depending on the particular characteristics of a given corporation; it is obvious that large and successful corporations with resources to fund a political war chest constitute a more potent threat to the political process than less successful business corporations or nonprofit corporations. It may also be that those supporting some nonbusiness corporations will identify with the corporations' political views more frequently than the average shareholder of General Motors would support the political activities of that corporation. These distinctions among corporations, however, are 'distinctions in degree' that do not amount to 'differences in kind.' *Buckley.* As such, they are more properly drawn by the legislature than by the judiciary. See *Buckley.* * * *

"The basically legislative character of the Court's decision is dramatically illustrated by its effort to carve out a constitutional niche for '[g]roups such as MCFL.' The three-part test gratuitously announced in today's dicta adds to a well-defined prohibition a vague and barely adumbrated exception certain to result in confusion and costly litigation." [d]

PACIFIC GAS & ELECTRIC CO. v. PUBLIC UTILITIES COMM'N

475 U.S. 1, 106 S.Ct. 903, 89 L.Ed.2d 1 (1986).

JUSTICE POWELL announced the judgment of the Court and delivered an opinion in which the CHIEF JUSTICE, JUSTICE BRENNAN, and JUSTICE O'CONNOR joined.

13. This restriction does not deprive such organizations of "members" that can be solicited for donations to a separate segregated fund that makes contributions to candidates, a fund that, under our decision in *National Right to Work Committee,* must be established by all corporations wishing to make such candidate contributions. *National Right to Work* requires that "members" have either a "financial or *organizational* attachment" to the corporation. Our decision today merely states that a corporation that does not have persons affiliated *financially* must fall outside § 441b's prohibition on direct expenditures if it also has the other two characteristics possessed by MCFL that we discuss in text.

c. In a section of the opinion joined only by Marshall, Powell, and Scalia, JJ., Brennan, J., argued that the various provisions including the reporting and disclosure requirements of the Act might create disincentives for an organization like MCFL to speak. O'Connor, J., joined most of the Court's opinion, but concurred to argue that the burden of the disclosure requirements was not undue.

d. In a brief separate statement, White, J., reaffirmed his commitment to the views he had previously expressed in *Buckley, Bellotti,* and *NCPAC.*

The question in this case is whether the California Public Utilities Commission may require a privately owned utility company to include in its billing envelopes speech of a third party with which the utility disagrees.

For the past 62 years, appellant Pacific Gas and Electric Company has distributed a newsletter in its monthly billing envelope. Appellant's newsletter, called *Progress*, reaches over three million customers. It has included political editorials, feature stories on matters of public interest, tips on energy conservation, and straightforward information about utility services and bills.[1]

In 1980, appellee Toward Utility Rate Normalization (TURN), an intervenor in a ratemaking proceeding before California's Public Utilities Commission, another appellee, urged the Commission to forbid appellant to use the billing envelopes to distribute political editorials, on the ground that the appellant's customers should not bear the expense of appellant's own political speech. The Commission decided that the envelope space that appellant had used to disseminate *Progress* is the property of the ratepayers.[3] This "extra space" was defined as "the space remaining in the billing envelope, after inclusion of the monthly bill and any required legal notices, for inclusion of other materials up to such total envelope weight as would not result in any additional postage cost."

In an effort to apportion this "extra space" between appellant and its customers, the Commission permitted TURN to use the "extra space" four times a year for the next two years. During these months, appellant may use any space not used by TURN and it may include additional materials if it pays any extra postage. [T]he Commission determined that ratepayers would benefit from permitting TURN to use the extra space in the billing envelopes to raise funds and to communicate with ratepayers: "Our goal [is] to change the present system to one which uses the extra space more efficiently for the ratepayers' benefit. It is reasonable to assume that the ratepayers will benefit more from exposure to a variety of views than they will from only that of PG&E." The Commission concluded that appellant could have no interest in excluding TURN's message from the billing envelope since appellant does not own the space that message would fill. The Commission placed no limitations on what TURN or appellant could say in the envelope, except that TURN is required to state that its messages are not those of appellant. The Commission reserved the right to grant other groups access to the envelopes in the future.[5] * * *

Compelled access like that ordered in this case both penalizes the expression of particular points of view and forces speakers to alter their speech to conform

1. For example, the December 1984 issue of *Progress* included a story on appellant's "automatic payment" and "balanced payment" plans, an article instructing ratepayers on how to weatherstrip their homes, recipes for holiday dishes, and a feature on appellant's efforts to help bald eagles in the Pit River area of California. * * *

3. The Commission summarized its reasoning as follows: "[E]nvelope and postage costs and any other costs of mailing bills are a necessary part of providing utility service to the customer. [However,] due to the nature of postal rates * * * extra space exists in these billing envelopes. * * * Mindful that the extra space is an artifact generated with ratepayer funds, and is not an intended or necessary item of rate base, and that the only alternative treatment would unjustly enrich

PG&E and simultaneously deprive the ratepayers of the value of that space, we concluded that the extra space in the billing envelope 'is properly considered as ratepayer property.'"

5. The Commission has already *denied* access to at least one group based on the content of its speech. The Commission denied the application of a taxpayer group—the "Committee of More than One Million Taxpayers to Save Proposition 13"—on the ground that that group neither wished to participate in Commission proceedings nor alleged that its use of the billing envelope space would improve consumer participation in those proceedings. The record does not reveal whether any other groups have sought access to the billing envelopes.

with an agenda they do not set. These impermissible effects are not remedied by the Commission's definition of the relevant property rights.

This Court has previously considered the question whether compelling a private corporation to provide a forum for views other than its own may infringe the corporation's freedom of speech. *Miami Herald Publishing Co. v. Tornillo;* see also *PruneYard Shopping Center v. Robins.*[6]

The concerns that caused us to invalidate the compelled access rule in *Tornillo* apply to appellant as well as to the institutional press.[7] See *First National Bank of Boston v. Bellotti.* Cf. *Lovell v. Griffin.* Just as the state is not free to "tell a newspaper in advance what it can print and what it cannot," *Pittsburgh Press,* the State is not free either to restrict appellant's speech to certain topics or views or to force appellant to respond to views that others may hold. Under *Tornillo* a forced access rule that would accomplish these purposes indirectly is similarly forbidden.

[*PruneYard*] is not to the contrary. [This] Court held that [a] shopping center did not have a constitutionally protected right to exclude [pamphleteers] from the area open to the public at large. Notably absent from *PruneYard* was any concern that access to this area might affect the shopping center owner's exercise of his own right to speak: the owner did not even allege that he objected to the content of the pamphlets; nor was the access right content-based. *PruneYard* thus does not undercut the proposition that forced associations that burden protected speech are impermissible.[8]

The Commission's order is inconsistent with these principles. The order does not simply award access to the public at large; rather, it discriminates on the basis of the viewpoints of the selected speakers. Two of the acknowledged purposes of the access order are to offer the public a greater variety of views in appellant's billing envelope, and to assist groups (such as TURN) that challenge appellant in the Commission's ratemaking proceedings in raising funds. Access to the envelopes thus is not content-neutral. [Access] is limited to persons or groups—such as TURN—who disagree with appellant's views as expressed in *Progress* and who oppose appellant in Commission proceedings.

Such one-sidedness impermissibly burdens appellant's own expression. *Tornillo* illustrates the point. Access to the newspaper in that case was content-based in two senses: (i) it was triggered by a particular category of newspaper

---

6. This Court has sustained a limited government-enforced right of access to broadcast media. *Red Lion Broadcasting Co. v. FCC.* Cf. *Columbia Broadcasting System, Inc. v. Democratic National Committee.* Appellant's billing envelopes do not, however, present the same constraints that justify the result in *Red Lion*: "[A] broadcaster communicates through use of a scarce, publicly owned resource. No person can broadcast without a license, whereas all persons are free to send correspondence to private homes through the mails." *Consolidated Edison Co. v. Public Service Comm'n of N. Y.*

7. Unlike the right-of-reply statute at issue in *Tornillo,* the Commission's order does not require appellant to place TURN's message in appellant's newsletter. Instead, the Commission ordered appellant to place TURN's message in appellant's envelope four months out of the year. Like the Miami Herald, however,

appellant is still required to carry speech with which it disagreed, and might well feel compelled to reply or limit its own speech in response to TURN's.

The Court's opinion in *Tornillo* emphasizes that the right-of-reply statute impermissibly deterred protected speech. In the last paragraph of the opinion, the Court concluded that an *independent* ground for invalidating the statute was its effect on editors' allocation of scarce newspaper space. That discussion in no way suggested that the State was free otherwise to burden the newspaper's speech as long as the actual paper on which the newspaper was printed was not invaded.

8. In addition, the relevant forum in *PruneYard* was the open area of the shopping center into which the general public was invited. This area was, almost by definition, peculiarly public in nature. * * *

speech, and (ii) it was awarded only to those who disagreed with the newspaper's views. The Commission's order is not, in *Tornillo*'s words, a "content-based penalty" in the first sense, because TURN's access to appellant's envelopes is not conditioned on any particular expression by appellant. But because access is awarded only to those who disagree with appellant's views and who are hostile to appellant's interests, appellant must contend with the fact that whenever it speaks out on a given issue, it may be forced—at TURN's discretion—to help disseminate hostile views. Appellant "might well conclude" that, under these circumstances, "the safe course is to avoid controversy," thereby reducing the free flow of information and ideas that the First Amendment seeks to promote.

Appellant does not, of course, have the right to be free from vigorous debate. But it *does* have the right to be free from government restrictions that abridge its own rights in order to "enhance the relative voice" of its opponents. *Buckley v. Valeo.* The Commission's order requires *appellant* to assist in disseminating *TURN*'s views; it does not equally constrain both sides of the debate about utility regulation.[10] This kind of favoritism goes well beyond the fundamentally content-neutral subsidies that we sustained in *Buckley* and in *Regan v. Taxation With Representation.* See *Buckley* (sustaining funding of general election campaign expenses of major party candidates); *Regan* (sustaining tax deduction for contributors to veterans' organizations). Unlike these permissible government subsidies of speech, the Commission's order identifies a favored speaker "based on the identity of the interests that [the speaker] may represent," *Bellotti,* and forces the speaker's opponent—not the taxpaying public—to assist in disseminating the speaker's message. Such a requirement necessarily burdens the expression of the disfavored speaker.

The Commission's access order also impermissibly requires appellant to associate with speech with which appellant may disagree.[11] * * *.[12] [Especially] since TURN has been given access in part to create a multiplicity of views in the envelopes, there can be little doubt that appellant will feel compelled to

10. Justice Stevens analogizes this aspect of the Commission's order to Securities and Exchange Commission regulations that require management to transmit proposals of minority shareholders in shareholder mailings. The analogy is inappropriate. The regulations Justice Stevens cites differ from the Commission's order in two important ways. First, they allocate shareholder property between management and certain groups of shareholders. Management has no interest in corporate property except such interest as derives from the shareholders; therefore, regulations that limit management's ability to exclude some shareholders' views from corporate communications do not infringe corporate First Amendment rights. Second, the regulations govern speech by a corporation *to itself.* *Bellotti* and *Consolidated Edison* establish that the Constitution protects corporations' right to speak to the public based on the informational value of corporate speech. Rules that define how corporations govern themselves do not limit the range of information that the corporation may contribute to the public debate. The Commission's order, by contrast, burdens appellant's right freely to speak to the public at large.

11. The presence of a disclaimer on TURN's messages does not suffice to eliminate the impermissible pressure on appellant to respond to TURN's speech. The disclaimer serves only to avoid giving readers the mistaken impression that TURN's words are really those of appellant. It does nothing to reduce the risk that appellant will be forced to respond when there is strong disagreement with the substance of TURN's message.

12. The Commission's order is thus readily distinguishable from orders requiring appellant to carry various legal notices, such as notices of upcoming Commission proceedings or of changes in the way rates are calculated. The State, of course, has substantial leeway in determining appropriate information disclosure requirements for business corporations. See *Zauderer.* Nothing in *Zauderer* suggests, however, that the State is equally free to require corporations to carry the messages of third parties, where the messages themselves are biased against or are expressly contrary to the corporation's views.

respond to arguments and allegations made by TURN in its messages to appellant's customers.

That kind of forced response is antithetical to the free discussion that the First Amendment seeks to foster. *Harper & Row.* See also *Wooley v. Maynard.*[13] For corporations as for individuals, the choice to speak includes within it the choice of what not to say. [Were] the government freely able to compel corporate speakers to propound political messages with which they disagree, this protection would be empty, for the government could require speakers to affirm in one breath that which they deny in the next. * * *

The Commission has emphasized that appellant's customers own the "extra space" in the billing envelopes. * * *

The Commission expressly declined to hold that under California law appellant's customers own the entire billing envelopes and everything contained therein. [The] envelopes themselves, the bills, and *Progress* all remain appellant's property. The Commission's access order thus clearly requires appellant to use *its* property as a vehicle for spreading a message with which it disagrees. In *Wooley,* we held that New Hampshire could not require two citizens to display a slogan on their license plates and thereby "use their private property as a 'mobile billboard' for the State's ideological message." The "private property" that was used to spread the unwelcome message was the automobile, not the license plates. Similarly, the Commission's order requires appellant to use its property—the billing envelopes—to distribute the message of another. This is so whoever is deemed to own the "extra space."

A different conclusion would necessarily imply that our decision in *Tornillo* rested on the Miami Herald's ownership of the space that would have been used to print candidate replies. Nothing in *Tornillo* suggests that the result would have been different had the Florida Supreme Court decided that the newspaper space needed to print candidates' replies was the property of the newspaper's readers, or had the court ordered the Miami Herald to distribute inserts owned and prepared by the candidates together with its newspapers. The constitutional difficulty with the right-of-reply statute was that it required the newspaper to disseminate a message with which the newspaper disagreed. This difficulty did not depend on whether the particular paper on which the replies were printed belonged to the newspaper or to the candidate.

Appellees' argument suffers from the same constitutional defect. The Commission's order forces appellant to disseminate TURN's speech in envelopes that appellant owns and that bear appellant's return address. Such forced association with potentially hostile views burdens the expression of views different from TURN's and risks forcing appellant to speak where it would prefer to remain silent. Those effects do not depend on who "owns" the "extra space."[15]

* * *[a]

---

13. As we stated in *Wooley,* "[a] system which secures the right to proselytize religious, political, and ideological causes must also guarantee the concomitant right to decline to foster such concepts."

15. * * * "Extra space" exists not only in billing envelopes but also on billboards, bulletin boards, and sides of buildings and motor vehicles. Under the Commission's reasoning, a State could force business proprietors of such items to use the space for the dissemination of speech the proprietor op-

poses. At least where access to such fora is granted on the basis of the speakers' viewpoints, the public's ownership of the "extra space" does not nullify the First Amendment rights of the owner of the property from which that space derives.

a. Powell, J., denied that the Commission's order was a narrowly tailored means of serving a compelling state interest. He observed that the state interest in effective ratemaking proceedings and the state interest in making a variety of views available to the customers

JUSTICE BLACKMUN took no part in the consideration or decision of this case.

CHIEF JUSTICE BURGER, concurring.

I join Justice Powell's opinion, but think we need not go beyond the authority of *Wooley* to decide this case. I would not go beyond the central question presented by this case, which is the infringement of Pacific's right to be free from forced association with views with which it disagrees. I would also rely on that part of *Tornillo* holding that a forced right of reply violates a newspaper's right to be free from forced dissemination of views it would not voluntarily disseminate, just as we held that Maynard must be free from being forced by the State to disseminate views with which he disagreed. To compel Pacific to mail messages for others cannot be distinguished from compelling it to carry the messages of others on its trucks, its buildings, or other property used in the conduct of its business. For purposes of this case, those properties cannot be distinguished from property like the mailing envelopes acquired by Pacific from its income and resources.

JUSTICE MARSHALL, concurring in the judgment.

* * * Two significant differences between the State's grant of access in this case and the grant of access in *PruneYard* lead me to find a constitutional barrier here that I did not find in the earlier case.

The first difference is the degree of intrusiveness of the permitted access.

[In] the present case [appellant] has never opened up its billing envelope to the use of the public.[1] Appellant has not abandoned its right to exclude others from its property to the degree that the shopping center owner had done in *PruneYard*. Were appellant to use its billing envelope as a sort of community billboard, regularly carrying the messages of third parties, its desire to exclude a particular speaker would be deserving of lesser solicitude. As matters stand, however, appellant has issued no invitation to the general public to use its billing envelope, for speech or for any other purpose.[2] Moreover, the shopping

could be advanced by means that did not burden the utility company's expression. The lack of content neutrality was further said to undercut any contention that the Commission's order furthered the interest in making a variety of views available and also disposed of the suggestion that the Commission's order was a valid time, place, or manner regulation.

1. The State seizes upon appellant's status as a regulated monopoly in order to argue that the inclusion of postage and other billing costs in the utility's rate base demonstrates that these items "belong" to the public, which has paid for them. However, a consumer who purchases food in a grocery store is "paying" for the store's rent, heat, electricity, wages, etc., but no one would seriously argue that the consumer thereby acquires a property interest in the store. That the utility passes on its overhead costs to rate payers at a rate fixed by law rather than the market cannot affect the utility's ownership of its property, nor its right to use that property for expressive purposes, see *Consolidated Edison Co. v. Public Service Comm'n*. The State could have concluded that the public interest would be best served by state ownership of utilities. Having chosen to keep utilities in private hands, how-

ever, the State may not arbitrarily appropriate property for the use of third parties by stating that the public has "paid" for the property by paying utility bills.

I hasten to add that nothing in this opinion nor, as I understand it, the plurality's opinion, addresses the issue whether the State may exclude the cost of mailing *Progress* from petitioner's rate base. Indeed, appellant concedes that the State may force its shareholders to bear those costs.

2. The State also argues that it frequently requires appellant to carry messages concerning utility ratemaking and the rights of utility consumers. These messages, however, do not include political speech, and are directly relevant to commercial transactions between the ratepayer and the utility. The State's interest in requiring appellant to carry such messages is therefore particularly compelling. Somewhat analogously, the State could not argue that, because it may demand access for the State's agents to a private home to monitor compliance with health or safety regulations, it may also grant access to third parties for nongovernmental purposes.

center in *PruneYard* bore a strong resemblance to the streets and parks that are traditional public forums. People routinely gathered there, at the owner's invitation, and engaged in a wide variety of activities. Adding speech to the list of those activities did not in any great way change the complexion of the property. The same is not true in this case.

The second difference between this case and *PruneYard* is that the State has chosen to give TURN a right to speak at the expense of appellant's ability to use the property in question as a forum for the exercise of its own First Amendment rights. While the shopping center owner in *PruneYard* wished to be free of unwanted expression, he nowhere alleged that his own expression was hindered in the slightest. In contrast, the present case involves a forum of inherently limited scope. By appropriating, four times a year, the space in appellant's envelope that appellant would otherwise use for its own speech, the State has necessarily curtailed petitioner's use of its own forum. The regulation in this case, therefore, goes beyond a mere infringement of appellant's desire to remain silent.

While the interference with appellant's speech is, concededly, very slight, the State's justification—the subsidization of another speaker chosen by the State—is insufficient to sustain even that minor burden. We have held that the State may use its own resources for subsidization, *Regan v. Taxation With Representation,* but that interest, standing alone, cannot justify interference with the speech of others. See *Buckley; Bellotti.*

[In] the present case, the State has redefined a property right in the extra space in appellant's billing envelope in such a way as to achieve a result— burdening the speech of one party in order to enhance the speech of another— that the First Amendment disallows. In doing so, moreover, it has sanctioned an intrusion onto appellant's property that exceeds the slight incursion permitted in *PruneYard.* Under these circumstances, I believe that the State has crossed the boundary between constitutionally permissible and impermissible redefinitions of private property. * * *

JUSTICE REHNQUIST, with whom JUSTICE WHITE and JUSTICE STEVENS join as to Part I, dissenting. * * *

I. This Court established in *Bellotti* that the First Amendment prohibits the Government from *directly* suppressing the affirmative speech of corporations. A newspaper publishing corporation's right to express itself freely is also implicated by governmental action that penalizes speech, see *Tornillo,* because the deterrent effect of a penalty is very much like direct suppression. Our cases cannot be squared, however, with the view that the First Amendment prohibits governmental action that only *indirectly* and *remotely* affects a speaker's contribution to the overall mix of information available to society. * * *

Of course, the First Amendment does prohibit governmental action affecting the mix of information available to the public if the effect of the action approximates that of direct content-based suppression of speech. [*Tornillo*] held that a governmentally imposed "penalty" for the exercise of protected speech is sufficiently like direct suppression to trigger heightened First Amendment scrutiny. * * *

Although the plurality draws its deterrence rationale from *Tornillo,* it does not even attempt to characterize the right of access as a "penalty"; indeed, such a Procrustean effort would be doomed to failure. Instead, the plurality stretches *Tornillo* to stand for the general proposition that the First Amendment prohibits any regulation that deters a corporation from engaging in some expressive behavior. But the deterrent effect of any statute is an empirical question of degree. When the potential deterrent effect of a particular state law is remote and speculative, the law simply is not subject to heightened First Amendment scrutiny. The plurality does not adequately explain how the potential deterrent effect of the right of access here is sufficiently immediate and direct to warrant strict scrutiny. While a statutory penalty, like the right of reply statute in *Tornillo*, may sufficiently deter speech to trigger such heightened First Amendment scrutiny, the right of access here will not have such an effect on PG&E's incentives to speak.

The record does not support the inference that PUC issued its order to penalize PG&E because of the content of its inserts or because PG&E included the inserts in its billing envelopes in the first place. The order does not prevent PG&E from using the billing envelopes in the future to distribute inserts whenever it wishes. Nor does its vitality depend on whether PG&E includes inserts in any future billing envelopes. Moreover, the central reason for the access order—to provide for an effective ratepayer voice—would not vary in importance if PG&E had never distributed the inserts or ceased distributing them tomorrow. The most that can be said about the connection between the inserts and the order is that the existence of the inserts quite probably brought to TURN's attention the possibility of requesting access.

Nor does the access order create any cognizable risk of deterring PG&E from expressing its views in the most candid fashion. Unlike the reply statute in *Tornillo*, which conditioned access upon discrete instances of certain expression, the right of access here bears no relationship to PG&E's future conduct. PG&E cannot prevent the access by remaining silent or avoiding discussion of controversial subjects. The plurality suggests, however, that the possibility of minimizing the undesirable content of TURN's speech may induce PG&E to adopt a strategy of avoiding certain topics in hopes that TURN will not think to address them on its own. But this is an extremely implausible prediction. The success of such a strategy would depend on any group given access being little more than a reactive organization. TURN or any other group eventually given access will likely address the controversial subjects in spite of PG&E's silence. I therefore believe that PG&E will have no incentive to adopt the conservative strategy. Accordingly, the right of access should not be held to trigger heightened First Amendment scrutiny on the ground that it somehow might deter PG&E's right to speak.

II. The plurality argues, however, that the right of access also implicates PG&E's right not to speak or to associate with the speech of others, thereby triggering heightened scrutiny. [There is a] fundamental flaw with the plurality's analysis. This Court has recognized that natural persons enjoy negative free speech rights because of their interest in self-expression; an individual's right not to speak or to associate with the speech of others is a component of the broader constitutional interest of natural persons in freedom of conscience. *Barnette; Wooley.* * * *

In *Tornillo*, the Court extended negative free speech rights to newspapers without much discussion. The Court stated that the right of reply statute not only deterred affirmative speech, but it "fail[ed] to clear the barriers of the First Amendment because of its intrusion into the function of editors." The Court explained that interference with "the exercise of editorial control and judgment" creates a peril for the liberty of the press like government control over "what is to go into a newspaper." The Court did not elaborate further on the justification for its holding.

Extension of the individual freedom of conscience decisions to business corporations strains the rationale of those cases beyond the breaking point. To ascribe to such artificial entities an "intellect" or "mind" for freedom of conscience purposes is to confuse metaphor with reality. Corporations generally have not played the historic role of newspapers as conveyers of individual ideas and opinion. In extending positive free speech rights to corporations, this Court drew a distinction between the First Amendment rights of corporations and those of natural persons. It recognized that corporate free speech rights do not arise because corporations, like individuals, have any interest in self-expression. It held instead that such rights are recognized as an instrumental means of furthering the First Amendment purpose of fostering a broad forum of information to facilitate self-government.

The interest in remaining isolated from the expressive activity of others, and in declining to communicate at all, is for the most part divorced from this "broad public forum" purpose of the First Amendment. The right of access here constitutes an effort to facilitate and enlarge public discussion; it therefore furthers rather than abridges First Amendment values. See *Harper & Row.* [B]ecause the interest on which the constitutional protection of corporate speech rests is the societal interest in receiving information and ideas, the constitutional interest of a corporation in not permitting the presentation of other distinct views clearly identified as those of the speaker is *de minimis.* This is especially true in the case of PG&E, which is after all a regulated public utility. Any claim it may have had to a sphere of corporate autonomy was largely surrendered to extensive regulatory authority when it was granted legal monopoly status. * * *

JUSTICE STEVENS, dissenting.

* * * The narrow question we must address is whether a state public utility commission may require the fund-raising solicitation of a consumer advocacy group to be carried in a utility billing envelope. Since the utility concedes that *it* has no right to use the extra space in the billing envelope for its own newsletter, the question is limited to whether the Commission's requirement that it be the courier for the message of a third party violates the First Amendment. In my view, this requirement differs little from regulations applied daily to a variety of commercial communications that have rarely been challenged—and to my knowledge never invalidated—on First Amendment grounds. * * *[b]

I assume that the plurality would not object to a utility commission rule dictating the format of the bill, even as to required warnings and the type size of various provisos and disclaimers.[3] Such regulation is not too different from that applicable [under federal regulations] to credit card bills, loan forms, and media advertising. I assume also the plurality would permit the Commission to require the utility to disseminate legal notices of public hearings and ratemaking proceedings written by it.[5] These compelled statements differ little from mandating disclosure of information in the bill itself, as the plurality recognizes.

b. Stevens, J., next argued that TURN had been given only a limited editorial license to explain its program, to describe pending and anticipated PG&E applications likely to have a significant effect on customers' rates and services, and to invite financial support for TURN's advocacy before the Commission. He denied that TURN had been granted the "postal equivalent of a soap box in the park."

3. Since 1919 the predecessor to the California Public Utility Commission ordered that each electric bill reprint the regulations "regarding payment of bills, disputed bills and discontinuance of service." Other States have similar requirements.

5. At various times the Commission has required that inserts be placed in billing envelopes to "explai[n] the reasons behind [a] gas

Given that the Commission can require the utility to make certain statements and to carry the Commission's own messages to its customers, it seems but a small step to acknowledge that the Commission can also require the utility to act as the conduit for a public interest group's message that bears a close relationship to the purpose of the billing envelope.[7] An analogue to this requirement appears in securities law: the Securities and Exchange Commission requires the incumbent board of directors to transmit proposals of dissident shareholders which it opposes.[8] Presumably the plurality does not doubt the constitutionality of the SEC's requirement under the First Amendment, and yet—although the analogy is far from perfect—it performs the same function as the Commission's rule by making accessible the relevant audience, whether it be shareholders investing in the corporation or consumers served by the utility, to individuals or groups with demonstrable interests in reaching that audience for certain limited and approved purposes.

If the California Public Utility Commission had taken over company buildings and vehicles for propaganda purposes, or even engaged in viewpoint discrimination among speakers desirous of sending messages via the billing envelope, I would be concerned. But nothing in this case presents problems even remotely resembling or portending the ones just mentioned. Although the plurality's holding may wisely forestall serious constitutional problems that are likely to arise in the future, I am not convinced that the order under review today has crossed the threshold of unconstitutionality. * * *

rate increase," and to "describe the components of utility costs." See *Pacific Gas & Electric Co.,* 7 P.U.C.2d 349, 518 (1981) ("By March 1, 1982, PG&E shall mail to all its customers a bill insert which describes the components of the utility's costs. The complete bill insert to be sent is given in Appendix G of this decision. Its size and form shall be approved by the Executive Director in writing prior to inclusion with any customer's bill.").

California has also enacted legislation requiring that utilities notify their customers of rate increases. These notices, which by statute must be included in utility bill envelopes, "shall state the amount of the proposed increase expressed in both dollar and percentage terms, a brief statement of the reasons the increase is required or sought, and the mailing address of commission to which any customer inquiries relative to the proposed increase [may] be directed." Other states likewise require certain service-related communications to be carried in a utility company's billing envelope.

7. Because TURN's purpose is to solicit funds to fight utility rate increases, the success of its appeal bears directly on the size of the bill which, after all, the billing envelope contains.

8. This regulation cannot be justified on the basis of the commercial character of the communication, because the Rule can and has been used to propagate purely political proposals. See, e.g., *Medical Committee for Human Rights v. SEC,* 432 F.2d 659, 662 (1970) (shareholder proposal to stop sale of napalm in part because of use in Vietnam), vacated as moot, 401 U.S. 973, 91 S.Ct. 1191, 28 L.Ed.2d 322 (1971).

Even if the SEC Rule were justified largely on the basis of the commercial character of the communication, that justification is not irrelevant in this case. The messages that the utility disseminates in its newsletter are unquestionably intended to advance the corporation's commercial interests and its objections to the public interest groups messages are based on their potentially adverse impact on the utility's ability to obtain rate increases. These commercial factors do not justify an abridgment of the utility's constitutionally protected right to communicate in *its* newsletter, but they do provide a legitimate and an adequate justification for the Commission's action in giving TURN access to the same audience that receives the utility's newsletter.

Chapter

FREEDOM OF RELIGION

SECTION: ESTABLISHMENT CLAUSE

RELIGION AND PUBLIC SCHOOLS

CON LAW: P. 1048, before note 4

AMER CON: P. 807, before note 4

RTS & LIB: P. 715, before note 4

EDWARDS v. AGUILLARD, 482 U.S. 578, 107 S.Ct. 2573, 96 L.Ed.2d 510 (1987), per BRENNAN, J., held that a Louisiana statute, which forebade "the teaching of the theory of evolution in public schools unless accompanied by instruction in 'creation science,'" "'no clear secular purpose'": "True, the Act's stated purpose is to protect academic freedom. [While] the Court is normally deferential to a State's articulation of a secular purpose, it is required that the statement of such purpose be sincere and not a sham. See *Jaffree; Stone v. Graham; Schempp.* [It] is clear from the legislative history that the purpose [was] to narrow the science curriculum. [It] is equally clear that requiring schools to teach creation science with evolution does not advance academic freedom. The Act does not grant teachers a flexibility that they did not already possess to supplement the present science curriculum with the presentation of theories, besides evolution, about the origin of life. * * *

"Furthermore, the goal of basic 'fairness' is hardly furthered by the Act's discriminatory preference for the teaching of creation science and against the teaching of evolution. While requiring that curriculum guides be developed for creation science, the Act says nothing of comparable guides for evolution. [The] Act forbids school boards to discriminate against anyone who 'chooses to be a creation-scientist' or to teach 'creationism,' but fails to protect those who choose to teach evolution or any other non-creation science theory, or who refuse to teach creation science.

"If the Louisiana legislature's purpose was solely to maximize the comprehensiveness and effectiveness of science instruction, it would have encouraged the teaching of all scientific theories about the origins of humankind. But [the] legislative history documents that the Act's primary purpose was to change the science curriculum of public schools in order to provide persuasive advantage to a particular religious doctrine that rejects the factual basis of evolution in its entirety [and that] embodies the religious belief that a supernatural creator was responsible for the creation of humankind. * * *

305

"We do not imply that a legislature could never require that scientific critiques of prevailing scientific theories be taught. [T]eaching a variety of scientific theories about the origins of humankind to school children might be validly done with the clear secular intent of enhancing the effectiveness of science instruction. But, because the primary purpose of the Creationism Act is to endorse a particular religious doctrine, the Act furthers religion in violation of the Establishment Clause." [a]

SCALIA, J., joined by Rehnquist, C.J., dissented: "Even if I agreed with the questionable premise that legislation can be invalidated under the Establishment Clause on the basis of its motivation alone, without regard to its effects, I would still find no justification for today's decision. [The] Louisiana Legislature explicitly set forth its secular purpose ('protecting academic freedom') [which] meant: *students'* freedom from *indoctrination.* The legislature wanted to ensure that students would be free to decide for themselves how life began, based upon a fair and balanced presentation of the scientific evidence. [The] legislature did not care *whether* the topic of origins was taught; it simply wished to ensure that *when* the topic was taught, students would receive 'all of the evidence.' * * *

"If one adopts the obviously intended meaning of the statutory terms 'academic freedom,' there is no basis whatever for concluding that the purpose they express is a 'sham.' To the contrary, the Act pursues that purpose plainly and consistently. It requires that, whenever the subject of origins is covered, evolution be 'taught as a theory, rather than as proven scientific fact' and that scientific evidence inconsistent with the theory of evolution (viz., 'creation science') be taught as well. Living up to its title of *'Balanced Treatment* for Creation-Science and Evolution-Science Act,' it treats the teaching of creation the same way. It does *not* mandate instruction in creation science; *forbids* teachers to present creation science 'as proven scientific fact'; and *bans* the teaching of creation science unless the theory [is] 'discredit[ed] at every turn' with the teaching of evolution. It surpasses understanding how the Court can see in this a purpose 'to restructure the science curriculum to conform with a particular religious viewpoint,' 'to provide a persuasive advantage to a particular religious doctrine,' 'to promote the theory of creation science which embodies a particular religious tenet,' and 'to endorse a particular religious doctrine.'

"[The] Louisiana legislators had been told repeatedly that creation scientists were scorned by most educators and scientists, who themselves had an almost religious faith in evolution. It is hardly surprising, then, that in seeking to achieve a balanced, 'nonindoctrinating' curriculum, the legislators protected from discrimination only those teachers whom they thought were *suffering* from discrimination. [The] two provisions respecting the development of curriculum guides are also consistent with 'academic freedom' as the Louisiana Legislature understood the term. [In] light of the unavailability of works on creation science suitable for classroom use (a fact appellees concede) and the existence of ample materials on evolution, it was entirely reasonable for the Legislature to conclude that science teachers attempting to implement the Act would need a curriculum guide on creation science, but not on evolution. [Thus,] the provisions of the Act of so much concern to the Court *support* the conclusion that the Legislature acted to advance 'academic freedom.' * * *

a. Powell, J., joined by O'Connor, J., joined the Court's opinion but wrote separately "to emphasize that nothing in the Court's opinion diminishes the traditionally broad discretion accorded state and local school officials in the selection of the public school curriculum." White, J., concurred only in the judgment, with which he agreed "unless [we] are to reconsider the Court's decisions interpreting the Establishment Clause."

"It is undoubtedly true that what prompted the Legislature to direct its attention to the misrepresentation of evolution in the schools (rather than the inaccurate presentation of other topics) was its awareness of the tension between evolution and the religious beliefs of many children. But even appellees concede that a valid secular purpose is not rendered impermissible simply because its pursuit is prompted by concern for religious sensitivities. [I] am astonished by the Court's unprecedented readiness to [disbelieve] the secular purpose set forth in the Act [and to conclude] that it is a sham enacted to conceal the legislators' violation of their oaths of office. [I] can only attribute [this] to an intellectual predisposition [and] an instinctive reaction that any governmentally imposed requirements bearing upon the teaching of evolution must be a manifestation of Christian fundamentalist repression. In this case, however, it seems to me the Court's position is the repressive one. The people of Louisiana, including those who are Christian fundamentalists, are quite entitled, as a secular matter, to have whatever scientific evidence there may be against evolution presented in their schools, just as Mr. Scopes was entitled to present whatever scientific evidence there was for it. Perhaps what the Louisiana Legislature has done is unconstitutional because there *is* no such evidence, and the scheme they have established will amount to no more than a presentation of the Book of Genesis. But we cannot say that on the evidence before us in this summary judgment context, which includes ample uncontradicted testimony that 'creation science' is a body of scientific knowledge rather than revealed belief.[b] *Infinitely less* can we say (or should we say) that the scientific evidence for evolution is so conclusive that no one could be gullible enough to believe that there is any real scientific evidence to the contrary, so that the legislation's stated purpose must be a lie. Yet that illiberal judgment, that *Scopes*-in-reverse, is ultimately the basis on which the Court's facile rejection of the Louisiana Legislature's purpose must rest. * * *

"I have to this point assumed the validity of the *Lemon* 'purpose' test. In fact, however, I think [it] is 'a constitutional theory [that] has no basis in the history of the amendment it seeks to interpret, is difficult to apply and yields unprincipled results.' *Jaffree* (Rehnquist, J., dissenting).

"Our cases interpreting and applying the purpose test have made such a maze of the Establishment Clause that even the most conscientious governmental officials can only guess what motives will be held unconstitutional. We have said essentially the following: Government may not act with the purpose of advancing religion, except when forced to do so by the Free Exercise Clause (which is now and then); or when eliminating existing governmental hostility to religion (which exists sometimes); or even when merely accommodating governmentally uninhibited religious practices, except that at some point (it is unclear where) intentional accommodation results in the fostering of religion, which is of course unconstitutional.

"[D]iscerning the subjective motivation of those enacting the statute is, to be honest, almost always an impossible task. The number of possible motivations, to begin with, is not binary, or indeed even finite. In the present case, for example, a particular legislator need not have voted for the Act either because he wanted to foster religion or because he wanted to improve education. He

---

b. "The only evidence in the record [defining] 'creation science' is found in five affidavits filed by appellants. In those affidavits, two scientists, a philosopher, a theologian, and an educator, all of whom claim extensive knowledge of creation science, swear that it is essentially a collection of scientific data supporting the theory that the physical universe and life within it appeared suddenly and have not changed substantially since appearing."

may have thought the bill would provide jobs for his district, or may have wanted to make amends with a faction of his party he had alienated on another vote, or he may have been a close friend of the bill's sponsor, or he may have been repaying a favor he owed the Majority Leader, or he may have hoped the Governor would appreciate his vote and make a fundraising appearance for him, or he may have been pressured to vote for a bill he disliked by a wealthy contributor or by a flood of constituent mail, or he may have been seeking favorable publicity, or he may have been reluctant to hurt the feelings of a loyal staff member who worked on the bill, or he may have been settling an old score with a legislator who opposed the bill, or he may have been mad at his wife who opposed the bill, or he may have been intoxicated and utterly *un*motivated when the vote was called, or he may have accidentally voted 'yes' instead of 'no,' or, of course, he may have had (and very likely did have) a combination of some of the above and many other motivations. To look for *the sole purpose* of even a single legislator is probably to look for something that does not exist."

FINANCIAL AID TO RELIGION

CON LAW: P. 1067, add to last ¶ of fn. 10

AMER CON: P. 815, add to last ¶ of fn. 10

RTS & LIB: P. 734, add to last ¶ of fn. 10

[In BENDER v. WILLIAMSPORT AREA SCHOOL DIST., 475 U.S. 534, 106 S.Ct. 1326, 89 L.Ed.2d 501 (1986), in which the Court did not reach the merits, Burger, C.J., and White, Powell and Rehnquist, JJ., expressed the view that "*Widmar* clearly controls the resolution of this case."]

CON LAW: P. 1074, before *Grand Rapids*

AMER CON: P. 822, at end

RTS & LIB: P. 741, before *Grand Rapids*

TEXAS MONTHLY, INC. v. BULLOCK, ___ U.S. ___, 109 S.Ct. 890, 103 L.Ed.2d 1 (1989), held violative of the establishment clause a Texas sales tax exemption for "periodicals that are published or distributed by a religious faith and that consist wholly of writings promulgating the teaching of the faith and books that consist wholly of writings sacred to a religious faith." BRENNAN, J., joined by Marshall and Stevens, JJ., reasoned that *Walz, Widmar,* and *Mueller* "emphasized that the benefits derived by religious organizations flowed to a large number of nonreligious groups as well": "However, when government directs a subsidy exclusively to religious organizations that is not required by the Free Exercise Clause and that either burdens nonbeneficiaries markedly or cannot reasonably be seen as removing a significant state-imposed deterrent to the free exercise of religion, as Texas has done, it 'provide[s] unjustifiable awards of assistance to religious organizations' and cannot but 'conve[y] a message of endorsement' to slighted members of the community. This is particularly true where, as here, the subsidy is targeted at writings that *promulgate* the teachings of religious faiths. It is difficult to view Texas' narrow exemption as anything but state sponsorship of religious belief [which] lacks a secular objective."

BLACKMUN, J., joined by O'Connor, J., concurred: "[A] tax exemption *limited* to the sale of religious literature * * * offends our most basic understanding of what the Establishment Clause is all about." [a]

a. White, J., concurred on the ground that the law "discriminates on the basis of the content of publications [and] is plainly forbid-den by the Press Clause of the First Amendment [under] *Arkansas Writer's Project v. Ragland,*" p. 285 of this Supplement.

SCALIA, J., joined by Rehnquist, C.J., and Kennedy, J., pointing out that "at least 45 state [tax] codes contain exemptions for religious groups without analogous exemptions for other types of nonprofit institutions," dissented: *Walz* "is utterly dispositive" and Brennan, J.'s distinction of *Walz* "is not a plausible reading of the opinion. [*Walz*] is just one of a long line of cases in which we have recognized that the government may (and sometimes must) accommodate religious practices and that it may do so without violating the Establishment Clause." [b]

CON LAW: P. 1083, before note (b)

AMER CON: P. 831, at end of note 2(a)

RTS & LIB: P. 750, before note (b)

WITTERS v. WASHINGTON DEP'T OF SERVICES, 474 U.S. 481, 106 S.Ct. 748, 88 L.Ed.2d 846 (1986), per MARSHALL, J.—focusing on the second prong of the *Lemon* test—unanimously upheld "assistance under a state vocational rehabilitation assistance program to a blind person studying at a Christian college and seeking to become a pastor, missionary, or youth director": Assistance "is paid directly to the student, who transmits it to the educational institution of his or her choice. Any aid [that] ultimately flows to religious institutions does so only as a result of the genuinely independent and private choices of aid recipients. Washington's program is 'made available generally without regard to the sectarian-nonsectarian, or public-nonpublic nature of the institution benefitted,' and is in no way skewed towards religion. [Further], nothing in the record indicates that [any] significant portion of the aid expended under the Washington program as a whole will end up flowing to religious education. [No] evidence has been presented indicating that any other person has ever sought to finance religious education or activity pursuant to the State's program."

POWELL, J., joined by Burger, C.J., and Rehnquist, J., concurred "to emphasize that *Mueller* strongly supports the result": "state programs that are wholly neutral in offering educational assistance to a class defined without reference to religion do not violate the second part of the *Lemon* test, because any aid to religion results from the private choices of individual beneficiaries." O'CONNOR, J., concurred, specifically subscribing to this statement. WHITE, J., concurred "with respect to the relevance of *Mueller*," as stated by Powell, J.

CON LAW: P. 1086, before Sec IV

AMER CON: P. 833, before Sec IV

RTS & LIB: P. 753, before Sec IV

BOWEN v. KENDRICK, ___ U.S. ___, 108 S.Ct. 2562, 101 L.Ed.2d 520 (1988), per REHNQUIST, C.J., held that the Adolescent Family Life Act (AFLA)—which grants funds to a variety of public and private agencies (including religious organizations) to provide counseling for prevention of adolescent sexual relations and care for pregnant adolescents and adolescent parents—did not, on its face, violate the establishment clause:

"AFLA was motivated primarily, if not entirely, by a legitimate secular purpose—the elimination or reduction of social and economic problems caused by teenage sexuality, pregnancy, and parenthood. [Although] two of its stated purposes are to 'promote self discipline and other prudent approaches to the

b. Scalia, J.'s reasoning continues at pp. 316, 325 of this Supplement, where the case is also discussed.

problem of adolescent premarital sexual relations,' and to 'promote adoption as an alternative,' [this] approach is not inherently religious, although it may coincide with the approach taken by certain religions."

As for the role of religious organizations, "when, as Congress found, 'prevention of adolescent sexual activity depends primarily upon developing strong family values and close family ties,' it seems quite sensible for Congress to recognize that religious organizations can influence values and can have some influence on family life, including parents' relations with their adolescent children. To the extent that this Congressional recognition has any effect of advancing religion, the effect is at most 'incidental and remote.' * * *

"incidental and remote" relation to RELIGION

"[T]his Court has never held that religious institutions are disabled by the First Amendment from participating in publicly sponsored social welfare programs [*Bradfield v. Roberts*, and] nothing on the face of the AFLA indicates that a significant proportion of the federal funds will be disbursed to 'pervasively sectarian' institutions. Indeed, the contention that there is a substantial risk of such institutions receiving direct aid is undercut by the AFLA's facially neutral grant requirements, the wide spectrum of public and private organizations which are capable of meeting the AFLA's requirements, and the fact that, of the eligible religious institutions, many will not deserve the label of 'pervasively sectarian.' [As] in *Tilton* and *Roemer*, we do not think the possibility that AFLA grants may go to religious institutions that can be considered 'pervasively sectarian' is sufficient to conclude that no grants whatsoever can be given under the statute to religious organizations. We think that the District Court was wrong in concluding otherwise [and in presuming] that religiously affiliated AFLA grantees are not capable of carrying out their functions under the AFLA in a lawful, secular manner. * * *

"Here, [there] is no reason to assume that the religious organizations which may receive grants are 'pervasively sectarian' in the same sense as the Court has held parochial schools to be. There is accordingly no reason to fear that the less intensive monitoring involved here will cause the Government to intrude unduly in the day-to-day operation of the religiously affiliated AFLA grantees. Unquestionably, the Secretary will review the programs set up and run by the AFLA grantees, and undoutedly this will involve a review of, for example, the educational materials that a grantee proposes to use. The Secretary may also wish to have government employees visit the clinics or offices where AFLA programs are being carried out to see whether they are in fact being administered in accordance with statutory and constitutional requirements. But in our view, this type of grant monitoring does not amount to 'excessive entanglement,' at least in the context of a statute authorizing grants to religiously affiliated organizations that are not necessarily 'pervasively sectarian.'

No excessive entanglement

"[I]t will be open to appellees on remand to show that AFLA aid is flowing to grantees that can be considered 'pervasively sectarian' religious institutions, such as we have held parochial schools to be. The District Court should also consider on remand whether in particular cases AFLA aid has been used to fund 'specifically religious activit(ies) in an otherwise substantially secular setting,' [for example], whether the Secretary has permitted AFLA grantees to use materials that have an explicitly religious content or are designed to inculcate the views of a particular religious faith."

O'CONNOR, J., who joined the Court's opinion, concurred: "Using religious organizations to advance the secular goals of the AFLA, without thereby permitting religious indoctrination, is inevitably more difficult than in other projects, such as ministering to the poor and the sick. I nonetheless agree with the Court that the partnership between governmental and religious institutions contemplated by the AFLA need not result in constitutional violations, despite an undeniably greater risk than is present in cooperative undertakings that involve less sensitive objectives."

KENNEDY, J., joined by Scalia, J., joined the Court's opinion, adding that "where, as in this case, a statute provides that the benefits of a program are to be distributed in a neutral fashion to religious and non-religious applicants alike, and the program withstands a facial challenge, it is not unconstitutional as applied solely by reason of the religious character of a specific recipient. The question in an as-applied challenge is not whether the entity is of a religious character, but how it spends its grant."

BLACKMUN, J., joined by Brennan, Marshall and Stevens, JJ., dissented: "The majority's holding that the AFLA is not unconstitutional on its face marks a sharp departure from our precedents. While aid programs providing nonmonetary, verifiably secular aid have been upheld notwithstanding the indirect effect they might have on the allocation of an institution's own funds for religious activities, see, e.g., *Allen*; *Everson*, direct cash subsidies have always required much closer scrutiny into the expected and potential uses of the funds, and much greater guarantees that the funds would not be used inconsistently with the Establishment Clause. [Here, for example, the] teaching materials that may be purchased, developed, or disseminated with AFLA funding are in no way restricted to those already selected and approved for use in secular contexts.

"Notwithstanding the fact that government funds are paying for religious organizations to teach and counsel impressionable adolescents on a highly sensitive subject of considerable religious significance, often on the premises of a church or parochial school and without any effort to remove religious symbols from the sites, the majority concludes that the AFLA is not facially invalid. The majority acknowledges the constitutional proscription on government-sponsored religious indoctrination but, on the basis of little more than an indefensible assumption that AFLA recipients are not pervasively sectarian and consequently are presumed likely to comply with statutory and constitutional mandates, dismisses as insubstantial the risk that indoctrination will enter counseling. [Whereas] there may be secular values promoted by the AFLA, including the encouragement of adoption and premarital chastity and the discouragement of abortion, it can hardly be doubted that when promoted in theological terms by religious figures, those values take on a religious nature. Not surprisingly, the record is replete with observations to that effect. It should be undeniable by now that religious dogma may not be employed by government even to accomplish laudable secular purposes such as 'the promotion of moral values, the contradiction to the materialistic trends of our times, the perpetuation of our institutions and the teaching of literature.' *Schempp*.

"[O]ur cases do not require a plaintiff to demonstate that a government action *necessarily* promotes religion, but simply that it creates such a substantial risk. [After] such further proceedings as are now to be deemed appropriate, and after the District Court enters findings of fact on the basis of the testimony and documents entered into evidence, it may well decide, as I would today, that the AFLA as a whole indeed has been unconstitutionally applied."

OFFICIAL ACKNOWLEDGMENT OF RELIGION

CON LAW: P. 1095, before Sec. 2

AMER CON: P. 842, before Sec. 2

RTS & LIB: P. 762, before Sec. 2

ALLEGHENY COUNTY v. ACLU, ___ U.S. ___, 109 S.Ct. ___, ___ L.Ed.2d ___ (1989), per BLACKMUN, J., held that the display during the Christmas season of a creche (with a banner proclaiming "Gloria in Excelsis Deo") in the courthouse in Pittsburgh had "the effect of endorsing a patently Christian message" and thus violated the establishment clause: "The creche [uses] words, as well as the picture of the nativity scene, to make its religious meaning unmistakably clear. 'Glory to God in the Highest!' [Here,] unlike in *Lynch*, nothing in the context of the display detracts from the creche's religious message. [The] floral decoration surrounding the creche [serves] only to draw one's attention to the message inside the frame. [Furthermore], the creche sits on the Grand Staircase, the 'main' and 'most beautiful part' of the building that is the seat of county government. No viewer could reasonably think that it occupies this location without the support and approval of the government. Thus, by permitting the 'display of the creche in this particular physical setting,' *Lynch*, (O'Connor, J., concurring), the county sends an unmistakable message that it supports and promotes the Christian praise to God that is the creche's religious message. [The] fact that the creche bears a sign disclosing its ownership by a Roman Catholic organization does not alter this conclusion. On the contrary, the sign simply demonstrates that the government is endorsing the religious message of that organization, rather than communicating a message of its own." [a]

Six justices also held that the holiday display of a Chanukah menorah, owned by a Jewish group but erected each year by the city (along with a Christmas tree and a sign stating the city's "salute to liberty"), did not violate the establishment clause. BLACKMUN, J., reasoning that a "Christmas tree, unlike the menorah, is not itself a religious symbol," found that "the tree [is] clearly the predominant element in the city's display. The 45-foot tree occupies the central position [in] front of [the] City-County Building; the 18-foot menorah is positioned to one side. Given this configuration, it is much more sensible to interpret the meaning of the menorah in light of the tree, rather than vice versa. In the shadow of the tree, the menorah is readily understood as simply a recognition that Christmas is not the only traditional way of observing the winter-holiday season. In these circumstances, then, the combination of the tree and the menorah communicates, not a simultaneous endorsement of both Christian and Jewish faith, but instead, a secular celebration of Christmas coupled with an acknowledgment of Chanukah as a contemporaneous alternative tradition.

"Although the city has used a symbol with religious meaning as its representation of Chanukah, this is not a case in which the city has reasonable alternatives that are less religious in nature. * * * [68] The Mayor's sign

a. In a separate part of the opinion, Blackmun, J., joined by Stevens, J., expressed approval of O'Connor, J.'s concurrence in *Lynch*: "[D]espite divergence at the bottom line, the five Justices in concurrence and dissent in *Lynch* agreed upon the relevant constitutional principles: the government's use of religious symbolism is unconstitutional if it has the effect of endorsing religious belief, and the effect of the government's use of religious symbolism depends upon its context."

68. [In] displaying the menorah next to the tree, the city has demonstrated no preference

further diminishes the possibility that the tree and the menorah will be interpreted as a dual endorsement of Christianity and Judaism. The sign states that during the holiday season the city salutes liberty. Moreover, the sign draws upon the theme of light, common to both Chanukah and Christmas as winter festivals, and links that theme with this Nation's legacy of freedom, which allows an American to celebrate the holiday season in whatever way he wishes, religiously or otherwise."

O'CONNOR, J., concurred: "[The city's sign had] the following message: 'During this holiday season, the City of Pittsburgh salutes liberty. Let these festive lights remind us that we are the keepers of the flame of liberty and our legacy of freedom.' [By] accompanying its display of a Christmas tree—a secular symbol of the Christmas holiday season—with a salute to liberty, and by adding a religious symbol from a Jewish holiday also celebrated at roughly the same time of year, I conclude that the city did not endorse Judaism or religion in general, but rather conveyed a message of pluralism and freedom of belief during the holiday season."

BRENNAN, J., joined by Marshall and Stevens, JJ., dissented as to the menorah: "The decision [rests] on three premises: the Christmas tree is a secular symbol; Chanukah is a holiday with secular dimensions, symbolized by the menorah; and the government may promote pluralism by sponsoring or condoning displays having strong religious associations on its property. None of these is sound. [Blackmun and O'Connor, JJ.,] appear to believe that, where seasonal displays are concerned, more is better. Whereas a display might be constitutionally problematic if it showcased the holiday of just one religion, those problems vaporize as soon as more than one religion is included. I know of no principle under the Establishment Clause, however, that permits us to conclude that governmental promotion of religion is acceptable so long as one religion is not favored."

STEVENS, J., joined by Brennan and Marshall, JJ., also dissented as to the menorah: "In my opinion the Establishment Clause should be construed to create a strong presumption against the display of religious symbols on public property. There is always a risk that such symbols will offend nonmembers of the faith being advertised as well as adherents who consider the particular advertisement disrespectful. [Even] though '[p]assersby who disagree with the message conveyed by these displays are free to ignore them, or even turn their backs,' displays of this kind inevitably have a greater tendency to emphasize sincere and deeply felt differences among individuals than to achieve an ecumenical goal. The Establishment Clause does not allow public bodies to foment such disagreement."

KENNEDY, J., joined by Rehnquist, C.J., and White and Scalia, JJ.,—"content for present purposes to remain within the *Lemon* framework, but [not wishing] to be seen as advocating, let alone adopting, that test as our primary guide"— concurred in the judgment as to the menorah but dissented as to the creche: "The ability of the organized community to recognize and accommodate religion in a society with a pervasive public sector requires diligent observance of the border between accommodation and establishment. Our cases disclose two limiting principles: government may not coerce anyone to support or participate in any religion or its exercise; and it may not, in the guise of avoiding hostility

for the *religious* celebration of the holiday season. This conclusion, however, would be untenable had the city substituted a creche for its Christmas tree or if the city had failed to substitute for the menorah an alternative, more secular, representation of Chanukah."

or callous indifference, give direct benefits to religion in such a degree that it in fact 'establishes a [state] religion or religious faith, or tends to do so.' *Lynch.* These two principles, while distinct, are not unrelated, for it would be difficult indeed to establish a religion without some measure of more or less subtle coercion, be it in the form of taxation to supply the substantial benefits that would sustain a state-established faith, direct compulsion to observance, or governmental exhortation to religiosity that amounts in fact to proselytizing. * * * Absent coercion, the risk of infringement of religious liberty by passive or symbolic accommodation is minimal.[b] Our cases reflect this reality by requiring a showing that the symbolic recognition or accommodation advances religion to such a degree that it actually 'establishes a religion or religious faith, or tends to do so.' *Lynch.* * * * Non-coercive government action within the realm of flexible accommodation or passive acknowledgment of existing symbols does not violate the Establishment Clause unless it benefits religion in a way more direct and more substantial than practices that are accepted in our national heritage.[c]

"[In] permitting the displays on government property of the menorah and the creche, the city and county sought to do no more [than] acknowledge, along with many of their citizens, the historical background and the religious as well as secular nature of the Chanukah and Christmas holidays. [If] government is to participate in its citizens' celebration of a holiday that contains both a secular and a religious component, enforced recognition of only the secular aspect would signify the callous indifference toward religious faith that our cases and traditions do not require * * *.

"There is no suggestion here that the government's power to coerce has been used to further the interests of Christianity or Judaism in any way. No one was compelled to observe or participate in any religious ceremony or activity. Neither the city nor the county contributed significant amounts of tax money to serve the cause of one religious faith. The creche and the menorah are purely passive symbols of religious holidays. Passersby who disagree with the message conveyed by these displays are free to ignore them, or even to turn their backs, just as they are free to do when they disagree with any other form of government speech.

"There is no realistic risk that the creche or the menorah represent an effort to proselytize * * *.[d] *Lynch* is dispositive of this claim with respect to the

b. In his opinion for the Court, Blackmun, J., observed that "an accommodation of religion, in order to be permitted under the Establishment Clause, must lift 'an identifiable burden *on the exercise of religion.*' * * * Prohibiting the display of a creche at this location, [does] not impose a burden on the practice of Christianity (except to the extent some Christian sect seeks to be an officially approved religion), and therefore permitting the display is not an 'accommodation' of religion in the conventional sense."

c. The Court's opinion responded: "[Kennedy, J.] argues that *Marsh* legitimates all 'practices with no greater potential for an establishment of religion' than those 'accepted traditions dating back to the Founding.' [But, however] history may affect the constitutionality of nonsectarian references to religion by the government, history cannot legitimate practices that demonstrate the government's allegiance to a particular sect or creed."

d. The Court's opinion commented that "when all is said and done, Justice Kennedy's effort to abandon the 'endorsement' inquiry in favor of his 'proselytization' test seems nothing more than an attempt to lower considerably the level of scrutiny in Establishment Clause cases." In a separate opinion, O'CONNOR, J., joined by Brennan and Stevens, JJ., agreed: "An Establishment Clause standard that prohibits only 'coercive' practices or overt efforts at government proselytization, but fails to take account of the numerous more subtle ways that government can show favoritism to particular beliefs or convey a message of disapproval to others, would not, in my view, adequately protect the religious liberty or respect the religious diversity of the members of our pluralistic political community."

creche, and I find no reason for reaching a different result with respect to the menorah. [Crucial in *Lynch*] was not the number, prominence, or type of secular items contained in the holiday display but the simple fact that, when displayed by government during the Christmas season, a creche presents no realistic danger of moving government down the forbidden road toward an establishment of religion. Whether the creche be surrounded by poinsettias, talking wishing wells, or carolers, the conclusion remains the same, for the relevant context is not the items in the display itself but the season as a whole. * * *

"Even if *Lynch* did not control, I would not commit this Court to the test applied by the majority today. The notion that cases arising under the Establishment Clause should be decided by an inquiry into whether a 'reasonable observer' may 'fairly understand' government action to 'sen[d] a message to nonadherents that they are outsiders, not full members of the political community,' is a recent, and in my view most unwelcome, addition to our tangled Establishment Clause jurisprudence. [If] the endorsement test, applied without artificial exceptions for historical practice, reached results consistent with history, my objections to it would have less force. But [f]ew of our traditional practices recognizing the part religion plays in our society can withstand scrutiny under a faithful application of this formula [referring to many of the observances listed in *Lynch*].

"If there be such a person as the 'reasonable observer,' I am quite certain that he or she will take away a salient message from our holding in this case: the Supreme Court of the United States has concluded that the First Amendment creates classes of religions based on the relative numbers of their adherents. Those religions enjoying the largest following must be consigned to the status of least-favored faiths so as to avoid any possible risk of offending members of minority religions. I would be the first to admit that many questions arising under the Establishment Clause do not admit of easy answers, but whatever the Clause requires, it is not the result reached by the Court today."

SECTION: FREE EXERCISE CLAUSE AND RELATED PROBLEMS

CONFLICT WITH STATE REGULATION

CON LAW: P. 1101, add to fn. e

AMER CON: P. 847, add to fn. e

RTS & LIB: P. 768, add to fn. e

In a factual situation nearly identical to *Sherbert*, *Hobbie v. Unemployment Appeals Comm'n of Florida*, 480 U.S. 136, 107 S.Ct. 1046, 94 L.Ed.2d 190 (1987), per Brennan, J., specifically reaffirmed *Sherbert* and *Thomas*. Only Rehnquist, C.J., dissented.

In *Oregon Dept. of Human Resources v. Smith*, 485 U.S. 660, 108 S.Ct. 1444, 99 L.Ed.2d 753 (1988), a drug rehabilitation counselor, who was fired for ingesting peyote as part of his Native American religion, was denied unemployment compensation. The Court remanded to the state courts for a determination of whether religious use of peyote was illegal under state law: In *Sherbert*, *Thomas* and *Hobbie*, "the conduct that gave rise to the termination of employment was perfectly legal. [I]f Oregon does prohibit the religious use of peyote, and if that prohibition is consistent with the Federal Constitution, [the] State is free to withhold unemployment compensation from respondents for engaging in work-related misconduct, despite its religious motivation."

CON LAW: P. 1102, at end of note 3

RTS & LIB: P. 769, at end of note 3

In TEXAS MONTHLY, INC. v. BULLOCK, p. 308 of this Supplement, BRENNAN, J., joined by Marshall and Stevens, JJ., read *Murdock* and *Follett* narrowly as forbidding either "a special occupation tax exclusively on those who devote their days to spreading religious messages," or "a facially neutral license fee [that imposes a] tax burden [that] is far from negligible [on] religious activity [that] is deemed central to a given faith, as the Court found this form of proselytizing to be in *Murdock* and *Follett*": "To the extent that our opinions in *Murdock* and *Follett* might be read, however, to suggest that the States and the Federal Government may never tax the sale of religious or other publications, we reject those dicta."

BLACKMUN, J., joined by O'Connor, J., felt that "defining the ultimate scope of *Follett* and *Murdock* may be left for another day."

SCALIA, J., joined by Rehnquist, C.J., and Kennedy, J., was "willing to acknowledge that *Murdock* and *Follett* are narrowly distinguishable." [c]

CON LAW: P. 1109, after *Lee*

AMER CON: P. 854, after *Lee*

RTS & LIB: P. 775, after *Lee*

See also *Hernandez v. Commissioner,* p. 320 of this Supplement.

CON LAW: P. 1110, after *Bob Jones*

AMER CON: P. 855, after *Bob Jones*

RTS & LIB: P. 777, after *Bob Jones*

GOLDMAN v. WEINBERGER, 475 U.S. 503, 106 S.Ct. 1310, 89 L.Ed.2d 478 (1986), per REHNQUIST, J.—relying on "military" decisions such as *Parker v. Levy,* 417 U.S. 733, 94 S.Ct. 2547, 41 L.Ed.2d 439 (1974), and *Rostker v. Goldberg* [CON LAW p. 1303, AMER CON p. 1010, RTS & LIB p. 969]—rejected an Orthodox Jewish psychologist's claim that the free exercise clause "requires the Air Force to make an exception to its uniform dress requirements" so as to permit him to wear a yarmulke while on duty in uniform at a military hospital; "[W]hen evaluating whether military needs justify a particular restriction on religiously motivated conduct, courts must give great deference to the professional judgment of military authorities concerning the relative importance of a particular military interest."

STEVENS, J., joined by White and Powell, JJ., all of whom joined the Court's opinion, concurred: Although this was "an especially attractive case for an exception" because it "creates almost no danger of impairment of the Air Force's military mission," the "claim creates the danger that a similar claim on behalf of a Sikh [to wear a turban] or a Rastafarian [to wear a dreadlock] might readily be dismissed as 'so extreme, so unusual, or so faddish an image that public confidence in his ability to perform his duties will be destroyed.' [The] Air Force has no business drawing distinctions between such persons when it is enforcing commands of universal application."

5-4   Brennan, Marshall, Blackmun and O'Connor, JJ., dissented.

---

c. This case is also discussed at p. 325 of this Supplement.

In BOWEN v. ROY, 476 U.S. 693, 106 S.Ct. 2147, 90 L.Ed.2d 735 (1986), the parents of a two year old girl (named Little Bird of the Snow), for whom a social security number had been assigned at birth, contended that federal requirements—that recipients of AFDC and Food Stamps must submit their social security numbers, which shall be used by the government to prevent welfare fraud—violated their Native American religious beliefs. Five justices found that *Sherbert* and *Thomas* sustained the parents' claim that this violated free exercise. The principal opinion was by O'CONNOR, J., joined by Brennan, and Marshall, JJ.: "Our precedents have long required the Government to show that a compelling state interest is served by its refusal to grant a religious exemption. The Government here has [met] its burden of showing that the prevention of welfare fraud is a compelling governmental goal. If the Government could meet its compelling needs only by refusing to grant a religious exemption, and chose a narrowly tailored means to do so, then the Government would prevail. But [g]ranting an exemption to Little Bird of the Snow, and to the handful of others who can be expected to make a similar religious objection to providing the social security number in conjunction with receipt of welfare benefits, will not demonstrably diminish the Government's ability to combat welfare fraud." Blackmun, J.—who would have remanded to determine whether the case is moot (as would Stevens, J.)—agreed with O'Connor, J.; White, J., stated only that *Sherbert* and *Thomas* "control this case."

BURGER, C.J., joined by Powell and Rehnquist, JJ., rejected the claim: "[G]overnment regulation that indirectly and incidentally calls for a choice between securing a governmental benefit and adherence to religious beliefs is wholly different from government [action] that criminalizes religiously inspired activity or inescapably compels conduct that some find objectionable for religious reasons. Although the denial of governmental benefits over religious objection can raise serious Free Exercise problems, these two very different forms of government action are not governed by the same constitutional standard. * * * Absent proof of an intent to discriminate against particular religious beliefs or against religion in general, the Government meets its burden when it demonstrates that a challenged requirement for governmental benefits, neutral and uniform in its application, is a reasonable means of promoting a legitimate public interest." [a]

CON LAW: P. 1112, after note 2

AMER CON: P. 856, at end

RTS & LIB: P. 779, after note 2

LYNG v. NORTHWEST INDIAN CEMETERY PROTECTIVE ASS'N, 485 U.S. 439, 108 S.Ct. 1319, 99 L.Ed.2d 534 (1988), per O'CONNOR, J., held the federal government's building a road and allowing timber harvesting in a national forest did not violate the free exercise rights of American Indian tribes even though this would "virtually destroy the Indians' ability to practice their religion" because it would irreparably damage "sacred areas which are an integral and necessary part of [their] belief systems": "In *Bowen v. Roy*, we considered a challenge to a federal statute that required the States to use Social Security numbers in administering certain welfare programs. Two applicants for benefits under these programs contended that their religious beliefs prevented them from acceding to the use of a Social Security number for their two-year-

a. Another issue in the case is discussed in *Lyng*, infra.

old daughter because the use of a numerical identifier would ' "rob the spirit" of [their] daughter and prevent her from attaining greater spiritual power.' [The] Court rejected this kind of challenge in *Roy:* 'The Free Exercise Clause simply cannot be understood to require the Government to conduct its own internal affairs in ways that comport with the religious beliefs of particular citizens. Just as the Government may not insist that [the Roys] engage in any set form of religious observance, so [they] may not demand that the Government join in their chosen religious practices by refraining from using a number to identify their daughter. [The] Free Exercise Clause affords an individual protection from certain forms of governmental compulsion; it does not afford an individual a right to dictate the conduct of the Government's internal procedures.'

"The building of a road or the harvesting of timber on publicly owned land cannot meaningfully be distinguished from the use of a Social Security number in *Roy.* In both cases, the challenged government action would interfere significantly with private persons' ability to pursue spiritual fulfillment according to their own religious beliefs. In neither case, however, would the affected individuals be coerced by the Government's action into violating their religious beliefs; nor would either governmental action penalize religious activity by denying any person an equal share of the rights, benefits, and privileges enjoyed by other citizens.

"[It] is true that this Court has repeatedly held that indirect coercion or penalties on the free exercise of religion, not just outright prohibitions, are subject to scrutiny under the First Amendment. [*Sherbert.*] This does not and cannot imply that incidental effects of government programs, which may make it more difficult to practice certain religions but which have no tendency to coerce individuals into acting contrary to their religious beliefs, require government to bring forward a compelling justification for its otherwise lawful actions. The crucial word in the constitutional text is 'prohibit': 'For the Free Exercise Clause is written in terms of what the government cannot do to the individual, not in terms of what the individual can exact from the government.'

"[However] much we might wish that it were otherwise, government simply could not operate if it were required to satisfy every citizen's religious needs and desires. A broad range of government activities—from social welfare programs to foreign aid to conservation projects—will always be considered essential to the spiritual well-being of some citizens, often on the basis of sincerely held religious beliefs. Others will find the very same activities deeply offensive, and perhaps incompatible with their own search for spiritual fulfillment and with the tenets of their religion. The First Amendment must apply to all citizens alike, and it can give to none of them a veto over public programs that do not prohibit the free exercise of religion. The Constitution does not, and courts cannot, offer to reconcile the various competing demands on government, many of them rooted in sincere religious belief, that inevitably arise in so diverse a society as ours. That task, to the extent that it is feasible, is for the legislatures and other institutions. * * *

"The Constitution does not permit government to discriminate against religions that treat particular physical sites as sacred, and a law forbidding the Indian respondents from visiting the Chimney Rock area would raise a different set of constitutional questions. Whatever rights the Indians may have to the use of the area, however, those rights do not divest the Government of its right to use what is, after all, *its* land.

"[The] dissent now offers to distinguish [*Roy*] by saying that the Government was acting there 'in a purely internal manner,' whereas land-use decisions 'are likely to have substantial external effects.' [But robbing] the spirit of a child, and preventing her from attaining greater spiritual power, is both a 'substantial external effect' and one that is remarkably similar to the injury claimed by respondents in the case before us today. * * *

"Perceiving a 'stress point in the longstanding conflict between two disparate cultures,' the dissent attacks us for declining to 'balanc[e] these competing and potentially irreconcilable interests, choosing instead to turn this difficult task over to the federal legislature.' Seeing the Court as the arbiter, the dissent proposes a legal test under which it would decide which public lands are 'central' or 'indispensable' to which religions, and by implication which are 'dispensable' or 'peripheral,' and would then decide which government programs are 'compelling' enough to justify 'infringement of those practices.' We would accordingly be required to weigh the value of every religious belief and practice that is said to be threatened by any government program. Unless a 'showing of "centrality"' is nothing but an assertion of centrality, the dissent thus offers us the prospect of this Court holding that some sincerely held religious beliefs and practices are not 'central' to certain religions, despite protestations to the contrary from the religious objectors who brought the lawsuit. In other words, the dissent's approach would require us to rule that some religious adherents misunderstand their own religious beliefs. We think such an approach cannot be squared with the Constitution or with our precedents, and that it would cast the judiciary in a role that we were never intended to play."

BRENNAN, J., joined by Marshall and Blackmun, JJ., dissented: "The Court does not for a moment suggest that the interests served by the G–O road are in any way compelling, or that they outweigh the destructive effect construction of the road will have on respondents' religious practices. [Indeed,] the Government's proposed activities will restrain religious practice to a far greater degree here than in any of the cases cited by the Court today. None of the religious adherents in *Hobbie*, *Thomas*, and *Sherbert*, for example, claimed or could have claimed that the denial of unemployment benefits rendered the practice of their religions impossible; at most, the challenged laws made those practices more expensive. Here, in stark contrast, respondents have claimed—and proved— that the desecration of the high country will prevent religious leaders from attaining the religious power or medicine indispensable to the success of virtually all their rituals and ceremonies. [And] of course respondents here do not even have the option, however unattractive it might be, of migrating to more hospitable locales; the site-specific nature of their belief system renders it non-transportable.

"[Both] common sense and our prior cases teach us, therefore, that governmental action that makes the practice of a given faith more difficult necessarily penalizes that practice and thereby tends to prevent adherence to religious belief. The harm to the practitioners is the same regardless of the manner in which the Government restrains their religious expression, and the Court's fear that an 'effects' test will permit religious adherents to challenge governmental actions they merely find 'offensive' in no way justifies its refusal to recognize the constitutional injury citizens suffer when governmental action not only offends but actually restrains their religious practices. Here, respondents have demonstrated that the Government's proposed activities will completely prevent them from practicing their religion, and such a showing, no less than those made out in *Hobbie, Thomas, Sherbert,* and *Yoder,* entitles them to the protections of the Free Exercise Clause.

"[A]dherents challenging a proposed use of federal land should be required to show that the decision poses a substantial and realistic threat of frustrating their religious practices. Once such a showing is made, the burden should shift to the Government to come forward with a compelling state interest sufficient to justify the infringement of those practices.

"The Court today suggests that such an approach would place courts in the untenable position of deciding which practices and beliefs are 'central' to a given faith and which are not, and invites the prospect of judges advising some religious adherents that they 'misunderstand their own religious beliefs.' In fact, however, courts need not undertake any such inquiries: like all other religious adherents, Native Americans would be the arbiters of which practices are central to their faith, subject only to the normal requirement that their claims be genuine and sincere. [T]oday's ruling sacrifices a religion at least as old as the Nation itself, along with the spirtual well-being of its approximately 5,000 adherents, so that the Forest Service can build a six-mile segment of road that two lower courts found had only the most marginal and speculative utility, both to the Government itself and to the private lumber interests that might conceivably use it."

Kennedy, J., did not participate.

CON LAW: P. 1112, add to fn. j

AMER CON: P. 856, add at end of fn. i

RTS & LIB: P. 779, add to fn. j

O'LONE v. ESTATE OF SHABAZZ, 482 U.S. 342, 107 S.Ct. 2400, 96 L.Ed.2d 282 (1987), per Rehnquist, C.J.—stressing that "courts afford appropriate deference to prison officials"—held that a prison regulation that conflicts with the free exercise of a prisoner's religion "is valid if it is reasonably related to legitimate penological interests." Prison officials need *not* prove "that no reasonable method exists by which [prisoners'] religious rights can be accommodated without creating bona fide security problems."

Brennan, J., joined by Marshall, Blackmun and Stevens, JJ., dissented, agreeing to the Court's standard of review only when "exercise of the asserted right [is] presumptively dangerous [and] the prison has [not] completely deprived an inmate of that right." Otherwise, "prison officials [should be required] to demonstrate that the restrictions they have imposed are necessary to further an important government interest, and that these restrictions are no greater than necessary to achieve prison objectives."

SECTION: PREFERENCE FOR AND AMONG RELIGIONS

CON LAW: P. 1122, at end of note 2

AMER CON: P. 864, at end of note 2

RTS & LIB: P. 789, at end of note 2

HERNANDEZ v. COMMISSIONER, ___ U.S. ___, 109 S.Ct. 2136, 104 L.Ed.2d 766 (1989), per MARSHALL, J., held that the government did not violate the establishment clause by not permitting federal taxpayers to deduct as "charitable contributions" payments to the Church of Scientology for "auditing" and "training" sessions. A central tenet of the Church requires "fixed donations" for these sessions to study the faith's tenets and to increase spiritual awareness. The proceeds are the Church's primary source of income.

"Unlike the Minnesota statute at issue in *Larson*," IRS disallowance for payments made "with some expectation of a quid pro quo in terms of goods or services [makes] no 'explicit and deliberate distinctions between different religious organizations,' applying instead to all religious entities. [It] may be that a consequence of

the quid pro quo orientation of the 'contribution or gift' requirement is to impose a disparate burden on those charitable and religious groups that rely on sales of commodities or services as a means of fund-raising, relative to those groups that raise funds primarily by soliciting unilateral donations. But a statute primarily having a secular effect does not violate the Establishment Clause merely because it 'happens to coincide or harmonize with the tenets of some or all religions.' *McGowan*."

Because of the absence of "a proper factual record," the Court did not consider the contention of O'CONNOR, J., joined by Scalia, J., dissenting, that "at least some of the fixed payments which the IRS has treated as charitable deductions [are as much a 'quid pro quo exchange'] as the payments [here]": "In exchange for their payment of pew rents, Christians receive particular seats during worship services. Similarly, in some synagogues attendance at the worship services for Jewish High Holy Days is often predicated upon the purchase of a general admission ticket or a reserved seat ticket. Religious honors such as publicly reading from Scripture are purchased or auctioned periodically in some synagogues of Jews from Morocco and Syria. Mormons must tithe ten percent of their income as a necessary but not sufficient condition to obtaining a 'temple recommend,' i.e., the right to be admitted into the temple. A Mass stipend—a fixed payment given to a Catholic priest, in consideration of which he is obliged to apply the fruits of the Mass for the intention of the donor—has similar overtones of exchange. [Thus, the case] involves the differential application of a standard based on constitutionally impermissible differences drawn by the Government among religions."

Brennan and Kennedy, JJ., did not participate.

CON LAW: P. 1129, at end

AMER CON: P. 871, at end

RTS & LIB: P. 795, at end

CORPORATION OF THE PRESIDING BISHOP OF THE CHURCH OF JESUS CHRIST OF LATTER-DAY SAINTS v. AMOS

483 U.S. 327, 107 S.Ct. 2862, 97 L.Ed.2d 273 (1987).

JUSTICE WHITE delivered the opinion of the Court.

Section 702 of the Civil Rights Act of 1964 exempts religious organizations from Title VII's prohibition against discrimination in employment on the basis of religion. The question presented is whether applying the § 702 exemption to the secular nonprofit activities of religious organizations violates the Establishment Clause of the First Amendment. The District Court held that it [does].

The Deseret Gymnasium (Gymnasium) in Salt Lake City, Utah, is a nonprofit facility, open to the public, run by [an] unincorporated religious association sometimes called the Mormon or LDS Church.

Appellee Mayson worked at the Gymnasium for some 16 years as an assistant building engineer and then building engineer. He was discharged in

1981 because he failed to qualify for a temple recommend, that is, a certificate that he is a member of the Church and eligible to attend its temples.

Mayson [contended] that if construed to allow religious employers to discriminate on religious grounds in hiring for nonreligious jobs, § 702 violates the Establishment Clause. * * *

"This Court has long recognized that the government may (and sometimes must) accommodate religious practices and that it may do so without violating the Establishment Clause." It is well established, too, that "[t]he limits of permissible state accommodation to religion are by no means co-extensive with the noninterference mandated by the Free Exercise Clause." *Walz.* [At] some point, accommodation may devolve into "an unlawful fostering of religion," but this is not such a case, in our view. * * *

Lemon requires first that the law at issue serve a "secular legislative purpose." This does not mean that the law's purpose must be unrelated to [religion]. Rather, *Lemon*'s "purpose" requirement aims at preventing the relevant governmental decisionmaker—in this case, Congress—from abandoning neutrality and acting with the intent of promoting a particular point of view in religious matters.

Under the *Lemon* analysis, it is a permissible legislative purpose to alleviate significant governmental interference with the ability of religious organizations to define and carry out their religious missions. Appellees argue that there is no such purpose here because § 702 provided adequate protection for religious employers prior to the 1972 amendment, when it exempted only the religious activities of such employers from the statutory ban on religious discrimination. We may assume for the sake of argument that the pre-1972 exemption was adequate in the sense that the Free Exercise Clause required no more. Nonetheless, it is a significant burden on a religious organization to require it, on pain of substantial liability, to predict which of its activities a secular court will consider religious. The line is hardly a bright one, and an organization might understandably be concerned that a judge would not understand its religious tenets and sense of mission. Fear of potential liability might affect the way an organization carried out what it understood to be its religious mission.

After a detailed examination of the legislative history of the 1972 amendment, the District Court concluded that Congress' purpose was to minimize governmental "interfer[ence] with the decision-making process in religions." We agree with the District Court that this purpose does not violate the Establishment Clause.

The second requirement under *Lemon* is that the law in question have "a principal or primary effect [that] neither advances nor inhibits religion." Undoubtedly, religious organizations are better able now to advance their purposes than they were prior to the 1972 amendment to § 702. But religious groups have been better able to advance their purposes on account of many laws that have passed constitutional muster: for example, the property tax exemption at issue in *Walz,* or the loans of school books to school children, including parochial school students, upheld in *Allen.* A law is not unconstitutional simply because it *allows* churches to advance religion, which is their very purpose. For a law to have forbidden "effects" under *Lemon,* it must be fair to say that the *government itself* has advanced religion through its own activities and influence. [Moreover,] we find no persuasive evidence in the record before us that the Church's ability to propagate its religious doctrine through the Gymnasium is any greater now than it was prior to the passage of the Civil Rights Act in 1964. In such circumstances, we do not see how any advancement of religion achieved by the Gymnasium can be fairly attributed to the Government, as opposed to the Church.[15]

We find unpersuasive the District Court's reliance on the fact that § 702 singles out religious entities for a benefit. [The Court] has never indicated that statutes that give special consideration to religious groups are per se invalid. That would run contrary to the teaching of our cases that there is ample room for accommodation of religion under the Establishment Clause. Where, as here, government acts with the proper purpose of lifting a regulation that burdens the exercise of religion, we see no reason to require that the exemption come packaged with benefits to secular entities. * * *

Appellees argue that § 702 offends equal protection principles by giving less protection to the employees of religious employers than to the employees of secular employers. Appellees rely on *Larson* for the proposition that a law drawing distinctions on religious grounds must be strictly scrutinized. But *Larson* indicates that laws discriminating *among* religions are subject to strict scrutiny, and that laws "affording a uniform benefit to all religions" should be analyzed under *Lemon*. In a case such as this, where a statute is neutral on its face and motivated by a permissible purpose of limiting governmental interference with the exercise of religion, we see no justification for applying strict scrutiny to a statute that passes the *Lemon* test. [A]s applied to the nonprofit activities of religious employers, § 702 is rationally related to the legitimate purpose of alleviating significant governmental interference with the ability of religious organizations to define and carry out their religious missions. * * *

The judgment of the District Court is reversed * * *.

JUSTICE BRENNAN, with whom JUSTICE MARSHALL joins, concurring in the judgment.

[Any] exemption from Title VII's proscription on religious discrimination necessarily has the effect of burdening the religious liberty of prospective and current employees. An exemption says that a person may [be] put to the choice of either conforming to certain religious tenets or losing a job opportunity, a promotion, or, as in this case, employment itself. The potential for coercion created by such a provision is in serious tension with our commitment to individual freedom of conscience in matters of religious belief.

At the same time, religious organizations have an interest in autonomy in ordering their internal [affairs]. Determining that certain activities are in furtherance of an organization's religious mission, and that only those committed to that mission should conduct them, is thus a means by which a religious community defines itself. Solicitude for a church's ability to do so reflects the idea that furtherance of the autonomy of religious organizations often furthers individual religious freedom as well. * * *

This rationale suggests that, ideally, religious organizations should be able to discriminate on the basis of religion *only* with respect to religious activities, so that a determination should be made in each case whether an activity is

---

15. Undoubtedly, Mayson's freedom of choice in religious matters was impinged upon, but it was the Church [and] not the Government, who put him to the choice of changing his religious practices or losing his job. This is a very different case than *Caldor*. [In] effect, Connecticut had given the force of law to the employee's designation of a Sabbath day and required accommodation by the employer regardless of the burden which that constituted for the employer or other employees. In the present case, appellee was not legally obligated to take the steps necessary to qualify for a temple recommend, and his discharge was not required by statute. * * *

religious or secular. This is because the infringement on religious liberty that results from conditioning performance of *secular* activity upon religious belief cannot be defended as necessary for the community's self-definition. Furthermore, the authorization of discrimination in such circumstances is not an accommodation that simply enables a church to gain members by the normal means of prescribing the terms of membership for those who seek to participate in furthering the mission of the community. Rather, it puts at the disposal of religion the added advantages of economic leverage in the secular realm. As a result, the authorization of religious discrimination with respect to nonreligious activities goes beyond reasonable accommodation, and has the effect of furthering religion in violation of the Establishment Clause.

What makes the application of a religious-secular distinction difficult is that the character of an activity is not self-evident. As a result, determining whether an activity is religious or secular requires a searching case-by-case analysis. This results in considerable ongoing government entanglement in religious affairs. Furthermore, this prospect of government intrusion raises concern that a religious organization may be chilled in its Free Exercise activity. While a church may regard the conduct of certain functions as integral to its mission, a court may disagree. A religious organization therefore would have an incentive to characterize as religious only those activities about which there likely would be no dispute, even if it genuinely believed that religious commitment was important in performing other tasks as well. As a result, the community's process of self-definition would be shaped in part by the prospects of litigation.

* * *

The risk of chilling religious organizations is most likely to arise with respect to *nonprofit* activities. The fact that an operation is not organized as a profit-making commercial enterprise makes colorable a claim that it is not purely secular in orientation. * * *

Sensitivity to individual religious freedom dictates that religious discrimination be permitted only with respect to employment in religious activities. Concern for the autonomy of religious organizations demands that we avoid the entanglement and the chill on religious expression that a case-by-case determination would produce. We cannot escape the fact that these aims are in tension. Because of the nature of nonprofit activities, I believe that a categorical exemption for such enterprises appropriately balances these competing concerns.

* * *

JUSTICE BLACKMUN, concurring in the judgment.

Essentially for the reasons set forth in JUSTICE O'CONNOR's [opinion,] I too, concur in the judgment of the Court. * * *

JUSTICE O'CONNOR, concurring in the judgment.

[While] acknowledging that "[u]ndoubtedly, religious organizations are better able now to advance their purposes than they were prior to the 1972 amendment to § 702," the Court seems to suggest that the "effects" prong of the *Lemon* test is not at all implicated as long as the government action can be characterized as "allowing" religious organizations to advance religion, in contrast to government action directly advancing religion. This distinction seems to me to obscure far more than to enlighten. Almost any government benefit to religion could be recharacterized as simply "allowing" a religion to better advance itself, unless perhaps it involved actual proselytization by government agents. In nearly every case of a government benefit to religion, the religious mission would not be advanced if the religion did not take advantage of the benefit; even a direct financial subsidy to a religious organization would not advance religion if for some reason the organization failed to make any use of the [funds.]

The necessary first step in evaluating an Establishment Clause challenge to a government action lifting from religious organizations a generally applicable regulatory burden is to recognize that such government action *does* have the effect of advancing religion. The necessary second step is to separate those benefits to religion that constitutionally accommodate the free exercise of religion from those that provide unjustifiable awards of assistance to religious organizations. As I have suggested in earlier opinions, the inquiry framed by the *Lemon* test should be "whether government's purpose is to endorse religion and whether the statute actually conveys a message of endorsement." To ascertain whether the statute conveys a message of endorsement, the relevant issue is how it would be perceived by an objective observer, acquainted with the text, legislative history, and implementation of the statute. [This] case involves a government decision to lift from a nonprofit activity of a religious organization the burden of demonstrating that the particular nonprofit activity is religious as well as the burden of refraining from discriminating on the basis of religion. Because there is a probability that a nonprofit activity of a religious organization will itself be involved in the organization's religious mission, in my view the objective observer should perceive the government action as an accommodation of the exercise of religion rather than as a government endorsement of religion.

It is not clear, however, that activities conducted by religious organizations solely as profit-making enterprises will be as likely to be directly involved in the religious mission of the organization. While I express no opinion on the issue, I emphasize that under the holding of the Court, and under my view of the appropriate Establishment Clause analysis, the question of the constitutionality of the § 702 exemption as applied to for-profit activities of religious organizations remains open.

In TEXAS MONTHLY, INC. v. BULLOCK, pp. 308 and 316 of this Supplement, SCALIA, J., joined by Rehnquist, C.J., and Kennedy, J., charged that according to Brennan, J.'s plurality opinion, "no law is constitutional whose 'benefits [are] confined to religious organizations,' except, of course, those laws that are unconstitutional *unless* they contain benefits confined to religious organizations. [But] 'the limits of permissible state accommodation to religion are by no means co-extensive with the noninterference mandated by the Free Exercise Clause.' [*Walz*] Breadth of coverage is essential to constitutionality whenever a law's benefiting of religious activity is sought to be defended not specifically (or not exclusively) as an intentional and reasonable accommodation of religion, but as merely the incidental consequence of seeking to benefit *all* activity that achieves a particular secular goal. But that is a different rationale—more commonly invoked than accommodation of religion but, as our cases show, not preclusive of it. Where accommodation of religion is the justification, by definition religion is being singled out." Finally, "the proper lesson to be drawn from" the fact that the free exercise clause may not require the Texas sales tax exemption and "that *Murdock* and *Follett* are narrowly distinguishable" is that "if the exemption comes so close to being a constitutionally required accommodation, there is no doubt that it is at least a permissible one."

BRENNAN, J., joined by Marshall and Stevens, JJ., responded: "Contrary to the dissent's claims, we in no way suggest that *all* benefits conferred exclusively upon religious groups or upon individuals on account of their religious beliefs are forbidden by the Establishment Clause unless they are mandated by the Free Exercise Clause. Our decisions in *Zorach* and *Amos* offer two examples. Similarly, if the Air Force provided a sufficiently broad exemption from its dress requirements for servicemen whose religious faiths commanded them to wear certain headgear or other attire, see *Goldman v. Weinberger,* that exemption presumably would not be invalid under the Establishment Clause even though this Court has not found it to be required by the Free Exercise Clause.

"All of these cases, however, involve legislative exemptions that did not or would not impose substantial burdens on nonbeneficiaries while allowing others to act according to their religious beliefs, or that were designed to alleviate government intrusions that might significantly deter adherents of a particular faith from conduct protected by the Free Exercise Clause. New York City's decision to release students from public schools so that they might obtain religious instruction elsewhere, which we upheld in *Zorach,* was found not to coerce students who wished to remain behind to alter their religious beliefs, nor did it impose monetary costs on their parents or other taxpayers who opposed or were indifferent to the religious instruction given to students who were released. The hypothetical Air Force uniform exemption also would not place a monetary burden on those required to conform to the dress code or subject them to any appreciable privation. And the application of Title VII's exemption for religious organizations that we approved in *Amos* though it had some adverse effect on those holding or seeking employment with those organizations (if not on taxpayers generally), prevented potentially serious encroachments on protected religious freedoms.

"Texas' tax exemption, by contrast, does not remove a demonstrated and possibly grave imposition on religious activity sheltered by the Free Exercise Clause. Moreover, it burdens nonbeneficiaries by increasing their tax bills by whatever amount is needed to offset the benefit bestowed on subscribers to religious publications."

Chapter

EQUAL PROTECTION

SECTION: TRADITIONAL APPROACH

CON LAW: P. 1148, add to fn. d

AMER CON: P. 887, add to fn. d

RTS & LIB: P. 814, add to fn. d

See also *Bowen v. Owens,* 476 U.S. 340, 106 S.Ct. 1881, 90 L.Ed.2d 316 (1986), for a dissent by Blackmun, J., finding no "rational basis" for a Social Security Act classification. Marshall and Brennan, JJ., also dissented on the ground that Congress had no "actual purpose" "for drawing this line other than its desire to find a point of compromise between the two Houses."

See also *Lyng v. Int'l Union,* 485 U.S. 360, 108 S.Ct. 1184, 99 L.Ed.2d 380 (1988), for a dissent by Marshall, J., joined by Brennan and Blackmun, JJ., finding that Congress' denial of food stamps to persons who meet the low income test because they are on strike "cannot survive even rational basis scrutiny"; *Bankers Life & Casualty Co. v. Crenshaw,* ___ U.S. ___, 108 S.Ct. 1645, 100 L.Ed.2d 62 (1988), for a dissent by Blackmun, J., finding that a statutory classification was not "reasonably related" to the asserted state interests and was thus "arbitrary and irrational."

CON LAW: P. 1148, at end of note 3

AMER CON: P. 887, at end of note 3

RTS & LIB: P. 814, at end of Sec. 1

ALLEGHENY PITTSBURGH COAL CO. v. COUNTY COMM'N, ___ U.S. ___, 109 S.Ct. 633, 102 L.Ed.2d 688 (1989), per REHNQUIST, C.J., unanimously found an equal protection violation when a West Virginia county tax assessor "valued petitioners' real property on the basis of its recent purchase price, but made only minor modifications in the assessments of land which had not been recently sold," resulting in the fact that "petitioners' property has been assessed at roughly 8 to 35 times more than comparable neighboring property, and these discrepancies have continued for more than 10 years with little change." The Court, noting that it was not passing on a scheme like California's that deliberately reassessed the value of property only when it was transferred, held that the county assessor's practice was not "rationally related" to West Virginia's rule "that all property of the kind held by petitioners shall be taxed at a rate uniform throughout the state according to its estimated market value."

327

SECTION: RACE AND ETHNIC ANCESTRY

DE JURE vs. DE FACTO DISCRIMINATION

CON LAW: P. 1171, after note 3

RTS & LIB: P. 837, after note 3

BATSON v. KENTUCKY, 476 U.S. 79, 106 S.Ct. 1712, 90 L.Ed.2d 69 (1986), per POWELL, J.—declining to follow *Swain* because it "has placed on defendants a crippling burden of proof"—held that, using the same "combination of factors" as in cases like *Castaneda*, "a defendant may establish a prima facie case of purposeful discrimination in selection of the petit jury solely on evidence concerning the prosecutor's exercise of peremptory challenges at the defendant's trial. [Then], the burden shifts to the State to come forward with a neutral explanation for challenging black jurors. [T]he prosecution's explanation need not rise to the level justifying exercise of a challenge for cause. [B]ut the prosecutor may not rebut the defendant's prima facie case of discrimination by stating merely that he challenged jurors of the defendant's race on the assumption—or his intuitive judgment—that they would be partial to the defendant because of their shared race, [because the] core guarantee of equal protection, ensuring citizens that their State will not discriminate on account of race, would be meaningless" if this were permitted.

REHNQUIST, J., joined by Burger, C.J., dissented: "[T]here is simply nothing 'unequal' about the State using its peremptory challenges to strike blacks from the jury in cases involving black defendants, so long as such challenges are also used to exclude whites in cases involving white defendants, Hispanics in cases involving Hispanic defendants, Asians in cases involving Asian defendants, and so on. This case-specific use of peremptory challenges by the State does not single out blacks, or members of any other race for that matter, for discriminatory treatment."

CON LAW: P. 1171, after *Batson*

AMER CON: P. 903, after note (b)

RTS & LIB: P. 837, after *Batson*

Capital sentencing McCLESKEY v. KEMP, whose facts are set forth in detail at p. 159 of this Supplement, per POWELL, J., rejected petitioner's claim "that the Baldus study compels an inference that his sentence rests on purposeful discrimination." Unlike the jury selection cases, where "the factors that may be considered are limited, usually by state [statute], each particular decision to impose the death penalty is made by a [jury] unique in its composition, and the Constitution requires that its decision rest on consideration of innumerable factors that vary according to the characteristics of the individual defendant and the facts of the particular capital offense." Further, unlike the jury selection context, "here, the State has no practical opportunity to rebut the Baldus study" because "policy considerations" (1) "dictate that jurors [not] be called [to] testify to the motives and influences that led to their verdict" and (2) "suggest the impropriety of our requiring prosecutors to defend their decisions to seek death penalties, often years after they were made." [17] Finally, implementation of laws against murder, which are "at the heart of the State's criminal justice system,

---

17. Requiring a prosecutor to rebut a study that analyzes the past conduct of scores of prosecutors is quite different from requiring a prosecutor to rebut a contemporaneous challenge to his own acts. See *Batson*.

[requires] discretionary judgments. [W]e would demand exceptionally clear proof before we would infer that the discretion has been abused."

BLACKMUN, J., joined by Brennan, Marshall and Stevens, JJ., dissented, reviewing parts of the Baldus study in detail: "I concentrate on the decisions within the prosecutor's office through which the State decided to seek the death penalty and, in particular, the point at which the State proceeded to the penalty phase after conviction. This is a step at which the evidence of the effect of the racial factors was especially strong" and not adequately rebutted by the state.

"I agree [as] to the difficulty of examining the jury's decisionmaking process [but not with the] Court's refusal to require that the prosecutor provide an explanation for his actions * * *. Prosecutors undoubtedly need adequate discretion to allocate the resources of their offices and to fulfill their responsibilities to the public in deciding how best to enforce the law, but this does not place them beyond the constraints imposed on state action under the Fourteenth Amendment. Cf. *Ex parte Virginia*."

REMEDYING SEGREGATION

CON LAW: P. 1216, after note (c)

AMER CON: P. 937, after note (c)

RTS & LIB: P. 882, after note (c)

4. *Beyond schools.* BAZEMORE v. FRIDAY, 478 U.S. 385, 106 S.Ct. 3000, 92 L.Ed.2d 315 (1986), per WHITE, J., held that *Green*'s "affirmative duty to desegregate" has "no application" to the 4–H and Homemaker Clubs (which had been deliberately segregated until 1965) operated by the North Carolina Agricultural Extension Service, despite the fact that a majority of the clubs remained uniracial in 1980: "Even if the Service in effect assigned blacks and whites to separate clubs prior to 1965, it did not do so after that time. While school children must go to school, there is no compulsion to join 4–H or Homemaker Clubs, and while School Boards customarily have the power to create school attendance areas and otherwise designate the school that particular students may attend, there is no statutory or regulatory authority to deny a young person the right to join any Club he or she wishes to join."

BRENNAN, J., joined by Marshall, Blackmun and Stevens, JJ., dissented: "Nothing in our earlier cases suggests that the State's obligation to desegregate is confined only to those activities in which members of the public are compelled to participate."

AFFIRMATIVE ACTION AND "BENIGN" DISCRIMINATION

CON LAW: P. 1247, before note (c)

AMER CON: P. 962, after note (b)

RTS & LIB: P. 913, before note (c)

JOHNSON v. TRANSPORTATION AGENCY, 480 U.S. 616, 107 S.Ct. 1442, 94 L.Ed.2d 615 (1987), per BRENNAN, J., relied on *Weber* to hold that a county agency's [a] voluntary affirmative action plan—which "set aside no specific number of positions for minorities or women, but authorized the consideration of

---

a. Although the case involved a public employer subject to the equal protection clause, "no constitutional issue was either raised or addressed in the litigation below." Thus, the Court decided "only the issue of the prohibitory scope of Title VII," observing that "the *statutory* prohibition [was] not intended to extend as far as that of the Constitution."

ethnicity or sex as a factor when evaluating qualified candidates for jobs in which members of such groups were poorly represented"—did not violate Title VII.[b]

CON LAW: P. 1267, before Sec. 3

AMER CON: P. 980, before Sec. 3

RTS & LIB: P. 933, before Sec. 3

WYGANT v. JACKSON BD. OF EDUC., 476 U.S. 267, 106 S.Ct. 1842, 90 L.Ed.2d 260 (1986), invalidated a layoff provision (Article XII) of a collective bargaining agreement—between a Michigan school board (that had not been found to have previously engaged in racially discriminatory hiring practices) and a teacher's union—that "teachers with the most seniority [shall] be retained, except that at no time will there be a greater percentage of minority personnel laid off than the current percentage of minority personnel [defined as "those employees who are Black, American Indian, Oriental, or of Spanish descendancy"] employed at the time of the layoff." POWELL, J., announced the judgment and an opinion joined by Burger, C.J., and Rehnquist and O'Connor, JJ.: "We must decide whether the layoff provision is supported by a compelling state purpose and whether the means chosen to accomplish that purpose are narrowly tailored. * * *

"This Court never has held that societal discrimination alone is sufficient to justify a racial classification. Rather, the Court has insisted upon some showing of prior discrimination by the governmental unit involved before allowing limited use of racial classifications in order to remedy such discrimination. [See] *Swann*. [The theory of the courts below—] that the Board's interest in providing minority role models for its minority students, as an attempt to alleviate the effects of societal discrimination, was sufficiently important to justify the racial classification embodied in the layoff provision [—] has no logical stopping point. The role model theory allows the Board to engage in discriminatory hiring and layoff practices long past the point required by any legitimate remedial purpose. Indeed, by tying the required percentage of minority teachers to the percentage of minority students, it requires just the sort of year-to-year calibration the Court stated was unnecessary in [*Swann*].

"Moreover, because the role model theory does not necessarily bear a relationship to the harm caused by prior discriminatory hiring practices, it actually could be used to escape the obligation to remedy such practices by justifying the small percentage of black teachers by reference to the small percentage of black students. Carried to its logical extreme, the idea that black students are better off with black teachers could lead to the very system the Court rejected in *Brown*. [No] one doubts that there has been serious racial discrimination in this country. But as the basis for imposing discriminatory *legal* remedies that work against innocent people, societal discrimination is insufficient and over expansive. * * *

"Respondents [*now*] argue that their purpose in adopting the layoff provision was to remedy prior discrimination against minorities by the Jackson School

---

b. Stevens, J., joined the Court's opinion but concurred to emphasize that Title VII permits employers to consider a broad range of "legitimate reasons to give preferences to members of under-represented groups." O'Connor, J., concurred only in the judgment, believing that an employer must be able to "point to a statistical disparity sufficient to support a prima facie claim under Title VII by the employee beneficiaries of the affirmative action plan of a pattern or practice claim of discrimination." Rehnquist, C.J., and Scalia and White, JJ., dissented, urging that *Weber* be overruled.

District in hiring teachers. * * * Evidentiary support for the conclusion that remedial action is warranted becomes crucial when the remedial program is challenged in court by nonminority employees. [Although the] ultimate burden remains with the employees to demonstrate the unconstitutionality of an affirmative action program, [the] trial court must make a factual determination that the employer had a strong basis in evidence for its conclusion that remedial action was necessary.[a] [Nor] can the respondent unilaterally insulate itself from this key constitutional question by conceding that it has discriminated in the past, now that it is in its interest to make such a concession."

Finally, Powell, J.'s opinion (this part not joined by O'Connor, J.) noted that none of the prior decisions recognizing that "innocent persons may be called upon to bear some of the burden [b] [to] remedy the effects of prior discrimination [8] involved layoffs. * * * We have previously expressed concern over the burden that a preferential layoffs scheme imposes on innocent persons. See *Stotts*; see also *Weber*. * * *

"While hiring goals impose a diffuse burden, often foreclosing only one of several opportunities,[11] layoffs impose the entire burden of achieving racial equality on particular individuals, often resulting in serious disruption of their lives. That burden is too intrusive. We therefore hold that, as a means of accomplishing purposes that otherwise may be legitimate, the Board's layoff plan

a. O'Connor, J.'s separate concurring opinion stressed that when public employers "act on the basis of information which gives them a sufficient basis for concluding that remedial action is necessary, a contemporaneous findings requirement should not be necessary. [Such requirement] would severely undermine public employers' incentive to meet voluntarily their civil rights obligations."

b. Compare Scalia, *The Disease as Cure*, 1979 Wash.U.L.Q. 147, 152: "There [are] many white ethnic groups that came to this country in great numbers relatively late in its history—Italians, Jews, Irish, Poles—who not only took no part in, and derived no profit from, the major historic suppression of the currently acknowledged minority groups, but were, in fact, themselves the object of discrimination by the dominant Anglo-Saxon majority. [To] be sure, in relatively recent years some or all of these groups have been the beneficiaries of discrimination against blacks, or have themselves practiced discrimination. But to compare their racial debt—I must use that term, since the concept of "restorative justice" implies it; there is no creditor without a debtor—with that of those who plied the slave trade, and who maintained a formal caste system for many years thereafter, is to confuse a mountain with a molehill. Yet [it] is precisely *these* groups that do most of the restoring. It is they who, to a disproportionate degree, are the competitors with the urban blacks and Hispanics for jobs, housing, education—all those things that enable one to scramble to the top of the social heap where one can speak eloquently (and quite safely) of restorative justice."

8. Of course, when a state implements a race-based plan that requires such a sharing of the burden, it cannot justify the discriminatory effect on some individuals because other individuals had approved the plan. Any "waiver" of the right not to be dealt with by the government on the basis of one's race must be made by those affected. Yet Justice Marshall repeatedly contends that the fact that Article XII was approved by a majority vote of the Union somehow validates this plan. [In] view of the way union seniority works, it is not surprising that while a straight freeze on minority layoffs was overwhelmingly rejected, a "compromise" eventually was reached that placed the entire burden of the compromise on the most junior union members. The more senior union members simply had nothing to lose from such a compromise. [The] Constitution does not allocate constitutional rights to be distributed like bloc grants within discrete racial groups; and until it does, petitioners' more senior union colleagues cannot vote away petitioners' rights. * * *

11. The "school admission" cases, which involve the same basic concepts as cases involving hiring goals, illustrate this principle. For example, in *DeFunis*, while petitioner's complaint alleged that he had been denied admission to the University of Washington Law School because of his race, he also had been accepted at the Oregon, Idaho, Gonzaga, and Willamette Law Schools. The injury to DeFunis was not of the same kind or degree as the injury that he would have suffered had he been removed from law school in his third year. Even this analogy may not rise to the level of harm suffered by a union member who is laid off.

is not sufficiently narrowly tailored.[12]   Other, less intrusive means of accomplishing similar purposes—such as the adoption of hiring goals—are available. For these reasons, the Board's selection of layoffs as the means to accomplish even a valid purpose cannot satisfy the demands of the Equal Protection Clause.[13]

WHITE, J., concurred in the judgment: "Whatever the legitimacy of hiring goals or quotas may be, the discharge of white teachers to make room for blacks, none of whom has been shown to be a victim of any racial discrimination, is quite a different matter. I cannot believe that in order to integrate a work force, it would be permissible to discharge whites and hire blacks until the latter comprised a suitable percentage of the work force. [The] layoff policy of this case [has] the same effect and is equally violative of the Equal Protection Clause."

MARSHALL, J., joined by Brennan and Blackmun, JJ., dissented: "[W]e need not rely on any general awareness of 'societal discrimination' to conclude that the Board's purpose is of sufficient importance to justify its limited remedial efforts. There are allegations that the imperative to integrate the public schools was urgent. Racially motivated violence had erupted at the schools, interfering with all educational objectives. We are told that, having found apparent violations of the law and a substantial underrepresentation of minority teachers, the state agency responsible for ensuring equality [had] instituted a settlement that required the Board to adopt affirmative hiring practices in lieu of further enforcement proceedings. [Surely,] if properly presented to the District Court, this would supply the '[e]videntiary support for the conclusion that remedial action is warranted' that the plurality purports to seek. Since the District Court did not permit submission of this evidentiary support, I am at a loss as to why Justice Powell so glibly rejects the obvious solution of remanding for the factfinding he appears to recognize is necessary. * * *

"Under Justice Powell's approach, the community of Jackson, having painfully watched the hard-won benefits of its integration efforts vanish as a result of massive layoffs, would be informed today, simply, that preferential layoff protection is never permissible because hiring policies serve the same purpose at a lesser cost. As a matter of logic as well as fact, a hiring policy achieves no purpose at all if it is eviscerated by layoffs. [N]either petitioners nor any Justice of this Court has suggested an alternative to Article XII that would have attained the stated goal in any narrower or more equitable fashion. Nor can I conceive of one."

STEVENS, J., also dissented: "[T]he collective-bargaining agreement [stated] a valid public purpose—'recognition of the desirability of multi-ethnic representation on the teaching faculty.' [Thus], there was a rational and unquestionably legitimate basis for the Board's decision to enter into the [agreement,] even though the agreement required special efforts to recruit and retain minority teachers. [T]he question that remains is whether that public purpose transcends the harm to the white teachers who are disadvantaged by the special preference

12. We have recognized, however, that in order to provide make-whole relief to the actual, identified victims of individual discrimination, a court may in an appropriate case award competitive seniority. See *Franks* v. *Bowman Transportation Co.*

13. The Board's definition of minority to include blacks, Orientals, American Indians, and persons of Spanish descent, further illus-trates the undifferentiated nature of the plan. There is no explanation of why the Board chose to favor these particular minorities or how in fact members of some of the categories can be identified. Moreover, respondents have never suggested—much less formally found—that they have engaged in prior, purposeful discrimination against members of each of these minority groups.

the Board has given to its most recently hired minority teachers. In my view, there are two important inquiries in assessing the harm to the disadvantaged teacher. The first is an assessment of the procedures that were used to adopt, and implement, the race-conscious action. The second is an evaluation of the nature of the harm itself.

"[As] Justice Marshall has demonstrated, the procedures for adopting this provision were scrupulously fair. The Union that represents the petitioners negotiated the provision and agreed to it; the agreement was put to a vote of the membership, and overwhelmingly approved. [Similarly], the provision is specifically designed to achieve its objective—retaining the minority teachers that have been specially recruited to give the Jackson schools, after a period of racial unrest, an integrated faculty. * * *[14]"

SHEET METAL WORKERS v. EEOC, 478 U.S. 421, 106 S.Ct. 3019, 92 L.Ed.2d 344 (1986): In 1975, a federal district court, having found that petitioner union had discriminated against nonwhites in violation of Title VII of the Civil Rights Act of 1964, ordered a 29% nonwhite membership goal (based on the percentage of nonwhites in the labor pool) to be achieved by 1981, subsequently extended to 1982. In both 1982 and 1983, the district court held the union in contempt for "egregious noncompliance" with the various remedial orders over the years. It also amended the nonwhite membership goal to 29.23%, to be met by 1987. The Supreme Court affirmed.

BRENNAN, J., joined by Marshall, Stevens and Blackmun, JJ., first held that § 706(g) of the Civil Rights Act—"No order of the court shall require the admission or reinstatement of an individual as a member of a union, or the hiring, reinstatement, or promotion of an individual as an employee, or the payment to him of back pay, if such individual was refused admission, suspended, or expelled, or was refused employment or advancement for any reason other than discrimination on account of race, color, religion, sex or national origin in violation [of] this title"—"does not, as petitioners and the Solicitor General suggest, say that a court may order relief only for actual victims of past discrimination. The sentence on its face addresses only the situation where a plaintiff demonstrates that a union (or an employer) has engaged in unlawful discrimination, but the union can show that a particular individual would have been refused admission even in the absence of discrimination, for example because that individual was unqualified. In these circumstances, § 706(g) confirms that a court could not order the union to admit the unqualified individual. [Where] an employer or union has engaged in particularly longstanding or egregious discrimination, * * * requiring recalcitrant employers or unions to hire and to admit qualified minorities roughly in proportion to the number of qualified minorities in the work force may be the only effective way to ensure the full enjoyment of the rights protected by Title VII.[a] [W]hile Congress

---

14. The fact that the issue arises in a lay-off context, rather than a hiring context, has no bearing on the equal protection question. [Powell, J.] seems to assume that a teacher who has been working for a few years suffers a greater harm when he is laid off than the harm suffered by an unemployed teacher who is refused a job for which he is qualified. In either event, the adverse decision forecloses "only one of several opportunities" that may be available to the disappointed teacher.

Moreover, the distinction is artificial, for the layoff provision at issue in this case was included as part of the terms of the *hiring* of minority and other teachers under the collective-bargaining agreement.

a. Brennan, J.'s opinion subsequently emphasized that the membership goal did not establish an "inflexible racial quota": "The record shows that the District Court has been willing to accommodate *legitimate* reasons for

opposed the use of quotas or preferences merely to maintain racial balance, it gave no intimation as to whether such measures would be acceptable as *remedies* for Title VII violations."[b]

Second, as for equal protection, "we conclude that the relief ordered in this case passes even the most rigorous test—it is narrowly tailored to further the Government's compelling interest in remedying past discrimination. [T]here is no problem, as there was in *Wygant*, with a proper showing of prior discrimination that would justify the use of remedial racial classifications. [T]he District Court considered the efficacy of alternative remedies, and concluded that, in light of petitioners' long record of resistance to official efforts to end their discriminatory practices, stronger measures were necessary. The court devised the temporary membership goal [for] remedying past discrimination. More importantly, the District Court's orders will have only a marginal impact on the interests of white workers. [T]he District Court's orders did not disadvantage *existing* union members. While white applicants for union membership may be denied certain benefits available to their nonwhite counterparts, the court's orders do not stand as an absolute bar to the admission of such individuals; again, a majority of those entering the union after entry of the court's orders have been white."

POWELL, J., concurred in the judgment, relying on five factors to conclude that the "remedy is 'narrowly tailored' to the goal of eradicating the discrimination engaged in by petitioners": "First, it is doubtful, given petitioners' history in this litigation, that the District Court has available to it any other effective remedy. * * * Second, the goal was not imposed as a permanent requirement, but is of limited duration. Third, the goal is directly related to the percentage of nonwhites in the relevant workforce. [Fourth, the] flexible application of the goal requirement in this case demonstrates that it is not a means to achieve racial balance. [Finally, it was] conceded at oral argument that imposition of the goal would not require the layoff of nonminority union workers, and that therefore the District Court's order did not disadvantage existing union members. This case is thus distinguishable from [*Wygant*].[3]

"My view that the imposition of flexible goals as a remedy for past discrimination may be permissible under the Constitution is not an endorsement of their indiscriminate use. Nor do I imply that the adoption of such a goal will always pass constitutional muster."[c]

---

petitioner's failure to comply with court orders, and we have no reason to expect that this will change in the future."

b. Powell, J., concurred in this result "in cases [such as this] involving particularly egregious conduct." White, J., "general[ly] agreed," but dissented because he interpreted the district court's remedy in this case as establishing "not just a minority membership goal but also a strict racial quota that the union was required to attain. We have not heretofore approved this kind of racially discriminatory hiring practice, and I would not do so now." O'Connor, J., agreed with White, J.'s latter point as a matter of statutory interpretation. Rehnquist, J., joined by Burger, C.J., also dissented because "§ 706(g) does not allow us [to] sanction the granting of relief to those who were not victims at the expense of

innocent minority workers injured by racial preferences."

3. Of course, it is too simplistic to conclude from the combined holdings in *Wygant* and this case that hiring goals withstand constitutional muster whereas layoff goals and fixed quotas do not. There may be cases, for example, where a hiring goal in a particularly specialized area of employment would have the same pernicious effect as the layoff goal in *Wygant*. The proper constitutional inquiry focuses on the effect, if any, and the diffuseness of the burden imposed on innocent nonminorities, not on the label applied to the particular employment plan at issue.

c. Burger, C.J., and White, Rehnquist and O'Connor, JJ., found it unnecessary to reach the issue of constitutionality.

UNITED STATES v. PARADISE, 480 U.S. 149, 107 S.Ct. 1053, 94 L.Ed.2d 203 (1987): In 1972, a federal district court found that the Alabama Department of Public Safety had intentionally excluded all blacks from employment as state troopers during its entire 37 year history. The court enjoined the Department, inter alia, from engaging in any promotional practices "for the purpose or with the effect of discriminating against any employee [on] the ground of race or color." During the next eleven years, the court issued a series of further orders dealing with "attempts by the Department to delay or frustrate compliance." This included a consent decree in 1979—when "out of 232 state troopers at the rank of corporal or above, there is still not one black"—by which "the Department agreed to develop within one year [a] promotion procedure with little or no adverse impact on blacks." In 1983, "confronted with the Department's failure to develop promotion procedures" and with only four black corporals out of 66 and no blacks at any higher ranks, "the District Court ordered the promotion of one black trooper for each white trooper elevated in rank, as long as qualified black candidates were available, until the Department implemented an acceptable promotion procedure." The Supreme Court affirmed.

BRENNAN, J., joined by Marshall, Blackmun and Powell, JJ., found "that the relief ordered survives even strict scrutiny analysis." In response to the contention "that the Department was found guilty only of discrimination in hiring, and not in its promotional practices," the plurality held that "the race-conscious relief at issue here is justified by a compelling interest in remedying the discrimination that permeated entry-level hiring practices and the promotional process alike. [It] is also supported by the societal interest in compliance with the judgments of federal courts. The relief at issue was imposed upon a defendant with a consistent history of resistance to the District Court's orders, and only *after* the Department failed to live up to its court-approved commitments."

In addition, the plurality found "that the one-for-one promotion requirement was narrowly tailored to serve its several purposes, both as applied to the initial set of promotions to the rank of corporal and as a continuing contingent order with respect to the upper ranks"—stressing that "it was *necessary* [in order] to eliminate the effects of the Department's 'long term, open, and pervasive' discrimination" without further delay.

"The feature of the one-for-one requirement and its actual operation indicate that it is flexible ["waivable and temporary"] in application at all ranks. The requirement may be waived if no qualified black candidates are available. The Department has, for example, been permitted to promote only white troopers to the ranks of lieutenant and captain since no black troopers have qualified for those positions. Further, it applies only when the Department needs to make promotions. Thus, if external forces, such as budget cuts, necessitate a promotion freeze, the Department will not be required to make gratuitous promotions to remain in compliance with the court's order.

"Most significantly, [the] requirement endures only until the Department comes up with a procedure that does not have [an] adverse impact, demonstrating that it is not a disguised means to achieve racial balance. [When] the District Court imposed the provision, the judge expressed the hope that its use would be 'a one-time occurrence.' [Four months later, the Department] submitted procedures for promotions to corporal and sergeant, and the court has consequently suspended application of the promotional order with respect to those ranks. * * *

"The Government suggests that the one-for-one requirement is arbitrary because it bears no relationship to the 25% minority labor pool relevant here. This argument ignores that the 50% figure is not itself the goal; rather it represents the speed at which the goal of 25% will be achieved. [T]he District Court, with its first-hand experience of the parties and the potential for resistance, imposed the requirement that it determined would compensate for past delay and prevent future recalcitrance, while not unduly burdening the interests [of] white applicants for promotion. It was used only once at the rank of corporal and may not be utilized at all in the upper ranks. Nor has the court imposed an 'absolute bar' to white advancement. *Sheet Metal Workers.* In the one instance in which the quota was employed, 50% of those elevated were white.

"The one-for-one requirement does not require the layoff and discharge of white employees and therefore does not impose burdens of the sort that concerned the plurality in *Wygant.* Because the one-for-one requirement is so limited in scope and duration, it only postpones the promotions of qualified whites. Consequently, like a hiring goal, it 'impose[s] a diffuse burden, * * * foreclosing only one of several opportunities.' Id. 'Denial of a future employment opportunity is not as intrusive as loss of an existing job,' *Wygant,* and plainly postponement imposes a lesser burden still.

"Finally, the basic limitation, that black troopers promoted must be qualified, remains. Qualified white candidates simply have to compete with qualified black candidates. To be sure, should the District Court's promotion requirement be applied, black applicants would receive some advantage. But this situation is only temporary, and is subject to amelioration by the action of the Department itself.

"Accordingly, the one-for-one promotion requirement imposed in this case does not disproportionately harm the interests, or unnecessarily trammel the rights, of innocent individuals.

"In determining whether this order was 'narrowly tailored,' we must acknowledge the respect owed a District Court's judgment that specified relief is essential to cure a violation of the Fourteenth Amendment. [Nor] have we in all situations 'required remedial plans to be limited to the least restrictive means of implementation. We have recognized that the choice of remedies to redress racial discrimination is "a balancing process left, within appropriate constitutional or statutory limits, to the sound discretion of the trial court." ' *Fullilove* (Powell, J., concurring). [The] District Judge determined that the record demonstrated that 'without promotional quotas the continuing effects of [the Department's] discrimination cannot be eliminated.' His proximate position and broad equitable powers mandate substantial respect for this judgment."

POWELL, J., also filed a concurrence: "The District Court imposed the one-for-one promotion requirement only on one occasion, when it ordered the promotion of eight blacks and eight whites to the rank of corporal in February 1984. Because the Department urgently needed at least fifteen additional corporals, there appears to have been no alternative remedy that would have met the then-existing need. Given the findings of persistent discrimination, the Department's longstanding resistance to necessary remedies, and the exigent circumstances presented to the District Court, the imposition of a one-for-one requirement for the particular promotions at issue did not violate the Equal Protection Clause."

STEVENS, J., concurred in the judgment: "[T]he record discloses an egregious violation of the Equal Protection Clause. It follows, therefore, [from *Swann*,] that the District Court had broad and flexible authority to remedy wrongs resulting from this violation * * *.

"A party who has been found guilty of repeated and persistent violations of the law bears the burden of demonstrating that the chancellor's efforts to fashion effective relief exceed the bounds of 'reasonableness.' The burden of proof in a case like this is precisely the opposite of that in cases such as *Wygant* and *Fullilove,* which did not involve any proven violations of law.[3] In such cases the governmental decisionmaker who would make race-conscious decisions must overcome a strong presumption against them. No such burden rests on a federal district judge who has found that the governmental unit before him is guilty of racially discriminatory conduct that violates the Constitution."

O'CONNOR, J., joined by Rehnquist, C.J., and Scalia, J., although agreeing that "the Federal Government has a compelling interest in remedying past and present discrimination by the Department," dissented "because the Court adopts a standardless view of 'narrowly tailored' far less stringent than that required by strict scrutiny."

In the dissent's view, "the order at issue [clearly had] one purpose only—to compel the Department to develop a promotion procedure that would not have an adverse impact on blacks. [The] District Court had available several alternatives that would have achieved full compliance with the consent decrees without trammelling on the rights of nonminority troopers. The court, for example, could have appointed a trustee to develop a promotion procedure that would satisfy the terms of the consent decrees. [Or it] could have found the recalcitrant Department in contempt of court, and imposed stiff fines or other penalties for the contempt. [What] is most disturbing [is] that the District Court imposed the promotion quota *without consideration of any of the available alternatives.* [If this] can survive strict scrutiny as narrowly tailored, the requirement that a racial classification be 'narrowly tailored' for a compelling governmental purpose has lost most of its meaning. * * *

"Moreover, even if the one-for-one quota had the purpose of eradicating the effects of the Department's delay, [it] far exceeded the percentage of blacks in the trooper force, and there is no evidence in the record that such an extreme quota was [necessary]. The Court attempts to defend this one-for-one promotion quota as merely affecting the speed by which the Department attains the goal of 25% black representation in the upper ranks. Such a justification, however, necessarily eviscerates any notion of 'narrowly tailored' because it has no stopping point; even a 100% quota could be defended on the ground that it merely 'determined how quickly the Department progressed toward' some ultimate goal."

WHITE, J., "agreeing with much of" O'Connor, J.'s opinion, found "it evident that the District Court exceeded its equitable powers in devising a remedy in this case."

---

3. The law violator who would oppose a remedy imposed against him as itself a violation of the law does not stand in the same position as an innocent party; those whom the court has found in the wrong may not oppose a remedy on the ground that it would constitute a wrong if leveled at a nonparticipant in the litigation. * * *

RICHMOND v. J.A. CROSON CO.

— U.S. —, 109 S.Ct. 706, 102 L.Ed.2d 854 (1989).

JUSTICE O'CONNOR announced the judgment of the Court and delivered the opinion of the Court with respect to Parts I, III–B, and IV, an opinion with respect to Part II, in which THE CHIEF JUSTICE and JUSTICE WHITE join, and an opinion with respect to Parts III–A and V, in which THE CHIEF JUSTICE, JUSTICE WHITE and JUSTICE KENNEDY join. * * *

I. On April 11, 1983, the Richmond City Council adopted the Minority Business Utilization Plan (the Plan). The Plan required prime contractors to whom the city awarded construction contracts to subcontract at least 30% of the dollar amount of the contract to one or more Minority Business Enterprises (MBEs) [defined] as "[a] business at least fifty-one (51) percent of which is owned and controlled [by] minority group members." "Minority group members" were defined as "[c]itizens of the United States who are Blacks, Spanish-speaking, Orientals, Indians, Eskimos, or Aleuts." [The] Plan declared that it was "reme-dial" in nature, and enacted "for the purpose of promoting wider participation by minority business enterprises in the construction of public projects." The Plan expired on June 30, 1988, and was in effect for approximately five years.

The Plan authorized the Director of the Department of General Services to promulgate rules which "shall allow waivers in those individual situations where a contractor can prove to the satisfaction of the director that the requirements herein cannot be achieved." * * * .

The Plan was adopted by the Richmond City Council after a public hearing. Seven members of the public spoke to the merits of the ordinance: five were in opposition, two in favor. Proponents of the set-aside provision relied on a study which indicated that, while the general population of Richmond was 50% black, only .67% of the city's prime construction contracts had been awarded to minority businesses in the 5-year period from 1978 to 1983. It was also established that a variety of contractors' associations, whose representatives appeared in opposition to the ordinance, had virtually no minority businesses within their membership. * * *

There was no direct evidence of race discrimination on the part of the city in letting contracts or any evidence that the city's prime contractors had discrimi-nated against minority-owned subcontractors. * * * Representatives of var-ious contractors' associations questioned whether there were enough MBEs in the Richmond area to satisfy the 30% set-aside requirement. Mr. Murphy noted that only 4.7% of all construction firms in the United States were minority owned and that 41% of these were located in California, New York, Illinois, Florida, and Hawaii. He predicted that the ordinance would thus lead to a windfall for the few minority firms in Richmond. Councilperson Gillespie indicated his concern that many local labor jobs, held by both blacks and whites, would be lost because the ordinance put no geographic limit on the MBEs eligible for the 30% set-aside. Some of the representatives of the local contrac-tors organizations indicated that they did not discriminate on the basis of race and were in fact actively seeking out minority members. * * *

[The case was brought by a contractor whose low bid on a city project was not accepted because of failure to comply with the Plan's requirements. Relying on *Wygant*,] a divided panel of the Court of Appeals struck down the Richmond set-aside program as violating both prongs of strict scrutiny under the Equal Protection [Clause].

II. The parties and their supporting amici fight an initial battle over the scope of the city's power to adopt legislation designed to address the effects of past discrimination. Relying on our decision in *Wygant,* appellee argues that the city must limit any race-based remedial efforts to eradicating the effects of its own prior discrimination. This is essentially the position taken by the Court of Appeals below. Appellant argues that our decision in *Fullilove* is controlling, and that as a result the city of Richmond enjoys sweeping legislative power to define and attack the effects of prior discrimination in its local construction industry. We find that neither of these two rather stark alternatives can withstand analysis. * * *

Appellant and its supporting amici rely heavily on *Fullilove* for the proposition that a city council, like Congress, need not make specific findings of discrimination to engage in race-conscious relief. Thus, appellant argues "[i]t would be a perversion of federalism to hold that the federal government has a compelling interest in remedying the effects of racial discrimination in its own public works program, but a city government does not."

What appellant ignores is that Congress, unlike any State or political subdivision, has a specific constitutional mandate to enforce the dictates of the Fourteenth Amendment. The power to "enforce" may at times also include the power to define situations which *Congress* determines threaten principles of equality and to adopt prophylactic rules to deal with those situations. See *Katzenbach v. Morgan.* See also *South Carolina v. Katzenbach* * * *.

That Congress may identify and redress the effects of society-wide discrimination does not mean that, a fortiori, the States and their political subdivisions are free to decide that such remedies are appropriate. Section 1 of the Fourteenth Amendment is an explicit *constraint* on state power, and the States must undertake any remedial efforts in accordance with that provision. To hold otherwise would be to cede control over the content of the Equal Protection Clause to the 50 state legislatures and their myriad political subdivisions. The mere recitation of a benign or compensatory purpose for the use of a racial classification would essentially entitle the States to exercise the full power of Congress under § 5 of the Fourteenth Amendment and insulate any racial classification from judicial scrutiny under § 1. We believe that such a result would be contrary to the intentions of the Framers of the Fourteenth Amendment, who desired to place clear limits on the States' use of race as a criterion for legislative action, and to have the federal courts enforce those limitations. * * *

It would seem equally clear, however, that a state or local subdivision (if delegated the authority from the State) has the authority to eradicate the effects of private discrimination within its own legislative jurisdiction. This authority must, of course, be exercised within the constraints of § 1 of the Fourteenth Amendment. Our decision in *Wygant* is not to the contrary. *Wygant* addressed the constitutionality of the use of racial quotas by local school authorities pursuant to an agreement reached with the local teachers' union. It was in the context of addressing the school board's power to adopt a race-based layoff program affecting its own work force that the *Wygant* plurality indicated that the Equal Protection Clause required "some showing of prior discrimination by the governmental unit involved." As a matter of state law, the city of Richmond has legislative authority over its procurement policies, and can use its spending powers to remedy private discrimination, if it identifies that discrimination with the particularity required by the Fourteenth Amendment. To this extent, on the question of the city's competence, the Court of Appeals erred in following

Wygant by rote in a case involving a state entity which has state-law authority to address discriminatory practices within local commerce under its jurisdiction.

Thus, if the city could show that it had essentially become a "passive participant" in a system of racial exclusion practiced by elements of the local construction industry, we think it clear that the city could take affirmative steps to dismantle such a system. It is beyond dispute that any public entity, state or federal, has a compelling interest in assuring that public dollars, drawn from the tax contributions of all citizens, do not serve to finance the evil of private prejudice. Cf. *Norwood v. Harrison.*

III. A. [The] Richmond Plan denies certain citizens the opportunity to compete for a fixed percentage of public contracts based solely upon their race. To whatever racial group these citizens belong, their "personal rights" to be treated with equal dignity and respect are implicated by a rigid rule erecting race as the sole criterion in an aspect of public decisionmaking.

Absent searching judicial inquiry into the justification for such race-based measures, there is simply no way of determining what classifications are "benign" or "remedial" and what classifications are in fact motivated by illegitimate notions of racial inferiority or simple racial politics. Indeed, the purpose of strict scrutiny is to "smoke out" illegitimate uses of race by assuring that the legislative body is pursuing a goal important enough to warrant use of a highly suspect tool. The test also ensures that the means chosen "fit" this compelling goal so closely that there is little or no possibility that the motive for the classification was illegitimate racial prejudice or stereotype.

Classifications based on race carry a danger of stigmatic harm. Unless they are strictly reserved for remedial settings, they may in fact promote notions of racial inferiority and lead to a politics of racial hostility. We thus reaffirm the view expressed by the plurality in *Wygant* that the standard of review under the Equal Protection Clause is not dependent on the race of those burdened or benefited by a particular classification. * * *

Under the standard proposed by Justice Marshall's dissent, "[r]ace-conscious classifications designed to further remedial goals" are forthwith subject to a relaxed standard of review. How the dissent arrives at the legal conclusion that a racial classification is "designed to further remedial goals," without first engaging in an examination of the factual basis for its enactment and the nexus between its scope and that factual basis we are not told. However, once the "remedial" conclusion is reached, the dissent's standard is singularly deferential, and bears little resemblance to the close examination of legislative purpose we have engaged in when reviewing classifications based either on race or gender. The dissent's watered-down version of equal protection review effectively assures that race will always be relevant in American life, and that the "ultimate goal" of "eliminat[ing] entirely from governmental decisionmaking such irrelevant factors as a human being's race," *Wygant* (Stevens, J., dissenting), will never be achieved.

Even were we to accept a reading of the guarantee of equal protection under which the level of scrutiny varies according to the ability of different groups to defend their interests in the representative process, heightened scrutiny would still be appropriate in the circumstances of this case. One of the central arguments for applying a less exacting standard to "benign" racial classifications is that such measures essentially involve a choice made by dominant racial groups to disadvantage themselves. If one aspect of the judiciary's role under the Equal Protection Clause is to protect "discrete and insular minorities" from majoritarian prejudice or indifference, see *United States v. Carolene Products Co.,* some maintain that these concerns are not implicated when the "white majority" places burdens upon itself. See Ely, *Democracy and Distrust* 170 (1980).

In this case, blacks comprise approximately 50% of the population of the city of Richmond. Five of the nine seats on the City Council are held by blacks. The concern that a political majority will more easily act to the disadvantage of a minority based on unwarranted assumptions or incomplete facts would seem to militate for, not against, the application of heightened judicial scrutiny in this case. * * *

B. [The] District Court found the city council's "findings sufficient to ensure that, in adopting the Plan, it was remedying the present effects of past discrimination in the *construction industry.*" Like the "role model" theory employed in *Wygant,* a generalized assertion that there has been past discrimination in an entire industry provides no guidance for a legislative body to determine the precise scope of the injury it seeks to remedy. It "has no logical stopping point." *Wygant.* "Relief" for such an ill-defined wrong could extend until the percentage of public contracts awarded to MBEs in Richmond mirrored the percentage of minorities in the population as a whole.

Appellant argues that it is attempting to remedy various forms of past discrimination that are alleged to be responsible for the small number of minority businesses in the local contracting industry. Among these the city cites the exclusion of blacks from skilled construction trade unions and training programs. This past discrimination has prevented them "from following the traditional path from laborer to entrepreneur." The city also lists a host of nonracial factors which would seem to face a member of any racial group attempting to establish a new business enterprise, such as deficiencies in working capital, inability to meet bonding requirements, unfamiliarity with bidding procedures, and disability caused by an inadequate track record.

While there is no doubt that the sorry history of both private and public discrimination in this country has contributed to a lack of opportunities for black entrepreneurs, this observation, standing alone, cannot justify a rigid racial quota in the awarding of public contracts in Richmond, Virginia. Like the claim that discrimination in primary and secondary schooling justifies a rigid racial preference in medical school admissions, an amorphous claim that there has been past discrimination in a particular industry cannot justify the use of an unyielding racial quota.

It is sheer speculation how many minority firms there would be in Richmond absent past societal discrimination, just as it was sheer speculation how many minority medical students would have been admitted to the medical school at Davis absent past discrimination in educational opportunities. Defining these sorts of injuries as "identified discrimination" would give local governments license to create a patchwork of racial preferences based on statistical generalizations about any particular field of endeavor.

These defects are readily apparent in this case. The 30% quota cannot in any realistic sense be tied to any injury suffered by anyone. The District Court relied upon five predicate "facts" [discussed below] in reaching its conclusion that there was an adequate basis for the 30% quota * * *.

None of these "findings," singly or together, provide the city of Richmond with a "strong basis in evidence for its conclusion that remedial action was necessary." *Wygant.* There is nothing approaching a prima facie case of a constitutional or statutory violation by *anyone* in the Richmond construction industry. *Id.*

The District Court accorded great weight to the fact that the city council designated the Plan as "remedial." But the mere recitation of a "benign" or legitimate purpose for a racial classification, is entitled to little or no weight. Racial classifications are suspect, and that means that simple legislative assurances of good intention cannot suffice.

The District Court also relied on the highly conclusionary statement of a proponent of the Plan that there was racial discrimination in the construction industry "in this area, and the State, and around the nation." It also noted that the city manager had related his view that racial discrimination still plagued the construction industry in his home city of Pittsburg. These statements are of little probative value in establishing identified discrimination in the Richmond construction industry. The fact-finding process of legislative bodies is generally entitled to a presumption of regularity and deferential review by the judiciary. But when a legislative body chooses to employ a suspect classification, it cannot rest upon a generalized assertion as to the classification's relevance to its goals.

* * *

Reliance on the disparity between the number of prime contracts awarded to minority firms and the minority population of the city of Richmond is similarly misplaced. * * *

In the employment context, we have recognized that for certain entry level positions or positions requiring minimal training, statistical comparisons of the racial composition of an employer's workforce to the racial composition of the relevant population may be probative of a pattern of discrimination. See *Teamsters v. United States.* But where special qualifications are necessary, the relevant statistical pool for purposes of demonstrating discriminatory exclusion must be the number of minorities qualified to undertake the particular task.

In this case, the city does not even know how many MBEs in the relevant market are qualified to undertake prime or subcontracting work in public construction projects. Compare *Ohio Contractors Assn. v. Keip,* 713 F.2d, at 171 (relying on percentage of minority *businesses* in the State compared to percentage of state purchasing contracts awarded to minority firms in upholding set-aside). Nor does the city know what percentage of total city construction dollars minority firms now receive as subcontractors on prime contracts let by the city.

To a large extent, the set-aside of subcontracting dollars seems to rest on the unsupported assumption that white prime contractors simply will not hire minority firms.[3] Indeed, there is evidence in this record that overall minority participation in city contracts in Richmond is seven to eight percent, and that minority contractor participation in Community Block Development Grant *construction* projects is 17% to 22%. Without any information on minority participation in subcontracting, it is quite simply impossible to evaluate overall minority representation in the city's construction expenditures.

---

3. Since 1975 the city of Richmond has had an ordinance on the books prohibiting both discrimination in the award of public contracts and employment discrimination by public contractors. The city points to no evidence that its prime contractors have been violating the ordinance in either their employment or subcontracting practices. The complete silence of the record concerning enforcement of the city's own anti-discrimination ordinance flies in the face of the dissent's vision of a "tight-knit industry" which has prevented blacks from obtaining the experience necessary to participate in construction contracting.

The city and the District Court also relied on evidence that MBE membership in local contractors' associations was extremely low. Again, standing alone this evidence is not probative of any discrimination in the local construction industry. There are numerous explanations for this dearth of minority participation, including past societal discrimination in education and economic opportunities as well as both black and white career and entrepreneurial choices. [The] mere fact that black membership in these trade organizations is low, standing alone, cannot establish a prima facie case of discrimination.

For low minority membership in these associations to be relevant, the city would have to link it to the number of local MBEs eligible for membership. If the statistical disparity between eligible MBEs and MBE membership were great enough, an inference of discriminatory exclusion could arise. In such a case, the city would have a compelling interest in preventing its tax dollars from assisting these organizations in maintaining a racially segregated construction market. See *Norwood; Ohio Contractors* (upholding minority set-aside based in part on earlier District Court finding that "the state had become 'a joint participant' with private industry and certain craft unions in a pattern of racially discriminatory conduct which excluded black laborers from work on public construction contracts").

Finally, the city and the District Court relied on Congress' finding in connection with the set-aside approved in *Fullilove* that there had been nationwide discrimination in the construction industry. The probative value of these findings for demonstrating the existence of discrimination in Richmond is extremely limited. By its inclusion of a waiver procedure in the national program addressed in *Fullilove,* Congress explicitly recognized that the scope of the problem would vary from market area to market area.

Moreover, as noted above, Congress was exercising its powers under § 5 of the Fourteenth Amendment in making a finding that past discrimination would cause federal funds to be distributed in a manner which reinforced prior patterns of discrimination. While the States and their subdivisions may take remedial action when they possess evidence that their own spending practices are exacerbating a pattern of prior discrimination, they must identify that discrimination, public or private, with some specificity before they may use race-conscious relief. Congress has made national findings that there has been societal discrimination in a host of fields. If all a state or local government need do is find a congressional report on the subject to enact a set-aside program, the constraints of the Equal Protection Clause will, in effect, have been rendered a nullity. [The] "evidence" relied upon by the dissent, the history of school desegregation in Richmond and numerous congressional reports, does little to define the scope of any injury to minority contractors in Richmond or the necessary remedy. The factors relied upon by the dissent could justify a preference of any size or duration. * * *

In sum, none of the evidence presented by the city points to any identified discrimination in the Richmond construction industry. We, therefore, hold that the city has failed to demonstrate a compelling interest in apportioning public contracting opportunities on the basis of race. To accept Richmond's claim that past societal discrimination alone can serve as the basis for rigid racial preferences would be to open the door to competing claims for "remedial relief" for every disadvantaged group. The dream of a Nation of equal citizens in a society where race is irrelevant to personal opportunity and achievement would be lost in a mosaic of shifting preferences based on inherently unmeasurable claims of past wrongs. * * *

The foregoing analysis applies only to the inclusion of blacks within the Richmond set-aside program. There is *absolutely no evidence* of past discrimination against Spanish-speaking, Oriental, Indian, Eskimo, or Aleut persons in any aspect of the Richmond construction industry. * * *

If a 30% set-aside was "narrowly tailored" to compensate black contractors for past discrimination, one may legitimately ask why they are forced to share this "remedial relief" with an Aleut citizen who moves to Richmond tomorrow? The gross overinclusiveness of Richmond's racial preference strongly impugns the city's claim of remedial motivation.

IV. As noted by the court below, it is almost impossible to assess whether the Richmond Plan is narrowly tailored to remedy prior discrimination since it is not linked to identified discrimination in any way. We limit ourselves to two observations in this regard.

First, there does not appear to have been any consideration of the use of race-neutral means to increase minority business participation in city contracting. Many of the barriers to minority participation in the construction industry relied upon by the city to justify a racial classification appear to be race neutral. If MBEs disproportionately lack capital or cannot meet bonding requirements, a race-neutral program of city financing for small firms would, a fortiori, lead to greater minority participation. The principal opinion in *Fullilove* found that Congress had carefully examined and rejected race-neutral alternatives before enacting the MBE set-aside.

Second, the 30% quota cannot be said to be narrowly tailored to any goal, except perhaps outright racial balancing. It rests upon the "completely unrealistic" assumption that minorities will choose a particular trade in lockstep proportion to their representation in the local population.

Since the city must already consider bids and waivers on a case-by-case basis, it is difficult to see the need for a rigid numerical quota. As noted above, the congressional scheme upheld in *Fullilove* allowed for a waiver of the set-aside provision where an MBE's higher price was not attributable to the effects of past discrimination. Based upon proper findings, such programs are less problematic from an equal protection standpoint because they treat all candidates individually, rather than making the color of an applicant's skin the sole relevant consideration. Unlike the program upheld in *Fullilove,* the Richmond Plan's waiver system focuses solely on the availability of MBEs; there is no inquiry into whether or not the particular MBE seeking a racial preference has suffered from the effects of past discrimination by the city or prime contractors.

Given the existence of an individualized procedure, the city's only interest in maintaining a quota system rather than investigating the need for remedial action in particular cases would seem to be simple administrative convenience. But the interest in avoiding the bureaucratic effort necessary to tailor remedial relief to those who truly have suffered the effects of prior discrimination cannot justify a rigid line drawn on the basis of a suspect classification. Under Richmond's scheme, a successful black, Hispanic, or Oriental entrepreneur from anywhere in the country enjoys an absolute preference over other citizens based solely on their race. We think it obvious that such a program is not narrowly tailored to remedy the effects of prior discrimination.

V. Nothing we say today precludes a state or local entity from taking action to rectify the effects of identified discrimination within its jurisdiction. If the city of Richmond had evidence before it that nonminority contractors were systematically excluding minority businesses from subcontracting opportunities it could take action to end the discriminatory exclusion. Where there is a significant statistical disparity between the number of qualified minority contractors willing and able to perform a particular service and the number of such contractors actually engaged by the locality or the locality's prime contractors, an inference of discriminatory exclusion could arise. Under such circumstances, the city could act to dismantle the closed business system by taking appropriate measures against those who discriminate on the basis of race or other illegitimate criteria. In the extreme case, some form of narrowly tailored racial preference might be necessary to break down patterns of deliberate exclusion.

* * *

Proper findings in this regard are necessary to define both the scope of the injury and the extent of the remedy necessary to cure its effects. Such findings also serve to assure all citizens that the deviation from the norm of equal treatment of all racial and ethnic groups is a temporary matter, a measure taken in the service of the goal of equality itself. Absent such findings, there is a danger that a racial classification is merely the product of unthinking stereotypes or a form of racial politics. * * *

Affirmed.

JUSTICE STEVENS, concurring in part and concurring in the judgment.

* * * I believe the Constitution requires us to evaluate our policy decisions—including those that govern the relationships among different racial and ethnic groups—primarily by studying their probable impact on the future. I therefore do not agree with the premise that seems to underlie today's decision, as well as the decision in *Wygant*, that a governmental decision that rests on a racial classification is never permissible except as a remedy for a past wrong.[1] I do, however, agree with the Court's explanation of why the Richmond ordinance cannot be justified as a remedy for past discrimination, and therefore join Parts I, III–B, and IV of its opinion. I write separately to emphasize [views stated in Stevens, J.'s opinions in *Wygant, Paradise* and *Fullilove*].

JUSTICE KENNEDY, concurring in part and concurring in the judgment.

I join all but Part II of Justice O'Connor's opinion * * *.

[The] process by which a law that is an equal protection violation when enacted by a State becomes transformed to an equal protection guarantee when enacted by Congress poses a difficult proposition for me; but as it is not before us, any reconsideration of that issue must await some further case. * * *

The moral imperative of racial neutrality is the driving force of the Equal Protection Clause. Justice Scalia's opinion underscores that proposition, quite properly in my view. The rule suggested in his opinion, which would strike

---

1. In my view the Court's approach to this case gives unwarranted deference to race-based legislative action that purports to serve a purely remedial goal, and overlooks the potential value of race-based determinations that may serve other valid purposes. With regard to the former point—as I explained at some length in *Fullilove*—I am not prepared to assume that even a more narrowly tailored set-aside program supported by stronger findings would be constitutionally justified. Unless the legislature can identify both the particular victims and the particular perpetrators of past discrimination, which is precisely what a court does when it makes findings of fact and conclusions of law, a *remedial* justification for race-based legislation will almost certainly sweep too broadly. With regard to the latter point: I think it unfortunate that the Court in neither *Wygant* nor this case seems prepared to acknowledge that some race-based policy decisions may serve a legitimate public purpose. I agree, of course, that race is so seldom relevant to legislative decisions on how best to foster the public good that legitimate justifications for race-based legislation will usually not be available. But unlike the Court, I would not totally discount the legitimacy of race-based decisions that may produce tangible and fully justified future benefits.

down all preferences which are not necessary remedies to victims of unlawful discrimination, would serve important structural goals, as it would eliminate the necessity for courts to pass upon each racial preference that is enacted. Structural protections may be necessities if moral imperatives are to be obeyed. His opinion would make it crystal clear to the political branches, at least those of the States, that legislation must be based on criteria other than race.

Nevertheless, given that a rule of automatic invalidity for racial preferences in almost every case would be a significant break with our precedents that require a case-by-case test, I am not convinced we need adopt it at this point. On the assumption that it will vindicate the principle of race neutrality found in the Equal Protection Clause, I accept the less absolute rule contained in Justice O'Connor's opinion, a rule based on the proposition that any racial preference must face the most rigorous scrutiny by the courts. My reasons for doing so are as follows. First, I am confident that, in application, the strict scrutiny standard will operate in a manner generally consistent with the imperative of race neutrality, because it forbids the use even of narrowly drawn racial classifications except as a last resort. Second, the rule against race-conscious remedies is already less than an absolute one, for that relief may be the only adequate remedy after a judicial determination that a State or its instrumentality has violated the Equal Protection Clause. I note, in this connection, that evidence which would support a judicial finding of intentional discrimination may suffice also to justify remedial legislative action, for it diminishes the constitutional responsibilities of the political branches to say they must wait to act until ordered to do so by a court. Third, the strict scrutiny rule is consistent with our precedents, as Justice O'Connor's opinion demonstrates. * * *

JUSTICE SCALIA, concurring in the judgment.

I agree with much of the Court's opinion, and, in particular, with its conclusion that strict scrutiny must be applied to all governmental classification by race, whether or not its asserted purpose is "remedial" or "benign." I do not agree, however, with the Court's dicta suggesting that, despite the Fourteenth Amendment, state and local governments may in some circumstances discriminate on the basis of race in order (in a broad sense) "to ameliorate the effects of past discrimination." The benign purpose of compensating for social disadvantages, whether they have been acquired by reason of prior discrimination or otherwise, can no more be pursued by the illegitimate means of racial discrimination than can other assertedly benign purposes we have repeatedly rejected. See, e.g., [Wygant]. At least where state or local action is at issue, only a social emergency rising to the level of imminent danger to life and limb—for example, a prison race riot, requiring temporary segregation of inmates, cf. Lee v. Washington—can justify an exception to the principle embodied in the Fourteenth Amendment that "[o]ur Constitution is color-blind, and neither knows nor tolerates classes among citizens," Plessy (1896) (Harlan, J., dissenting) * * *.

A sound distinction between federal and state (or local) action based on race rests not only upon the substance of the Civil War Amendments, but upon social reality and governmental theory. It is a simple fact that what Justice Stewart described in Fullilove as "the dispassionate objectivity [and] the flexibility that are needed to mold a race-conscious remedy around the single objective of eliminating the effects of past or present discrimination"—political qualities already to be doubted in a national legislature—are substantially less likely to exist at the state or local level. The struggle for racial justice has historically been a struggle by the national society against oppression in the individual States. * * *

In my view there is only one circumstance in which the States may act *by race* to "undo the effects of past discrimination": where that is necessary to eliminate their own maintenance of a system of unlawful racial classification. [This] distinction explains our school desegregation cases, in which we have made plain that States and localities sometimes have an obligation to adopt race-conscious remedies. While there is no doubt that those cases have taken into account the continuing "effects" of previously mandated racial school assignment, we have held those effects to justify a race-conscious remedy only because we have concluded, in that context, that they perpetuate a "dual school system." We have stressed each school district's constitutional "*duty to dismantle* its dual system," and have found that "[e]ach instance of a failure or refusal to fulfill this affirmative duty *continues the violation* of the Fourteenth Amendment." *Columbus.*

Our analysis in *Bazemore v. Friday,* reflected our unwillingness to conclude, outside the context of school assignment, that the continuing effects of prior discrimination can be equated with state maintenance of a discriminatory system. * * *

I agree with the Court's dictum that a fundamental distinction must be drawn between the effects of "societal" discrimination and the effects of "identified" discrimination, and that the situation would be different if Richmond's plan were "tailored" to identify those particular bidders who "suffered from the effects of past discrimination by the city or prime contractors." In my view, however, the reason that would make a difference is not, as the Court states, that it would justify race-conscious action but rather that it would enable race-neutral remediation. Nothing prevents Richmond from according a contracting preference to identified victims of discrimination. While most of the beneficiaries might be black, neither the beneficiaries nor those disadvantaged by the preference would be identified *on the basis of their race*. In other words, far from justifying racial classification, identification of actual victims of discrimination makes it less supportable than ever, because more obviously unneeded. * * *

It is plainly true that in our society blacks have suffered discrimination immeasurably greater than any directed at other racial groups. But those who believe that racial preferences can help to "even the score" display, and reinforce, a manner of thinking by race that was the source of the injustice and that will, if it endures within our society, be the source of more injustice still. The relevant proposition is not that it was blacks, or Jews, or Irish who were discriminated against, but that it was individual men and women, "created equal," who were discriminated against. And the relevant resolve is that that should never happen again. Racial preferences appear to "even the score" (in some small degree) only if one embraces the proposition that our society is appropriately viewed as divided into races, making it right that an injustice rendered in the past to a black man should be compensated for by discriminating against a white. Nothing is worth that embrace. Since blacks have been disproportionately disadvantaged by racial discrimination, any race-neutral remedial program aimed at the disadvantaged *as such* will have a disproportionately beneficial impact on blacks. Only such a program, and not one that operates on the basis of race, is in accord with the letter and the spirit of our Constitution. * * *

JUSTICE MARSHALL, with whom JUSTICE BRENNAN and JUSTICE BLACKMUN join, dissenting.

* * * My view has long been that race-conscious classifications designed to further remedial goals "must serve important governmental objectives and must be substantially related to achievement of those objectives" in order to withstand constitutional scrutiny. * * * Analyzed in terms of this two-prong standard, Richmond's set-aside, like the federal program on which it was modeled, is "plainly constitutional." *Fullilove* (Marshall, J., concurring in judgment).

Turning first to the governmental interest inquiry, Richmond has two powerful interests in setting aside a portion of public contracting funds for minority-owned enterprises. The first is the city's interest in eradicating the effects of past racial discrimination. * * *

Richmond has a second compelling interest in setting aside, where possible, a portion of its contracting dollars. [When] government channels all its contracting funds to a white-dominated community of established contractors whose racial homogeneity is the product of private discrimination, it does more than place its imprimatur on the practices which forged and which continue to define that community. It also provides a measurable boost to those economic entities that have thrived within it, while denying important economic benefits to those entities which, but for prior discrimination, might well be better qualified to receive valuable government contracts. In my view, the interest in ensuring that the government does not reflect and reinforce prior private discrimination in dispensing public contracts is every bit as strong as the interest in eliminating private discrimination—an interest which this Court has repeatedly deemed compelling. See, e.g., *Roberts v. United States Jaycees*, [CON LAW p. 977, AMER CON p. 741, RTS & LIB p. 644]; *Bob Jones University v. United States*, [CON LAW p. 1110, AMER CON p. 855, RTS & LIB p. 776]; *Runyon v. McCrary*, [CON LAW p. 1517, AMER CON p. 1172, RTS & LIB p. 1183].

The remaining question with respect to the "governmental interest" prong of equal protection analysis is whether Richmond has proffered satisfactory proof of past racial discrimination to support its twin interests in remediation and in governmental nonperpetuation. * * * Richmond acted against a backdrop of congressional and Executive Branch studies which demonstrated with such force the nationwide pervasiveness of prior discrimination that Congress presumed that " 'present economic inequities' " in construction contracting resulted from " 'past discriminatory systems.' " The city's local evidence confirmed that Richmond's construction industry did not deviate from this pernicious national pattern. The fact that just .67% of public construction expenditures over the previous fives years had gone to minority-owned prime contractors, despite the city's racially mixed population, strongly suggests that construction contracting in the area was rife with "present economic inequities." To the extent this enormous disparity did not itself demonstrate that discrimination had occurred, the descriptive testimony of Richmond's elected and appointed leaders drew the necessary link between the pitifully small presence of minorities in construction contracting and past exclusionary practices. That *no one* who testified challenged this depiction of widespread racial discrimination in area construction contracting lent significant weight to these accounts. The fact that area trade associations had virtually no minority members dramatized the extent of present inequities and suggested the lasting power of past discriminatory systems. In sum, to suggest that the facts on which Richmond has relied do not provide a sound basis for its finding of past racial discrimination simply blinks credibility.

Richmond's reliance on localized, industry-specific findings is a far cry from the reliance on generalized "societal discrimination" which the majority decries as a basis for remedial action. But [the] majority also takes the disingenuous approach of disaggregating Richmond's local evidence, attacking it piecemeal, and thereby concluding that no *single* piece of evidence adduced by the city, "standing alone," suffices to prove past discrimination. But items of evidence do not, of course, "stan[d] alone" or exist in alien juxtaposition; they necessarily work together, reinforcing or contradicting each other.

In any event, the majority's criticisms of individual items of Richmond's evidence rest on flimsy foundations. The majority states, for example, that reliance on the disparity between the share of city contracts awarded to minority firms (.67%) and the minority population of Richmond (approximately 50%) is "misplaced." * * * First, considering how miniscule the share of Richmond public construction contracting dollars received by minority-owned businesses is, it is hardly unreasonable to conclude that this case involves a "gross statistical disparit[y]." There are roughly equal numbers of minorities and nonminorities in Richmond—yet minority-owned businesses receive *one-seventy-fifth* the public contracting funds that other businesses receive.

Second, and more fundamentally, where the issue is not present discrimination but rather whether *past* discrimination has resulted in the *continuing exclusion* of minorities from an historically tight-knit industry, a contrast between population and work force is entirely appropriate to help gauge the degree of the exclusion. [This] contrast is especially illuminating in cases like this, where a main avenue of introduction into the work force—here, membership in the trade associations whose members presumably train apprentices and help them procure subcontracting assignments—is itself grossly dominated by nonminorities. The majority's assertion that the city "does not even know how many MBE's in the relevant market are qualified," is thus entirely beside the point. [The Plan] is designed precisely to ease minority contractors into the industry.

The majority's perfunctory dismissal of the testimony of Richmond's appointed and elected leaders is also deeply disturbing. [By] disregarding the testimony of local leaders and the judgment of local government, the majority does violence to the very principles of comity within our federal system which this Court has long championed. Local officials, by virtue of their proximity to, and their expertise with, local affairs, are exceptionally well-qualified to make determinations of public good "within their respective spheres of authority." * * *

Had the majority paused for a moment on the facts of the Richmond experience, it would have discovered that the city's leadership is deeply familiar with what racial discrimination is. The members of the Richmond City Council have spent long years witnessing multifarious acts of discrimination, including, but not limited to, the deliberate diminution of black residents' voting rights, resistance to school desegregation, and publicly sanctioned housing discrimination. Numerous decisions of federal courts chronicle this disgraceful recent history. * * *

When the legislatures and leaders of cities with histories of pervasive discrimination testify that past discrimination has infected one of their industries, armchair cynicism like that exercised by the majority has no [place.] Disbelief is particularly inappropriate here in light of the fact that appellee Croson, which had the burden of proving unconstitutionality at trial, *Wygant,* has *at no point* come forward with *any* direct evidence that the City Council's motives were anything other than sincere.[9]

9. Compare *Fullilove* (Stevens, J., dissenting) (noting statements of sponsors of federal set-aside that measure was designed to give their constituents "a piece of the action").

Finally, I vehemently disagree with the majority's dismissal of the congressional and Executive Branch findings noted in *Fullilove* as having "extremely limited" probative value in this case. [In] thus requiring that Richmond's local evidence be severed from the context in which it was prepared, the majority would require cities seeking to eradicate the effects of past discrimination within their borders to reinvent the evidentiary wheel and engage in unnecessarily duplicative, costly, and time-consuming factfinding.

No principle of federalism or of federal power, however, forbids a state or local government from drawing upon a nationally relevant historical record prepared by the Federal Government.[10] Of course, Richmond could have built an even more compendious record of past discrimination, one including additional stark statistics and additional individual accounts of past discrimination. But nothing in the Fourteenth Amendment imposes such onerous documentary obligations upon States and localities once the reality of past discrimination is apparent.

In my judgment, Richmond's set-aside plan also comports with the second prong of the equal protection inquiry, for it is substantially related to the interests it seeks to serve in remedying past discrimination and in ensuring that municipal contract procurement does not perpetuate that discrimination. The most striking aspect of the city's ordinance is the similarity it bears to the "appropriately limited" federal set-aside provision upheld in *Fullilove*. [The] majority takes issue, however, with two aspects of Richmond's tailoring: the city's refusal to explore the use of race-neutral measures to increase minority business participation in contracting, and the selection of a 30% set-aside figure. The majority's first criticism is flawed in two respects. First, the majority overlooks the fact that since 1975, Richmond has barred both discrimination by the city in awarding public contracts and discrimination by public contractors. The virtual absence of minority businesses from the city's contracting rolls, indicated by the fact that such businesses have received less than 1% of public contracting dollars, strongly suggests that this ban has not succeeded in redressing the impact of past discrimination or in preventing city contract procurement from reinforcing racial homogeneity. Second, the majority's suggestion that Richmond should have first undertaken such race-neutral measures as a program of city financing for small firms ignores the fact that such measures, while theoretically appealing, have been discredited by Congress as ineffectual in eradicating the effects of past discrimination in this very industry. For this reason, this Court in *Fullilove* refused to fault Congress for not undertaking race-neutral measures as precursors to its race-conscious set-aside. ∗ ∗ ∗

As for Richmond's 30% target, the majority states that this figure "cannot be said to be narrowly tailored to any goal, except perhaps outright racial balancing." The majority ignores two important facts. First, the set-aside measure affects only 3% of overall city contracting; thus, any imprecision in tailoring has far less impact than the majority suggests. But more important, the majority ignores the fact that Richmond's 30% figure was patterned directly on the *Fullilove* precedent. Congress' 10% figure fell "roughly halfway between the present percentage of minority contractors and the percentage of minority

---

10. Although the majority sharply criticizes Richmond for using data which it did not itself develop, it is noteworthy that the federal set-aside program upheld in *Fullilove* was adopted as a floor amendment "without any congressional hearings or investigation whatsoever." L. Tribe, *American Constitutional Law* 345 (2d ed. 1988). The principal opinion in *Fullilove* justified the set-aside by relying heavily on the aforementioned studies by agencies like the Small Business Administration and on legislative reports prepared in connection with prior, failed legislation.

group members in the Nation." The Richmond City Council's 30% figure similarly falls roughly halfway between the present percentage of Richmond-based minority contractors (almost zero) and the percentage of minorities in Richmond (50%). In faulting Richmond for not presenting a different explanation for its choice of a set-aside figure, the majority honors *Fullilove* only in the breach. * * *

Today, for the first time, a majority of this Court has adopted strict scrutiny as its standard of Equal Protection Clause review of race-conscious remedial measures. This is an unwelcome development. * * *

I am also troubled by the majority's assertion that, even if it did not believe generally in strict scrutiny of race-based remedial measures, "the circumstances of this case" require this Court to look upon the Richmond City Council's measure with the strictest scrutiny. The sole such circumstance which the majority cites, however, is the fact [that] "blacks comprise approximately 50% of the population of the city of Richmond" and that "[f]ive of the nine seats on the City Council are held by blacks."

While I agree that the numerical and political supremacy of a given racial group is a factor bearing upon the level of scrutiny to be applied, this Court has never held that numerical inferiority, standing alone, makes a racial group "suspect" and thus entitled to strict scrutiny review. Rather, we have identified *other* "traditional indicia of suspectness": whether a group has been "saddled with such disabilities, or subjected to such a history of purposeful unequal treatment, or relegated to such a position of political powerlessness as to command extraordinary protection from the majoritarian political process."

It cannot seriously be suggested that nonminorities in Richmond have any "history of purposeful unequal treatment." Nor is there any indication that they have any of the disabilities that have characteristically afflicted those groups this Court has deemed suspect. Indeed, the numerical and political dominance of nonminorities within the State of Virginia and the Nation as a whole provide an enormous political check against the "simple racial politics" at the municipal level which the majority fears. If the majority really believes that groups like Richmond's nonminorities, which comprise approximately half the population but which are outnumbered even marginally in political fora, are deserving of suspect class status for these reasons alone, this Court's decisions denying suspect status to women stand on extremely shaky ground.

In my view, the "circumstances of this case," underscore the importance of *not* subjecting to a strict scrutiny straitjacket the increasing number of cities which have recently come under minority leadership and are eager to rectify, or at least prevent the perpetuation of, past racial discrimination. In many cases, these cities will be the ones with the most in the way of prior discrimination to rectify. * * *

Richmond's own recent political history underscores the facile nature of the majority's assumption that elected officials' voting decisions are based on the color of their skins. In recent years, white and black councilmembers in Richmond have increasingly joined hands on controversial matters. When the Richmond City Council elected a black man Mayor in 1982, for example, his victory was won with the support of the City Council's four white members. The vote on the set-aside plan a year later also was not purely along racial lines. Of the four white councilmembers, one voted for the measure and another abstained. The majority's view that remedial measures undertaken by municipalities with black leadership must face a stiffer test of Equal Protection Clause scrutiny than remedial measures undertaken by municipalities with white leadership implies a lack of political maturity on the part of this Nation's elected minority officials that is totally unwarranted. Such insulting judgments have no place in constitutional jurisprudence.

Today's decision, finally, is particularly noteworthy for the daunting standard it imposes upon States and localities contemplating the use of race-conscious measures to eradicate the present effects of prior discrimination and prevent its perpetuation. * * *

Nothing in the Constitution or in the prior decisions of this Court supports limiting state authority to confront the effects of past discrimination to those situations in which a prima facie case of a constitutional or statutory violation can be made out. By its very terms, the majority's standard effectively cedes control of a large component of the content of that constitutional provision to Congress and to state legislatures. If an antecedent Virginia or Richmond law had defined as unlawful the award to nonminorities of an overwhelming share of a city's contracting dollars, for example, Richmond's subsequent set-aside initiative would then satisfy the majority's standard. But without such a law, the initiative might not withstand constitutional scrutiny. The meaning of "equal protection of the laws" thus turns on the happenstance of whether a State or local body has previously defined illegal discrimination. Indeed, given that racially discriminatory cities may be the ones least likely to have tough, antidiscrimination laws on their books, the majority's constitutional incorporation of state and local statutes has the perverse effect of inhibiting those States or localities with the worst records of official racism from taking remedial action.

Similar flaws would inhere in the majority's standard even if it incorporated only federal anti-discrimination statutes. If Congress tomorrow dramatically expanded Title VII of the Civil Rights Act of 1964—or alternatively, if it repealed that legislation altogether—the meaning of equal protection would change precipitously along with it. Whatever the Framers of the Fourteenth Amendment had in mind in 1868, it certainly was not that the content of their Amendment would turn on the amendments to or the evolving interpretations of a federal statute passed nearly a century later. * * *[a]

SECTION: SPECIAL SCRUTINY FOR OTHER CLASSIFICATIONS

ILLEGITIMACY

CON LAW: P. 1285, add at end of fn. b

AMER CON: P. 995, add at end of fn. b

RTS & LIB: P. 951, add at end of fn. b

See also *Clark v. Jeter,* ___ U.S. ___, 108 S.Ct. 1910, 100 L.Ed.2d 465 (1988), using a similar analysis to invalidate Pennsylvania's six-year statute of limitation, and unanimously stating the level of scrutiny as "substantially related to an important governmental objective."

a. Blackmun, J.'s brief dissent, joined by Brennan, J., is omitted.

SECTION: "FUNDAMENTAL RIGHTS"

DISCRIMINATION IN RESPECT TO VOTING

"DILUTION" OF THE RIGHT: APPORTIONMENT

CON LAW: P. 1345, after note (d)

AMER CON: P. 1044, after note (c)

RTS & LIB: P. 1011, after note (d)

DAVIS v. BANDEMER

478 U.S. 109, 106 S.Ct. 2797, 92 L.Ed.2d 85 (1986).

[Democrats challenged Indiana's 1981 state apportionment—enacted by Republican majorities in both houses of the legislature and signed by a Republican governor—on the ground that it "constituted a political gerrymander intended to disadvantage Democrats on a statewide basis." A majority of the Court, per White, J.—relying on cases such as *Baker* and *Reynolds* (indicating "the justiciability of claims going to the adequacy of state representation in state legislatures"); *Mobile, Whitcomb, Regester* and *Rogers* ("racial gerrymandering presents a justiciable equal protection claim"); and, particularly, *Gaffney*—held that a "political gerrymandering claim [is] justiciable."]

JUSTICE WHITE announced the judgment of the Court and delivered [an] opinion in which JUSTICE BRENNAN, JUSTICE MARSHALL, and JUSTICE BLACKMUN joined * * *.

We [agree] with the District Court that in order to succeed the Bandemer plaintiffs were required to prove both intentional discrimination against an identifiable political group and an actual discriminatory effect on that group. [As] long as redistricting is done by a legislature, it should not be very difficult to prove that the likely political consequences of the reapportionment were intended.

We do not accept, however, the District Court's legal and factual bases for concluding that the 1981 Act visited a sufficiently adverse effect on the appellees' constitutionally protected rights to make out a violation of the Equal Protection Clause. The District Court held that because any apportionment scheme that purposely prevents proportional representation is unconstitutional, Democratic voters need only show that their proportionate voting influence has been adversely affected. Our cases, however, clearly foreclose any claim that the Constitution requires proportional representation or that legislatures in reapportioning must draw district lines to come as near as possible to allocating seats to the contending parties in proportion to what their anticipated statewide vote will be. *Whitcomb; Regester.*

The typical election for legislative seats in the United States is conducted in described geographical districts, with the candidate receiving the most votes in each district winning the seat allocated to that district. If all or most of the districts are competitive, [even] a narrow statewide preference for either party would produce an overwhelming majority for the winning party in the state legislature. This consequence, however, is inherent in winner-take-all, district-based elections, and we cannot hold that such a reapportionment law would violate the Equal Protection Clause because the voters in the losing party do not have representation in the legislature in proportion to the statewide vote received by their party candidates. * * *

In cases involving individual multi-member districts, we have required a substantially greater showing of adverse effects than a mere lack of proportional representation to support a finding of unconstitutional vote dilution. Only where there is evidence that excluded groups have "less opportunity to participate in the political processes and to elect candidates of their choice" have we refused to approve the use of multi-member districts. *Rogers.* See also *United Jewish Orgs. v. Carey; Register; Whitcomb.* In these cases, we have also noted the lack of responsiveness by those elected to the concerns of the relevant groups.

These holdings rest on a conviction that the mere fact that a particular apportionment scheme makes it more difficult for a particular group in a particular district to elect the representatives of its choice does not render that scheme constitutionally infirm. This conviction, in turn, stems from a perception that the power to influence the political process is not limited to winning elections. An individual or a group of individuals who votes for a losing candidate is usually deemed to be adequately represented by the winning candidate and to have as much opportunity to influence that candidate as other voters in the district. We cannot presume in such a situation, without actual proof to the contrary, that the candidate elected will entirely ignore the interests of those voters. This is true even in a safe district where the losing group loses election after election. * * *

As with individual districts, where unconstitutional vote dilution is alleged in the form of statewide political gerrymandering, the mere lack of proportional representation will not be sufficient to prove unconstitutional discrimination. Again, without specific supporting evidence, a court cannot presume in such a case that those who are elected will disregard the disproportionately under-represented group. Rather, unconstitutional discrimination occurs only when the electoral system is arranged in a manner that will consistently degrade a voter's or a group of voters' influence on the political process as a whole.
* * *

Based on these views, we would reject the District Court's apparent holding that *any* interference with an opportunity to elect a representative of one's choice would be sufficient to allege or make out an equal protection violation, unless justified by some acceptable state interest that the State would be required to demonstrate. [S]uch a low threshold for legal action would invite attack on all or almost all reapportionment statutes. District-based elections hardly ever produce a perfect fit between votes and representation. [Inviting] attack on minor departures from some supposed norm would too much embroil the judiciary in second-guessing what has consistently been referred to as a political task for the legislature * * *.

The District Court's findings do not satisfy this threshold condition to stating and proving a cause of action. In reaching its conclusion, the District Court relied primarily on the results of the 1982 elections: Democratic candidates for the State House of Representatives had received 51.9% of the votes cast statewide and Republican candidates 48.1%; yet, out of the 100 seats to be filled, Republican candidates won 57 and Democrats 43. In the Senate, 53.1% of the votes were cast for Democratic candidates and 46.9% for Republicans; of the 25 Senate seats to be filled, Republicans won 12 and Democrats 13. The court also relied upon the use of multi-member districts in Marion and Allen counties, where Democrats or those inclined to vote Democratic in 1982 amounted to 46.6% of the population of those counties but Republicans won 86 percent—18 of 21—seats allocated to the districts in those counties. These disparities were enough to require a neutral justification by the State, which in the eyes of the District Court was not forthcoming.[15]

Relying on a single election to prove unconstitutional discrimination is unsatisfactory. The District Court observed, and the parties do not disagree, that Indiana is a swing State. Voters sometimes prefer Democratic candidates, and sometimes Republican. The District Court did not find that because of the 1981 Act the Democrats could not in one of the next few elections secure a sufficient vote to take control of the assembly. Indeed, the District Court declined to hold that the 1982 election results were the predictable consequences of the 1981 Act and expressly refused to hold that those results were a reliable prediction of future ones. The District Court did not ask by what percentage the statewide Democratic vote would have had to increase to control either the House or the Senate. The appellants argue here, without a persuasive response from appellees, that had the Democratic candidates received an additional few percentage points of the votes cast statewide, they would have obtained a majority of the seats in both houses. Nor was there any finding that the 1981 reapportionment would consign the Democrats to a minority status in the Assembly throughout the 1980's or that the Democrats would have no hope of doing any better in the reapportionment that would occur after the 1990 census. Without findings of this nature, the District Court erred in concluding that the 1981 Act violated the Equal Protection Clause.

The District Court's discussion of the multi-member districts created by the 1981 Act does not undermine this conclusion. For the purposes of the statewide political gerrymandering claim, these districts appear indistinguishable from safe Republican and safe Democratic single-member districts. Simply showing that there are multi-member districts in the State and that those districts are constructed so as to be safely Republican or Democratic in no way bolsters the contention that there has been *statewide* discrimination against Democratic voters. It could be, were the necessary threshold effect to be shown, that multi-member districts could be demonstrated to be suspect on the ground that they are particularly useful in attaining impermissibly discriminatory ends; at this stage of the inquiry, however, the multi-member district evidence does not materially aid the appellees' case. * * *

In response to our approach, Justice Powell suggests an alternative method for evaluating equal protection claims of political gerrymandering. In his view, courts should look at a number of factors in considering these claims: the nature of the legislative procedures by which the challenged redistricting was accomplished and the intent behind the redistricting; the shapes of the districts and their conformity with political subdivision boundaries; and "evidence concerning population disparities and statistics tending to show vote dilution." [T]he crux of Justice Powell's analysis seems to be that—at least in some cases—the intentional drawing of district boundaries for partisan ends and for no other

---

15. The District Court apparently thought that the political group suffering discrimination was all those voters who voted for Democratic Assembly candidates in 1982. Judge Pell, in dissent, argued that the allegedly disfavored group should be defined as those voters who could be counted on to vote Democratic from election to election, thus excluding those who vote the Republican ticket from time to time. He would have counted the true believers by averaging the Democratic vote cast in two different elections for those state-wide offices for which party-line voting is thought to be the rule and personality and issue-oriented factors are relatively unimportant. Although accepting Judge Pell's definition of Democratic voters would have strongly suggested that the 1981 reapportionment had no discriminatory effect at all, there was no response to his position. The appellees take up the challenge in this Court, claiming that Judge Pell chose the wrong election years for the purpose of averaging the Democratic votes. The dispute need not now be resolved.

reason violates the Equal Protection Clause in and of itself. We disagree, however, with this conception of a constitutional violation. Specifically, even if a state legislature redistricts with the specific intention of disadvantaging one political party's election prospects, we do not believe that there has been an unconstitutional discrimination against members of that party unless the redistricting does in fact disadvantage it at the polls.

Moreover, as we discussed above, a mere lack of proportionate results in one election cannot suffice in this regard. [E]qual protection violations may be found only where a history (actual or projected) of disproportionate results appears in conjunction with ["strong indicia of lack of political power and the denial of fair representation."] The mere lack of control of the General Assembly after a single election does not rise to the requisite level. [But] Justice Powell's view would allow a constitutional violation to be found where the only proven effect on a political party's electoral power was disproportionate results in one (or possibly two) elections. * * *

In rejecting Justice Powell's approach, we do not mean to intimate that the factors he considers are entirely irrelevant. The election results obviously are relevant to a showing of the effects required to prove a political gerrymandering claim under our view. And the district configurations may be combined with vote projections to predict future election results, which are also relevant to the effects showing. The other factors, even if not relevant to the effects issue, might well be relevant to an equal protection claim. The equal protection argument would proceed along the following lines: If there were a discriminatory effect and a discriminatory intent, then the legislation would be examined for valid underpinnings. Thus, evidence of exclusive legislative process and deliberate drawing of district lines in accordance with accepted gerrymandering principles would be relevant to intent, and evidence of valid and invalid configuration would be relevant to whether the districting plan met legitimate state interests.

This course is consistent with our equal protection cases generally and is the course we follow here: We assumed that there was discriminatory intent, found that there was insufficient discriminatory effect to constitute an equal protection violation,[19] and therefore did not reach the question of the state interests (legitimate or otherwise) served by the particular districts as they were created by the legislature. Consequently, the valid or invalid configuration of the districts was an issue we did not need to consider.

* * * We recognize that our own view may be difficult of application. Determining when an electoral system has been "arranged in a manner that will consistently degrade a voter's or a group of voters' influence on the political process as a whole" is of necessity a difficult inquiry. Nevertheless, we believe that it recognizes the delicacy of intruding on this most political of legislative functions and is at the same time consistent with our prior cases regarding individual multi-member districts, which have formulated a parallel standard. * * *

JUSTICE POWELL, with whom JUSTICE STEVENS joins, concurring [on the issue of justiciability], and dissenting.

[T]he plurality expresses the view, with which I agree, that a partisan political gerrymander violates the Equal Protection Clause only on proof of "both intentional discrimination against an identifiable political group and an

---

19. In most equal protection cases, it is true, a discriminatory effect will be readily apparent, and no heightened effect will be required, but that is the only real difference between this type of equal protection claim and others.

actual discriminatory effect on that group." The plurality acknowledges that the record in this case supports a finding that the challenged redistricting plan was adopted for the purpose of discriminating against Democratic voters. The plurality argues, however, that appellees failed to establish that their voting strength was diluted statewide despite uncontradicted proof that certain key districts were grotesquely gerrymandered to enhance the election prospects of Republican candidates. * * *

The Equal Protection Clause guarantees citizens that their state will govern them impartially. See *Karcher* (Stevens, J., concurring). In the context of redistricting, that guarantee is of critical importance because the franchise provides most citizens their only voice in the legislative process. Since the contours of a voting district powerfully may affect citizens' ability to exercise influence through their vote, district lines should be determined in accordance with neutral and legitimate criteria. When deciding where those lines will fall, the state should treat its voters as standing in the same position, regardless of their political beliefs or party affiliation. [*Reynolds*] contemplated that "one person, one vote" would be only one among several neutral factors that serve the constitutional mandate of fair and effective representation. * * *

The [most] basic flaw in the plurality's opinion is its failure to enunciate any standard that affords guidance to legislatures and courts.[10] [This] places the plurality in the curious position of inviting further litigation even as it appears to signal the "constitutional green light" to would-be gerrymanderers. * * *

A court should look first to the legislative process by which the challenged plan was adopted. Here, the District Court found that the procedures used in redistricting Indiana were carefully designed to exclude Democrats from participating in the legislative process [which] consisted of nothing more than the majority party's private application of computer technology to mapmaking. [T]he only data used in the computer program were precinct population, race of precinct citizens, precinct political complexion, and statewide party voting trends. * * *

Next, the District Court found [how] the mapmakers carved up counties, cities, and even townships in their effort to draw lines beneficial to the majority party. [The] redistricting dissects counties into strange shapes lacking in common interests, on one occasion even placing the seat of one county in a voting district composed of townships from other counties. Under these conditions, the District Court expressly found that "the potential for voter disillusion and nonparticipation is great," as voters are forced to focus their political activities in artificial electoral units. Intelligent voters, regardless of party affiliation, resent this sort of political manipulation of the electorate for no public purpose. * * *

[When] the plan was completed, Republican leaders announced that the House map was designed to yield 56 "safe" Republican seats and 30 Democratic seats, with the remainder being "tossups." Republicans expected that their Senate map would regularly produce 30 Republican seats and 8 to 10 Democratic

---

10. * * * I cannot agree, as the plurality suggests, that a standard requiring proof of "heightened effect," where invidious intent has been established directly, has support in any of our cases, or that an equal protection violation can be established "only where a history (actual or projected) of disproportionate results appears." If a racial minority es- tablished that the legislature adopted a redistricting law for no purpose other than to disadvantage that group, the plurality's new and erroneous standard would require plaintiffs to wait for the results of several elections, creating a history of discriminatory effect, before they can challenge the law in court.

seats so that Republicans would maintain their grip on the Senate even if Democrats won the remaining seats. In short, the record unequivocally demonstrates that in 1981 the Republican-dominated General Assembly deliberately sought to design a redistricting plan under which members of the Democratic party would be deprived of a fair opportunity to win control of the General Assembly at least until 1991, the date of the next redistricting. * * *

Appellees further demonstrated through a statistical showing that the House Plan debased the effectiveness of their votes [reciting the 1982 election statistics in White, J.'s opinion. Moreover, since] half of the Senate membership is up for election every two years, the only election results under the challenged plan available at trial [showed] that, of the seats up for election in 1982, Democrats were elected to 13 seats and Republicans to 12. [It] was appellees' contention that most of the Senate seats won by Democrats in 1982 were "safe" Democratic seats so that their party's success at the polls in that year was fully consistent with the statewide Republican gerrymander. This contention is borne out by the results of the 1984 Senate election. In that election, Democratic candidates received 42.3 percent of the vote, and Republicans 57.7 percent. Yet, of the 25 Senate positions up for election, only 7 were captured by Democrats.

The District Court found, and I agree, that appellants failed to justify the discriminatory impact of the plan by showing that the plan had a rational basis in permissible neutral criteria. [As] the plurality opinion makes clear, [a] colorable claim of discriminatory gerrymandering presents a justiciable controversy under the Equal Protection Clause. Federal courts in exercising their duty to adjudicate such claims should impose a heavy burden of proof on those who allege that a redistricting plan violates the Constitution. [T]his case presents a paradigm example of unconstitutional discrimination against the members of a political party that happened to be out of power. The well-grounded findings of the District Court to this effect have not been, and I believe cannot be, held clearly erroneous. * * *[25]

JUSTICE O'CONNOR, with whom THE CHIEF JUSTICE and JUSTICE REHNQUIST join, concurring in the judgment.

[T]he legislative business of apportionment is fundamentally a political affair, and challenges to the manner in which an apportionment has been carried out—by the very parties that are responsible for this process—present a political question in the truest sense of the term.

To turn these matters over to the federal judiciary is to inject the courts into the most heated partisan issues. It is predictable that the courts will respond by moving away from the nebulous standard a plurality of the Court fashions today and toward some form of rough proportional representation for all political groups. The consequences of this shift will be as immense as they are unfortunate. I do not believe, and the Court offers not a shred of evidence to suggest, that the Framers of the Constitution intended the judicial power to encompass the making of such fundamental choices about how this Nation is to be governed. Nor do I believe that the proportional representation towards which the Court's

---

25. As is evident from the several opinions filed today, there is no "Court" for a standard that properly should be applied in determining whether a challenged redistricting plan is an unconstitutional partisan political gerrymander. The standard proposed by the plu-

rality is explicitly rejected by two Justices, and three Justices also have expressed the view that the plurality's standard will "prove unmanageable and arbitrary." (O'Connor, J., joined by Burger, C.J., and Rehnquist, J., concurring in the judgment).

expansion of equal protection doctrine will lead is consistent with our history, our traditions, or our political institutions.[a] * * *

The step taken today is a momentous one, which if followed in the future can only lead to political instability and judicial malaise. [Federal] courts will have no alternative but to attempt to recreate the complex process of legislative apportionment in the context of adversary litigation in order to reconcile the competing claims of political, religious, ethnic, racial, occupational, and socioeconomic groups. Even if there were some way of limiting such claims to organized political parties, the fact remains that the losing party or the losing group of legislators in every reapportionment will now be invited to fight the battle anew in federal court. [The] Equal Protection Clause does not supply judicially manageable standards for resolving purely political gerrymandering claims, and no group right to an equal share of political power was ever intended by the Framers. [Unlike racial minorities], members of the Democratic and Republican parties cannot claim that they are a discrete and insular group vulnerable to exclusion from the political process by some dominant group: these political parties *are* the dominant groups, and the Court has offered no reason to believe that they are incapable of fending for themselves through the political process. Indeed, there is good reason to think that political gerrymandering is a self-limiting enterprise. See Cain, *The Reapportionment Puzzle* 151–159 (1984). In order to gerrymander, the legislative majority must weaken some of its safe seats, thus exposing its own incumbents to greater risks of defeat—risks they may refuse to accept past a certain point. Similarly, an overambitious gerrymander can lead to disaster for the legislative majority: because it has created more seats in which it hopes to win relatively narrow victories, the same swing in overall voting strength will tend to cost the legislative majority more and more seats as the gerrymander becomes more ambitious. More generally, each major party presumably has ample weapons at its disposal to conduct the partisan struggle that often leads to a partisan apportionment, but also often leads to a bipartisan one. * * *

Furthermore, the Court fails to explain why a bipartisan gerrymander—which is what was approved in *Gaffney*—affects individuals any differently than a partisan gerrymander. [As] the plurality acknowledges, the scheme upheld in *Gaffney* tended to "deny safe district minorities any realistic chance to elect their own representatives." If this bipartisan arrangement between two groups of self-interested legislators is constitutionally permissible, as I believe and as the Court held in *Gaffney,* then—in terms of the rights of individuals—it should be equally permissible for a legislative majority to employ the same means to pursue its own interests over the opposition of the other party.

* * * [The] Court has in effect decided that it is constitutionally acceptable for both parties to "waste" the votes of individuals through a bipartisan gerrymander, so long as the *parties* themselves are not deprived of their group voting strength to an extent that will exceed the plurality's threshold requirement. This choice confers greater rights on powerful political groups than on individuals; that cannot be the meaning of the Equal Protection Clause. * * *

Vote dilution analysis is far less manageable when extended to major political parties than if confined to racial minority groups. First, [d]esigning an

a. Burger, C.J.'s separate opinion, relying on Frankfurter, J.'s dissent in *Baker v. Carr,* is omitted.

apportionment plan that does not impair or degrade the voting strength of several groups is more difficult than designing a plan that does not have such an effect on one group for the simple reason that, as the number of criteria the plan must meet increases, the number of solutions that will satisfy those criteria will decrease. * * *

Second, while membership in a racial group is an immutable characteristic, voters can—and often do—move from one party to the other or support candidates from both parties. Consequently, the difficulty of measuring voting strength is heightened in the case of a major political party. * * *

Moreover, any such intervention is likely to move in the direction of proportional representation for political parties. This is clear by analogy to the problem that arises in racial gerrymandering cases: "in order to decide whether an electoral system has made it harder for minority voters to elect the candidates they prefer, a court must have an idea in mind of how hard it 'should' be for minority voters to elect their preferred candidates under an acceptable system." Any such norm must make some reference, even if only a loose one, to the relation between the racial minority group's share of the electorate and its share of the elected representatives. In order to implement the plurality's standard, it will thus be necessary for courts to adopt an analogous norm, in order to assess whether the voting strength of a political party has been "degraded" by an apportionment, either on a state-wide basis or in particular districts. Absent any such norm, the inquiry the plurality proposes would be so standardless as to make the adjudication of political gerrymandering claims impossible.

* * * [Because] the most easily measured indicia of political power relate solely to winning and losing elections, there is a grave risk that the plurality's various attempts to qualify and condition the group right the Court has created will gradually pale in importance. What is likely to remain is a loose form of proportionality, under which *some* deviations from proportionality are permissible, but any significant, persistent deviations from proportionality are suspect. Courts will be forced to look for some form of "undue" disproportionality with respect to electoral success if political gerrymandering claims are justiciable, because otherwise they will find their decisions turning on imponderables such as whether the legislators of one party have fairly represented the voters of the other.

Of course, in one sense a requirement of proportional representation, whether loose or absolute, is judicially manageable. If this Court were to declare that the Equal Protection Clause required proportional representation within certain fixed tolerances, I have no doubt that district courts would be able to apply this edict. The flaw in such a pronouncement, however, would be the use of the Equal Protection Clause as the vehicle for making a fundamental policy choice that is contrary to the intent of its Framers and to the traditions of this republic. The political question doctrine as articulated in *Baker* rightly requires that we refrain from making such policy choices in order to evade what would otherwise be a lack of judicially manageable standards. * * *

* * * [To] allow district courts to strike down apportionment plans on the basis of their prognostications as to the outcome of future elections or future apportionments invites "findings" on matters as to which neither judges nor anyone else can have any confidence. Once it is conceded that "a group's electoral power is not unconstitutionally diminished by the simple fact of an apportionment scheme that makes winning elections more difficult," the virtual

impossibility of reliably predicting how difficult it will be to win an election in 2, or 4, or 10 years should, in my view, weigh in favor of holding such challenges nonjusticiable. Racial gerrymandering should remain justiciable, for the harms it engenders run counter to the central thrust of the Fourteenth Amendment. But no such justification can be given for judicial intervention on behalf of mainstream political parties, and the risks such intervention poses to our political institutions are unacceptable. * * *

RESTRICTIONS ON PARTIES AND CANDIDATES

CON LAW: P. 1357, after *American Party of Texas*

RTS & LIB: P. 1023, after *American Party of Texas*

See also *Munro v. Socialist Workers Party*, 479 U.S. 189, 107 S.Ct. 533, 93 L.Ed.2d 499 (1986), upholding a requirement that minor-party candidates receive at least 1% of all votes cast for the office sought in the primary in order to get on the general election ballot. Brennan and Marshall, JJ., dissented.[a]

DISCRIMINATION IN RESPECT TO TRAVEL

CON LAW: P. 1371, before Part III

AMER CON: P. 1061, before Part III

RTS & LIB: P. 1037, before Part III

ATTORNEY GENERAL v. SOTO-LOPEZ, 476 U.S. 898, 106 S.Ct. 2317, 90 L.Ed.2d 899 (1986), held violative of equal protection a New York civil service employment preference for residents who served in the military during time of war and who were New York residents when they entered the service. Brennan, J., joined by Marshall, Blackmun and Powell, JJ., recognized that "the benefit sought here may not rise to the same level of importance as the necessities of life and the right to vote, [but such] a permanent deprivation of a significant benefit, based only on the fact of nonresidence at a past point in time, clearly operates to penalize appellees' for exercising their rights to migrate. [The] State has not met its heavy burden of proving that it has selected a means of pursuing a compelling state interest which does not impinge unnecessarily on constitutionally protected interests."

Burger, C.J.—with whom White, J., agreed—concurred in the judgment because, under *Zobel* and *Hooper*—in which "we had no occasion to reach the issues whether the classifications would survive heightened scrutiny or whether the right to travel was violated"—"the statutory scheme cannot pass even the minimum rationality test."

O'Connor, J., joined by Rehnquist and Stevens, JJ., dissented, reasoning along the lines of her concurrence in *Zobel* and the dissents in *Zobel* and *Hooper*: "[F]inding that this scheme in theory or practical effect constitutes a 'penalty' on appellees' fundamental right to settle in New York or on their 'right to migrate' seems to me ephemeral, and completely unnecessary to safeguard the constitutional purpose of 'maintaining a Union rather than a mere "league of states." ' *Zobel* (O'Connor, J., concurring in judgment). Thus, heightened scrutiny, either under the 'right to migrate' or the Equal Protection Clause is inappropriate. Under rational basis review, New York [is] attempting to say 'thank you' to

---

a. On the question of whether state laws that conflict with a political party's rules violate the party's first amendment right of association, see *Tashjian v. Republican Party*, p. 282 of this Supplement.

those who personified New York's sacrifice and effort to 'do its part' in supporting this Nation's war efforts."

CONFINEMENT OF "FUNDAMENTAL RIGHTS"

CON LAW: P. 1393, before Notes and Questions

AMER CON: P. 1079, before Notes and Questions

RTS & LIB: P. 1058, before Notes and Questions

For a holding (Powell, J., joined by Burger, C.J., and Rehnquist, J., dissenting) that a complaint—alleging an equal protection violation because of "a state decision to divide state resources unequally among school districts"—should survive a motion to dismiss, see *Papasan v. Allain*, 478 U.S. 265, 106 S.Ct. 2932, 92 L.Ed.2d 209 (1986).

CON LAW: P. 1400, before note 3

AMER CON: P. 1085, before note 3

RTS & LIB: P. 1065, before note 3

KADRMAS v. DICKINSON PUBLIC SCHOOLS, __ U.S. __ 108 S.Ct. 2481, 101 L.Ed.2d 399 (1988), upheld a North Dakota statute, as applied to an indigent family, that allowed some school boards to assess a fee for school bus transportation. The Court, per O'CONNOR, J., concluded that the statute "discriminates against no suspect class and interferes with no fundamental right," and "appellants have failed to carry the heavy burden of demonstrating that the statute is arbitrary and irrational. * * *

"We have not extended [*Plyler*] beyond the 'unique circumstances' that provoked its 'unique confluence of theories and rationales.' [Unlike] the children in that case, Sarita Kadrmas has not been penalized by the government for illegal conduct by her parents. On the contrary, Sarita was denied access to the school bus only because her parents would not agree to pay the same user fee charged to all other families that took advantage of the service."

As for cases such as *Griffin v. Illinois, Boddie v. Connecticut* and *Little v. Streater*, "each involved a rule that barred indigent litigants from using the judicial process in circumstances where they had no alternative to that process. [In] contrast to the 'utter exclusiveness of court access and court remedy,' *Kras*, North Dakota does not maintain a legal or a practical monopoly on the means of transporting children to school. Thus, unlike the complaining parties in all the cases cited by appellants, the Kadrmas family could and did find a private alternative to the public school bus service for which Dickinson charged a fee. That alternative was more expensive, to be sure, and we have no reason to doubt that genuine hardships were endured by the Kadrmas family when Sarita was denied access to the bus. Such facts, however, do not imply that the Equal Protection Clause has been violated."

MARSHALL, J., joined by Brennan, J., dissented, relying on Marshall, J.'s dissent in *Rodriquez* and finding that, as in *Plyler*, the "State in this case has acted to burden the educational opportunities of a disadvantaged group of children, who need an education to become full participants in society."

STEVENS, J., joined by Blackmun, J., also dissented, relying largely on the approach of Stevens, J.'s concurrence in *Cleburne*.

CON LAW: P. 1402, add to fn. b

AMER CON: P. 1086, add to fn. b

RTS & LIB: P. 1067, add to fn. b

Compare LYNG v. CASTILLO, 477 U.S. 635, 106 S.Ct. 2727, 91 L.Ed.2d 527 (1986), per STEVENS, J., holding that a Food Stamp Act provision—which treated "parents, children, and siblings who live together" *less* favorably than "distant relatives, or groups of unrelated persons who live together"—had a "rational basis": "Congress could reasonably determine that close relatives sharing a home—almost by definition—tend to purchase and prepare meals together while distant relatives and unrelated individuals might not be so inclined. [And] Congress might have reasoned that it would be somewhat easier for close relatives—again, almost by definition—to accommodate their living habits to a federal policy favoring common meal preparation than it would be for more distant relatives or unrelated persons to do so." Brennan, Marshall and White, JJ., dissented.

SECTION: IRREBUTTABLE PRESUMPTIONS

CON LAW: P. 1405, ater note 1(a)

AMER CON: P. 1088, after note 1(a)

RTS & LIB: P. 1070, after note 1(a)

MICHAEL H. v. GERALD D., __ U.S. __, 109 S.Ct. 2333, __ L.Ed.2d __ (1989) upheld a California statute (§ 621) establishing an irrebuttable presumption (with narrow exceptions) that a child born to a married woman living with her husband, who is neither impotent nor sterile, is a child of the marriage. SCALIA, J., joined by Rehnquist, C.J., and O'Connor and Kennedy, JJ., argued that decisions such as *Stanley, Vlandis* and *La Fleur* did not "rest upon *procedural* due process. A conclusive presumption does, of course, foreclose the person against whom it is invoked from demonstrating, in a particularized proceeding, that applying the presumption to him will in fact not further the lawful governmental policy the presumption is designed to effectuate. But the same can be said of any legal rule that establishes general classifications, whether framed in terms of a presumption or not. In this respect there is no difference between a rule which says that the marital husband shall be irrebuttably presumed to be the father, and a rule which says that the adulterous natural father shall not be recognized as the legal father. *Both* rules deny someone in Michael's situation a hearing on whether, in the particular circumstances of his case, California's policies would best be served by giving him parental rights. [Thus,] our 'irrebuttable presumption' cases must ultimately be analyzed as calling into question not the adequacy of procedures [but] the adequacy of the 'fit' between the classification and the policy that the classification serves."

BRENNAN, J., joined by Marshall and Blackmun, JJ., dissenting, responded "that the defect from which conclusive presumptions suffer is a *procedural* one: the State has declared a certain fact relevant, indeed controlling, yet has denied a particular class of litigants a hearing to establish that fact. [It] may be that all conclusive presumptions are, in a sense, substantive rules of law; but § 621 then belongs in that special category of substantive rules that presumes a fact relevant to a certain class of litigation, and it is that feature that renders § 621 suspect under our prior cases. To put the point differently, a conclusive presumption takes the form of 'no X's are Y's,' and is typically accompanied by a rule such as, 'and only Y's may obtain a driver's license.' (There would be no need for the presumption unless something hinged on the fact presumed.) Ignoring the fact that § 621 takes the form of 'no X's are Y's,' Gerald D. and the plurality fix upon the rule following § 621—only Y's may assert parental rights—and call § 621 a substantive rule of law. This strategy ignores both the form and the effect of § 621."

Chapter

THE CONCEPT OF STATE ACTION

SECTION: RECENT DEVELOPMENTS

CON LAW: P. 1463, before *Flagg Bros.*

AMER CON: P. 1127, before *Flagg Bros.*

RTS & LIB: P. 1129, before *Flagg Bros.*

In SAN FRANCISCO ARTS & ATHLETICS, INC. v. UNITED STATES OLYMPIC COMM., 483 U.S. 522, 107 S.Ct. 2971, 97 L.Ed.2d 427 (1987), respondent USOC, to which Congress granted the right to prohibit certain commercial and promotional uses of the word "Olympic," secured relief enjoining petitioner from calling its athletic competitions the "Gay Olympic Games." Petitioner claimed that USOC's enforcement discriminated in violation of equal protection. The Court, per POWELL, J.—relying mainly on *Rendell-Baker, Blum* and *Jackson*—held that USOC is not a "governmental actor."

BRENNAN, J., joined by Marshall, J.—and "largely" by O'Connor and Blackmun, JJ.—dissented[a] on the basis of *Burton*:

"The USOC and the Federal Government exist in a symbiotic relationship sufficient to provide a nexus between the USOC's challenged action and the Government. First, as in *Burton*, the relationship here confers a variety of mutual benefits. [T]he Act gave the USOC authority and responsibilities that no private organization in this country had ever held. The Act also conferred substantial financial resources on the USOC, authorizing it to seek up to $16 million annually in grants from the Secretary of Commerce, and affording it unprecedented power to control the use of the word 'Olympic' and related emblems to raise additional funds. As a result of the Act, the United States obtained, for the first time in its history, an exclusive and effective organization

a. Brennan, J., joined only by Marshall, J., also argued that unlike the entities in the cases relied on by the Court, "which merely provided public services, the USOC has been endowed by the Federal Government with the exclusive power to serve a unique national, administrative, adjudicative, and representational role"—"it represents this Nation to the world community." The Court responded that "absent the additional element of governmental control, this representational function can hardly be called traditionally governmental. All sorts of private organizations send 'national representatives' to participate in world competitions. Although many are of interest only to a select group, others, like the Davis Cup Competition, the America's Cup, and the Miss Universe Pageant, are widely viewed as involving representation of our country. The organizations that sponsor United States participation in these events all perform 'national representational,' as well as 'administrative [and] adjudicative role[s],' in selecting and presenting the national representatives."

to coordinate and administer all amateur athletics related to international competition, and to represent that program abroad.

"Second, in the eye of the public, both national and international, the connection between the decisions of the United States Government and those of the United States Olympic Committee is profound. The President of the United States has served as the Honorary President of the USOC. The national flag flies both literally and figuratively over the central product of the USOC, the United States Olympic Team. * * *

"If petitioner is correct in its allegation that the USOC has used its discretion to discriminate against certain groups, then the situation here, as in *Burton*, is that 'profits earned by discrimination not only contribute to, but also are indispensable elements in, the financial success of a governmental agency.' Indeed, the required nexus between the challenged action and the Government appears even closer here than in *Burton*. While in *Burton* the restaurant was able to pursue a policy of discrimination because the State had failed to impose upon it a policy of non-discrimination, the USOC could pursue its alleged policy of selective enforcement only because Congress *affirmatively* granted it power that it would not otherwise have to control the use of the word 'Olympic.'" [b]

CON LAW: p. 1470, after note 1(b)

AMER CON: p. 1133, after note 1(b)

RTS & LIB: p. 1136, after note 1(b)

(c) NATIONAL COLLEGIATE ATHLETIC ASS'N v. TARKANIAN, ___ U.S. ___, 109 S.Ct. 454, 102 L.Ed.2d 469 (1988): The NCAA is an association of virtually all colleges with major athletic programs, and its rules governing these programs are binding on its members. After its investigation that found 38 recruitment violations by the staff of the University of Nevada, Las Vegas, including 10 by Tarkanian, who was UNLV's basketball coach, NCAA imposed a number of sanctions on UNLV and requested it to show cause why additional penalties should not be imposed if it failed to suspend Tarkanian. The Court, per STEVENS, J., conceded that UNLV's suspension of Tarkanian, which was clearly state action, "was influenced by the rules and recommendations of the NCAA," but held that this did not turn the NCAA's conduct into "state action" and thus the NCAA did not violate Tarkanian's right to procedural due process: Although, as a member of the NCAA, UNLV played a role in formulating its rules, "UNLV delegated no power to the NCAA to take specific action against any University employee. The commitment by UNLV to adhere to NCAA enforcement procedures was enforceable only by sanctions that the NCAA might impose on UNLV," and which UNLV could choose to ignore by withdrawing from the NCAA. And even if "the power of the NCAA is so great that the UNLV had no practical alternative to compliance with its demands," "it does not follow that such a private party [is] acting under color of state law." Finally, "in the case before us the state and private parties' relevant interests do not coincide, as they did in *Burton*; rather, they have clashed throughout the investigation, the attempt to discipline Tarkanian, and this litigation. UNLV and the NCAA were antagonists, not joint participants, and the NCAA may not be deemed a state actor on this ground."

b. The Court responded that petitioner "has failed to demonstrate that the Federal Government can or does exert any influence over the exercise of the USOC's enforcement decisions. Absent proof of this type of 'close nexus between the [Government] and the challenged action of the [USOC],' the challenged action may not be 'fairly treated as that of the [Government] itself.' *Jackson*."

WHITE, J., joined by Brennan, Marshall and O'Connor, JJ.,—emphasizing that UNLV, a public university is a "state actor"—dissented: "[I]t was the NCAA's findings that Tarkanian had violated NCAA rules, made at NCAA-conducted hearings, all of which were agreed to by UNLV in its membership agreement with the NCAA, that resulted in Tarkanian's suspension by UNLV. On these facts, the NCAA was 'jointly engaged with [UNLV] officials in the challenged action,' and therefore was a state actor."

Chapter

CONGRESSIONAL ENFORCEMENT
OF CIVIL RIGHTS

SECTION: MODERN DEVELOPMENTS

CON LAW: P. 1520, add to fn. e

AMER CON: P. 1173, add to fn. e

RTS & LIB: P. 1185, add to fn. e

The Court has interpreted § 1981 "to protect from discrimination identifiable classes of persons who are subjected to intentional discrimination solely because of their ancestry of ethnic characteristics." *Saint Francis College v. Al-Khazraji*, 481 U.S. 604, 107 S.Ct. 2022, 95 L.Ed.2d 582 (1987) (Arabs); *Shaare Tefila Congregation v. Cobb*, 481 U.S. 615, 107 S.Ct. 2019, 95 L.Ed.2d 594 (1987) (Jews).

Chapter

LIMITATIONS ON JUDICIAL POWER AND REVIEW

SECTION: CASE OR CONTROVERSY STANDING AND RIPENESS

INJURY REQUIRED FOR STANDING: SUITS BY TAXPAYERS AND CITIZENS

CON LAW: P. 1530, before *Doremus*

AMER CON: P. 1181, before *Doremus*

RTS & LIB: P. 1193, before *Doremus*

ASARCO INC. v. KADISH, ___ U.S. ___, 109 S.Ct. 2037, 104 L.Ed.2d 696 (1989), per KENNEDY, J., held that the exception from the *Frothingham* rule for municipal taxpayers does not apply to state taxpayers: "we have refused to confer standing upon a state taxpayer absent a showing of 'direct injury,' pecuniary or otherwise." Brennan, J., joined by White, Marshall and Blackmun, JJ., did not join this part of the Court's opinion.

CON LAW: P. 1530, after Tribe in fn. c

AMER CON: P. 1181, after Tribe in fn. c

RTS & LIB: P. 1193, after Tribe in fn. c

See *Asarco Inc. v. Kadish,* above (Court has jurisdiction to review state judgment under such circumstances).

SECTION: CHALLENGES TO STATE ACTION IN FEDERAL COURTS

ELEVENTH AMENDMENT

CON LAW: P. 1581, add to 1st ¶ of fn. 6

AMER CON: P. 1221, add to 1st ¶ of fn. 6

RTS & LIB: P. 1233, add to 1st ¶ of fn. 6

Welch v. State Dep't of Highways, 483 U.S. 468, 107 S.Ct. 2941, 97 L.Ed.2d 389 (1987), held that "to the extent that *Parden* is inconsistent with the requirement that an abrogation of Eleventh Amendment immunity by Congress must be expressed in unmistakably clear language, it is overruled."

CON LAW: P. 1584, at end of note 1(c)

AMER CON: P. 1224, at end

RTS & LIB: P. 1236, at end

PENNSYLVANIA v. UNION GAS CO., ___ U.S. ___, 109 S.Ct. 2273, ___ L.Ed.2d ___ (1989), significantly limited *Hans v. Louisiana*. BRENNAN, J., joined by Marshall, Blackmun and Stevens, JJ., reasoned that Congress possesses the same power under the commerce clause as it has under § 5 of the fourteenth amendment to abrogate state immunity from federal court suits for money damages, "but it must make its intent to do so, 'unmistakably clear.' [I]n approving the commerce power, the States consented to suits against them based on congressionally created causes of actions." WHITE, J., agreed with Brennan, J.'s conclusion "that Congress has the authority under Article I to abrogate the Eleventh Amendment immunity of the States, although I do not agree with much of his reasoning."

SCALIA, J., joined by Rehnquist, C.J., and O'Connor and Kennedy, JJ., dissenting, found this conclusion "contrary to the clear understanding of a century of cases": "An interpretation of the original Constitution which permits Congress to eliminate sovereign immunity only if it wants to render the doctrine a practical nullity and is therefore unreasonable."

INJUNCTIONS, DECLARATORY JUDGMENTS, AND THE "ABSTENTION DOCTRINE"

CON LAW: P. 1595, after note (b)

In PENNZOIL CO. v. TEXACO, INC., 481 U.S. 1, 107 S.Ct. 1519, 95 L.Ed.2d 1 (1987), Pennzoil obtained a state court judgment of over $11 billion against Texaco. State law permitted Pennzoil to execute a lien against Texaco's property unless Texaco filed a bond in the amount of the judgment. Being financially unable to do so, Texaco secured a federal preliminary injunction against the state lien and bond provisions on the ground that they probably violated due process and equal protection. The Court, per POWELL, J., reversed, relying on *Juidice*: "There is little difference between the State's interest in forcing persons to transfer property in response to a court's judgment and in forcing persons to respond to the court's process on pain of contempt. Both *Juidice* and this case involve challenges to the processes by which the State compels compliance with the judgment of its courts." [a]

CON LAW: P. 1596, after note (d)

(e) OHIO CIVIL RIGHTS COMM'N v. DAYTON CHRISTIAN SCHOOLS, INC., 477 U.S. 619, 106 S.Ct. 2718, 91 L.Ed.2d 512 (1986), per REHNQUIST, J., held that *Younger* applied to "pending state administrative proceedings in which an important state interest is involved" (the commission's complaint against a religious school for sex discrimination), adding that "it is sufficient [that] constitutional claims may be raised in state court judicial review of the administrative proceeding." [a]

a. Brennan and Marshall, JJ., concurred on the substantive ground that there was no violation of the fourteenth amendment, but dissented as to *Younger*'s applicability: "The State's interest in this case in negligible." Stevens, J., agreed. Blackmun, J., agreed as to *Younger*, but would have abstained "under the principles announced in *Pullman*."

a. Stevens, J., joined by Brennan, Marshall and Blackmun, JJ., concurred in the judgment on other grounds but disagreed with the Court's abstention reasoning, particularly the last point.

†